Pascal Reference Chart (cont.)

Program Composition (Page in Text)	Example

Variable section (54, 80)
(predefined types)
  integer
  real
  character
  boolean
  text file
(user-defined types)
	var
	  Count, I, Number : integer;
	  Hours, Rate, Wages : real;
	  DeptCode, FirstInit, SecondInit : char;
	  OverTime : boolean;
	  OutFile : text;
	  Dept : DepartmentName;
	  EmpCode : Digit;
	  Product, Item : List;
	  ProductName : String;
	  Letters : CapLetterSet;
	  EmpRec : InfoRecord;
	  InFile : EmployeeFile;
	  FirstPtr, TempPtr : ListPointer;

Subprogram section (152)
  Function definition (173)
	function *RoundCents (Amount : real) : real;*
	(∗ Round *Amount* to nearest cent ∗)
	begin (∗ *RoundCents* ∗)
	  RoundCents := *round*(100 ∗ *Amount*) / 100
	end (∗ *RoundCents* ∗);

Procedure definition (152)	**procedure** *ReadCodes* (**var** *Department,*
	                              Employee : char);
	(∗ Read department & employee codes ∗)
	begin (∗ *ReadCodes* ∗)
	  write ('Enter dept. & employee codes: ');
	  readln (*Department, Employee*)
	end (∗ *ReadCodes* ∗);

Statement part (51, 81)	**begin** (∗ main program ∗)
	  statement-1;
	    .
	    .
	    .
	  statement-n
	end (∗ main program ∗).

PASCAL
Programming and Problem Solving

SANFORD LEESTMA
LARRY NYHOFF
Department of Mathematics and Computer Science
Calvin College

PASCAL
Programming and Problem Solving

SECOND EDITION

Macmillan Publishing Company
NEW YORK

Collier Macmillan Publishers
LONDON

Macmillan Publishing Company
866 Third Avenue, New York, New York 10022

Collier Macmillan Canada, Inc.

Library of Congress Cataloging-in-Publication Data

Leestma, Sanford.
  Pascal : programming and problem solving.

  Includes index.
  1. PASCAL (Computer program language)   I. Nyhoff,
Larry R.   II. Title.
QA76.73.P2L44 1987   005.13'3   86-21692
ISBN 0-02-369690-7

Printing: 2 3 4 5 6 7 8   Year: 7 8 9 0 1 2 3 4 5

ISBN   0-02-369690-7

PREFACE

Pascal was developed in the late 1960s and early 1970s by Niklaus Wirth, a Swiss computer scientist at the Eidgenössische Technishe Hochshule (ETH) in Zurich, Switzerland. His primary goal was to develop a language that makes it possible "to teach programming as a systematic discipline based on certain fundamental concepts clearly and naturally reflected by the language." *The Pascal User Manual and Report,* written by Wirth and K. Jensen and published in 1974, serves as the basic definition of the Pascal language. As the use of Pascal grew, some differences appeared in various implementations. To ensure that Pascal programs written on one system can be executed on another, national and international standards for the language have been formulated. A recent standard is *An American National Standard IEEE Standard Pascal Computer Programming Language,* which was published in 1983 by Institute of Electrical and Electronics Engineers (IEEE). This standard was approved by the IEEE Standards Board and the American National Standards Institute (ANSI) and serves as the basis for this text. Differences between this standard and other popular versions of Pascal are described in brief sections at the ends of appropriate chapters and in Appendix G.

This text is a complete introduction to the Pascal programming language and is designed to meet the objectives of the course CS1: *Introduction to Programming Methodology* as described in the Curriculum '84 recommendations of the Association of Computing Machinery (ACM). The course objectives as described in this curriculum guideline are (cf. "Recommended Curriculum for CS1, 1984," *Communications of the ACM,* October, 1984):

- to introduce a disciplined approach to problem-solving methods and algorithm development;
- to introduce procedural and data abstraction;
- to teach program design, coding, debugging, testing, and documentation using good programming style;
- to teach a block-structured high-level programming language;
- to provide a familiarity with the evolution of computer hardware and software technology;
- to provide a foundation for further studies in computer science.

To meet these objectives, this text emphasizes problem solving using structured algorithm and program design throughout and illustrates these with a large number of complete examples and applications, many of which include algorithms given in pseudocode and/or structure diagrams, complete Pascal programs implementing the algorithms, and sample runs. Each of the examples is intended to demonstrate good algorithm design and programming style. At the end of each chapter a Programming Pointers section summarizes the main points regarding structure and style as well as language features presented and some problems that beginning programmers may experience. In addition to presenting the basic features of Pascal, the text introduces such topics as data representation, machine language, and compilers, and the last two chapters introduce some elementary data structures, such as stacks, queues, linked lists, and trees.

Like the first edition, this text is intended for an introductory computer programming course using Pascal. Thus, the level is the same as that of the first edition, with the intended audience being freshman and/or sophomore college students whose mathematical background includes high school algebra. The first edition was written for the course CS1 as described in the Curriculum '78 guidelines of the ACM. A new course description appeared in 1984, however, and the new text has been carefully revised to implement these recommendations. We have also benefited from constructive comments of instructors and students who used the first edition and we have incorporated many of these suggestions in this second edition. Specifically, the changes in the new edition include the following:

- Procedures are introduced earlier in the text (before functions). The discussion of scope rules is simplified, and more difficult and less frequently used material has been relegated to an appendix. The introduction to recursion is expanded and improved.
- More examples and exercises from nonmathematical applications have been included.
- Material in Chapter 4 has been reorganized so that selection structures are considered before repetition structures; in the case of the latter, **while** and **repeat** statements are considered before the **for** statement.
- Introduction to data structure design and algorithm analysis (Chapters 13 and 14) has been improved.
- Presentation of structured data types has been improved with a new introduction to and better examples of multidimensional arrays in Chapter 9, consideration of records before sets in Chapters 10 and 11, and a simplified treatment of files in Chapter 12.
- The discussion of problem solving and algorithm development in Chapter 2 has been expanded, and additional material on testing and debugging has been included in Chapter 4. More structure diagrams have been used to display the structure of more complicated programs.
- The discussion of data representation and other basic concepts of computer systems (including machine language, assembly language, and compilers) in Chapter 1 has been expanded so that it conforms to the CS1 guidelines.
- A second color has been used to highlight important concepts and to improve readability.
- Brief sections describing common variations of and extensions to standard Pascal have been added at the ends of chapters where appropriate.

- A new appendix details these variations and extensions as implemented in Macintosh™ Pascal Turbo Pascal™, and UCSD™ Pascal.

Revised and expanded supplementary materials available from the publisher include the following:

- An instructor's manual containing lecture notes, solutions to exercises, sample test questions, and transparency masters.
- Data disks containing all the sample programs and data files used in the text. Standard Pascal and Turbo Pascal versions are available.
- A test bank and test generation software for microcomputers.

Acknowledgments

We express our appreciation to all those who were involved in the preparation of this text: to our colleagues who have used this material in their classes and whose suggestions have strengthened the presentation; to our students, who have served as test subjects; to David Johnstone, Ron Harris, and all other Macmillan personnel who initiated, supervised, produced, or in some other way contributed to the finished product; to the several reviewers of the manuscript, whose comments were encouraging, helpful, and sincerely appreciated; and to Marge, Michelle, Sandy, Michael, Shar, Jeff, Dawn, Jim, Julie, and Joan, whose patience, love, support, and understanding during the preparation of this text and others has exceeded what we have any right to expect.

S.C.L.
L.R.N.

CONTENTS

1

Introduction and History

The modern electronic computer is one of the most important products of the twentieth century. It is an essential tool in many areas, including business, industry, government, science, and education; indeed, it has touched nearly every aspect of our lives. The impact of this twentieth-century information revolution brought about by the development of high-speed computing systems has been nearly as widespread as the impact of the nineteenth-century industrial revolution. This chapter gives a summary of the history of computer systems and briefly describes their components.

1.1 History of Computing Systems

There are two important concepts in the history of computation: the *mechanization of arithmetic* and the concept of a *stored program* for the automatic control of computations. We shall focus our attention on some of the devices that have implemented these concepts.

A variety of computational devices were used in ancient civilizations. One of the earliest, which might be considered a forerunner of the modern computer, is the *abacus* (Figure 1.1), which has movable beads strung on rods to count and make computations. Although its exact origin is unknown, the abacus was used by the Chinese perhaps three to four thousand years ago and is still used today.

1

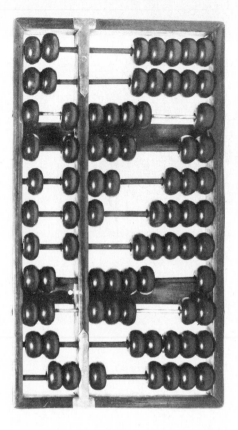

Figure 1.1
Abacus.

The ancient British stone monument ***Stonehenge*** (Figure 1.2a), located in southern England, was built between 1900 and 1600 B.C. and evidently was an astronomical calculator used to predict the changes of the seasons. Five hundred years ago, the Inca Indians of South America used a system of knotted cords called ***quipus*** (Figure 1.2b) to count and record divisions of land among the various tribal groups. In Western Europe, ***Napier's bones*** (Figure 1.2c) and tables of ***logarithms*** were designed by the Scottish mathematician John Napier (1550–1617) to simplify calculations. These led to the subsequent invention of the ***slide rule*** (Figure 1.2d).

In 1642, the young French mathematician ***Blaise Pascal*** (1623–1662) invented one of the first mechanical adding machines (Figure 1.3). This device used a system of gears and wheels similar to that used in odometers and other modern counting devices. ***Pascal's adder*** could both add and subtract, and was invented to calculate taxes. Pascal's announcement of his invention reveals the labor-saving motivation for its development:

> Dear reader, this notice will serve to inform you that I submit to the public a small machine of my invention, by means of which you alone may, without any effort, perform all the operations of arithmetic, and may be relieved of the work which has often times fatigued your spirit, when you have worked with the counters or with the pen. As for simplicity of movement of the operations, I have so devised it that, although the operations of arithmetic are in a way opposed the one to the other—as addition to subtraction, and multiplication to division—nevertheless they are all performed on this ma-

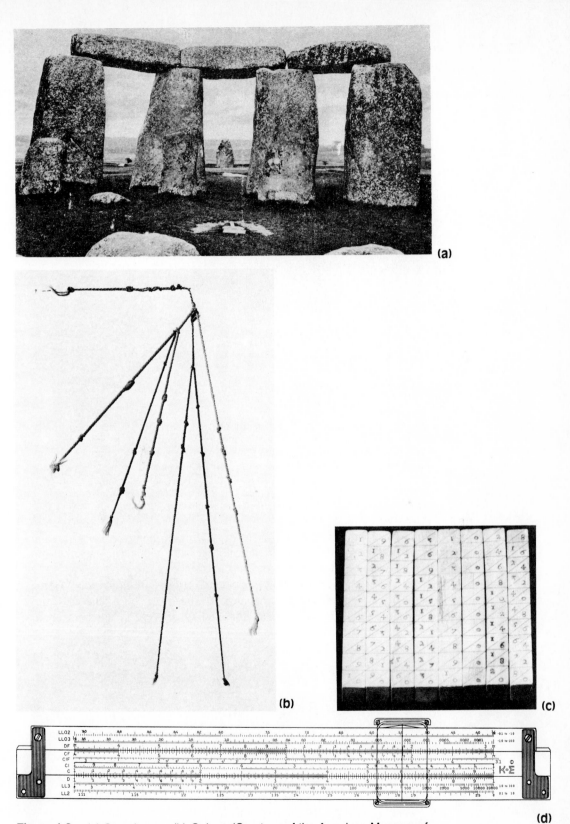

Figure 1.2. (a) Stonehenge. (b) Quipus (Courtesy of the American Museum of Natural History). (c) Napier's bones (Courtesy of the Smithsonian Institution). (d) Slide rule.

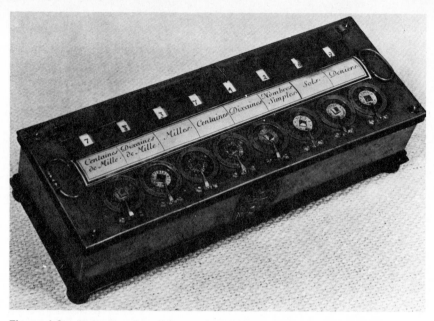

Figure 1.3. Pascal's adder. (Courtesy of IBM.)

chine by a single movement. The facility of this movement of operation is very evident since it is just as easy to move one thousand or ten thousand dials, all at one time, if one desires to make a single dial move, although all accomplish the movement perfectly. The most ignorant find as many advantages as the most experienced. The instrument makes up for ignorance and for lack of practice, and even without any effort of the operator, it makes possible shortcuts by itself, whenever the numbers are set down.

Although Pascal built more than fifty of his adding machines, his commercial venture failed because the devices could not be built with sufficient precision for practical use.

In the 1670s, the German mathematician ***Gottfried Wilhelm von Leibniz*** (1646–1716) produced a machine that was similar in design to Pascal's, but somewhat more reliable and accurate (Figure 1.4). Leibniz's calculator could

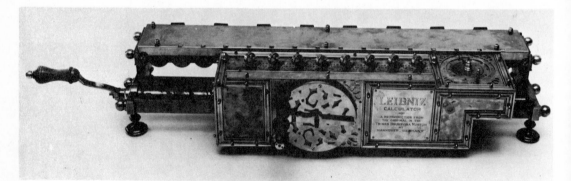

Figure 1.4. Leibniz's calculator. (Courtesy of IBM.)

perform all four of the basic arithmetic operations: addition, subtraction, multiplication, and division.

A number of other mechanical calculators followed that further refined the designs of Pascal and Leibniz. By the end of the nineteenth century, these calculators had become important tools in science, business, and commerce.

As noted earlier, the second idea to emerge in the history of computing was the concept of a stored program to control the calculations. One early example of an automatically controlled device is the weaving loom (Figure 1.5) invented by the Frenchman *Joseph Marie Jacquard* (1752–1834). This automatic loom, introduced at a Paris exhibition in 1801, used metal cards punched with holes to position threads for the weaving process. A collection of these cards made up a program that directed the loom. Within a decade, 11,000 of these machines were in use in French textile plants, resulting in what may have been the first incidence of unemployment caused by automation. Unemployed workers rioted and destroyed several of the new looms and cards. Jacquard wrote: ''The iron was sold for iron, the wood for wood, and I its inventor delivered up to public ignominy.'' The *Jacquard loom* is still used today, although modern versions are controlled by magnetic tape rather than punched cards.

Figure 1.5.
Jacquard loom. (Courtesy of IBM.)

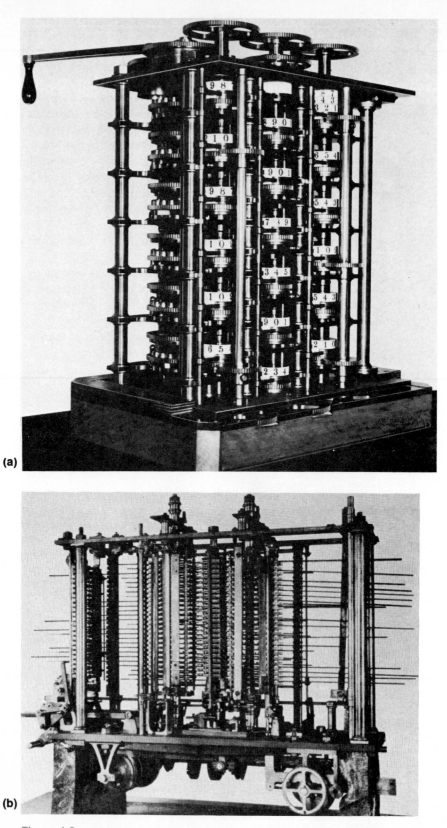

Figure 1.6. (a) Babbage's Difference Engine. (b) Babbage's Analytical Engine. (Courtesy of IBM.)

These two concepts, mechanized calculation and stored program control, were combined by the English mathematician **Charles Babbage** (1792–1871), who began work in 1822 on a machine that he called the **Difference Engine** (Figure 1.6a). This machine was designed to compute polynomials for the preparation of mathematical tables. Babbage continued his work until 1833 with support from the British government, which was interested in possible military applications of the Difference Engine. But Babbage later abandoned this project since the metal-working technology of that time was not sufficiently advanced to manufacture the required precision gears and linkages. Babbage was not discouraged, however, but designed a more sophisticated machine that he called his **Analytical Engine** (Figure 1.6b). This machine had several special-purpose components that were intended to work together. The ''mill'' was supposed to carry out the arithmetic computations; the ''store'' was the machine's memory for storing data and intermediate results; and other components were designed for the input and output of information and for the transfer of information between components. The operation of this machine was to be fully automatic, controlled by punched cards, an idea based on Jacquard's earlier work. In fact, Babbage himself said, ''The analogy of the Analytical Engine with this well-known process is nearly perfect.'' **Ada Augusta**, Lord George Byron's daughter and the Countess of Lovelace, understood how the device was to work and supported Babbage. Considered by some to be the first programmer, Lady Lovelace described the similarity of Jacquard's and Babbage's inventions: ''The Analytical Engine weaves algebraic patterns just as the Jacquard loom weaves flowers and leaves.'' Although Babbage's machine was not built during his lifetime, it is nevertheless part of the history of computing because many of the concepts of its design are used in modern computers.

A related development in the United States was the census bureau's use of punched-card systems to help compile the 1890 census (Figure 1.7). These systems, designed by **Herman Hollerith**, a young mathematician employed by the bureau, used electrical sensors to interpret the information stored on the punched cards. In 1896, Hollerith left the census bureau and formed his own tabulating company, which in 1924 became the International Business Machines Corporation (IBM).

The development of computing devices continued at a rapid pace in the United States. Some of the pioneers in this effort were Howard Aiken, J. P. Eckert, J. W. Mauchly, and John von Neumann. Repeating much of the work of Babbage, Aiken designed a system consisting of several mechanical calculators working together. This work, which was supported by IBM, led to the invention in 1944 of the electromechanical **Mark I** computer (Figure 1.8). This machine is the best-known computer built before 1945 and may be regarded as the first realization of Babbage's Analytical Engine.

The best known of the early fully electronic computers was the **ENIAC** (Electronic Numerical Integrator and Computer), constructed in 1946 by J. P. Eckert and J. W. Mauchly at the Moore School of Electrical Engineering of the University of Pennsylvania (Figure 1.9). This extremely large machine contained over 18,000 vacuum tubes and 1,500 relays and nearly filled a room 20 feet by 40 feet in size. It could multiply numbers approximately 1,000 times faster than the Mark I could, though it was quite limited in its applications and was used primarily by the Army Ordnance Department to calculate firing tables

Figure 1.7. Hollerith equipment. (Courtesy of IBM.)

Figure 1.8. Mark I. (Courtesy of IBM.)

Figure 1.9. ENIAC. (Courtesy of Sperry Corporation.)

and trajectories for various types of shells. Eckert and Mauchly later left the University of Pennsylvania to form the Eckert-Mauchly Computer Corporation, which built the **UNIVAC** (Universal Automatic Computer), the first commercially available computer designed for both scientific and business applications. The first UNIVAC was sold to the census bureau in 1951.

The instructions, or program, that controlled the ENIAC's operation were entered into the machine by rewiring some parts of the computer's circuits. This complicated process was very time-consuming, sometimes taking several people several days, and during this time, the computer was idle. In other early computers, the instructions were stored outside the machine on punched cards or some other medium and were transferred into the machine one at a time for interpretation and execution. A new scheme, developed by Princeton mathematician John von Neumann and others, used internally stored commands. The advantages of this stored program concept are that internally stored instructions can be processed more rapidly, and, more importantly, that they can be modified by the computer itself while computations are taking place. The stored program concept makes possible the general-purpose computers so commonplace today.

The actual physical components used in constructing a computer system are its **hardware**. Several generations of computers can be identified by the type of hardware used. The ENIAC and UNIVAC are examples of **first-generation** computers, which are characterized by their extensive use of vacuum tubes. Advances in electronics brought changes in computing systems, and in 1958, IBM introduced the first of the **second-generation** computers, the

IBM 7090. These computers were built between 1959 and 1965 and used transistors in place of vacuum tubes. Consequently, these computers were smaller and less expensive, required less power, generated far less heat, and were more reliable than their predecessors. The ***third-generation*** computers that followed used integrated circuits and introduced new techniques for better system utilization, such as multiprogramming and time-sharing. The IBM System/360 introduced in 1964 is commonly accepted as the first of this generation of computers. Computers of the 1980s, commonly called ***fourth-generation*** computers, used very-large-scale integrated circuits (VLSI) on silicon chips and other microelectronic advances to shrink their size and cost still more while enlarging their capability. A typical memory chip is equivalent to many thousands of transistors, is smaller than a baby's fingernail, weighs a small fraction of an ounce, requires only a trickle of power, and costs but a few dollars. Such miniaturization made possible the development of the personal computers so popular today (Figure 1.10). One of the pioneers in the development of microcomputers, Robert Noyce, contrasted them to the ENIAC as follows:

> An individual integrated circuit on a chip perhaps a quarter of an inch square now can embrace more electronic elements than the most complex piece of electronic equipment that could be built in 1950. Today's microcomputer, at a cost of perhaps $300, has more computing capacity than the first electronic computer, ENIAC. It is twenty times faster, has a larger memory, consumes the power of a light bulb rather than that of a locomotive, occupies 1/30,000 the volume and costs 1/10,000 as much. It is available by mail order or at your local hobby shop.

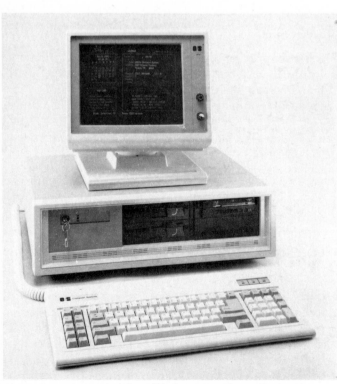

Figure 1.10. A modern personal computer. (Courtesy of OnSite Business Systems, a Division of Dale Computer Corporation.)

The stored program concept was a significant improvement over manual programming methods, but early computers were still difficult to use because of the complex coding schemes required for the representation of programs and data. Consequently, in addition to improved hardware, computer manufacturers began to develop collections of programs known as *system software*, which makes computers easier to use. One of the more important advances in this area was the development of *high-level languages*, which allow users to write programs in a language similar to natural language. A program written in a high-level language is known as a *source program*. For most high-level languages, the instructions that make up a source program must be translated into *machine language*, that is, the language used directly by a particular computer in all its calculations and processing. This machine language program is called an *object program*. The programs that translate source programs into object programs are called *compilers*. Another part of the system software, the *operating system*, controls the translation of the source program, allocates storage for the program and data, and carries out many other supervisory functions.

One of the first high-level languages to gain widespread acceptance was FORTRAN (FORmula TRANslation). It was developed for the IBM 704 computer by John Backus and a team of thirteen other programmers at IBM over a three-year period (1954–1957). Since that time many other high-level languages have been developed, including ALGOL, BASIC, COBOL, Pascal, C, Ada, and Modula-2. In this text we shall discuss the Pascal programming language.

Pascal, named in honor of the French mathematician Blaise Pascal, was designed by Niklaus Wirth at the Eidgenössische Technishe Hochshule (ETH) in Zurich, Switzerland. The first Pascal compiler appeared in 1970, and the first report on the language was published in 1971.[1] A revised user manual and report was published in 1974.[2] The first two paragraphs of the introduction to this report describe Wirth's reasons for developing Pascal:

> The development of the language Pascal is based on two principal aims. The first is to make available a language suitable to teach programming as a systematic discipline based on certain fundamental concepts clearly and naturally reflected by the language. The second is to develop implementations of this language which are both reliable and efficient on presently available computers.
>
> The desire for a new language for the purpose of teaching programming is due to my dissatisfaction with the presently used major languages whose features and constructs too often cannot be explained logically and convincingly and which too often defy systematic reasoning. Along with this dissatisfaction goes my conviction that the language in which the student is taught to express his ideas profoundly influences his habits of thought and invention, and that the disorder governing these languages directly imposes itself onto the programming style of the students.

For Pascal, Wirth used much of the framework of ALGOL. Pascal itself has served as the basis for more recent programming languages such as Ada (named after Ada Augusta) and Modula-2 (also developed by Wirth).

---

[1] N. Wirth, ''The Programming Language Pascal,'' *Acta-Informatica* 1 (1971):35–63.
[2] K. Jensen and N. Wirth, *Pascal User Manual and Report* (Heidelberg: Springer-Verlag, 1974).

In summary, the history of computation and computational aids began several thousands of years ago, and in some cases, the theory underlying such devices developed much more rapidly than did the technical skills required to produce working models. Although the modern electronic computer with its mechanized calculation and automatic program control has its roots in the mid-nineteenth-century work of Charles Babbage, the electronic computer is a fairly recent development. The rapid changes that have marked its progression since its inception in 1945 can be expected to continue into the future.

1.2   Computing Systems

In our discussion of the history of computing, we noted that Babbage designed his Analytical Engine as a system of several separate components, each with its own particular function. This general scheme was incorporated in many later computers and is, in fact, a common feature of most modern computers. In this section we briefly describe the major components of a modern computing system.

The heart of any computing system is its *central processing unit*, or *CPU*. The CPU controls the operation of the entire system, performs the arithmetic and logic operations, stores and retrieves instructions and data. The instructions and data are stored in a high-speed *memory unit*, and the *control unit* fetches these instructions from memory, decodes them, and directs the system to execute the operations indicated by the instructions. Those operations that are arithmetical or logical in nature are carried out using special registers and circuits of the *arithmetic-logic unit (ALU)* of the CPU.

The memory unit is called the *internal* or *main* or *primary memory* of the computer system. In older machines this memory usually consisted of magnetic

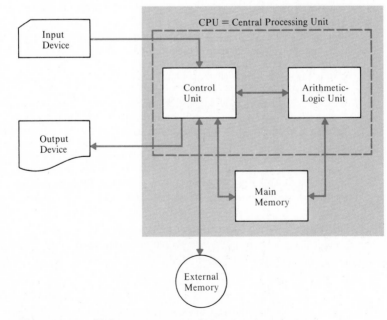

Figure 1.11.   Major components of a computing system.

Figure 1.12. A typical minicomputer system. (Courtesy of Prime Computer Corporation.)

cores, whereas newer machines use semiconductors (although memory is still sometimes referred to as *core memory*). Information stored in these devices can be retrieved rapidly, but since they are rather expensive, most computing systems also contain components that serve as *external* or *auxiliary* or *secondary memory*. Common forms of this type of memory are magnetic disks and magnetic tapes. These *peripheral devices* provide relatively inexpensive storage for large collections of information, but the rate of transfer of information to and from them is considerably slower than that for internal memory.

Other peripherals are used to transmit instructions, data, and computed results between the user and the CPU. These are the *input/output devices* and may take a variety of forms such as card readers, remote terminals, paper tape readers, optical scanners, voice input devices, and high-speed printers. Their function is to convert information from an external form understandable to the user to a form that can be processed by the computer system, and vice versa.

The diagram in Figure 1.11 shows the relationship between these components in a computer system, and Figure 1.12 shows these components as they appear in a modern computer system.

1.3 Internal Representation

The devices that comprise the memory unit of a computer are two-state devices. If one of the states is interpreted as 0 and the other as 1, then it is natural to use a *binary scheme*, using only the two binary digits (*bits*) 0 and 1 for representation within a computer. These two-state devices are organized into groups called *bytes*, each of which contains a fixed number of these devices, usually eight, and thus can store a fixed number of bits. Memory is commonly measured in bytes; for example, a 256K memory usually refers to a memory that consists of $2^8 \times 2^{10} = 2^{18} = 262,144$ bytes ($1K = 2^{10} = 1,024$), or, equivalently, $2^{21} = 2,097,152$ bits.

A larger grouping of bits and bytes is into *words*. Word sizes vary with computers, but common sizes are 16 bits ($= 2$ bytes) and 32 bits ($= 4$ bytes). Each word is identified by an *address* and can be directly accessed using this address. This makes it possible to store information in a specific memory word and then retrieve it later. To understand how this is done, we must first examine the binary number system.

The number system that we are accustomed to using is a *decimal* or *base-10* number system, which uses the digits 0, 1, 2, 3, 4, 5, 6, 7, 8, and 9. The significance of these digits in a numeral depends on the positions that they occupy in that numeral. For example, in the numeral

$$485$$

the digit 4 is interpreted as

$$4 \text{ hundreds}$$

and the digit 8 as

$$8 \text{ tens}$$

and the digit 5 as

$$5 \text{ ones}$$

Thus, the numeral 485 represents the number four-hundred eighty-five and can be written in *expanded form* as

$$(4 \times 100) + (8 \times 10) + (5 \times 1)$$

or

$$(4 \times 10^2) + (8 \times 10^1) + (5 \times 10^0)$$

The digits that appear in the various positions of a decimal (base-10) numeral thus represent coefficients of powers of 10.

Similar positional number systems can be devised using numbers other than 10 as a base. The *binary* number system uses 2 as the base and has only two digits, 0 and 1. As in a decimal system, the significance of the bits in a binary numeral is determined by their positions in that numeral. For example, the binary numeral

$$101$$

can be written in expanded form (using decimal notation) as

$$(1 \times 2^2) + (0 \times 2^1) + (1 \times 2^0)$$

that is, the binary numeral 101 has the decimal value

$$4 + 0 + 1 = 5$$

Similarly, the binary numeral 111010 has the decimal value

$$(1 \times 2^5) + (1 \times 2^4) + (1 \times 2^3) + (0 \times 2^2) + (1 \times 2^1) + (0 \times 2^0)$$
$$= 32 + 16 + 8 + 2$$
$$= 58$$

When necessary, to avoid confusion about which base is being used, it is customary to write the base as a subscript for nondecimal numerals. Using this convention, we could indicate that 5 and 58 have the binary representations just given by writing

$$5 = 101_2$$

and

$$58 = 111010_2$$

When an integer value such as 5 or 58 must be stored in the computer's memory, the binary representation of that value is typically stored in one memory word. To illustrate, consider a computer whose word size is sixteen, and suppose that the integer value 58 is to be stored. A memory word is selected and a sequence of sixteen bits formed from the binary representation 111010 of 58 is stored there:

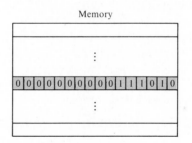

Negative integers must also be stored in a binary form in which the sign of the integer is part of the representation. There are several ways this can be done, but one of the most common is the *two's complement* representation. In this scheme, positive integers are represented in binary form as just described, with the leftmost bit set to 0 to indicate that the value is positive. The representation of a negative integer $-n$ is obtained by first finding the binary representation of n, complementing it, that is, changing each 0 to 1 and each 1 to 0, and then adding 1 to the result. For example, the two's complement representation of -58 using a string of sixteen bits is obtained as follows:

1. Represent 58 by a 16-bit binary numeral:

   0000000000111010

2. Complement this bit string:

   1111111111000101

3. Add 1:

   1111111111000110

Note that the leftmost bit in this two's complement representation of a negative integer will always be 1, indicating that the number is negative.

The fixed word size limits the range of the integers that can be stored internally. For example, the largest positive integer that can be stored in a 16-bit word is

$$0111111111111111_2 = 2^{15} - 1 = 32767$$

and the smallest negative integer is

$$1000000000000000_2 = -2^{15} = -32768$$

The range of integers that can be represented using a 32-bit word is

$$10000000000000000000000000000000_2 = -2^{31} = -2147483648$$

through

$$01111111111111111111111111111111_2 = 2^{31} - 1 = 2147483647$$

An attempt to store an integer outside the allowed range will result in the loss of some of the bits of its binary representation, a phenomenon known as **overflow**. This limitation may be partially overcome by using more than one word to store an integer. Although this technique enlarges the range of integers that can be stored exactly, it does not resolve the problem of overflow; the range of representable integers is still finite.

Numbers that contain decimal points are called **real numbers** or **floating point numbers**. In the decimal representation of such numbers, each digit is the coefficient of some power of 10. Digits to the left of the decimal point are coefficients of nonnegative powers of 10, while those to the right are coefficients of negative powers of 10. For example, the decimal numeral 56.317 can be written in expanded form as

$$(5 \times 10^1) + (6 \times 10^0) + (3 \times 10^{-1}) + (1 \times 10^{-2}) + (7 \times 10^{-3})$$

or, equivalently, as

$$(5 \times 10) + (6 \times 1) + \left(3 \times \frac{1}{10}\right) + \left(1 \times \frac{1}{100}\right) + \left(7 \times \frac{1}{1000}\right)$$

Digits in the binary representation of a real number are coefficients of powers of two. Those to the left of the **binary point** are coefficients of nonnegative powers of two, and those to the right are coefficients of negative powers of two. For example, the expanded form of 110.101 is

$$(1 \times 2^2) + (1 \times 2^1) + (0 \times 2^0) + (1 \times 2^{-1}) + (0 \times 2^{-2}) + (1 \times 2^{-3})$$

and thus has the decimal value

$$4 + 2 + 0 + \frac{1}{2} + 0 + \frac{1}{8} = 6.625$$

There is some variation in the schemes used for storing real numbers in computer memory, but one common method is the following. The binary representation

$$110.101_2$$

of the real number 6.625 can be written equivalently as

$$0.110101_2 \times 2^3$$

Typically, one part of a memory word (or words) is used to store a fixed number of bits of the **mantissa** or **fractional part** 0.110101_2, and another part to store the **exponent** $3 = 11_2$. For example, if the leftmost eleven bits in a 16-bit word are used for the mantissa and the remaining five bits for the exponent, 6.625 could be stored as

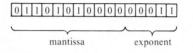

where the first bit in each part is reserved for the sign.

Since the binary representation of the exponent may require more than the available number of bits, we see that the overflow problem discussed in connection with integer representation may also occur in storing a real number. Also, there obviously are some real numbers whose mantissas have more than the allotted number of bits; consequently, some of these bits will be lost in storing such numbers. In fact, most real numbers do not have finite binary representations and thus cannot be stored exactly in any computer. For example, the binary representation of the real number 0.7 is

$$(0.10110011001100110 \ldots)_2$$

where the block 0110 is repeated indefinitely. If only the first eleven bits are stored and all remaining bits are truncated, then the stored representation of 0.7 is

$$0.10110011002$$

which has the decimal value 0.69921875. If the binary representation is rounded to eleven bits, then the stored representation for 0.7 is

$$0.10110011012.$$

which has the decimal value 0.700195312. In either case, the stored value is not exactly 0.7. This error, called **roundoff error**, can be reduced, but not eliminated, by using a larger number of bits to store the binary representation of real numbers.

Computers store and process not only numeric data but also boolean or logical data (false or true), character data, and other types of nonnumeric information. Storing boolean values is easy; false can be encoded as 0, true as 1, and these bits stored. The schemes used for the internal representation of character data are based on the assignment of a numeric code to each of the characters in the character set. Several standard coding schemes have been developed, such as **ASCII** (American Standard Code for Information Interchange) and **EBCDIC** (Extended Binary Coded Decimal Interchange Code). Table 1.1 shows these codes for capital letters. A complete table of ASCII and EBCDIC codes for all characters is given in Appendix A.

TABLE 1.1   Character codes

Character	ASCII		EBCDIC	
	Decimal	Binary	Decimal	Binary
A	65	01000001	193	11000001
B	66	01000010	194	11000010
C	67	01000011	195	11000011
D	68	01000100	196	11000100
E	69	01000101	197	11000101
F	70	01000110	198	11000110
G	71	01000111	199	11000111
H	72	01001000	200	11001000
I	73	01001001	201	11001001
J	74	01001010	209	11010001
K	75	01001011	210	11010010
L	76	01001100	211	11010011
M	77	01001101	212	11010100
N	78	01001110	213	11010101
O	79	01001111	214	11010110
P	80	01010000	215	11010111
Q	81	01010001	216	11011000
R	82	01010010	217	11011001
S	83	01010011	226	11100010
T	84	01010100	227	11100011
U	85	01010101	228	11100100
V	86	01010110	229	11100101
W	87	01010111	230	11100110
X	88	01011000	231	11100111
Y	89	01011001	232	11101000
Z	90	01011010	233	11101001

Characters are represented internally using these binary codes. A byte consisting of eight bits can thus store the binary representation of one character, and a 16-bit word consisting of two bytes can store two characters. For example, the character string HI can be stored in a single 16-bit word with the code for H in the left byte and the code for I in the right byte; with ASCII code, the result would be as follows:

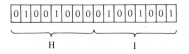

Memory words of size 32 (bits) are usually divided into four bytes and thus can store four characters. Character strings of a length greater than the number of bytes in a word are usually stored in two or more consecutive memory words.

We have now seen how various types of data can be stored in a computer's memory. Program instructions for processing data must also be stored in memory. As an example, suppose three values $8 = 1000_2$, $24 = 11000_2$, and $58 = 111010_2$ have been stored in memory locations with addresses 4, 5, and 6, and we want to multiply the first two values, add the third, and store the result in memory word 7.

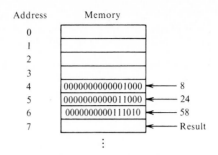

To perform this computation, the following instructions must be executed:

1. Fetch the contents of memory word 4 and load it into the accumulator register of the ALU.
2. Fetch the contents of memory word 5 and compute the product of this value with the value in the accumulator.
3. Fetch the contents of memory word 6 and add this value to the value in the accumulator.
4. Store the contents of the accumulator in memory word 7.

In order to store these instructions in computer memory, they must be represented in binary form. The addresses of the data values present no problem, since they can easily be converted to binary addresses:

$$4 = 100_2$$
$$5 = 101_2$$
$$6 = 110_2$$
$$7 = 111_2$$

The operations load, multiply, add, store, and other basic machine instructions are represented by numeric codes, called *opcodes*; for example,

$$\text{LOAD} = 16 = 10000_2$$
$$\text{STORE} = 17 = 10001_2$$
$$\text{ADD} = 35 = 100011_2$$
$$\text{MULTIPLY} = 36 = 100100_2$$

Using part of a word to store the opcode and another part for the address of the *operand*, we could represent our sequence of instructions in *machine language* as

1. 0001000000000100
2. 0010010000000101
3. 0010001100000110
4. 0001000100000111

  opcode   operand

These instructions can then be stored in four (consecutive) memory words. When the program is executed, the control unit will fetch each of these instructions, decode it to determine the operation and the address of the operand, fetch the operand, and then perform the required operation, using the ALU if necessary.

Programs for early computers had to be written in such machine language. Later it became possible to write programs in ***assembly language***, which uses mnemonics (names) in place of numeric opcodes and variable names in place of numeric addresses. For example, the preceding sequence of instructions might be written in assembly language as

1. LOAD *A*
2. MULT *B*
3. ADD *C*
4. STORE *X*

An ***assembler***, part of the system software, translates such assembly language instructions into machine language.

Today, most programs are written in a high-level language such as Pascal, and a ***compiler*** translates each statement in this program into a sequence of basic machine (or assembly) language instructions.

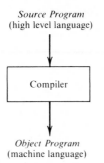

Source Program
(high level language)

Compiler

Object Program
(machine language)

For example, for the preceding problem, the programmer could write the Pascal statement

$$X := A * B + C$$

which instructs the computer to multiply the values of *A* and *B*, add the value of *C*, and assign the value to *X*. The compiler would then translate this statement into the sequence of four machine (or assembly) language instructions considered earlier.

As the preceding diagram indicates, a compiler translates the entire source program into an equivalent object program consisting of machine language instructions. After this translation is complete, this object program is executed by the computer. Some languages are processed using an ***interpreter*** rather than a compiler. An interpreter also examines a source program statement by statement. However, after each statement is translated, the resulting machine language instructions are immediately executed, before the next statement is examined; no object program is actually produced. Still another approach is to compile the source program into a simple machine-independent language called ***intermediate code***. The resulting program might be either interpreted or compiled. In any case, the original source program in a high-level language must be translated into strings of 0s and 1s that represent machine instructions.

Exercises

1. Describe the importance of each of the following persons to the history of computing:

   (a) Charles Babbage   (b) Blaise Pascal
   (c) John von Neumann   (d) Herman Hollerith
   (e) Joseph Jacquard   (f) Gottfried Wilhelm von Leibniz

2. Describe the importance of each of the following devices to the history of computing:

   (a) ENIAC   (b) Analytical Engine
   (c) Jacquard loom   (d) UNIVAC
   (e) Mark I

3. Distinguish the four different generations of computers.

4. Briefly define each of the following terms:

   (a) stored program concept   (b) FORTRAN
   (c) Pascal   (d) CPU
   (e) ALU   (f) peripheral devices
   (g) bit   (h) byte
   (i) word   (j) overflow
   (k) roundoff error   (l) ASCII
   (m) EBCDIC   (n) source program
   (o) object program   (p) compiler
   (q) assembler   (r) assembly language
   (s) machine language

5. Convert each of the following unsigned binary numerals into base 10:

   (a) 1001   (b) 110010
   (c) 1000000   (d) 111111111111111 (fifteen 1's)
   (e) 1.1   (f) 1010.10101

6. An *octal* numeration system uses a base of 8 and the digits 0, 1, 2, 3, 4, 5, 6, and 7. In an octal numeral such as 1703_8, the digits represent coefficients of powers of 8, and so this numeral is an abbreviation for the expanded form

   $$(1 \times 8^3) + (7 \times 8^2) + (0 \times 8^1) + (3 \times 8^0)$$

   and hence has the decimal value

   $$512 + 448 + 0 + 3 = 963$$

   Convert each of the following octal numerals to base 10:

   (a) 123   (b) 2705   (c) 10000
   (d) 77777   (e) 7.2   (f) 123.45

7. A *hexadecimal* numeration system uses a base of 16 and the digits 0, 1, 2, 3, 4, 5, 6, 7, 8, 9, A (ten), B (eleven), C (twelve), D (thirteen), E (fourteen), and F (fifteen). The hexadecimal numeral $5E4_{16}$ has the expanded form

$$(5 \times 16^2) + (14 \times 16^1) + (4 \times 16^0)$$

which has the decimal value

$$1280 + 224 + 4 = 1508$$

Convert each of the following hexadecimal numerals to base 10:

(a) 12   **(b)** 1AB   **(c)** ABC
(d) FFF   **(e)** 8.C   **(f)** AB.CD

8. Conversion from octal representation (see Exercise 6) to binary representation is easy, as we need only replace each octal digit with its three-bit binary equivalent. For example, to convert 617_8 to binary, replace 6 with 110, 1 with 001, and 7 with 111 to obtain 110001111_2. Convert each of the octal numerals in Exercise 6 to binary numerals.

9. Imitating the conversion scheme in Exercise 8, convert each of the hexadecimal numerals in Exercise 7 to binary numerals.

10. To convert a binary numeral to octal, place the digits in groups of three, starting from the binary point, or from the right end if there is no binary point and replace each group with the corresponding octal digit. For example, $10101111_2 = 010\ 101\ 111_2 = 257_8$. Convert each of the binary numerals in Exercise 5 to octal numerals.

11. Imitating the conversion scheme in Exercise 10, convert each of the binary numerals in Exercise 5 to hexadecimal numerals.

12. One method for finding the **base-b** representation of a whole number given in base-10 notation is to divide the number repeatedly by b until a quotient of zero results. The successive remainders are the digits from right to left of the base-b representation. For example, the binary representation of 26 is 11010_2, as the following computation shows:

$$
\begin{array}{r}
0\ R\ 1 \\
2\overline{)1}\ R\ 1 \\
2\overline{)3}\ R\ 0 \\
2\overline{)6}\ R\ 1 \\
2\overline{)13}\ R\ 0 \\
2\overline{)26}
\end{array}
$$

Convert each of the following base-10 numerals to (i) binary, (ii) octal, (iii) hexadecimal:

(a) 27   **(b)** 99   **(c)** 314   **(d)** 5280

13. To convert a decimal fraction to its base-b equivalent, repeatedly multiply the fractional part of the number by b. The integer parts are the digits from left to right of the base-b representation. For example, the decimal numeral 0.6875 corresponds to the binary numeral 0.1011_2, as the following computation shows:

$$
\begin{array}{c|l}
 & .6875 \\
\hline
 & \times 2 \\
\hline
1 & .375 \\
\hline
 & \times 2 \\
\hline
0 & .75 \\
\hline
 & \times 2 \\
\hline
1 & .5 \\
\hline
 & \times 2 \\
\hline
1 & .0 \\
\end{array}
$$

Convert the following base-10 numerals to (i) binary, (ii) octal, (iii) hexadecimal:

(a) 0.5   **(b)** 0.25   **(c)** 0.625
(d) 16.0625   **(e)** 8.828125

14. Even though the base-10 representation of a fraction may terminate, its representation in some other base need not terminate. For example, the following computation shows that the binary representation of 0.7 is $(0.1011001100110011001100110 \ldots)_2$, where the block of bits 0110 is repeated indefinitely. This representation is commonly written as $0.1\overline{0110}_2$.

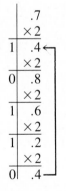

Convert the following base-10 numerals to (i) binary, (ii) octal, (iii) hexadecimal:

(a) 0.3   **(b)** 0.6   **(c)** 0.05   **(d)** $0.\overline{3} = 0.33333 \cdots = 1/3$

15. Find the decimal value of each of the following 16-bit integers, assuming a two's complement representation:

(a) 0000000001000000   **(b)** 1111111111111110
(c) 1111111110111111   **(d)** 0000000011111111
(e) 1111111100000000   **(f)** 1000000000000001

16. Find the 16-bit two's complement representation for each of the following integers:

    (a) 255   (b) 1K
    (c) -255 (d) -256
    (e) -34567_8 (f) $-3ABC_{16}$

17. Assuming two's complement representation, what range of integers can be represented in 8-bit words?

18. Assuming an 11-bit mantissa and a 5-bit exponent as described in the text, and assuming that two's complement representation is used for each, indicate how each of the following real numbers would be stored in a 16-bit word if extra bits in the mantissa are (i) truncated or (ii) rounded:

    (a) 0.375   (b) 37.375
    (c) 0.03125   (d) 63.84375
    (e) 0.1   (f) 0.01

19. Using the tables for ASCII and EBCDIC in Appendix A, indicate how each of the following character strings would be stored in 2-byte words using (i) ASCII and (ii) EBCDIC:

    (a) TO   (b) FOUR   (c) AMOUNT
    (d) ETC.   (e) J. DOE   (f) A#∗4−C

20. Using the instruction mnemonics and opcodes given in the text, write a sequence of (a) assembly language and (b) machine language instructions equivalent to the Pascal statement

    $$X := (A + B) * C$$

    For the machine language instructions, assume that the values of A, B, and C are stored in memory words 15, 16, and 17, respectively, and the value of X is to be stored in memory word 23.

21. Repeat Exercise 20 for the Pascal statement

    $$X := (A + B) * (C + D)$$

    assuming that the value of D is stored in memory word 18.

2

Program Development

People always get what they ask for; the only trouble is that they never know, until they get it, what it actually is that they have asked for.

ALDOUS HUXLEY

The main reason that people learn programming languages is to use the computer as a problem-solving tool. At least four steps can be identified in the computer-aided problem-solving process:

1. Problem analysis and specification.
2. Algorithm development.
3. Program coding.
4. Program execution and testing.

In this chapter we describe and illustrate each of these steps. In the last section, we discuss one additional step that is particularly important in the *life cycle* of programs developed in real-world applications:

5. Program maintenance.

2.1 Problem Analysis and Specification

The first step in the problem-solving process is to review the problem carefully in order to determine its *input*—what information is given and which items are important in solving the problem—and its *output*—what information must be produced to solve the problem. For a problem that appears as an exercise in a programming text, its input and output are the two major parts of the problem's *specification* and are usually not too difficult to identify. In a real-world problem encountered by a professional programmer, the problem's specification often includes other items, as described in Section 2.5, and may require considerable effort to formulate. In this section we consider three problems and illustrate what is involved in their analyses.

PROBLEM 1: Calculating Wages. John Doe is a chocolate chip counter at the Celestial Cookie Company and earns $4.50 per hour. During the week of June 22–26, he worked 38.5 hours. The total tax withheld from his paycheck will be 17.5 percent of his gross pay. What will be his gross pay, how much tax will be withheld for this pay period, and what will be his net pay?

Identifying the input and output in this textbook problem is easy:

Input	Output
Hours worked: 38.5	Gross pay
Hourly rate: $4.50	Amount of tax withheld
Tax-withholding rate: 17.5%	Net pay

The other given items of information—the employee's name, his job, the company name, and the date—are not relevant (at least not for this problem) and can be ignored.

Determining John Doe's gross pay, tax withheld, and net pay can be easily done by hand, or still more easily by using a calculator, and does not warrant the development of a computer program for its solution. A program written to solve this particular problem would probably be used just once; if John Doe works 42 hours next week, or if he receives a raise, or if the tax withholding rate changes, we would have a new problem requiring the development of a new program. This is obviously a waste of effort, since it is clear that each such problem is a special case of the more general problem of finding the gross pay, tax withheld, and net pay for any employee. A program that solves the general problem can be used in a variety of situations and is consequently more useful than is one designed for solving only the original special problem.

One important aspect of problem analysis, therefore, is *generalization*. The effort involved in later phases of the problem-solving process demands that the program eventually developed be sufficiently flexible, that it solve not only the given specific problem but also any related problem of the same kind with little, if any, modification required. In this example, therefore, the specification of the problem could better be formulated in general terms:

Input	Output
Hours worked	Gross pay
Hourly rate	Amount of tax withheld
Tax-withholding rate	Net pay

Obviously, we could generalize still more—allow overtime, allow both salaried and hourly wages, other types of withholding, and so on—but the line must be drawn somewhere or we could go on generalizing forever. In this elementary introduction to the problem-solving process, we wish to keep our examples quite simple.

PROBLEM 2: Pollution Indices.   The level of air pollution in the city of Dogpatch is measured by a pollution index. Readings are made at 12:00 P.M. at three locations: the Abner Coal Plant, downtown at the corner of Daisy Avenue and 5th Street, and at a randomly selected location in a residential area. The average of these three readings is the pollution index, and a value of 50 or greater for this index indicates a hazardous condition, whereas values less than 50 indicate a safe condition. Since this calculation must be done daily, the Dogpatch Environmental Statistician would like a program that calculates the pollution index and then determines the appropriate condition, safe or hazardous.

The relevant given information consists of the three pollution readings and the cutoff value used to distinguish between safe and hazardous conditions. A solution to the problem consists of the pollution index and a message indicating the condition. Generalizing so that any cutoff value, not just 50, can be used, we could specify the problem as follows:

Input	Output
Three pollution readings	Pollution index = the average of the pollution readings
Cutoff value to distinguish between safe and hazardous conditions	Condition—safe or hazardous

PROBLEM 3: Summation.   When the famous mathematician Carl Friedrich Gauss was a young student, his teacher instructed him to add the first 100 positive integers, 1, 2, 3, . . ., 100. (Perhaps this was a form of punishment comparable to "writing lines" today.) What is the value of this sum,

$$1 + 2 + 3 + \cdots + 100 = ?$$

Here the problem analysis is straightforward. Generalizing to find the sum

$$1 + 2 + 3 + \cdots + LastNumber$$

for any positive integer *LastNumber*, we can specify the problem by

Input	Output
LastNumber	Value of $1 + 2 + \cdots + LastNumber$

2.2 Algorithm Development

Once a problem has been specified, a procedure to produce the required output from the given input must be designed. Since the computer is a machine possessing no inherent problem-solving capabilities, this procedure must be formulated as a detailed sequence of simple steps. Such as procedure is called an *algorithm*.

The steps that comprise an algorithm must be organized in a logical and clear manner so that the program that implements this algorithm is similarly well structured. ***Structured algorithms and programs*** are designed using three basic methods of control:

1. ***Sequential***:   Steps are performed in a strictly sequential manner, each step being executed exactly once.
2. ***Selection***:   One of a number of alternative actions is selected and executed.
3. ***Repetition***:   One or more steps is performed repeatedly.

These three structures appear to be very simple, but in fact they are sufficiently powerful that any algorithm can be constructed using them.

Programs to implement algorithms must be written in a language that can be understood by the computer. It is natural, therefore, to describe algorithms in a language that resembles the language used to write computer programs, that is, in a "pseudoprogramming language," or as it is more commonly called, ***pseudocode***.

Unlike high-level programming languages such as Pascal, there is no set of rules that defines precisely what is and what is not pseudocode. It varies from one programmer to another. Pseudocode is a mixture of natural language and symbols, terms, and other features commonly used in one or more high-level languages. Typically one finds the following features in the various pseudocodes that appear in textbooks.

1. The usual computer symbols are used for arithmetic operations: $+$ for addition, $-$ for subtraction, $*$ for multiplication, and $/$ for division.
2. Symbolic names (variables) are used to represent the quantities being processed by the algorithm.
3. Some provision is made for including comments. This is done by enclosing each comment between a pair of special symbols such as $(*$ and $*)$ or $\{$ and $\}$.
4. Certain key words that are common in high-level languages may be used; for example, *read* or *enter* to indicate an input operation; *display*, *print* or *write* for output operations.
5. Indentation is used to indicate certain key blocks of instructions.

The details of an algorithm or part of an algorithm can also be displayed graphically using a ***flowchart***. A flowchart is a diagram that uses the standard symbols shown in Figure 2.1. Each step of the algorithm is displayed within the appropriate symbol, and the order in which these steps are to be carried out is indicated by connecting them with arrows called ***flow lines***.

The structure of an algorithm can also be displayed in a ***structure diagram*** that shows the various tasks that must be performed and their relation to one another. These diagrams are especially useful in describing algorithms for more complex problems and will be described in more detail in Section 2.5. In this section we restrict our attention to the three simple examples introduced in the preceding section. Using these examples, we illustrate the three basic control structures—sequential, selection, and repetition—and how to present algorithms using both pseudocode and flowcharts.

PROBLEM 1: Wage Calculation—Sequential Structure. As we noted in the preceding section, the input for this problem consists of the hours worked, hourly rate, and tax-withholding rate for some employee; the output to be produced consists of the employee's gross pay, amount of tax withheld, and net pay.

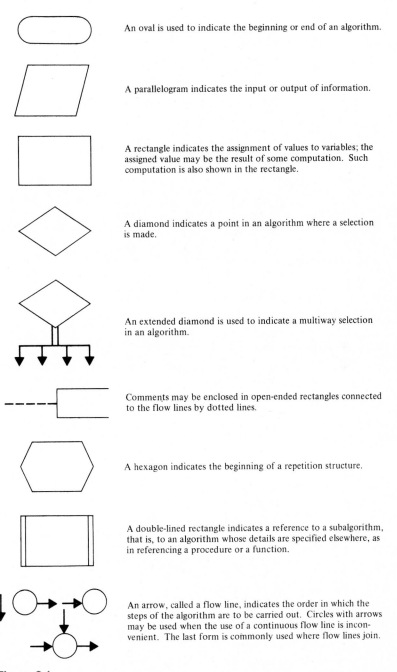

An oval is used to indicate the beginning or end of an algorithm.

A parallelogram indicates the input or output of information.

A rectangle indicates the assignment of values to variables; the assigned value may be the result of some computation. Such computation is also shown in the rectangle.

A diamond indicates a point in an algorithm where a selection is made.

An extended diamond is used to indicate a multiway selection in an algorithm.

Comments may be enclosed in open-ended rectangles connected to the flow lines by dotted lines.

A hexagon indicates the beginning of a repetition structure.

A double-lined rectangle indicates a reference to a subalgorithm, that is, to an algorithm whose details are specified elsewhere, as in referencing a procedure or a function.

An arrow, called a flow line, indicates the order in which the steps of the algorithm are to be carried out. Circles with arrows may be used when the use of a continuous flow line is inconvenient. The last form is commonly used where flow lines join.

Figure 2.1.

The first step in an algorithm for solving this problem is to obtain the values for the input items—hours worked, hourly rate, and tax-withholding rate. The next step is to calculate the gross pay by multiplying the hours worked by the hourly rate. The amount of tax withheld can then be obtained by multiplying the gross pay by the tax rate expressed in decimal form. The net pay is then obtained by subtracting the tax withheld from the gross pay. Finally, the output values—gross pay, tax withheld, and net pay—must be displayed.

This algorithm can be expressed in pseudocode as follows:

ALGORITHM FOR WAGE CALCULATION

(* This algorithm calculates *GrossPay*, *Withhold* (dollar amount of tax withheld), and *NetPay* for a given number of hours worked (*Hours*), a given hourly rate (*HourlyRate*), and a given tax-withholding rate (*TaxRate*) expressed in decimal form *)

1. Enter *Hours, HourlyRate, TaxRate*.
2. Calculate *GrossPay = Hours * HourlyRate*.
3. Calculate *Withhold = GrossPay * TaxRate*.
4. Calculate *NetPay = GrossPay − Withhold*.
5. Display *GrossPay, Withhold, NetPay*.

A flowchart representation of this algorithm might be as follows:

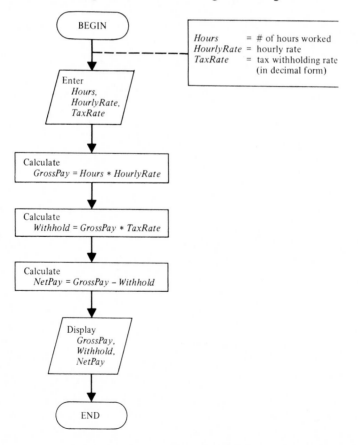

In this example, the steps of the algorithm must be performed in sequence, from beginning to end, with each step being performed exactly once. For other problems, however, the solution may require that some of the steps be performed in some situations and bypassed in others. This is illustrated by our second example.

PROBLEM 2: Pollution Index—Selection Structure.   Recall that, for this problem, the input consists of three pollution readings and a cutoff value that distinguishes between safe and hazardous conditions. The output to be produced consists of the pollution index, which is the average of the three readings, and a message indicating the appropriate condition.

Once again, the first step in an algorithm to solve this problem is to obtain values for the input items—the three pollution readings and the cutoff value. The next step is to calculate the pollution index by averaging the three readings. Now, one of two possible actions must be selected; either a message indicating a safe condition must be displayed or a message indicating a hazardous condition must be displayed. The appropriate action is selected by comparing the pollution index with the cutoff value. In the pseudocode description of this algorithm that follows, this selection is indicated by

>If Index < Cutoff then
>   Display 'Safe condition'
>Else
>   Display 'Hazardous condition'

ALGORITHM FOR POLLUTION INDEX PROBLEM

(∗ This algorithm reads three pollution levels, *Level1*, *Level2*, and *Level3*, and a *Cutoff* value. It then calculates the pollution *Index*. If the value of *Index* is less than *Cutoff*, a message indicating a safe condition is displayed; otherwise, a message indicating a hazardous condition is displayed. ∗)

1. Enter *Level1*, *Level2*, *Level3*, and *Cutoff*.
2. Calculate

$$Index = \frac{Level1 \ + \ Level2 \ + \ Level3}{3}$$

3. If *Index* < *Cutoff* then
>   Display 'Safe condition'
>Else
>   Display 'Hazardous condition'

In a flowchart, a diamond is used to represent a selection (see Figure 2.1). Thus, a flowchart representation of this algorithm might be as follows:

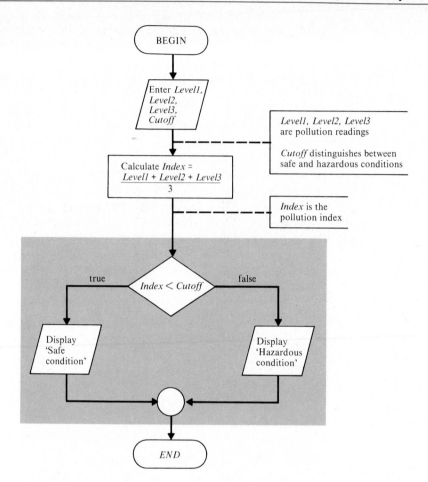

In addition to sequential processing and selection illustrated in the preceding two examples, the solution of other problems may require that a step or a collection of steps be repeated. This is illustrated in our third example.

PROBLEM 3: Summation—Repetition Structure. For this problem, the input consists simply of some positive integer *LastNumber*, and the output is the value of the sum $1 + 2 + \cdots + LastNumber$. To solve this problem in a "brute force" manner (and not using the clever technique discovered by Gauss), we might begin as follows:

$$
\begin{array}{r}
0 \\
+\ 1 \\
\hline
1 \\
+\ 2 \\
\hline
3 \\
+\ 3 \\
\hline
6 \\
+\ 4 \\
\hline
10 \\
+\ 5 \\
\hline
15 \\
\cdot \\
\cdot \\
\cdot
\end{array}
$$

(Although we might not actually write down the first two lines, but rather only "think" them, they are included here for completeness.) We see that the procedure involves two quantities:

1. A counter that is incremented by 1 at each step.
2. The sum of the integers from 1 up to that counter.

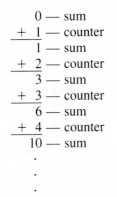

$$
\begin{array}{rl}
0 & - \text{ sum} \\
+ \ 1 & - \text{ counter} \\
\hline
1 & - \text{ sum} \\
+ \ 2 & - \text{ counter} \\
\hline
3 & - \text{ sum} \\
+ \ 3 & - \text{ counter} \\
\hline
6 & - \text{ sum} \\
+ \ 4 & - \text{ counter} \\
\hline
10 & - \text{ sum} \\
\end{array}
$$

.
.
.

The procedure begins with 1 as the value of the counter and with 0 as the initial value of the sum. At each stage, the value of the counter is added to the sum, producing a new sum, and the value of the counter is increased by 1. These steps are repeated until eventually we reach

.
.
.

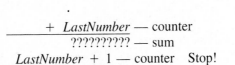

$$
\begin{array}{rl}
+ \ LastNumber & - \text{ counter} \\
\hline
?????????? & - \text{ sum} \\
LastNumber + 1 & - \text{ counter} \quad \text{Stop!}
\end{array}
$$

When the value of the counter exceeds *LastNumber*, the value of the sum is the desired answer, and the computation stops.

In the pseudocode description of this algorithm that follows, the repetition is indicated by

While *Counter* ≤ *LastNumber* do the following:
    a. Add *Counter* to *Sum*.
    b. Increment *Counter* by 1.

This instruction specifies that statements a and b are to be repeated as long as the condition *Counter* ≤ *LastNumber* remains true. Thus, when the value of *Counter* exceeds *LastNumber*, this repetition is terminated and Statement 5 is executed.

ALGORITHM FOR SUMMATION PROBLEM

(∗ This algorithm calculates the value of the sum

$$1 + 2 + \cdots + LastNumber$$

for some positive integer *LastNumber*. It uses the variable *Counter* as a counter and the variable *Sum* for this sum. ∗)

1. Enter *LastNumber*.
2. Set *Counter* to 1.
3. Set *Sum* to 0.
4. While *Counter* ≤ *LastNumber* do the following:
   a. Add *Counter* to *Sum*.
   b. Increment *Counter* by 1.
5. Display *Sum*.

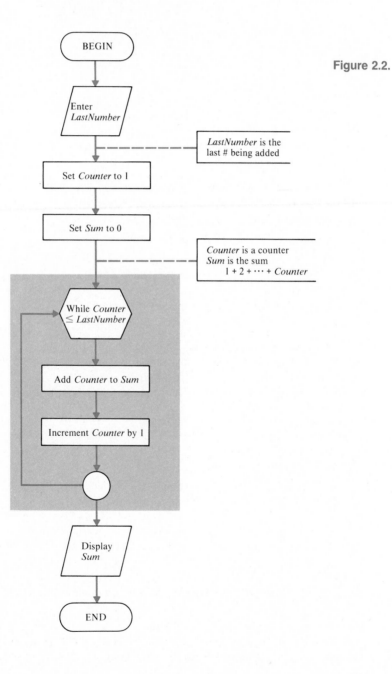

Figure 2.2.

In a flowchart, repetition can be indicated by using a hexagon containing the information that controls the repetition at the beginning of the steps to be repeated, a small circle after these statements, and an arrow from this circle back to the hexagon. Thus, in the flowchart of Figure 2.2, which represents the algorithm for the summation problem, repetition is indicated by

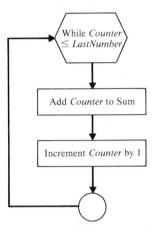

The three control structures in these examples, **sequential, selection**, and **repetition**, are used throughout this text in designing algorithms to solve problems. The implementation of each of them in a Pascal program is considered in detail in later chapters.

2.3   Program Coding

The third step in using the computer to solve a problem is to express the algorithm in a programming language. In the second step, the algorithm may be described in a natural language or pseudocode, but the program that implements that algorithm must be written in the vocabulary of a programming language and must conform to the **syntax**, or grammatical rules, of that language. The major portion of this text is concerned with the vocabulary and syntax of the programming language Pascal. In this section we introduce some elementary features of this language and give an example of a simple Pascal program. These features will be discussed in detail in subsequent chapters.

In the three examples in the preceding section, we used names to identify various quantities. These names are called **variables**. In the first example, the variables *Hours, HourlyRate,* and *TaxRate* represented the hours worked, hourly rate, and tax-withholding rate, respectively. The output in this example was the employee's gross pay, dollar amount of tax withheld, and net pay, as represented by the variables *GrossPay, Withhold,* and *NetPay,* respectively. In the second example, the variables *Level1, Level2, Level3, Cutoff,* and *Index* were used, and in the third example, our variables were *LastNumber, Counter,* and *Sum.*

In Pascal, variable names must begin with a letter, which may be followed by any combination of letters and digits. This allows us to choose names that suggest what the variable represents, for example, *Hours, HourlyRate, Tax-*

Rate, GrossPay, Level1, LastNumber, and *Sum. Meaningful variable names should always be used because they make the program easier to read and understand.*

In the examples we have been considering, two types of numbers are used. The values of *Level1, Level2, Level3, Cutoff,* and *Index* in the second example, and *LastNumber, Counter,* and *Sum* in the third example, are integers, whereas the values of *Hours, HourlyRate, TaxRate, GrossPay, Withhold,* and *NetPay* in the first example are real; that is, they have fractional parts. Pascal distinguishes between these two types of numeric data, and the types of the values that each variable may have must be specified. This is done by placing declarations of the form

> **var**
>   *list1* : *integer*;
>   *list2* : *real*;

at the beginning of the program, where *list1* is a list of the variable names of integer type and *list2* is a list of variable names of real type. Thus, the types of the Pascal variables in the first example can be specified by

> **var**
>   *Hours, HourlyRate, TaxRate,*
>   *GrossPay, Withhold, NetPay* : *real*;

and those in the third example by

> **var**
>   *Counter, Sum* : *integer*;

Notice that **var** is shown here in boldface. In this text, the words printed in boldface are ***reserved words*** in Pascal. They may not be used for any purpose other than those designated by the rules of the language. For example, reserved words may not be used as variable names.

Addition and subtraction are denoted in Pascal by the usual + and − symbols. Multiplication is denoted by ∗ and division by /. The assignment operation is denoted by := in Pascal programs. For example, the statement

> *GrossPay* := *Hours* ∗ *HourlyRate*

calculates the value of the product

> *Hours* ∗ *HourlyRate*

and assigns this value to the variable *GrossPay.*

In the pseudocode description of an algorithm in the preceding section, we used the words "enter" and "read" for input operations and "display," "print," and "write" for output operations. In a flowchart, a parallelogram is used to indicate the input or output of information. One Pascal statement that may be used for input is the *readln* statement. A simple form of this statement is

    readln (list)

where *list* is a list of variables for which values are to be read. For example, the statement

    readln (Hours, HourlyRate, TaxRate)

reads values for the variables *Hours, HourlyRate,* and *TaxRate* from some input device.

    A simple output statement in Pascal is the *writeln* statement of the form

    writeln (list)

where *list* is a list of items to be displayed. For example, the statement

    writeln ('Gross wages =', GrossPay)

displays the label

    Gross wages =

followed by the value of the variable *GrossPay*.

    Comments can also be incorporated into Pascal programs. They are indicated by enclosing them within (∗ and ∗)

    (∗ comment ∗)

or within braces

    { comment }

    Figure 2.3 shows a Pascal program for the algorithm to solve the wage calculation problem considered earlier in this chapter. The program begins with the **program heading**

    program *Wages (input, output)*;

```
PROGRAM Wages (input, output);
(*******************************************************************

   Program to read the hours worked, hourly rate, and a tax
   withholding rate for an employee, then calculate and
   display his/her gross pay, tax withheld, and net pay.

*****************************************************************)
```
Figure 2.3.

Figure 2.3. (cont.)

```
VAR
    Hours,              (* hours worked *)
    HourlyRate,         (* hourly pay rate *)
    TaxRate,            (* tax-withholding rate *)
    GrossPay,           (* gross wages *)
    Withhold,           (* amount of tax withheld *)
    NetPay : real;      (* net pay *)

BEGIN
    writeln ('Enter hours worked, hourly rate, and tax rate');
    readln (Hours, HourlyRate, TaxRate);
    GrossPay := Hours * HourlyRate;
    Withhold := GrossPay * TaxRate;
    NetPay := GrossPay - Withhold;
    writeln ('Gross pay = $', GrossPay:6:2);
    writeln ('Amount of tax withheld = $', Withhold:6:2);
    writeln ('Net pay =   $', NetPay:6:2)
END.



Sample run:
```

```
Enter hours worked, hourly rate, and tax rate
38.5 4.50 0.175
Gross pay = $173.25
Amount of tax withheld = $ 30.32
Net pay =   $142.93
```

where *Wages* is the name assigned to the program by the programmer, and *input* and *output* indicate that certain information will be input to the program from an external source and that the program will also produce some output.

The first step in the algorithm is an input instruction to enter values for the variables *Hours*, *HourlyRate*, and *TaxRate*:

1. Enter *Hours, HourlyRate, TaxRate*.

This is translated into two statements in the program:

writeln ('Enter hours worked, hourly rate, and tax rate');
readln (*Hours, HourlyRate, TaxRate*);

The *writeln* statement is used to prompt the user that the values are to be entered. The *readln* statement actually assigns the three values entered by the user to the three variables *Hours*, *HourlyRate*, and *TaxRate*. Thus, in the sample run shown, when the user enters

38.5   4.50   0.175

the value 38.5 is assigned to *Hours*, 4.50 to *HourlyRate*, and 0.175 to *TaxRate*. The next three steps in the algorithm

2. Calculate *GrossPay* = *Hours* ∗ *HourlyRate*.
3. Calculate *Withhold* = *GrossPay* ∗ *TaxRate*.
4. Calculate *NetPay* = *GrossPay* − *Withhold*.

translate into the Pascal assignment statements

GrossPay := *Hours* * *HourlyRate*;
Withhold := *GrossPay* * *TaxRate*;
NetPay := *GrossPay* − *Withhold*;

The output instruction

5. Display *GrossPay*, *Withhold*, *NetPay*.

is translated into the three Pascal statements

writeln ('Gross pay = $', *GrossPay*:6:2);
writeln ('Amount of tax withheld = $', *Withhold*:6:2);
writeln ('Net pay = $', *Netpay*:6:2)

As the sample run shows, each *writeln* statement produces one line of output. Each line consists of an appropriate label followed by the value, rounded to two decimal places, of the corresponding variable in a six-space zone:

Gross pay = $173.25
Amount of tax withheld = $ 30.32
Net pay = $142.93

The end of the program is indicated by the Pascal reserved word **end** followed by a period. Note that the statements in the program are separated by semicolons.

2.4   Program Execution and Testing

The fourth step in using the computer to solve a problem is to execute and test the program. The procedure for submitting a program to a computer varies from one system to another; the details regarding your particular system can be obtained from your instructor, computer center personnel, or user manuals supplied by the manufacturer.

Access to the computer system must first be obtained. In the case of a personal computer, this may require turning the machine on and inserting the appropriate diskette in the disk drive. For a larger system, some *login* procedure may be required to establish contact between a remote terminal and the computer. Once access has been gained, the program must be entered, often using an *editor* provided in the system's software. For example, to enter a program like that in Figure 2.3, the user might access an editor for entering Pascal programs and then enter the program as follows:

```
OK, EDPAS                                                              |
INPUT                                                                  |
PROGRAM Wages (input, output);                                         |
                                                                       |
(**************************************************************        |
                                                                       |
  Program to read the hours worked, hourly rate, and a tax            |
  withholding rate for an employee, then calculate and                |
  display his/her gross pay, tax withheld, and net pay.               |
                                                                       |
*************************************************************)         |
```

```
VAR
    Hours,            (* hours worked *)
    HourlyRate,       (* hourly pay rate *)              |--> Using a
    TaxRate,          (* tax-withholding rate *)         |--> system
    GrossPay,         (* gross wages *)                  |--> editor
    Withhold,         (* amount of tax withheld *)       |--> to create
    NetPay : real;    (* net pay *)                      |--> the Pascal
                                                         |--> program
BEGIN                                                    |
    writeln ('Enter hours worked, hourly rate, and tax rate');|
    readln (Hours, HourlyRate, TaxRate)                  |
    GrossPay := Hours * HourlyRate;                      |
    Withhold := GrosPay * TaxRate;                       |
    NetPay := GrossPay - Withhold;                       |
    writeln ('Gross pay = $', GrossPay:6:2);             |
    writeln ('Amount of tax withheld = $', Withhold:6:2);|
    writeln ('Net pay =    $', NetPay:6:2)               |
END.                                                     |
                                                         |
EDIT                                                     |
FILE SAMPLE.PASCAL                                       |
                                                        /
OK,
```

Once the program has been entered, it is compiled and executed by giving appropriate system commands; for example,

```
OK, RUN SAMPLE.PASCAL
No errors reported.

Executing WAGES

Enter hours worked, hourly rate, and tax rate
38.5 4.50 0.175
Gross pay = $173.25
Amount of tax withheld = $ 30.32
Net pay =    $142.93
```

Here the user gave the RUN command to compile the program, which had previously been saved on disk under the name SAMPLE.PASCAL. Since no errors were detected during compilation, execution of the resulting object program was initiated. A message prompting the user for three input values was displayed by the program, and after these values were entered, the desired output values were calculated and displayed.

In this example, we have illustrated the *interactive mode* of processing, in which the user entered data values 38.5, 4.50, and 0.175 from a terminal during program execution, and the output produced by the program was also displayed at the terminal. Another common mode of operation is *batch processing*. In this mode, a file containing the program, the data, and certain command lines must be prepared by the user. This file is then submitted to the system, and execution proceeds without any user interaction. For some systems, programs, data, and command lines may be entered using punched cards. These cards are prepared using a keypunch, which has a typewriter-like keyboard and which codes the information entered from the keyboard by punching holes in a card. The information from these cards is then entered into a computer via a card reader, and the results are returned to the user via an output device such as a line printer.

In this example, the program was entered, compiled, and executed without error. Usually, however, the beginning programmer will make some errors in designing the program or in attempting to enter and execute it. Errors may be detected at various stages of program processing and may cause the processing to be terminated ("aborted"). For example, an incorrect system command will be detected early in the processing and will usually prevent compilation and execution of the program. Errors in the program's syntax, such as incorrect punctuation or misspelled key words, will be detected during compilation. (In some systems, syntax errors may be detected while the program is being entered.) Such errors are called **syntax errors** or **compile-time errors** and will usually make it impossible to complete the compilation and execution of the program. For example, if the output statement that prompts the user to enter values was mistakenly entered as

writeln ('Enter hours worked, hourly rate, and tax rate';

with a missing right parenthesis, an attempt to compile and execute the program might result in a message like the following, signaling a "fatal" error:

```
OK, RUN SAMPLE.PASCAL
   20    writeln ('Enter hours worked, hourly rate, and tax rate';
*****                                                              ↑
***** Symbol expected was ")"

1 error reported.
```

Less severe errors may generate "warning" messages, but the compilation will be continued and execution of the resulting object program attempted.

Other errors, such as an attempt to divide by zero in an arithmetic expression, may not be detected until the execution of the program has begun. Such errors are called **run-time errors**. The error messages displayed by your particular system can be found in the user manuals supplied by the manufacturer. In any case, the errors must be corrected by replacing the erroneous statements with correct ones, and the modified program must be recompiled and then reexecuted.

Errors that are detected by the computer system are relatively easy to identify and correct. There are, however, other errors that are more subtle and difficult to identify. These are **logical errors** that arise in the design of the algorithm or in the coding of the program that implements the algorithm. For example, if the statement

GrossPay := *Hours * HourlyRate*

in the program of Figure 2.3 were mistakenly entered as

GrossPay := *Hours + HourlyRate*

with the multiplication symbol (*) replaced by the symbol for addition (+), the program would still be syntactically correct. No error would occur during the compilation or execution of the program. But the results produced by the program would be incorrect because an incorrect formula would have been used to calculate the gross pay. Thus, if the values 38.5, 4.50, and 0.175 were entered for the variables *Hours, HourlyRate*, and *TaxRate*, respectively, the output produced by the program would be

    Gross pay = $ 43.00
    Amount of tax withheld = $ 7.52
    Net pay = $ 35.48

instead of the correct output

    Gross pay = $173.25
    Amount of tax withheld = $ 30.32
    Net pay = $142.93

as shown in the sample run in Figure 2.3.

Since it may not be obvious whether the results produced by a program are correct, *it is important that the user run a program several times with input data for which the correct results are known in advance.* For the preceding example, it is easy to calculate by hand the correct answer for values such as 10.0, 2.00, and 0.25 for *Hours, HourlyRate*, and *TaxRate*, respectively, to check the output produced by the program. This process of **program validation** is extremely important, as a *program cannot be considered to be correct if it has not been validated with several sets of test data.* The test data should be carefully selected so that each part of the program can be checked.

2.5 Software Engineering

Programming and problem-solving is an art in that it requires a good deal of imagination, ingenuity, and creativity. But it is also a science in that certain techniques and methodologies are commonly used. The term **software engineering** has come to be applied to the study and use of these techniques.

As we noted in the introduction to this chapter, the **life cycle** of software, that is, programs, consists of five basic phases:

1. Problem analysis and specification.
2. Algorithm development.
3. Program coding.
4. Program execution and testing.
5. Program maintenance.

In the preceding sections we have described the first four phases and illustrated them with some examples. It must be emphasized, however, that these examples were deliberately kept simple so the main ideas could be emphasized without getting lost in a maze of details. In real-world applications and in later problems in this text, these phases may be considerably more complex. In this section we reexamine each of these phases and describe some of the additional questions and complications that face professional programmers, and some of the software engineering techniques used in dealing with them.

Problem Analysis and Specification. Like exercises and problems in most programming texts, the examples we have considered thus far were quite simple and, we hope, clearly stated. Analysis of these problems to identify the input and output was, therefore, quite easy. This is not the case, however, in most real-world problems. These problems are often stated vaguely and imprecisely, since the person posing the problem often does not fully understand it. For example, the wage calculation problem considered in Section 2.1 might have been presented to the programmer as a request to "computerize the payroll system for the Celestial Cookie Company."

In these situations, there are many questions that must be answered in order to complete the problem's specification. Some of these answers are required to describe the problem's input and output more completely. What information is available for each employee? How is the program to access this data? Has this information been validated or must the program provide error checking? In what format should the output be displayed? Are paychecks being printed? Must additional reports be generated for company executives and/or government agencies?

Other questions deal more directly with the processing that is required. Are employees paid on an hourly or a salaried basis, or are there some of each? What premium, if any, is paid for overtime? What items must be withheld— for federal, state, and city income taxes, retirement plans, insurance, etc.— and how are they to be computed?

Many other questions must be answered before the specification of the problem is complete and before design of the algorithms and programs can begin. Will the users of the program be technically sophisticated or must the program be made very user friendly to accommodate novice users? How often will the program be used? What are the response time requirements? What is the expected life of the program, that is, how long will it be used and what changes can be expected in the future? What hardware and software are available?

Although this list is by no means exhaustive, it does indicate the wide range of information that must be obtained in analyzing and specifying the problem. In some situations this is done by a *systems analyst*, while in others it is part of the programmer's responsibility.

Algorithm Design. The solution of a complex problem may require so many steps in the final algorithm that they cannot all be anticipated at the outset. To attack such problems, a *top-down* approach is commonly used. We begin by identifying the major tasks to be performed to solve the problem and arranging them in the order in which they are to be carried out. These tasks and their relation to one another can be displayed in a one-level *structure diagram*. For example, a first structure diagram for the wage calculation problem might have the form

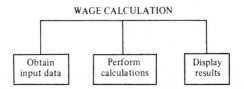

Usually one or more of these first-level tasks are still quite complex and must be divided into subtasks. For example, in the wage calculation problem, some of the input data, such as the employee's name, social security number, and number of dependents, are permanent information and may be stored in a system file, while other information, such as hours worked, will be entered during program execution. Consequently, the task "Obtain input data" can be subdivided into two subtasks:

1. Obtain permanent employee information.
2. Obtain current information.

Similarly, the task "Perform calculations" may be split into three subtasks:

1. Calculate gross pay.
2. Calculate withholding.
3. Calculate net pay.

Finally, the third task, "Display results," might be subdivided into

1. Print paychecks.
2. Print summary reports.

In a structure diagram, these subtasks are placed on a second level below the corresponding main task as pictured in the first diagram on page 45.

These subtasks may require further division into still smaller subtasks, resulting in additional levels as illustrated in the second diagram on page 45. This *successive refinement* continues until each subtask is sufficiently simple that design of an algorithm for that subtask is straightforward.

This *divide-and-conquer* approach can thus be used to divide a complex problem into a number of simpler subproblems. This allows the programmer to design and test an algorithm and a corresponding program *module* for each subproblem independently of the others. For very large projects, a team approach might be used in which the low-level subtasks are assigned to different programmers. The individual program modules developed by them are eventually combined into one complete program that solves the original problem.

Program Coding.   The first decision that must be made in translating an algorithm into a program is what programming language to use. This obviously depends on the languages available to the programmer, but other factors also influence the decision. There may be characteristics of the problem that make one language more appropriate than another. For example, if the problem involves scientific computations requiring extended precision and/or complex arithmetic, FORTRAN may be the most suitable language. Problems that involve a large amount of file input/output and report generation can perhaps best be handled in COBOL. Structured algorithms, especially those developed in a top-down manner, can be implemented most easily in a structured language like Pascal.

Regardless of which language is used, there are certain programming principles that have been developed to assist in designing programs that can be easily read and understood. The first principle is that each program should contain *documentation*, that is, information that explains what the program

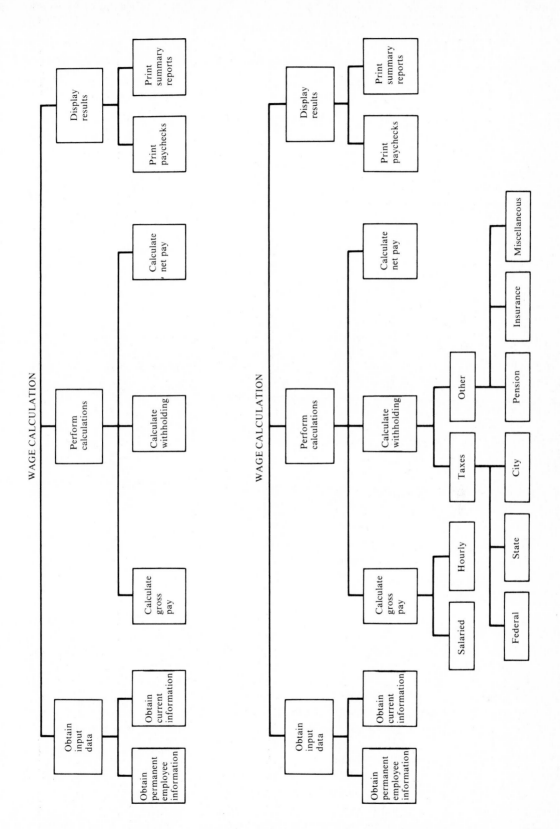

does, how it works, what variables it uses, any special algorithms it implements, and so on. There are two simple guidelines that are especially useful in this regard:

1. Each variable name should suggest the quantity it represents.

For example, the statement

$$Distance := Rate * Time$$

means more than does

$$X7 := R * Zeke$$

2. The program should include comments that make it easier to understand.

This may include comments at the beginning of the program that identify the author of the program, indicate the date it was written, and briefly describe the variables and the purpose of the program. In addition, comments should be used throughout the program to explain the purpose of the main sections of the program. Such comments should be few and brief. Too many or too detailed comments clutter the program, making it more difficult to read.

A second principle is that the program should be readable, and its physical appearance should reflect its structure. Three simple guidelines that are useful in this regard are the following:

1. Spaces between items in a Pascal statement should be used as needed to improve its readability.

For example, the statement

$$Sum := Sum + Counter;$$

is more readable and pleasing to the eye than either

$$Sum:=Sum+Counter;$$

or

$$Sum \qquad := Sum+ \qquad Counter;$$

2. Blank lines should be used to separate program sections.
3. Statements making up a block should be indented to emphasize this relationship.

As we discuss features of the Pascal language in the chapters that follow, additional principles for program design will be given. It is important for the beginning programmer to follow these guidelines, even in early simple programs, so that good habits are established and carried on into the design of more complex programs.

Program Execution and Testing.   Obviously, the most important characteristic of any program is that it be *correct*. No matter how well structured, how well documented, or how nice the program looks, if it does not produce correct results, it is worthless. As we have seen, the fact that a program executes with no error messages produced is no guarantee that it is correct. The results produced may be erroneous due to logical errors that the computer system cannot detect. It is the responsibility of the programmer to test each program in order to ensure that it is correct. (See Section 4.8 for more about program testing.)

Program Maintenance. The life cycle of a program written by a student programmer normally ends with the fourth phase; that is, once the program has been written, executed, and tested, the assignment is complete. Programs in real-world applications, however, will likely be used for a number of years and will probably require some modification as time passes. Especially in large programs developed for complex projects, there will usually be obscure bugs that do not become apparent until after the program has been placed in use. Correction of these flaws is obviously one aspect of program maintenance. It may also be necessary or desirable to modify the program in order to improve its performance, add new features, and so on. Other modifications may be required due to changes in the computer hardware and/or the system software such as the operating system. External factors may also force program modification; for example, changes in the tax laws may require revision of part of a payroll program.

Software maintenance is, in fact, a major component of the life cycle of a program and may account for as much as 80 percent of its total cost. This fact, combined with the fact that most program maintenance is done by someone not involved in the original design, makes it mandatory that the programmer do his or her utmost to design a program that is readable, documented, and well structured so that it is easy to understand and modify.

Exercises

For each of the problems described in Exercises 1 through 10, identify the information that must be produced to solve the problem and the given information that will be useful in obtaining the solution. Then design an algorithm to solve the problem.

1. Calculate and display the circumference and area of a circle with a given radius.

2. Two common temperature scales are the Fahrenheit and Celsius scales. The boiling point of water is 212° on the Fahrenheit scale and 100° on the Celsius scale. The freezing point of water is 32° on the Fahrenheit scale and 0° on the Celsius scale. Assuming a linear relationship $(F = a \cdot C + b)$ between these two temperature scales, convert a temperature on the Celsius scale to the corresponding Fahrenheit temperature.

3. Calculate and display the largest and smallest of three given test scores.

4. Calculate and display the largest, the smallest, and the range (largest − smallest) of any given set of test scores.

5. The business manager of a certain company desires a program to calculate the wages for the company's employees. This program should accept an employee number, his or her base pay rate per hour, and the number of hours worked. All hours above 40 are to be paid at the overtime rate of 1.5 times the base rate. For each employee, the program should print his or her number, total number of hours worked, base pay rate, and total wages, and it should also print the total of all wages paid by the company.

6. A certain city classifies a pollution index of less than 35 as "pleasant," 35 through 60 as "unpleasant," and above 60 as "hazardous." The city pollution control office desires a program that will accept several values of the pollution index and will produce the appropriate classification for each.

7. Suppose that a professor gave a quiz to her class and compiled a list of scores ranging from 50 through 100. She intends to use only three grades: A if the score is 90 or greater, B if it is below 90 but above or equal to 75, and C if it is below 75. She would like a program to assign the appropriate letter grades to the numeric scores.

8. The "divide and average" algorithm for approximating the square root of any positive number A is as follows: Take any initial approximation X that is positive and then find a new approximation by calculating the average of X and A/X, that is, $(X + A/X)/2$. Repeat this procedure with X replaced by this new approximation, stopping when X and A/X differ in absolute value by some specified error allowance, such as 0.00001.

9. The quadratic equation $Ax^2 + Bx + C = 0$ has no real roots if the discriminant $B^2 - 4AC$ is negative; it has one real root, $-B/2A$, if the discriminant is zero; and it has two real roots given by the quadratic formula

$$\frac{-B \pm \sqrt{B^2 - 4AC}}{2A}$$

if the discriminant is positive. A program is to be developed to solve several different quadratic equations or to indicate that there are no real solutions.

10. The Rinky Dooflingy Company currently sells 200 dooflingies per month at a profit of $300 per dooflingy. The company now spends $2000 per month on advertising and has a fixed operating cost of $10,000 per month that does not depend on the volume of sales. If the company doubles the amount spent on advertising, its sales will increase by 20 percent. The company president would like to know, beginning with the company's current status and successively doubling the amount spent on advertising, at what point the net profit will "go over the hump," that is, begin to decline.

11. Enter and execute the following short Pascal program on your computer system:

    program *Exercise11* (*input, output*);
    (* Program to perform various arithmetic
        operations on two numbers *X* and *Y*. *)

    var
        X, Y, Sum : *integer*;

    begin
        X := 214;
        Y := 2057;
        Sum := *X* + *Y*;
        writeln ('Sum of', *X, Y,* ' is', *Sum*)
    end.

12. Make the following changes in the program in Exercise 11 and execute the modified program:

    (a) Change 214 to 1723 in the statement assigning a value to *X*.
    (b) Change the variable names *X* and *Y* to *Alpha* and *Beta* throughout.
    (c) Insert the comment

    (* Calculate the sum *)

    before the statement

    Sum := *Alpha* + *Beta*;

    (d) Insert the following comment and statement before the *writeln* statement:

    (* Now calculate the differcence *)
    Difference := *Alpha* − *Beta*;

    change the variable declaration to

    var
        Alpha, Beta, Sum, Difference : *integer*;

    and add the following statement after the *writeln* statement:

    writeln ('Difference of', *Alpha, Beta,* ' is', *Difference*)

    Note: For the modified program to work correctly, you must also insert a semicolon at an appropriate location.

13. Using the program in Figure 2.3 as a guide, write a Pascal program for the algorithm in Exercise 1.

14. Using the program in Figure 2.3 as a guide, write a Pascal program for the algorithm in Exercise 2.

3

Basic Pascal

Kindly enter them in your note-book.
And, in order to refer to them
conveniently, let's call them A, B, and Z.

THE TORTOISE IN LEWIS CARROLL'S
What the Tortoise Said to Achilles

In language, clarity is everything.

CONFUCIUS

One important phase in using the computer to solve a problem is the implementation of the algorithm for solving that problem as a program. Whereas algorithms can be described somewhat informally in a pseudoprogramming language, the corresponding program must be written in strict compliance with the rules of some programming language. There are two important aspects of any programming language, its syntax and its semantics. The *syntax* of a language is its grammar, that is, the set of rules for forming words and statements in that language. The interpretation or meaning of the statements in a language is called its *semantics*. In this chapter we begin our study of these two aspects of the Pascal language.

As we noted in Chapter 1, the programming language Pascal was developed in the late 1960s and early 1970s by the Swiss computer scientist Niklaus Wirth. Different versions of Pascal have appeared since its introduction, and for several years the *Pascal User Manual and Report* written by Wirth and Kathleen Jensen and published in 1974 served as the *de facto* standard. In 1983 an official standard was prepared by committees of the American National Standards Institute (ANSI) and the Institute of Electrical and Electronic Engineers (IEEE) and was published as the *American National Standard Pascal Computer Programming Language*. This ANSI/IEEE standard is the basis for this text. However, a number of other versions of Pascal that provide useful variations of and extensions to the standard have become popular. Some of these features are summarized in the Variations and Extensions sections at the chapter ends, and Appendix G gives additional details.

3.1   From Algorithms to Programs

An algorithm for the solution of a problem is a sequence of steps that must be performed in order to obtain the solution of the problem from the information given in the problem's specification. Thus, a computer program that implements such an algorithm must accept and store the given information, perform the sequence of steps required to solve the problem (which may also require calculating and storing some intermediate results), and finally, display the results. This general structure is reflected in the organization of a Pascal program.

The first statement of a Pascal program is a ***program heading***. This statement gives the program a name and, more importantly, indicates the kinds of input/output operations that will be performed. The second part is a ***declaration part*** in which variables (among other things) that will be used to store input and output values as well as intermediate results are listed. The last part of a Pascal program is the ***statement part***. It is this part that contains the statements that actually carry out the steps of the alogrithm.

A Pascal program thus has the general form

    program heading
    declaration part
    statement part.

(Note the required period that follows the statement part.) Each of these parts is described in detail in the following sections.

3.2   Data Types

Computer programs, regardless of the language in which they are written, are designed to manipulate some kind of data. Thus we begin by considering the types of data that can be processed in a Pascal program.

Pascal provides four standard types of data:

    integer
    real
    char
    boolean

The first two are numeric types and are used to process different kinds of numbers. The *char* type is used to process character data. The *boolean* type is used to process so-called boolean or logical data; such data may have either the value true or the value false.

Constants.   *Constants* are quantities whose values do not change during program execution. They may be of numeric, character, or boolean type. An *integer* constant is a string of digits that does not include commas or a decimal point; negative integer constants must be preceded by a negative sign, but a plus sign is optional for nonnegative integers. Thus

$$
\begin{aligned}
&0\\
&137\\
&-2516\\
&+17745
\end{aligned}
$$

are valid integer constants, whereas the following are invalid for the reasons indicated:

    5,280   (Commas are not allowed in integer constants.)
    16.0   (Integer constants may not contain decimal points.)
    − −5   (Only one algebraic sign is allowed.)
    7 −   (The algebraic sign must precede the string of digits.)

Another type of numeric data is the *real* type. Constants of this type may be represented as ordinary decimal numbers or in scientific notation. The *decimal* representation of real constants must include exactly one decimal point, but the constant may not begin or end with a decimal point. As in the case of integer constants, no commas are allowed. Negative real constants must be preceded by a negative sign, but the plus sign is optional for nonnegative reals. Thus

$$
\begin{aligned}
&1.234\\
&-0.1536\\
&+56473.0
\end{aligned}
$$

are valid real constants, whereas the following are invalid for the reasons indicated:

    1,752.63   (Commas are not allowed in real constants.)
    82   (Real constants in decimal form must contain a decimal point.)
    .01   (Real constants may not begin with a decimal point.)
    24.   (Real constants may not end with a decimal point.)

The *scientific* or *floating point* representation of a real constant consists of an integer or real constant in decimal form followed by the letter E (or e) followed by integer constant that is interpreted as an exponent on the base 10. For example, the real constant 337.456 may also be written as

$$3.37456E2$$

which means

$$3.37456 \times 10^2$$

or it may be written in a variety of other forms, such as

$$0.337456E3$$
$$337.456E0$$
$$33745.6E-2$$
$$337456E-3$$

A *character* is one of the symbols in the Pascal character set. Although this character set may vary from one Pascal implementation to another, it usually includes digits 0 through 9; upper-case letters A through Z; lower-case letters a through z; usual punctuation symbols such as the semicolon (;), comma (,), and period (.); and special symbols such as $+$, $=$, $>$, and $\uparrow$. In fact, many Pascal implementations allow a character to be any symbol from the character set for that machine. (See Appendix A for two commonly used character sets, ASCII and EBCDIC.)

A *character constant* consists of a character enclosed within single quotes (apostrophes); for example,

'A', '+', '3', ':'

If a character constant is to consist of an apostrophe, it must appear as a pair of apostrophes enclosed within single quotes (apostrophes):

''''

A sequence of characters is commonly called a *string*, and a *string constant* consists of a string enclosed within single quotes. Thus

'John Q. Doe'

and

'PDQ123−A'

are valid string constants. Again, if an apostrophe is one of the characters in a string constant, it must appear as a pair of apostrophes; for example,

'Don''t'

The type *boolean* is named after the nineteenth-century mathematician George Boole, who originated the logical calculus. There are only two *boolean constants*,

true

and

false

These constants are called *logical* constants in some programming languages.

Identifiers. *Identifiers* are names given to programs, constants, variables, and other entities in a program. Identifiers may contain any number of letters or digits, but must begin with a letter. *This allows one to choose meaningful identifiers that suggest what they represent.*

Pascal *reserved words* such as **var**, **begin**, and **end** may not be used as identifiers, since they have a special meaning in Pascal. A complete list of reserved words is given in Appendix B. There are also certain *standard identifiers* in Pascal, such as *integer, real, true, false, read, readln, write,* and *writeln. These identifiers have predefined meaning, but they are not reserved words. Consequently, they may be redefined by the programmer, but it is not good practice to do so.* A complete list of standard identifiers is given in Appendix B.

Since *Pascal makes no distinction between upper case and lower case* (except in character and string constants), one may use upper- and lower-case letters in any way that will improve the program's readability. A common practice, and one that we use in the sample programs of this text, is to write all reserved words in upper case and all identifiers in lower case, usually capitalizing the first letter if it is user defined. If the identifier is made up of several words, we usually capitalize the first letter of each. For example, *HourlyRate* is a valid identifier and will not be distinguished from *HOURLYRATE, hourlyrate,* or *HoURlyRaTE,* even if one form is used one place in the program and another is used somewhere else.

Variables. In mathematics, a symbolic name is often used to refer to a quantity. For example, the formula

$$A = l \cdot w$$

is used to calculate the area (denoted by A) of a rectangle with a given length (denoted by l) and a given width (denoted by w). These symbolic names, A, l, and w, are called *variables*. If specific values are assigned to l and w, this formula can be used to calculate the value of A, which then represents the area of a particular rectangle.

Variables were also used in Chapter 2 in the discussion of algorithms and programs. When a variable is used in a Pascal program, the compiler associates it with a particular memory location. The value of a variable at any time is the value stored in the associated memory location at that time. Variable names are identifiers and thus must follow the rules for forming valid identifiers.

The type of a Pascal variable must be one of the four data types described earlier (or one of the other data types discussed later), and the type of each variable determines the type of value that may be stored in that variable. It is therefore necessary to specify the type of each variable in a Pascal program. This is done in the *variable section* of the declaration part of the program. This section begins with the reserved word **var** and has the form

> **var**
>   *variable-list-1* : *type-1*;
>   *variable-list-2* : *type-2*;
>   ⋮
>   *variable-list-m* : *type-m*;

where each *variable-list-i* is a single variable or a list of variables separated by commas, and each *type-i* is one of the Pascal data types *integer, real, char,* or *boolean* (or one of the other types discussed later). For example, the variable declaration section

>   **var**
>   *EmpNumber* : *integer*;
>   *Hours* : *real*;
>   *Rate* : *real*;
>   *Wages* : *real*;

or equivalently,

>   **var**
>   *EmpNumber* : *integer*;
>   *Hours, Rate, Wages* : *real*;

declares that only the four variables *EmpNumber, Hours, Rate*, and *Wages* may be used in the program and that *EmpNumber* is of type *integer*, whereas *Hours, Rate*, and *Wages* are of type *real*.

It is good programming practice to use meaningful variable names that suggest what they represent since this makes the program more readable and easier to understand. It is also good practice to include brief comments that indicate how the variable is to be used. These comments may be included in the variable declaration section. The following illustrates:

>   **var**
>   *EmpNumber* : *integer*;   (* employee number *)
>   *Hours*,   (* hours worked *)
>   *Rate*,   (* hourly pay rate *)
>   *Wages* : *real*;   (* total wages *)

Named Constants.   Certain constants occur so frequently that names are often given to them. For example, the name "pi" is commonly given to the constant 3.14159 . . . and "e" to the base 2.71828 . . . of natural logarithms. Pascal allows the programmer to assign identifiers to certain constants in the **constant section** of the program's declaration part. This section, if present, must precede the variable section and must begin with the reserved word **const**; it has the form

>   **const**
>   *identifier-1* = *constant-1*;
>   *identifier-2* = *constant-2*;
>   ⋮
>   *identifier-k* = *constant-k*;

For example, the constant section

> **const**
> $Pi = 3.14159$;
> $NegPi = -Pi$;
> $MyName = $ 'John Doe';
> $CurrentYear = 1987$;

associates the names *Pi* and *NegPi* with the real constants 3.14159 and -3.14159, respectively, *MyName* with the string constant 'John Doe', and *CurrentYear* with the integer 1987. These names can then be used anywhere in the program that the corresponding constant value can be used.

One reason for using named constants is to make the program easier to read and to modify. Programmers should not use "magic numbers" that suddenly appear without explanation, as in

> $PopChange := (0.1758 - 0.1257) * Population$;

If these numbers must be changed, someone must search through the program to determine what they represent and which are the appropriate ones to change, and to locate all the places where they appear. It is better to use named constants, as in

> **const**
> $BirthRate = 0.1758$;
> $DeathRate = 0.1257$;
> $\vdots$
> $PopChange := (BirthRate - DeathRate) * Population$;

Readability is improved and the flexibility of the program is increased, because if these constants must be changed, one need only change the definitions of *BirthRate* and *DeathRate* in the constant section at the beginning of the program.

Pascal also includes three predefined constant identifiers: the boolean constant identifiers *true* and *false* and the integer constant identifier *maxint*. The value of *maxint* is the largest integer that can be represented in the particular computer being used. Typical values are 32767 ($2^{15} - 1$) or 2147483647 ($2^{31} - 1$).

Exercises

1. Which of the following are legal Pascal identifiers?

(a) *XRay*	**(b)** *X-Ray*	**(c)** *Jeremiah*	**(d)** *R2D2*
(e) *3M*	**(f)** *PDQ123*	**(g)** *PS.175*	**(h)** *x*
(i) *4*	**(j)** *N/4*	**(k)** *$M*	**(l)** *ZZZZZZ*
(m) *night*	**(n)** *ngiht*	**(o)** *nite*	**(p)** *to day*

2. Classify each of the following as an integer constant, real constant, or neither:

(a)	12	**(b)**	12.	**(c)**	12.0	**(d)**	'12'
(e)	8 + 4	**(f)**	− 3.7	**(g)**	3.7 −	**(h)**	1,024
(i)	+ 1	**(j)**	$3.98	**(k)**	0.357E4	**(l)**	24E0
(m)	E3	**(n)**	five	**(o)**	3E.5	**(p)**	.000001
(q)	1.2 × 10	**(r)**	−(− 1)	**(s)**	0E0	**(t)**	1/2

3. Which of the following are legal string constants?

(a)	'X'	**(b)**	'123'	**(c)**	IS'	**(d)**	'too yet'
(e)	'DO''ESNT'	**(f)**	'isn''t'	**(g)**	'constant'	**(h)**	'$1.98'
(i)	'DON'T'	**(j)**	'12 + 34'	**(k)**	'''twas'	**(l)**	'A''B''C'

4. Write variable sections to declare:

(a) *Item, Number,* and *Job* to be of real type.

(b) *ShoeSize* to be of integer type.

(c) *Mileage* to be of real type and *Cost* and *Distance* to be of integer type.

(d) *Alpha* and *Beta* to be of integer type, *Code* to be of character type, *Root* to be of real type, and *RootExists* to be of boolean type.

5. For each of the following, write constant sections to name each given constant with the specified name:

(a) 1.25 with the name *Rate.*

(b) 40.0 with the name *RegHours* and 1.5 with the name *Overtime-Factor.*

(c) 1984 with the name *Year,* 'F' with *Female,* and a blank character with *Blank.*

(d) *true* with the name *Exists,* 0 with *Zero,* ∗ with *Asterisk,* an apostrophe with *Apostrophe,* and the string CPSC151A with *Course.*

3.3 Arithmetic Operations and Functions

In the preceding section we considered variables and constants of various types. These variables and constants can be processed by using operations and functions appropriate to their types. In this section we discuss the arithmetic operations and functions that are used with numeric data.

In Pascal, addition and subtraction are denoted by the usual plus (+) and minus (−) signs. Multiplication is denoted by an asterisk (∗). This symbol must be used to denote every multiplication; thus to multiply *n* by 2, we must use 2 ∗ *n* or *n* ∗ 2, not 2*n*. There are three other arithmetic operations in Pascal: a real division operation denoted by a slash (/); an integer division operation denoted by the reserved word **div**; and an integer operation denoted by the reserved word **mod** that yields the remainder that results from an integer division. The following table summarizes these arithmetic operations:

Operator	Operation
+	addition
−	subraction, unary minus
*	multiplication
/	real divison
div	integer divison
mod	remainder in integer division

For the operators +, −, and *, the operands may be of either integer or real type. If both are integer, the result is integer; but if either is of real type, the result is real. For example,

$$2 + 3 = 5$$

$$2 + 3.0 = 5.0$$

$$2.0 + 3 = 5.0$$

$$2.0 + 3.0 = 5.0$$

The division operator / produces a real result, regardless of the type of the operands, for example,

$$7 / 2 = 3.5$$

$$7.0 / 2 = 3.5$$

$$7 / 2.0 = 3.5$$

$$7.0 / 2.0 = 3.5$$

For the operators **div** and **mod**, the operands must both be of integer type, and the result is also of integer type. If x and y are of integer type, then x **div** y produces the integer quotient obtained when x is divided by y, and x **mod** y produces the remainder. For example,

7 **div** 2 =	3		7 **mod** 2 = 1	
12 **div** 3 =	4		12 **mod** 3 = 0	
0 **div** 5 =	0		0 **mod** 5 = 0	
4 **div** 5 =	0		4 **mod** 5 = 4	
−8 **div** 3 =	−2		−8 **mod** 3 = 1	

The expression x **div** y is defined for all nonzero integers y, but x **mod** y is defined only for positive values of y.

There are two *precedence levels* for these arithmetic operators: high and low. The high-priority operators are, *, /, **div**, and **mod**, and the low-priority operators are + and −. When an expression containing several of these operators is evaluated, all high-priority operations are performed first in the order in which they occur, from left to right, and then all low-priority operations are carried out in the order in which they occur, from left to right.

To illustrate, consider the expression

$$7 * 10 - 5 \text{ \textbf{mod} } 3 * 4 + 9$$

The leftmost multiplication is performed first, giving the intermediate result

[handwritten marginal notes:]
In Turbo

$B = (B \text{ DIV } A) * A + (B \text{ MOD } A)$

$0 \le B \text{ MOD } A / < |A|$

$B < 0 \Rightarrow B \text{ MOD } A \le 0$
$B > 0 \Rightarrow B \text{ MOD } A \ge 0$

$(B \text{ DIV } A) * A$ is the multiple of A that is in $[0,B]$ or $[B,0]$, depending on B, and nearest B.

$$70 - 5 \textbf{ mod } 3 * 4 + 9$$

The next high-priority operator encountered is **mod**, which gives

$$70 - 2 * 4 + 9$$

The second multiplication is the final operation of high priority; when it is performed, it yields

$$70 - 8 + 9$$

Next, the low-priority operations are performed in the order in which they occur, from left to right. The subtraction is thus performed first, giving

$$62 + 9$$

and then the addition is carried out, giving the final result

$$71$$

The standard order of evaluation can be modified by using parentheses to enclose subexpressions within an expression. These subexpressions are first evaluated in the standard manner, and the results are then combined to evaluate the complete expression. If the parentheses are "nested," that is, if one set of parentheses is contained within another, the computations in the innermost parentheses are performed first.

For example, consider the expression

$$(7 * (10 - 5) \textbf{ mod } 3) * 4 + 9$$

The subexpression $10 - 5$ is evaluated first, producing

$$(7 * 5 \textbf{ mod } 3) * 4 + 9$$

Next the subexpression $7 * 5 \textbf{ mod } 3$ is evaluated in the standard order, giving

$$2 * 4 + 9$$

Now the multiplication is performed, giving

$$8 + 9$$

and the addition produces the final result

$$17$$

Care must be taken in writing expressions containing two or more operations to ensure that they are evaluated in the order intended. Even though parentheses may not be required, they should be used freely to clarify the intended order of evaluation and to write complicated expressions in terms of simpler subexpressions. One must make sure, however, that the parentheses balance, that is, that they occur in pairs, since an unpaired parenthesis results in an error.

The symbols $+$ and $-$ can also be used as ***unary operators***; for example, $-x$ and $+(a + b)$ are allowed. But unary operators must be used carefully, since Pascal does not allow two operators to follow in succession. For example, the expression $n * -2$ is not allowed; rather, it must be written $n * (-2)$. These unary operations have low priority, as do the corresponding binary operations.

In summary, the following rules govern the evaluation of arithmetic expressions:

1. The high-priority operators $*$, $/$, **div**, and **mod** are performed first. The low-priority operators $+$ and $-$ (both binary and unary) are performed last. Operators having the same priority are evaluated from left to right.
2. If an expression contains subexpressions enclosed within parentheses, these are evaluated first, using the standard order specified in Rule 1. If there are nested parentheses, the innermost subexpressions are evaluated first.

There are also a number of predefined arithmetic functions in the Pascal language, as given in Table 3.1. To use any of these functions, we simply give the function name followed by the constant, variable, or expression to which the function is to be applied enclosed within parentheses. Thus, to calculate the square root of 5, we write

$$sqrt(5)$$

and to calculate $\sqrt{b^2 - 4ac}$, we could use

$$sqrt(sqr(b) - 4 * a * c)$$

If the value of the expression $sqr(b) - 4 * a * c$ is negative, an error results because the square root of a negative number is not defined.

TABLE 3.1   Predefined Arithmetic Functions

Function	Description	Type of Parameter	Type of Value
$abs(x)$	Absolute value of x	Integer or real	Same as argument
$arctan(x)$	Inverse tangent of x (value in radians)	Integer or real	Real
$cos(x)$	Cosine of x (in radians)	Integer or real	Real
$exp(x)$	Exponential function e^x	Integer or real	Real
$ln(x)$	Natural logarithm of x	Integer or real	Real
$round(x)$	x rounded to nearest integer	Real	Integer
$sin(x)$	Sine of x (in radians)	Integer or real	Real
$sqr(x)$	x^2	Integer or real	Same as argument
$sqrt(x)$	Square root of x	Integer or real	Real
$trunc(x)$	x truncated to its integer part	Real	Integer

Exercises

1. Find the value of each of the following expressions or explain why it is not a valid expression.

   (a) $9 - 5 - 3$
   (b) 2 **div** $3 + 3 / 5$
   (c) 9 **div** $2 / 5$

    (d) 9 / 2 **div** 5
    (e) 2.0 / 4
    (f) (2 + 3) **mod** 2
    (g) 7 **mod** 5 **mod** 3
    (h) (7 **mod** 5) **mod** 3
    (i) 7 **mod** (5 **mod** 3)
    (j) (7 **mod** 5 **mod** 3)
    (k) 25 * 1 / 2
    (l) 25 * 1 **div** 2
    (m) 25 * (1 **div** 2)
    (n) − 3.0 * 5.0
    (o) 5.0 * − 3.0
    (p) 12 / 2 * 3
    (q) ((12 + 3) **div** 2) / (8 − (5 + 1))
    (r) ((12 + 3) **div** 2) / (8 − 5 + 1)
    (s) (12 + 3 **div** 2) / (8 − 5 + 1)
    (t) *sqrt(sqr(4))*
    (u) *sqrt(sqr(− 4))*
    (v) *sqr(sqrt(4))*
    (w) *sqr(sqrt(− 4))*
    (x) *trunc(8 / 5) + round(8 / 5)*

2. If *zwei* = 2.0, *drei* = 3.0, *vier* = 4, *funf* = 5, and *acht* = 8, find the value of each of the following:

    (a) *zwei + drei + drei*
    (b) *acht* **div** 3
    (c) *acht* / 3
    (d) *(drei + zwei) * vier*
    (e) *acht* **div** *funf* * 5.1
    (f) *sqr(vier) / sqr(zwei)*
    (g) *sqr(funf) / sqr(zwei)*
    (h) *sqrt(zwei + drei + vier)*

3. Write Pascal expressions to compute the following:

    (a) $10 + 5B - 4AC$.
    (b) Three times the difference $4 - n$ divided by twice the quantity $m^2 + n^2$.
    (c) The square root of $a + 3b^2$.
    (d) The real quantity *Amount* rounded to the nearest hundredth.

3.4 The Assignment Statement

The ***assignment statement*** is used to assign values to variables and has the form

    variable := *expression*

where *expression* may be a constant, another variable to which a value has previously been assigned, or a formula to be evaluated. For example, suppose that *xCoord* and *yCoord* are real variables, *Number* and *Position* are integer variables, *Code* is a character variable, and *Done* is a boolean variable as declared by the following variable section:

> **var**
>> *xCoord, y Coord : real;*
>> *Number, Position : integer;*
>> *Code : char;*
>> *Done : boolean;*

These declarations associate memory locations with the six variables. This might be pictured as follows, where the question marks indicate that these variables are initially undefined:

xCoord	?
yCoord	?
Number	?
Position	?
Code	?
Done	?

Now consider the following assignment statements:

> *xCoord* := 5.23;
> *yCoord* := *sqrt*(25.0);
> *Number* := 17;
> *Code* := 'M';
> *Done* := *false*;
> *Position* := *Number* **div** 3 + 2;
> *xCoord* := 2.0 * *xCoord*;

The first assignment statement assigns the real constant 5.23 to the real variable *xCoord*, the second assigns the real constant 5.0 to the real variable *yCoord*. The next three assignment statements assign the integer constant 17 to the integer variable *Number*, the character M to the character variable *Code*, and the boolean value *false* to the boolean variable *Done*. Thus the memory locations named by the variables *xCoord, yCoord, Number, Code,* and *Done* contain the values 5.23, 5.0, 17, M, and *false*, respectively; the variable *Position* is still undefined.

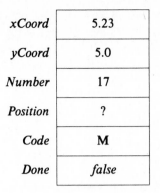

xCoord	5.23
yCoord	5.0
Number	17
Position	?
Code	M
Done	false

This means that until the contents of these memory locations are changed, these values are substituted for the variables in any subsequent expression containing these variables. Thus, in the sixth assignment statement, the value 17 is substituted for the variable *Number*, the expression *Number* **div** 3 + 2 is evaluated yielding 7, and this value is then assigned to the integer variable *Position*; the value of *Number* is unchanged.

xCoord	5.23
yCoord	5.0
Number	17
Position	7
Code	M
Done	false

In the last assignment statement, the variable *xCoord* appears on both sides of the assignment operator (: =). In this case, the current value 5.23 for *xCoord* is used in evaluating the expression 2.0 ∗ *xCoord*, yielding the value 10.46; this value is then assigned to *xCoord*. The old value 5.23 is lost because it has been replaced with the new value 10.46.

xCoord	10.46
yCoord	5.0
Number	17
Position	7
Code	M
Done	false

In every assignment statement, the variable to be assigned a value must appear on the left of the assignment operator (:=), and a legal expression must appear on the right. Furthermore, both the variable and the expression must be of the same type. However, *it is legal to assign an integer value to a real variable;* the integer value will be converted to the corresponding real value. *One may not, however, assign a real value to an integer variable.*

The following are examples of invalid Pascal assignment statements. A reason is given for each to explain why it is not valid. The variables in these statements are assumed to have the types specified earlier.

Statement	Error
5 := *Number*	Variable must appear on the left of the assignment operator.
xCoord + 3.5 := 2.7	Arithmetic expressions may not appear on the left of the assignment operator.
Code := 5	Numeric value may not be assigned to a character variable.
Number := '5'	Character constant may not be assigned to a numeric variable.
Number := 3.4	Real value may not be assigned to an integer variable.
Number := '2' + '3'	'2' + '3' is not a legal expression.
Position := *Number* := 1	*Number* := 1 is not a legal expression.
Done := 'F'	'F' is not a boolean expression.

It is important to remember that the *the assignment statement is a replacement statement.* Some beginning programmers forget this and write an assignment statement like

$A := B$

when the statement

$B := A$

is intended. These two statements produce very different results: the first assigns the value of B to A, leaving B unchanged, and the second assigns the value of A to B, leaving A unchanged.

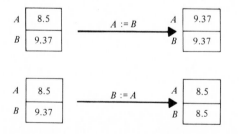

To illustrate further that an assignment statement is a replacement statement, suppose that *Alpha* and *Beta* are integer variables with values 357 and 59, respectively. The following statements interchange the values of *Alpha* and *Beta*, using the auxiliary integer variable *Temp*:

$Temp := Alpha;$
$Alpha := Beta;$
$Beta := Temp;$

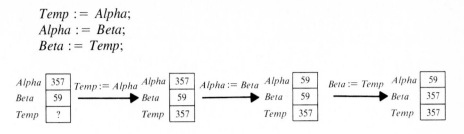

As another example, consider the statement

$Sum := Sum + Counter$

Such a statement, in which the same variable appears on both sides of the assignment operator, often confuses beginning programmers. Execution of this statement causes the values of *Sum* and *Counter* to be substituted for these variables to evaluate the expression *Sum + Counter*, and the resulting value is then assigned to *Sum*. The following diagram illustrates this for the case in which the integer variables *Sum* and *Counter* have the values 120 and 16, respectively.

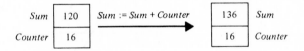

Note that the old value of the variable *Sum* is lost because it was replaced with a new value.

Another statement in which the same variable appears on both sides of the assignment operator is

$Counter := Counter + 1$

This statement implements the operation "increment *Counter* by 1." When it is executed, the current value of *Counter* is substituted for this variable to evaluate the expression *Counter + 1*, and this new value is then assigned to *Counter*. For example, if *Counter* has the value 16, the value of *Counter + 1* is $16 + 1 = 17$, which is then assigned as the new value for *Counter*:

Note once again that the old value of the variable has been lost because it was replaced with a new value.

In a Pascal program, *variables are undefined until their values have been explicitly specified* by an assignment statement or by one of the other statements discussed later. The results of attempting to use undefined variables are unpredictable and depend on the particular Pascal compiler being used.

Exercises

1. Assuming that *Number* is of integer type, *xValue* and *yValue* are of
   real type, *Grade* is of character type, and *Found* is of boolean type,
   determine which of the following are valid Pascal assignment statements. If they are not valid, explain why they are not.

   (a) *xValue* := 2.71828   (b) 3 := *Number*
   (c) *Grade* := 'B+'   (d) *Number* := Number +   1
   (e) *xValue* := 1   (f) *Grade* := A
   (g) *Number* + 1 := *Number*   (h) *xValue* := '1'
   (i) *Found* := *Grade*   (j) *yValue* := *yValue*
   (k) *xValue* := A   (l) *Grade* := *Grade* + 10
   (m) *Found* := 'true'   (n) *xValue* := *Number*
   (o) *Number* := *yValue*

2. Given that *two, tri, four,* and *xCoord* are real variables with *two* =
   2.0, *tri* = 3.0, and *four* = 4.0; *acht, funf,* and *zahl* are integer variables
   with *acht* = 8 and *funf* = 5; and *Numeral* and *Symbol* are character
   variables with *Numeral* = '2', find the value assigned to the given
   variable by each of the following, or indicate why the statement is not
   valid.

   (a) *xCoord* := (*two* + *tri*) * *tri*
   (b) *xCoord* := (*tri* + *two* / *four*) * 2
   (c) *xCoord* := *acht* / *funf* + 5
   (d) *zahl* := *acht* **div** *funf* + 5
   (e) *xCoord* := sqr(*funf*) / sqr(*acht*)
   (f) *zahl* := sqr(*funf*) / sqr(*acht*)
   (g) *Symbol* := 4
   (h) *Symbol* := *Numeral*
   (i) *Symbol* := '4'
   (j) *Symbol* := *four*
   (k) *two* := 2
   (l) *two* := '2'
   (m) *two* := *Numeral*
   (n) *acht* := *acht* + 2
   (o) *zahl* := 1 + *Numeral*
   (p) *zahl* := round(sqr(*acht* **mod** *funf*) / *four*)

3. Write a Pascal assignment statement for each of the following that
   calculates the given expression and assigns the result to the specified
   variable:

   (a) *Rate* times *Time* to *Distance*.
   (b) *Tax* rounded to the nearest dollar to *Tax*.
   (c) $\dfrac{1}{\dfrac{1}{R1} + \dfrac{1}{R2} + \dfrac{1}{R3}}$ to *Resistance*.
   (d) Area of a triangle of base *b* and height *h* (one-half base times
        height) to *Area*.

(e) The last three digits of the integer *StockNumber* with a decimal point before the last two digits to *Price* (e.g., if *StockNumber* is 1758316, *Price* is assigned the value of 3.16).

4. For each of the following, give values for the integer variables *a*, *b*, and *c* for which the two given expressions have different values.

(a) *a* ∗ (*b* **div** *c*) and *a* ∗ *b* **div** *c*

(b) *a* **div** *b* and *a* ∗ (1 / *b*)

(c) (*a* + *b*) **div** *c* and *a* **div** *c* + *b* **div** *c*

3.5 Input/Output

In the preceding section we considered the assignment statement, which enables us to calculate the values of expressions and store the results of these computations by assigning them to variables. An assignment statement does not, however, display these results on some output device, nor does it allow the user to enter new values during execution. For example, a program to calculate the wages earned by John Doe, employee #31564, for 38.5 hours of work at an hourly rate of $8.75 could contain the variable section

```
var
    EmpNumber : integer;      (* employee number *)
    Hours,                    (* hours worked *)
    Rate,                     (* hourly pay rate *)
    Wages : real;             (* total wages *)
```

and the statement part

```
begin
    EmpNumber := 31564;
    Hours := 38.5;
    Rate := 8.75;
    Wages := Hours * Rate
end.
```

The value of *Wages* is calculated as desired but is stored only internally in the memory location associated with *Wages* and is not displayed to the user. Moreover, if the same wage calculation is to be done for Mary Smith, employee #31565, who worked 37.5 hours at an hourly rate of $9.25, the statement part of the program must be almost completely rewritten as follows:

```
begin
    EmpNumber := 31565;
    Hours := 37.5;
    Rate := 9.25;
    Wages := Hours * Rate
end.
```

The output statement that we consider in this section provides a method for easily displaying information. We also consider an input statement to provide a convenient method of assigning values from an external source to variables during execution of the program.

Program Heading.   Any collection of data to be input to a program or output from a program is called a **file**. There are programs that do not require any input from a file, since all values to be processed are assigned within the program. This is true, for example, in the preceding program segments. All useful programs, however, do produce some output, because the results obtained would not otherwise be displayed to the user.

The program heading in a Pascal program has the form

    program *name (file-list)*;

where *name* is a valid Pascal identifier used to name the program and *file-list* is a list of files used in the program. Two standard files provided by the Pascal language are *input* and *output*. The file *input* refers to a system input device, such as a terminal or a card reader, and the file *output* refers to a system output device, such as a terminal or a printer. An appropriate program heading for a Pascal program that does not require input could have the form

    program *name (output)*;

A program that requires input and produces output could have a program heading of the form

    program *name (input, output)*;

Output.   There are two output statements in Pascal, the *write* and the *writeln* (read "write-line") statements. A simple form of the *writeln* statement is

    writeln (output-list)

where *output-list* is a single expression or a list of expressions separated by commas. Each of these expressions can be a constant, a variable, or a formula. Execution of a *writeln* statement displays the values of the items in the output list on the current line and then advances to the next line so that subsequent output will appear on a new line. For example, the statements

    writeln (Alpha, Beta);
    writeln (Gamma, Delta);

display the values of *Alpha* and *Beta* on one line and the values of *Gamma* and *Delta* on the next line. Subsequent output would begin on yet another line.

The values of the expressions in the output list of a *writeln* statement are displayed in *fields*, which are zones of consecutive positions in the output line. To illustrate, suppose that *Counter*, *RealNum*, *Code*, and *BooleVar* are variables declared by

    var
        Counter : integer;
        RealNum : real;
        Code : char;
        BooleVar : boolean;

and consider the following statements:

```
Counter := 16;
RealNum := 123.456;
Code := 'A';
BooleVar := true;
writeln ('Counter');
writeln (Counter);
writeln (Counter, ' is even', Counter + 1, ' is odd');
writeln (RealNum, RealNum / 70000);
writeln (Code, 'B', 'C', '***');
writeln (BooleVar, false);
```

These statements produce output similar to the following:

```
Counter
         16
         16 is even         17 is odd
 1.234560000E+02 1.763657143E-03
ABC***
TRUE FALSE
```

The format of the output will vary from one system to another since the field widths used for integer, real, and boolean values are compiler dependent. For a character or a string value, however, the field width is the number of characters in that value. Note that numeric values are ***right-justified*** in their fields, that is, they are placed so that the last digit is in the rightmost position of the field, and that real values are displayed in floating point notation.

The *write* statement has the form

write (output-list)

where the output list has the same form as for *writeln*. When this statement is executed, the values are displayed on the current line, but *there is no advance to a new line.*[1] Consequently, any subsequent output will be displayed on this same line. For example, the statements

```
write ('A');
write ('B');
write ('C');
writeln ('DEF');
writeln ('GHI')
```

produce as output

```
ABCDEF
GHI
```

The *writeln* statement, but not *write*, may also be used with no output list to advance to a new line. In this case, the parentheses used to enclose the

[1]In some implementations of Pascal, *write* may not produce immediate output but rather "buffer" it (store it temporarily) for output at a later time. In fact, this may also be true for *writeln*. In this text we assume that both *write* and *writeln* produce immediate output.

output list are also omitted, so the statement has the form

writeln

Execution of this statement produces a blank line unless the last preceding output statement was a *write* statement, in which case output to the current line is terminated and subsequent output begins on a new line. For example, consider the statements

Counter := 16;
write (*Counter*, ' is even');
write (*Counter* + 1, ' is odd');
writeln;
writeln ('*********');
writeln ('*   *');
writeln ('*********');
writeln;
writeln (2 * *Counter*, ' is even');

These statements produce output similar to the following:

```
_____16_is_even_____17_is_odd

*********_____

*_____*_____

*********_____

_____

_____32_is_even_____
```

In an earlier example in this section we considered the problem of calculating wages for an employee. To display some of the relevant information from this example, we might add several *writeln* statements, as shown in the program in Figure 3.1.

```
PROGRAM WageCalculation (output);

(*******************************************************************

    This program calculates wages as hours * rate for a given number
    of hours worked and a given hourly rate for some employee
    identified by his/her employee number.

*****************************************************************)
VAR
    EmpNumber : integer;    (* employee number *)
    Hours,                  (* hours worked *)
    Rate,                   (* hourly rate *)
    Wages : real;           (* gross wages earned *)

BEGIN
    EmpNumber := 31564;
    Hours := 38.5;
    Rate := 8.75;
    Wages := Hours * Rate;
```

Figure 3.1

Figure 3.1 (cont.)

```
    writeln ('Employee #', EmpNumber);
    writeln ('Hours worked:   ', Hours);
    writeln ('Hourly rate:  $', Rate);
    writeln ('Total Wages:  $', Wages)
END.

Sample run:


Employee #   31564
Hours worked:   3.850000000E+01
Hourly rate:  $ 8.750000000E+00
Total Wages:  $ 3.368750000E+02
```

The output produced by this program is not really satisfactory for two reasons. First, too many spaces are used to display the values; second, the real values are displayed in scientific form that is not appropriate for monetary values. These deficiencies can be remedied by specifying the format of the output by appending *format descriptors* to the items in the output list.

A format descriptor can have one of two forms

   :*w*

or

   :*w*:*d*

In both forms, *w* is a positive integer expression that specifies the field width to be used in displaying the corresponding value. For example, in the statement

   writeln (*Counter*:2, ' is even', *Counter* + 1 : 5, ' is odd')

the format descriptor :2 specifies that the value of *Counter* is to be displayed in a field of width 2, and the format descriptor :5 specifies that the value of *Counter* + 1 is to be displayed in a field of width 5. If *Counter* has the value 16, the output produced by this statement is

```
    16_is_even___17_is_odd
```

If *Zone* is an integer variable with value 2, the statement

   writeln (*Counter*:*Zone*, ' is even', *Counter* + 1 : *Zone* + 3, ' is odd')

produces this same output. The statement

   writeln (*Counter*:1, ' is even', *Counter* + 1 : 1, ' is odd')

produces

```
    16_is_even17_is_odd
```

As this last example demonstrates, if a numeric value is too large for the specified field, then the field is automatically enlarged to accommodate it. Thus, because the value 16 of *Counter* has two digits, the field of size 1 specified for it by *Counter*:1 is enlarged so that both digits are displayed. But if a field is too small for a character, string, or boolean value, it is not enlarged, and only the leftmost *w* characters are displayed where *w* is the specified field width. Consequently, the output produced by the statement

   writeln (*Counter*:1, ' is even':7, *Counter* + 1 : 1,' is odd':5)

is

```
16_is_eve17_is_o
```

If the field width is larger than necessary, the value is *right-justified* in the field. Thus, the output produced by the statement

   writeln (*Counter*:5, 'is even':8, *Counter* + 1 : 10, 'is odd':8)

is

```
___16_is_even_____17__is_odd
```

If a real value is output using the format descriptor :*w*, it is displayed in scientific form. If the usual decimal form for a real value is desired, the format descriptor :*w*:*d* must be used. In this descriptor, *d* is an integer expression specifying the number of digits to be displayed to the right of the decimal point. The value to be displayed is *rounded* to *d* decimal places, with zeros added as necessary. To illustrate, suppose that *Alpha* and *Beta* are real variables with the values 3.51 and 123.47168, respectively, and that *Zone* and *NumDigits* are integer variables with the values 8 and 2, respectively. Consider the following statements:

```
write(Alpha:4:2);
write(Beta:11:5);
writeln;
writeln;
writeln (Alpha:8:4, Beta:12:6);
writeln;
writeln (Alpha:8:2, Beta:12:3);
writeln (Alpha:8:1, Beta:12:1);
writeln;
writeln (Alpha:3:1, Beta:3:1);
writeln;
writeln (Alpha + 3 : Zone : NumDigits);
writeln (Beta − 1 : Zone + 1 : NumDigits + 1);
```

The output produced by these statements is

```
3.51  123.47168_____

-------------------------

  3.5100  123.471680

-------------------------

    3.51      123.472
      3.5       123.5

-------------------------

3.5123.5_____

-------------------------

    6.51_____
  122.472_____
```

We remarked earlier that the output produced by the program in Figure 3.1 is not really satisfactory. The program in Figure 3.2 is a modification that uses format descriptors to display the results in a more acceptable format.

```
PROGRAM WageCalculation (output);

(*************************************************************************

   This program calculates wages,as hours * rate for a given number
   of hours worked and a given hourly rate for some employee
   identified by his/her employee number.

*************************************************************************)

VAR
    EmpNumber : integer;   (* employee number *)
    Hours,                 (* hours worked *)
    Rate,                  (* hourly rate *)
    Wages : real;          (* gross wages earned *)

BEGIN
    EmpNumber := 31564;
    Hours := 38.5;
    Rate := 8.75;
    Wages := Hours * Rate;
    writeln ('Employee # ', EmpNumber:1);
    writeln ('Hours worked:   ', Hours:7:2);
    writeln ('Hourly rate:  $', Rate:7:2);
    writeln ('Total wages:  $', Wages:7:2)
END.


Sample run:


Employee # 31564
Hours worked:    38.50
Hourly rate:  $   8.75
Total wages:  $ 336.88
```

Figure 3.2

Input. There are two input statements in Pascal, the *read* and the *readln* (read "read line") statements. Here we restrict our attention to numeric input, since these statements cannot be used for boolean values and the input of character strings is somewhat tricky.

A simple form of the *readln* statement is

readln (input-list)

where *input-list* consists of a single variable or a list of variables separated by commas. A *readln* statement reads values from the standard file *input* and assigns them to the variables in the input list. Recall that the standard file *input* refers to a system input device, such as a terminal or a card reader. The examples in this text assume interactive input, so that data values are entered by the user during program execution rather than from some file or collection of data cards prepared before execution begins.

To illustrate, consider the statement

readln (EmpNumber, Hours, Rate)

where *EmpNumber* is an integer variable and *Hours* and *Rate* are real variables. If the data values

31564 38.5 8.75

are entered, the value 31564 is assigned to the variable *EmpNumber*, 38.5 to *Hours*, and 8.75 to *Rate*. Thus this single *readln* statement can replace the three assignment statements

EmpNumber := 31564;
Hours := 38.5;
Rate := 8.75;

used in the programs of Figures 3.1 and 3.2. The modified program is shown in Figure 3.3. Note that because the program involves both input and output, the program heading includes both of the standard files *input* and *output*.

```
PROGRAM WageCalculation (input, output);

(*********************************************************************

   This program calculates wages as hours * rate for an employee
   identified by his/her employee number.  The employee number,
   hours worked, and hourly rate are read during execution.

*********************************************************************)

VAR
    EmpNumber : integer;    (* employee number *)
    Hours,                  (* hours worked *)
    Rate,                   (* hourly rate *)
    Wages : real;           (* gross wages earned *)
```

Figure 3.3

Figure 3.3 (cont.)

```
BEGIN
    readln (EmpNumber, Hours, Rate);
    Wages := Hours * Rate;
    writeln ('Employee # ', EmpNumber:1);
    writeln ('Hours worked:  ', Hours:7:2);
    writeln ('Hourly rate:  $', Rate:7:2);
    writeln ('Total wages:  $', Wages:7:2)
END.
```

Sample run:

```
31564 38.5 8.75
Employee # 31564
Hours worked:    38.50
Hourly rate:  $   8.75
Total wages:  $ 336.88
```

Data values entered for the variables in the input list of a *readln* statement must be constants, and consecutive numbers should be separated by one or more blanks. (An algebraic sign may also be used to separate consecutive numbers). They must be arranged so that the type of each value agrees with that of the variable to which it is to be assigned. Assignment of a real value to an integer variable is not allowed, although an integer value may be read and assigned to a real variable.

After values have been read for all of the variables in the input list, a *readln* statement causes an advance to a new input line from which subsequent values will be read. Consequently, if there are more values in the current input line than there are variables in the input list, the first data values are read, but all remaining values are ignored.

If there are fewer entries in a line of input data than variables in the input list, successive lines of input data are processed until values for all variables in the input list have been obtained. Thus for the statement

readln (*EmpNumber, Hours, Rate*)

the values for *EmpNumber, Hours,* and *Rate* can all be entered on the same line

31564 38.5 8.75

or on three separate lines

31564
38.5
8.75

or with the value for *EmpNumber* on the first line and the values for *Hours* and *Rate* on the next line

    31564
    38.5 8.75

and so on.

In a batch mode of operation, these lines of input data are obtained from some previously prepared data file. When a *readln* statement is encountered, the values from this file are retrieved automatically and assigned to the variables in the input list.

In an interactive mode of operation, the values assigned to variables in an input list are entered by the user. In this case, when a *readln* statement is encountered, program execution is suspended until the user enters values for all variables in the input list. Program execution then automatically resumes. Because execution is interrupted and because the correct number and types of values must be entered before execution can resume, *it is good practice to provide some message to prompt the user when it is necessary to enter data values*. This is accomplished by preceding input statements with output statements that display appropriate prompts. The program in Figure 3.4 illustrates this by prompting the user when values for *EmpNumber*, *Hours*, and *Rate* are to be entered; it is a modification of the program in Figure 3.3.

```
PROGRAM WageCalculation (input, output);

(*********************************************************************

   This program calculates wages as hours * rate for an employee
   identified by his/her employee number.  The employee number,
   hours worked, and hourly rate are read during execution.

*********************************************************************)

VAR
    EmpNumber : integer;    (* employee number *)
    Hours,                  (* hours worked *)
    Rate,                   (* hourly rate *)
    Wages : real;           (* gross wages earned *)

BEGIN
    write ('Enter employee number:   ');
    readln (EmpNumber);
    write ('Enter hours worked and hourly rate:   ');
    readln (Hours, Rate);
    Wages := Hours * Rate;
    writeln ('Employee # ', EmpNumber:1);
    writeln ('Hours worked:   ', Hours:7:2);
    writeln ('Hourly rate:   $', Rate:7:2);
    writeln ('Total wages:   $', Wages:7:2)
END.
```

Figure 3.4

Figure 3.4 (cont.)

Sample run:

```
Enter employee number:   31564
Enter hours worked and hourly rate:   38.5 8.75
Employee # 31564
Hours worked:      38.50
Hourly rate:   $    8.75
Total wages:   $ 336.88
```

Another input statement is a *read* statement of the form

read (input-list)

where *input-list* has the same form as for *readln*. This statement is similar to the *readln* statement except that it does *not* advance to a new input line after values have been read for the variables in the input list. To illustrate, consider the statement

read (EmpNumber, Hours, Rate)

and suppose that the data are entered as follows:

31564 38.5 8.75 31523
40.0   8.75

As in the case of the earlier *readln* statement, the values read for *EmpNumber*, *Hours*, and *Rate* are 31564, 38.5, and 8.75, respectively. However, if this statement is executed again, the value 31523 will be read for *EmpNumber*, 40.0 for *Hours* (ends of lines are ignored for numeric input), and 8.75 for *Rate*.

Another distinction between the *read* and *readln* statements is that *readln* but not *read* may be used with no input list:

readln

Note that in this case the parentheses are also omitted. Execution of this statement terminates input from the current line, so that subsequent input begins with a new line. It may thus be used to skip a line of input or to skip over values that remain in the current line.

Exercises

1. Assuming that *Alpha* and *Beta* are real variables with values -567.392 and 0.00004, respectively, and that *Rho* is an integer variable with a value 436, show precisely the output that each of the following sets of statements produces, or explain why an error occurs.

(a) *writeln (Rho);*
writeln (Rho + 1);
writeln (Rho + 2);

(b) *write (Rho);*
write (Rho + 1);
writeln (Rho + 2);

(c) *write ('Alpha = ');*
write (Alpha:9:3);
write ('Beta = ':7);
writeln (Beta:7:4);

(d) *write (Rho:5, 2 ∗ Rho:5);*
writeln;
writeln (Beta:10:5);

(e) *writeln (Alpha:8:1, Rho:5);*
writeln ('Tolerance:', Beta:8:5);

(f) *writeln ('Alpha =', Alpha:12:5);*
writeln ('Beta =', Beta:6:2, ' ':4, 'Rho =', Rho:6);
writeln (Alpha + 4.0 + Rho:15:3);

(g) *write ('Tolerance =' :8);*
writeln (Beta:5:3);
writeln;
writeln;
writeln (Rho:2, Alpha:4:2);

(h) *writeln (10 ∗ Alpha:8:1, trunc(10 ∗ Alpha):8, round(10 ∗ Alpha):8);*
*writeln (sqr(Rho **div** 100):5, sqrt(Rho **div** 100):5);*

(i) *writeln ('Rho =':7, Rho:8:2);*
writeln ('∗∗∗∗∗');

(j) *write (Alpha:10);*
write;
writeln (Beta:10);

2. Assuming that *I* and *J* are integer variables with *I* = 15 and *J* = 8, that *C* and *D* are character variables with *C* = 'C' and *D* = ' − ', and that *X* and *Y* are real variables with *X* = 2559.50 and *Y* = 8.015, show precisely the output that each of the following sets of statements produce:

(a) *writeln ('New balance =':I, X:J:2);*
*writeln (C:I **mod** 10, Y:J:J − 6);*

(b) *write ('I =' :I);*
write (I:I);
writeln ('J =' :J, J:J);
writeln;
writeln (I:J, J:I);
*writeln (trunc(X / J):J, J − Y:I:J, D:J **div** 7)*

3. Assume that *N1* and *N2* are integer variables with values 39 and −5117, respectively; that *R1* and *R2* are real variables with values 56.7173 and −0.00247, respectively; and that *C* is a character variable with value F. For each of the following, write a set of output statements that use these variables to produce the given output:

(a)   <u>__56.7173___F___39</u>
    <u>−5117PDQ−0.00247__</u>

(b) __56.717_____-0.0025***39__F
     ____56.72__39-5117_____

(c) ROOTS_ARE__56.717_AND_-0.00247

(d) APPROXIMATE_ANGLES:__56.7_AND_-0.0
     MAGNITUDES_ARE_____39_AND__5117___

4. Assuming that *A*, *B*, and *C* are integer variables and *X*, *Y*, and *Z* are real variables, tell what value, if any, will be assigned to each of these variables, or explain why an error occurs, when each of the following sets of statements is executed with the given input data.

(a) *readln* (*A*, *B*, *C*, *X*, *Y*, *Z*);   Input: 1   2   3
                                               4 5.5 6.6

(b) *readln* (*A*, *B*, *C*);   Input: 1
    readln (*X*, *Y*, *Z*);   2
                                                 3
                                                 4
                                                 5
                                                 6

(c) *read* (*A*, *X*);   Input: 1 2.2
    read (*B*, *Y*);   3 4.4
    read (*C*, *Z*);   5 6.6

(d) *read* (*A*, *B*, *C*);   Input: 1 2.2
    readln (*X*, *Y*, *Z*);   3 4.4
                                                 5 6.6

(e) *read* (*A*);   Input: 1   2   3
    readln (*B*, *C*);   4 5.5 6.6
    read (*X*, *Y*);
    readln (*Z*);

(f) *readln* (*A*);   Input: 1   2   3
    read (*B*, *C*);   4 5.5 6.6
    readln (*X*, *Y*);
    read (*Z*);

(g) *read* (*A*, *B*);   Input: 1   2   3
    readln;   4 5.5 6.6
    read (*C*);   7 8.8 9.9
    read (*X*);   10 11.11 12.12
    readln;   13 14.14 15.15
    readln (*Y*);
    readln:
    readln (*Z*);

3.6   Program Composition

As noted in Section 3.1, a Pascal program consists of three parts:

> program heading
> declaration part
> statement part.

These three parts *must* appear in the order shown. The ***program heading*** is a single statement of the form

> **program** *name* (*file-list*);

as described in the preceding section. The name assigned to the program must be a legal Pascal identifier, distinct from any other identifier used in the program.

The ***declaration part*** of a Pascal program may contain up to five sections that define various entities used in the program. These sections in the order in which they must appear are

> label section
> constant section
> type section
> variable section
> subprogram section

The ***constant section*** has the form

> **const**
>   *identifier-1* = *constant-1*;
>   *identifier-2* = *constant-2*;
>   ⋮
>   *identifier-k* = *constant-k*;

and is used to assign names to constants, as described in Section 3.2. The ***variable section*** has the form

> **var**
>   *variable-list-1* : *type-1*;
>   *variable-list-2* : *type-2*;
>   ⋮
>   *variable-list-m* : *type-m*;

and is used to declare *all* variables used in the program, that is, to specify their names and types. This also was discussed in Section 3.2. The other sections of the declaration part are discussed later.

The *statement part* of the program has the form

begin
   statement-1;
   statement-2;
     ⋮
   statement-n
end

This part of the program contains the statements that implement the steps of an algorithm. It may include such statements as assignment statements, input/output statements, and other statements considered in subsequent chapters of this book.

Correct punctuation is critical in a Pascal program, and each of the sections must be punctuated exactly as indicated. In particular, the program heading, each constant definition, and each variable declaration must end with a semicolon. In the statement part, the statements are *separated* by semicolons, but there need be no semicolon following the last statement. Finally, note that a period must follow the reserved word **end** that closes the statement part of the program.

We have seen that comments are indicated in Pascal program by enclosing them between (∗ and ∗)

(∗ *comment* ∗)

or within braces

{ *comment* }

These comments are not program statements and may be placed anywhere in the program, except, of course, in the middle of a reserved word, an identifier, a constant, and so on. As discussed in Section 2.5, comments should be used to explain the use of variables, to explain the purpose of the program or a program segment, and to provide other pertinent information about the program. Such documentation is intended to clarify the purpose and structure of the program. It is invaluable if revisions and modifications are made to the program in the future, especially if such maintenance is done by persons other than the original programmer.

3.7 Example: Truck Fleet Accounting

Suppose that a manufacturing company maintains a fleet of trucks to deliver its products. On each trip, the driver records the distance traveled in miles, the number of gallons of fuel used, the cost of the fuel, and the other costs of operating the truck. As part of the accounting process, the comptroller needs to calculate and record for each truck and for each trip the miles per gallon, the total cost of that trip, and the cost per mile. A simple program is to be designed to carry out these calculations.

The input to the program is the miles traveled, gallons of fuel used, fuel cost, and other operating costs, and the output must include the miles per gallon, the total cost of the trip, and the cost per mile. The calculations required to solve this program are quite simple. The miles per gallon is obtained by dividing the number of miles traveled by the number of gallons of fuel used. The total cost is obtained by adding the cost of fuel to the other operating costs. This sum is divided by the number of miles traveled to yield the cost per mile.

Expressing this algorithm in pseudocode is quite straightforward once we select the appropriate variable names to represent the quantities involved. Selecting names that are somewhat self-documenting, we use the following:

Miles	Total miles traveled
Fuel	Total gallons of fuel used
FuelCost	Total cost of fuel
OperCost	Total of other operating costs
Mpg	Miles per gallon
TotalCost	Total cost of the trip
CostPerMile	Cost per mile

A pseudocode description of the algorithm is the following:

ALGORITHM TO CALCULATE TRUCK COSTS:

(* This algorithm calculates miles per gallon (*Mpg*), total cost of the trip (*TotalCost*), and cost per mile (*CostPerMile*), given the number of miles traveled (*Miles*), gallons of fuel used (*Fuel*), cost of the fuel (*FuelCost*) and other operating costs (*OperCost*). *)

1. Enter *Miles, Fuel, FuelCost*, and *OperCost*.
2. Calculate *Mpg = Miles / Fuel*.
3. Calculate *TotalCost = FuelCost + OperCost*.
4. Calculate *CostPerMile = TotalCost / Miles*.
5. Display *Mpg, TotalCost*, and *CostPerMile*.

A Pascal program implementing this algorithm with two sample runs using test data to verify its correctness are shown in Figure 3.5.

```
PROGRAM TruckCosts (input, output);

(*************************************************************************

   This program calculates the miles per gallon, total cost, and cost
   per mile for the operation of a vehicle based on the miles traveled,
   fuel consumed, cost of fuel, and other operating costs.

*************************************************************************)
```

Figure 3.5

Figure 3.5 (cont.)

```
VAR
    Miles : integer;        (* total miles traveled *)
    Fuel,                   (* total gallons of fuel used *)
    FuelCost,               (* total cost of fuel *)
    OperCost,               (* total of other operating costs *)
    Mpg,                    (* miles per gallon *)
    TotalCost,              (* total cost of the trip *)
    CostPerMile : real;     (* cost per mile *)

BEGIN
    writeln ('Enter miles traveled, gallons of fuel used,');
    writeln ('total cost of fuel, and total of other costs:');
    readln (Miles, Fuel, FuelCost, OperCost);
    Mpg := Miles / Fuel;
    TotalCost := FuelCost + OperCost;
    CostPerMile := TotalCost / Miles;
    writeln ('Miles per gallon:', Mpg:7:2);
    writeln ('Total cost:      $', TotalCost:7:2);
    writeln ('Cost per mile:   $', CostPerMile:7:2)
END.



Sample runs:
```

```
Enter miles traveled, gallons of fuel used,
total cost of fuel, and total of other costs:
10 1 1.50 3.50
Miles per gallon:  10.00
Total cost:     $   5.00
Cost per mile:  $   0.50



Enter miles traveled, gallons of fuel used,
total cost of fuel, and total of other costs:
100 10 15 10
Miles per gallon:  10.00
Total cost:     $  25.00
Cost per mile:  $   0.25
```

3.8 Syntax Diagrams

In Section 3.2 we specified the syntax of a Pascal identifier by stating that it
may consist of any number of letters or digits, but it must begin with a letter.

This syntax rule can also be given by a *syntax diagram*:

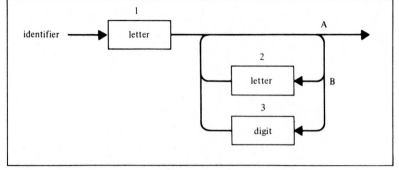

To use this diagram as a syntax rule for forming identifiers, we begin on the left and proceed to the right. Each time we pass through one of the boxes, we record a character of the specified type. At a junction in the diagram, any one of the paths may be followed. When we exit from the right, we will have formed a legal identifier. For example, the identifier *x14a* can be formed as follows: Beginning on the left and passing through the first box, we record the letter *x*. Moving to the right, at Junction A we loop back, passing through Box 3, and record the digit *1*. When we return to Junction A, we loop back again and record the digit *4* when we pass through Box 3. At Junction A we loop back one final time, but this time at Junction B we take the path through Box 2 and record the letter *a*. Finally, at Junction A we proceed to the right and exit, having formed the identifier *x14a*. (We labeled the boxes and junctions of the syntax diagram to facilitate our discussion, though normally such labels are not used.)

A syntax diagram may also be used to specify the syntax of a Pascal statement. For example, a syntax diagram specifying the correct form of an assignment statement is the following:

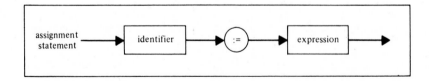

In a syntax diagram such as this one, the rectangular boxes indicate a language construct for which syntax rules must be specified, perhaps using syntax diagrams like that for an identifier. The circles or oval figures indicate symbols or reserved words in Pascal that must appear exactly as shown. For example, : = is a symbol that must be used to represent the assignment operator in an assignment statement.

Syntax diagrams may also be used to specify the form of a Pascal program and its various parts. The basic structure of a Pascal program is pictured in the following syntax diagram:

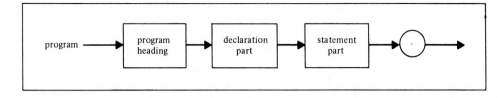

Each of the three parts of a program can also be described by a syntax diagram. For example,

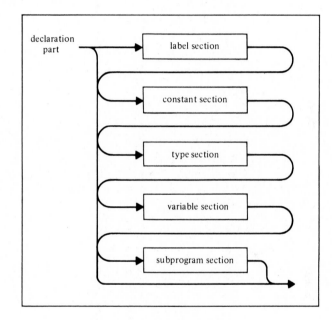

specifies the structure of the declaration part and

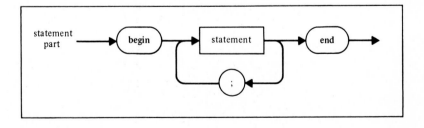

specifies the syntax of the statement part.

These syntax diagrams provide a convenient mechanism for defining precisely the syntax rules for Pascal and provide a quick reference for these rules. A complete set of syntax diagrams for the various components of a Pascal program is given in Appendix C.

Exercises

1. A "thing" is defined by the following syntax diagrams:

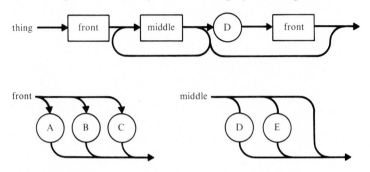

Determine which of the following are valid things.

(a) ADDDDDDA **(b)** ADDA **(c)** ADA **(d)** ABC **(e)** ADC **(f)** A

2. A widget is defined by the following syntax rules:

(a) A widget is a jabber followed by a wocky followed by a slash (/).
(b) A jabber is a thunk or a thunk followed by * or a thunk followed by a wocky.
(c) A thunk is the letter T followed by one of the digits 1, 2, or 3.
(d) A wocky is a thunk or a list of thunks separated by commas.

Give a complete set of syntax diagrams for widgets.

3. Write a program heading for a program named *Sample*, which will involve both input and output, a constant section to name 1900 with the name *Year* and the string Nat'l Science with *FieldOfStudy*, and a variable section that declares *Number* and *Prime* to be of integer type and *Initial* to be of character type.

4. Describe the syntax errors in the following program:

```
(*  1 *)   PROGRAM Eror (output; input)
(*  2 *)       (* 'Example BEGIN END' *)
(*  3 *)   VAR
(*  4 *)       Alpha, Beta, Rho
(*  5 *)       : real;
(*  6 *)       Add, Sub, Mult, Div : integer
(*  7 *)   CONST Year := 1776;
(*  8 *)   BEGIN
(*  9 *)       Mult := 3.14;
(* 10 *)       readln (Div);
(* 11 *)       ALPha := 3;
(* 12 *)       Beta = Alpha + 1;
(* 13 *)       Rho := Beta MOD 3;
(* 14 *)       writeln ('Value is, Alpha:3:1);
(* 15 *)       writeln ('Gamma isn''t' negative');
(* 16 *)       writeln (Mult:3:1);
(* 17 *)       Year := Year + 1
(* 18 *)   END
```

5. Write a program that reads two three-digit integers and then calculates and prints their product and the quotient and the remainder that result when the first is divided by the second. The output should be formatted to appear as follows:

```
        739                      61  R    7
     X   12                   -----
     -----              12  )  739
      8868
```

6. Write a program to read the lengths of the two legs of a right triangle, and calculate and print the area of the triangle (one half of the product of the legs) and the length of the hypotenuse (square root of the sum of the squares of the legs).

7. Write a program to read values for the coefficients A, B, and C of the quadratic equation $Ax^2 + Bx + C = 0$, and then find the two roots of this equation by using the quadratic formula

$$\frac{-B \pm \sqrt{B^2 - 4AC}}{2A}$$

Execute the program with several values of A, B, and C for which the quantity $B^2 - 4AC$ is nonnegative including $A = 4$, $B = 0$, $C = -36$; $A = 1$, $B = 5$, $C = -36$; $A = 2$, $B = 7.5$, $C = 6.25$.

8. Write a program to convert a measurement given in feet to the equivalent number of (a) yards, (b) inches, (c) centimeters, and (d) meters. (1 ft = 12 in., 1 yd = 3 ft, 1 in. = 2.54 cm, 1 m = 100 cm). Read the number of feet, and print the number of yards, number of feet, number of inches, number of centimeters, and number of meters, with appropriate labels.

9. Write a program to read a student's number, his or her old GPA (grade point average), and old number of course credits (for example, 31479, 3.25, 66), and then print these with appropriate labels. Finally, read the course credit and grade for each of four courses; for example, *Course1* = 5.0, *Grade1* = 3.7, *Course2* = 3.0, *Grade2* = 4.0, and so on. Calculate:

old # of honor points = (old # of course credits) * (old GPA)

new # of honor points = *Course1* * *Grade1* + *Course2* * *Grade2* + $\cdots$

total # of new course credits = *Course1* + *Course2* + $\cdots$

$$\text{current GPA} = \frac{\text{\# of new honor prints}}{\text{\# of new course credits}}$$

Print the current GPA with appropriate label. Then calculate cumulative GPA =

$$\frac{(\# \text{ of old honor prints}) + (\# \text{ of new honor points})}{(\# \text{ of old course credits}) + (\# \text{ of new course credits})}$$

and print this with a label.

10. The shipping clerk at the Rinky Dooflingy Company (Exercise 10 of Section 2.4) is faced with the following problem. Dooflingies are very delicate and must be shipped in special containers. These containers are available in four sizes, huge, large, medium, and small, which can hold 50, 20, 5, and 1 dooflingy, respectively. Write a program that reads the number of dooflingies to be shipped and prints the number of huge, large, medium, and small containers needed to send the shipment in the minimum number of containers. Use constant definitions for the number of dooflingies each type of container can hold. The output should be similar to the following:

```
Container   Number
=========   ======
   Huge       21
   Large       2
   Medium      1
   Small       3
```

Execute the program for 3, 18, 48, 78, and 10,598 dooflingies.

11. Write a program that reads the amount of a purchase and the amount received in payment, (both amounts in cents) and then computes the change in dollars, half dollars, quarters, dimes, nickels, and pennies.

12. Angles are often measured in degrees (°), minutes ('), and seconds ("). There are 360 degrees in a circle, 60 minutes in one degree, and 60 seconds in one minute. Write a program that reads two angular measurements given in degrees, minutes, and seconds, and then calculates and prints their sum. Use the program to verify each of the following:

$74°29'13'' + 105°8'16'' = 179°37'29''$
$7°14'55'' + 5°24'55'' = 12°39'50''$
$20°31'19'' + 0°31'30'' = 21°2'49''$
$122°17'48'' + 237°42'12'' = 0°0'0''$

13. Write a program that reads two three-digit integers and then prints their product in the following format:

```
          749
   X      381
       -------
          749
         5992
         2247
       -------
       285369
```

Execute the program with the following values: 749 and 381; -749 and 381; 749 and -381; -749 and -381; 999 and 999.

Programming Pointers

In this section we consider some aspects of program design and suggest guidelines for good programming style. We also point out some errors that may occur in writing Pascal programs.

Program Design

1. *Programs cannot be considered correct if they have not been validated using test data.* Test all programs with data for which the results are known or can be checked by hand calculations.

2. *Programs should be readable and understandable.*

   ● *Use meaningful identifiers.*

   For example,

   > *Wages* := *Hours* ∗ *Rate*

   is more meaningful than

   > *W* := *H* ∗ *R*

   or

   > *Z7* := *Alpha* ∗ *X*

   Also, avoid "cute" identifiers, as in

   > *BaconBroughtHome* := *HoursWasted* ∗ *Pittance*

   ● *Use comments to describe the purpose of a program or other key program segments.* However, don't clutter the program with needless comments; for example, the comment in the statement

   > *Counter* := *Counter* + 1 (∗ add 1 to counter ∗)

   is not helpful and should be omitted.

   ● *Label all output produced by a program.* For example,

   > *writeln* ('Employee #', *EmpNumber*:5, ' Wages = $', *Wages*:8:2)

   produces more informative output than

   > *writeln* (*EmpNumber*:5, *Wages*:8:2)

3. *Programs should be efficient.* For example, unnecessary computations such as

   > *Root1* := ($-B$ + *sqrt*(B ∗ B $-$ 4 ∗ A ∗ C)) / (2 ∗ A);
   > *Root2* := ($-B$ $-$ *sqrt*(B ∗ B $-$ 4 ∗ A ∗ C)) / (2 ∗ A);

should be avoided. It is not efficient to calculate $B * B - 4 * A * C$ or its square root twice; calculate it once, assign it to a variable, and then use this variable in these calculations.

4. *Programs should be general and flexible.* They should solve a class of problems rather than one specific problem. It should be relatively easy to modify a program to solve a related problem without changing much of the program. Using named constants instead of "magic numbers" as described in Section 3.2 is helpful in this regard.

Potential Problems

1. *Real constants must have at least one digit before and at least one digit after the decimal point.* Thus, 2. and .1 are not valid real constants.

2. *String constants must be enclosed within single quotes.* If either the beginning or ending quote is missing, an error will result. An apostrophe is represented in a character constant or a string constant as a pair of apostrophes, for example, 'isn''t'.

3. *The boolean constants* true *and* false *are not the same as the string constants 'true' and 'false'.*

4. *Parentheses within expressions must be paired.* For each left parenthesis there must be exactly one matching right parenthesis.

5. *Real division is denoted by* /, *integer division by* **div**. Thus 8 / 5 = 1.6, 8 **div** 5 = 1, 8.0 / 4.0 = 2.0, but 8.0 **div** 4.0 is not a valid expression.

6. *All multiplications must be indicated by* ∗. For example, $2 * n$ is valid, but $2n$ is not.

7. *A semicolon must appear*

   - *at the end of the program heading.*
   - *at the end of each constant declaration.*
   - *at the end of each variable declaration.*
   - *between statements.*

   No semicolon is necessary after the last statement of a program. However, it is not an error if one is used; for example,

   begin
   ⋮
   writeln ('Hourly rate: $', *Rate*);
   writeln ('Total Wages: $', *Wages*);
   end.

The semicolon at the end of the last *writeln* statement produces an **empty statement** between this statement and the reserved word **end**.

8. *Comments are enclosed within (* and *) or { and }*. Each beginning delimiter (* must have a matching end delimiter *). Failure to use these in pairs can produce strange results. For example, in the statement part

   begin
       (* Read employee data)
       readln (EmpNumber, Hours, Rate);
       (* Calculate wages *)
       *Wages := Hours * Rate*
   end

   everything from "Read employee data . . ." through "Calculate wages," including the *readln* statement, is a single comment. No values are read for *EmpNumber*, *Hours*, and *Rate*, and so *Hours* and *Rate* are undefined when the statement *Wages := Hours * Rate* is executed.

9. *There must be a period after the reserved word* **end** *at the end of the program*. Failure to include it usually causes an error.

10. *All identifiers must be declared*. Failure to declare an identifier used in a program is an error.

11. *Pascal does not distinguish between upper-case and lower-case letters except in string constants*. For example, *Sum*, *sum*, and *SUM* all represent the same identifier. Thus, variable declarations such as

    var
        Sum : integer;
        SUM : real;

    produce an error, since the same identifier is declared more than once.

12. *All variables are initially undefined*. Although some compilers may initialize variables to specific values (e.g., 0 for numeric variables), it should be assumed that all variables are initially undefined. For example, the statement $y := x + 1$ usually produces a "garbage" value for y if x has not previously been assigned a value.

13. *The type of a variable and the type of its value must be the same*. Thus, entering the value 2.7 for the integer variable *Counter* in the statement

    readln (Counter)

    may generate an error message such as

    *** I/O error while reading input from the terminal.
    '.' found where ' + ', ' − ', or digit expected.

Similarly, the assignment statement

  Counter : = 2.7

is also incorrect. An integer value may, however, be assigned to a real variable and is automatically converted to real type.

14. *Reserved words, identifiers, and constants, as well as the assignment operator, may not be broken at the end of a line, nor may they contain blanks (except, of course, a string constant may contain blanks).* Thus, the statements

  EmpNumber : = 12345;
  writeln ('Employee number is ',
        EmpNumber:5)

are valid, whereas the statements

  Emp Number : = 12 345;
  writeln ('Employee number
        is ', *EmpNumber*:5)

are not valid.

15. *An equal sign* (=) *is used in constant declarations to associate an identifier with a constant. The assignment operator* (:=) *is used in assignment statements to assign a value to a variable.* These two operators are not interchangeable; do not confuse them. Also, note that : = is a single operator; : and = may not be separated by a blank.

Program Style

In the examples in this text, we adopt certain stylistic guidelines for Pascal programs, and you should write your program in a similar style. In this text the following standards are used; others are described in the Programming Pointers of subsequent chapters.

1. *Put each statement of the program on a separate line.*

2. *Use upper-case and lower-case letters in a way that contributes to program readability;* for example, put reserved words in upper case and identifiers in lower case, capitalizing the first letter if it is user defined.

3. *Put the program heading and the reserved words* **begin, end, const,** *and* **var** *on separate lines.*

4. *When a statement is continued from one line to another, indent the continuation line(s).*

5. *Each* **begin** *and its corresponding* **end** *should be aligned. The statements enclosed by* **begin** *and* **end** *are indented.*

    begin
      statement-1;
          ⋮
      statement-n
    end

6. *Indent each constant declaration and each variable declaration;* for example,

    const
      TaxRate = 0.1963;
      InterestRate = 0.185;
    var
      EmpNumber : *integer*;
      Hours, Rate, Wages : *real*;

7. *Insert a blank line before the* **const** *section, the* **var** *section, the beginning of the statement part of the program, and wherever appropriate in a sequence of statements to set off blocks of statements.*

8. *Use spaces between the items in a statement to make it more readable.*

Variations and Extensions

Variations and extensions of the features described in this chapter are provided in many versions of Pascal (see Appendix G for details). Some of these are:

- Additional data types (*byte, longint*).

- Alternative representations of numbers (hexadecimal).

- Specified values for predefined constants (*maxint* = 32767) and/or additional predefined constants (*Pi* = 3.1415926536E + 00).

- Additional reserved words (**shl, shr, otherwise**).

- Other characters (underscore) allowed in identifiers and/or limits on the number of characters.

- Additional arithmetic operators (**shl, shr, not, and, or, xor**) and functions (*frac, int, log, pwroften*).

- Optional and/or modified forms of the program heading.

- Alternative forms of the declaration part.

4

Control Structures

A journey of a thousand miles begins with a single step.

ANCIENT PROVERB

Then Logic would take you by the throat, and force you to do it!

ACHILLES IN LEWIS CARROLL'S
What the Tortoise Said to Achilles

But what has been said once can always be repeated.

ZENO OF ELEA

In Chapter 2 we described several techniques that assist in the design of programs that are easy to understand and whose logical flow is easy to follow. Such programs are more likely to be correct when first written than are poorly structured programs; and if they are not correct, the errors are easier to find and correct. Such programs are also easier to modify, which is especially important, since such modifications are often made by someone other than the original programmer.

In a ***structured program,*** the logical flow is governed by the three basic control structures, ***sequential, selection,*** and ***repetition.*** In this chapter we review these control structures and describe in detail their implementations in Pascal.

4.1 Sequential Structure: Compound Statements; *begin* and *end*

Sequential structure, as illustrated in Fig. 4.1, refers to the execution of statements in the order in which they appear. The sample programs in Chapter 3 are all "straight-line" programs in which the only control used is sequential.

94

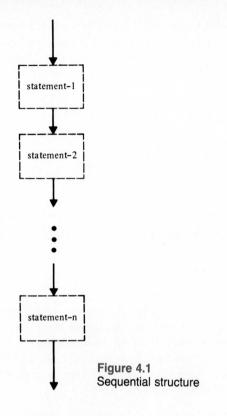

Figure 4.1
Sequential structure

In this section we consider the implementation of sequential structure as a compound statement in Pascal.

The following syntax diagram displays the form of a *compound statement.*

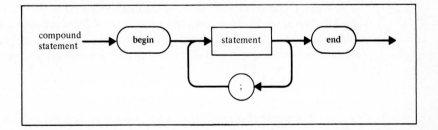

A compound statement thus consists of the reserved word **begin,** followed by a sequence of statements, followed by the reserved word **end,** and so has the form

> **begin**
>   *statement*-1;
>   *statement*-2;
>   ⋮
>   *statement*-n
> **end**

Note that semicolons are used to separate the statements that make up a compound statement.

Execution of the statements in a compound statement proceeds sequentially. For example, the compound statement

> **begin**
>   *write* ('Enter two numbers: ');
>   *readln* (*Number1, Number2*);
>   *Sum* := *Number1* + *Number2*;
>   *writeln* ('Sum =', *Sum*)
> **end**

first displays a prompt to the user and then reads two numbers; next, it calculates their sum; and finally, it displays the result.

4.2   The Boolean Data Type

Several of the Pascal statements that implement selection and repetition structures involve boolean expressions. Consequently, before we can describe these statements, we must examine in more detail the **boolean** data type.

Recall that there are two boolean constants, *true* and *false,* and that boolean variables may have only these values. The standard type identifier *boolean* is used to specify the type of a boolean variable; for example,

> **var**
>   *Male, Graduate, OnDeansList, OddValue* : *boolean;*

declares that *Male, Graduate, OnDeansList,* and *OddValue* are boolean variables.

Three predefined boolean-valued functions are provided in Pascal. One is the function *odd,* which returns the value *true* or *false* according to whether its integer parameter is an odd or even number. For example, if the integer variable *Number* has the value 17, then the value of the boolean expression

> *odd(Number)*

is *true*. The other two predefined boolean-valued functions, *eoln* and *eof,* are used in connection with file processing and are described in Chapter 6.

Boolean values may be displayed with *write* or *writeln* statements, as described in Section 3.5, but values for boolean variables cannot be read (except from certain types of files, as described in Chapter 12). A Boolean variable may, however, be assigned a value with an assignment statement of the form

> *boolean-variable* := *boolean-expression*

For example,

> *Male* := *true;*

assigns the boolean constant *true* to the boolean variable *Male,* and

$$OddValue := odd(5 * Number + 1);$$

assigns *false* to *OddValue* if the integer variable *Number* has the value 3.

Boolean expressions may be either **simple** or **compound.** Boolean constants and variables, as well as references to boolean-valued functions, are simple boolean expressions, as are expressions of the form

expression-1 relational-operator expression-2

where *expression-1* and *expression-2* are of the same type and the **relational operator** may be any of the following:

Relational Operator	Definition
<	is less than (or precedes)
>	is greater than (or follows)
=	is equal to
<=	is less than or equal to
>=	is greater than or equal to
<>	is not equal to

These relational operators may be applied to any of the four standard data types: integer, real, boolean, and character. The following are examples of boolean expressions formed using these relational operators:

$$x < 5.2$$
$$sqr(b) >= 4*a*c$$
$$Number = 500$$
$$Initial <> 'Q'$$

For numeric data, the relational operators are the standard ones used to compare numbers. Thus, if x has the value 4.5, the expression $x < 5.2$ is true. If *Number* has the value 400, the expression *Number* $= 500$ is false.

When using the relational operators $=$ and $<>$ to compare numeric quantities, it is important to remember that *most real values cannot be stored exactly* (see Section 1.3). *Consequently, boolean expressions formed by comparing real quantities with $=$ are often evaluated as false, even though these quantities are algebraically equal.* The program in Figure 4.2 demonstrates this by showing that for most real values X, the value of Y computed by

$$Y := X * (1.0 / X);$$

is not 1. In this program, the assignment statement

$$EqualsOne := (Y = 1.0);$$

assigns the value *true* to the boolean variable *EqualsOne* if the value of *Y* is equal to 1.0, and *false* otherwise.

```
PROGRAM Roundoff (input, output);

(**********************************************************************

        Program to show inexact representation of reals.

********************************************************************)

VAR
    X,                      (* real number entered *)
    Y : real;               (* Y = X * (1 / X) *)
    EqualsOne : boolean;    (* indicates if value of Y is 1 *)

BEGIN
    write ('Enter real # :   ');
    readln (X);
    Y := X * (1.0 / X);
    writeln ('X = ', X:7:5, '    Y = X*(1/X) = ', Y:7:5,
            '    1.0 - Y = ', 1.0 - Y:12);
    EqualsOne := (Y = 1.0);
    writeln ('Y equals 1?    ', EqualsOne)
END.



Sample runs:


Enter real # :   0.5
X = 0.50000    Y = X*(1/X) = 1.00000    1.0 - Y =  0.00000E+00
Y equals 1?    TRUE


Enter real # :   0.1
X = 0.10000    Y = X*(1/X) = 1.00000    1.0 - Y =  7.10543E-15
Y equals 1?    FALSE


Enter real # :   0.2
X = 0.20000    Y = X*(1/X) = 1.00000    1.0 - Y =  7.10543E-15
Y equals 1?    FALSE


Enter real # :   6.39631
X = 6.39631    Y = X*(1/X) = 1.00000    1.0 - Y =  7.10543E-15
Y equals 1?    FALSE
```

Figure 4.2

For character data, a **collating sequence** is used to establish an ordering for the character set. This sequence varies from one machine to another, but in all cases, letters are in alphabetical order and digits are in numerical order. Thus

'A' < 'F'
'6' > '4'

are true boolean expressions. Comparison of characters and strings is discussed in more detail in Chapter 8.

For boolean values, the constant *false* is less than the constant *true*. Thus,

false < *true*
true > *false*

are true boolean expressions.

Compound boolean expressions are formed by combining boolean expressions using the **boolean operators**

not
and
or

These operators are defined as follows:

Boolean Operator	Boolean Expression	Definition
not	**not** *p*	*negation* of *p*: **not** *p* is false if *p* is true; **not** *p* is true if *p* is false.
and	*p* **and** *q*	*conjunction* of *p* and *q*: *p* **and** *q* is true if *p* and *q* both are true; it is false otherwise.
or	*p* **or** *q*	*disjunction* of *p* and *q*: *p* **or** *q* is true if either *p* or *q* or both are true; it is false otherwise.

These definitions are summarized by the following **truth tables,** which display all possible values for *p* and *q* and the corresponding values of the boolean expression:

p	**not** *p*
true	false
false	true

p	*q*	*p* **or** *q*
true	true	true
true	false	true
false	true	true
false	false	false

p	*q*	*p* **and** *q*
true	true	true
true	false	false
false	true	false
false	false	false

In a boolean expression containing several of these operators, the operations are performed in the order **not, and, or.** Parentheses may be used to indicate subexpressions that should be evaluated first. For example, given the boolean variables *Male, OnDeansList,* and *Graduate,* we can form boolean expressions such as

Male **and** *OnDeansList*
not *Male* **and** *Graduate*
Male **and** (*OnDeansList* **or** *Graduate*)

The first expression *Male* **and** *OnDeansList* is true only in the case that *Male* and *OnDeansList* both are true. In the second example, the subexpression **not**

Male is evaluated first, and this result is then combined with the value of *Graduate,* using the operator **and.** The entire expression is therefore true only in the case that *Male* is false and *Graduate* is true. In the last example, the subexpression *OnDeansList* **or** *Graduate* is evaluated first, and this result is then combined with the value of *Male,* using the operator **and.** Thus, the entire expression is true only in the case that *Male* is true and either *OnDeansList* or *Graduate* (or both) is true. This is summarized in the following truth table:

Male	*OnDeansList*	*Graduate*	*Male* **and** *(OnDeansList* **or** *Graduate)*
true	true	true	true
true	true	false	true
true	false	true	true
true	false	false	false
false	true	true	false
false	true	false	false
false	false	true	false
false	false	false	false

The evaluation of a boolean expression that contains an assortment of arithmetic operators, boolean operators, and relational operators is carried out using the following *precedence levels:*

Operator	Priority
not	highest (performed first)
/, *, div, mod, and	
+, −, or	lowest (performed last)
<, >, =, <=, >=, <>	

As an example, suppose that we wish to determine whether the value of the real variable x is strictly between 1.0 and the real value $z + 7.0$. The appropriate boolean expression is

$$(1.0 < x) \text{ and } (x < z + 7.0)$$

The parentheses may not be omitted, for the resulting expression

$$1.0 < x \text{ and } x < z + 7.0$$

would be equivalent to the expression

$$1.0 < (x \text{ and } x) < (z + 7.0)$$

since the highest-priority operator **and** is evaluated first. This is clearly not a valid expression because the boolean operator **and** cannot be applied to numeric operands.

Exercises

1. Assuming that a, b, and c are boolean variables, use truth tables to display the values of the following boolean expressions for all possible values of a, b, and c:

   (a) a **or not** b **(b)** **not**(a **and** b)
   (c) **not** a **or not** b **(d)** a **and** *true* **or** $(1 + 2 = 4)$
   (e) a **and** (b **or** c)   **(f)** (a **and** b) **or** (a **and** c)

2. Write boolean expressions to express the following conditions:

   (a) x is greater than 3.
   (b) y is strictly between 2 and 5.
   (c) r is negative and z is positive.
   (d) *Alpha* and *Beta* both are positive.
   (e) *Alpha* and *Beta* have the same sign (both are negative or both are positive).
   (f) $-5 < x < 5$.
   (g) a is less than 6 or is greater than 10.
   (h) $p = q = r$.
   (i) x is less than 3, or y is less than 3, but not both.

3. Given the boolean variables a, b, and c, write a boolean expression that is

   (a) true if and only if a and b are true and c is false.
   (b) true if and only if a is true and at least one of b or c is true.
   (c) true if and only if exactly one of a and b is true.

4. The Cawker City Credit Company approves a loan application if the applicant's income is at least \$25,000 or the value of his assets is at least \$100,000; in addition, his total liabilities must be less than \$50,000. Write a program that accepts three numbers representing income, assets, and liabilities, assigns the value *true* or *false* to the boolean variable *CreditOK* according to these criteria, and displays this value.

5. Write a program that reads three real numbers and assigns the appropriate value *true* or *false* to the following boolean variables:

Triangle:	*true* if the three real numbers can represent lengths of the sides of a triangle, and *false* otherwise. (The sum of any two of the numbers must be greater than the third.)
Equilateral:	*true* if *Triangle* is *true* and the triangle is equilateral (three sides are equal).
Isosceles:	*true* if *Triangle* is *true* and the triangle is isosceles (at least two sides are equal).
Scalene:	*true* if *Triangle* is *true* and the triangle is scalene (no two sides are equal).

The output from your program should have a format like the following:

```
For A = 2.00, B = 3.00, C = 3.00
Triangle is:    TRUE
Equilateral is: FALSE
Isosceles is:   TRUE
Scalene is:     FALSE
```

4.3 Selection Structure: The *if* Statement

A *selection structure* makes possible the selection and execution of one of a number of alternative actions. This enables the programmer to introduce decision points in a program, that is, points at which a decision is made *during program execution* to follow one of several courses of action. In this section we consider the simple selection structures in which there are two possible courses of action. These are illustrated in Figure 4.3.

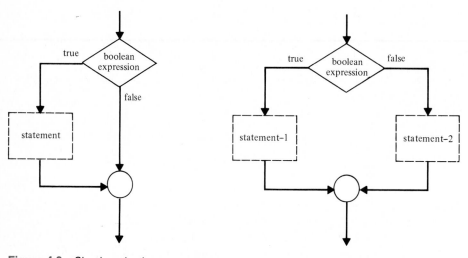

Figure 4.3   Simple selection structures

These selection structures are implemented in Pascal using the **if** statement. This statement has one of the forms

> **if** *boolean-expression* **then**
>   *statement*

or

> **if** *boolean-expression* **then**
>   *statement-1*
> **else**
>   *statement-2*

Both forms are summarized in the following syntax diagram:

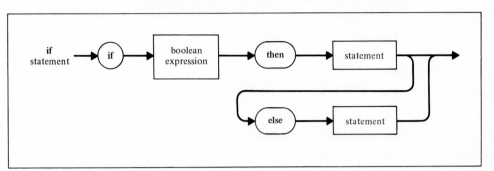

In the first form of the **if** statement, the specified statement is executed if the boolean expression is true, otherwise, it is bypassed, and execution continues with the next statement in the program. For example, in the statement

> **if** *Score* <= 60 **then**
> *writeln* ('F');

the boolean expression *Score* <= 60 is evaluated, and if it is true, the letter F is displayed. Otherwise, the *writeln* statement is bypassed. In either case, execution continues with the statement following this **if** statement. The statement that appears in an **if** statement may be a compound statement, for example

> **if** *Hours* > 40 **then**
> **begin**
>   *Overtime* := *Hours* − 40;
>   *OvertimePay* := 1.5 ∗ *Overtime* ∗ *Rate*
> **end** (∗ **if** ∗);

Here the values of *Overtime* and *OvertimePay* are calculated only in the case that the boolean expression *Hours* > 40 is true.

The second form of the **if** statement allows the programmer not only to specify the statement selected for execution when the boolean expression is true but also to indicate an alternative statement for execution when it is false. If the boolean expression is true, *statement-1* is executed and *statement-2* is bypassed. Otherwise, *statement-1* is bypassed and *statement-2* is executed. In either case, execution continues with the statement following the **if** statement.

A problem that requires this type of selection structure is the pollution index problem considered in Chapter 2. In this problem, a pollution index is to be calculated, and if this index is less than some cutoff value, a message indicating a safe condition must be displayed; if not, a message indicating a hazardous condition must be displayed. This selection was indicated in the algorithm for solving this problem (see Section 2.2) by

> If *Index* < *Cutoff* then
> Display 'Safe condition'
> Else
> Display 'Hazardous condition'

and is implemented in the Pascal program in Figure 4.4 by the following Pascal statement:

> **if** *Index* < *Cutoff* **then**
>   *writeln* ('Safe condition')
> **else**
>   *writeln* ('Hazardous condition')

```
PROGRAM PollutionIndex (input, output);

(*********************************************************************

   Program that reads 3 pollution levels, calculates a pollution
   index as their average, and then displays a "safe condition"
   message if this index is less than some cutoff value, otherwise
   displays a "hazardous condition" message.

*********************************************************************)

CONST
    Cutoff = 50;                 (* bottom line for a safe condition *)

VAR
    Level1, Level2, Level3,      (* three pollution readings *)
    Index : integer;             (* pollution index *)

BEGIN
    write ('Enter 3 pollution readings:   ');
    readln (Level1, Level2, Level3);
    Index := (Level1 + Level2 + Level3) DIV 3;
    IF Index < Cutoff THEN
        writeln ('Safe condition')
    ELSE
        writeln ('Hazardous condition')
END.



Sample runs:



Enter 3 pollution readings:   55 39 48
Safe condition


Enter 3 pollution readings:   68 49 57
Hazardous condition
```

Figure 4.4

As another illustration of this form of the **if** statement, suppose that the company in the wage calculation example of Section 3.5 pays its employees an hourly wage, with all hours over 40 paid at 1.5 times the regular hourly rate. A program is to be written to calculate the wages for an employee of this company. An algorithm for calculating wages is as follows:

WAGE CALCULATION ALGORITHM—VERSION 1

(* Algorithm to calculate *Wages* for an employee whose employee number (*EmpNumber*), *Hours* worked, and hourly *Rate* are read; *RegWages* denotes regular wages, *OverWages* are overtime wages paid at 1.5 times the hourly rate for hours over 40. *)

1. Read *EmpNumber, Hours,* and *Rate* for the employee.
2. If *Hours* > 40 then calculate
    RegWages = *Rate* * 40, and
    OverWages = 1.5 * *Rate* * (*Hours* − 40).
   Else
    Calculate *RegWages* = *Rate* * *Hours,* and
    set *OverWages* equal to 0.
3. Calculate *Wages* = *RegWages* + *OverWages.*
4. Display *EmpNumber* and *Wages.*

A Pascal program to implement this algorithm is given in Fig. 4.5. An **if** statement is used to implement the selection structure that selects the method of calculating wages depending on the boolean expression *Hours* > 40. Note the use of the two constant identifiers *OvertimeFactor* and *HoursLimit* in place of the constants 1.5 and 40. These identifiers are defined in the constant section and then used throughout the program. If the program has to be modified to handle overtime paid at a rate different from 1.5 or for hours above some number other than 40, we need change only the definitions of *OvertimeFactor* and *HoursLimit;* the statement part of the program need not be modified.

```
PROGRAM WageCalculation (input, output);

(*****************************************************************************

   Program to read an employee's number, hours worked, and hourly
   rate and then calculate his or her wages.  Hours above HoursLimit
   are paid at OvertimeFactor times the hourly rate.

*****************************************************************************)

CONST
   OvertimeFactor = 1.5;   (* overtime multiplication factor *)
   HoursLimit = 40.0;      (* overtime hours limit *)

VAR
   EmpNumber : integer;    (* employee number *)
   Hours,                  (* hours worked *)
   Rate,                   (* hourly pay rate *)
   RegWages,               (* regular wages *)
   OverWages,              (* overtime pay *)
   Wages : real;           (* total wages for employee *)
```

Figure 4.5

Figure 4.5 (cont.)

```
BEGIN
   writeln ('Enter employee #, hours worked, hourly rate:');
   readln (EmpNumber, Hours, Rate);
   IF Hours > HoursLimit THEN
      BEGIN (* Overtime *)
         RegWages := Rate * HoursLimit;
         OverWages := OvertimeFactor * Rate * (Hours - HoursLimit)
      END (* Overtime *)
   ELSE
      BEGIN (* No overtime *)
         RegWages := Rate * Hours;
         OverWages := 0
      END (* No overtime *);
   Wages := RegWages + OverWages;
   writeln;
   writeln ('Employee #', EmpNumber:1, '  Wages = $', Wages:4:2);
END.
```

Sample runs:
_____

```
Enter employee #, hours worked, hourly rate:
1234 30.0 10.00

Employee #1234  Wages = $300.00


Enter employee #, hours worked, hourly rate:
1235 45.0 10.00

Employee #1235  Wages = $475.00


Enter employee #, hours worked, hourly rate:
2775 43.5 8.55

Employee #2775  Wages = $386.89


Enter employee #, hours worked, hourly rate:
2884 38.25 9.45

Employee #2884  Wages = $361.46
```

The statements in an **if** statement may themselves contain other **if** statements. In this case, one **if** statement is said to be *nested* within the other **if** statement. To illustrate, suppose that in the preceding problem, each employee with a number greater than or equal to 1000 is paid weekly an amount equal to his or her annual salary divided by 52 but that all other employees are paid on an hourly basis. The following algorithm solves this problem:

WAGE CALCULATION ALGORITHM—VERSION 2

(* Algorithm to calculate wages for employees. Those with an employee number (*EmpNumber*) of 1000 or above are salaried and receive weekly *Wages* of *Salary*/52. All others are paid according to *Hours* worked at a given hourly *Rate*. For these employees, *RegWages* denotes regular wages and *OverWages* denotes overtime wages paid at 1.5 times the hourly rate for hours above 40. *)

1. Read *EmpNumber* for an employee.
2. If *EmpNumber* ≥ 1000 then   (* salaried employee *)
   a. Read *Salary*.
   b. Calculate *Wages* = *Salary* / 52.
   Else   (* hourly employee *)
   a. Read *Hours* and *Rate*.
   b. If *Hours* > 40 then   (* overtime *)
      i. Calculate *RegWages* = *Rate* * 40.
      ii. Calculate *OverWages* = 1.5 * *Rate* * (*Hours* − 40).
      Else   (* no overtime *)
      i. Calculate *RegWages* = *Rate* * *Hours*.
      ii. Set *OverWages* equal to 0.
   c. Calculate *Wages* = *RegWages* + *OverWages*.
3. Display *EmpNumber* and *Wages*.

This pseudocode description of the algorithm clearly shows the selection structure for calculating wages based on the condition *Hours* > 40 nested within the larger selection structure based on the condition *EmpNumber* ≥ 1000. This nested selection structure is implemented in the Pascal program in Figure 4.6 by nested **if** statements.

```
PROGRAM WageCalculation (input, output);

(*********************************************************************

   Program to calculate wages for an employee.  An employee's number
   is read.  If this number is greater than WageTypeLine, an annual
   salary for this employee is then read, and wages are calculated
   by dividing this salary by NumPayPeriods.  Otherwise, the number
   of hours worked and the rate per hour are read and wages are
   calculated with hours above HoursLimit paid at OvertimeFactor
   times the hourly rate.

*********************************************************************)

CONST
    WageTypeLine = 1000;    (* dividing-line for salaried & hourly type *)
    NumPayPeriods = 52;     (* number of pay periods *)
    OvertimeFactor = 1.5;   (* overtime multiplication factor *)
    HoursLimit = 40.0;      (* overtime hours limit *)
```

Figure 4.6

Figure 4.6   (cont.)

```
VAR
   EmpNumber : integer;      (* employee number *)
   Salary,                   (* annual salary *)
   Hours,                    (* hours worked *)
   Rate,                     (* hourly pay rate *)
   RegWages,                 (* regular wages *)
   OverWages,                (* overtime pay *)
   Wages : real;             (* total wages for employee *)

BEGIN
   write('Enter employee #:  ');
   readln (EmpNumber);
   IF EmpNumber >= WageTypeLine THEN
      BEGIN (* salaried *)
         write ('Enter salary:  ');
         readln (Salary);
         Wages := Salary / NumPayPeriods
      END (* salaried *)
   ELSE
      BEGIN (* hourly *)
         write ('Enter hours & rate:  ');
         readln (Hours, Rate);
         IF Hours > HoursLimit THEN
            BEGIN (* Overtime *)
               RegWages := Rate * HoursLimit;
               OverWages := OvertimeFactor * Rate * (Hours - HoursLimit)
            END (* Overtime *)
         ELSE
            BEGIN (* No overtime *)
               RegWages := Rate * Hours;
               OverWages := 0
            END (* No overtime *);
         Wages := RegWages + OverWages;
      END (* hourly *);
   writeln ('Employee #', EmpNumber:1, '  Wages = $', wages:4:2);
END.
```

```
Sample runs:


Enter employee #:  12345
Enter salary:  52000
Employee #12345  Wages = $1000.00


Enter employee #:  375
Enter hours & rate:  42.0 10.00
Employee #375  Wages = $430.00


Enter employee #:  2253
Enter salary:  25900
Employee #2253  Wages = $498.08


Enter employee #:  410
Enter hours & rate:  37.4 8.35
Employee #410  Wages = $313.12
```

In a nested **if** *statement, each* **else** *clause is matched with the nearest preceding unmatched* **if.** For example, in the statement

> **if** $x > 0$ **then**
>   **if** $y > 0$ **then**
> $z := sqrt(x) + sqrt(y)$
>   **else**
>   *readln* (z);

the **else** clause is associated with the **if** statement containing the boolean expression $y > 0$. Consequently, the *readln* statement is executed only in the case that x is positive and y is nonpositive. If we wish to associate this **else** clause with the outer **if** statement, we can write

> **if** $x > 0$ **then**
>   **begin**
>   **if** $y > 0$ **then**
> $z := sqrt(x) + sqrt(y)$
>   **end** (* **if** x *)
> **else**
>   *readln* (z);

Here the *readln* statement is executed whenever x is nonpositive.

In these examples, note that each **else** clause is aligned with the corresponding **if.** This alignment emphasizes the relationship between each **if** and its associated **else.**

4.4 Multialternative Selection Structure: *if–else if* Constructs and the *case* Statement

The selection structure considered in the preceding section involved selecting one of two alternatives. It is also possible to use the **if** statement to design selection structures that contain more than two alternatives. The program for wage calculation in Figure 4.6 is, in fact, an example of a three-way selection structure in which a selection was made from the following three alternatives:

1. Salaried wages.
2. Hourly wages with overtime.
3. Hourly wages with no overtime.

This three-way selection structure was implemented with a nested **if** statement of the form

> **if** *boolean-expression-1* **then**
>   *statement-1*
> **else**
>   **if** *boolean-expression-2* **then**
>   *statement-2*
>   **else**
>   *statement-3*

In general, any *n-way selection structure* can be constructed using a nested **if** statement, but such compound **if** statements may become quite complex, and the correspondence between **if**s and **else**s may not be clear if indentation is not used properly. When implementing an *n*-way selection structure with a compound **if** statement, we prefer to write it as an **if–else if** construct of the form

> **if** *boolean-expression-1* **then**
>   *statement-1*
> **else if** *boolean-expression-2* **then**
>   *statement-2*
>   ⋮
> **else**
>   *statement-n*

This format clarifies the correspondence between **if**s and **else**s and also emphasizes that the statement implements an *n*-way selection structure in which exactly one of *statement-1, statement-2, . . . , statement-n* is executed.

As an illustration of multialternative selection, consider the problem of assigning letter grades to test scores and honors credit as indicated in the following table:

Numeric Score	Letter Grade	Honors Credit
score $\geq$ 90	A	true
$80 \leq$ score < 90	B	true
$70 \leq$ score < 80	C	false
$60 \leq$ score < 70	D	false
score < 60	F	false

The program in Figure 4.7 uses an **if–else if** construct to implement the five-way selection structure given in this table.

```
PROGRAM Grader (input, output);

(*****************************************************************************

   Program to assign a letter grade to an integer test score and
   determine if student is to be designated as an honors student.

*****************************************************************************)
CONST
    ABLine = 90;      (* dividing line between A and B *)
    BCLine = 80;      (*      "        "       "   B and C *)
    CDLine = 70;      (*      "        "       "   C and D *)
    DFLine = 60;      (*      "        "       "   D and F *)

VAR
    Grade : char;     (* letter grade *)
    Score : integer;  (* test score *)
    Honors : boolean; (* indicates if honors credit to be given *)
```

Figure 4.7

Figure 4.7 (cont.)

```
BEGIN
   write('Enter score:   ');
   readln (Score);
   Honors := false;
   IF Score >= ABLine THEN
      BEGIN
         Grade := 'A';
         Honors := true
      END (* IF *)
   ELSE IF Score >= BCLine THEN
      BEGIN
         Grade := 'B';
         Honors := true
      END (* ELSE IF *)
   ELSE IF Score >= CDLine THEN
      Grade := 'C'
   ELSE IF Score >= DFLine THEN
      Grade := 'D'
   ELSE
      Grade := 'F';
   writeln ('Grade = ', Grade);
   IF Honors THEN
      writeln ('Honors student')
END.
```

```
Sample runs:


Enter score:   100
Grade = A
Honors student


Enter score:   30
Grade = F


Enter score:   65
Grade = D


Enter score:   89
Grade = B
Honors student

Enter score:   100
Grade = A
Honors student


Enter score:   30
Grade = F


Enter score:   65
Grade = D
```

Pascal also provides a **case** statement that is useful in implementing some multialternative selection structures. This statement has the form

    case *selector* **of**
        label-list-1 : *statement-1;*
        label-list-2 : *statement-2;*
                ⋮
        label-list-n : *statement-n*
    end

where *selector* is an expression of integer, boolean, or character type (or of enumerated or subrange type, as defined in Chapter 7). Note that the selector may not be of real type. Each *label-list-i* is a list of one or more possible values of the selector. When a **case** statement is executed, the selector is evaluated; if this value is in *label-list-i,* then *statement-i* is executed and execution continues with the statement following the reserved word **end** that marks the end of the **case** statement. It is an error if the selector's value is not in any of the label lists.[1] A syntax diagram for the case statement is

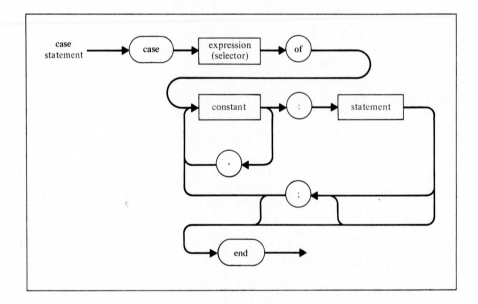

---

[1] Many implementations of Pascal allow execution of a **case** statement to "fall through" if the value of the selector is not in any of the label lists; that is, execution continues with the statement following the **case** statement. Many implementations also allow an **otherwise** or **else** clause that is executed if the value of the selector does not appear in any of the label lists.

    case *selector* **of**
        label-list-1 : *statement-1;*
                ⋮
        label-list-n : *statement-n*
    otherwise (∗ **else** in some versions ∗)
        statement
    end

As an application of the **case** statement, consider the problem of converting an integer class code to a class name. If the value of the variable *Class* is 1, 2, 3, or 4, the following **case** statement is appropriate:

```
case Class of
    1: writeln ('Freshman');
    2: writeln ('Sophomore');
    3: writeln ('Junior');
    4: writeln ('Senior')
end (* case *);
```

To ensure that the value of the selector *Class* is in the range from 1 through 4, an **if** statement should be used:[2]

```
if (Class < 1) or (Class > 4) then
    writeln ('Illegal class code')
else
    case Class of
        1: writeln ('Freshman');
        2: writeln ('Sophomore');
        3: writeln ('Junior');
        4: writeln ('Senior')
    end (* case *);
```

Occasionally, no action is required for certain values of the selector in a **case** statement. In such situations, these values may be placed in a label list for which the corresponding statement is empty. For example, a program to count aces and face cards might use the **case** statement

```
case Card of
                'A': ace := ace + 1;
        'J', 'Q', 'K': face := face + 1;
    '2', '3', '4', '5', '6',
        '7', '8', '9', 'T': (* no action required *)
end (* case *);
```

The grading program in Figure 4.7 used an **if–else if** construct to implement a five-way selection structure. The program in Figure 4.8 does the same processing but implements the selection structure using a **case** statement.

---

[2] If an **otherwise** or **else** clause as described in the previous footnote is available, it can be used to check that the selector is in range; for example,

```
case Class of
    1: writeln ('Freshman');
    2: writeln ('Sophomore');
    3: writeln ('Junior');
    4: writeln ('Senior')
    otherwise (* or else *)
        writeln ('Illegal class code')
end (* case *);
```

```
PROGRAM Grader (input, output);

(*********************************************************************

    Program to assign a letter grade to an integer test score and
    determine if student is to be designated as an honors student.

*********************************************************************)

CONST
    MaxScore = 100;     (* maximum score *)
    ABLine = 90;        (* dividing line between A and B *)
    BCLine = 80;        (*       "         "       "   B and C *)
    CDLine = 70;        (*       "         "       "   C and D *)
    DFLine = 60;        (*       "         "       "   D and F *)

VAR
    Grade : char;       (* letter grade *)
    Score : integer;    (* test score *)
    Honors : boolean;   (* indicates if honors credit to be given *)

BEGIN
    Honors := false;
    write ('Score:   ');
    readln (Score);
    IF Score > MaxScore THEN
        writeln ('*** Illegal Score *** ')
    ELSE
        BEGIN
            CASE Score DIV 10 OF
                          9, 10 : BEGIN
                                      Grade := 'A';
                                      Honors := true
                                  END;
                              8 : BEGIN
                                      Grade := 'B';
                                      Honors := true
                                  END;
                              7 : Grade := 'C';
                              6 : Grade := 'D';
                0, 1, 2, 3, 4, 5 : Grade := 'F'
            END (* CASE *);
            writeln ('Grade = ', Grade);
            IF Honors THEN
                writeln ('Honors student')
        END (* ELSE *)
END.
```

Figure 4.8

Exercises

1. Write a Pascal statement for each of the following:

   (a) If *TaxCode* is 'T', increase *Price* by adding *TaxRate* percentage of *Price* to it.

   (b) If *Code* has the value 1, read values for *x* and *y* and calculate and print the sum of *x* and *y*.

(c) If A is strictly between 0 and 5, set B equal to $1/A^2$; otherwise set B equal to A^2.

(d) Assign *true* to the boolean variable *LeapYear* if the integer variable *Year* is the number of a leap year. (A leap year is a multiple of 4, and if it is a multiple of 100, it must also be a multiple of 400.)

(e) Assign the value to *Cost* corresponding to the value of *Distance* given in the following table:

Distance	Cost
0 through 100	5.00
More than 100 but not more than 500	8.00
More than 500 but less than 1000	10.00
1000 or more	12.00

(f) Display the number of days in the month corresponding to the value of *Month* (1, 2, . . . , 12). Use part (d) to determine the number of days if the value of *Month* is 2, assuming that a value has been assigned to *Year*.

2. Describe the output produced by the following poorly indented program segment:

```
Number := 4;
Alpha := −1.0;
if Number > 0 then
   if Alpha > 0 then
      writeln ('First writeln')
else
   writeln ('Second writeln');
writeln ('Third writeln');
```

3. Replace the following **if** statement with a single assignment statement:

```
if Honors = true then
   if Awards = true then
      GoodStudent := true
   else
      GoodStudent := false
else if Honors = false then
   GoodStudent := false;
```

4. Write a program to check a quadratic equation of the form $Ax^2 + Bx + C = 0$ to see if it has real roots, and if so, find these roots. If there are no real roots, print an appropriate message. (See Exercise 9 of Chapter 2.)

5. A certain city classifies a pollution index less than 35 as "pleasant," 35 through 60 as "unpleasant," and above 60 as "hazardous." Write a program that reads a real number representing a pollution index and displays the appropriate classification for it.

6. Write a program that reads one of the numbers 2 through 13 representing a TV channel and then uses a **case** statement to print the call letters of the station that corresponds to that number or some message indicating that the channel is not used. Use the following channel numbers and call letters:

    2:   WCBS
    4:   WNBC
    5:   WNEW
    7:   WABC
    9:   WOR
  11:   WPIX
  13:   WNET

7. A wholesale office supply company discounts the price of each of its products depending on the number of units bought and the price per unit. The discount increases as the numbers of units bought and/or the unit price increases. These discounts are given in the following table.

| Number | Unit Price (dollars) | | |
Bought	0–10.00	10.01–100.00	100.01–
1–10	0%	2%	5%
11–100	5%	7%	9%
101–500	9%	15%	21%
501–1000	14%	23%	32%
1001–	21%	32%	43%

Write a program that reads the number of units bought and the unit price, and then calculates and prints the total full cost, the total amount of the discount, and the total discounted cost.

8. Locating avenues' addresses in mid-Manhattan is not easy; for example, the nearest cross street to 866 3rd Avenue is 53rd Street, whereas the nearest cross street to 866 2nd Avenue is 46th Street. To locate approximately the nearest numbered cross street for a given avenue address, the following algorithm can be used:

Cancel the last digit of the number, divide by 2, and add or subtract the number given in the following (abbreviated) table:

1st Ave.	Add 3
2nd Ave.	Add 3
3rd Ave.	Add 10
4th Ave.	Add 8
5th Ave. up to 200	Add 13
5th Ave. up to 400	Add 16
6th Ave. (Ave. of the Americas)	Subtract 12
7th Ave.	Add 12
8th Ave.	Add 10
10th Ave.	Add 14

Write a program that reads an avenue address and then uses a **case** statement to determine the number of the nearest cross street according to the preceding algorithm.

9. An airline vice president in charge of operations needs to determine whether or not the current estimates of flight times are accurate. Since there is a larger possibility of variations due to weather and air traffic in the longer flights, he allows a larger error in the time estimates for them. He compares an actual flight time with the estimated flight time and considers the estimate to be too large, acceptable, or too small, depending on the following table of acceptable error margins.

Estimated Flight Time in Minutes	Acceptable Error Margin in Minutes
0–29	1
30–59	2
60–89	3
90–119	4
120–179	6
180–239	8
240–359	13
360–479	17

For example, if an estimated flight time is 106 minutes, the acceptable error margin is 4 minutes. Thus, the estimated flight time is too large if the actual flight time is less than 102 minutes, or the estimated flight time is too small if the actual flight time is greater than 110 minutes; otherwise, the estimate is acceptable. Write a program that reads an estimated flight time and an actual flight time, uses a **case** statement to determine the acceptable error according to this table, and then prints whether the estimated time is too large, acceptable, or too small. If the estimated flight time is either too large or too small, the program should also print the amount of the overestimate or underestimate.

4.5 Repetition Structure: The *while* Statement

A *repetition structure* or *loop* makes possible repeated execution of one or more statements. This repetition must be controlled so that these statements are executed only a finite number of times. Pascal provides three statements that implement repetition structures: the **while** statement, the **repeat** statement, and the **for** statement. In this section we consider the first of these statements, which can be used to implement a repetition structure called a *while loop* and pictured in Figure 4.9, in which repetition continues while some boolean expression remains true.

The **while** statement has the form

while *boolean-expression* **do**
    statement

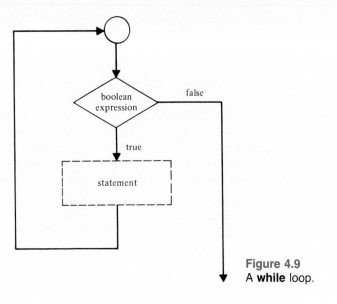

Figure 4.9
A **while** loop.

Its syntax diagram is

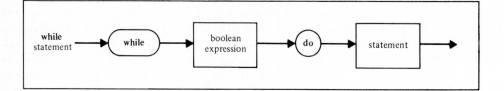

When a **while** statement is executed, the boolean expression is evaluated, and if true, the statement following the **do** is executed. The boolean expression is then reevaluated, and if still true, the statement is executed again. This process of evaluating the boolean expression and executing the specified statement is repeated as long as the boolean expression is true. When it becomes false, repetition is terminated. Note that this means that execution of the statement within the **while** statement must eventually cause the value of the boolean expression to become false, since otherwise repetition would continue *ad infinitum*.

To demonstrate the use of the **while** statement, consider the following problem:

For a given value of *Limit*, what is the smallest positive integer *Number* for which the sum

$$1 + 2 + \cdots + Number$$

is greater than *Limit*, and what is the value of this sum?

The following algorithm solves this problem:

ALGORITHM FOR SUMMATION PROBLEM

(* Algorithm to find the smallest positive integer *Number* for which the sum $1 + 2 + \cdots + Number$ is greater than *Limit*. *)

1. Enter *Limit*.
2. Set *Number* equal to 0.
3. Set *Sum* equal to 0.
4. While *Sum* ≤ *Limit* do the following:
   a. Increment *Number* by 1.
   b. Add *Number* to *Sum*.
5. Display *Number* and *Sum*.

In this algorithm, the **body** of the while loop in Step 4 consists of two statements, but in Pascal, a **while** statement may only contain one statement. Consequently, we must combine two statements into one compound statement:

> **while** *Sum* <= *Limit* **do**
>   **begin**
>   *Number* := *Number* + 1;
>   *Sum* := *Sum* + *Number*
>   **end** (* **while** *);

The program in Figure 4.10 uses this **while** statement in implementing this algorithm.

```
PROGRAM Summation (input, output);

(*********************************************************************

   Program to find the smallest positive integer Number for which
   the sum
                    1 + 2 + ... + Number
   is greater than the value of a specified number Limit.  It also
   displays the value of this sum.

*********************************************************************)

VAR
   Number,            (* positive integer added to the sum *)
   Sum,               (* 1 + 2 + .. + Number *)
   Limit : integer;   (* limit for sum *)

BEGIN
   write ('Enter value that 1 + 2 + ... + ? is to exceed:  ');
   readln (Limit);
   Number := 0;
   Sum := 0;
   WHILE Sum <= Limit DO
      BEGIN
         Number := Number + 1;
         Sum := Sum + Number
      END (* WHILE *);
   writeln ('1 + ... + ', Number:1, ' = ', Sum:1, ' > ', Limit:1)
END.
```

Figure 4.10

Figure 4.10   (cont.)

Sample runs:

```
Enter value that 1 + 2 + ... + ? is to exceed:   10
1 + ... + 5 = 15 > 10


Enter value that 1 + 2 + ... + ? is to exceed:   10000
1 + ... + 141 = 10011 > 10000


Enter value that 1 + 2 + ... + ? is to exceed:   -1
1 + ... + 0 = 0 > -1
```

In the first sample run of Figure 4.10 in which the value 10 is entered for *Limit,* the body of the while loop is executed five times, as indicated in the following table, which traces its execution:

Number	Sum	Sum <= Limit	Action
0	0	true	Execute body of while loop
1	1	true	Execute body of while loop
2	3	true	Execute body of while loop
3	6	true	Execute body of while loop
4	10	true	Execute body of while loop
5	15	false	Terminate repetition

A similar trace table for the second sample run would show that the loop body is executed 141 times. The third sample run demonstrates that, as illustrated in Figure 4.9, the boolean expression in a **while** statement is evaluated before repetition begins. When the value −1 is entered for *Limit,* the **while** statement causes an immediate transfer of control to the *writeln* statement that displays the value 0 for both *Number* and *Sum.*

As another example of a repetition structure, we develop a program to calculate the mean of a set of test scores. The program is to be used with sets of scores from various classes. Since the number of students in each class is not known in advance, the program should count the scores being averaged.

In this problem, the input is a set of real scores, one for each student in the class. The output is the number of students in the class and the mean score. An algorithm for solving the problem consists of reading a score, counting it, and adding it to the sum of scores previously read. This must be repeated for each student. In this example, we append to the data an artificial value called a *flag* or *sentinel,* which is distinct from any possible valid data item. As each data item is read, it is checked to determine if it is this end-of-data flag. When the end of data is reached, the repetition is terminated, the mean is calculated, and the desired information is displayed.

ALGORITHM TO FIND MEAN SCORE

(∗ Algorithm to read a list of scores, count them, and find the mean score (*MeanScore*); *Score* represents the current score read, *NumScores* is the number of scores, and *Sum* is the sum of the scores. Scores are read until the end-of-data flag is encountered. *)

1. Set *Sum* equal to 0.
2. Set *NumScores* equal to 0.
3. Read first *Score*.
4. While *Score* is not the end-of-data flag, do the following:
   a. Add 1 to *NumScores*.
   b. Add *Score* to *Sum*.
   c. Read next *Score*.
5. Calculate *MeanScore* = *Sum* / *NumScores*.
6. Display *MeanScore* and *NumScores*.

In the Pascal program in Figure 4.11 that implements this algorithm, a negative score is used as an end-of-data flag, and the repetition structure in Step 4 is inplemented as a **while** statement controlled by the boolean expression *Score* >= 0.

```
PROGRAM CalculateMeanScore (input, output);

(*****************************************************************

   This program reads a list of scores, counts them, and
   calculates the mean score.  Any negative number serves
   as an end-of-data flag.

****************************************************************)

VAR
    NumScores : integer;   (* number of scores *)
    Sum,                   (* sum of the scores *)
    Score,                 (* current score being processed *)
    MeanScore : real;      (* mean of the scores *)

BEGIN
    writeln ('*** Enter a negative score to signal the end of input.');
    writeln;
    Sum := 0;
    NumScores := 0;
    write ('Score:   ');
    readln (Score);
    WHILE Score >= 0 DO
       BEGIN
          NumScores := NumScores +1;
          Sum := Sum + Score;
          write ('Score:   ');
          readln (Score)
       END (* WHILE *);
    MeanScore := Sum / NumScores;
    writeln;
    writeln (NumScores:1, ' scores with mean = ', MeanScore:5:2)
END.
```

Figure 4.11

Figure 4.11   (cont.)

Sample runs:
_____

*** Enter a negative score to signal the end of input.

Score: 60
Score: 70
Score: 80
Score: -1

3 scores with mean = 70.00

*** Enter a negative score to signal the end of input.

Score: 55
Score: 86.5
Score: 79.5
Score: 86
Score: 84
Score: 55
Score: 97.5
Score: 100
Score: 57
Score: 83.5
Score: 72
Score: -1

11 scores with mean = 77.82

4.6   Repetition Structure: The *repeat* Statement

Recall that in a **while** statement, the boolean expression is evaluated *before* execution of the specified statement begins (see Fig. 4.7), and thus a while loop might be called a ***pretest loop***. In some situations, however, it may be more appropriate to use a ***posttest loop*** in which the boolean expression that controls repetition is tested *after* the statement(s) that comprise the body of the loop are executed. This repetition structure called a ***repeat loop*** is illustrated in Figure 4.12 and can be implemented in Pascal by using a **repeat** statement.

The **repeat** statement has the form

> **repeat**
>   *statement-1*;
>   *statement-2*;
>   ⋮
>   *statement-n*
> **until** *boolean expression*

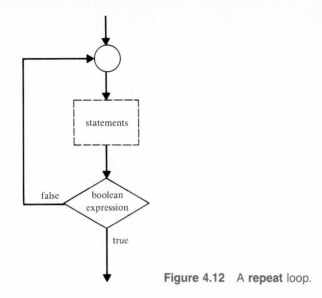

Figure 4.12 A **repeat** loop.

A syntax diagram for this statement is

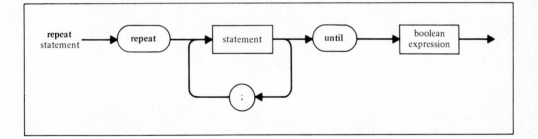

When a **repeat** statement is executed, the specified statements *statement-1*, *statement-2*, . . . , *statement-n* are executed, and the *boolean expression* is evaluated. If its value is true, execution continues with the next statement in the program; otherwise, the specified statements are executed again. This repetition continues until the boolean expression becomes true.

To illustrate the **repeat** statement, we reconsider the problem of finding the smallest positive integer *Number* for which the sum $1 + 2 + \cdots + Number$ is greater than some specified value *Limit*. Suppose that the algorithm given earlier is modified as follows:

MODIFIED SUMMATION ALGORITHM

(∗ Algorithm to find the smallest positive integer *Number* for which the sum $1 + 2 + \cdots + Number$ is greater than *Limit*. ∗)

1. Enter *Limit*.
2. Set *Number* equal to 0.
3. Set *Sum* equal to 0.

4. Repeat the following until *Sum* > *Limit*.
   a. Increment *Number* by 1.
   b. Add *Number* to *Sum*.
5. Display *Number* and *Sum*.

For this algorithm, it is appropriate to implement the repetition structure in Step 4 by a **repeat** statement, as shown in the program in Figure 4.13.

> **repeat**
>   *Number* := *Number* + 1;
>   *Sum* := *Sum* + *Number*
> **until** *Sum* > *Limit*;

```
PROGRAM Summation (input, output);

(*********************************************************************

   Program to find the smallest positive integer Number for which
   the sum
                      1 + 2 + ... + Number
   is greater than the value of a specified number Limit.  It also
   displays the value of this sum.

*********************************************************************)

VAR
   Number,            (* positive integer added to the sum *)
   Sum,               (* 1 + 2 + ... + Number *)
   Limit : integer;   (* limit for sum *)

BEGIN
   write ('Enter value that 1 + 2 + ... + ? is to exceed:   ');
   readln (Limit);
   Number := 0;
   Sum := 0;
   REPEAT
      Number := Number + 1;
      Sum := Sum + Number;
   UNTIL Sum > Limit;
   writeln ('1 + ... + ', Number:1, ' = ', Sum:1, ' > ', Limit:1)
END.


Sample runs:


Enter value that 1 + 2 + ... + ? is to exceed:   10
1 + ... + 5 = 15 > 10


Enter value that 1 + 2 + ... + ? is to exceed:   10000
1 + ... + 141 = 10011 > 10000


Enter value that 1 + 2 + ... + ? is to exceed:   -1
1 + ... + 1 = 1 > -1
```

Figure 4.13

Any number of statements separated by semicolons may be placed between the reserved words **repeat** and **until.** Since these reserved words clearly mark the beginning and the end of this statement, it is not necessary to use the reserved words **begin** and **end** for this purpose, as was required for the **while** statement.

A more important feature that distinguishes the **repeat** statement from the **while** statement is that the boolean expression is evaluated *after* the specified statements, *not before*. This means that *these statements are always executed at least once*. Thus, in the program in Figure 4.13, the two statements *Number* := *Number* + 1 and *Sum* := *Sum* + *Number* are always executed at least once, regardless of the value of *Limit*. Compare the third sample run here with that in Figure 4.10, where a **while** statement was used.

4.7   Repetition Structure: The *for* Statement

A third Pascal statement that can be used to implement some repetition structures is the **for** statement. This statement is not as generally applicable as the **while** and **repeat** statements, but it is convenient for implementing repetition structures in which the body of the loop is executed once for each value of some *control variable* in a specified range of values.

The syntax diagram for a **for** statement is

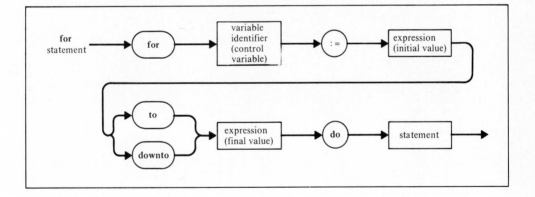

From this diagram we see that it has two forms:

> **for** *control-variable* := *initial-value* **to** *final-value* **do**
>   *statement*

or

> **for** *control-variable* := *initial-value* **downto** *final-value* **do**
>   *statement*

In these forms, the control variable, the initial value, and the final value must all be of the same type, which may be integer, character, or boolean (or other types as described in Chapter 7). In the examples in this chapter, they are always of integer type. The initial and final values may be any valid Pascal expressions.

A **for** statement of the form

> **for** *control-variable* := *initial value* **to** *final-value* **do**
>   *statement*

implements the repetition structure shown in Figure 4.14. As the flowchart shows, when a **for** statement of this form is executed, the control variable is assigned the initial value, and the specified statement is executed unless the initial value is greater than the final value. The control variable is incremented, and if this new value does not exceed the final value, the statement is executed again. Thus, the specified statement is executed for each value of the control variable from the initial value up to and including the final value.

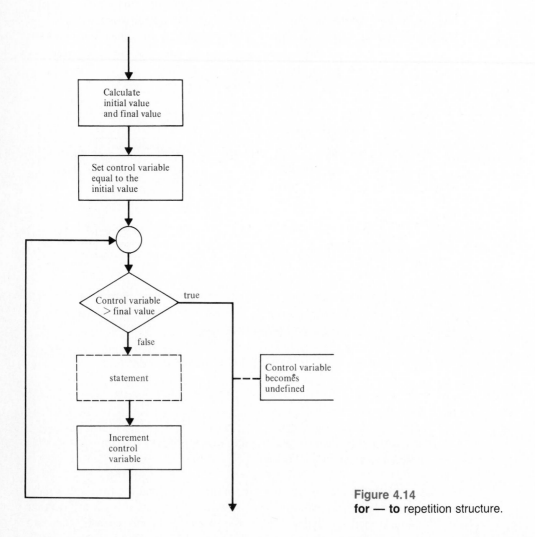

Figure 4.14
for — to repetition structure.

To illustrate, consider the statement

for *Number* := 1 **to** 10 **do**
    writeln (*Number*:2, *sqr*(*Number*):5);

where *Number* is of integer type. In this statement, *Number* is the control variable, the initial value is 1, and the final value is 10. When this statement is executed, the initial value 1 is assigned to *Number,* and the *writeln* statement is executed. The value of *Number* is then incremented by 1, and because this new value 2 is less than the final value 10, the *writeln* statement is executed again. This repetition continues as long as the value of the control variable *Number* is less than or equal to the final value 10. Thus, the output produced by this statement is

```
 1    1
 2    4
 3    9
 4   16
 5   25
 6   36
 7   49
 8   64
 9   81
10  100
```

To repeat more than one statement using a **for** loop, we combine them into a single compound statement. For example, to double space the preceding output, we might use

for *Number* := 1 **to** 10 **do**
    begin
        writeln (*Number*:2, *sqr*(*Number*):5);
        writeln
    end (∗ **for** ∗);

In the second form of the **for** statement

for *control-variable* := *initial-value* **downto** *final-value* **do**
    statement

the control variable is decremented rather than incremented, and repetition continues as long as the value of the control variable is greater than or equal to the final value. This is illustrated in the flowchart in Figure 4.15.

For example, consider the statement

for *Number* := 10 **downto** 1 **do**
    writeln (*Number*:2, *sqr*(*Number*):5);

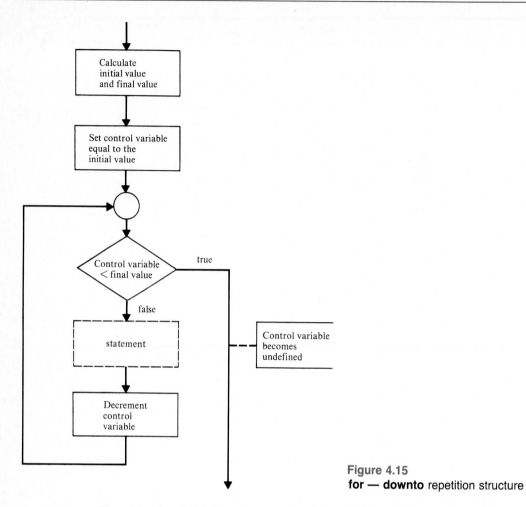

Figure 4.15
for — downto repetition structure

The control variable *Number* is assigned the initial value 10, and because this value is greater than the final value 1, the *writeln* statement is executed. The value of *Number* is then decreased to 9, and because this new value is greater than the final value, the *writeln* statement is executed again. This process continues as long as the value of *Number* is greater than or equal to the final value 1. Thus, the output produced is

       10   100
        9   81
        8   64
        7   49
        6   36
        5   25
        4   16
        3   9
        2   4
        1   1

Note that in this form of the **for** statement, **downto** is a single word.
    As Figures 4.14 and 4.15 illustrate, the value of the control variable is

compared with the final value *before* the specified statement is executed. Thus, in the first form of the **for** statement, if the initial value is greater than the final value, the specified statement is never executed. This is also the case in the second form if the initial value is less than the final value.

The initial and/or final values in a **for** statement may be variables or expressions. To illustrate, consider the statements

> *write* ('Enter table size: ');
> *readln* (*TableSize*);
> **for** *Number* := 1 **to** *TableSize* **do**
>   *writeln* (*Number*:4, *sqr(Number)*:8);

The value entered for *TableSize* is the final value in this **for** statement. These statements are used in the program of Figure 4.16 to print a table of squares whose size is read during program execution.

```
PROGRAM TableOfSquares (input, output);

(*******************************************************************

    This program prints a table of integers and their squares.
    The size of the table is entered during execution.

 *****************************************************************)

VAR
    TableSize,          (* number of rows in table *)
    Number : integer;   (* number whose square is calculated *)

BEGIN
    write ('Enter table size:   ');
    readln (TableSize);
    writeln;
    writeln ('Number   Square');
    writeln ('------   ------');
    FOR Number := 1 TO TableSize DO
        writeln (Number:4, sqr(Number):8)
END.


Sample run:

Enter table size:   10

Number   Square
------   ------
   1        1
   2        4
   3        9
   4       16
   5       25
   6       36
   7       49
   8       64
   9       81
  10      100
```

Figure 4.16

The initial and final values are determined before repetition begins and changing them during execution of the **for** *statement does not affect the number of repetitions.* Also, the statement within a **for** statement may use the value of the control variable, though *it must not modify the value of the control variable. When execution of the* **for** *statement is completed, the control variable becomes undefined.* Using this variable before assigning it a value yields unpredictable results.

The statement that appears within a **for** statement may itself be a **for** statement, that is, one **for** statement may be nested within another **for** statement. As an example, consider the program in Figure 4.17 that calculates and displays products of the form $X * Y$ for X ranging from 1 through *LastX* and Y ranging from 1 through *LastY* for integers *LastX* and *LastY*. The table of products is generated by the **for** statement

```
for X := 1 to LastX do
   for Y := 1 to LastY do
      begin
         Product := X * Y;
         writeln (X:2, '*', Y:2, '=', Product:3)
      end (* for *)
```

In the sample run, *LastX* and *LastY* are both assigned the value 4. The control variable X is assigned its initial value 1, and the statement

```
for Y := 1 to LastY do
   begin
      Product := X * Y;
      writeln (X:2, '*', Y:2, '=', Product:3)
   end (* for *)
```

is executed. This calculates and displays the first four products $1 * 1$, $1 * 2$, $1 * 3$, and $1 * 4$. The value of X is then incremented by 1, and the preceding **for** statement is executed again. This calculates and displays the next four products, $2 * 1$, $2 * 2$, $2 * 3$, and $2 * 4$. The control variable X is then incremented to 3, producing the next four products, $3 * 1$, $3 * 2$, $3 * 3$, and $3 * 4$, and finally X is incremented to 4, giving the last four products, $4 * 1$, $4 * 2$, $4 * 3$, and $4 * 4$.

```
PROGRAM Products (input, output);

(*********************************************************************

   This program calculates and displays a list of products
   of two numbers.

*********************************************************************)

VAR
   X, Y,                  (* two numbers being multiplied *)
   LastX, LastY,          (* last values of X and Y, respectively *)
   Product : integer;     (* product of X and Y *)
```

Figure 4.17

Figure 4.17 (cont.)

```
BEGIN
    write ('Enter upper limits for factors of product:   ');
    readln (LastX, LastY);
    writeln;
    FOR X := 1 TO LastX DO
        FOR Y := 1 TO LastY DO
            BEGIN
                Product := X * Y;
                writeln (X:2, ' *', Y:2, ' =', Product:3)
            END (* FOR *)
END.
```

Sample run:

```
Enter upper limits for factors of product:   4 4

1 * 1 =  1
1 * 2 =  2
1 * 3 =  3
1 * 4 =  4
2 * 1 =  2
2 * 2 =  4
2 * 3 =  6
2 * 4 =  8
3 * 1 =  3
3 * 2 =  6
3 * 3 =  9
3 * 4 = 12
4 * 1 =  4
4 * 2 =  8
4 * 3 = 12
4 * 4 = 16
```

4.8 Program Testing and Debugging Techniques: An Example

In Section 2.4 we noted that there are three types of errors that may occur in developing a program to solve a problem: syntax or compile-time errors, run-time errors, and logical errors. *Syntax errors* such as incorrect punctuation, unbalanced parentheses, and misspelled reserved words will be detected during compilation of the program, and an appropriate error message will usually be displayed. *Run-time errors* such as division by zero and integer overflow are detected during execution of the program, and again, a suitable error message will often be displayed. These two types of errors are, for the most part, relatively easy to correct, since the system error messages displayed will often indicate the type of error and where it occurred. *Logical errors,* on the other hand, are usually more difficult to detect, since they arise in the design of the algorithm or in coding the algorithm as a program, and in most cases, no error messages are displayed to assist the programmer in identifying such errors.

In this text, the Programming Pointers at the end of each chapter include warnings about some of the more common errors. As programs become increasingly complex, however, logical errors that occur are more subtle and consequently more difficult to identify and correct. In this section we consider an example of a program that contains logical errors and describe techniques that are useful in detecting them.

Suppose that, as a programming exercise, students were asked to write a program to read a list of positive integers representing employee salaries in thousands of dollars and determine the salary range, that is, the difference between the largest salary and the smallest. The following program heading and declaration part were given, and the students were asked to write the statement part of the program.

```
PROGRAM SalaryRange (input, output);

(*********************************************************************

   Program to read a list of salaries in thousands of dollars and
   determine the range of salaries.  A negative value for the
   salary is used to signal the end of data.

*********************************************************************)

VAR
   Salary,                 (* the current salary being processed *)
   MaxSalary,              (* largest salary read so far *)
   MinSalary : integer;    (* smallest   "      "   "   "  *)
```

One attempted solution was the following (where the lines have been numbered for easy reference):

```
(1)    BEGIN
(2)       writeln ('Enter salaries in thousands of dollars.  ',
(3)                'Enter a negative salary to stop.');
(4)       MaxSalary := 0;        (* initialize max. salary very small *)
(5)       MinSalary := maxint;   (* and min. salary very large *)
(6)       REPEAT
(7)          write ('Enter salary:  ');
(8)          readln (Salary);
(9)          IF Salary > MaxSalary THEN
(10)             MaxSalary := Salary
(11)          ELSE IF Salary < MinSalary THEN
(12)             MinSalary := Salary
(13)       UNTIL Salary < 0;
(14)       writeln ('Salary range = ', MaxSalary - MinSalary:1, ' thousand')
(15)    END.
```

Execution of the program produced

```
Enter salaries in thousands of dollars.  Enter a negative salary to stop.
Enter salary:   10
Enter salary:   7
Enter salary:   15
Enter salary:   -1
Salary range = 16 thousand
```

Although no error messages were displayed, the output produced clearly indicates that the program is not correct, since the correct salary range for this set of data is $8000.

One common technique used to locate logical errors is to construct manually a *trace trable* of the segment of the program that is suspect. This technique is also known as *walking through the code* or *desk checking,* and consists of recording in a table the values of all or certain key variables in the program segment, step by step. In this example, the following trace table for the repeat loop might be obtained:

Statements	Salary	MaxSalary	MinSalary	
	—	0	32767	← Initial values ($maxint = 32767$)
7–8	10	0	32767	First pass through the loop
9–10	10	10	32767	
7–8	7	10	32767	Second pass through the loop
11–12	7	10	7	
7–8	15	10	7	Third pass through the loop
9–10	15	15	7	
7–8	−1	15	7	Fourth pass through the loop
11–12	−1	15	−1	

The last line in this trace table shows why the salary range was incorrect; the value of *MinSalary* became −1 on the last pass through the loop, and this occurred because the value −1 used to signal the end of data was read and processed as a salary.

The execution of a program segment can also be traced automatically by inserting temporary output statements or by using special system-debugging software to display the values of key variables at selected stages of program execution. For example, we might insert the statement

> *writeln* ('Salary ', *Salary*);

after the *readln* statement to echo the data values as they are entered, and the statement

> *writeln* ('Max ', *MaxSalary, ' Min ', MinSalary*)

at the bottom of the loop to display the values of these variables at the end of each pass through the loop. (Note that a semicolon must also be appended to the statement preceding this last *writeln* statement.) The resulting output then is

```
Enter salaries in thousands of dollars.  Enter a negative salary to stop.
Enter salary:  10
Salary        10
Max        10 Min     32767
Enter salary:  7
Salary         7
Max        10 Min         7
Enter salary:  15
Salary        15
Max        15 Min         7
Enter salary:  −1
Salary        −1
Max        15 Min        −1
Salary range = 16 thousand
```

This technique must not be used indiscriminately, however, since incorrect placement of such temporary debug statements may display output that is not helpful in locating the source of the error. Also, if too many such statements are used, so much output may be produced that it is difficult to isolate the error.

Using either manual or automatic tracing of this program reveals that the source of difficulty is that the value -1 used to signal the end of data is processed as an actual salary. A first reaction might be to fix this error by using a nested **if** statement:

> **if** *Salary* > 0 **then**
> > **if** *Salary* $>$ *MaxSalary* **then**
> > > *MaxSalary* $:=$ *Salary*
> >
> > **else if** *Salary* $<$ *MinSalary* **then**
> > > *MinSalary* $:=$ *Salary*

Such "quick and dirty patches" are usually not recommended, however, since they often fail to address the real source of the problem and make the program unnecessarily complicated and messy.

The real source of difficulty in the preceding example is the repetition structure used. The value -1 was read and processed as an actual salary because the boolean expression in a repeat loop is tested at the end of the loop, *after* the statements in the body of the loop are executed. A better repetition structure would have been a while loop in which the boolean expression is tested at the beginning of the loop, *before* the loop body is executed.

```
(1)    BEGIN
(2)       writeln ('Enter salaries in thousands of dollars.  ',
(3)                'Enter a negative salary to stop.');
(4)       MaxSalary := 0;       (* initialize max. salary very small *)
(5)       MinSalary := maxint;  (* and min. salary very large *)
(6)       write ('Enter salary:  ');
(7)       readln (Salary);
(8)       WHILE Salary >= 0 DO
(9)          BEGIN
(10)            IF Salary > MaxSalary THEN
(11)               MaxSalary := Salary
(12)            ELSE IF Salary < MinSalary THEN
(13)               MinSalary := Salary;
(14)            write ('Enter salary:  ');
(15)            readln (Salary)
(16)         END (* WHILE *);
(17)      writeln ('Salary range = ', MaxSalary - MinSalary:1, ' thousand')
(18)   END.
```

A sample run using the same data values now produces the correct output:

```
Enter salaries in thousands of dollars.  Enter a negative salary to stop.
Enter salary:  10
Enter salary:  7
Enter salary:  15
Enter salary:  -1
Salary range = 8 thousand
```

The student may now be tempted to conclude that the program is correct. However, to establish one's confidence in the correctness of a program, it is necessary to test it with several sets of data. For example, the following sample run reveals that the program still contains a logical error:

```
Enter salaries in thousands of dollars.  Enter a negative salary to stop.
Enter salary:   7
Enter salary:   10
Enter salary:   15
Enter salary:   -1
Salary range = -32752 thousand
```

Tracing the execution of the while loop produces the following:

Statements	Salary	MaxSalary	MinSalary	
	7	0	32767	← Initial values
10–11	7	7	32767	} First pass through the loop
14–15	10	7	32767	
10–11	10	10	32767	} Second pass through the loop
14–15	15	10	32767	
10–11	15	15	32767	} Third pass through the loop
14–15	−1	15	32767	

This trace table reveals that the value of *MinSalary* never changes, suggesting that the statement

$$MinSalary := Salary$$

is never executed. This is because the boolean expression *Salary* > *MaxSalary* is true for each data value, since these values are entered in increasing order; consequently, the **else if** part of the **if** statement is never executed. This error can be corrected by using two **if** statements:

> **if** *Salary* > *MaxSalary* **then**
>   *MaxSalary* := *Salary;*
> **if** *Salary* < *MinSalary* **then**
>   *MinSalary* := *Salary;*

The resulting program is then correct, but is not as efficient as it could be since the boolean expressions in both of these **if** statements must be evaluated on each pass through the loop. A more efficient alternative is described in the exercises.

In summary, logical errors may be very difficult to detect, especially as programs become more complex, and it is very important that test data be carefully selected so that each part of the program is thoroughly tested. The program should be executed with data values entered in several different orders, with large data sets and with small data sets, with extreme values, and with "bad" data. For example, entering the salaries in increasing order revealed the existence of a logical error in the program considered earlier. Also, even though the last version of the program produces correct output if legitimate data values are read, the output

Salary range = − 32767 thousand

would be produced if a negative value was entered immediately. Although it may not be necessary to guard against invalid data input in student programs, those written for the public domain, especially programs used by computer novices, should be as *robust* as possible and should not "crash" or produce "garbage" results when unexpected data values are read.

When a logical error is detected, a trace table is an effective tool for locating the source of the error. Once it has been found, the program must be corrected and then tested again. It may be necessary to repeat this cycle of testing, tracing, and correcting many times before the program produces correct results for a wide range of test data, allowing us to be reasonably confident of its correctness. It is not possible, however, to check a program with every possible set of data, and thus obscure bugs may still remain. In some applications, this may not be critical, but in others, for example, in programs used to guide a space shuttle, errors cannot be tolerated. Certain formal techniques have been developed for proving that a program is correct and will always execute correctly (assuming no system malfunction), but a study of these techniques is beyond the scope of this introductory text.

Exercises

1. Assuming that I, J, and K are integer variables, describe the output produced by each of the following program segments:

   (a) $K := 5$;
   $\quad I := -2$;
   $\quad$ **while** $I <= K$ **do**
   $\quad\quad$ **begin**
   $\quad\quad\quad I := I + 2$;
   $\quad\quad\quad K := K - 1$;
   $\quad\quad\quad writeln\ (I + K{:}2)$
   $\quad\quad$ **end** (∗ **while** ∗);

   (b) $I := -2$;
   $\quad$ **repeat**
   $\quad\quad K := I * I * I - 3 * I + 1$;
   $\quad\quad writeln\ (I{:}3,\ K{:}3)$
   $\quad$ **until** $I > 2$;

   (c) **for** $I := 1$ **to** 3 **do**
   $\quad$ **for** $J := 1$ **to** 3 **do**
   $\quad\quad$ **for** $K := I$ **to** J **do**
   $\quad\quad\quad writeln\ (I{:}1,\ J{:}1,\ K{:}1)$;

(d) $K := 5$;
  for $I := 1$ **to** K **do**
    begin
      writeln $(I + K{:}2)$;
      $K := 2$
    end (∗ **for** ∗);

2. Write a Pascal statement to

  (a) Print the value of x and decrease x by 0.5 as long as x is positive.
  (b) Read values for a, b, and c and print their sum, repeating this as long as none of a, b, or c is negative.
  (c) Read values for a, b, and c, and print their sum, repeating this until at least one of a, b, or c is negative.
  (d) Print the squares of the first 100 positive integers in increasing order.
  (e) Print the cubes of the first 50 positive integers in decreasing order.
  (f) Print the square roots of the first 25 odd positive integers.
  (g) Calculate and print the squares of consecutive positive integers until the difference between a square and the preceding one is greater than 50.
  (h) Print a list of points (x, y) on the graph of $y = x^3 - 3x + 1$ for x ranging from -2 to 2 in steps of 0.1.

3. Describe the output produced by the following poorly indented program segments:

  (a) *Number* $:= 4$;
    while *Number* > 0 **do**
      Number $:=$ *Number* $- 1$;
      writeln (*Number*:1);
      writeln;
    writeln ('∗∗∗∗∗');

  (b) **for** *Number* $:= 1$ **to** 4 **do**
      writeln (*Number*:1);
      writeln (' squared $=$', *sqr(Number)*:1);
      writeln;

4. Write a program to read data values as shown in the following table, calculate the miles per gallon in each case, and print the values with appropriate labels.

Miles Traveled	Gallons of Gasoline Used
231	14.8
248	15.1
302	12.8
147	9.25
88	7
265	13.3

5. Write a program to read several values representing miles, convert miles to kilometers (1 mile = 1.60935 kilometers), and print all values with appropriate labels.

6. A certain product is to sell for *UnitPrice* dollars. Write a program that reads values for *UnitPrice* and *TotalNumber* and then produces a table showing the total price of from 1 through *TotalNumber* units. The table should have a format like the following:

```
Number  of  Units    Total  Price
================     ===========
       1             $  1.50
       2             $  3.00
       3             $  4.50
       4             $  6.00
       5             $  7.50
```

Design the program so that after a table is printed, it calls for the input of new values for *UnitPrice* and *TotalNumber* and generates a new table. Execute the program using the following pairs of values for *UnitPrice* and *TotalNumber:* 1.20, 5; 15.49, 8; 4.99, 15; 177.89, 10.

7. Write a program that reads the exchange rate for converting English currency to U.S. currency and then reads several values for *Pounds, Shillings,* and *Pence* and converts the amount of currency represented into the equivalent amount of U.S. dollars and cents. Display all amounts with appropriate labels.

8. Proceed as in Exercise 7, but convert several values from U.S. currency to English currency.

9. (a) Write a program that solves the salary range problem discussed in Section 4.8 but is more efficient than those described in the text. (*Hint:* Initialize *MaxSalary* and *MinSalary* to the first data value.)
   (b) For each of the following data sets, construct a trace table for the repetition structure used in your program and determine the salary range that will be computed by your program:

   (i) 7, 15, 10, −1   (ii) 7, 10, 15, −1   (iii) 15, 10, 7, −1
   (iv) 7, −1   (v) −1

10. Write a program to read a set of numbers, count them, and calculate and display the mean, variance, and standard deviation of the set of numbers. The **mean** and **variance** of numbers $x_1, x_2, \ldots, x_n$ can be calculated using the formulas

$$\text{mean} = \frac{1}{n} \sum_{i=1}^{n} x_i, \quad \text{variance} = \frac{1}{n} \sum_{i=1}^{n} x_i^2 - \frac{1}{n^2} \left(\sum_{i=1}^{n} x_i \right)^2$$

The **standard deviation** is the square root of the variance.

11. Write a program that implements the "divide and average" algorithm for approximating square roots (see Exercise 8 of Section 2.5). It should accept positive real values for the variables *PosReal, Approx,* and *Epsilon,* and approximate the square root of *PosReal* by repeatedly replacing *Approx* by the average of *Approx* and *PosReal / Approx,* until *Approx* and *PosReal / Approx* differ in absolute value by less than *Epsilon,* where the value of *Epsilon* is small. Have the program display each of the successive values of *Approx.*

12. In an ***infinite series,*** the *n*th ***partial sum*** is the sum of the first *n* terms of the series; The infinite series $\sum_{k=0}^{\infty} \frac{1}{k!}$ converges to the number *e*. [For a positive integer *n*, *n*! (read "*n factorial*") is the product of the integers from 1 through *n*; 0! is defined as 1.] Write a program to calculate and print the first 10 partial sums of this series.

13. Write a program to calculate and print the first 20 partial sums of the ***continued fraction***

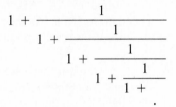

If S_k is the *k*th partial sum, then $S_1 = 1$, $S_2 = 1 + \frac{1}{1}$,

$$S_3 = 1 + \cfrac{1}{1 + \cfrac{1}{1}}, \text{ and so on. } (Hint: \text{ Find a relationship between } S_{k+1}$$

and S_k.)

14. Write a program that uses nested **for** statements to print the following multiplication table:

```
       1   2   3   4   5   6   7   8  9
   1   1
   2   2   4
   3   3   6   9
   4   4   8  12  16
   5   5  10  15  20  25
   6   6  12  18  24  30  36
   7   7  14  21  28  35  42  49
   8   8  16  24  32  40  48  56  64
   9   9  18  27  36  45  54  63  72 81
```

15. Suppose that at a given time, genotypes AA, AB, and BB appear in the proportions x, y, and z, respectively, where $x = 0.25$, $y = 0.5$, and $z = 0.25$. If individuals of type AA cannot reproduce, then the probability that one parent will donate gene A to an offspring is

$$p = \frac{1}{2}\left(\frac{y}{y + z}\right)$$

since $y/(y + z)$ is the probability that the parent is of type AB and $1/2$ is the probability that such a parent will donate gene A. Then the proportions x', y', and z' of AA, AB, and BB, respectively, in the succeeding generation are given by

$$x' = p^2, \; y' = 2p(1 - p), \; z' = (1 - p)^2$$

and the new probability is given by

$$p' = \frac{1}{2}\left(\frac{y'}{y' + z'}\right)$$

Write a program to calculate and print the generation number and the proportions of AA, AB, and BB under appropriate headings for 30 generations. (Note that the proportions of AA and AB should approach 0, since gene A will gradually disappear.)

16. Write a program that reads an amount of a loan, an annual interest rate, and a monthly payment and then displays under appropriate headings the payment number, the interest for that month, and the balance remaining after that payment. The monthly interest is $R/12$ percent of the unpaid balance after the payment is subtracted, where R is the annual interest rate. Also, keep a running total of the interest and display this after the last payment with an appropriate label. Design the program so that it will automatically construct such tables for several different loan amounts, interest rates, and monthly payments; in particular, execute it with the following triples of values: $100, 18 percent, $10 and $500, 12 percent, $25. (*Note:* In general, the last payment will not be the same as the monthly payment; design the program so that it will display the exact amount of the last payment due.)

17. Proceed as in Exercise 16, but with the following modifications. During program execution, have the user enter a payment amount and the day of the month from 1 through 30. The monthly interest is to be calculated on the *average daily balance* for that month. (Assume that each month has 30 days and that the billing date is the first of the month.) For example, if the balance on June 1 is $500 and a payment of $20 is received on the 12th, the interest is computed on $(500 * 11 + 480 * 19)/30$ dollars, which represents the average daily balance for that month.

18. Suppose that on January 1, April 1, July 1, and October 1 of each year, some fixed *Amount* is invested and earns interest at some annual

interest rate R compounded quarterly (that is, $R/4$ percent at the end of each quarter). Write a program to calculate and display for a specified number of years, the year, the yearly dividend (total interest earned for that year), and the total savings accumulated through that year.

   A possible modification/addition to your program: Instead of investing *Amount* dollars each quarter, invest *Amount*/3 dollars on the first of each month. Then in each quarter, the first payment earns interest for three months ($R/4$ percent), the second for two months ($R/6$ percent), and the third for one month ($R/12$ percent).

19. One method of calculating depreciation is the ***sum-of-the-years-digits*** method. To illustrate, suppose that \$15,000 is to be depreciated over a five-year period. We first calculate the sum $1 + 2 + 3 + 4 + 5 = 15$. Then 5/15 of \$15,000 (\$5,000) is depreciated the first year, 4/15 of \$15,000 (\$4,000) is depreciated the second year, 3/15 the third year, and so on. Write a program that reads the current year, an amount to be depreciated, and the number of years over which it is to be depreciated. Then display a depreciation table with suitable headings that shows the year number and the amount to be depreciated for that year for the specified number of years, beginning with the current year.

   A possible addition to your program: To find how much is saved in taxes, assume a fixed tax rate over these years, and assume that the amounts saved in taxes by claiming the depreciation as a deduction are invested and earn interest at some fixed annual rate.

20. The sequence of ***Fibonacci numbers*** begins with the integers

   1, 1, 2, 3, 5, 8, 13, 21, . . .

where each number after the first two is the sum of the two preceding numbers. In this sequence, the ratios of consecutive Fibonacci numbers (1/1, 1/2, 2/3, 3/5, . . .) approach the ''golden ratio''

$$\frac{\sqrt{5} - 1}{2}$$

Write a program to calculate all the Fibonacci numbers smaller than 5000 and the decimal values of the ratios of consecutive Fibonacci numbers.

21. The Rinky Dooflingy Company (Exercise 10 of Chapter 2) currently sells 200 dooflingies per month at a profit of \$300 per dooflingy. The company now spends \$2000 per month on advertising and has fixed operating costs of \$1000 per month that do not depend on the volume of sales. If the company doubles the amount spent on advertising, sales will increase by 20 percent. Write a program that prints under appropriate headings the amount spent on advertising, the number of sales made, and the net profit. Begin with the company's current status and successively double the amount spent on advertising until the net profit "goes over the hump," that is, begins to decline. The output should include the amounts up through the first time that the net profit begins to decline.

22. The proper divisors of an integer *n* are the positive divisors less than *n*. A positive integer is said to be a *deficient, perfect,* or *abundant* number if the sum of its proper divisors is less than, equal to, or greater than the number, respectively. For example, 8 is deficient, because its proper divisors are 1, 2, and 4, and $1 + 2 + 4 < 8$; 6 is perfect, because $1 + 2 + 3 = 6$; and 12 is abundant, because $1 + 2 + 3 + 4 + 6 > 12$. Write a program that classifies *n* as being deficient, perfect, or abundant for $n = 20$ to 30, then for $n = 490$ to 500, and finally for $n = 8120$ to 8130. Extra: Find the smallest odd abundant number.

23. Write a program that accepts a positive integer and gives its prime factorization, that is, expresses the integer as a product of primes or indicates that it is a prime.

Programming Pointers

Program Design

1. *All programs can be written using the three control structures considered in this chapter: sequential, selection, and repetition.*

2. *Use constant identifiers in place of specific constants for values that may need to be changed in a revision of a program.* For example, the statements

   Tax := 0.1963 * *Wages*;

   and

   NewBalance := *OldBalance* + 0.185 * *OldBalance*;

   are better expressed without the magic numbers 0.1963 and 0.185 as

   Tax := *TaxRate* * *Wages*;

   and

   NewBalance := *OldBalance* + *InterestRate* * *OldBalance*;

   where *TaxRate* and *InterestRate* are constants defined by

   const
       TaxRate = 0.1963;
       InterestRate = 0.185;

3. *Multialternative selection structures can be implemented more efficiently with a* **case** *statement or a compound* **if** *statement than with a sequence of* **if** *statements.* For example, using the statements

```
if Score < 60 then
    Grade := 'F';
if (Score >= 60) and (Score < 70) then
    Grade := 'D';
if (Score >= 70) and (Score < 80) then
    Grade := 'C';
if (Score >= 80) and (Score < 90) then
    Grade := 'B';
if Score >= 90 then
    Grade := 'A';
```

is less efficient than

```
if Score < 60 then
    Grade := 'F'
else if Score < 70 then
    Grade := 'D'
else if Score < 80 then
    Grade := 'C'
else if Score < 90 then
    Grade := 'B'
else
    Grade := 'A';
```

In the first case, all of the **if** statements are executed for each score processed, and three of the boolean expressions are compound expressions. In the second case, each boolean expression is simple and not all of them are evaluated for each score; for example, for a score of 65, only the boolean expressions *Score* < 60 and *Score* < 70 are evaluated.

Potential Problems

1. *Semicolons must be used to separate the statements in a compound statement.* For many compilers, a missing semicolon at the end of a line will not be detected until the next line. For example, compiling the erroneous compound statement

```
begin
    Number := Number + 1
    Sum := Sum + Number
end
```

may produce the error message

```
Sum := Sum + Number
↑
*** Unexpected symbol
```

Since a statement may be continued from one line to the next, the absence of a semicolon at the end of the statement

```
Number := Number + 1
```

is not detected until the next line is examined, and "S" is not a symbol that can legally follow this statement.

2. *Each* **begin** *must have a matching* **end.** A missing **end** may be rather difficult to detect. The compiler may even search to the end of the program for an **end** to match an earlier **begin** and produce an error message such as

> END.
> ↑
> *** Unexpected symbol
> *** End of source file—missing "." or unclosed comment?

3. *Parentheses must be used within boolean expressions to indicate those subexpressions that are to be evaluated first.* The precedence of operators that may appear in boolean expressions is

> **not**   —— highest priority (performed first)
> *, /, **div, mod, and**
> +, −, **or**
> <,>,=,<=,>=,<>   —— lowest priority (performed last)

To illustrate, consider the statement

> **if** $1 < x$ **and** $x < 10$ **then**
>   *writeln* (x)

where x is of real type. The first operation performed in evaluating the boolean expression is the **and** operation. However, the subexpression x **and** x is not a valid boolean expression, because boolean operators cannot be applied to numeric quantities; thus an error message such as the following results:

> *** Illegal types of operand(s). Types of operands conflict.

4. *Real quantities that are algebraically equal may yield a false boolean expression when compared with* =, *because most real values are not stored exactly.* For example, even though the two real expressions $x * (1/x)$ and 1.0 are algebraically equal, the boolean expression $x * (1/x) = 1.0$ is usually false.

5. *In an* **if** *statement containing an* **else** *clause, there is no semicolon before the* **else.** A statement such as

> **if** $x > 0$ **then**
>   *writeln* (x);
> **else**
>   *writeln* $(2 * x)$

results in an error. A semicolon following **then** or **else** as in

> **if** $x > 0$ **then**;
>   *writeln* (x);

or

if $x > 0$ **then**
   $x := abs(x)$
else;
   writeln (x);

is syntactically correct, but it is almost surely a mistake since it indicates an empty statement. For both of these examples, the statement *writeln* (x) is executed, regardless of whether x is positive or not.

6. *In a nested* **if** *statement, each* **else** *clause is matched with the nearest preceding unmatched* **if.** For example, consider the following statements, which are given without indentation:

if $x > 0$ **then**
if $y > 0$ **then**
$z := x + y$
else
$z := x + abs(y)$;
$w := x * y * z$;

With which **if** is the **else** associated? According to the rule just stated, these statements are executed as

if $x > 0$ **then**
   if $y > 0$ **then**
      $z := x + y$
   else
      $z := x + abs(y)$;
$w := x * y * z$;

where the **else** clause matches the **if** statement containing the boolean expression $y > 0$.

7. *It should be assumed that all subexpressions are evaluated in determining the value of a compound boolean expression.* Suppose, for example, we write the statement

if $(x >= 0)$ **and** $(sqrt(x) < 5.0)$ **then**
   writeln ('Square root is less than 5')

where the subexpression $x >= 0$ is intended to prevent an attempt to calculate the square root of a negative number when x is negative. Some Pascal compilers may evaluate the subexpression $x >= 0$ and if it is false, will not evaluate the second subexpression $sqrt(x) < 5.0$. Other compilers evaluate both parts, and thus an error results when x is negative. This error can be avoided by rewriting the statement as

if $x >= 0$ **then**
   if $sqrt(x) < 5.0$ **then**
      writeln ('Square root is less than 5')

8. *The statement within a* **while** *statement must eventually cause the boolean expression controlling repetition to become false. The statements within a* **repeat** *statement must eventually cause the boolean expression in the* **until** *clause to become true.* An ***infinite loop*** is the result otherwise. For example, if x is a real variable, the statements

    $x := 0$;
    repeat
        writeln $(x:4:1)$;
        $x := x + 0.3$
    until $x = 1.0$

produce an infinite loop.

    Output:
    0.0
    0.3
    0.6
    0.9
    1.2
    1.5
    1.8
        $\vdots$

Since the value of x is never equal to 1.0, repetition is not terminated. In view of Potential Problem 3, the statements

    $x := 0$;
    repeat
        writeln $(x:4:1)$;
        $x := x + 0.2$
    until $x = 1.0$

may also produce an infinite loop.

    Output:
    0.0
    0.2
    0.4
    0.6
    0.8
    1.0
    1.2
    1.4
    1.6
        $\vdots$

Since x is initialized to 0 and 0.2 is added to x five times, x should have the value 1.0. But the boolean expression $x = 1.0$ may be false, because most real values are not stored exactly.

9. *In a* **while** *statement, the boolean expression is evaluated before execution of the statement within the* **while** *statement. In a* **repeat** *state-*

ment, the boolean expression is evaluated after execution of the statements within the **repeat** *statement.* Thus, the statement within a **while** statement is not executed if the boolean expression is false, but the statements within a **repeat** statement are always executed at least once.

10. *The* **repeat** *statement controls repetition of all statements between* **repeat** *and* **until,** *but* **for** *and* **while** *statements control repetition of only one statement.* For example, the statements

```
Count := 1;
while Count <= 10 do
    begin
        writeln (Count:2, sqr(Count):5);
        Count := Count + 1
    end (* while *)
```

display a list of the integers from 1 through 10 and their squares. The statements

```
Count := 1;
while Count <= 10 do
    writeln (Count:2, sqr(Count):5);
    Count := Count + 1
```

produce an infinite loop.

Output:
```
1    1
1    1
1    1
⋮    ⋮
```

11. *The control variable, initial value, and final value of a* **for** *statement cannot be modified within the body of the* **for** *statement.* For example, the statements

```
k := 5;
for i := 1 to k do
    begin
        writeln (k);
        k := k - 1
    end
```

produce the output
```
5
4
3
2
1
```

The statement

for $i := 1$ **to** 5 **do**
  begin
    writeln (i);
    $i := i - 1$
  end

is an error and produces a message such as

***A control variable must not be altered in its "FOR" loop.

Program Style

In this text, we use the following conventions for formatting the statements considered in this chapter.

1. *In a compound statement,* **begin** *and* **end** *are aligned and the statements they enclose are indented.*

  begin
    statement-1;
      ⋮
    statement-n
  end

2. *For an* **if** *statement,* **if** *. . .* **then** *is on one line, with its statement indented on the next line. If there is an* **else** *clause,* **else** *is on a separate line, aligned with* **if,** *and its statement indented on the next line.*

  if . . . **then**
    statement-1
  else
    statement-2

  if . . . **then**
    begin
      statement-1;
        ⋮
      statement-k
    end (∗ **if** ∗)
  else
    begin
      statement-k + 1;
        ⋮
      statement-n
    end(∗ **else** ∗)

An exception is made when an **if - else if** *construct is used to implement a multialternative selection structure. In this case the format used is*

> **if . . . then**
>   *statement-1*
> **else if . . . then**
>   *statement-2*
> **else if . . . then**
>   *statement-3*
>   ⋮
> **else**
>   *statement-n*

3. *In* **case** *statements,* **case** *is aligned with its corresponding* **end** *and the lines within the* **case** *statement are indented and the colons or the label lists are aligned.*

> **case** *selector* **of**
>   *label-list-1* : *statement-1*;
>   ⋮
>   *label-list-n* : *statement-n*
> **end** (∗ **case** ∗)

4. *In a* **while** *statement,* **while . . . do** *is on one line, with the body of the loop indented on the next line(s).*

> **while . . . do**
>   *statement*

> **while . . . do**
>   **begin**
>   *statement-1*;
>   ⋮
>   *statement-n*
>   **end** (∗ **while** ∗)

5. *In a* **repeat** *statement,* **repeat** *is aligned with the corresponding* **until** *and the body of the loop indented.*

> **repeat**
>   *statement-1*;
>   ⋮
>   *statement-n*
> **until . . .**

6. *In a* **for** *statement,* **for . . . do** *is on one line, with the body of the loop indented on the next line(s).*

> **for . . . do**
>   *statement*

> **for . . . do**
>   **begin**
>   *statement-1*;
>   ⋮
>   *statement-n*
>   **end** (∗ **for** ∗)

Variations and Extensions

The standard Pascal control structures described in this chapter are provided in nearly every version of Pascal. In some versions, however:

- It may not be possible to display boolean values. (UCSD)
- Boolean operators/functions may be applied (bitwise) to integer values. (Macintosh, Turbo)
- Execution of a **case** statement may fall through if the value of the selector is not in any of the label lists. (Turbo, UCSD)
- The **case** statement may have an **otherwise** (Macintosh) or **else** (Turbo) clause.
- The value of the control variable in a **for** loop may retain its last value rather than become undefined when repetition terminates. (Turbo)

See Appendix G for details.

5

Procedures and Functions

Great things can be reduced to small things, and small things can be reduced to nothing.

CHINESE PROVERB

The problems we have considered thus far have been simple enough that algorithms for their complete solution were quite straightforward. As we noted in Chapter 2, more complex problems are best solved using a ***top-down*** approach that uses a ***divide-and-conquer*** strategy to divide a problem into a number of simpler subproblems. Each of these subproblems is then considered individually, and in some cases it may be necessary to divide them further until the resulting subproblems are simple enough that algorithms for their solution can be easily designed. The complete algorithm for the original problem is then described in terms of these subalgorithms. ***Subprograms*** or ***modules*** can be written to implement each of these subalgorithms, and these subprograms combined to give a complete program that solves the original problem. In Pascal, these subprograms are ***procedures*** and ***functions*** whose execution is controlled by some other program unit, either the main program or some other subprogram.

Because the program units in this modular style of programming are independent of one another, the programmer can write each module and test it without worrying about the details of other modules. This makes it considerably easier to locate an error when it arises, since it often occurs in the module most recently written and added to the program and since the effects of these modules are easily isolated. Programs developed in this manner are also usually easier to understand because the structure of each program unit can be studied independently of that of the other program units.

5.1   Procedures

As noted in the introduction, a ***procedure*** is a subprogram designed to perform a particular task whose execution is controlled by some other program unit. In a Pascal program, procedures are defined in the **subprogram section,** which is the last section in the declaration part of the program (see the syntax diagram in Section 3.8). Once defined, they may be referenced in other parts of the program, with information being passed to and from these procedures by means of ***parameters.***

A procedure definition has a syntax that is very similar to that of a Pascal program in that it consists of a heading, a declaration part, and a statement part. A procedure is thus often said to be a ***subprogram*** of the ***main program.*** Its syntax diagram is

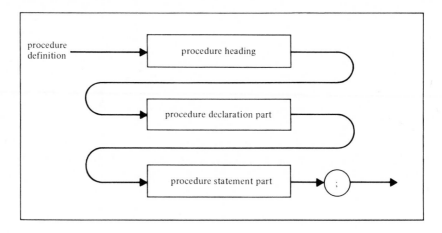

The syntax diagram for the procedure heading is

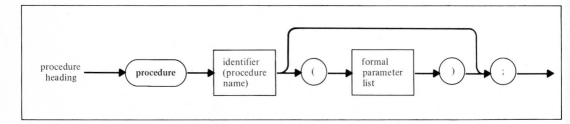

From this diagram we see that a procedure heading may have the form

> **procedure** *name*;

or

> **procedure** *name* (*formal-parameter-list*);

Here *name* is the name of the procedure and may be any legal Pascal identifier. The first form of the procedure heading is appropriate when it is not necessary to pass information to or from the procedure. The second form is more common, and in it the *formal-parameter-list* specifies the formal parameters of the procedure. These parameters are used to pass information to the procedure and/or to return information from it to the program unit that references it. This formal parameter list has the form

ind-1 list-1 : type-1; *ind-2 list-2 : type-2*; . . . ; *ind-k list-k : type-k*

where each *list-i* is a single identifier or a list of identifiers separated by commas, and *type-i* specifies their types; *ind-i* indicates how the identifiers in *list-i* are to be used. If this indicator is the reserved word **var,** then the identifiers in the list are ***variable parameters,*** sometimes called ***in-out parameters,*** which may be used *both* to transfer information to the procedure from the program unit that references it *and* to return information from the procedure. If this indicator is omitted, then the identifiers in the list may be used *only* to pass information to this procedure and not to return information; such parameters are called ***value parameters*** or ***in parameters.*** The following syntax diagram displays this form for the formal parameter list. (A more general form is given in Appendix C.)

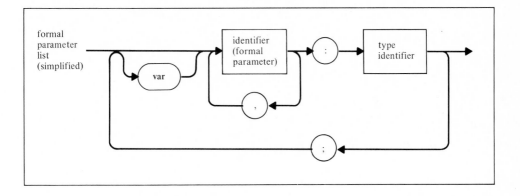

The statement part of a procedure definition has the same form as the statement part of a Pascal program. However, a semicolon rather than a period follows the reserved word **end** marking the end of the procedure definition.

To illustrate, suppose we wish to develop a procedure that accepts from the main program a month number, a day number, and a year number, and displays them in the form

mm/dd/yy

For example, the values 8, 14, 1941 are to be displayed as

8/14/41

and the values 9, 3, 1905 as

9/3/05

This procedure must have three formal parameters, each of integer type, representing the number of the month, day, and year, respectively. Since these parameters are used only to pass values to the procedure, they need not be designated as variable parameters. Thus, an appropriate procedure heading is

    procedure *DisplayDate* (*Month, Day, Year* : *integer*);

Only the last two digits of the year are to be displayed, and these can be obtained using the statement

    Year := *Year* **mod** 100;

For example, if the value passed to *Year* is 1941, this statement assigns the value 41 to *Year,* which can then be displayed. If, however, the value passed to *Year* is 1905, this statement assigns the value 5 to *Year;* displaying this value produces 5 rather than 05. Thus, we must calculate and display each digit individually. An appropriate output statement is therefore

    writeln (*Month*:1, '/', *Day*:1, '/', *Year* **div** 10 : 1, *Year* **mod** 10 : 1)

Using these two statements in the statement part of the procedure *DisplayDate,* we obtain the following complete procedure:

    procedure *DisplayDate* (*Month, Day, Year* : *integer*);

        (∗ Procedure to accept a *Month* number, a *Day* number, and
          a *Year* number and display the date in the form *mm/dd/yy* ∗)

    begin (∗ *DisplayDate* ∗)
      Year := *Year* **mod** 100;
      writeln (*Month*:1, '/', *Day*:1 '/', *Year* **div** 10 : 1,
           Year **mod** 10 : 1)
    end (∗ *DisplayDate* ∗);

Note that a comment is included to describe the procedure. It is good practice to include such documentation to briefly describe what the procedure does, what its parameters represent, and other information that explains the procedure definition.

    This procedure definition is placed after the variable section in the declaration part of a Pascal program. The procedure *DisplayDate* can then be called with a ***procedure reference statement*** of the form

    name (*actual-parameter-list*)

where *name* is the name of the procedure and *actual-parameter-list* is a list of **actual parameters** that are to be associated with the parameters in the formal parameter list of the procedure heading. For example, the procedure *DisplayDate* is called by the statement

    DisplayDate (*TheMonth, TheDay, TheYear*)

in the program of Figure 5.1. This statement causes the values of the actual parameters *TheMonth, TheDay,* and *TheYear* to be assigned to the formal parameters *Month, Day,* and *Year,* respectively, of the procedure *DisplayDate,* and initiates execution of the procedure. When the end of the procedure is reached, execution resumes with the statement following this procedure reference statement in the main program.

```
PROGRAM Date (input, output);

(*******************************************************************

   Program demonstrating use of  a procedure to display a given date
   in the form:        mm/dd/yy

*******************************************************************)

VAR
   TheMonth, TheDay, TheYear : integer;     (* month, day, year *)

PROCEDURE DisplayDate (Month, Day, Year : integer);

   (****************************************************************

           Displays a date in the form mm/dd/yy.

   ****************************************************************)

   BEGIN (* DisplayDate *)
      Year := Year MOD 100;
       writeln (Month:1, '/', Day:1, '/', Year DIV 10 : 1, Year MOD 10 : 1);
   END (* DisplayDate *);
BEGIN (* main program *)
   write ('Enter month, day, and year:  ');
   readln (TheMonth, TheDay, TheYear);
   writeln;
   DisplayDate (TheMonth, TheDay, TheYear)
END (* main program *).


Sample runs:

Enter month, day, and year:  8 14 1941

8/14/41


Enter month, day, and year:  9 3 1905

9/3/05
```

Figure 5.1

In this example, the procedure *DisplayDate* does not return any values to the main program; it only displays information that is passed to it. Thus, its formal parameters *Month, Day,* and *Year* are value parameters. Before a procedure is referenced, its value parameters are undefined. At the time of reference, memory locations are associated with them, and the values of the corresponding actual parameters are copied into these locations. Thus, for the procedure *DisplayDate*, the formal parameters *Month, Day,* and *Year* are undefined until the procedure reference statement

    DisplayDate (TheMonth, TheDay, TheYear)

is encountered. The values of the actual parameters *TheMonth, TheDay,* and *TheYear* are then copied to *Month, Day,* and *Year,* respectively.

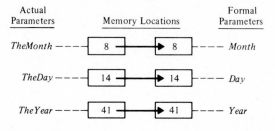

After execution of the procedure, these value parameters once again become undefined so that any values they had during execution of the procedure or function are lost.

    We noted earlier that variable parameters may be used to return values from a procedure. A variable formal parameter and the corresponding actual parameter are associated with the same memory location, and thus a variable formal parameter is merely a temporary **alias** or **synonym** for the actual parameter it represents. Consequently, any modification of a variable formal parameter in a procedure changes the value of the corresponding actual parameter. The actual parameter must therefore be a variable; constants and expressions are not allowed. Also, actual parameters must be of the same type as the corresponding formal parameters.

    As a simple example of variable parameters, consider the problem of determining which of two real numbers is the larger and which is the smaller. The following procedure solves this problem:

       procedure *FindMaxAndMin (Num1, Num2 : real*;
                            var *Max, Min : real*);

      (* Procedure to find and return the *Max*imum and the
        *Min*inum of two real numbers *Num1* and *Num2* *)

     begin (* *FindMaxAndMin* *)
       if *Num1 > Num2* **then**
         begin
           Max := Num1;
           Min := Num2
         end (* **if** *)
       else
         begin
           Max := Num2;
           Min := Num1
         end (* **else** *)
     end (* *FindMaxAndMin* *);

Because the values of *Max* and *Min* are to be returned by the procedure, they must be declared to be variable parameters. Figure 5.2 shows a complete program that reads a pair of real numbers, calls procedure *FindMaxAndMin* to find the largest and the smallest number in the pair, and displays these numbers with appropriate labels.

```
PROGRAM MaxMin (input, output);

(***************************************************************

  Program demonstrating use of a procedure to find the
  maximum and the minimum of two real numbers.

*************************************************************)

VAR
   X, Y,                        (* two real numbers *)
   Largest, Smallest : real;    (* largest and smallest of the numbers *)

PROCEDURE FindMaxAndMin (Num1, Num2 : real; VAR Max, Min : real);

   (***********************************************************

      Procedure to find and return the Maximum and the
      Minimum of two real numbers Num1 and Num2.

   *********************************************************)

   BEGIN (* FindMaxAndMin *)
      IF Num1 > Num2 THEN
         BEGIN
            Max := Num1;
            Min := Num2
         END (* IF *)
      ELSE
         BEGIN
            Max := Num2;
            Min := Num1
         END (* ELSE *)
   END (* FindMaxAndMin *);

BEGIN (* main program *)
   write ('Enter two numbers:  ');
   readln (X, Y);
   FindMaxAndMin (X, Y, Largest, Smallest);
   writeln ('Largest is ', Largest:4:1, ' and smallest is ', Smallest:4:1)
END (* main *).


Sample runs:

Enter two numbers:  2.0  1.1
Largest is  2.0 and smallest is  1.1


Enter two numbers:  -33.6  25.5
Largest is 25.5 and smallest is -33.6
```
Figure 5.2

In this program, the variable declarations

var
    X, Y,   (∗ two real numbers ∗)
    Largest, Smallest : *real*;   (∗ largest and smallest of the numbers ∗)

associate memory locations with the four variables *X, Y, Largest* and *Smallest*.

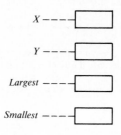

When the statement

    FindMaxAndMin (X, Y, Largest, Smallest);

is executed, new memory locations are associated with the value parameters *Num1* and *Num2*, and the values of *X* and *Y* are copied into these locations. No new memory locations are obtained for the variable parameters *Max* and *Min;* instead these formal parameters are associated with the existing memory locations of the corresponding actual parameters *Largest* and *Smallest*.

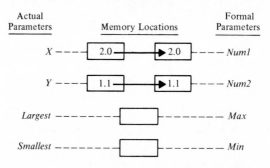

When the procedure *FindMaxAndMin* is executed, values are determined for *Max* and *Min*, and because *Max* and *Min* are associated with the same memory locations as *Largest* and *Smallest*, these values are also the values of *Largest* and *Smallest*.

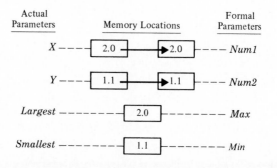

Because the memory locations associated with *Num1* and *Num2* are distinct from those for *X* and *Y*, changes to *Num1* and *Num2* in procedure *FindMaxAndMin* could not change the values of *X* and *Y*. When execution of the procedure is completed, the association of memory locations with *Num1*, *Num2*, *Max*, and *Min* is terminated, and these formal parameters become undefined.

When a procedure is referenced, the number of actual parameters must be the same as the number of formal parameters, and the type of each actual parameter must be the same as the type of the corresponding formal parameter. One exception is that an actual parameter of integer type may be associated with a value parameter of real type. Thus, in a program in which variables *N1* and *N2* have been declared to be of integer type and *R1* and *R2* of real type, the procedure *FindMaxAndMin* could be called with either of the statements

> *FindMaxAndMin (N1, N2, R1, R2)*;
>
> *FindMaxAndMin (N1 / 4, 7.5, R1, R2)*;

The following would not be valid, however, for the reasons indicated:

> *FindMaxAndMin (R1, R2)*;   (The number of actual parameters does not agree with the number of formal parameters.)
>
> *FindMaxAndMin (N1, R1, 5.1, R2)*;   (The constant 5.1 may not be associated with the variable parameter *Max*.)
>
> *FindMaxAndMin (N1, R1, N2, R2)*;   (The integer actual parameter *N2* may not be associated with the real variable parameter *Max*.)

The following rules summarize the relation between actual and formal parameters:

Rules for Parameter Association

1. There must be the same number of formal parameters as there are actual parameters.
2. The types of associated formal and actual parameters must agree; however, an actual parameter of integer type may be associated with a formal value parameter of real type.
3. An actual parameter associated with a variable formal parameter must be a variable; it may not be a constant or an expression.

Some procedure definitions may require the use of constants and/or variables in addition to the formal parameters. These are usually defined and declared within the procedure itself, in the constant and variable sections of the procedure's declaration part, which has the same form as the declaration part of a Pascal program. For example, suppose we wish to develop a program that reads the amount of a purchase and the amount tendered in payment, calls a procedure to determine the change in dollars, half-dollars, quarters, dimes, nickels, and pennies, and then displays these values.

A procedure *MakeChange* to calculate the required change will have two value parameters, *Purchase* and *Payment*, of real type, whose values will be passed from the main program. It will also have variable parameters *Dollars*, *Halves*, *Quarters*, *Dimes*, *Nickels*, and *Pennies* of integer type, whose values must be returned to the main program. An appropriate procedure heading is therefore

> **procedure** *MakeChange* (*Purchase*, *Payment* : *real*;
>   **var** *Dollars*, *Halves*, *Quarters*, *Dimes*,
>   *Nickels*, *Pennies* : *integer*);

In addition, an auxiliary variable *Change* is needed to store intermediate results; this variable is declared in the declaration part of this procedure:

> **var**
>   *Change* : integer;

In the statement part of procedure *MakeChange*, *Change* is initially calculated by

> *Change* := *round*(100 * (*Payment* − *Purchase*));

(The function *round* is used because the real values *Payment* and *Purchase* may not be stored exactly.) In subsequent calculations, *Change* represents the change yet to be dispensed. The program in Figure 5.3 shows the complete procedure.

```
PROGRAM ChangeMaker (input, output);

(************************************************************************

    Program to read a given Purchase and Payment, and call the
    procedure MakeChange to determine change to be tendered.

 ************************************************************************)
VAR
    Purchase,          (* purchase made *)
    Payment : real;    (* payment received; assumed >= Purchase *)
    Dollars, Halves,   (* numbers of bills and coins to be *)
    Quarters, Dimes,   (* returned in change *)
    Nickels, Pennies : integer;

PROCEDURE MakeChange (Purchase, Payment : real;
                      VAR Dollars, Halves, Quarters, Dimes,
                          Nickels, Pennies : integer);

    (*********************************************************************

        Procedure to determine various denominations of change to be
        tendered for a given Purchase and Payment.

     *********************************************************************)
    VAR
        Change : integer;   (* amount of change to be tendered *)
```

Figure 5.3

Figure 5.3 (cont.)

```
   BEGIN (* MakeChange *)
      Change := round (100 * (Payment - Purchase));
      Dollars := Change DIV 100;
      Change := Change MOD 100;
      Halves := Change DIV 50;
      Change := Change MOD 50;
      Quarters := Change DIV 25;
      Change := Change MOD 25;
      Dimes := Change DIV 10;
      Change := Change MOD 10;
      Nickels := Change DIV 5;
      Pennies := Change MOD 5
   END (* MakeChange *);

BEGIN (* main program *)
   write ('Purchase and payment?  ');
   readln (Purchase, Payment);
   MakeChange (Purchase, Payment, Dollars, Halves, Quarters,
               Dimes, Nickels, Pennies);
   writeln ('Change tendered:');
   writeln (Dollars:1, ' Dollars');
   writeln (Halves:1, ' Halves');
   writeln (Quarters:1, ' Quarters');
   writeln (Dimes:1, ' Dimes');
   writeln (Nickels:1, ' Nickels');
   writeln (Pennies:1, ' Pennies')
END (* main program *).


Sample runs:


Purchase and payment?  1.01 5.00
Change tendered:
3 Dollars
1 Halves
1 Quarters
2 Dimes
0 Nickels
4 Pennies


Purchase and payment?  1.99 2.00
Change tendered:
0 Dollars
0 Halves
0 Quarters
0 Dimes
0 Nickels
1 Pennies
```

In this example, the variables *Purchase, Payment, Dollars, Halves, Quarters, Dimes, Nickels, Pennies,* and *Change* have values only when the procedure *MakeChange* is referenced, and these values are accessible only within this procedure. These variables are therefore said to be **local** to the procedure. The portion of a program in which a variable is accessible is called the **scope** of that variable. Thus the scope of these variables is the procedure *MakeChange*.

One consequence of this scope rule for local variables is that the same identifier can be used without conflict in two different program units. For example, the procedure *MakeChange* and some other procedure can both be used in the same program, even though both procedures use the variable name *Payment*. When these procedures are referenced, the variable *Payment* in procedure *MakeChange* is associated with a different memory location than is the variable *Payment* in the other procedure. Thus, changing the value of one does not change the value of the other. Similarly, any of the other local variables in procedure *MakeChange* may be used without conflict elsewhere in the program.

5.2 Example of Modular Programming: Menu-Driven Checkbook-Balancing Program

In the introduction to this chapter, we claimed that one of the advantages of procedures is that they enable a programmer to develop programs in a ***modular*** fashion. This means that the major tasks to be performed by the program can be identified and individual procedures for these tasks can then be designed and tested. Programs written in this manner are not only easier to develop and test and easier to understand, but also easier to modify since individual modules can be added, deleted, or altered. In this section we illustrate this technique of modular programming by developing a simple checkbook-balancing program.

Suppose we wish to develop a program that allows the user to reconcile his checkbook with a monthly statement received from the bank. There are three main tasks that must be performed:

1. Deposits must be added to the current balance.
2. The amount of each check written and a check-processing charge must be subtracted from the current balance.
3. A summary of the month's activity must be printed. This summary should include the initial balance, number of checks, total amount of checks, number of deposits, total deposits, total service charges, and the final balance.

One procedure of the program will be an initialization module that obtains a value for *InitialBalance* and initializes the variable *Balance* to *InitialBalance*, the variables *TotalDeposits*, *TotalChecks*, *TotalServiceCharges*, *NumberOf-Checks*, and *NumberOfDeposits* to 0, and a boolean variable *DoneProcessing* to false. A second procedure will be designed to process deposits and a third to process checks. There will also be another procedure to print the monthly summary. The main program will first reference the procedure *Initialize* and then repeatedly call four other procedures, *DisplayMenu*, *ProcessDeposit*, *ProcessCheck*, and *PrintSummary*, as necessary. The following ***structure diagram*** summarizes the structure of the program.

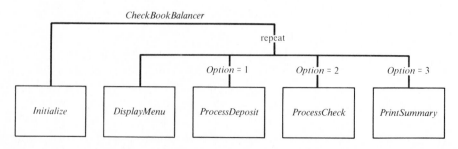

The user will select an option from a ***menu*** and the appropriate procedure will be called. The statement part of the main program will thus have the form

```
begin (* main program *)
    Initialize (InitialBalance, Balance, TotalDeposits, TotalChecks,
                TotalServiceCharges, NumberOfDeposits,
                NumberOfChecks, DoneProcessing);
    repeat
        write ('Enter Option:    ');
        readln (Option);
        if (Option >= 0) and (Option <= NumberOfOptions) then
            case Option of
                0 : DoneProcessing := true;
                1 : ProcessDeposit (Balance, TotalDeposits,
                                        NumberOfDeposits);
                2 : ProcessCheck (Balance, TotalChecks,
                                    TotalServiceCharges,
                                    NumberOfChecks);
                3 : PrintSummary (InitialBalance, Balance, TotalDeposits,
                                    TotalChecks, TotalServiceCharges,
                                    NumberOfDeposits, NumberOfChecks)
            end (* case *)
        else
            writeln ('*** Invalid Option ***')
    until DoneProcessing
end (* main program *).
```

For the procedure *Initialize*, all of the parameters must be variable parameters since each of the values must be returned. An appropriate procedure heading is therefore

```
procedure Initialize (var InitialBalance, Balance, TotalDeposits,
                            TotalChecks, TotalServiceCharges : real;
                       var NumberOfChecks, NumberOfDeposits : integer;
                       var DoneProcessing : boolean);
```

Note that although in previous examples we used different names for the actual parameters and the corresponding formal parameters, this is not necessary, as this example illustrates.

The procedure *DisplayMenu* simply displays the menu of options available to the user; no information is passed to or from it. Its heading thus requires no formal parameter list:

```
procedure DisplayMenu;
```

The parameters for procedure *ProcessDeposit* must be in-out parameters, that is, variable parameters, because current values for *Balance*, *TotalDeposits*, and *NumberOfDeposits* will be passed to the procedure, which must then update them and return those new values. Similarly, each of the parameters for procedure *ProcessCheck* must be variable parameters. Appropriate headings for these procedures are therefore

> **procedure** *ProcessDeposit* (**var** *Balance, TotalDeposits* : *real*;
>   **var** *NumberOfDeposits* : *integer*);

and

> **procedure** *ProcessCheck* (**var** *Balance, TotalChecks,*
>   *TotalServiceCharges* : *real*;
>   **var** *NumberOfChecks* : *integer*);

The procedure *PrintSummary* simply displays information that is passed to it. Its formal parameters are thus in parameters, that is, value parameters, so that its heading is

> **procedure** *PrintSummary* (*InitialBalance, FinalBalance, TotalDeposits,*
>   *TotalChecks, TotalServiceCharges* : *real*;
>   *NumberOfDeposits, NumberOfChecks* : *integer*);

Figure 5.4 shows the complete ***menu-driven program*** with complete procedures. Although the final program is given here, it could well have been developed in a piecewise manner by writing and testing only some of the procedures before writing the others. In this case, undeveloped procedures could simply have empty statement parts:

> **begin** (∗ *ProcessCheck* ∗)
> **end** (∗ *ProcessCheck* ∗);

Usually, however, they would be ***program stubs*** that at least signal execution of these procedures:

> **begin** (∗ *ProcessCheck* ∗)
>   *writeln* ('Executing Processcheck')
> **end** (∗ *ProcessCheck* ∗);

and they might also produce temporary printouts to assist in checking other procedures.

```
PROGRAM CheckbookBalancer (input, output);

(*******************************************************************
   Menu-driven program for reconciling a checkbook with a monthly
   statement.
 *******************************************************************)

CONST
   NumberOfOptions = 3;          (* # of options in menu *)
```

Figure 5.4

Figure 5.4 (cont.).

```
VAR
    InitialBalance,             (* beginning balance in checking account *)
    Balance,                    (* current balance *)
    TotalDeposits,              (* sum of all deposits for the month *)
    TotalChecks,                (* sum of all checks processed *)
    TotalServiceCharges : real; (* total check-processing charges *)
    NumberOfDeposits,           (* total number of deposits made *)
    NumberOfChecks,             (*            and checks written *)
    Option : integer;           (* option selected by user *)
    DoneProcessing : boolean;   (* indicates if processing completed *)

PROCEDURE Initialize (VAR InitialBalance, Balance, TotalDeposits,
                          TotalChecks, TotalServiceCharges : real;
                      VAR NumberOfDeposits, NumberOfChecks : integer;
                      VAR DoneProcessing : boolean);

    (**********************************************************************

           Procedure to get initial balance from user and
           initialize variables.

     *********************************************************************)

    BEGIN (* Initialize *)
       write ('Enter beginning balance:   $');
       readln (InitialBalance);
       Balance := InitialBalance;
       TotalDeposits := 0;
       TotalChecks := 0;
       TotalServiceCharges := 0;
       NumberOfDeposits := 0;
       NumberOfChecks := 0;
       DoneProcessing := false;
    END (* Initialize *);

PROCEDURE DisplayMenu;

    (**********************************************************************

           Procedure to display the menu of options.

     *********************************************************************)

    BEGIN (* DisplayMenu *)
       writeln;
       writeln ('Options available are:');
       writeln ('0.  Quit processing');
       writeln ('1.  Process a deposit.');
       writeln ('2.  Process a check.');
       writeln ('3.  Print summary of month''s activities');
    END (* DisplayMenu *);
```

Figure 5.4 (cont.)

```
PROCEDURE ProcessDeposit (VAR Balance, TotalDeposits : real;
                          VAR NumberOfDeposits : integer);

   (*******************************************************************

      Procedure to process a deposit.  Returns updated values of
      Balance, TotalDeposits, and NumberOfDeposits.

    *****************************************************************)

   VAR
      Deposit : real;          (* amount of deposit *)

   BEGIN (* ProcessDeposit *)
      write ('Enter deposit:  $');
      readln (Deposit);
      Balance := Balance + Deposit;
      TotalDeposits := TotalDeposits + Deposit;
      NumberOfDeposits := NumberOfDeposits + 1
   END (* ProcessDeposit *);

PROCEDURE ProcessCheck (VAR Balance, TotalChecks, TotalServiceCharges : real;
                        VAR NumberOfChecks : integer);

   (*******************************************************************

      Procedure to process a check.  Returns updated values of
      Balance, TotalChecks, and NumberOfChecks.

    *****************************************************************)

   CONST
      CheckCharge = 0.20;     (* per check processing charge *)

   VAR
      Check : real;           (* amount of check *)

   BEGIN (* ProcessCheck *)
      write ('Enter check:  $');
      readln (Check);
      Balance := Balance - Check - CheckCharge;
      TotalChecks := TotalChecks + Check;
      TotalServiceCharges := TotalServiceCharges + CheckCharge;
      NumberOfChecks := NumberOfChecks + 1
   END (* ProcessCheck *);

PROCEDURE PrintSummary (InitialBalance, Balance, TotalDeposits,
                        TotalChecks, TotalServiceCharges : real;
                        NumberOfDeposits, NumberOfChecks : integer);

   (*******************************************************************

      Procedure to print summary of month's transactions.

    *****************************************************************)
```

Figure 5.4 (cont.)

```
BEGIN (* PrintSummary *)
   writeln;
   writeln ('Initial Balance  . . . . . . . . $', InitialBalance:8:2);
   writeln ('Total Deposits . . . . . . . . $', TotalDeposits:8:2);
   writeln ('Total Checks . . . . . . . . . $', TotalChecks:8:2);
   writeln ('Total Service Charges  . . . . $', TotalServiceCharges:8:2);
   writeln ('Final Balance  . . . . . . . . $', Balance:8:2);
   writeln ('Number of Deposits:  ', NumberOfDeposits:1);
   writeln ('Number of Checks:    ', NumberOfChecks:1)
END (* PrintSummary *);

BEGIN (* main program *)
   Initialize (InitialBalance, Balance, TotalDeposits, TotalChecks,
               TotalServiceCharges, NumberOfDeposits, NumberOfChecks,
               DoneProcessing);
   REPEAT
      DisplayMenu;
      write ('Enter Option:  ');
      readln (Option);
      IF (Option >= 0) AND (Option <= NumberOfOptions) THEN
         CASE Option OF
            0 : DoneProcessing := true;
            1 : ProcessDeposit (Balance, TotalDeposits, NumberOfDeposits);
            2 : ProcessCheck (Balance, TotalChecks, TotalServiceCharges,
                              NumberOfChecks);
            3 : PrintSummary (InitialBalance, Balance, TotalDeposits,
                              TotalChecks, TotalServiceCharges,
                              NumberOfDeposits, NumberOfChecks)
         END (* CASE *)
      ELSE
         writeln ('*** Invalid Option ***')
   UNTIL DoneProcessing
END (* main program *).
```

```
Sample run:


Enter beginning balance:  $357.40

Options available are:
0.  Quit processing
1.  Process a deposit.
2.  Process a check.
3.  Print summary of month's activities
Enter Option:  1
Enter deposit:  $250.00

Options available are:
0.  Quit processing
1.  Process a deposit.
2.  Process a check.
3.  Print summary of month's activities
Enter Option:  2
Enter check:  $35.00
```

Figure 5.4 (cont.)

```
Options available are:
0.   Quit processing
1.   Process a deposit.
2.   Process a check.
3.   Print summary of month's activities
Enter Option:   2
Enter check:   $14.00

Options available are:
0.   Quit processing
1.   Process a deposit.
2.   Process a check.
3.   Print summary of month's activities
Enter Option:   3

Initial Balance  . . . . . . . .  $   357.40
Total Deposits . . . . . . . . .  $   250.00
Total Checks . . . . . . . . . .  $    49.00
Total Service Charges  . . . . .  $     0.40
Final Balance  . . . . . . . . .  $   558.00
Number of Deposits:   1
Number of Checks:     2

Options available are:
0.   Quit processing
1.   Process a deposit.
2.   Process a check.
3.   Print summary of month's activities
Enter Option:   0
```

A major advantage of the modular design of a program such as this is that it is relatively easy to modify when necessary. For example, if the bank changes the amount charged for processing checks, we know immediately that procedure *ProcessCheck* is the one to modify; we simply change the value of *CheckCharge* to the new value. Similarly, if a charge is to be made for processing deposits, procedure *ProcessDeposit* is the one requiring modification. Some changes may require modification of more than one procedure, but the task is still considerably easier than in a nonmodular program, since one can usually determine which procedures require change and which ones must be added or deleted. For example, suppose we wish to modify the program to handle cash withdrawals as well, such as those from an automatic teller machine for which no processing charge is made. We could design a new procedure *ProcessATM* with variable parameters *Balance*, *TotalATMs*, and *NumberOfATMs*. To incorporate this procedure into the program, we need only do the following:

1. Change *NumberOfOptions* to 4.
2. Add a call to procedure *ProcessATM* in the case statement with a new option number 4 (or perhaps renumber *PrintSummary* with 4 and use 3 for *ProcessATM*).
3. Add another *writeln* statement to procedure *DisplayMenu* to display this new option.
4. Modify the heading of and the reference to procedure *Initialize* to include *TotalATMs* and *NumberOfATMs* as variable parameters and add statements in *Initialize* to set these to 0.

5. Modify the heading of and the reference to procedure *PrintSummary* to include *TotalATMs* and *NumberOfATMs* as parameters and add statements in *PrintSummary* to display their values.

Exercises

1. Consider the following program skeleton:

   program *Demo* (*input, output*);

   const
      pi = 3.14159;
      two = 2;

   var
      Month, Day, Year, p, q : *integer*;
      Hours, Rate, Amount, u, v : *real*;
      Code, Class : *char*;

      procedure *Calculate* (*a* : *real*; **var** *b* : *real*;
                          m : *integer*; **var** *k, n* : *integer*;
                          var *c* : *char*);
                        ⋮

   Determine whether each of the following statements can be used in the statement part of the program. If it cannot be used, explain why.

   (a) *Calculate* (*u, v, two, p, q, Code*);
   (b) *Calculate* (*pi, u, two, p, v, Class*);
   (c) *Calculate* (*Hours, pi, two, Day, Year, Class*);
   (d) **while** *u* > 0 **do**
       Calculate (*Rate, u, Day* + 2, *p, q,* 'M');
   (e) *Calculate* (0, *Hours,* (*p* + 1)/2, *Day, Year, Code*);
   (f) **repeat**
       Calculate (*two, Amount, Day, p* + *q, Day, Class*)
     until *Amount* > 0;

2. Write a procedure *CalculateWages* that calculates and returns the wages for a given number of hours worked and a given hourly pay rate. Hours over 40 should be paid at 1.5 times the regular hourly rate.

3. Write a procedure *DisplayMonth* that displays the name of a month whose number is passed to it.

4. Write a procedure *Switch* that interchanges the values of two variables. For example, if *a* has the value 3 and *b* has the value 4, then the reference *Switch* (*a, b*) causes *a* to have the value 4 and *b* the value 3.

5. With **polar coordinates** (*r*, θ) of a point *P*, the first polar coordinate *r* is the distance from the origin to *P*, and the second polar coordinate θ is the angle from the positive *x* axis to the ray joining the origin with *P*.

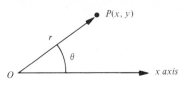

The formulas that relate polar coordinates of a point to **rectangular coordinates** are

$$x = r \cos \theta$$
$$y = r \sin \theta$$

Write a procedure *Convert* that converts polar coordinates to rectangular coordinates. Use it in a program that reads the polar coordinates for several points, calls *Convert* to find the rectangular coordinates for each point, and then displays both pairs of coordinates.

6. Write a procedure that calculates the amount of city income tax and the amount of federal income tax to be withheld from an employee's pay for one pay period. Assume that city income tax withheld is computed by taking 1.15 percent of gross pay on the first $15,000 earned per year and that federal income tax withheld is computed by taking the gross pay less $15 for each dependent claimed and multiplying by 20 percent.

   Use this procedure in a program that for each of several employees reads his or her employee number, number of dependents, hourly pay rate, city income tax withheld to date, federal income tax withheld to date, and hours worked for this pay period, and then calculates and prints the employee number, gross pay and net pay for this pay period, the amount of city income tax and amount of federal income tax withheld for this pay period, and the total amounts withheld through this pay period.

7. One simple method of calculating depreciation is the **straight-line** method. If the value of the asset being depreciated is *Amount* dollars and it is to be depreciated over *NumberOfYears* years, then *Amount* / *NumberOfYears* dollars is depreciated in each year. Write a program that reads values for *Amount* and *NumberOfYears*, calls a procedure to calculate the annual depreciation, and then displays this value.

8. Another method of calculating depreciation is the **double declining balance** method. For an asset with value *Amount* dollars that is to be depreciated over *NumberOfYears* years, 2 / *NumberOfYears* times the undepreciated balance is depreciated annually. Since in each year only a fraction of the remaining balance is depreciated, the entire amount would never be depreciated. Consequently, it is permissible to switch to the straight-line method (see Exercise 7) at any time. Write a program that reads values for *Amount, NumberOfYears,* and the year in which to switch to the straight-line method, and calls a procedure to

print a table showing the year number and the amount to be depreciated in that year.

9. The **greatest common divisor** of two integers a and b, GCD(a,b), not both of which are zero, is the largest positive integer that divides both a and b. The **Euclidean Algorithm** for finding this greatest common divisor of a and b is as follows: Divide a by b to obtain the integer quotient q and remainder r, so that $a = bq + r$ (if $b = 0$, interchange a and b). Then GCD(a,b) = GCD(b,r). Replace a with b and b with r and repeat this procedure. Since the remainders are decreasing, eventually a remainder of 0 results. The last nonzero remainder is GCD(a,b). For example:

$$
\begin{aligned}
1260 &= 198 \cdot 6 + 72 & \text{GCD}(1260, 198) &= \text{GCD}(198, 72) \\
198 &= 72 \cdot 2 + 54 & &= \text{GCD}(72, 54) \\
72 &= 54 \cdot 1 + 18 & &= \text{GCD}(54, 18) \\
54 &= 18 \cdot 3 + 0 & &= 18
\end{aligned}
$$

(Note: If either a or b is negative, we replace them with their absolute values.) The **least common multiple** of a and b, LCM (a,b), is the smallest nonnegative integer that is a multiple of both a and b and can be calculated using

$$
\text{LCM}(a,b) = \frac{|a \cdot b|}{\text{GCD}(a,b)}
$$

Write a program that reads two integers, calls a procedure that calculates and returns their greatest common divisor and least common multiple, and then displays these two values.

10. Write a program that reads two positive integers n and b and then calls a procedure *ChangeBase* to calculate and display the base b representation of n. Assume that b is not greater than 10 (see Exercise 12 of Chapter 1 for one method for converting from base 10 to another base).

11. Write a program that reads a positive integer n and then calls a procedure *Hexadecimal* to display the base-16 representation of n. The symbols A, B, C, D, E, and F should be displayed for 10, 11, 12, 13, 14, and 15, respectively (see Exercises 7 and 12 of Chapter 1 and the preceding exercise).

12. Write a menu-driven program that allows the user to convert measurements from either minutes to hours or feet to meters (1 foot = 0.3048 meter), or from degrees Fahrenheit to degrees Celsius ($C = \frac{5}{9}(F - 32)$). Use procedures to implement the various options. A sample run of the program should proceed somewhat as follows:

   Available options are:
   0. Display this menu.
   1. Convert minutes to hours.

2. Convert feet to meters.
3. Convert degrees Fahrenheit to degrees Celsius.
4. Quit

Enter an option (0 to see menu): 3
Enter degrees Fahrenheit: 212
This is equivalent to 100.0 degrees Celsius

Enter an option (0 to see menu): 5
*** 5 is not a valid option ***

Enter an option (0 to see menu): 0
Available options are:
0. Display this menu.
1. Convert minutes to hours.
2. Convert feet to meters.
3. Convert degrees Fahrenheit to degrees Celsius.
4. Quit

Enter an option (0 to see menu): 1
Enter minutes: 360
This is equivalent to 60.0 hours

Enter an option (0 to see menu): 2
Enter number of feet: 1
This is equivalent to 0.3048 meters

Enter an option (0 to see menu): 4

13. Write a menu-driven program that allows the user to select one of the following methods of depreciation:
   1. Straight-line (see Exercise 7).
   2. Double-declining balance (see Exercise 8).
   3. Sum-of-the-years-digits (see Exercise 19 of Section 4.8)
Design the program to be modular, using procedures to implement the various options.

5.3 Functions

As we have seen, Pascal provides several ***predefined functions*** such as *sqr*, *round*, and *odd*. Recall that to use any of these functions to calculate some value in an expression, one need only give its name followed by the actual parameter to which it is to be applied, enclosed in parentheses. For example, the statements

writeln (sqr(x));

Alpha := *round*(100 * *Beta*) / 100;

if *odd*(*Number*) **then**
  writeln (*Number*);

display the square of *x*, assign to *Alpha* the value of *Beta* rounded to the nearest hundredth, and display the value of *Number* provided it is an odd integer.

In some programs it may be convenient for the user to define additional functions. Such **user-defined functions** are possible in Pascal, and once defined, they are used in the same way as the predefined functions.

Like procedures, functions are defined in the subprogram section of a program and consist of a heading, a declaration part, and a statement part. The syntax diagram for a function definition is

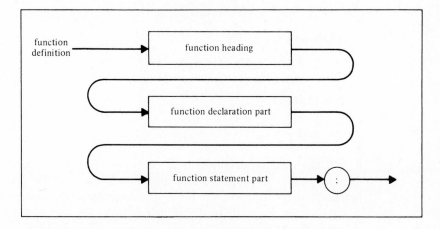

The function heading has the form

function *name* (*formal-parameter-list*) : *result-type*;

where *name* is the name of the function and may be any legal Pascal identifier. The type of the function value, *result-type,* may be any of the standard Pascal data types (or certain other data types considered later). The *formal-parameter-list* has the same form as for a procedure heading. The syntax diagram for a function heading is

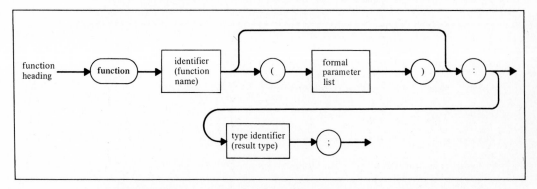

The declaration and statement parts of a function definition have the same forms as for procedures, with the additional stipulation that at least one of the statements in the statement part must assign a value to the identifier that names the function.

To illustrate, suppose that we wish to define the trigonometric tangent function, which is an important function in mathematics but which is not one of the predefined functions in Pascal. This function has a single formal parameter, which is of real type, and the result type is also real. Thus an appropriate function heading is

function *tan*(*x* : *real*) : *real*;

and the complete function definition for *tan* is

function *tan*(*x* : *real*) : *real*;

 (∗ Function *tan* returns the tangent
 of *x* (which is in radians). ∗)

 begin (∗ *tan* ∗)
  tan := *sin*(*x*) / *cos*(*x*)
 end (∗ *tan* ∗);

If this function definition is placed in the subprogram section of the declaration part of a program, the function *tan* can then be referenced in the statement part of the program (or in later functions and procedures) in the same manner as are the predefined Pascal functions. The simple program in Figure 5.5 provides an illustration.

```
PROGRAM TangentTable (input, output);

(*******************************************************************

  Program to print a table of values of the tangent function.

*****************************************************************)

VAR
    Lower, Upper,   (* bounds on range of values *)
    Step,           (* increment *)
    Theta : real;   (* actual argument *)

FUNCTION tan (x : real) : real;

  (*****************************************************************

    Function tan returns the tangent of x (which is in radians).

  ***************************************************************)

  BEGIN (* tan *)
    tan := sin(x) / cos(x)
  END (* tan *);
```

Figure 5.5

Figure 5.5 (cont.)

```
BEGIN (* main program *)
   write ('Enter range of values and step size: ');
   readln (Lower, Upper, Step);
   writeln;
   writeln ('Theta   tan(Theta)');
   writeln ('─────   ───────────');
   Theta := Lower;
   WHILE Theta <= Upper DO
      BEGIN
          writeln (Theta:5:2, tan(Theta):10:4);
          Theta := Theta + Step
      END (* WHILE *)
END (* main program *).
```

Sample run:

```
Enter range of values and step size: 0 1.5 0.25

Theta   tan(Theta)
─────   ───────────
 0.00    0.0000
 0.25    0.2553
 0.50    0.5463
 0.75    0.9316
 1.00    1.5574
 1.25    3.0096
 1.50   14.1014
```

Several of the sample programs in the preceding chapters calculated wages. In these examples, as in most programs involving monetary calculations, the amounts should be rounded to the nearest cent. A function to do this is the following:

> **function** *RoundCents(Amount : real) : real*;
>
> (* Function to round *Amount* to the nearest cent. *)
>
> **begin** (* *RoundCents* *)
>   *RoundCents* := *round*(100 * *Amount*) / 100
> **end** (* *RoundCents* *);

A statement such as

> *GrossPay* := *RoundCents(Wages)*;

can then be used to reference this function.

As another example, consider a function to find the maximum of two integers. If we name the function *Maximum* and its formal parameters *Number1* and *Number2*, then the function definition is

function *Maximum(Number1, Number2 : integer) : integer;*

(* Function returns the maximum of two
    integers *Number1* and *Number2.* *)

begin (* *Maximum* *)
    if *Number1* >= *Number2* **then**
        Maximum := *Number1*
    else
        Maximum := *Number2*
end (* *Maximum* *);

Some function definitions may require the use of local variables other than
the formal parameters to calculate the function value. For example, consider
the operation of exponentiation, which, unfortunately, is not a standard operation in Pascal. The following function can be used to calculate x^n for a real
variable x and an integer variable n:

function *Power(x : real; n : integer) : real;*

(* Function returns the nth power of x for any real value
    x and any integer value n (positive, zero, or negative). *)

var
    i : *integer;*
    Prod : *real;*

begin (* *Power* *)
    if $x = 0$ **then**
        Power := 0
    else
        begin
            Prod := 1;
            for i := 1 **to** *abs(n)* **do**
                Prod := *Prod* * *x;*
            if n >= 0 **then**
                Power := *Prod*
            else
                Power := 1 / *Prod*
        end (* **else** *)
end (* *Power* *);

Functions and procedures have many similarities; in particular:

1. The definition of each appears in the subprogram section of the declaration
   part of a program and in each case consists of a heading, a declaration part,
   and a statement part, followed by a semicolon.
2. Each of them is an independent program unit. Parameters, constants, and
   variables declared within a function or procedure are local to that function
   or procedure; they are accessible only within that subprogram.
3. When a function or procedure is referenced, the number of actual parameters

must be the same as the number of formal parameters, and the types of actual parameters must agree with the types of the corresponding formal parameters, with one exception: an actual parameter of integer type may be associated with a value parameter of real type.

There are also a number of differences between functions and procedures:

1. Functions usually return a single value to the program unit that references them. Procedures often return more than one value, or they may return no value at all but simply perform some task such as an input/output operation.
2. Since a value must be assigned to a function name, a type must also be associated with it. Thus, a function heading must include a type identifier that specifies the type of the result. A procedure name, however, is not assigned a value; hence, no type is associated with it.
3. Whereas a procedure is referenced by a procedure reference statement, a function is referenced by using its name in an expression.

Exercises

1. Consider the following program skeleton:

> **program** *Demo* (*input, output*);
>
> **const**
> > *pi* = 3.14159;
> > *two* = 2;
>
> **var**
> > *Month, Day, Year, p, q* : *integer*;
> > *Hours, Rate, Amount, u, v* : *real*;
> > *Code, Class* : *char*;
>
> **function** *f(x, y* : *real*; *d* : *integer*) : *real*;
> > ⋮
>
> **procedure** *Calculate* (*a* : *real*; **var** *b* : *real*; *m* : *integer*;
> > > > > **var** *k, n* : *integer*; **var** *c* : *char*);
> > ⋮

Determine whether each of the following statements can be used in the statement part of the program. If it cannot be used, explain why.

(a) *Amount* := *f(pi, Rate, Month)*;
(b) *Rate* := *f(Hours, Day, two)*;
(c) *writeln (f(0, 0, 0))*;
(d) *f(Hours, Rate, Month)*;
(e) *Calculate (x, y, m, d, Day, Code)*;
(f) *Hours* := *two* * *f(pi, Amount)* / (2.71828 * *Rate*);
(g) *Amount* := *f(pi* * *Hours,* (2.71828 + *Day*) / *Rate, two)*;
(h) **if** *Month* = *two* **then**
> > *Year* := *f(Hours, f(Rate, pi, two), Day)*;
(i) **if** *u* > 0 **then**
> > *Amount* := *Calculate (u, v, two, p, q, Code)*;

    (j) **if** *Calculate* (0, *u*, 1, *p*, *Year*, *Class*) > 0 **then**
        writeln ('Okay');
    (k) **while** *f*(*Amount*, 0, 0) < *pi* **do**
        Amount := *f*(*Amount*, *pi*, 1);
    (l) **repeat**
        Amount := *f*(*Amount*, 0, *Code*)
        until *Amount* > 0;
    (m) *Calculate* (*f*(*u*, *v*, *Day*), *Rate*, 7, *p*, *q*, *Code*);
    (n) *Amount* := *f*(*a*, *b*, *Day*);

2. Write a function *Range* that calculates the range between two integers, that is, the larger integer minus the smaller integer.

3. Write a function that converts a temperature given in degrees Celsius to degrees Fahrenheit. (The conversion formula is $F = \frac{9}{5}C + 32$.)

4. Write a boolean-valued function *IsADigit* that determines whether a character is one of the digits 0 through 9.

5. Write a function *RoundOff* that accepts a real value *Amount* and an integer value *NumPlaces* and returns the value of *Amount* rounded to the specified number of places. For example, the function references *RoundOff*(10.536, 0), *Roundoff*(10.536, 1), and *Roundoff*(10.536, 2) should give the values 11.0, 10.5, and 10.54, respectively.

6. Write a function *GPA* that accepts a letter grade and returns the corresponding numeric value (A = 4.0, B = 3.0, C = 2.0, D = 1.0, F = 0.0).

7. The number of bacteria in a culture can be estimated by

$$N \cdot e^{kt}$$

where *N* is the initial population, *k* is a rate constant, and *t* is time. Write a function to calculate the number of bacteria present at time *t* for given values of *k* and *N*; use it in a program that reads values for the initial population, the rate constant, and the time (e.g., 1000, 0.15, 100), and displays the number of bacteria at that time.

8. Write a program that uses the function *Power* given in the text to calculate a monthly loan payment given by

$$\frac{r \cdot A/n}{1 - \left(1 + \dfrac{r}{n}\right)^{-n \cdot y}}$$

where *A* is the amount borrowed, *r* is the interest rate (expressed as a decimal), *y* is the number of years, and *n* is the number of payments per year. Design the program to read values for the amount borrowed, the interest rate, the number of years, and the number of payments per year, and display the corresponding monthly payment.

9. Write a character-valued function *LetterGrade* that assigns a letter grade to an integer score using the following grading scale:

    90–100: A
    80–89: B
    70–79: C
    60–69: D
    Below 60: F

Use the function in a program that reads several scores and displays the corresponding letter grades.

10. Write two boolean-valued functions that have formal parameters p and q of boolean type and that compute the logical expressions

$$\sim p \wedge \sim q \quad \text{(not } p \text{ and not } q\text{)}$$

and

$$\sim(p \vee q) \quad \text{(not } (p \text{ or } q)\text{)}$$

Write a program that uses these functions to print truth tables for these expressions.

11. A ***prime number*** is an integer $n > 1$ whose only positive divisors are 1 and n itself. Write a predicate (boolean-valued function) that determines whether n is a prime number. Use it in a program that reads several integers, uses the function to determine whether each is prime, and displays each number with the appropriate label "is prime" or "is not prime."

12. It is often necessary to find a ***zero*** of a function f, that is, a value c where $f(c) = 0$. Geometrically, we are looking for a point c on the x axis at which the graph of $y = f(x)$ crosses the x axis. If f is a continuous function between $x = a$ and $x = b$, that is, if there is no break in the graph of $y = f(x)$ between these two values, and $f(a)$ and $f(b)$ are of opposite signs, then f must have at least one zero between $x = a$ and $x = b$. One method for finding such a zero, or at least an approximation to it, is the ***bisection method.*** For this, bisect the interval $[a, b]$ and determine in which half f changes sign; then f must have a zero in that half of the interval. Now bisect this subinterval and determine in which half f changes sign. Repeating this process gives a sequence of smaller and smaller subintervals, each of which contains a zero of the function (see Figure 5.6). The process can be terminated when a small subinterval, say of length less than 0.0001, is obtained or f has the value 0 at one of the endpoints.

    Define a Pascal function to compute $x - \cos x$, and then write a program to find a zero of this function in the interval $\left[0, \dfrac{\pi}{2} \right]$.

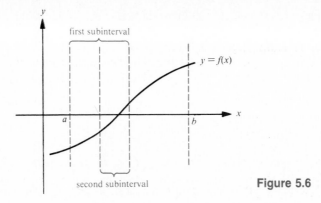

Figure 5.6

13. Another method used to locate a zero of a function f is ***Newton's method.*** This method consists of taking an initial approximation x_1 and constructing a tangent line to the graph of f at that point. The point x_2 where this tangent line crosses the x axis is taken as the second approximation to the zero. Then another tangent line is constructed at x_2, and the point x_3 where this tangent line crosses the x axis is the next approximation. Figure 5.7 shows this process.

If x is an approximation to the zero of f, then the formula for obtaining the next approximation by Newton's method is

$$\text{new approximation} = x - \frac{f(x)}{f'(x)}$$

where f' is the derivative of f. Using Pascal functions to define a function f and its derivative f', write a program to locate a zero of f, using Newton's method. The process should terminate when a value of $f(x)$ is sufficiently small in absolute value or when the number of iterations exceeds some upper limit. Display the sequence of successive approximations.

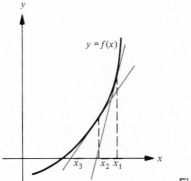

Figure 5.7

5.4   Examples: Numerical Integration, Simulation

EXAMPLE 1: Numerical Integration.   One problem in which numerical methods are often used is that of approximating the area under the graph of a nonnegative function $y = f(x)$ from $x = a$ to $x = b$, thus obtaining an approximate value for the integral

$$\int_a^b f(x) \, dx$$

One simple method is to divide the interval $[a, b]$ into n subintervals each of length $\Delta x = (b - a)/n$ and then form rectangles having these subintervals as bases and with altitudes given by the values of the function at the midpoints (or left or right endpoints) $x_1, x_2, \ldots, x_n$ of the subintervals. This is illustrated in Figure 5.8. The sum of the areas of these rectangles

$$f(x_1) \, \Delta x + f(x_2) \, \Delta x + \cdots + f(x_n) \, \Delta x$$

which is the same as

$$[f(x_1) + f(x_2) + \cdots + f(x_n)] \, \Delta x$$

or, written more concisely using Σ (sigma) notation,

$$\left[\sum_{i=1}^{n} f(x_i) \right] \Delta x$$

is then an approximation to the area under the curve.

Figure 5.8 illustrates this method for a curve lying above the x axis. It may also be used to approximate the integral of a function whose graph falls below the x axis. In this case, the integral does not give the total area between the curve and the axis, but rather gives the area of the region(s) above the axis minus the area of the region(s) below the axis.

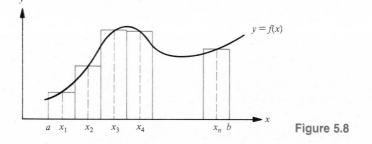

Figure 5.8

The program in Figure 5.9 uses this rectangle method to approximate an integral. The endpoints a and b of the interval of integration and the number n of subintervals are read during execution.

```
PROGRAM Area (input, output);

(************************************************************************

    Program to approximate the integral of a function f over the
    interval [a,b] using the rectangle method with altitudes chosen
    at the midpoints of the subintervals.

***********************************************************************)

VAR
    a, b,                   (* endpoints of interval of integration *)
    x,                      (* the midpoint of one of the subintervals *)
    Deltax,                 (* the length of the subintervals *)
    Sum : real;             (* the approximating sum *)
    n,                      (* number of subintervals used *)
    i : integer;            (* counter *)

FUNCTION f(x : real) : real;

    (**********************************************************************

                The function being integrated

    *********************************************************************)

    BEGIN (* f *)
        f := sqr(x) + 1
    END (* f *);

BEGIN (* main program *)
    write ('Enter interval endpoints and # of subintervals: ');
    readln (a, b, n);
    Deltax := (b - a) / n;
    Sum := 0;
    x := a + Deltax / 2;
    FOR i := 1 TO n DO
        BEGIN
            Sum := Sum + f(x);
            x := x + Deltax
        END (* FOR *);
    Sum := Deltax * Sum;
    writeln ('Approximate value using ', n:1, ' subintervals is ', Sum:8:4)
END (* main program *).
```

Sample runs:

```
Enter interval endpoints and # of subintervals: 0 1 10
Approximate value using 10 subintervals is   1.3325


Enter interval endpoints and # of subintervals: 0 1 20
Approximate value using 20 subintervals is   1.3331


Enter interval endpoints and # of subintervals: 0 1 100
Approximate value using 100 subintervals is   1.3333
```

Figure 5.9

EXAMPLE 2: Simulation. The term *simulation* refers to modeling a dynamic process and using this model to study the behavior of the process. The behavior of some *deterministic* processes can be modeled with an equation or a set of equations. For example, processes that involve exponential growth or decay are commonly modeled with an equation of the form

$$A(t) = A_0 e^{kt}$$

where $A(t)$ is the amount of some substance present at time t, A_0 is the initial amount of the substance, and k is some constant.

In many problems, however, the process being studied involves *randomness,* for example, Brownian motion, arrival of airplanes at an airport, number of defective parts manufactured by a machine, and so on. Computer programs that simulate such processes use a *random number generator,* which is a subprogram that produces a number selected from some fixed range in such a way that a sequence of these numbers tends to be uniformly distributed over the given range. Although it is not possible to develop an algorithm that produces truly random numbers, there are some methods that produce sequences of *pseudorandom numbers* that are adequate for most purposes.

Many computer systems provide a random number generator that produces random real numbers uniformly distributed over the range 0 to 1. The numbers produced by such a generator can be used to generate random real numbers in other ranges or to generate random integers. To demonstrate the way in which this is done, suppose that the random number generator is implemented as a function *Random* having no arguments. The expression

$$a + (b - a) * Random$$

can be used to generate random real numbers in the range a to b, and the expression

$$m + trunc(n * Random)$$

can be used to generate random integers in the range m through $m + n - 1$.

To illustrate, suppose we wish to model the random process of tossing a pair of dice. Using the preceding expression for generating random integers, we might define the following function:

function *RandomInteger*(*m, n* : *integer*) : *integer*;

   (∗ Function returns an integer randomly selected
      from $m, m + 1, \ldots, m + n - 1$. It uses the
      function *Random* that generates a random
      real number in the interval from 0 to 1. ∗)

  begin (∗ *RandomInteger* ∗)
     RandomInteger := $m + trunc(n * Random)$
  end (∗ *RandomInteger* ∗);

and then use the statements

> $Die1 := RandomInteger(1, 6);$
> $Die2 := RandomInteger(1, 6);$
> $Pair := Die1 + Die2;$

to simulate one roll of two dice; the value of *Pair* is the total number of spots showing.

If the random number generator is suitably constructed, the relative frequency of each value from 2 through 12 for *Pair* should correspond to the probability of that number occurring on one throw of a pair of dice. These probabilities (rounded to three decimal places) are given in the following table:

Outcome	Probability
2	0.028
3	0.056
4	0.083
5	0.111
6	0.139
7	0.167
8	0.139
9	0.111
10	0.083
11	0.056
12	0.028

The program in Figure 5.10 reads an integer indicating a possible outcome of a roll of two dice and an integer indicating the number of times the dice are to be tossed, and displays the relative frequency of this outcome. It assumes that a system function *Random* for generating random real numbers in the range 0 to 1 is available, as is a system procedure *Randomize* to initialize the random number generator. (If your system does not provide a random number generator, you might use the random number function described in Appendix F.)

```
PROGRAM DiceRoll (input, output);

(*******************************************************************

   Program that uses a random number generator to simulate
   rolling a pair of dice, counting the number of times a
   specified number of spots occurs.

 *******************************************************************)

VAR
   Spots,          (* # of spots to be counted *)
   Count,          (* number of times Spots occurred *)
   Rolls,          (* # of rolls of dice *)
   Die1, Die2,     (* # of spots on die #1, #2, respectively *)
   Pair,           (* sum of Die1 and Die2 = total # of spots on the dice *)
   i : integer;    (* index variable *)
```

Figure 5.10

Figure 5.10 (cont.)

```
FUNCTION RandomInteger (m, n : integer) : integer;

   (****************************************************************

      Function to generate random integers in the range m through
      m + n - 1.  It uses the system random number generator Random.

      ***********************************************************)

   BEGIN (* RandomInteger *)
      RandomInteger := m + trunc(n * Random)
   END (* RandomInteger *);

BEGIN (* main program *)
   write ('# of spots to count: ');
   readln (Spots);
   write('# of times to roll the dice: ');
   readln (Rolls);
   Randomize;
   Count := 0;
   FOR i := 1 TO Rolls DO
      BEGIN
         Die1 := RandomInteger(1, 6);
         Die2 := RandomInteger(1, 6);
         Pair := Die1 + Die2;
         IF Pair = Spots THEN
            Count := Count + 1
      END (* FOR *);
   writeln;
   writeln ('Relative frequency of ', Spots:1, ' was ', Count / Rolls:5:3)
END (* main program *).


Sample run:
_____

# of spots to count: 6
# of times to roll the dice: 500

Relative frequency of 6 was 0.138
```

Exercises

1. In Example 1, we considered numerical approximation of integrals using rectangles. As Figure 5.11 indicates, a better approximation can usually be obtained using trapezoids rather than rectangles.

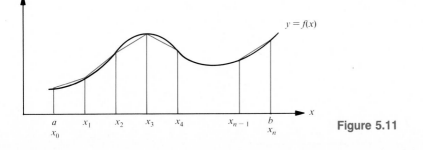

Figure 5.11

The sum of the areas of these trapezoids is given by

$$\sum_{i=1}^{n} [f(x_{i-1}) + f(x_i)] \frac{\Delta x}{2}$$

which can also be written

$$\frac{\Delta x}{2} [f(x_0) + 2f(x_1) + 2f(x_2) + \cdots + 2f(x_{n-1}) + f(x_n)]$$

or

$$\Delta x \left[\frac{f(a) + f(b)}{2} + \sum_{i=1}^{n-1} f(x_i) \right]$$

Write a program to approximate an integral using this *trapezoidal method.*

2. Another method of numerical integration that in general produces better approximations than the rectangle method described in Example 1 or the trapezoidal method described in Exercise 1 is based on the use of parabolas and is known as *Simpson's Rule.* In this method, the interval $[a, b]$ is divided into an even number n of subintervals, each of length Δx, and the sum

$$\frac{\Delta x}{3} [f(x_0) + 4f(x_1) + 2f(x_2) + 4f(x_3)$$
$$+ 2f(x_4) + \cdots + 2f(x_{n-2}) + 4f(x_{n-1}) + f(x_n)]$$

is used to approximate the integral of f over the interval $[a, b]$. Write a program to approximate an integral using Simpson's Rule.

Simulation Exercises

3. A coin is tossed repeatedly and a payoff of 2^n dollars is made, where n is the number of the toss on which the first head appears. For example, TTH pays $8, TH pays $4, and H pays $2. Write a program to simulate playing this game 100 times, and print the average payoff for these games.

4. Suppose that a gambler places a wager of $5 on the following game: A pair of dice is tossed, and if the result is odd, the gambler loses his wager. If the result is even, a card is drawn from a standard deck of fifty two playing cards. If the card drawn is an ace, 3, 5, 7, or 9, the gambler wins the value of the card; otherwise, he loses. What will be the average winnings for this game? Write a program to simulate the game.

5. Johann VanDerDoe, centerfielder for the Klavin Klodhoppers, has the following lifetime hitting percentages:

Out	63.4%
Walk	10.3%
Single	19.0%
Double	4.9%

| Triple | 1.1% |
| Home run | 1.3% |

Write a program to simulate 1000 times at bat for Johann, counting the number of outs, walks, singles, and so on, and calculating his batting average $((\#\text{ of hits})/(1000 - \#\text{ of walks}))$.

6. The classic **drunkard's walk problem** is as follows: Over an 8-block line, the home of an intoxicated chap is at block 8, and a pub is at block 1. Our poor friend starts at block n, $1 < n < 8$, and wanders at random, one block at a time, either toward or away from home. At any intersection, he moves toward the pub with a certain probability, say 2/3, and toward home with a certain probability, say 1/3. Having gotten either home or to the pub, he remains there. Write a program to simulate 500 trips in which he starts at block 2, another 500 in which he starts at block 3, and so forth up to block 7. For each starting point, calculate and print the percentage of the time he ends up at home and the average number of blocks he walked on each trip.

7. The famous **Buffon Needle Problem** is as follows: A board is ruled with equidistant parallel lines, and a needle of length equal to the distance between these lines is dropped at random on the board. Write a program to simulate this experiment and estimate the probability p that the needle crosses one of these lines. Display the values of p and $2/p$. (The value of $2/p$ should be approximately equal to a well-known constant. What constant is it?)

8. An unusual method for approximating the area under a curve is the following **Monte Carlo technique.** As illustrated in Figure 5.12, consider a rectangle with base $[a,b]$ and height m, where $f(x) \leq m$ for all x in $[a,b]$. Imagine throwing q darts at rectangle $ABCD$ and counting the total number p that hit the shaded region. For a large number of throws, we would expect

$$\frac{p}{q} \simeq \frac{\text{area of shaded region}}{\text{area of rectangle } ABCD}$$

Write a program to calculate areas using this Monte Carlo method. To simulate throwing a dart, generate two random numbers, X from $[a,b]$ and Y from $[0,m]$, and consider the point (X,Y) to be the point where the dart hits.

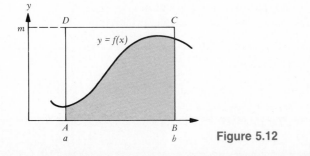

Figure 5.12

9. Figure 5.13 shows a cross section of the lead-shielding wall of a nuclear reactor. A neutron enters the wall at a point E and then follows a random path by moving forward, backward, right, or left, in jumps of one unit. A change of direction is interpreted as a collision with an atom of lead. Suppose that after 10 such collisions the neutron's energy is dissipated and that it dies within the lead shielding, provided that it has not already passed back inside the reactor or outside the shielding (by moving forward a net distance of 4 units). Write a program to simulate 100 neutrons entering this shield, and calculate how many reach the outside of the reactor.

Outside

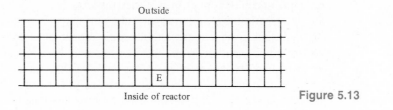

Inside of reactor   **Figure 5.13**

5.5 Scope Rules

As we have seen, functions and procedures are program units whose structures are similar to that of a Pascal program. Each consists of a heading followed by a declaration part followed by a statement part. Consequently, in a program that contains functions and/or procedures, there may be several points at which identifiers are declared. The portion of the program in which an identifier is accessible is called its *scope*. In this section we describe the rules that govern the scopes of identifiers.

There is one basic principle that prescribes the scope of an identifier. All of the other scope rules are consequences of this general principle.

Fundamental Scope Principle

The scope of an identifier is the program unit in which it is declared.

Recall that identifiers may be declared in either the heading of a program unit or its declaration part. Thus this scope principle applies both to formal parameters that appear in a heading and to constants, variables, function and procedure names (and user-defined types as discussed in Chapter 7) that appear in the declaration part of a program unit.

An immediate consequence of this principle is

Scope Rule 1

An identifier declared in a program unit is not accessible outside that unit.

To illustrate, consider the problem of calculating **binomial coefficients** $\binom{n}{k}$

defined for nonnegative integers n and k by

$$\binom{n}{k} = \frac{n!}{k!(n - k)!}$$

Here the expressions $n!$, $k!$, and $(n - k)!$ represent factorials defined in general
by

$$m! = \begin{cases} 1 \text{ if } m = 0 \\ 1 \times 2 \times \cdots \times m \text{ if } m > 0 \end{cases}$$

The program in Figure 5.14 reads values for n and k and then displays the
value of the binomial coefficient $\binom{n}{k}$, using the function *Factorial* to calculate

the necessary factorials.

```
PROGRAM BinomialCoefficients (input, output);

(*************************************************************************

                                              n!
   Program to calculate binomial coefficients (n:k) = ───────
                                              k!*(n-k)!
   for various values of n and k.

*************************************************************************)

VAR
   n, k,                     (* values entered *)
   BinomCoeff : integer;     (* binomial coefficient *)

FUNCTION Factorial (m : integer) : integer;

   (*********************************************************************

      Function to calculate m! = the factorial of m.  This is
      defined to be 1 if m = 0, and 1 * 2 * ... * m for m >= 1.

   *********************************************************************)

   VAR
      k,                     (* index *)
      Fac : integer;         (* partial factorial *)

   BEGIN (* Factorial *)
      Fac := 1;
      FOR k := 2 TO m DO
         Fac := Fac * k;
      Factorial := Fac
   END (* Factorial *);
```

Figure 5.14

Figure 5.14 (cont.)

```
BEGIN (* main program *)
   writeln ('Enter negative values for n and k to stop.');
   writeln;
   write ('Enter n and k:');
   readln (n,k);
   WHILE n >= 0 DO
      BEGIN
         BinomCoeff := Factorial(n) DIV (Factorial(k) * Factorial(n-k));
         writeln ('(', n:1, ':', k:1, ') = ', BinomCoeff:1);
         writeln;
         write ('Enter n and k:');
         readln (n, k)
      END (* WHILE *)
END (* main program *).
```

According to the Fundamental Scope Principle, the scope of the formal parameter *m* and the variables *k* and *Fac* is the function *Factorial,* and by Scope Rule 1, they are not accessible outside this function. Such identifiers are **local** to the function, and any attempt to use them outside the function is an error.

The Fundamental Scope Principle states that the scope of an identifier is the program unit in which it is declared. In particular, the main program is a program unit. The identifiers listed in the heading of the main program or declared in its declaration part are called **global identifiers** since they are accessible throughout the entire program, except within program units in which they are declared locally.

> ### Scope Rule 2
>
> A global identifier is accessible in any program unit in which that identifier is not declared locally.

For example, in the program in Figure 5.14, the global identifiers *n* and *BinomCoeff* are accessible to both the main program and the function *Factorial.* The global variable *k* is not accessible to the function *Factorial,* however, since *k* is declared locally in *Factorial*. Reference to the variable *k* within the function *Factorial* yields the value of the local variable *k*, whereas a reference to *k* outside the function gives the value of the global variable *k*. Thus these *k*'s represent two different variables that are associated with two different memory locations.

There is one important exception to this scope rule: *Variables used as control variables in* **for** *statements must be declared within the program unit in which they are used.* Consequently, a global variable may not be used for this purpose. In the preceding example, therefore, it was necessary to declare the loop control variable *k* used in the function *Factorial* as a variable local to that function.

Although global variables can be used to share data between program units, it is usually unwise to do so since this practice reduces the independence of the various program units and thus makes modular programming more difficult. Changing the value of a global variable in one program unit has the ***side effect*** of changing the value of that variable in all of the other program units. Consequently, it is difficult to determine the value of that variable at any particular point in the program.

Scope Rule 2 applies to identifiers in a main program and their accessibility in a subprogram. Recall that functions and procedures have declaration parts in which other functions and/or procedures may be defined. Scope Rule 3 applies to such nested functions and procedures.

Scope Rule 3

An identifier declared in a subprogram can be accessed by any subprogram defined within it, provided that the identifier is not declared locally in the internal subprogram.

To illustrate this scope rule, we consider the problem of calculating binomial probabilities. Such probabilities arise in analyzing an experiment consisting of a sequence of trials, each of which has two possible outcomes, "success" and "failure." An example is a sequence of coin tosses in which the appearance of a head is considered a success and the appearance of a tail a failure. The probability of success on each trial of such an experiment is assumed to be some constant p, and the probability of failure is then $1 - p$. The probability of exactly k successes in n trials is given by

$$\binom{n}{k} p^k (1 - p)^{n-k}$$

The program in Figure 5.15 reads values for n, k, and p. It uses the function *Binomial* to calculate the binomial coefficient $\binom{n}{k}$ and the function *Power* to calculate p^k and $(1 - p)^{n-k}$. The function *Binomial* in turn references the function *Factorial* to calculate $n!$, $k!$, and $(n - k)!$. The relationship among these program units is indicated by the diagram in Figure 5.16, which shows clearly the nesting of the function *Factorial* within *Binomial*, and *Binomial* within the main program.

```
PROGRAM Probability (input, output);

(******************************************************************

   Program to calculate binomial probabilities.  Functions Binomial,
   Factorial and Power are used.

******************************************************************)

VAR
    n,                    (* number of trials *)
    k : integer;          (* number of successes *)
    p,                    (* probability of success *)
    Prob : real;          (* probability of k successes in n trials *)
```
Figure 5.15

Figure 5.15 (cont.)

```
FUNCTION Binomial (n, k : integer) : integer;

   (***********************************************************************
                                              n!
       Returns the binomial coefficient (n:k) = ————————
                                            k!*(n-k)!

   ***********************************************************************)

   VAR
       Fact1, Fact2, Fact3 : integer;   (* Factorials *)

   FUNCTION Factorial (m : integer) : integer;

      (********************************************************************

          Function to calculate m! = the factorial of m.  This is
          defined to be 1 if m = 0, and 1 * 2 * ... * m for m >= 1.

      ********************************************************************)

      VAR
          k,               (* index *)
          Fac : integer;  (* partial factorial *)

      BEGIN (* Factorial *)
          Fac := 1;
          FOR k := 2 TO m DO
              Fac := Fac * k;
          Factorial := Fac
      END (* Factorial *);

   BEGIN (* Binomial *)
      Fact1 := Factorial(n);
      Fact2 := Factorial(k);
      Fact3 := Factorial(n - k);
      Binomial := Fact1 DIV (Fact2 * Fact3)
   END (* Binomial *);
```

Figure 5.15 (cont.)

```
FUNCTION Power(x : real; n : integer) : real;

   (*********************************************************************

      Function returns the n-th power of x for any real value x and
      any integer value n (positive, zero, or negative).

   *********************************************************************)

   VAR
      i : integer;      (* index *)
      Prod : real;      (* product of x's *)

BEGIN (* Power *)
   IF x = 0 THEN
      Power := 0
   ELSE
      BEGIN
         Prod := 1;
         FOR i := 1 to abs(n) DO
            Prod := Prod * x;
         IF n >= 0 THEN
            Power := Prod
         ELSE
            Power := 1 / Prod
      END (* ELSE *)
END (* Power *);

BEGIN (* main program *)
   writeln ('Enter number of trials, number of successes desired,');
   writeln ('and probability of success (all 0''s to stop):');
   readln (n, k, p);
   WHILE n <> 0 DO
      BEGIN
         Prob := Binomial(n, k) * Power(p, k) * Power(1 - p, n - k);
         writeln ('Probability of ', k:1, ' successes in ', n:1,
                  ' trials is ', Prob:5:4);
         writeln;
         write ('# trials, # successes, probability of success? ');
         readln (n, k, p)
      END (* WHILE *)
END (* main program *).
```

program *Probability*

```
parameters: input, output
var n, k, p, Prob
function Binomial

    parameters: n, k
    var Fact1, Fact2, Fact3
    function Factorial

        parameters: m
        var k, Fac
        begin (* Factorial *)
            ⋮
        end(* Factorial *);

    begin (* Binomial *)
        ⋮
        Fact1 := Factorial (n);
        Fact2 := Factorial (k);
        Fact3 := Factorial (n − k);
        ⋮
    end (* Binomial *);

function Power

    parameters: x, n
    var i, Prod
    begin (* Power *)
        ⋮
    end (* Power *);

begin (* main program *)
    ⋮
    Prob := Binomial (n, k) * Power (p, k) * Power (1 − p, n − k);
    ⋮
end (* main program *).
```

Figure 5.16

Scope Rule 3 states that identifiers declared in a subprogram can be accessed in a subprogram contained within it, provided that they are not declared locally in the internal subprogram (and are not used as control variables in **for**-loops). Thus, in this example, the local variables *n*, *Fact1*, *Fact2*, and *Fact3* of the function *Binomial* are accessible within it as well as within the function *Factorial*. The formal parameter *k* in *Binomial*, however, is not accessible to the function *Factorial*, because *k* is declared as a local variable within *Factorial*.

According to Scope Rule 2, the global variables *n*, *p*, and *Prob* (as well as the files *input* and *output*) are accessible to both of the functions *Binomial* and *Factorial*. On the other hand, the global variable *k* is not accessible to the function *Binomial* and thus not to *Factorial*, since it is a local variable in

Binomial. Similarly, the global variables *p*, *k*, and *Prob* are accessible to the function *Power*, whereas *n* is not.

It should be noted in this example that the function *Factorial* is not accessible to the main program or to the function *Power*, since it is defined within the function *Binomial*. This is undesirable if factorials need to be calculated in the main program, because the function *Factorial* is not available. This limitation can be removed by defining all of the functions *Power*, *Binomial*, and *Factorial* in the main program so that the program has the structure shown in Figure 5.17.

program *Probability*

```
    parameters: input, output
    var n, k, p, Prob
    function Factorial

        parameters: m
        var k, Fac
        begin (* Factorial *)
            ⋮
        end (* Factorial *);

    function Binomial

        parameters: n, k
        var Fact1, Fact2, Fact3
        begin (* Binomial *)
            ⋮
            Fact1 := Factorial (n);
            Fact2 := Factorial (k);
            Fact3 := Factorial (n − k);
            ⋮
        end (* Binomial *);

    function Power

        parameters: x, n
        var i, Prod
        begin (* Power *)
            ⋮
        end (* Power *);

    begin (* main program *)
        ⋮
        Prob := Binomial (n, k) * Power (p, k) * Power (1 − p, n − k);
        ⋮
    end (* main program *).
```

Figure 5.17

Since the function *Factorial* is referenced by the function *Binomial*, it must be defined before *Binomial*. In general, a function or procedure must be defined before it can be referenced by another function or procedure at the same level. This is Scope Rule 4.

Scope Rule 4

If *SubA* and *SubB* are subprograms defined in the same program unit and if *SubA* is referenced by *SubB*, then *SubA* must be defined before *SubB*.

According to this scope rule, the program structure in Figure 5.17 is an acceptable alternative to that in Figure 5.16 because the functions are arranged in the order *Factorial, Binomial, Power*. Other acceptable orderings of these functions are *Factorial, Power, Binomial* and *Power, Factorial, Binomial*. However, the ordering *Binomial, Factorial, Power* would not be valid since *Binomial* references *Factorial*, thus violating Scope Rule 4.

5.6   Example of Top-Down Design: Determining Eligibility

The athletic department at a certain university wants a program for its secretarial staff that can be used to determine the academic eligibility of its athletes for the next academic year. This eligibility check is made at the end of each of the first three years of the student's academic career. Eligibility is determined by two criteria: the number of hours that the student has successfully completed and his or her cumulative grade point average (GPA). To maintain eligibility, the student must have completed at least 25 hours with a minimum GPA of 1.7 by the end of the first year. At the end of the second year, 50 hours must have been completed with a cumulative GPA of 1.85 or higher, and at the end of the third year, 85 hours must have been completed with a minimum cumulative GPA of 1.95.

The program should display the student's number, class, cumulative hours, GPA for the current year, and cumulative GPA, as well as an indication of his or her eligibility. At the end of this report, the program should also display the total number of students processed, the number who are eligible, and the average current GPA for all students. The information to be supplied to the program is the student's number, class level, hours accumulated, cumulative GPA, and hours and grades for courses taken during the current year.

Since this program will be used by personnel who are generally not regular users of a computer system, some instructions should be displayed each time the program is used. The first module in the program will be designed to carry out this task. The second task is to accept the given information for each student, calculate the relevant statistics, and determine eligibility. The final task is to generate and display the desired summary statistics after all the student information has been processed. The following outline, along with the structure diagram in Figure 5.18, summarizes this analysis:

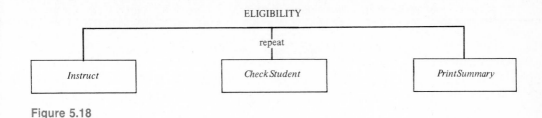

Figure 5.18

INPUT DATA

student's number.
class level (1, 2, or 3).
cumulative hours.
cumulative GPA.
hours and grade for each course completed in the current year.

OUTPUT DATA

student's number.
current GPA.
updated cumulative hours and cumulative GPA.
indication of eligibility.
number of students processed.
number of students eligible.
average of all current GPAs.

LEVEL-1 ALGORITHM

1. Provide instructions to the user.
2. Repeat the following until the end-of-data flag is encountered:

    Read the given information for a student, calculate statistics, determine eligibility, and display report.

3. Calculate and display summary statistics.

The three tasks we have identified can be implemented as three procedures: *Instruct, CheckStudent,* and *Summary.* Since the procedure *Instruct* simply displays instructions to the user, it requires no information from other program units. The procedure *PrintSummary* requires the total number of students processed (*StudentCount*), the total number who are eligible to participate in athletics (*EligibleCount*), and the sum of all the current GPAs (*SumOfGpas*). These values must be calculated by the procedure *CheckStudent* and shared with *PrintSummary.* Thus, the entire program has the form

```
program Eligibility (input, output);

var
    StudentCount, EligibleCount : integer;
    SumOfGpas : real;
    Response : char;

procedure Instruct;
        ⋮
procedure CheckStudent (var StudentCount, EligibleCount : integer;
        ⋮                    var SumOfGpas : real);
procedure PrintSummary (StudentCount, EligibleCount : integer;
                                SumOfGpas : real);
        ⋮
begin (* main program *)
    Instruct;
    StudentCount := 0;
    EligibleCount := 0;
    SumOfGpas := 0;
    repeat
        CheckStudent (StudentCount, EligibleCount, SumOfGpas);
        writeln;
        write ('More (Y or N)? ');
        readln (Response)
    until Response <> 'Y';
    PrintSummary (StudentCount, EligibleCount, SumOfGpas)
end (* main program *).
```

Since *CheckStudent* is central to the entire program and is the most complex of the three procedures, we begin with its development. We can identify three main subtasks. The first is to read the information for a student and calculate the relevant statistics. The second subtask is to use these statistics to determine whether the student is eligible for athletics. The third subtask is to generate a report displaying some of these statistics and an indication of eligibility. Using the second-level procedures *ReadAndCalculate*, *CheckEligibility*, and *Report* to carry out these subtasks within the procedure *Check-Student*, we obtain the structure diagram in Figure 5.19.

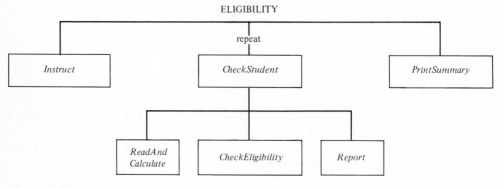

Figure 5.19

The development of the procedure *ReadAndCalculate* and its implementation as a Pascal procedure are relatively straightforward. This procedure must read a student's number (*Snumb*), class level (*Class*), cumulative hours (*CumHours*), and cumulative GPA (*CumGpa*), and then calculate the student's current GPA (*CurrGpa*) and update the values of *CumHours, CumGpa, StudentCount, SumOfGpas*. Because these are to be shared with other program units, they must be variable parameters for this procedure.

Once the procedure *ReadAndCalculate* has been written, it can be incorporated into the program and tested before the other procedures are developed, as shown in Figure 5.20. We simply insert *writeln* statements in the statement parts of the undeveloped procedures to signal when they are called. In this program, the procedures *Instruct, PrintSummary,* and *CheckEligibility* contain such **program stubs** to signal their execution, and *Report* produces a temporary printout to enable us to verify the correctness of *ReadAndCalculate*. The procedure *ReadAndCalculate* is in its final form, as is the statement part of the main program.

```
PROGRAM Eligibility (input, output);

(***********************************************************************

  Program to determine academic eligibility of athletes according to
  two criteria:  cumulative hours and cumulative gpa.   It also
  determines the total number of students checked, the number found to
  be eligible and calculates the average current gpa for all students.

***********************************************************************)

VAR
    StudentCount,                (* count of all students processed *)
    EligibleCount : integer;     (* count of those found to be eligible *)
    SumOfGpas : real;            (* sum of current gpas of all students *)
    Response : char;             (* user response *)

PROCEDURE Instruct;

    BEGIN (* Instruct *)
       writeln ('*********** Instruct called ***********')
    END (* Instruct *);

PROCEDURE CheckStudent (VAR StudentCount, EligibleCount : integer;
                        VAR SumOfGpas : real);

    (*******************************************************************

      Accepts student information, determines eligibility, maintains
      counts of students processed and those found to be eligible
      and a sum of the current gpa's.

    *******************************************************************)
```

Figure 5.20

Figure 5.20 (cont.)

```
VAR
    Snumb,                  (* student number *)
    Class : integer;        (* student's class level — 1, 2, or 3 *)
    CumHours,               (* cumulative hours *)
    CumGpa,                 (* cumulative grade point average *)
    CurrGpa : real;         (* current grade point average *)
    Eligible : boolean;     (* true if student eligible, else false *)

PROCEDURE ReadAndCalculate ( VAR Snumb, Class, StudentCount : integer;
                    VAR CumHours, CumGpa, CurrGpa, SumOfGpas : real);

    (****************************************************************

        Procedure to read a student's number, class, cumulative
        hours and cumulative gpa; then read hours and grades
        for courses taken during the current year, and calculate
        current gpa, update cumulative hours, cumulative gpa,
        and count of students processed.  Hours = 0 and grade = 0
        are used to signal the end of data for a student.

    ****************************************************************)

    VAR
        Hours,              (* hours of credit for a course *)
        Grade,              (* numeric grade for that course *)
        NewHours,           (* total hours earned during current year *)
        NewHonorPts,        (* honor points earned in current year *)
        OldHonorPts : real; (* honor points earned in past years *)

    BEGIN (* ReadAndCalculate *)
        writeln ('Enter student number, class, cum. hours, cum. gpa:');
        readln (Snumb, Class, CumHours, CumGpa);
        OldHonorPts := CumHours * CumGpa;
        NewHours := 0;
        NewHonorPts := 0;
        write ('Hours and grade? ');
        readln (Hours, Grade);
        WHILE Hours > 0 DO
            BEGIN
                NewHours := NewHours + Hours;
                NewHonorPts := NewHonorPts + Hours * Grade;
                write ('Hours and grade? ');
                readln (Hours, Grade);
            END (* WHILE *);
        IF NewHours = 0 THEN
            CurrGpa := 0
        ELSE
            CurrGpa := NewHonorPts / NewHours;
        SumOfGpas := SumOfGpas + CurrGpa;
        CumHours := CumHours + NewHours;
        CumGpa := (OldHonorPts + NewHonorPts) / CumHours;
        StudentCount := StudentCount + 1;
    END (* ReadAndCalculate *);
```

Figure 5.20 (cont.)

```
PROCEDURE CheckEligibility;

   BEGIN (* CheckEligibility *)
      writeln ('********** CheckEligibility called ***********');
   END (* CheckEligibility *);

PROCEDURE Report (Snumb, class : integer;
                  CumHours, CurrGpa, CumGpa : real);

   BEGIN (* Report *)
      writeln ('********** Report called ***********');
      (***** Temporary printout *****)
      writeln ('Snumb:  ', Snumb:1);
      writeln ('Class:  ', Class:1);
      writeln ('Cum. hours:  ', CumHours:4:2);
      writeln ('Curr. gpa:   ', CurrGpa:4:2);
      writeln ('Cum. gpa:    ', CumGpa:4:2);
   END (* Report *);

BEGIN (* CheckStudent *)
   ReadAndCalculate (Snumb, Class, StudentCount, CumHours, CumGpa,
                     CurrGpa, SumOfGpas);
   CheckEligibility;
   Report (Snumb, Class, CumHours, CurrGpa, CumGpa)
END (* CheckStudent *);

PROCEDURE PrintSummary (StudentCount, EligibleCount : integer;
                        SumOfGpas : real);

   BEGIN (* PrintSummary *)
      writeln ('********** PrintSummary called ***********')
   END (* PrintSummary *);

BEGIN (* main program *)
   Instruct;
   StudentCount := 0;
   EligibleCount := 0;
   SumOfGpas := 0;
   REPEAT
      Checkstudent (StudentCount, EligibleCount, SumOfGpas);
      writeln;
      write ('More (Y or N)? ');
      readln (Response)
   UNTIL Response <> 'Y';
   PrintSummary (StudentCount, EligibleCount, SumOfGpas)
END (* main program *).
```

Figure 5.20 (cont.)

Sample run:

```
********** Instruct called **********
Enter student number, class, cum. hours, cum. gpa:
12345 1 0 0
Hours and grade? 5 3.0
Hours and grade? 4 3.0
Hours and grade? 3.5 3.0
Hours and grade? 4 3.0
Hours and grade? 3 3.0
Hours and grade? 2 3.0
Hours and grade? 0 0
********** CheckEligibility called **********
********** Report called **********
Snumb:   12345
Class:   1
Cum. hours:   21.50
Curr. gpa:   3.00
Cum. gpa:   3.00

More (Y or N)? N
********** PrintSummary called **********
```

The sample run of this program indicates that the procedure *ReadAnd-Calculate* is correct. Therefore, we may now turn to the development of the other procedures. A further analysis of the subtask of determining the student's eligibility reveals that there are two criteria used: an hours condition and a GPA condition. Figure 5.21 shows the two corresponding subtasks in a refined

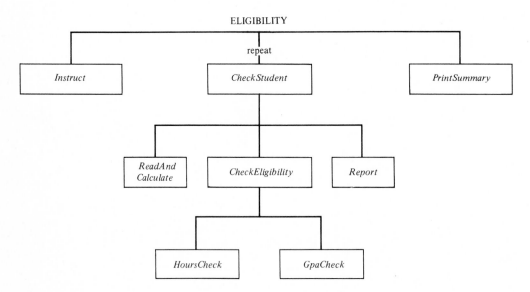

Figure 5.21

structure diagram. These can be conveniently implemented as boolean-valued functions *HoursCheck* and *GpaCheck* that return the value *true* or *false*, depending on whether the student satisfies the corresponding eligibility criterion. Replacing the temporary version of *CheckEligibility* and the reference to it in the statement part of procedure *CheckStudent* in the preceding program produces the refined program in Figure 5.22. Note that we have also modified the temporary version of *Report* and the reference to it in order to display the value of *Eligible*.

```
PROGRAM Eligibility (input, output);

              .
              .
              .

    PROCEDURE CheckEligibility (Class: integer; CumHours, CumGpa : real;
                                VAR Eligible : boolean;
                                VAR EligibleCount : integer);

    (*********************************************************************

        Procedure to check eligibility.  Two criteria are used:
        cumulative hours, and cumulative gpa.  Functions HoursCheck
        GpaCheck implement these.

    *********************************************************************)

        FUNCTION HoursCheck(Class : integer; CumHours : real) : boolean;

        (*****************************************************************

                Check student's cumulative hours.

        *****************************************************************)

            CONST
                Freshman = 25;
                Sophomore = 50;
                Junior = 85;

            BEGIN (* HoursCheck *)
                CASE Class OF
                    1 : HoursCheck := CumHours >= Freshman;
                    2 : HoursCheck := CumHours >= Sophomore;
                    3 : HoursCheck := CumHours >= Junior
                END (* CASE *)
            END (* HoursCheck *);
```

Figure 5.22

Figure 5.22 (cont.)

```
    FUNCTION GpaCheck(Class : integer; CumGpa : real) : boolean;

    (***************************************************************

            Check student's cumulative gpa.

    **************************************************************)

        CONST
            Gpa1 = 1.7;
            Gpa2 = 1.85;
            Gpa3 = 1.95;

        BEGIN (* GpaCheck *)
            CASE Class OF
                1 : GpaCheck := CumGpa >= Gpa1;
                2 : GpaCheck := CumGpa >= Gpa2;
                3 : GpaCheck := CumGpa >= Gpa3
            END (* CASE *)
        END (* GpaCheck *);

    BEGIN (* CheckEligibility *)
        IF (Class < 1) OR (Class > 3) THEN
            BEGIN
                writeln ('*** Illegal class code ***');
                Eligible := false
            END (* IF *)
        ELSE
            Eligible := HoursCheck(Class, CumHours)
                        AND GpaCheck(Class, CumGpa);
        IF Eligible THEN
            EligibleCount := EligibleCount + 1
    END (* CheckEligibility *);

    PROCEDURE Report (Snumb, Class : integer;
                      CumHours, CurrGpa, CumGpa : real;
                      Eligible : boolean);
                      .
                      .
                      .
        writeln ('Eligible:   ', Eligible);
    END (* Report *);
                      .
                      .
                      .
END (* main program *).
```

Figure 5.22 (cont.)

Sample run:

```
********** Instruct called **********
Enter student number, class, cum. hours, cum. gpa:
12345 1 0 0
Hours and grade? 5 3.0
Hours and grade? 4 3.0
Hours and grade? 3.5 3.0
Hours and grade? 4 3.0
Hours and grade? 3 3.0
Hours and grade? 2 3.0
Hours and grade? 0 0
********** Report called **********
Snumb:  12345
Class:  1
Cum. hours:  21.50
Curr. gpa:   3.00
Cum. gpa:    3.00
Eligible:  FALSE

More (Y or N)? Y
Enter student number, class, cum. hours, cum. gpa:
55555 5 0 0
Hours and grade? 3 3.0
Hours and grade? 0 0
********** Illegal class code **********
********** Report called **********
Snumb:  55555
Class:  5
Cum. hours:  3.00
Curr. gpa:   3.00
Cum. gpa:    3.00
Eligible:  FALSE

More (Y or N)? N
********** PrintSummary called **********
```

We observe that the newly added procedure appears to be correct, and consequently, we proceed to develop the remaining procedures *Report, Instruct,* and *PrintSummary*. The final version of the complete program is shown in Figure 5.23.

```
PROGRAM Eligibility (input, output);

(*****************************************************************************

   Program to determine academic eligibility of athletes according to
   two criteria:  cumulative hours and cumulative gpa.  It also
   determines the total number of students checked, the number found to
   be eligible and calculates the average current gpa for all students.

******************************************************************************)

VAR
   StudentCount,                (* count of all students processed *)
   EligibleCount : integer;     (* count of those found to be eligible *)
   SumOfGpas : real;            (* sum of current gpas of all students *)
   Response : char;             (* user response *)

PROCEDURE Instruct;

   (**************************************************************************

              Print instructions to the user.

   **************************************************************************)

   BEGIN (* Instruct *)
      writeln ('You will first be asked to enter the student''s');
      writeln ('number, class, cumulative hours, and cumulative gpa.');
      writeln ('Enter these with at least one space separating them.');
      writeln;
      writeln ('You will then be asked to enter the number of hours and');
      writeln ('the numeric grade earned for each of the courses the');
      writeln ('student took during the current year.  Separate the');
      writeln ('number of hours from the grade by at least one space.');
      writeln ('Enter 0 for hours and 0 for grades when you are finished');
      writeln ('entering the information for each student.');
      writeln;
      writeln;
      writeln;
      writeln
   END (* Instruct *);

PROCEDURE CheckStudent (VAR StudentCount, EligibleCount : integer;
                        VAR SumOfGpas : real);

   (**************************************************************************

      Accepts student information, determines eligibility, maintains
      counts of students processed and those found to be eligible
      and a sum of the current gpa's.


   **************************************************************************)
```

Figure 5.23

Figure 5.23 (cont.)

```
VAR
    Snumb,                  (* student number *)
    Class : integer;        (* student's class level — 1, 2, or 3 *)
    CumHours,               (* cumulative hours *)
    CumGpa,                 (* cumulative grade point average *)
    CurrGpa : real;         (* current grade point average *)
    Eligible : boolean;     (* true if student eligible, else false *)

PROCEDURE ReadAndcalculate ( VAR Snumb, Class, StudentCount : integer;
                    VAR CumHours, CumGpa, CurrGpa, SumOfGpas : real);

(**************************************************************

    Procedure to read a student's number, class, cumulative
    hours and cumulative gpa; then read hours and grades
    for courses taken during the current year, and calculate
    current gpa, update cumulative hours, cumulative gpa,
    and count of students processed.  Hours = 0 and grade = 0
    are used to signal the end of data for a student.

**************************************************************)

    VAR
        Hours,              (* hours of credit for a course *)
        Grade,              (* numeric grade for that course *)
        NewHours,           (* total hours earned during current year *)
        NewHonorPts,        (* honor points earned in current year *)
        OldHonorPts : real; (* honor points earned in past years *)

BEGIN (* ReadAndCalculate *)
    writeln ('Enter student number, class, cum. hours, cum. gpa:');
    readln (Snumb, Class, CumHours, CumGpa);
    OldHonorPts := CumHours * CumGpa;
    NewHours := 0;
    NewHonorPts := 0;
    write ('Hours and grade? ');
    readln (Hours, Grade);
    WHILE Hours > 0 DO
        BEGIN
            NewHours := NewHours + Hours;
            NewHonorPts := NewHonorPts + Hours * Grade;
            write ('Hours and grade? ');
            readln (Hours, Grade);
        END (* WHILE *);
    IF NewHours = 0 THEN
        CurrGpa := 0
    ELSE
        CurrGpa := NewHonorPts / NewHours;
    SumOfGpas := SumOfGpas + CurrGpa;
    CumHours := CumHours + NewHours;
    CumGpa := (OldHonorPts + NewHonorPts) / CumHours;
    StudentCount := StudentCount + 1;
END (* ReadAndCalculate *);
```

Figure 5.23 (cont.)

```
PROCEDURE CheckEligibility (Class: integer; CumHours, CumGpa : real;
                           VAR Eligible : boolean;
                           VAR EligibleCount : integer);

(*******************************************************************

   Procedure to check eligibility.  Two criteria are used:
   cumulative hours, and cumulative gpa.  Functions HoursCheck
   GpaCheck implement these.

******************************************************************)

FUNCTION HoursCheck(Class : integer; CumHours : real) : boolean;

(*****************************************************************

      Check student's cumulative hours.

****************************************************************)

   CONST
      Freshman = 25;
      Sophomore = 50;
      Junior = 85;

   BEGIN (* HoursCheck *)
      CASE Class OF
         1 : HoursCheck := CumHours >= Freshman;
         2 : HoursCheck := CumHours >= Sophomore;
         3 : HoursCheck := CumHours >= Junior
      END (* CASE *)
   END (* HoursCheck *);

FUNCTION GpaCheck(Class : integer; CumGpa : real) : boolean;

(*****************************************************************

      Check student's cumulative gpa.

****************************************************************)

   CONST
      Gpa1 = 1.7;
      Gpa2 = 1.85;
      Gpa3 = 1.95;

   BEGIN (* GpaCheck *)
      CASE Class OF
         1 : GpaCheck := CumGpa >= Gpa1;
         2 : GpaCheck := CumGpa >= Gpa2;
         3 : GpaCheck := CumGpa >= Gpa3
      END (* CASE *)
   END (* GpaCheck *);
```

Figure 5.23 (cont.)

```
BEGIN (* CheckEligibility *)
    IF (Class < 1) OR (Class > 3) THEN
        BEGIN
            writeln ('*** Illegal class code ***');
            Eligible := false
        END (* IF *)
    ELSE
        Eligible := HoursCheck(Class, CumHours)
                    AND GpaCheck(Class, CumGpa);
    IF Eligible THEN
        EligibleCount := EligibleCount + 1
END (* CheckEligibility *);

PROCEDURE Report (Snumb, Class : integer;
                  CumHours, CurrGpa, CumGpa : real;
                  Eligible : boolean);

(*******************************************************************

    Display the statistics for a given student.

*******************************************************************)

  BEGIN (* Report *)
      writeln;
      writeln ('***** Report for student ', Snumb:1, '  *****');
      writeln ('Class:              ', Class:1);
      writeln ('Cumulative hours:  ', CumHours:4:2);
      writeln ('Current gpa:        ', CurrGpa:4:2);
      writeln ('Cumulative gpa:     ', CumGpa:4:2);
      IF Eligible THEN
          writeln ('ELIGIBLE')
      ELSE
          writeln ('*** NOT ELIGIBLE ***');
      writeln ('*************************************');
      writeln
  END (* Report *);

BEGIN (* CheckStudent *)
    ReadAndCalculate (Snumb, Class, StudentCount, CumHours, CumGpa,
                CurrGpa, SumOfGpas);
    CheckEligibility (Class, CumHours, CumGpa, Eligible, EligibleCount);
    Report (Snumb, Class, CumHours, CurrGpa, CumGpa, Eligible)
END (* CheckStudent *);

PROCEDURE PrintSummary (StudentCount, EligibleCount : integer;
                        SumOfGpas : real);

  (*******************************************************************

            Print summary statistics.

  *******************************************************************)
```

Figure 5.23 (cont.)

```
   BEGIN (* PrintSummary *)
      writeln;
      writeln;
      writeln ('*************************************************************');
      writeln ('*                     SUMMARY STATISTICS                    *');
      writeln ('*************************************************************');
      writeln;
      writeln ('NUMBER OF STUDENTS PROCESSED:      ', StudentCount:1);
      writeln ('AVERAGE CURRENT GPA OF STUDENTS:  ',
                  SumOfGpas / StudentCount : 4:2);
      writeln ('NUMBER FOUND TO BE ELIGIBLE:       ', EligibleCount:1)
   END (* PrintSummary *);

BEGIN (* main program *)
   Instruct;
   StudentCount := 0;
   EligibleCount := 0;
   SumOfGpas := 0;
   REPEAT
      Checkstudent (StudentCount, EligibleCount, SumOfGpas);
      writeln;
      write ('More (Y or N)? ');
      readln (Response)
   UNTIL Response <> 'Y';
   PrintSummary (StudentCount, EligibleCount, SumOfGpas)
END (* main program *).
```

Sample run:

```
You will first be asked to enter the student's
number, class, cumulative hours, and cumulative gpa.
Enter these with at least one space separating them.

You will then be asked to enter the number of hours and
the numeric grade earned for each of the courses the
student took during the current year.  Separate the
number of hours from the grade by at least one space.
Enter 0 for hours and 0 for grades when you are finished
entering the information for each student.




Enter student number, class, cum. hours, cum. gpa:
12345 1 0 0
Hours and grade? 5 3.0
Hours and grade? 4 3.0
Hours and grade? 3.5 3.0
Hours and grade? 4 3.0
Hours and grade? 3 3.0
Hours and grade? 2 3.0
Hours and grade? 0 0
```

Figure 5.23 (cont.)

```
***** Report for student 12345  *****
Class:            1
Cumulative hours: 21.50
Current gpa:      3.00
Cumulative gpa:   3.00
*** NOT ELIGIBLE ***
**************************************


More (Y or N)? Y
Enter student number, class, cum. hours, cum. gpa:
33333 2 30 3.3
Hours and grade? 5 3.3
Hours and grade? 5 4.0
Hours and grade? 5 2.7
Hours and grade? 5 3.0
Hours and grade? 3 3.7
Hours and grade? 0 0

***** Report for student 33333  *****
Class:            2
Cumulative hours: 53.00
Current gpa:      3.31
Cumulative gpa:   3.30
ELIGIBLE
**************************************


More (Y or N)? Y
Enter student number, class, cum. hours, cum. gpa:
44444 3 60 2.0
Hours and grade? 5 1.0
Hours and grade? 5 1.3
Hours and grade? 4 0.7
Hours and grade? 3 0.7
Hours and grade? 5 1.0
Hours and grade? 0 0

***** Report for student 44444  *****
Class:            3
Cumulative hours: 82.00
Current gpa:      0.97
Cumulative gpa:   1.72
*** NOT ELIGIBLE ***
**************************************


More (Y or N)? N


*********************************************************
*                SUMMARY STATISTICS                     *
*********************************************************

NUMBER OF STUDENTS PROCESSED:     3
AVERAGE CURRENT GPA OF STUDENTS:  2.43
NUMBER FOUND TO BE ELIGIBLE:      1
```

Exercises

1. Use a top-down design strategy to develop a menu-driven program that computes any one of the following five quantities, given values for the other four:

   Amount: original amount (in dollars) deposited in a savings account or the original amount borrowed.
   Balance: the final amount (in dollars)
   Payment: periodic payment made some specified number of times per year.
   IntRate: annual interest rate (percent).
   Years: number of years.

   In each case, the user also enters the number of times per year payments are made and indicates whether these payments are loan payments or deposits into a savings account.

2. A *complex number* is a number of the form $a + bi$, where a and b are real numbers and $i^2 = -1$. Using a top-down approach, develop a menu-driven program that reads two complex numbers (where $a + bi$ is entered simply as the pair of real numbers a and b) and allows the user to select one of the operations of addition, subtraction, multiplication, or division to be performed. The program should then call an appropriate procedure to perform the specified arithmetic operation and display the result in the form $a + bi$. The four operations are defined as follows:

$$(a + bi) + (c + di) = (a + c) + (b + d)i$$

$$(a + bi) - (c + di) = (a - c) + (b - d)i$$

$$(a + bi) * (c + di) = (ac - bd) + (ad + bc)i$$

$$(a + bi) / (c + di) = \left(\frac{ac + bd}{c^2 + d^2}\right) + \left(\frac{bc - ad}{c^2 + d^2}\right)i$$

   provided c and d are not both zero in the case of division.

3. Many everyday situations involve *queues* (waiting lines): at supermarket checkout lanes, at ticket counters, at bank windows, at gas stations, and so on. Consider the following example: An airport has one runway. Each airplane takes 3 minutes to land and 2 minutes to take off. On the average 8 planes land and 8 take off in 1 hour. Assume that the planes arrive at random instants of time. (Delays make the assumption of randomness quite reasonable.) There are two types of queues: airplanes waiting to land and airplanes waiting to take off. Because it is more expensive to keep a plane airborne than to have one waiting on the ground, we assume that an airplane waiting to land has priority over one waiting to take off.

   Write a computer simulation of this airport's operation. To simulate landing arrivals, generate a random number corresponding to a 1-minute interval: if it is less than 8/60, then a ''landing arrival'' occurs and joins the queue of planes waiting to land. Generate another random number to determine if a ''take-off arrival'' occurs; if so, it joins the take-off queue. Next, check to determine if the runway is free. If so, first check the landing queue, and if planes are waiting, allow the first airplane in the landing queue to land; otherwise, consider the queue of planes waiting to take off. Have the program calculate the average queue lengths and the average time an airplane spends in a queue. For this, you might simulate a 24-hour day. You might also investigate the effect of varying arrival and departure rates to simulate prime and slack times of day, or what happens if the amount of time it takes to land or take off is increased or decreased.

5.7 Introduction to Recursion

We have seen in previous sections that a function or procedure may reference other functions and/or procedures. A function or procedure may even reference itself, a phenomenon known as *recursion.*

A function or procedure that references itself is said to be *recursive.* Recursion may be *direct,* that is, the function or procedure references itself directly, or it may be *indirect,* where the function or procedure references other functions and/or procedures that eventually reference this function or procedure again.

The definition of a recursive function (or procedure) consists of two parts: (1) an *anchor* in which one or more values of the function (or parameters being returned) are given, and (2) an *inductive step* in which other values of the function (or parameters) are defined in terms of previously defined values. The classic example is the factorial function that is defined in Section 5.3 by

$$n! = \begin{cases} 1 \text{ if } n = 0 \\ 1 \times 2 \times \cdots \times n \text{ if } n > 0 \end{cases}$$

but that is commonly defined recursively by

$0! = 1$
If $n > 0$, $n! = n \times (n - 1)!$

Here the first statement is the anchor and defines the value of the factorial function for 0. The second statement is the inductive step; it defines $n!$ for $n > 0$ in terms of n and the factorial of $n - 1$.

To calculate 5! using this definition, we must first calculate 4! since the definition specifies that 5! is the product of 5 and 4!. Similarly, to calculate 4!, we must first calculate 3! since 4! is defined as 4 × 3!. We continue applying the inductive step of the definition until the anchor case is reached:

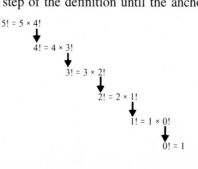

Since the value of 0! is given, we can ***backtrack*** to find the value of 1!:

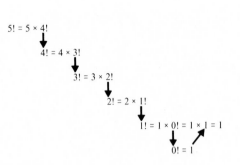

This value can then be used to find the value of 2!:

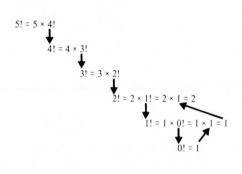

Backtracking continues until we finally obtain the value 120 for 5!:

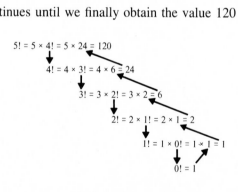

This recursive definition of the factorial function can be implemented as a recursive function in Pascal:

function *Factorial*(*n* : *integer*) : *integer*;

(∗ Recursive function to calculate the factorial *n*! ∗)

begin (∗ *Factorial* ∗)
  if *n* = 0 **then**
    Factorial := 1
  else
    Factorial := *n* ∗ *Factorial*(*n* − 1)
end (∗ *Factorial* ∗);

When this function is referenced, the inductive step

> **else**
> *Factorial* := *n* * *Factorial*(*n* − 1)

causes the function to reference itself repeatedly, each time with a smaller parameter, until the anchor case

> **if** *n* = 0 **then**
> *Factorial* := 1

is reached.

For example, the function reference *Factorial*(5) generates a function reference with parameter 5 − 1 = 4, which we might picture as follows:

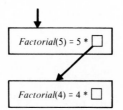

This second function reference, *Factorial*(4), then generates another reference with parameter 4 − 1 = 3, and so on until a reference with 0 is produced:

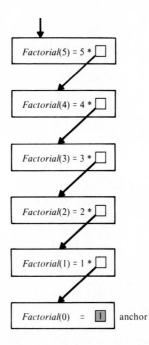

Since the anchor condition is now satisfied, no additional function references are generated. The value 1 is returned for the function reference *Factorial*(0), which is then used to calculate the value of *Factorial*(1), and so on until the value 120 is eventually returned as the value of the original function reference *Factorial*(5):

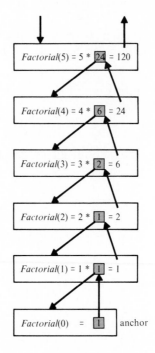

As a second example of a recursive function, consider the operation of exponentiation that can be defined recursively by

$$x^0 = 1 \quad \text{(anchor)}$$
$$\text{If } n > 0, \, x^n = x * x^{n-1} \text{ (inductive step)}$$

Like the factorial definition, this definition leads naturally to a recursive Pascal function:

```
function Power(x : real; n : integer) : real;

    (* Recursive function to calculate
       nth power of x (n >= 0). *)
    begin (* Power *)
      if n = 0 then
        Power := 1
      else
        Power := x * Power( x, n − 1)
    end (* Power *);
```

The following diagram pictures the five levels of function references generated by the initial reference *Power*(2, 4):

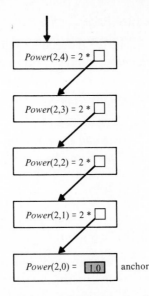

In the function reference with actual parameters 2 and 0, the value 1.0 is assigned to *Power*. This fifth function reference is thus completed, and control returns to the preceding reference in which the actual parameters are 2 and 1. This fourth reference is completed by calculating the expression $2 * Power(2, 0) = 2 * 1.0 = 2.0$, and this value is returned to the previous function reference. Eventually the expression $2 * Power(2, 3) = 2 * 8.0 = 16.0$ is calculated in the first function reference, and 16.0 is returned as the value for the initial function reference $Power(2, 4)$. The following diagram summarizes:

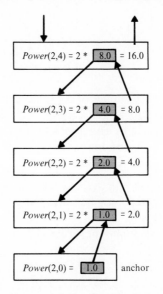

Procedures may also be recursive. To illustrate, consider the problem of printing the digits of a nonnegative integer in order from right to left. Although this problem can easily be solved without recursion (as the exercises ask you to do), it can also be solved by a recursive procedure.

procedure *Reverse* (*Number* : *integer*);

  (∗ Recursive procedure to display the digits of
    Number in order (from right to left). ∗)

var
  LeftDigits : *integer;*   (∗ the leftmost digits of *Number* ∗)

begin (∗ *Reverse* ∗)
  write (*Number* **mod** 10);
  LeftDigits := *Number* **div** 10;
  if *LeftDigits* = 0 **then**
    writeln   (∗ reversal complete ∗)
  else
    Reverse (*LeftDigits*)
end (∗ *Reverse* ∗);

The following diagram illustrates the procedure references generated by the initial call *Reverse* (6285):

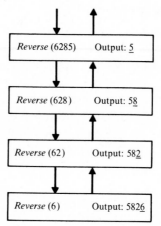

A classic example of a problem that can be solved quite easily by using recursion, but for which a nonrecursive solution is quite difficult, is the ***Towers of Hanoi*** problem. This problem involves solving the puzzle shown in Figure 5.24, in which one must move the disks from the left peg to the right peg according to the following rules:

1. When a disk is moved, it must be placed on one of the three pegs.
2. Only one disk may be moved at a time, and it must be the top disk on one of the pegs.
3. A larger disk may never be placed on top of a smaller one.

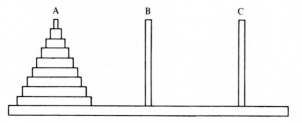

Figure 5.24

Legend has it that the priests in the Temple of Bramah were given a puzzle consisting of a golden platform with 3 golden needles on which were placed 64 golden disks. The world was to end when they had successfully finished moving the disks to another needle, following the rules just given. (Query: If the priests moved 1 disk per second and began their work in the year 0, when would the world come to an end?)

The Towers of Hanoi puzzle with only one disk is easy to solve: simply move the disk from peg A to peg C. This obviously does not violate any of the three rules. A solution for the problem of moving $n > 1$ disks can easily be described recursively:

1. Move the topmost $n - 1$ disks from peg A to peg B, using C as an auxiliary peg.
2. Move the large disk remaining on peg A to peg C.
3. Move the $n - 1$ disks from peg B to peg C, using peg A as an auxiliary peg.

This recursive scheme is implemented by the procedure *Move* in the program of Figure 5.25, which solves the Towers of Hanoi problem.

```
PROGRAM TowersOfHanoi (input, output);

(*********************************************************************

    Program using the recursive procedure Move to solve the
    Towers Of Hanoi puzzle.

*********************************************************************)
CONST
    Peg1 = 'A';
    Peg2 = 'B';
    Peg3 = 'C';

VAR
    NumDisks : integer;      (* number of disks *)

PROCEDURE Move (n : integer; StartPeg, AuxPeg, EndPeg : char);

    (*************************************************************

        Procedure to move n disks from StartPeg to EndPeg using
        AuxPeg as an auxiliary peg.

    *************************************************************)
```

Figure 5.25

Figure 5.25 (cont.)

```
    BEGIN (* Move *)
       IF n = 1 THEN
          writeln ('Move disk from ', StartPeg, ' to ', EndPeg)
       ELSE
         BEGIN
            (* Move n—1 disks from StartPeg to AuxPeg using EndPeg *)

            Move (n — 1, StartPeg, EndPeg, AuxPeg);

            (* Move disk from StartPeg to EndPeg *)

            Move (1, StartPeg, ' ', EndPeg);

            (* Move n—1 disks from AuxPeg to EndPeg using StartPeg *)

            Move (n — 1, AuxPeg, StartPeg, EndPeg)
         END (* ELSE *)
    END (* Move *);

BEGIN (* main program *)
   write ('# of disks:  ');
   readln (NumDisks);
   Move (NumDisks, Peg1, Peg2, Peg3);
END (* main program *).
```

Sample run:

```
# of disks:   4

Move disk from A to B
Move disk from A to C
Move disk from B to C
Move disk from A to B
Move disk from C to A
Move disk from C to B
Move disk from A to B
Move disk from A to C
Move disk from B to C
Move disk from B to A
Move disk from C to A
Move disk from B to C
Move disk from A to B
Move disk from A to C
Move disk from B to C
```

Many problems can be solved with equal ease using either a recursive or a nonrecursive algorithm. For example, the factorial algorithm was implemented in this section as a recursive function and in Section 5.3 as a nonrecursive one. Nonrecursive functions and procedures may execute more rapidly and utilize memory more efficiently than corresponding recursive subprograms. Thus, if an algorithm can be described either recursively or nonrecursively with little difference in effort, it is usually appropriate to use the nonrecursive formulation.

For some problems, such as the Towers of Hanoi problem, recursion is the most natural and straightforward technique. Nonrecursive algorithms often are not obvious, are more difficult to develop, and are less readable than recursive ones. For such problems, the simplicity of the recursive algorithms compensates for any inefficiency. Unless the programs are to be executed many times, the extra effort required to develop nonrecursive solutions is not warranted. Recursion is also appropriate when the problem's data are organized in a data structure that is defined recursively. Such data structures are considered in Chapter 14.

The examples of recursion in this section have illustrated direct recursion, in which a function or procedure references itself directly. Indirect recursion occurs when a subprogram references other subprograms, and some chain of subprogram references eventually results in a reference to the first subprogram again. For example, function A may reference function B, which calls procedure C, which references A again. The implementation of such indirect recursion in Pascal is discussed in Appendix F.

Exercises

1. Write a nonrecursive version of the recursive procedure *Reverse* in the text.

2. The ***Euclidean Algorithm*** for calculating the greatest common divisor GCD(a,b) of two integers a and b is described in Exercise 9 of Section 5.2. Write a recursive function or procedure to calculate GCD(a,b). Also, draw a diagram like those in the text to show the references generated by the initial reference GCD(1260,198).

3. The sequence of ***Fibonacci numbers*** 1, 1, 2, 3, 5, 8, 13, 21, . . . (see Exercise 20 of Section 4.8) can be defined recursively by

$$\left. \begin{array}{l} f_1 = 1 \\ f_2 = 1 \end{array} \right\} \text{(anchor)}$$
$$\text{For } n > 2, \ f_n = f_{n-1} + f_{n-2} \text{ (inductive step)}$$

where f_k denotes the kth Fibonacci number.

   (a) Write a recursive function *Fibonacci* to calculate the kth Fibonacci number for a positive integer k.
   (b) Draw a diagram like those in the text showing the function references generated by the initial reference *Fibonacci*(5). Since there will be two function references at each stage after the first reference, the diagram has a treelike structure.
   (c) Write a nonrecursive function to calculate the kth Fibonacci number.
   (d) Which of the two subprograms in (a) and (c) is more efficient?

4. A ***palindrome*** is a numeral that has the same value whether it is read from left to right or from right to left. For example, 121, 356653, and 1 are palindromes. Write a recursive function or procedure to determine whether a given number is a palindrome. Write a program to read an integer, call the subprogram to determine whether it is a palindrome, and display an appropriate message.

5. ***Binomial coefficients*** can be defined recursively as follows:

$$\left.\begin{array}{c} \dbinom{n}{0} = 1 \\[2mm] \dbinom{n}{n} = 1 \end{array}\right\} \text{(anchor)}$$

For $0 < k < n$, $\dbinom{n}{k} = \dbinom{n-1}{k-1} + \dbinom{n-1}{k}$ (inductive step)

a. Write a recursive function or procedure to calculate binomial coefficients.

b. Draw a treelike diagram like that in Exercise 3, showing the subprogram references and returns involved in calculating the binomial coefficient $\dbinom{4}{2}$.

c. Use your recursive subprogram in a program that reads values for n and k and displays the value of $\dbinom{n}{k}$, using the subprogram to obtain this value.

Programming Pointers

Program Design

1. *Programs for solving complex problems should be designed in a modular fashion.*

- *A problem should be divided into simpler subproblems so that a function or procedure can be written to solve each of these subproblems.*
- *Local identifiers should be used whenever possible to avoid conflict with identifiers in other program units and to make the program as modular as possible.*
- *Formal parameters in subprograms should be declared as value parameters whenever possible so that subprograms cannot unexpectedly change the values of the actual parameters.*

2. *Recursive functions and procedures may be used when the problem's data are organized in a data structure that is defined recursively. They may also be used for problems for which a simple recursive algorithm can be given. If a nonrecursive algorithm can be given that is no more* *complex than the recursive one, it is usually best to use the nonrecursive version.*

Potential Problems

1. *When a procedure or function is referenced, the number of actual parameters must be the same as the number of formal parameters in the procedure or function heading, and the type of each actual parameter must be compatible with the type of the corresponding formal parameter.* For example, consider the function with the heading

    function *Maximum* (*Number1, Number2 : integer*) : *integer*;

    The statements

    Larger1 := *Maximum*(*k, m, n*);

    and

    Larger2 := *Maximum*(*Number*, 3.75);

    are incorrect. In the first case, the number of actual parameters does not agree with the number of formal parameters, and in the second, the real value 3.75 cannot be assigned to the integer parameter *Number2*.

2. *Parameters that are to return values from a procedure must be declared as variable parameters using the indicator* **var**. *The actual parameters that correspond to variable formal parameters must be variables; they may not be constants or expressions.* For example, the procedure whose heading is

    procedure *Taxes* (*Income : real*; **var** *NetIncome, Tax : real*);

    can return only values of *NetIncome* and *Tax* to the calling program unit, and it cannot be called by the statement

    Taxes (*Salary*, 3525.67, *IncomeTax*)

    because the constant 3525.67 cannot be associated with the variable parameter *NetIncome*.

3. *Formal parameters in procedures and functions are defined only during execution of that procedure or function; they are undefined both before and after execution.* Any attempt to use these parameters outside the function or procedure is an error.

4. *The scope of any identifier is the program unit in which it is declared.* For example, for the procedure

    procedure *Calculate* (*x : integer*; *y : real*);

    > **var**
    >   *a, b : integer*;
    >   ⋮

    the local variables *x, y, a,* and *b* cannot be accessed outside the procedure *Calculate*.

5. *A control variable for a* **for** *statement must be declared within the program unit in which it is used.* A global variable or any variable declared in some larger program unit may not be used for this purpose.

6. *Using global variables to share information between different program units should usually be avoided, since changing the value of such a variable in one program unit changes its value in all program units.* This may make it difficult to determine the value of such a variable at any point in the program because its value may have been changed by any of the program units.

7. *A procedure or function must be defined before it is referenced.* For example, if the procedure *Taxes* references the procedure *Calculate*, then *Calculate* must be defined before *Taxes*.

> **procedure** *Calculate* . . . ;
> ⋮
> **procedure** *Taxes* . . . ;
> ⋮

8. *Procedures and functions that have formal parameters cannot be referenced without corresponding actual parameters.* An error commonly made by beginning programmers is illustrated by the following attempt to define the function *Factorial:*

> **function** *Factorial*(*m* : *integer*) : *integer*;
>
> **var**
>   *k* : *integer*;
>
> **begin** (∗ *Factorial* ∗)
>   *Factorial* := 1;
>   **for** *k* := 1 **to** *m* **do**
>   *Factorial* := *Factorial* ∗ *k*
> **end** (∗ *Factorial* ∗);

In this example, the statement

> *Factorial* := *Factorial* ∗ *k*

is not valid since the right side of this assignment statement contains a reference to the function *Factorial* with no actual parameters.

Program Style

1. *Procedures and functions should be documented in the same way that programs are.* The documentation should include a brief description of the processing carried out by the function or procedure, the values passed to it, and the values returned by it.

2. *Procedures and functions are separate program units, and the program format should reflect this.* In this text we:

    (a) Insert a blank line before and after each procedure and function definition to separate it from other program units.

    (b) Indent the declarations and statements within each subprogram.

    (c) Follow the stylistic standards described in earlier chapters when writing subprograms.

Variations and Extensions

An assortment of additional predefined procedures and functions is usually provided in the various versions of Pascal. Typically included are:

- Additional arithmetic functions (e.g., *KeyPressed, BitShift, Log, PwrOfTen*).
- Random number generators.
- String functions and procedures (see the Variations and Extensions section of Chapter 8).
- Special graphics subprograms.

Such extended features are included in Macintosh, Turbo, and UCSD Pascal; see Appendix G for details.

6

Input/Output

When I read some of the rules for speaking and writing the English language correctly . . . I think
Any fool can make a rule
And every fool will mind it.

HENRY THOREAU

An average English word is four letters and a half. By hard, honest labor I've dug all the large words out of my vocabulary and shaved it down till the average is three and a half. . . .

MARK TWAIN

All useful programs involve the input and output of information, and therefore, these operations deserve special consideration. Up to now we have restricted our attention primarily to numeric input/output and merely noted in Chapter 4 that the boolean-valued functions *eof* and *eoln* may be used in conjunction with input. In this chapter we discuss these functions in more detail, and we also consider the input and output of nonnumeric data.

In our introduction to input/output in Chapter 3, we observed that these operations are carried out using *files.* We have thus far used only the standard system files *input* and *output* that are associated with the standard system input and output devices. In this chapter we introduce text files because interactive input is cumbersome for large data sets and may be quite difficult with some Pascal compilers.

6.1 Input/Output Procedures

Up to now we have used *read, readln, write,* and *writeln* statements to perform input/output. These statements are in fact procedure reference statements that call the predefined Pascal procedures *read, readln, write,* and *writeln,* respectively. The input/output lists are the parameters for these procedures. We begin by reviewing these four procedures.

The *writeln* procedure is called with a statement of the form

> *writeln* (*output-list*)

where *output-list* is an expression or a list of expressions separated by commas. Execution of such a statement displays the values of the expressions on a single line and then advances to a new line. For example, if the value of the integer variable *Number* is 27, the statements

> *writeln* ('Square of ', *Number*, ' is ', *sqr(Number)*);
> *writeln* ('and its square root is ', *sqrt(Number)*)

produce output like the following:

```
Square of        27 is      729
and its square root is  5.196152423E+00
```

The actual spacing within each line and the form in which real values are displayed are system dependent and may not be exactly as shown.

Recall that the format of the output can be specified by appending a format descriptor of the form :*w* or :*w:d* to the items in the output list. For example, the statements

> *writeln* ('Square of ', *Number*:2, ' is ', *sqr(Number)*:4);
> *writeln* ('and its square root is ', *sqrt(Number)*:8:3)

produce as output

```
Square of 27 is  729
and its square root is    5.196
```

The *writeln* procedure may also be called with no output list:

> *writeln*

and in this case the parentheses are also omitted. This statement serves simply to advance to the next line.

The *write* procedure is called with a statement of the form

> *write* (*output-list*)

where the output list has the same form as for the *writeln* statement; format descriptors may be used as just described. When this statement is executed, the values are displayed on the current line, but there is no advance to a new line. Consequently, any subsequent output will be displayed on this same line.

For example, the statements

> *write* ('The first 5 squares are:');
> **for** *i* : = 1 **to** 5 **do**
>   *write* (*sqr(i)*:3);
> *writeln* (' *****');
> *writeln* ('*****')

produce as output

```
The_first_5_squares_are:__1__4__9_16_25_*****
*****_____
```

The *readln* procedure is called with a statement of the form

readln (*input-list*)

where *input-list* is a variable or a list of variables of integer, real, or character type, separated by commas. When this statement is executed, values are read from the standard system file *input* and assigned to the variables in the input list. In a batch mode of operation, these values are typically obtained from a data file that accompanies the program. In an interactive mode, execution of the program is suspended while the user enters values for the variables. In this text the examples illustrate interactive input.

For example, when the statements

> *writeln* ('Enter employee number, hours worked, and hourly rate:');
> *readln* (*EmpNumber, Hours, Rate*)

are executed, the prompt

Enter employee number, hours worked, and hourly rate:

is displayed and execution of the program is interrupted. The user must enter values for the three variables before execution of the program can resume. To assign the values 31523, 38.5, and 7.50 to *EmpNumber, Hours,* and *Rate,* respectively, where *EmpNumber* is of integer type and *Hours* and *Rate* are of real type, the appropriate input is

31523 38.5 7.50

The values that are read are actually obtained from the standard system file *input*. Values are copied into this file sequentially as they are entered, and each time the end of a line of input is encountered, an **end-of-line mark** is placed in the file. Thus, if the user enters the values

31523 38.5 7.50
31564 40.0 8.75

the contents of the file *input* are

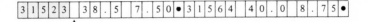

where we have used ● to indicate an end-of-line mark.

As values are read from this file by a *readln* statement, a data pointer, which is initially positioned at the beginning of the file, advances through the file. If we indicate the data pointer by ↑ , then the initial status of the file *input* is

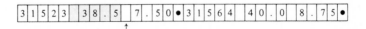

When a value for the integer variable *EmpNumber* is read from this file, the longest sequence of characters that forms an integer is read. That value is assigned to *EmpNumber,* and the data pointer advances to the first character that is not a digit. Thus, for the statement

   readln (EmpNumber, Hours, Rate)

the value read for *EmpNumber* is 31523, and the data pointer is advanced to the blank that follows the last digit of this number.

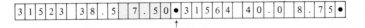

A value must now be read for the real variable *Hours.* The longest sequence of characters that represents a value that can be assigned to a real variable is read, with leading blanks ignored. Thus the value read for *Hours* is 38.5, and the data pointer advances to the blank following the last digit of this number.

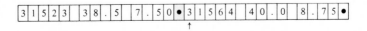

Similarly, the value 7.50 is read for *Rate,* and the data pointer is advanced to the end-of-line mark.

so that the values read for variables in subsequent *readln* statements begin at this point.

For the statement

readln (EmpNumber, Hours, Rate)

the values might be entered one per line:

31523
38.5
7.50
31564
40.0
8.75

In this case, the contents of the file *input* are

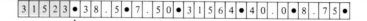

The value read for *EmpNumber* is 31523, and the data pointer advances to the end-of-line mark following the last digit of this number.

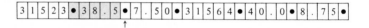

Next, a value must be read for *Hours;* the end-of-line mark is interpreted as a blank and is thus ignored, so that the value 38.5 is read and assigned to *Hours* and the data pointer is advanced.

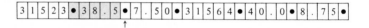

Similarly, the value 7.50 is read and assigned to *Rate,* and the data pointer is advanced.

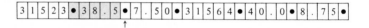

Because values have been read and assigned to each variable in the input list, the *readln* procedure now advances the data pointer past this end-of-line mark.

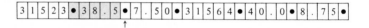

Suppose that the preceding data values are entered as

31523 38.5 7.50 31564
40.0   8.75

so that the contents of the file *input* are

When the statement

>   *readln* (*EmpNumber, Hours, Rate*)

is executed, the values 31523, 38.5, and 7.50 are read and assigned to *EmpNumber, Hours,* and *Rate,* respectively, as before. Because values have been read for each of the variables in the input list, the *readln* procedure now causes the data pointer to advance past the next end-of-line mark

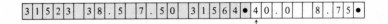

so that the value 31564 is not read. Subsequent input continues from this point. If the statement

>   *readln* (*EmpNumber, Hours, Rate*)

is executed again, the value read for *EmpNumber* is 40, since this is the longest sequence of characters that represents an integer; the data pointer advances to the decimal point following this integer.

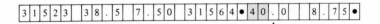

Next, a value must be read for the real variable *Hours.* An error occurs and execution terminates, however, since a real number may not begin with a decimal point. The error message displayed might be

>   *** I/O ERROR at character 3 of line 2;
>   '.' found where ' + ', ' − ', or digit expected.

The *read* procedure can also be used for input. It is called with a statement of the form

>   *read* (*input-list*)

where *input-list* is a variable or a list of variables separated by commas. The *read* procedure is similar to the *readln* procedure except that the *read* procedure does *not* advance the data pointer past an end-of-line mark after values have been read for the variables in the input list. To illustrate, consider the statement

>   *read* (*EmpNumber, Hours, Rate*)

and suppose that the data are entered as described previously:

    31523 38.5 7.50 31564
    40.0   8.75

As in the case of the *readln* statement, the values read for *EmpNumber, Hours,* and *Rate* are 31523, 38.5, and 7.50, respectively. For the *read* statement, however, the data pointer is not advanced past the end-of-line mark.

| 3 | 1 | 5 | 2 | 3 | | 3 | 8 | . | 5 | | 7 | . | 5 | 0 | | 3 | 1 | 5 | 6 | 4 | ● | 4 | 0 | . | 0 | | | 8 | . | 7 | 5 | ● |

Thus if the statement

    read (EmpNumber, Hours, Rate)

is executed again, the value 31564 is read for *EmpNumber,* 40.0 for *Hours* (the end-of-line mark preceding this number is ignored), and 8.75 for *Rate,* and the data pointer is advanced to the end-of-line mark following this last value.

| 3 | 1 | 5 | 2 | 3 | | 3 | 8 | . | 5 | | 7 | . | 5 | 0 | | 3 | 1 | 5 | 6 | 4 | ● | 4 | 0 | . | 0 | | | 8 | . | 7 | 5 | ● |

    A second distinction between the *read* and *readln* procedures is that *readln* but not *read* may be called with no input list:

    readln

Note that in this case the parentheses are also omitted. Execution of this statement advances the data pointer past the next end-of-line mark so that subsequent input begins with a new line. It may thus be used to skip a line of input or to skip over values that remain in the current line.

    When a value is read for a numeric variable, the longest sequence of characters that can be interpreted as a value for that variable is read, and the data pointer is advanced to the nondigit character that follows that value. The value of a character variable, however, is only a single character. Thus, when a value is read for a character variable, the next character is read and assigned to the variable, and the data pointer is advanced one position. Since blanks are legitimate characters, they are not ignored but, rather, are read and assigned as values for character variables. Similarly, end-of-line marks are not ignored but are read and interpreted as blanks when reading values for character variables.

    To illustrate, consider the statement

    read (Ch1, Ch2, Ch3, Ch4)

where *Ch1, Ch2, Ch3,* and *Ch4* are of character type. Suppose that the following data are entered:

    AB CD

so that the file *input* has the contents

When this statement is executed, the characters A and B are read and assigned to *Ch1* and *Ch2*, respectively; a blank is read and assigned to *Ch3*; C is read and assigned to *Ch4*; and the data pointer is advanced to the next character.

If characters are entered one per line

A
B
C
D

the contents of the file *input* are

When the preceding *read* statement is executed, the value read for *Ch1* is A. The next character read is an end-of-line mark; it is interpreted as a blank and assigned to *Ch2*. Similarly, the letter B is read and assigned to *Ch3*; an end-of-line mark is read, interpreted as a blank, and assigned to *Ch4*; and the data pointer is advanced to the next character.

If we wish to assign A, B, C, and D to the character variables *Ch1*, *Ch2*, *Ch3*, and *Ch4*, respectively, by using the statement

read (*Ch1*, *Ch2*, *Ch3*, *Ch4*)

the data should be entered on a single line with no intervening blanks:

ABCD

When this statement is executed, the data pointer advances to the end-of-line mark following the D.

Subsequent reading of values begins at this point. Thus, if a value is read for a character variable, this end-of-line mark is read and a blank is assigned to this variable.

It is important to remember how numeric and character values are read when variables of different types appear in the same input list. Suppose that *Num1* and *Num2* are integer variables and that *Ch1* and *Ch2* are character variables, and consider the statement

readln (Num1, Ch1, Num2, Ch2)

If the following data are entered on a single line

23A45B

then the values read and assigned are

Num1 ← 23
Ch1 ← A
Num2 ← 45
Ch2 ← B

If we enter the values on separate lines, however,

23
A
45
B

then the value 23 is read and assigned to *Num1* and an end-of-line mark is read and a blank is assigned to *Ch1*. But an error now occurs in reading a value for the integer variable *Num2* because the next character, A, is not a digit. The same error occurs if the data are entered as

23 A 45 B

with blanks separating the values.

If the data are entered as

23A 45B

then the values read and assigned are

Num1 ← 23
Ch1 ← A
Num2 ← 45
Ch2 ← B

No error occurs, since the blank separating A and 45 is ignored when reading a value for *Num2*. These same values are read and assigned if they are entered as

23A
45B

since in this case the end-of-line mark separating A and 45 is ignored when
reading a value for *Num2*.

Exercises

1. Suppose that *Num1*, *Num2*, *Num3*, and *Num4* are integer variables,
and that for each of the following *read* and *readln* statements, these
data are entered:

```
1   − 2 3
4 − 5 6
7        − 8     9
```

What values will be assigned to these variables when each of the following statements is executed?

(a) *read (Num1, Num2, Num3, Num4)*;

(b) *readln (Num1, Num2, Num3, Num4)*;

(c) *read (Num1, Num2)*;
   read (Num3);
   read (Num4);

(d) *readln (Num1, Num2)*;
   readln (Num3, Num4);

(e) *readln*;
   readln (Num1, Num2, Num3, Num4);

2. Assume the following declarations:

var
   N1, N2, N3 : integer;
   R1, R2, R3 : real;
   C1, C2, C3 : char;

and that for each of the following *read* and *readln* statements, the
following data are entered:

```
123   45.6
X78 − 909.8 7
− 65$     432.10
```

List the values that are assigned to each of the variables in the input
list, or explain why an error occurs:

(a) *readln (N1, R1)*;
   read (C1, N2);
   readln (R2);
   read (C2, N3, C3);

(b) *readln (N1)*;
   read (C1, C2, R1, R2);
   read (N2, N3, C3);
   read (R3);

(c) *read (N1, R1)*;
   readln (C1, C2, R2, N2, C3, R3)
   readln (N3);

(d) *readln;*
   read (C1, N1, C2, R1, R2);
   read (N2, C3, R3);

(e) *read (N1, R1, C1)*;
   read (C2, N2, R2);
   readln (N3, C3, R3);

(f) *readln (N1, R1, C1, C2, N2, R2, N3, R3, C3)*;

(g) *read (N1, R1)*;
   readln (C1, N2, R2, N3);
   readln (R3, C3);

(h) *readln (N1, R1)*;
   readln (C1, N2, N3, R2);
   readln (R3, C3);

3. Assume the following declarations:

   var
       N1, N2, N3 : integer;
       R1, R2, R3 : real;
       C1, C2, C3 : char;

   and that the contents of the file *input* are

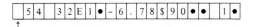

   List the values that are assigned to each of the variables in the input list for each of the following statements, or explain why an error occurs. Also, show the position of the data pointer after each of the sequences of statements is executed:

(a) *read (N1, N2, C1, C2, R1, C3, N3)*;

(b) *read (N1, R1, R2, C1, C2, C3, N2)*;

(c) *readln (N1, N2)*;
   readln (C1, R1, C2, R2);

(d) *read (N1)*;
   read (N2);
   read (C1);
   read (C2);

        read (R1);
        read (C3);
        read (N3);

(e) *readln (N1)*;
       readln (N2);
       readln (N3);

(f) *read (C1, C2, C3, N1)*;
       readln;
       readln (N2);

(g) *readln (R1, R2)*;
       readln (C1, N1, C2, N2, C3, N3);

(h) *read (R1, C1, N1, C2)*;
       readln (N2, C3, R2);

6.2   Introduction to Text Files; the *eof* and *eoln* Functions

Up to this point, we have assumed that the data for the sample programs were entered by the user during program execution. In this interactive mode, the data values are copied into the standard system file *input*, and values are obtained from this file by the *read* or *readln* procedures. In general, any collection of data items that are input to or output by a program is called a ***file***. It is possible to create a file before a program is executed and then to read values from this file during execution. There are several reasons that this may be desirable. It may be inconvenient for the user to enter the data each time the program is executed, especially if the volume of data is large; and, as we have noted, interactive input may be somewhat difficult with some systems. These problems can be avoided by preparing a data file in advance and designing the program to read the values from this file. In this section we introduce a simple kind of file called a ***text file*** and describe how input and output using such files are carried out.

    Files are usually stored on magnetic tape or magnetic disk or some other form of external (secondary) memory. Magnetic tape is coated with a substance that can be magnetized and stores information for computer processing in somewhat the same way that an audio tape stores sound information. Information can be written to or read from a tape using a device called a ***tape drive***. A standard tape drive can record 1600 bytes per inch of tape. This means that a 2400-foot reel of tape can store approximately 46 million characters. A magnetic disk is also coated with a substance that can be magnetized. Information is stored on such disks in tracks arranged in concentric circles and is written to or read from a disk using a ***disk drive***. This device transfers information by means of a read/write head that is positioned over one of the tracks of the rotating disks. Some disk packs consisting of several such disks can store more than a billion characters.

    To illustrate how text files are declared and accessed in Pascal programs, we consider the problem of processing employee wage information. Some employee information, such as the employee number and hourly pay rate, remains unchanged for long periods of time, and it is preferable to avoid entering this information each time programs for processing it are executed. Consequently, a file containing data such as the following might be created to store this permanent employee information:

```
31523  7.50
31564  8.75
31585  9.35
32012 10.50
35559  6.35
     ⋮
48813 11.60
```

This file might be created using a text editor and stored in secondary memory, or it might be produced by some other program. Here the information for each employee appears on a separate line, and one or more blanks separate the items in that line. A text file, like the standard system file *input*, is a sequence of characters, and thus this file should be viewed as having the form

```
3 1 5 2 3   7 . 5 0 ● 3 1 5 6 4   8 . 7 5 ●  ···  ● 4 8 8 1 3   1 1 . 6 0 ● ▼
```

where ● denotes an end-of-line mark and ▼ denotes an ***end-of-file mark.***

In Pascal, text files are accessed using ***file variables*** of type *text*. The type identifier *text* is quite different from those considered up to now. The data types *integer*, *real*, *boolean*, and *char* are called **simple** data types because a datum of one of these types consists of a single item that cannot be subdivided. The type *text*, however, is a ***structured*** data type in which a datum is a collection of items. For example, to process the text file containing the permanent employee information, we might use the file variable *EmpFile* declared by

var
    EmpFile : *text*;

Files that exist before and/or after execution of a program are called **permanent** (or **external**) files. Names of all permanent files used in a program, including the standard files *input* and *output*, must appear in the file list of the program heading. In our example, *EmpFile* is a permanent file and must, therefore, be listed in the program heading:

program *Payroll* (*input, output, EmpFile*);

Before the contents of a file can be read, the file must be *opened for input*, that is, a data pointer must be positioned at the beginning of the file. This is done by using the predefined Pascal procedure *reset*. This procedure is called with a statement of the form

    reset (*file-variable*)

Thus, for our example, the statement

    reset (*EmpFile*);

opens the employee information file for input, positioning the data pointer at the beginning of the file.[1]

```
| 3 | 1 | 5 | 2 | 3 |  | 7 | . | 5 | 0 |•| 3 | 1 | 5 | 6 | 4 |  | 8 | . | 7 | 5 |•|  ...  |•| 4 | 8 | 8 | 1 | 3 |  | 1 | 1 | . | 6 | 0 |•|▼|
  ↑
```

The data pointer is advanced sequentially through the file as the items are read, in the same manner as described for the file *input* in the preceding section.

    The values in a text file are read by using the standard input procedures *readln* and *read*. In this case, the input statements have the form

    readln (*file-variable, input-list*)

or

    read (*file-variable, input-list*)

where *file-variable* denotes the text file from which the values are to be read. If *file-variable* is omitted, the standard file *input* is assumed; thus the statements

    readln (*input-list*)   and   *read* (*input-list*)

are equivalent to

    readln (*input, input-list*)   and   *read* (*input, input-list*)

respectively.

    When an input statement is executed, values are read from the specified file and assigned to the variables in the input list. After each value is read, the data pointer is advanced in the same manner as described earlier for the standard file *input*. Thus, for the employee information file *EmpFile*, the statement

    readln (*EmpFile, EmpNumber, Rate*);

reads values for the integer variable *EmpNumber* and the real variable *Rate* from *EmpFile*. The data pointer is then advanced so that it is positioned after the next end-of-line mark. The first execution of this statement therefore assigns the value 31523 to *EmpNumber* and the value 7.50 to *Rate*, and then advances the data pointer past the first end-of-line mark.

---

[1] In some implementations of Pascal, the procedure *reset* is also used to associate the file name used in the program with the name of the actual data file stored in secondary memory, by allowing a second parameter:

    reset (*file-variable, file-name*)

In others, a separate procedure (e.g., *assign*) must be used to make this association. (See Appendix G for additional details.)

| 3 | 1 | 5 | 2 | 3 | | | 7 | . | 5 | 0 | ● | 3 | 1 | 5 | 6 | 4 | | | 8 | . | 7 | 5 | ● | ⋯ | ● | 4 | 8 | 8 | 1 | 3 | | 1 | 1 | . | 6 | 0 | ● | ▼ |
↑

The end of a file can be detected by using the boolean-valued function *eof*. This function is referenced by an expression of the form

eof(*file-variable*)

and has the value true if the data pointer is positioned at the end-of-file mark; otherwise, it has the value false.

If the file name and the parentheses are omitted, the standard system file *input* is assumed. Thus

eof

is equivalent to

eof (*input*)

The *eof* function can be used in a boolean expression to control repetition of an input loop, for example,

while not *eof(EmpFile)* **do**
   begin
      readln (EmpFile, EmpNumber, HourlyRate);
      ⋮
   end (* **while** *);

The program in Figure 6.1 uses this construction to read the contents of *EmpFile* and calculate the average hourly rate of all employees. After the last values 48813 and 11.60 are read from the file and assigned to *EmpNumber* and *HourlyRate*, respectively, the *readln* procedure advances the data pointer past the last end-of-line mark so that it is positioned at the end-of-file mark. The *eof* function now returns the value true, and execution of the while loop is terminated.

```
PROGRAM AverageHourlyRate (input, output, EmpFile);

(******************************************************************

   Program to determine the average hourly rate for employees whose
   employee numbers and hourly rates are stored in the file EmpFile.

******************************************************************)

VAR
    EmpFile : text;         (* the permanent employee file *)
    EmpNumber,              (* employee number *)
    Count : integer;        (* counts number of employees *)
    HourlyRate,             (* hourly pay rate *)
    Sum : real;             (* sum of hourly pay rates *)
```

Figure 6.1

Figure 6.1 (cont.)

```
BEGIN
    reset (EmpFile);
    Count := 0;
    Sum := 0;
    WHILE NOT eof(EmpFile) DO
        BEGIN
            readln (EmpFile, EmpNumber, HourlyRate);
            Count := Count + 1;
            Sum := Sum + HourlyRate
        END (* WHILE *);
    IF Count > 0 THEN
        writeln ('Average hourly rate is $', Sum / Count :4:2)
    ELSE
        writeln ('No employees listed in the file')
END.
```

Listing of EmpFile:
_____

```
31523   7.50
31564   8.75
31585   9.35
32102  10.50
35559   6.35
36800  10.85
40013   7.15
44009   9.15
47123   8.75
48813  11.60
```


Sample run:
_____

Average hourly rate is $8.99

Care must be taken to avoid attempting to read beyond the end of the file. To illustrate, if the *readln* statement in this program is replaced with

   read (*EmpFile, EmpNumber, HourlyRate*);

an error results. After the last data values 48813 and 11.60 are read, the data pointer is positioned at the end-of-line mark following these values.

Since *eof(EmpFile)* has the value false, the *read* statement is executed again. Attempting to read a value for *EmpNumber* results in an attempt to read beyond the end of the file. Execution of the program is terminated and an error message such as the following is displayed:

   ***I/O ERROR while reading EMPFILE,
       trying to read past end of file.

It is also possible to write to a user-defined text file so that the output can be stored for later processing. For example, suppose that all the employees listed in *EmpFile* are granted a 5 percent raise, and we wish to generate a new employee file *NewEmpFile* with the new hourly rates. In this case, the file variable *NewEmpFile* must also be listed in the program heading and declared to be of type *text:*

> **program** *Payroll* (*input, output, EmpFile, NewEmpFile*);
>   ⋮
>
> **var**
>   *EmpFile,*
>   *NewEmpFile* : *text*;

Before data can be written to a text file, the file must be opened for output by using the predefined procedure *rewrite*. A reference to this procedure has the form

> *rewrite (file-variable)*

This statement creates an empty file with the specified name, destroying any previous contents of the file.[2] In our example, we would thus include in the program the statement

> *rewrite* (*NewEmpFile*);

Output may be directed to a text file by using statements of the form

> *writeln (file-variable, output-list)*

or

> *write (file-variable, output-list)*

If *file-name* is omitted, the output is directed to the system file *output* and thus is displayed using the standard system output device. The statements

> *writeln (output-list)*   **and**   *write (output-list)*

are thus equivalent to

> *writeln (output, output-list)*   **and**   *write (output, output-list)*

respectively. In our example, the statement

---

[2] As in the case of the procedure *reset,* some implementations of Pascal also use the procedure *rewrite* to associate the file name used in the program with the name of the actual data file to be stored in secondary memory by allowing a second parameter,

> *rewrite (file-variable, file-name)*

and others use a separate procedure. (See Appendix G for details.)

> *writeln (NewEmpFile, EmpNumber*:5, *NewHourlyRate*:6:2)

is used in the program in Figure 6.2 to write the values of *EmpNumber* and *NewHourlyRate,* followed by an end-of-line mark to the text file *NewEmpFile.*

```
PROGRAM IncreaseHourlyRates (input, output, EmpFile, NewEmpFile);

(********************************************************************

    Program to read employee numbers and hourly rates from Empfile
    and generate NewEmpFile in which all hourly rates are increased
    by a specified percentage.

********************************************************************)

CONST
    Increase = 0.05;          (* percentage increase in decimal form *)

VAR
    EmpFile,                  (* the original permanent employee file *)
    NewEmpFile : text;        (* the new permanent file to be produced *)
    EmpNumber :integer;       (* employee number *)
    HourlyRate,               (* hourly pay rate *)
    NewHourlyRate : real;     (* new hourly rate *)

BEGIN
    reset (EmpFile);
    rewrite (NewEmpFile);
    WHILE NOT eof(EmpFile) DO
        BEGIN
            readln (EmpFile, EmpNumber, HourlyRate);
            NewHourlyRate := (1 + Increase) * HourlyRate;
            writeln (NewEmpFile, EmpNumber:5, NewHourlyRate:6:2)
        END (* WHILE *);
END.
```

Listing of EmpFile:

```
31523   7.50
31564   8.75
31585   9.35
32102  10.50
35559   6.35
36800  10.85
40013   7.15
44009   9.15
47123   8.75
48813  11.60
```

Figure 6.2

Figure 6.2 (cont.)

Listing of NewEmpFile:

```
31523   7.87
31564   9.19
31585   9.82
32102  11.02
35559   6.67
36800  11.39
40013   7.51
44009   9.61
47123   9.19
48813  12.18
```

A *writeln* statement of the form

writeln (*file-variable*)

in which the output list is omitted produces an advance to a new line in the specified text file. Such a statement can thus be used to write blank lines to this file. (The predefined procedure *page* can also be used with text files; it is described in Appendix F.)

File variables, like simple variables, may also be used as parameters in user-defined procedures and functions. In this case, they *must be variable parameters,* since allowing them to be value parameters would require assigning the value of one file variable to another file variable, and this is not allowed in Pascal.

To illustrate the use of file variables as parameters, consider the following problem. Wages are to be calculated for employees whose employee number and hourly rate are contained in the file *EmpFile* described earlier. For each of these employees, this information is to be read from the file, but the hours worked are to be entered by the user during program execution, since this value is usually not the same for all pay periods. The total of all employees' wages is also to be calculated and displayed. The program in Figure 6.3 solves this problem. The procedure *GetEmployeeInfo* reads an employee number and hourly rate from a file denoted by the formal parameter *InFile,* a file variable of type *text*. Since the corresponding actual parameter in the statement that calls this procedure in the main program is the file variable *EmpFile, GetEmployeeInfo* actually reads this information from the file *EmpFile*. It then prompts the user to enter the hours worked for this employee and returns this value, together with the employee's number and hourly rate, to the main program, which then calls procedure *CalculateWages* to determine the wages for this employee. When the end-of-file mark in *EmpFile* is encountered, the *eof* function causes repetition to terminate, and the main program then displays the total wages for all employees.

```
PROGRAM Payroll (input, output, EmpFile);

(************************************************************************

   Program to calculate wages for several employees whose employee
   numbers and hourly rates are read from the file EmpFile and
   whose hours are entered by the user during execution.  Total
   wages for this payroll are also calculated.

************************************************************************)

VAR
    EmpFile : text;         (* the permanent employee file *)
    EmpNumber : integer;    (* employee number *)
    Hours,                  (* hours worked *)
    HourlyRate,             (* hourly pay rate *)
    Wages,                  (* total wages for employee *)
    TotalPayroll : real;    (* total wages for this payroll *)

PROCEDURE GetEmployeeInfo (VAR InFile : Text; VAR EmpNumber : integer;
                           VAR HourlyRate, Hours : real);

    (*********************************************************************

       Procedure to read and return the employee number EmpNumber
       and HourlyRate from a text file InFile; the Hours worked is
       entered by the user and is also returned.

    *********************************************************************)

    BEGIN (* GetEmployeeInfo *)
       readln (InFile, EmpNumber, HourlyRate);
       write ('Hours worked for ', EmpNumber:1,':  ');
       readln (Hours);
    END (* GetEmployeeInfo *);


PROCEDURE CalculateWages (Hours, HourlyRate : real;
                          VAR Wages, TotalPayroll : real);

    (*********************************************************************

       Procedure to calculate and return Wages for employee who has
       worked the given number of Hours at the given HourlyRate.
       Hours above HoursLimit are paid at OvertimeFactor times
       the hourly rate.  Total wages for this payroll are also
       accumlated and returned.  The function RoundCents is used
       to round wages to the nearest cent.

    *********************************************************************)

    CONST
       OvertimeFactor = 1.5; (* overtime multiplication factor *)
       HoursLimit = 40.0;    (* overtime hours limit *)
```

Figure 6.3

Figure 6.3 (cont.)

```
    VAR
        RegWages,                  (* regular wages *)
        OverWages : real;          (* overtime pay *)

FUNCTION RoundCents (Amount : real) : real;

    (********************************************************************

            Returns Amount rounded to the nearest cent.

     *******************************************************************)

    BEGIN (* RoundCents *)
        RoundCents := round(100 * Amount) / 100
    END (* RoundCents *);

BEGIN (* CalculateWages *)
    IF Hours > HoursLimit THEN
        BEGIN (* Overtime *)
            RegWages := RoundCents(HourlyRate * HoursLimit);
            OverWages :=
                RoundCents(OvertimeFactor * HourlyRate * (Hours - HoursLimit))
        END (* Overtime *)
    ELSE
        BEGIN (* No overtime *)
            RegWages := RoundCents(HourlyRate * Hours);
            OverWages := 0
        END (* No overtime *);
    Wages := RegWages + OverWages;
    TotalPayroll := TotalPayroll + Wages
  END (* CalculateWages *);


BEGIN (* main program *)
    reset (EmpFile);
    TotalPayroll := 0;
    WHILE NOT eof(EmpFile) DO
        BEGIN
            GetEmployeeInfo (EmpFile, EmpNumber, HourlyRate, Hours);
            writeln ('Hourly rate:   $', HourlyRate:4:2);
            CalculateWages (Hours, HourlyRate, Wages, TotalPayroll);
            writeln ('Wages:  $', Wages:4:2);
            writeln;
        END (* WHILE *);
    writeln;
    writeln ('Total wages = $', TotalPayroll:4:2)
END (* main program *).



Listing of EmpFile:


31523   7.50
31564   8.75
31585   9.35
32102  10.50
35559   6.35
36800  10.85
```

Figure 6.3 (cont.)

```
Sample run:

Hours worked for 31523:   40
Hourly rate:    $7.50
Wages:  $300.00

Hours worked for 31564:   35.5
Hourly rate:    $8.75
Wages:  $310.63

Hours worked for 31585:   43.5
Hourly rate:    $9.35
Wages:  $423.09

Hours worked for 32102:   45
Hourly rate:    $10.50
Wages:  $498.75

Hours worked for 35559:   29.5
Hourly rate:    $6.35
Wages:  $187.32

Hours worked for 36800:   39
Hourly rate:    $10.85
Wages:  $423.15


Total wages = $2142.94
```

The preceding examples used the boolean-valued function *eof* to detect the end-of-file mark. End-of-line marks can be detected by using the boolean-valued function *eoln*. This function is referenced by an expression of the form

eoln(file-name)

and has the value true if the data pointer is positioned at an end-of-line mark; otherwise, it has the value false. As with the *eof* function, if the file name and the parentheses are omitted, the standard system file *input* is assumed; thus

eoln

is equivalent to

eoln(input)

To illustrate the use of the *eoln* function, consider the problem of reading a text file and replacing multiple blanks with a single blank. Each line of the input file *InFile* is read, character by character, and copied to the output file *OutFile*, except that multiple blanks are not written.

To read each character in a line of *InFile,* we use an input loop whose repetition is controlled by the boolean expression **not** *eoln(Infile)*:

while not *eoln(InFile)* **do**
  begin
    read (InFile, Character);
      ⋮
  end (* **while not** *eoln* *);

A character is written to *OutFile* if it is not a blank or if the preceding character is not a blank; otherwise, it is not written. The following statements, where *PreviousNotBlank* and *CurrentNotBlank* are boolean variables, accomplish this:

PreviousNotBlank := *false*;
while not eoln(*InFile*) **do**
  begin
    read (InFile, Character);
    CurrentNotBlank := *Character* <> *Blank;*
    if *CurrentNotBlank* **or** *PreviousNotBlank* **then**
      write (OutFile, Character);
    PreviousNotBlank := *CurrentNotBlank*
  end (* **while not** *eoln* *);
writeln (OutFile);
readln (InFile)

When an end-of-line mark is reached, the function *eoln* returns the value true, and no more characters are read from that line. The data pointer in *InFile* must be advanced past this end-of-line mark by using a *readln* statement with no input list:

readln (InFile)

An end-of-line mark must be written to *OutFile* by using the statement

writeln (OutFile)

containing no output list.

This processing can be repeated for each line of *InFile* by placing these statements within a **while** statement controlled by the boolean expression **not** *eof(InFile)*. The complete program together with listings of *InFile* and *OutFile* are shown in Figure 6.4.

```
PROGRAM BlankStripper (InFile, OutFile);

(***********************************************************************

    Program to read the file InFile character by character and
    copy each line to OutFile but with multiple blanks replaced
    by single blanks.

    *****************************************************************)

CONST
    Blank = ' ';

VAR
    InFile,                     (* the input file *)
    OutFile : text;             (* the output file *)
    Character : char;           (* character read from InFile *)
    PreviousNotBlank,           (* previous character was not a blank *)
    CurrentNotBlank : boolean;  (* current character is not a blank *)

BEGIN
    reset (InFile);
    rewrite (OutFile);
    WHILE NOT eof(InFile) DO
        BEGIN
            PreviousNotBlank := false;
            WHILE NOT eoln(InFile) DO
                BEGIN
                    read (InFile, Character);
                    CurrentNotBlank := Character <> Blank;
                    IF CurrentNotBlank OR PreviousNotBlank THEN
                        write (OutFile, Character);
                    PreviousNotBlank := CurrentNotBlank
                END (* WHILE NOT eoln *);
            writeln (OutFile);
            readln (InFile)
        END (* WHILE NOT eof *)
END.
```

Listing of InFile:

```
Fourscore and    seven    years ago,
our    fathers  brought
       forth
on              this continent    a      new        nation
conceived           in                              liberty
   and dedicated to the proposition
that
all           men
              are        created         equal.
```

Figure 6.4

Figure 6.4 (cont.)

Listing of OutFile:

Fourscore and seven years ago,
our fathers brought
forth
on this continent a new nation
conceived in liberty
and dedicated to the proposition
that
all men
are created equal.

Exercises

For descriptions of the files *UserFile, InventoryFile,* and *LeastSquares-File,* see Appendix E.

1. Suppose that *InFile* contains the following:

> I think that I shall never see
> A poem lovely as a tree
>
> −JOYCE KILMER (1914)

and that a program begins with

program *Echo* (*InFile, output*);

var
   Character : *char*;
   Infile : *text*;

What output will be produced by each of the following statement parts?

(a) begin
        reset (*InFile*);
        while not *eof*(*InFile*) **do**
           begin
              while not *eoln*(*InFile*) **do**
                 begin
                    read (*InFile, Character*);
                    write (*Character*)
                 end (∗ **while not** *eoln* ∗);
              readln (*InFile*);
              writeln
           end (∗ **while not** *eof* ∗)
     end.

(b) begin
    reset (*InFile*);
    while not *eof*(*InFile*) **do**
      begin
        while not *eoln*(*InFile*) **do**
          begin
            read (*InFile*, *Character*);
            write (*Character*)
          end (* **while not** *eoln* *);
        readln (*InFile*)
      end (* **while not** *eof* *)
end.

(c) begin
    reset (*InFile*);
    while not *eof*(*InFile*) **do**
      begin
        while not *eoln*(*InFile*) **do**
          begin
            read (*InFile*, *Character*);
            write (*Character*)
          end (* **while not** *eoln* *);
        writeln
      end (* **while not** *eof* *)
end.

2. Write a program to read a text file and copy it into another text file in which the lines are numbered 1, 2, 3, . . . with a number at the left of each line.

3. Write a program that reads a text file and counts the vowels in the file.

4. Write a program that reads a text file and counts the occurrences in the file of specified characters entered during execution of the program.

5. People from three different income levels A, B, and C rated each of two different products with a number from 0 through 10. Construct a text file in which each line contains the income level and product rankings for one respondent. Then write a program that reads this information and calculates

  (a) For each income bracket, the average rating for Product 1.
  (b) The number of persons in Income Bracket B who rated both products with a score of 5 or higher.
  (c) The average rating for Product 2 by persons who rated Product 1 lower than 3.

Label all output and design the program so that it automatically counts the number of respondents.

6. Write a program to search *UsersFile* to find and display the resources used to date for specified users whose identification numbers are entered during execution of the program.

7. Write a program to search *InventoryFile* to find an item with a specified item number. If a match is found, display the item number and the number currently in stock; otherwise, display a message indicating that it was not found.

8. At the end of each month, a report is produced that shows the status of the account of each user in *UsersFile*. Write a program to accept the current date and produce a report of the following form:

USER ACCOUNTS—09/30/87

USER-ID	RESOURCE LIMIT	RESOURCES USED
100101	$750	$380
100102	$650	$598***
⋮	⋮	⋮

where the three asterisks (***) indicate that the user has already used 90 percent or more of the resources available to him or her.

9. Suppose that a collection of data indicates that the relation between two quantities x and y is roughly linear; that is, if we plot the points (x, y), they tend to fall along a straight line. In this case, one may ask for the linear equation

$$y = mx + b$$

that "best fits" these observed points. This **regression equation** could then be used to predict the value of y by evaluating the equation for a given value of x. A standard method for finding the **regression coefficients** m and b is the **method of least squares,** so named because it produces the line $y = mx + b$, for which the sum of the squares of the deviations of the observed y values from the predicted y values (using the equation) is as small as possible. This least squares line has the equation $y = mx + b$, where

$$\text{slope} = m = \frac{(\Sigma xy) - (\Sigma x)\bar{y}}{(\Sigma x^2) - (\Sigma x)\bar{x}}$$

$$y \text{ intercept} = b = \bar{y} - m\bar{x}$$

where

Σx is the sum of the x values.
Σx^2 is the sum of the squares of the x values.
Σxy is the sum of the products xy of corresponding x and y values
$\bar{x}$ and $\bar{y}$ are the means of the x and y values, respectively.

Write a program to calculate the regression coefficients m and b for your own test data and then use the data in *LeastSquaresFile*. Design the program to count the number of values so that it can be used for any collection of data.

10. Related to Exercise 9 is the problem of determining whether there is a linear relationship between the two quantities x and y. One statistical measure used for this purpose is the ***correlation coefficient***. It is equal to 1 if there is a perfect positive linear relationship between x and y, that is, if y increases linearly as x increases. If there is a perfect negative linear relationship between x and y, that is, if y decreases linearly as x increases, then the correlation coefficient has the value -1. A value of zero for the correlation coefficient indicates that there is no linear relationship between x and y, and nonzero values between -1 and 1 indicate a partial linear relationship between the two quantities. The correlation coefficient for a set of n pairs of x and y values is calculated by

$$\frac{n(\Sigma xy) - (\Sigma x)(\Sigma y)}{\sqrt{(n\Sigma x^2 - (\Sigma x)^2)(n\Sigma y^2 - (\Sigma y)^2)}}$$

where

Σx is the sum of the x values.
Σy is the sum of the y values.
Σx^2 is the sum of the squares of the x values.
Σy^2 is the sum of the squares of the y values.
Σxy is the sum of the products of corresponding x and y values.

Write a program to calculate the correlation coefficient for the x and y values in *LeastSquaresFile*.

11. Write a program that reads a text file and counts the number of characters in each line. The program should display the line number and the length of the shortest and longest lines in the file, as well as the average number of characters per line.

12. Write a program that reads a text file and writes it to another text file, but with leading blanks and blank lines removed. Run this program using the last two Pascal programs you have written as input files, and comment on whether you think indenting Pascal programs makes them more readable.

13. Write a file pagination program that reads a text file and prints it in blocks of 20 lines. If after printing a block of lines there still are lines in the file, then the program should allow the user to indicate whether more output is desired; if so, the next block should be printed; otherwise, execution of the program should terminate.

14. Write a program that reads a text file, counts the nonblank characters, the nonblank lines, the words, and the sentences, and calculates the

average number of characters per word and the average number of words per sentence. You may assume the following: the file contains only letters, blanks, commas, periods, semicolons, and colons; a word is any sequence of letters that begins a line or is preceded by one or more blanks and that is terminated by a blank, comma, semicolon, colon, period, or the end of a line; a sentence is terminated by a period.

Programming Pointers

In this chapter we described the input/output operations in Pascal programs and noted several features and rules that must be remembered. The major points are the following:

1. *After values have been read for each variable in the input list, the readln procedure advances the data pointer past the next end-of-line mark.* Thus, if there are more values in a line of input data than there are variables in the input list, some data values are not read. For example, suppose that *Number* is an integer variable, *xCoord* is a real variable, and the file *input* from which values are to be read contains

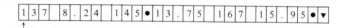

Then the statement

 readln (Number, xCoord)

reads the value 137 for *Number* and 8.24 for *xCoord* and advances the data pointer past the end-of-line mark.

Consequently, the value 145 is skipped. Moreover, if this statement is executed again, the value 13 is read for *Number*, but an error then occurs, since a real value cannot begin with a decimal point.

2. *After values have been obtained for each variable in the input list, the read procedure advances the data pointer so that it is positioned immediately after the last character read.* Thus, if the preceding *readln* statement is replaced with

 read (Number, xCoord)

the value 137 will be read for *Number*, 8.24 for *xCoord*, and the data pointer positioned at the blank following the character 4.

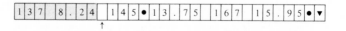

If the statement is executed again, the value 145 is read and assigned to *Number,* the end-of-line mark is ignored, and the value 13.75 is read for *xCoord*. The data pointer is then positioned at the blank following the character 5.

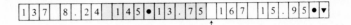

A potential problem in using the *read* statement is that an attempt to read beyond the end of the file may be made. For example, consider the following input loop:

while not *eof*(*input*) **do**
    begin
        read (*Number, xCoord*);
        ⋮
    end (* **while** *)

where the file *input* contains

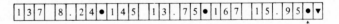

The values read and assigned to *Number* and *xCoord* are

Number	xCoord
137	8.24
145	13.75
167	15.95

After the last pair of values is obtained, the data pointer is positioned at the last end-of-line mark.

Because the data pointer is not positioned at the end-of-file mark, *eof*(*input*) is false, and so the *read* statement is executed again. This results in an attempt to read past the end of the file, which is an error. Note that the error does not occur if a *readln* statement is used, since after the last values 167 and 15.95 are read, the data pointer is advanced past the last end-of-line mark to the end-of-file mark. The boolean expression *eof*(*input*) is then true, and so execution of the while loop is terminated.

The way that the end-of-file mark is actually placed at the end of the file is system dependent. Usually in a batch mode of operation, it is automatically placed at the end of the file after the last data line has been entered. In an interactive mode, the user must usually enter some special control character from the keyboard to signal the end of the file.

3. *Leading blanks and leading end-of-line marks are ignored when reading numeric values but not when reading values for character variables.*
One consequence of this is that consecutive numeric values may be entered on separate lines. For example, if the data

   123
   456

are entered, the file *input* contains

The statement

   readln (Num1, Num2)

where *Num1* and *Num2* are integer variables, reads the value 123 for *Num1*, and advances the data pointer to the first end-of-line mark. This end-of-line mark is ignored when reading a value for *Num2* so that the value 456 is read. The *readln* procedure then advances the data pointer past the next end-of-line mark.

   In contrast, if *Ch1* and *Ch2* are character variables and the data

   A
   B

are entered so that the file *input* contains

```
A • B •
↑
```

the statement

   readln (Ch1, Ch2)

reads and assigns the letter A to *Ch1* and advances the data pointer to the first end-of-line mark. This end-of-line mark is then read, and a blank is assigned to *Ch2*. The data pointer is then advanced past the next end-of-line mark, and thus, the character B is not read.

4. *The data pointer in an input file always points to the next character to be read.* This "look-ahead" property of the data pointer is a common source of difficulty for beginning programmers. This is especially true for interactive input. To illustrate, consider the following statements:

```
Sum := 0;
while not eof(input) do
   begin
      writeln ('Enter number:');
      readln (Number);
      Sum := Sum + Number
   end (* while *);
```

On most systems, when the **while** statement is encountered, the boolean expression *eof(input)* cannot be evaluated since the system file *input* is empty because no values have yet been copied into it from the terminal. Before execution can proceed, the user must enter some value. As soon as the first character is entered, *eof(input)* can be evaluated and the statements within the loop executed. For example, if the user attempts to enter 123 as the first value for *Number*, the following may occur: As soon as the first character 1 is entered, the boolean expression *eof(input)* becomes false (since the data pointer is pointing at 1), and the *writeln* statement is executed:

1Enter number:

The remaining digits can then be entered and the return key depressed:

1Enter number:
23

The value 123 is then read for *Number* by the *readln* statement, the data pointer is advanced past the end-of-line mark, and the value 123 is added to *Sum*.

Since there is no character following this end-of-line mark, once again the boolean expression *eof(input)* cannot be evaluated, and the process is repeated. Thus, entering 456 as the second value for *Number* may result in

4Enter number:
56

One way to avoid this difficulty is to enter a blank as the first character to be read for *Number* so that the expression *eof(input)* can be evaluated and execution can proceed; this leading blank will be ignored in reading the value for *Number:*

bEnter number:
123

Of course, if a value for a character variable was being read, this leading blank would be read and assigned.

In summary, interactive input can be rather difficult with some systems, especially when the next character in the file *input* must be known so that some expression such as *eof(input)* can be evaluated. In the preceding example, perhaps the best solution is to use a data flag

```
Sum := 0;
writeln ('Enter number ( - 999 to stop):');
readln (Number);
while Number <> - 999 do
  begin
    Sum := Sum + Number;
    writeln ('Enter number:');
    readln (Number)
  end (* while *);
```

or to ask if there are more data values:

```
Sum := 0;
repeat
  writeln ('Enter number:');
  readln (Number);
  Sum := Sum + Number;
  write ('More (Y or N)? ');
  readln (Response)
until Response <> 'Y';
```

5. *Each file variable that names a permanent text file must appear in the file list of the program heading and must be declared in the variable section of the program to be of type text.*

6. *Before any data can be read from a user-defined text file, that file must be opened for input by using the procedure reset. Similarly, before any data can be written to a user-defined text file, it must be opened for output by using the procedure rewrite.* Remember the following, however:

   - Each call to *reset* positions the data pointer at the beginning of the file.
   - Each call to *rewrite* creates an empty file and any previous contents of the file are destroyed.

7. *File variables used as parameters must be variable parameters.*

Variations and Extensions

Input/output is one area in which some versions of Pascal may vary considerably from the standard. One finds such variations and extensions as the following:

- Output of boolean values to text files may not be allowed. (UCSD)
- Values entered from the keyboard for variables in a *read* or *readln* statement (or in a modified form of reference to these procedures) may not be echoed on the screen. (UCSD)
- The program heading may be optional (Turbo), or a modified form may be allowed or required (Macintosh, UCSD).
- The file *input* may not be a text file but rather a special file type (e.g., *interactive*). In particular, the difficulty caused by the look-

ahead property of the data pointer described in Programming Pointer 4 may not arise. (UCSD)

- As described in the footnotes on pages 239 and 242, modified references to procedures *reset* and *rewrite*,

  reset (file-variable, file-name)

  and

  rewrite (file-variable, file-name)

  may be required to open a file (Macintosh, UCSD), or it may be necessary to first call another procedure as in (Turbo)

  assign (file-variable, file-name);
  reset (file-variable)

  or

  assign (file-variable, file-name);
  rewrite (file-variable)

- It may be necessary to invoke a special *close* procedure to close a file before program execution is completed. (Macintosh, Turbo, UCSD)

See Appendix G for specific details.

7

Ordinal Data Types: Enumerated and Subrange

God created the integers; all the rest is the work of man.

LEOPOLD KRONECKER

The old order changeth, yielding place to new.

ALFRED LORD TENNYSON

In Chapter 3 we introduced the four predefined Pascal data types:

integer
boolean
char
real

These are called **simple** because a datum of one of these types is atomic, that is, it consists of a single item that cannot be subdivided. In addition to these simple data types, Pascal provides **structured** data types such as *text* in which a datum is a collection of items, and a **pointer** type used for data that are memory addresses. Figure 7.1 shows the various Pascal data types. The structured data types and pointers are discussed further in later chapters.

A simple data type is said to be an **ordinal** type if the values of that type are ordered so that each one except the first has an immediate predecessor, and each one except the last has an immediate successor. The type *integer* is an ordinal type since integer values are ordered by the natural ordering $-maxint$, . . . , -2, -1, 0, 1, 2, . . . , *maxint*. The type *boolean* is an ordinal type with the ordering *false, true*. The type *char* is also an ordinal type in which the ordering is that established by the collating sequence for the Pascal character set (see Section 4.2). The type *real* is not an ordinal type, however, because a given real number does not have an immediate predecessor or an immediate successor.

260

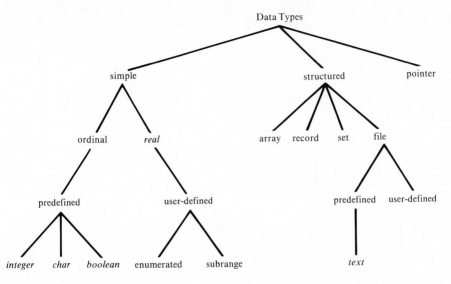

Figure 7.1

In addition to the predefined data types, Pascal allows user-defined data types. In this chapter we consider user-defined ordinal types.

7.1 The Type Section

The declaration part of a program consists of five sections arranged in the following order:

    label section
    constant section
    type section
    variable section
    subprogram section

We previously described the constant, variable, and subprogram sections, and we now consider the type section. (The label section is described in Appendix F.)

The type section is used to declare new data types or to rename previously defined types. It has the form

    type
        name-1 = *type-1*;
        name-2 = *type-2*;
            ⋮
        name-n = *type-n*;

where each *name-i* is a legal identifier that names the data type given by *type-i*. Each *type-i* is a predefined Pascal data type or a user-defined type.

For example, the type section

type
 Symbol = char;
 Logical = boolean;

declares *Symbol* and *Logical* to be synonyms for *char* and *boolean*, respectively. In the variable section we can then declare variables to be of type *Symbol* or *Logical*:

var
 Code, Class : Symbol;
 p, q, r : Logical;

Of course, the standard identifiers *char* and *boolean* may still be used in place of or in addition to the names *Symbol* and *Logical*, respectively.

Because the names of user-defined data types are Pascal identifiers, the scope rules for identifiers given in Section 5.5 apply to type identifiers as well. Recall that Scope Rule 1 states that an identifier declared in a program unit is not accessible outside that unit. Thus, the data type *Floating Point* declared in the function *Power* by

function *Power(x : real*; *n : integer) : real*;

 type
  FloatingPoint = real;

 var
  Prod : FloatingPoint;
   ⋮

may be used only to declare the types of local variables such as *Prod* within the function *Power*. It is not accessible outside this function and thus cannot be used to declare the type of *Power* itself or any identifiers outside this function.

Scope Rule 2 states that a global identifier is accessible within any subprogram in which that identifier is not declared locally. Thus any type declared in the type section of the main program is accessible within any subprogram that does not declare that identifier locally. This is one instance where the use of global identifiers is often necessary, since type identifiers may not be used as parameters for subprograms. For example, suppose that the type section

type
 Symbol = char;
 Logical = boolean;

appears in the declaration part of the main program, and consider the following procedure skeleton:

      procedure *Gamma* (*x, y* : *Logical*; **var** *c* : *char*);

        const
          Symbol = 'A';

        type
          Bit = *Logical*;
            ⋮

Since the global identifier *Logical* is not declared locally within procedure *Gamma*, it is accessible within *Gamma*. Thus parameters *x* and *y* may be declared of type *Logical*, and *Bit* may be declared as a synonym for *Logical* (and hence also *boolean*). The identifier *Symbol* is declared locally as the name of a constant in procedure *Gamma;* hence the global type identifier *Symbol* is not accessible within *Gamma*. Thus the type of the parameter *c* cannot be specified as *Symbol*.

    Scope Rule 3 asserts that identifiers declared in a subprogram can be accessed by any subprogram contained within it, provided that the identifier is not declared locally in the internal subprogram. Like the other scope rules, this rule also applies to type identifiers.

7.2 Enumerated Data Types

User-defined ordinal types can be divided into two classes: ***enumerated*** and ***subrange.*** Enumerated data types are considered in this section and subrange types in the next.

    Enumerated data types are defined simply by listing the values of that data type, separated by commas and enclosed in parentheses. These values must be legal identifiers, and no identifier may be listed in two different enumerated type definitions. For example,

    (*Sunday, Monday, Tuesday, Wednesday, Thursday, Friday, Saturday*)

defines an enumerated data type whose values are the identifiers *Sunday, Monday, Tuesday, Wednesday, Thursday, Friday*, and *Saturday*.

    The values of an enumerated data type are ordered by the listing of the values in the definition of that type. Thus, in this example, the predecessor of *Wednesday* is *Tuesday*, and *Thursday* is the successor of *Wednesday; Sunday* has no predecessor, and *Saturday* has no successor.

    The listing of values that defines an enumerated type can be associated with a type identifier in the type section; for example,

      type
        DaysOfWeek = (*Sunday, Monday, Tuesday, Wednesday, Thursday,*
                  Friday, Saturday);

This type identifier can then be used to specify the types of variables, formal parameters, and function values:

var
    Day : *DaysOfWeek*;
      ⋮

function *Convert*(*x*, *y* : *integer*) : *DaysOfWeek*;
      ⋮

procedure *Schedule* (*Day* : *DaysOfWeek*; **var** *NumberOfDay* : *integer*);
      ⋮

It is also possible to use the listing of values that define an enumerated type in the variable section to specify the type of a variable; for example,

var
    Day : (*Sunday, Monday, Tuesday, Wednesday, Thursday,*
          Friday, Saturday);

Such listings cannot be used, however, to declare the types of formal parameters or function values in function and procedure headings. Instead, a type identifier must be used; listing the values of an enumerated data type in a subprogram heading is *not* allowed.

Values of an enumerated type may be compared using the relational operators = and <>; for example,

if (*Day* <> *Sunday*) **and** (*Day* <> *Saturday*) **then**
    writeln ('Weekday');

Since the values of an enumerated type are ordered, they may also be compared by using <, >, <=, and >=. For example, the above **if** statement can also be written

if (*Monday* <= *Day*) **and** (*Day* < *Saturday*) **then**
    writeln ('Weekday');

The predefined Pascal functions *pred* and *succ* may be used to find the predecessor and successor, respectively, of a value of ordinal type. The following table gives several examples:

Function Reference	Value
pred(*Monday*)	*Sunday*
succ(*Friday*)	*Saturday*
succ(3)	4
pred(17)	16
pred('G')	'F'
succ('W')	'X'
succ(*false*)	*true*
pred(*true*)	*false*
pred(*Sunday*)	undefined
succ(*Saturday*)	undefined

Note that the function *pred* is undefined if its parameter is the first element of the ordinal type being considered, as is *succ* if its parameter is the last element.

Another predefined function used for processing ordinal data is *ord*. This function returns the **ordinal number** of an element; that is, its value is the number of the position of that element in the ordering for that type, with position numbering beginning with 0. Thus, for the data type *DaysOfWeek*,

ord(*Sunday*)

has the value 0, and

ord(*Tuesday*)

has the value 2. For the enumerated data type *FaceCard* defined by

type
    FaceCard = (*Jack, Queen, King*);

ord(*Jack*) = 0, ord(*Queen*) = 1, and ord(*King*) = 2.
For an integer *n*, $ord(n)$ has the value *n*. Thus

$ord(7) = 7$

$ord(-3) = -3$

For boolean type, ord(*false*) has the value 0 and ord(*true*) has the value 1. For character data, the ordinal number of a character is the number of its position in the collating sequence and is thus compiler dependent. If ASCII code is used, ord('A') = 65, ord('Z') = 90, and ord('2') = 50, whereas for EBCDIC, ord('A') = 193, ord('Z') = 233, and ord('2') = 242 (See the tables of ASCII and EBCDIC codes in Appendix A).

For character data the function *chr* is the inverse of *ord*. This function has an integer parameter and its value is the character whose ordinal number is that integer, provided that there is such a character. Thus $chr(65)$ = 'A' and $chr(50)$ = '2' if ASCII is used, whereas $chr(193)$ = 'A' and $chr(242)$ = '2' for EBCDIC. Note that for any element *c* of character type

$chr(ord(c)) = c$

and if *n* is the ordinal number of some character, then

$ord(chr(n)) = n$

One useful application of the functions *chr* and *ord* is in converting numerals to numbers and vice versa, as described in the exercises.

Because variables of an ordinal data type have values that are ordered, they may be used as control variables in **for** statements or as labels in a **case** statement. For example, if the variable *Day* is of type *DaysOfWeek*, described earlier, the statement

    case *Day* **of**
        Sunday   : *writeln* ('Sunday');
        Monday   : *writeln* ('Monday');
        Tuesday   : *writeln* ('Tuesday');
        Wednesday : *writeln* ('Wednesday');
        Thursday : *writeln* ('Thursday');
        Friday   : *writeln* ('Friday');
        Saturday : *writeln* ('Saturday')
    end (* **case** *)

can be used to display the day corresponding to the value of *Day*. The simple program in Figure 7.2 uses the variable *Day* of type *DaysOfWeek* in a **for** statement containing a similar **case** statement to display the names of the week-days.

```
PROGRAM DisplayWeekdays (input, output);

(*********************************************************************

   Program illustrating use of the enumerated data type DaysOfWeek.

********************************************************************)

TYPE
   DaysOfWeek = (Sunday, Monday, Tuesday, Wednesday, Thursday,
                 Friday, Saturday);

VAR
   Day : DaysOfWeek;

BEGIN
   FOR Day := Monday to Friday DO
      CASE Day OF
         Monday    : writeln ('Monday');
         Tuesday   : writeln ('Tuesday');
         Wednesday : writeln ('Wednesday');
         Thursday  : writeln ('Thursday');
         Friday    : writeln ('Friday');
      END (* CASE *)
END.


Sample run:


Monday
Tuesday
Wednesday
Thursday
Friday
```

Figure 7.2

A **while** statement can also be used in place of the **for** statement in this program. In this case, the function *succ* is used to "increment" the value of *Day:*

```
Day := Monday;
while Day <= Friday do
   begin
      case Day of
         Monday      : writeln ('Monday');
         Tuesday     : writeln ('Tuesday');
         Wednesday   : writeln ('Wednesday');
         Thursday    : writeln ('Thursday');
         Friday      : writeln ('Friday')
      end (* case *);
      Day := succ(Day)
   end (* while *)
```

If we attempt to print the names of all the days of the week by modifying this **while** statement as

```
Day := Sunday;
while Day <= Saturday do
   begin
      case Day of
         Sunday      : writeln ('Sunday');
         Monday      : writeln ('Monday');
         Tuesday     : writeln ('Tuesday');
         Wednesday   : writeln ('Wednesday');
         Thursday    : writeln ('Thursday');
         Friday      : writeln ('Friday');
         Saturday    : writeln ('Saturday')
      end (* case *);
      Day := succ(Day)
   end (* while *)
```

an error results. When the value of *Day* is *Saturday,* the value of *succ(Day)* is undefined.

Values of enumerated data types cannot be read from or written to text files, including the standard system files *input* and *output*. Nevertheless, it is sometimes convenient to use them to improve program readability by using a meaningful identifier rather than a cryptic code to represent an item. For example, using the values *Sunday, Monday, Tuesday,* . . . in place of the codes 0, 1, 2, . . . for the days of the week in a program obviously makes the program easier to read and understand. In such programs it may be necessary to use **case** statements like those described earlier to carry out the necessary conversion between the values of an enumerated data type and the numeric codes that can be input or character strings that can be displayed. The program in Figure 7.3 illustrates. It is a modification of the program in Figure 6.3 to read an employee number and an hourly rate from a permanent text file and calculate wages. During execution, the user enters the number of hours worked for each day from Sunday through Saturday. The procedure *PrintDay* is called by the procedure *GetEmployeeInfo* to display the character string corresponding to the value of *Day*.

```
PROGRAM Payroll (input, output, EmpFile);

(******************************************************************

    Program to calculate wages for several employees whose employee
    numbers and hourly rates are read from the file EmpFile and
    whose hours are entered by the user during execution.  Total
    wages for this payroll are also calculated.

******************************************************************)

VAR
    EmpFile : text;          (* the permanent employee file *)
    EmpNumber : integer;     (* employee number *)
    Hours,                   (* hours worked *)
    HourlyRate,              (* hourly pay rate *)
    Wages,                   (* total wages for employee *)
    TotalPayroll : real;     (* total wages for this payroll *)

PROCEDURE GetEmployeeInfo (VAR InFile : Text; VAR EmpNumber : integer;
                           VAR HourlyRate, WeekHours : real);

    (**************************************************************

        Procedure to read and return the employee number EmpNumber and
        HourlyRate from a text file InFile; Hours worked for each day
        are entered by the user and the total WeekHours is returned.
        The procedure PrintDay is used to print names of days.

    **************************************************************)

    TYPE
        DaysOfWeek = (Sunday, Monday, Tuesday, Wednesday,
                      Thursday, Friday, Saturday);

    VAR
        Day : DaysOfWeek;        (* day of the week *)
        DayHours : real;         (* hours worked each day *)

PROCEDURE PrintDay (Day : DaysOfWeek);

    (**************************************************************

        Procedure to print the name of the day corresponding to
        the value of Day of enumerated type DaysOfWeek.

    **************************************************************)
```

Figure 7.3

Figure 7.3 (cont.)

```
   BEGIN (* PrintDay *)
      CASE Day OF
         Sunday    : write ('Sunday:      ');
         Monday    : write ('Monday:      ');
         Tuesday   : write ('Tuesday:     ');
         Wednesday : write ('Wednesday:   ');
         Thursday  : write ('Thursday:    ');
         Friday    : write ('Friday:      ');
         Saturday  : write ('Saturday:    ');
      END (* CASE *)
   END (* PrintDay *);

BEGIN (* GetEmployeeInfo *)
   readln (InFile, EmpNumber, HourlyRate);
   writeln ('Hours worked for ', EmpNumber:1,' on   ');
   WeekHours := 0;
   FOR Day := Sunday TO Saturday DO
      BEGIN
         PrintDay (Day);
         readln (DayHours);
         WeekHours := WeekHours + DayHours
      END (* FOR *)
END (* GetEmployeeInfo *);

PROCEDURE CalculateWages (Hours, HourlyRate : real;
                          VAR Wages, TotalPayroll : real);

   (*****************************************************************

       Procedure to calculate and return Wages for employee who has
       worked the given number of Hours at the given HourlyRate.
       Hours above HoursLimit are paid at OvertimeFactor times
       the hourly rate.  Total wages for this payroll are also
       accumlated and returned.  The function RoundCents is used
       to round wages to the nearest cent.

   ****************************************************************)

   CONST
      OvertimeFactor = 1.5; (* overtime multiplication factor *)
      HoursLimit = 40.0;    (* overtime hours limit *)

   VAR
      RegWages,              (* regular wages *)
      OverWages : real;      (* overtime pay *)

   FUNCTION RoundCents (Amount : real) : real;

      (*************************************************************

           Returns Amount rounded to the nearest cent.

      ************************************************************)

      BEGIN (* RoundCents *)
         RoundCents := round(100 * Amount) / 100
      END (* RoundCents *);
```

Figure 7.3 (cont.)

```
    BEGIN (* CalculateWages *)
        IF Hours > HoursLimit THEN
            BEGIN (* Overtime *)
                RegWages := RoundCents(HourlyRate * HoursLimit);
                OverWages :=
                    RoundCents(OvertimeFactor * HourlyRate * (Hours - HoursLimit))
            END (* Overtime *)
        ELSE
            BEGIN (* No overtime *)
                RegWages := RoundCents(HourlyRate * Hours);
                OverWages := 0
            END (* No overtime *);
        Wages := RegWages + OverWages;
        TotalPayroll := TotalPayroll + Wages
    END (* CalculateWages *);

BEGIN (* main program *)
    reset (EmpFile);
    TotalPayroll := 0;
    WHILE NOT eof(EmpFile) DO
        BEGIN
            GetEmployeeInfo (EmpFile, EmpNumber, HourlyRate, Hours);
            writeln ('Hours worked:  ', Hours:4:2);
            writeln ('Hourly rate:   $', HourlyRate:4:2);
            CalculateWages (Hours, HourlyRate, Wages, TotalPayroll);
            writeln ('Wages:  $', Wages:4:2);
            writeln;
        END (* WHILE *);
    writeln;
    writeln ('Total wages = $', TotalPayroll:4:2)
END (* main program *).
```

```
Listing of EmpFile:
```

```
31523   7.50
31564   8.75
31585   9.35
32102  10.50
35559   6.35
36800  10.85
```

```
Sample run:
```

```
Hours worked by 31523 on
Sunday:       0
Monday:       8
Tuesday:      8
Wednesday:    8
Thursday:     8
Friday:       8
Saturday:     0
Hours worked:  40.00
Hourly rate:   $7.50
Wages:  $300.00
```

Figure 7.3 (cont.)

```
Hours worked by 31564 on
Sunday:      0
Monday:      7.5
Tuesday:     9.25
Wednesday:   8
Thursday:    8
Friday:      10
Saturday:    0
Hours worked:  42.75
Hourly rate:   $8.75
Wages:   $386.09

Hours worked by 31585 on
Sunday:      0
Monday:      8
Tuesday:     8
Wednesday:   9
Thursday:    8.5
Friday:      6
Saturday:    4
Hours worked:  43.50
Hourly rate:   $9.35
Wages:   $423.09

Hours worked by 32102 on
Sunday:      0
Monday:      0
Tuesday:     0
Wednesday:   0
Thursday:    8
Friday:      8
Saturday:    0
Hours worked:  16.00
Hourly rate:   $10.50
Wages:   $168.00


Total wages = $1277.18
```

7.3 Subrange Data Types

In the preceding section we considered the predefined ordinal data types *integer*, *boolean*, and *char*, and enumerated types. The set of values of each of these types is an ordered set. In some cases it may be convenient to use a data type that is a **subrange** of such a set. Subrange types are defined by specifying the first and last elements in the subrange in a declaration of the form

> *first-value .. last-value*

where *first-value* and *last-value* are values of some ordinal type called the **base type** and *first-value* ≤ *last-value*. A value of this subrange type may be any value *x* of the associated base type such that

first-value ≤ x ≤ last-value

Subrange definitions may be used in the variable section of a program unit to declare the type of a variable, or they may be associated with a type identifier in the type section. To illustrate, consider the following:

type
    DaysOfWeek = (*Sunday, Monday, Tuesday, Wednesday, Thursday,*
                Friday, Saturday);
    Weekdays = *Monday .. Friday*;
    WholeNumber = 0 .. *maxint*;
    Digit = '0' .. '9';

var
    SchoolDay : *Weekdays*;
    n : *WholeNumber*;
    DaysInMonth : 28..31;
    Cents : 0..99;

function *Factorial*(*n* : *WholeNumber*) : *WholeNumber*;
    ⋮

procedure *WorkSchedule* (*Day* : *Weekdays*; **var** *Code* : *Digit*);
    ⋮

Note that although the same value may not be listed in two different enumerated type definitions, it is permissible to use a value in two different subrange definitions.

A value to be assigned to a variable or function of a subrange type is checked to determine whether this value is in the specified range. If such ***range checking*** indicates that a value is out of range, an error message to that effect is displayed and execution is usually terminated. Thus, in the preceding example, if the value to be assigned to *n* is negative, then this value is out of range, and an out-of-range error occurs.

The main use of subrange types is to specify index types for arrays, as described in the next chapter. They can also be used to ensure that input data values are in a certain specified range, but in this case program execution will usually be terminated if an out-of-range error occurs. Thus it is perhaps better to allow invalid data values and use an **if** statement to check if they lie outside the given range; for example,

    readln (*Cents*);
    if (*Cents* < 0) **or** (*Cents* > 99) **then**
        writeln ('Data value ', *Cents*:1, ' out of range — ignored')
    else
        ⋮

The rules that govern the use of an ordinal type also apply to any subrange of that type. For example, because an integer value may be assigned to a real variable, it is also permissible to assign a value of type *WholeNumber* to a real variable in the preceding example. In general, two simple data types are said to be **compatible** if they are the same type, one is a subrange of the other, or both are subranges of the same base type. If *A* and *B* are two compatible data types, then wherever *A* may be used, *B* may also be used. Thus, in the preceding example, the function reference

> *Cents* := *Factorial(DaysInMonth)*

is valid, since the types of *Cents, Factorial,* and *DaysInMonth* are 0..99, *WholeNumber,* and 28..31, respectively, all of which are subranges of type *integer* and hence are compatible. Similarly, the statement

> *writeln* ('Number of cents = ', *Cents*:1)

is valid, since *Cents* is of type 0..99 which is compatible with type *integer*. It must be realized, of course, that range checking is performed. Thus, if the value of *Factorial* in this reference is 100 or larger, range checking of the value to be assigned to *Cents* indicates an error.

Exercises

1. **(a)** Write a type section that defines the enumerated type *MonthAbbrev*, whose values are abbreviations of the months of the year and consist of the first three letters of the months' names; also, define the subrange type *MonthNumber* consisting of the integers 1, 2, 3, . . . , 12.
   (b) Write a function whose parameter is the number of a month and whose value is the corresponding value of type *MonthAbbrev*.

2. **(a)** Write a type section that defines type *Numeral* to be the subrange of character type consisting of the characters '0', '1', '2', . . . , '9' and the type *Number* to be the subrange of integers consisting of the values 0, 1, 2, . . . , 9.
   (b) Write a function whose parameter is a variable of type *Numeral* and whose value is the corresponding numeric value. (*Hint:* Use the function *ord*.)
   (c) Write another function whose parameter is an integer in the range 0 through 9 and whose value is the corresponding numeral. (*Hint:* Use the functions *ord* and *chr*.)

3. For the enumerated type *MonthAbbrev* of Exercise 1, find the values of the following expressions:

   (a) *Jan < Aug*   **(b)** *Sep <= Sep*   **(c)** *succ(Sep)*
   (d) *pred(Apr)*   **(e)** *succ(succ(Aug))* **(f)** *pred(pred(Aug))*
   (g) *succ(pred(Mar))*   **(h)** *succ(pred(Jan))* **(i)** *ord(Jun)*
   (j) *ord(Sep) − ord(Jan)* **(k)** *ord(succ(May)) − ord(May)*
   (l) *chr(ord(Sep) + ord('0'))*

4. Write a function or procedure whose parameters are a nonnegative integer *n* and a month abbreviation *Abbrev,* like that in Exercise 1, and finds the "*n*th successor" of *Abbrev.* The 0th successor of *Abbrev* is *Abbrev* itself; for *n* > 0, the *n*th successor of *Abbrev* is the *n*th month following *Abbrev.* For example, the fourth successor of *Aug* is *Dec,* and the sixth successor of *Aug* is *Feb.*

5. Repeat Exercise 4 but define the function or procedure recursively.

6. Using the enumerated type *DaysOfWeek* in the text, write a program to read a customer's account number and current balance; then for each weekday (Monday through Friday) read a series of transactions by that customer of the form D (deposit) or W (withdrawal) followed by an amount, and update the balace with this amount. Display the new balance after all transactions for the week have been processed.

7. **(a)** Write a function whose parameters are a month of type *Month-Abbrev* (see Exercise 1) and a year in the range from 1538 through 1999 and whose value is the number of days in the month. Remember that February has 28 days, except in a leap year, when it has 29. A leap year is one in which the year number is divisible by 4, except for centesimal years (those ending in 00); these centesimal years are not leap years unless the year number is divisible by 400. (Thus 1950 and 1900 are not leap years, but 1960 and 1600 are.)

   (b) Use the function of part (a) in a program to read two dates in the form *mm dd yyyy* (such as 7 4 1776 and 1 1 1987), and calculate the number of days that have elapsed between the two dates.

Programming Pointers

In this chapter we discussed user-defined ordinal types. The following are some of the major points to remember when using them:

1. *Type identifiers must be used to declare formal parameters in a subprogram and the type of a function.* One may not list the values of an ordinal type in a function or procedure heading to specify the type of a parameter or the type of a function value. For example, the heading

   function *CardValue(Card* : *(Jack, Queen, King))* : 11..13;

is not valid. The enumerated type *(Jack, Queen, King)* and the subrange type 11..13 must be associated with type identifiers such as

   type
      FaceCard = *(Jack, Queen, King);*
      FaceValue = 11..13;

in a program unit that contains this function definition, and these type identifiers used in the heading:

   function *CardValue* *(Card* : *FaceCard)* : *FaceValue;*

2. *The scope rules given in Chapter 5 apply to type identifiers.*

3. *Values listed in an enumerated type definition must be legal identifiers and may not appear in any other enumerated type definition within that program unit.* For example, the declaration

type
    Assortment = (123A, 579, P-123, ABC-DE, 'Monday', 'A');

is not allowed, nor is

type
    Weekdays = (*Monday, Tuesday, Wednesday, Thursday,*
                Friday);
    VacationDays = (*Friday, Saturday, Sunday, Monday*);

4. *The function pred(x) is undefined if x is the first value of an ordinal type; succ(x) is undefined if x is the last value.*

5. *Values of an enumerated data type cannot be input from or output to text files, including the standard files input and output.*

6. *If a variable or function is declared to be of some subrange type, an error results if one attempts to assign it a value that is not in this subrange.* For example, if x and y are declared by

var
    x, y : 1..10;

the statement

for x := 1 **to** 10 **do**
    begin
        y := *x* * *x*;
        writeln (*y*)
    end

results in an error when x reaches the value 4 because the value of $x * x$ is then outside the range 1..10 and cannot be assigned to y.

Variations and Extensions

Most Pascal dialects are consistent with the standard in processing ordinal types. However, there are a few variations and extensions:

- Input/output of enumerated types may be allowed. (Macintosh)
- Special type-conversion features may be provided. (Turbo)
- Special compiler directives may be required to enable range-checking. (Turbo)

Appendix G contains details of these features.

One-Dimensional Arrays

With silver bells, and cockle shells,
And pretty maids all in a row.

MOTHER GOOSE

The simple data types we have considered thus far represent single values. In many situations, however, it is necessary to process a collection of values that are related in some way, for example, a list of test scores, a collection of measurements resulting from some experiment, or a sales-tax table. Processing such collections using only simple data types can be extremely cumbersome, and for this reason, most high-level languages include special features for structuring such data. As we noted in Chapter 7, Pascal provides four structured data types: arrays, files, records, and sets. In this chapter we consider arrays, their implementation in Pascal, and how they may be used to process lists and strings of characters.

8.1 Introduction to Arrays; Indexed Variables

In Chapter 6 we introduced files, which are collections of related data items used in input/output operations. In standard Pascal, these data items can be retrieved only *sequentially;* that is, an item can be accessed only by searching from the beginning of the file. This sequential character of files, together with the fact that they are usually stored in secondary memory from which data retrieval is rather slow, means that files are not practical in many applications. For some applications we prefer a ***direct access*** structure that is stored in main memory and has the property that a data item can be stored in or retrieved ·from the structure directly by specifying its location in the structure. One such data structure is an ***array*** in which a fixed number of data items, all of the same type, are organized in a sequence and direct access to each item is possible by specifying its position in this sequence.

Almost every high-level language provides a ***predefined data structure,*** also called a ***structured data type,*** that implements arrays. In Pascal, we can refer to an entire array using an ***array variable*** and can access each individual element or ***component*** of the array by an ***indexed variable*** formed by appending an ***index*** enclosed in brackets to the array variable. This index specifies the position of the array component to be accessed. Thus if X is an array variable, the indexed variable $X[3]$ refers to the third element in this array. (Indices are also called ***subscripts*** and indexed variables ***subscripted variables,*** since subscript notation such as X_3 is commonly used in mathematics to refer to a specified element in a sequence.)

For example, a program to process the test scores for ten students might use an array to store these scores. The computer must first be instructed to reserve a sequence of ten memory locations for the scores. The declarations

const
    NumScores = 10;

type
    ArrayOfScores = **array**[1..*NumScores*] **of** *integer*;

var
    Score : *ArrayOfScores*;

instruct the compiler to establish an array with name *Score* consisting of ten memory locations in which integer values will be stored and to associate the indexed variables *Score*[1], *Score*[2], . . . , *Score*[10] with these locations.

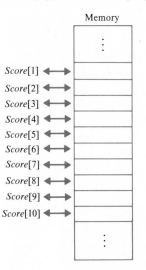

Each indexed variable names an individual memory location and hence can be used in much the same way as an ordinary variable can. For example, the assignment statement

    Score[4] := 83

stores the value 83 in the fourth location of the array *Score;* and the output statement

writeln (Score[10])

displays the value stored in the tenth location of the array *Score.*

As these examples illustrate, each component of the array *Score* is directly accessible. This direct access is accomplished by means of **address translation.** The address of the first word in the memory block reserved for an array, called the **base address** for the array, is used to store the first component, and the address of any other component is calculated in terms of this base address. For example, if the base address for the array *Score* is *b* and each score can be stored in a single memory word, then the address of *Score*[1] is *b*, the address of *Score*[2] is $b + 1$, that for *Score*[3] is $b + 2$, and in general, the address of *Score*[*i*] is $b + i - 1$.

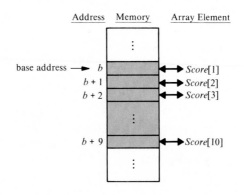

If *w* memory words are required for each component, then *Score*[1] would be stored in *w* consecutive words beginning at the word with address *b*, *Score*[2] in a block beginning at address $b + w$, and in general, *Score*[*i*] in a block of size *w* beginning at address $b + (i - 1)*w$. Each time an array component is accessed using an indexed variable, this address translation must be performed by the system software and/or hardware to determine the location of that component in memory.

Arrays such as *Score* involve only a single index and are commonly called **one-dimensional arrays.** Pascal programs, however, may process arrays of more than one dimension, in which case each element of the array is designated by attaching the appropriate number of indices to the array name. In this chapter we consider only one-dimensional arrays; multidimensional arrays are considered in the next chapter.

The name of a one-dimensional array, the type of its components, and the type of its index are declared by means of an **array declaration** of the form

array[*index-type*] **of** *component-type*

where *index-type* specifies the type of the indices and may be any ordinal type; *component-type* specifies the type of the array elements, or components, and may be any type. For example, the array declaration.

array[1..10] **of** *real*

specifies that the index may be any of the values 1, 2, 3, . . . , 10 and that the type of each array element is *real*. The array declaration

array['A'..'Z'] **of** *integer*

specifies a one-dimensional array whose index may be any of the characters A, B, . . . , Z, and whose components are of integer type.

Although array declarations may appear in the variable section of the declaration part of a program to specify the type of an array, it is preferable to associate them with type identifiers, as in

const
   NumLimit = 100;

type
   xRange = −5..10;
   Letter = 'A'..'Z';
   RealArray = **array**[*xRange*] **of** *real*;
   ArrayOfNumbers = **array**[0..*NumLimit*] **of** 1..999;
   FrequencyArray = **array**[*Letter*] **of** *integer*;
   Line = **array**[1..80] **of** *char*;

and then use these type identifiers to declare the types of arrays:

var
   Coordinate : *RealArray*;
   Number : *ArrayOfNumbers*;
   CharCount : *FrequencyArray*;
   TextLine : *Line*;

An important feature of the notation used for arrays is that the index attached to the array name may be a variable or an expression. For example, the statement

if *Score*[*n*] > 90 **then**
   writeln (*Score*[*n*]:3, ' = A')

retrieves the *n*th item of the array *Score,* compares it with 90, and prints it with a letter grade of A if it exceeds 90. The statement

if *Score*[*i*] > *Score*[*i* + 1] **then**
   begin
     Temp := *Score*[*i*];
     Score[*i*] := *Score*[*i* + 1];
     Score[*i* + 1] := *Temp*
   end

interchanges the contents of *Score*[*i*] and *Score*[*i* + 1] if the first is greater than the second.

Using an array reference in which the index is a variable or an expression within a loop that changes the value of the index on each pass through the loop is a convenient way to process each item in the array. Thus

> **for** *i* := 1 **to** *NumScores* **do**
> **if** *Score*[*i*] > 90 **then**
> *writeln* (*Score*[*i*], ' = A')

retrieves each item of the array *Score* in sequence, beginning with *Score*[1], compares it with 90, and prints it with a letter grade of A if it exceeds 90. It is equivalent to the following sequence of **if** statements:

> **if** *Score*[1] > 90 **then**
> *writeln* (*Score*[1], ' = A');
> **if** *Score*[2] > 90 **then**
> *writeln* (*Score*[2], ' = A');
> **if** *Score*[3] > 90 **then**
> *writeln* (*Score*[3], ' = A');
> ⋮
> **if** *Score*[10] > 90 **then**
> *writeln* (*Score*[10], ' = A')

Figure 8.1 illustrates.

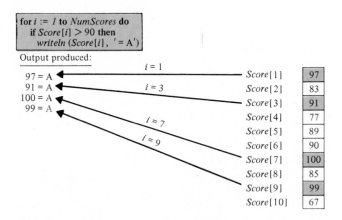

Figure 8.1. Using a variable index to access each element of array *Score*.

The syntax diagram for declarations of one-dimensional arrays is shown in the following display. Note that an array declaration may include the specification **packed.** This directs the compiler to store the data internally in a special compact format. Packed arrays are considered in more detail in Section 8.4.

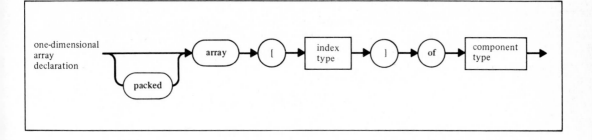

8.2   List Processing Using One-Dimensional Arrays

Many problems involve processing lists, a list of test scores, a list of names, a list of employee records, and so on. Such processing includes displaying all the items in the list, inserting new items, deleting items, searching the list for a specified item, and sorting the list so that the items are in a certain order. Since most programming languages do not provide a predefined list type (LISP, an acronym for LISt Processing, is one exception), lists must be processed using some other structure. This is commonly done using an array to store the list, storing the ith list item in the ith position of the array.

To illustrate, suppose we wish to process a list of test scores, as in the example of the preceding section. If we declare the array *Score* by

> **const**
>   *NumScores* = 10;
>
> **type**
>   *ListOfScores* = **array**[1..*NumScores*] **of** *integer*;
>
> **var**
>   *Score* : *ListOfScores*;

we can read the scores into the array *Score* by using an input statement within a repetition structure. For example, we might use a **for** statement

> **for** $i := 1$ **to** *NumScores* **do**
>   *read* (*Score*[i]);

where the type of the control variable i is compatible with the subrange type 1..*NumScores* specified for the array indices in the array declaration. A **while** statement

> $i := 1$;
> **while** $i <=$ *NumScores* **do**
>   **begin**
>   *read* (*Score*[i]);
> $i := i + 1$
>   **end**;

or a **repeat** statement

> *i* := 1;
> **repeat**
>   *read* (*Score*[*i*]);
>   *i* := *i* + 1
> **until** *i* > *NumScores*;

could also be used. If we wish to declare a larger array

> **const**
>   *ScoresLimit* = 100;
>
> **type**
>   *ListOfScores* = **array**[1..*ScoresLimit*] **of** *integer*;
>
> **var**
>   *Score* : *ListOfScores*;
>   *NumScores* : *integer*;

and use only part of it, the statements

> *readln* (*NumScores*);
> **if** *NumScores* > *ScoresLimit* **then**
>   *writeln* ('At most ', *ScoresLimit*:1, ' scores can be processed')
> **else**
>   **for** *i* := **to** *NumScores* **do**
>   *read* (*Score*[*i*]);

might be used. Note that after a value is read for *NumScores,* a check is made to ensure that this value is not too large, since *an error results if an attempt is made to use an index that is out of range.* If the value 15 is read for *NumScores,* the *read* statement is executed fifteen times, and values are assigned to the first fifteen positions *Score*[1], *Score*[2], . . . , *Score*[15] of the array. The rest of the array, *Score*[16], . . . , *Score*[100], is unchanged; these array elements are undefined unless values have previously been assigned to them.

The items in a list may be displayed by placing an output statement within a repetition structure. For example, the statement

> **for** *i* := 1 **to** *NumScores* **do**
>   *writeln* (*Score*[*i*]:3);

displays the first *NumScores* entries of the list *Score* on separate lines, one per line. The statement

> **for** *i* := 1 **to** *NumScores* **do**
>   *write* (*Score*[*i*]:3);

displays these entries on the same line. Note that subsequent output will also appear on this same line. This can be avoided by following the **for** statement with a *writeln* statement having no output list:

> **for** *i* := 1 **to** *NumScores* **do**
>   *write* (*Score*[*i*]:3);
> *writeln*;

Other kinds of list processing are also easy using repetition structures. For example, the mean of the scores in the list *Score* can be calculated by

> *Sum* := 0;
> **for** *i* := 1 **to** *NumScores* **do**
>   *Sum* := *Sum* + *Score*[*i*];
> *MeanScore* := *Sum* / *NumScores*;
> *writeln* ('Mean of the scores is: ', *MeanScore*:3:1);

To display the scores that are greater than the mean, we can use the statement

> **for** *i* := 1 **to** *NumScores* **do**
>   **if** *Score*[*i*] > *MeanScore* **then**
>   *writeln* (*Score*[*i*]:3)

The program in Figure 8.2 uses these statements to read a list of up to 100 scores, calculate their mean, and display a list of scores greater than the mean.

```
PROGRAM TestScores (input, output);

(*********************************************************************

  Program to read a list of test scores, calculate their mean,
  and print a list of scores greater than the mean.

*********************************************************************)
CONST
   ScoresLimit = 100;      (* maximum number of scores *)

TYPE
   ListOfScores = ARRAY[1..ScoresLimit] OF integer;

VAR
   Score : ListOfScores;   (* list of scores *)
   NumScores,              (* number of scores *)
   i : integer;            (* index *)
   Sum,                    (* sum of the scores *)
   MeanScore : real;       (* mean of the scores *)
```

Figure 8.2

Figure 8.2 (Cont.)

```
BEGIN
   write ('Enter number of scores:   ');
   readln (NumScores);
   IF NumScores > ScoresLimit THEN
      writeln ('At most ', ScoresLimit:1, ' scores can be processed')
   ELSE
      BEGIN
         (* Read the scores and store them in array Score *)

         writeln ('Enter the scores, as many per line as desired.');
         FOR i := 1 TO NumScores DO
            read (Score[i]);

         (* Calculate the mean of the scores *)

         Sum := 0;
         FOR i := 1 TO NumScores DO
            Sum := Sum + Score[i];
         MeanScore := Sum / NumScores;
         writeln ('Mean of the scores is ', MeanScore:3:1);

         (* Print list of scores greater than the mean *)

         writeln;
         writeln ('List of scores greater than the mean:');
         FOR i := 1 TO NumScores DO
            IF Score[i] > MeanScore THEN
               writeln (Score[i]:3)
      END (* ELSE *)
END.
```

```
Sample run:


Enter number of scores:   15
Enter the scores, as many per line as desired.
88 77 56 89 100 99 55 35 78 65
69 83 71 38 95
Mean of the scores is 73.2

List of scores greater than the mean:
 88
 77
 89
100
 99
 78
 83
 95
```

In most of our examples of arrays, the indices have been positive integers, ranging from 1 up through some upper limit. This is probably the most common index type, but as stated in the preceding section, the type of the index may be any ordinal type. For example, the declarations

type
    DaysOfWeek = (*Sunday, Monday, Tuesday, Wednesday, Thursday,*
                    Friday, Saturday);
    DaysArray = **array**[*DaysOfWeek*] **of** *real*;

var
    HoursWorked : *DaysOfWeek*;

establish a one-dimensional array *HoursWorked* with seven locations, each of which can store a real number:

Values can be read into these seven locations by the statement

    for *Day* := *Sunday* **to** *Saturday* **do**
      read (*HoursWorked*[*Day*]);

where the index *Day* is assumed to be of type *DaysOfWeek*, and the values read into the array are of real type. In general, the type of the indices in any array reference must be compatible with that specified in the array declaration, and the type of values stored in the array must be compatible with the component type. Recall that two ***types are compatible*** if they are the same, one is a subrange of the other, or both are subranges of the same underlying type.

To illustrate further the use of nonnumeric indices to access array elements, consider the problem of reading a line of upper-case text and counting the number of occurrences of each of the letters A, B, . . . , Z. The program in Figure 8.3 solves this problem by using the array *Frequency* declared by

type
    Letter = 'A'..'Z';
    CharCountArray = **array**[*Letter*] **of** *integer*;

var
    Frequency : *CharCountArray*;

The array *Frequency* is used to count the occurrences of each of the letters so that *Frequency*['A'] is the number of occurrences of A in the line of text, *Frequency*['B'] is the number of occurrences of B, and so on.

```
PROGRAM LetterCount (input, output);

(*************************************************************************

   Program to count the occurrences of each of the upper-case letters
   A, B, ..., Z in a line of text.  The array Frequency indexed by
   the subrange 'A'..'Z' is used for this.  If Character is any one
   of these 26 letters, Frequency[Character] is the number of
   occurrences of Character in the text line.

*************************************************************************)

TYPE
   Letter = 'A'..'Z';
   CharCountArray = ARRAY[Letter] OF integer;

VAR
   Frequency : CharCountArray;    (* frequencies of letters *)
   Character : char;              (* character from text line *)

BEGIN

   (* First initialize all frequencies to 0 *)

   FOR Character := 'A' TO 'Z' DO
      Frequency[Character] := 0;

   (* Read the line of text and count occurrences of letters *)

   writeln ('Enter the line of text:');
   WHILE NOT eoln DO
      BEGIN
         read (Character);
         IF ('A' <= Character) AND (Character <= 'Z') THEN
            Frequency[Character] := Frequency[Character] + 1
      END (* WHILE *);

   (* Print the frequencies *)

   writeln;
   FOR Character := 'A' TO 'Z' DO
      writeln ('Frequency of ', Character, ':  ', Frequency[Character]:2)
END.
```

Sample run:

Enter the line of text:
THE QUICK BROWN FOX JUMPED OVER THE LAZY DOGS AND RAN AWAY.

Frequency of A: 5
Frequency of B: 1
Frequency of C: 1
Frequency of D: 3
Frequency of E: 4

Figure 8.3

Figure 8.3 (Cont.)

```
Frequency of F:    1
Frequency of G:    1
Frequency of H:    2
Frequency of I:    1
Frequency of J:    1
Frequency of K:    1
Frequency of L:    1
Frequency of M:    1
Frequency of N:    3
Frequency of O:    4
Frequency of P:    1
Frequency of Q:    1
Frequency of R:    3
Frequency of S:    1
Frequency of T:    2
Frequency of U:    2
Frequency of V:    1
Frequency of W:    2
Frequency of X:    1
Frequency of Y:    2
Frequency of Z:    1
```

Sometimes it is necessary to copy the elements of one array into a second array. Suppose, for example, that arrays *Alpha* and *Beta* are declared by

type
    RealList = **array**[1..5] **of** *real*;

var
    Alpha, Beta : *RealList*;

If values have been assigned to the array *Alpha,* they can be copied to the array *Beta* by the statement

    for *i* := 1 **to** 5 **do**
        Beta[*i*] := *Alpha*[*i*]

This assignment of the elements of the array *Alpha* to the array *Beta* can be done more simply by the assignment statement

    Beta := *Alpha*

In general, one array may be assigned to another array only when they have the **same type.** This means that they must be declared by the same type identifier or by **equivalent** type identifiers. Two type identifiers are equivalent if their definitions can be traced back to a common *type identifier*. For example, consider the following type definitions:

type
    Aarray = **array**[1..5] **of** *real*;
    Barray = *Aarray*;
    Carray = *Aarray*;
    Darray = *Barray*;
    Earray = **array**[1..5] **of** *real*;

Type identifiers *Barray* and *Carray* are equivalent to *Aarray* and to each other since they are synonyms for the type *identifier Aarray*. Similarly, *Darray* is a synonym for *Barray* and is therefore equivalent to *Barray*. Type identifiers *Aarray, Carray,* and *Darray* are equivalent because their definitions can be traced back to a common type *identifier* (*Aarray*). It is important to note, however, that even though the definitions of *Aarray* and *Barray* are identical, these type identifiers are not equivalent because they are not defined using a common type *identifier*. Thus, if arrays *A, B, C, D,* and *E* are declared by

var
    A : *Aarray*;
    B : *Barray*;
    C : *Carray*;
    D : *Darray*;
    E : *Earray*;

the array assignment statements

    B := *A*;
    B := *C*;
    B := *D*;
    C := *D*;

are all valid because arrays *A, B, C,* and *D* all have the same type, but the assignment statement

    A := *E*;

is not valid.[1]

Arrays may also be used as parameters for functions and procedures, but the value of a function may not be an array. To illustrate, consider the following function:

---

[1] In some versions of Pascal, the definition of "same type" may be less restrictive; arrays *A* and *E* might be considered to have the same type.

```
function Mean (var Item : List; NumItems : integer) : real;

    (* Function to find the mean of a list of NumItems
       numbers stored in an array Item *)

    var
        i : integer; (* index *)
        Sum : real; (* sum of the numbers *)

    begin (* Mean *)
        if NumItems = 0 then
            begin
                writeln ('No elements—returning mean of 0');
                Mean := 0
            end (* if *)
        else
            begin
                Sum := 0;
                for i := 1 to NumItems do
                    Sum := Sum + Item[i];
                Mean := Sum / NumItems
            end (* else *)
    end (* Mean *);
```

Because the types of formal parameters must be specified by type identifiers, an array declaration such as **array**[1..100] **of** *integer* cannot be used to specify the type of the formal parameter *Item*.

When this function is referenced, the type of each actual parameter that is an array must be the same as the type of the corresponding formal parameter. Thus, to use this function in the program of Figure 8.2 (since type identifiers may *not* be passed as parameters), it would be necessary to make the type identifier *List* equivalent to the type identifier *ListOfScores* in the main program:

```
type
    ListOfScores = array[1..ScoresLimit] of integer;
    List = ListOfScores;
```

or use the same type identifier, either *ListOfScores* or *List*, both in the main program and in this function. The statement

```
MeanScore := Mean(Score, NumScores);
```

could then be used in the main program to calculate the mean score.

In this function *Mean*, the array *Item* is a variable parameter, although this is not required. If it were a value parameter, however, then a reference to this function would require copying the elements of the actual array into *Item*. This would produce two copies of the same list of values and would therefore not be an efficient use of memory. Moreover, the process of copying the elements of one array into another is time-consuming.

An array must be a variable parameter if the subprogram is to return the array to the program unit that calls it. For example, a procedure to read a list of items into **an** array *Item,* count the number of elements that were read, and return both **this** array and the count to the main program must declare both the array and the count as variable parameters:

> **procedure** *ReadList* (**var** *Item* : *List*; *ListLimit* : *integer*;
> **var** Count : *integer*);

> (∗ Procedure to read list elements into array *Item* that has
>   at most *ListLimit* elements and count the number of
>   elements read. Both *Item* and *Count* are returned. ∗)

> **var**
>   *Response* : *char*; (∗ user response ∗)

> **begin** (∗ *ReadList* ∗)
>   *writeln* ('Enter the list of items, as many per line as desired.');
>   *writeln* ('Note: At most ', *ListLimit*:1, ' items can be read.');
>   *writeln*;
>   *Count* := 0;
>   **repeat**
>   *write* ('Items: ');
>   **while not** *eoln* **do**
>   **begin**
>   *Count* := *Count* + 1;
>   *read* (*Item*[*Count*])
>   **end** (∗ **while** ∗);
>   *readln*;
>   *write* ('More (Y or N)? ');
>   *readln* (*Response*)
>   **until** *Response* <> 'Y'
> **end** (∗ *ReadList* ∗);

The examples in this section indicate that arrays are very useful for processing lists. The array implementation of lists does have its drawbacks, however. One is that whereas a list need not have a fixed length, an array must have a fixed number of elements. This means that it is possible to declare the array to have exactly the right size only if the list is *static,* that is, its size never changes. The common approach otherwise is to estimate the maximum size of the list and declare the array to have this number of components. However, if we declare the array too small, we run the risk of an error arising from indices that are out of range, or we may lose some of the list elements because there is no room for them in the array. If we make the array too large, then we may be wasting a considerable part of the memory allocated to it.

Another weakness of the array implementation of lists is that although algorithms for the insertion and deletion operations are quite easy to write (as the exercises ask you to do), they are not very efficient. For example, to insert the new value 75 at position 6 in the list of ten integers

23, 34, 48, 55, 68, 80, 82, 89, 91, 97

would require shifting the array elements in positions 6 through 10 into positions 7 through 11 to make room for the new value:

23, 34, 48, 55, 68, 80, 82, 84, 91, 97

23, 34, 48, 55, 68, 75, 80, 82, 84, 91, 97

Similarly, deleting an item requires moving array elements; for example, to remove the second number in this last list, we must shift the array elements in positions 3 through 11 into positions 2 through 10 to "close the gap":

23, 34, 48, 55, 68, 75, 80, 82, 84, 91, 97

23, 48, 55, 68, 75, 80, 82, 84, 91, 97

If insertions and deletions are restricted to the ends of the list, then array implementations that do not require moving array elements are possible. Two important special cases are stacks and queues. A **stack** is a list in which elements may be inserted (**pushed**) and deleted (**popped**) at only one end, called the **top** of the stack. If elements may be inserted only at one end (the **rear**) and deleted only at the other (the **front**), the list is called a **queue**. Array implementations of stacks and queues are described in the exercises at the end of the next section. Array implementations of stacks are considered in detail in Section 14.1, and this implementation is used in Section 14.2 to process arithmetic expressions. This application of arrays does not require any additional background, and those who are interested may wish to consider it in addition to the applications of arrays presented in the next section.

Arrays work very well for static lists and reasonably well for lists whose maximum sizes can be estimated and for which insertions and deletions are infrequent or are restricted to the ends of the list. **Dynamic** lists whose sizes may vary greatly during processing and those in which items are frequently inserted and/or deleted anywhere in the list are better implemented using a linked structure as described in Chapter 14.

8.3 Applications: Class Averages, Sorting, Searching

EXAMPLE 1: Class Averages. Consider the problem of calculating the average score received on a test by students in each of the four classes freshman, sophomore, junior, and senior. For each student, a score is to be read together with a class code of 1, 2, 3, or 4, representing the class to which the student belongs. For each class we must calculate the average score received by the students in that class. To do this, we must find the number of students in each class and the sum of the scores for all of the students in that class. To illustrate the use of arrays having an enumerated data type for indices, we use the following one-dimensional arrays:

Number: *Number*[*Class*] is the number of students in the class specified by the index *Class* where the value of *Class* is *Freshman, Sophomore, Junior,* or *Senior.*

SumOfScores: *SumOfScores*[*Class*] is the sum of the scores for all students in the class specified by the value of *Class*.

The program in Figure 8.4 solves this problem by using three procedures, *Initialize, ReadTheData,* and *Calculate,* and the function *ConvertCode.* The first procedure is used to initialize the arrays *Number* and *SumOfScores* to zero. The procedure *ReadTheData* then reads the pairs of class codes and scores, calls the function *ConvertCode* to convert the numeric class codes 1, 2, 3, 4 to *Freshman, Sophomore, Junior, Senior,* respectively, increases the appropriate counter *Number*[*Class*] by 1, and adds the test score to the appropriate sum *SumOfScores*[*Class*]. Finally, the procedure *Calculate* is called to find and display the class averages. The following diagram summarizes the program's structure:

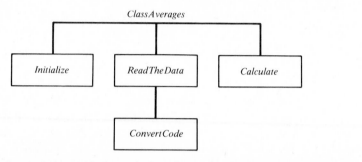

```
PROGRAM ClassAverages (input, output);

(*********************************************************************

   Program to calculate the average score received on a test by
   students in each of four classes:  Freshman (1), Sophomore (2),
   Junior (3) and Senior (4).

*********************************************************************)

TYPE
    ClassName = (Freshman, Sophomore, Junior, Senior);
    ClassList = ARRAY[ClassName] OF integer;

VAR
    Number,                    (* Number[Class] = number of students in Class *)
    SumOfScores : ClassList;   (* SumOfScores[Class] = sum of scores for
                                  students in Class *)
    Class : ClassName;         (* index *)

PROCEDURE Initialize (VAR Number, SumOfScores : ClassList);

   (*********************************************************************

      Procedure to initialize the arrays Number and SumOfScores to zero.

   *********************************************************************)

   VAR
      Class : ClassName;
```

Figure 8.4

Figure 8.4 (Cont.)

```
   BEGIN (* Initialize *)
      FOR Class := Freshman TO Senior DO
         BEGIN
            Number[Class] := 0;
            SumOfScores[Class] := 0
         END (* FOR *)
   END (* Initialize *);

PROCEDURE ReadTheData (VAR Number, SumOfScores : ClassList);

   (*******************************************************************

      Procedure to read each pair of class codes and scores, increase
      the appropriate counter Number[Class] by 1, and add the test
      score to SumOfScores[Class], the sum  of scores for this class.

   *******************************************************************)

   TYPE
      ClassNumber = 1..4;

   VAR
      ClassCode : integer;    (* class code *)
      Class : ClassName;      (* class name corresponding to class code *)
      Score : integer;        (* student's test score *)

   FUNCTION ConvertCode(ClassCode : ClassNumber) : ClassName;

      (****************************************************************

         Function to convert class code (1, 2, 3, 4) to the
         corresponding value of enumerated type ClassName.

      ****************************************************************)

      BEGIN (* ConvertCode *)
         CASE ClassCode OF
            1 : ConvertCode := Freshman;
            2 : ConvertCode := Sophomore;
            3 : ConvertCode := Junior;
            4 : ConvertCode := Senior
         END (* CASE *)
      END (* ConvertCode *);

   BEGIN (* ReadTheData *)
      writeln ('Enter the class codes and the test scores in pairs,');
      writeln ('as many per line as desired.  Enter 0''s to signal');
      writeln ('the end of data.');
      writeln;
      read (ClassCode, Score);
```

Figure 8.4 (Cont.)

```
      WHILE ClassCode <> 0 DO
         BEGIN
            IF (ClassCode < 1) OR (ClassCode > 4) THEN
               writeln ('** Illegal class code **')
            ELSE
               BEGIN
                  Class := ConvertCode(ClassCode);
                  Number[Class] := Number[Class] + 1;
                  SumOfScores[Class] := SumOfScores[Class] + Score
               END (* ELSE *);
            read (ClassCode, Score)
         END (* WHILE *)
   END (* ReadTheData *);

PROCEDURE Calculate (VAR Number, SumOfScores : ClassList);

   (*********************************************************************

      Procedure to calculate and display the average score for each
      of the four classes.

    *********************************************************************)

   VAR
      Class : ClassName;    (* index *)

   BEGIN (* Calculate *)
      writeln;
      writeln ('CLASS #  AVE. SCORE');
      writeln ('————   —————————');
      FOR Class := Freshman TO Senior DO
         BEGIN
            write (1 + ord(Class):4);
            IF Number[Class] = 0 THEN
               writeln ('     No scores')
            ELSE
               writeln (SumOfScores[Class] / Number[Class]:11:1)
         END (* FOR *)
   END (* Calculate *);

BEGIN (* main program *)
   Initialize (Number, SumOfScores);
   ReadTheData (Number, SumOfScores);
   Calculate (Number, SumOfScores)
END (* main program *).
```

Figure 8.4 (Cont.)

Sample run:

Enter the class codes and the test scores in pairs,
as many per line as desired.   Enter 0's to signal
the end of data.

```
1 95    1 88    3 77    4 100   4 67    1 58    3 62    3 99
3 87    4 72    4 58    1 66    4 89
0 0
```

CLASS #	AVE. SCORE
1	76.8
2	No scores
3	81.3
4	77.2

EXAMPLE 2: Sorting.   A common data-processing problem is *sorting* a list of items, that is, arranging these items so that they are in either ascending or descending order. There are many sorting methods, most of which use arrays to store the items to be sorted. In this section we describe the sorting method known as **bubble sort.** Although it is not the most efficient sorting method, it is quite easy to understand; more efficient sorting techniques are described in the exercises at the end of this chapter.

Suppose that the items to be sorted have been read and assigned to $X[1]$, $X[2]$, . . . , $X[NumItems]$. We scan the array, comparing $X[1]$ and $X[2]$, and interchanging them if they are in the wrong order. Then we compare $X[2]$ with $X[3]$, interchanging them if they are in the wrong order. This process of comparing and interchanging continues throughout the entire array. This constitutes one complete pass through the array. For example, suppose that the following list is to be sorted into increasing order:

$$77$$
$$30$$
$$89$$
$$54$$
$$62$$

We first compare 77 and 30 and interchange them, giving

$$30$$
$$77$$
$$89$$
$$54$$
$$62$$

Now we compare 77 and 89 but do not interchange them, since they are already in the correct order.

30
77
89
54
62

Next, 89 and 54 are compared and interchanged, giving

30
77
54
89
62

Finally, 89 and 62 are compared and interchanged, giving

30
77
54
62
89

This completes one pass through the list.

Note that the largest item in the list "sinks" to the bottom of the list and that some of the smaller items "bubble up" toward the top. We scan the list again, comparing consecutive items and interchanging them when they are out of order, but this time we leave the last item out of the pass, since it is already in its proper position. This pass produces

30
54
62
77
89

the second largest number sinks to its proper position, and more small numbers bubble up toward their proper positions.

For this short list, we can easily see that the sorting is now complete, but for a long list, this is not so easy to determine. One method for determining when the sorting is complete is simply to record on each pass through the list whether any interchanges take place. When we eventually scan the list and find that no interchanges have taken place, we know that the list is sorted, and so we can terminate the procedure.

BUBBLE SORT ALGORITHM

(* Algorithm to bubble sort the list of items $X[1]$, $X[2]$, . . . , $X[NumItems]$ so that they are in ascending order *)

1. Set *NumPairs* equal to *NumItems* $-$ 1; this is the number of pairs that must be examined in the current pass through the list.
2. Repeat the following until the boolean variable *Done* is true:
   a. Set *Done* to true. The value of *Done* will remain true if a pass through the list is made with no interchanges taking place, thus indicating that the items are in order; it will be set to false if interchanges are made.
   b. For each value of the index i from 1 through *NumPairs,* compare $X[i]$ with $X[i + 1]$. If $X[i] > X[i + 1]$, then interchange them and set *Done* to false; otherwise proceed to the next pair of items.
   c. Decrease *NumPairs* by 1. At the end of each pass through the list, the largest item will have sunk into place and thus need not be examined on the next pass.

This algorithm sorts the items into ascending order. To sort them into descending order, one need only change $>$ to $<$ in the comparison of $X[i]$ with $X[i + 1]$.

The program in Figure 8.5 implements this algorithm as the procedure *BubbleSort*. It reads a list of up to 100 items, sorts them using *BubbleSort,* and then displays the sorted list.

```
PROGRAM Sort (input, output);

(*******************************************************************

   Program to read and count a list of items
        Item[1], Item[2], ..., Item[NumItems],
   sort them in ascending order, and then display the sorted list.

********************************************************************)

CONST
   ListLimit = 100;      (* maximum number of items in the list *)

TYPE
   ItemType = integer;
   List = ARRAY[1..ListLimit] of ItemType;

VAR
   NumItems,             (* number of items *)
   i: integer;           (* index *)
   Item : List;          (* list of items to be sorted *)
```

Figure 8.5

Figure 8.5 (Cont.)

```
PROCEDURE ReadList (VAR Item : List; ListLimit : integer;
                    VAR Count : integer);

   (******************************************************************

      Procedure to read list elements into array Item which has at
      most ListLimit elements and to count the number of elements
      read.  Both Item and Count are returned.

   ******************************************************************)

   VAR
      Response : char;  (* user response *)

   BEGIN (* ReadList *)
      writeln ('Enter the list of items, as many per line as desired.');
      writeln ('Note:  At most ', ListLimit:1, ' items can be read.');
      writeln;
      Count := 0;
      REPEAT
         write ('Items:  ');
         WHILE NOT eoln DO
            BEGIN
               Count := Count + 1;
               read (Item[Count])
            END (* WHILE *);
         readln;
         write ('More (Y or N)?  ');
         readln (Response)
      UNTIL Response <> 'Y'
   END (* ReadList *);

PROCEDURE BubbleSort (VAR Item : List; N : integer);

   (******************************************************************

      Procedure to sort Item[1], ..., Item[N] into ascending order
      using the bubble sort algorithm.  For descending order,
      change > to < in the boolean expression Item[i] > Item[i+1].

   ******************************************************************)

   VAR
      i,                       (* index *)
      NumPairs : integer;      (* number of pairs examined in current scan *)
      Temporary : ItemType;    (* used to interchange two items *)
      Done : boolean;          (* indicates if sorting completed *)
```

Figure 8.5 (Cont.)

```
BEGIN (* BubbleSort *)
    NumPairs := N - 1;

    (* Scan the list comparing consecutive items *)

    REPEAT
        Done := true;
        FOR i := 1 TO NumPairs DO
            IF Item[i] > Item[i+1] THEN
                BEGIN
                    Temporary := Item[i];
                    Item[i] := Item[i+1];
                    Item[i+1] := Temporary;
                    Done := false  (* interchange occurred, so scan again *)
                END (* IF *);

        (* Largest item has sunk into place, so eliminate
           it from the next scan *)

        NumPairs := NumPairs - 1
    UNTIL Done
END (* BubbleSort *);

PROCEDURE PrintItems (VAR Item : List; NumItems : integer);

    (*****************************************************************

            Procedure to print the list of items.

    *****************************************************************)

    VAR
        i : integer;      (* index *)

    BEGIN (* PrintItems *)
        writeln;
        writeln ('Sorted list of ', Numitems:1, ' items:');
        writeln;
        FOR i := 1 TO NumItems DO
            writeln (Item[i])
    END (* PrintItems *);

BEGIN (* main program *)
    ReadList (Item, ListLimit, NumItems);
    BubbleSort (Item, NumItems);
    PrintItems (Item, NumItems)
END (* main *).
```

Figure 8.5 (Cont.)

<u>Sample run:</u>

```
Enter the list of items, as many per line as desired.
Note:  At most 100 items can be read.

Items:   55 88 34 85 21
More (Y or N)?   Y
Items:   99 5 83 71
More (Y or N)?   N

Sorted list of 9 items:

     5
    21
    34
    55
    71
    83
    85
    88
    99
```

EXAMPLE 3: Searching. Another important problem in data processing is *searching* a collection of data for a specified item and retrieving some information associated with that item. For example, one searches a telephone directory for a specific name in order to retrieve the phone number listed with that name. In a ***linear search,*** one begins with the first item in a list and searches sequentially until either the desired item is found or the end of the list is reached. The following algorithm describes this method of searching:

LINEAR SEARCH ALGORITHM

(∗ Algorithm to linear search a list $X[1]$, $X[2]$, . . . , $X[NumItems]$ for a specified *Item*. *Found* is set to true and *Location* to the position of *Item* if the search is successful; otherwise, *Found* is set to false. ∗)

1. Initialize *Location* to 1 and *Found* to false.
2. While *Location* ≤ *NumItems* and not *Found,* do the following:
   If *Item* = $X[Location]$ then
      Set *Found* to true.

   Else

      Increment *Location* by 1.

Although linear search may be an adequate method for small data sets, a more efficient technique is needed for large collections. If the list to be searched has been sorted, the ***binary search*** algorithm may be used. With this method, we first examine the middle item in the list; if this is the desired entry, the search is successful. Otherwise, we determine whether the item being sought is in the first half or the second half of the list and then repeat this process, using the middle entry of that sublist.

To illustrate, suppose that the list to be searched is

$$
\begin{array}{c}
1331 \\
1373 \\
1555 \\
1824 \\
1882 \\
\boxed{1898} \\
1987 \\
2002 \\
2335 \\
2665 \\
3103
\end{array}
$$

and that we are looking for 1987. We first examine the middle number, 1898, in the sixth position. Because 1987 is greater than 1898, we can disregard the first half of the list and concentrate on the second half:

$$
\begin{array}{c}
1987 \\
2002 \\
\boxed{2335} \\
2665 \\
3103
\end{array}
$$

The middle number is this sublist is 2335 and the desired item 1987 is less than 2335, so we discard the second half of this sublist and concentrate on the first half:

$$
\begin{array}{c}
\boxed{1987} \\
2002
\end{array}
$$

Since there is no middle number in this half, we examine the number immediately preceding the middle position, that is, 1987. In this case, we have located the desired entry with three comparisons rather than seven, as required in a linear search.

In general, the algorithm for binary search is as follows:

BINARY SEARCH ALGORITHM

(∗ Algorithm to binary search a list $X[1]$, $X[2]$, . . . , $X[NumItems]$ that has been ordered so the elements are in ascending order. *Found* is set to true and *Location* to the position of the *Item* being sought if the search is successful; otherwise, *Found* is set to false. ∗)

1. Initialize *First* to 1 and *Last* to *NumItems*. These represent the positions of the first and last items of the list or sublist being searched.
2. Initialize *Found* to false.

3. While *First* ≤ *Last* and not *Found,* do the following:
   a. Find the middle position in the sublist by setting *Middle* equal to the integer quotient of (*First* + *Last*) divided by 2.
   b. Compare the *Item* being searched for with *X*[*Middle*]. There are three possibilities:
      (i) *Item* < *X*[*Middle*]: *Item* is in the first half of the sublist; set *Last* equal to *Middle* − 1.
      (ii) *Item* > *X*[*Middle*]: *Item* is in the last half of the sublist; set *First* equal to *Middle* + 1.
      (iii) *Item* = *X*[*Middle*]: *Item* has been found; set *Location* equal to *Middle* and *Found* to true.

In the program of Figure 8.6, this algorithm is implemented as the procedure *BinarySearch*. The structure of this program is summarized by the following structure diagram:

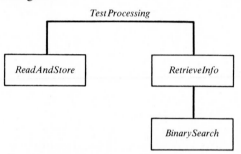

The procedure *ReadAndStore* reads student numbers, class codes, and test scores from a text file and stores these values in three arrays:

> *Snumb: Snumb*[*i*] is the *i*th student number.
> *Class: Class*[*i*] is the class code for the *i*th student.
> *TestScore: TestScore*[*i*] is the test score for the *i*th student.

The procedure *RetrieveInfo* then repeatedly accepts a student's number from the user and retrieves the class code and test score for that student. Since the three data items for the students are arranged in the file so that the student numbers are in ascending order, *RetrieveInfo* can call *BinarySearch* to perform the search.

```
PROGRAM TestProcessing (input, output,TestFile);

(************************************************************************

   This program reads in a list of student numbers, class codes,
   and test scores from TestFile and then sorts them so the student
   numbers are in ascending order.  A student number can then be
   input, the list searched using a binary search, and the
   corresponding class code and test score displayed.

*************************************************************************)

CONST
   ListLimit = 100;        (* maximum number of items in the list *)
```

Figure 8.6

Figure 8.6 (Cont.)

```
TYPE
   ItemType = integer;
   List = ARRAY[1..ListLimit] OF ItemType;

VAR
   Snumb,                 (* Snumb[i] = i-th student number *)
   Class,                 (* Class[i] = class code for i-th student *)
   TestScore: List;       (* TestScore[i] = test score for i-th student *)
   NumScores : integer;   (* number of test scores *)
   TestFile : text;       (* file from which student data is read *)

PROCEDURE ReadAndStore (VAR Snumb, Class, TestScore : List;
                        VAR Count : integer);

   (*********************************************************************

      Procedure to read the items from TestFile and store them in
      the arrays Snumb, Class, and TestScore.

   *********************************************************************)

   BEGIN (* ReadAndStore *)
      reset (TestFile);
      Count := 0;
      WHILE NOT eof(TestFile) DO
         BEGIN
            Count := Count + 1;
            readln (TestFile, Snumb[Count], Class[Count], TestScore[Count])
         END (* WHILE *)
   END (* ReadAndStore *);

PROCEDURE RetrieveInfo (VAR Snumb, Class, TestScore : List;
                        NumItems : integer);

   (*********************************************************************

      Procedure to accept a student number and then search the list
      Snumb for it.  If it is found, the class code and test score
      for that student are displayed.

   *********************************************************************)

   VAR
      SnumbDesired : ItemType;  (* student number to search for *)
      Found : boolean;          (* indicates if search was successful *)
      Location : integer;       (* location of number in the list *)

   PROCEDURE BinarySearch (VAR Item : List; NumItems : integer;
                           ItemSought : ItemType; VAR Found : boolean;
                           VAR Location : integer);

      (*********************************************************************

         Procedure to search the list Item for ItemSought using the
         binary search algorithm.  If ItemSought is found in the list,
         a value of true is returned for Found and the Location of the
         item is returned; otherwise, false is returned for Found and
         0 for Location.

      *********************************************************************)
```

Figure 8.6 (Cont.)

```
      VAR
         First,                (* first item in sublist being searched *)
         Last,                 (* last item in sublist *)
         Middle : integer;     (* middle item in sublist *)
   BEGIN (* BinarySearch *)
      First := 1;
      Last := NumItems;
      Found := false;
      WHILE (First <= Last) AND (NOT Found) DO
         BEGIN
            Middle := (First + Last) DIV 2;
            IF ItemSought = Item[Middle] THEN
               BEGIN
                  Found := true;
                  Location := Middle
               END (* IF *)
            ELSE IF ItemSought > Item[Middle] THEN
               First := Middle + 1  (* item in last half of sublist *)
            ELSE
               Last := Middle - 1   (* item in first half of sublist *)
         END (* WHILE *)
   END (* BinarySearch*);

BEGIN (* RetrieveInfo *)
   writeln ('To stop searching, enter student number of 0.');
   write ('Student number?  ');
   readln (SnumbDesired);
   WHILE SnumbDesired <> 0 DO
      BEGIN
         BinarySearch (Snumb, NumScores, SnumbDesired, Found, Location);
         IF Found THEN
            BEGIN
               writeln ('Student ', SnumbDesired:1, ' is in class ',
                        Class[Location]:1);
               writeln ('His/her test score was ', TestScore[Location]:1)
            END (* IF Found *)
         ELSE
            writeln ('Student ', SnumbDesired:1, ' not found');
         writeln;
         write ('Student number?  ');
         readln (SnumbDesired)
      END (* WHILE *)
END (* RetrieveInfo *);

BEGIN (* main program *)
   ReadAndStore (Snumb, Class, TestScore, NumScores);
   RetrieveInfo (Snumb, Class, TestScore, NumScores)
END (* main program *).
```

Figure 8.6 (Cont.)

Listing of TestFile:

```
11111 1  99
22222 2 100
33333 3  77
44444 1  55
55555 2  87
66666 1  63
77777 3  93
```

Sample run:

```
To stop searching, enter student number of 0.
Student number?  11111
Student 11111 is in class 1
His/her test score was 99

Student number?  55555
Student 55555 is in class 2
His/her test score was 87

Student number?  88888
Student 88888 not found

Student number?  33333
Student 33333 is in class 3
His/her test score was 77

Student number?  0
```

Exercises

1. Assume that the following declarations have been made:

type
    Color = (*red, yellow, blue, green, white, black*);
    ColorArray = **array**[*Color*] **of** *real*;
    LittleArray = **array**[1..10] **of** *integer*;
    CharCountArray = **array**['A'..'F'] **of** *integer*;

var
    Price : *ColorArray*;
    Number : *LittleArray*;
    LetterCount : *CharCountArray*;
    i : *integer*;
    Ch : *char*;
    Col : *Color*;

For each of the following, tell what value (if any) will be assigned to each array element, or explain why an error occurs.

(a) **for** $i := 1$ **to** 10 **do**
    $Number[i] := i$ **div** 2;

(b) **for** $i := 1$ **to** 6 **do**
    $Number[i] := i * i$;
  for $i := 7$ **to** 10 **do**
    $Number[i] := Number[i - 5]$;

(c) $i := 0$;
  while $i <> 10$ **do**
    begin
      if $(i$ **mod** $3) = 0$ **then**
        $Number[i] := 0$
      else
        $Number[i] := i$;
      $i := i + 1$
    end (* **while** *);

(d) $Number[1] := 1$;
  $i := 2$;
  repeat
    $Number[i] := 2 * Number[i - 1]$;
    $i := i + 1$
  until $i = 10$;

(e) **for** $Ch := $ 'A' **to** 'F' **do**
    if $Ch = $ 'A' **then**
      $LetterCount[Ch] := 1$
    else
      $LetterCount[Ch] := LetterCount[pred(Ch)] + 1$;

(f) **for** $Col := yellow$ **to** $white$ **do**
    $Price[Col] := 13.95$;

(g) **for** $Col := red$ **to** $black$ **do**
    case Col **of**
      $red, blue$: $Price[Col] := 19.95$;
      $yellow$: $Price[Col] := 12.75$;
      $green, black$: $Price[Col] := 14.50$;
      $white$:
    end (* **case** *);

2. For each of the following, write appropriate declarations and statements to create the specified array:

(a) An array whose indices are the integers from 0 through 5 and in which each element is the same as the index.

(b) An array whose indices are the integers from -5 through 5 and for which the elements are the indices in reverse order.

(c) An array whose indices are the upper-case letters and in which each element is the same as the index.

(d) An array whose indices are the integers from 1 through 20 and for which an array element has the value true if the corresponding index is even, and false otherwise.

(e) An array whose indices are the upper-case letters and for which each element is the letter preceding the index, except that the array element corresponding to A is Z.

(f) An array whose indices are the upper-case letters and in which each array element is the number of the position of the corresponding index in the sequence A, B, C, . . . , Z.

(g) An array whose indices are the lower-case letters and in which an array element has the value true if the index is a vowel, and false otherwise.

(h) An array whose indices are the names of the five subjects mathematics, chemistry, speech, history, and economics and in which the array elements are the letter grades received: A in mathematics and speech, B in chemistry, F in history, and C in economics.

3. Assuming that values of type *integer* and *char* are stored in one memory word and reals require two memory words, indicate with a diagram like that in Section 8.1 where each component of an array A of the following type would be stored if the base address of A is b; also, give the general address translation formula for $A[i]$.

(a) **array** [1..5] **of** *integer*.

(b) **array** [1..5] **of** *real*.

(c) **array** [−5..5] **of** *char*.

(d) **array** ['A'..'Z'] **of** *integer*. (*Hint:* use the *ord* function.)

4. Write a function *Max* that finds the largest value in an integer array *Number* of type *NumberArray* having *NumElements* components.

5. Write a procedure to locate and return the smallest and largest integers in an array *Number* as described in Exercise 4 and their positions in the array. It should also find and return the range of the numbers, that is, the difference between the largest number and the smallest.

6. Write a procedure to implement the linear search algorithm given in the text.

7. Write a procedure *Insert* for inserting an item at a specified position of a list implemented as an array and a procedure *Delete* for deleting an item at a specified position.

8. One possible implementation of a stack is to use an array *Stack* indexed 1..*StackLimit* with the top of the stack at position 1 of the array.

(a) Why is this not a good implementation?

(b) A better implementation is to let the stack grow from position 1 toward position *StackLimit* and maintain an integer variable *Top* to "point" to the current top of the stack. Write procedures for the push and pop operations in this implementation.

(c) Use the procedures of part (b) in a program that reads a command I (Insert) or D (Delete); for I, read an integer and push it onto the stack; for D, pop an integer from the stack and display it.

9. For a queue, we might imitate the array implementation of a stack in Exercise 8, using an array *Queue* indexed 1..*QueueLimit* and maintaining two "pointers," *Front* to the item at the front of the queue and *Rear* to the item at the rear. To add an item to the queue, simply increment *Rear* by 1 and store the item in *Queue*[*Rear*]; to remove an item, simply increment *Front* by 1.

(a) Describe the inadequacies of this implementation. Consider, for example, an integer array with five elements and the following sequence of queue operations: Insert 37, Insert 82, Insert 59, Delete an item, Delete an item, Insert 66, Insert 13, Insert 48.

(b) A better implementation is to think of the array as being circular, with the first element following the last. For this, index the array beginning with 0 and increment *Front* and *Rear* using addition **mod** *QueueLimit*. Write procedures for the insertion and deletion operations, assuming this implementation. Use these procedures in a program that reads a command I (Insert) or D (Delete); for I, read an integer and add it to the queue; for D, remove an integer from the queue and display it.

10. The Cawker City Candy Company records the number of cases of candy produced each day over a four-week period. Write a program that reads these production numbers and stores them in an array. The program should then accept from the user a week number and a day number and should display the production level for that day. Assume that each week consists of five work days.

11. The Cawker City Candy Company manufactures different kinds of candy, each identified by a product number. Write a program that reads in two arrays, *Number* and *Price,* where *Number*[1] and *Price*[1] are the product number and unit price for the first item, *Number*[2] and *Price*[2] are the product number and unit price for the second item, and so on. The program should then allow the user to select one of the following options:

1. Retrieve and display the price of a product whose number is entered by the user. (Use the linear search procedure developed in Exercise 7 to determine the index in the array *Number* of the specified item.)
2. Print a table displaying the product number and the price of each item.

12. The Cawker City Candy Company maintains two warehouses, one in Chicago and one in Detroit, each of which stocks, at most, 25 different items. Write a program that first reads the product numbers of items

stored in the Chicago warehouse and stores them in an array *Chicago*, and then repeats this for the items stored in the Detroit warehouse, storing these product numbers in an array *Detroit*. The program should then find and display the ***intersection*** of these two lists of numbers, that is, the collection of product numbers common to both lists. The lists should not be assumed to have the same number of elements.

13. Repeat Exercise 12 but find and display the ***union*** of the two lists, that is, the collection of product numbers that are elements of at least one of the lists.

14. If $\bar{x}$ denotes the mean of the numbers $x_1, x_2, \ldots, x_n$, the ***variance*** is the average of the squares of the deviations of the numbers from the mean:

$$\text{Variance} = \frac{1}{n} \sum_{i=1}^{n} (x_i - \bar{x})^2$$

and the ***standard deviation*** is the square root of the variance. Write a program that reads a list of real numbers, counts them, and then calculates their mean, variance, and standard deviation. Print with appropriate labels how many numbers there are, their mean, variance, and standard deviation. Use functions or procedures to calculate the mean, variance, and standard deviation.

15. Letter grades are sometimes assigned to numeric scores by using the grading scheme commonly called "grading on the curve." In this scheme, a letter grade is assigned to a numeric score according to the following table:

x = Numeric Score	Letter Grade
$x < m - \dfrac{3}{2}\sigma$	F
$m - \dfrac{3}{2}\sigma \leq x < m - \dfrac{1}{2}\sigma$	D
$m - \dfrac{1}{2}\sigma \leq x < m + \dfrac{1}{2}\sigma$	C
$m + \dfrac{1}{2}\sigma \leq x < m + \dfrac{3}{2}\sigma$	B
$m + \dfrac{3}{2}\sigma \leq x$	A

where m is the mean score and σ is the standard deviation. Extend the program of Exercise 14 to read a list of real numbers representing numeric scores, calculate their mean and standard deviation, and display the letter grade corresponding to each numeric score.

16. ***Insertion sort*** is an efficient sorting method for small data sets. It begins with the first item x_1, then inserts x_2 into this one-item list in

the correct position to form a sorted two-element list, then inserts x_3 into this two-element list in the correct position, and so on. For example, to sort the list 7, 1, 5, 2, 3, 4, 6, 0, the steps are as follows (the element being inserted is highlighted):

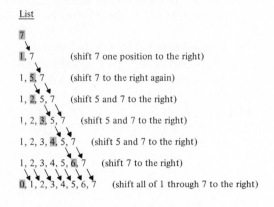

List

7

1, 7   (shift 7 one position to the right)

1, 5, 7   (shift 7 to the right again)

1, 2, 5, 7   (shift 5 and 7 to the right)

1, 2, 3, 5, 7   (shift 5 and 7 to the right)

1, 2, 3, 4, 5, 7   (shift 5 and 7 to the right)

1, 2, 3, 4, 5, 6, 7   (shift 7 to the right)

0, 1, 2, 3, 4, 5, 6, 7   (shift all of 1 through 7 to the right)

Write a program to sort a list of items, using this insertion sort method.

17. The investment company of Shyster and Shyster has been recording the trading price of a particular stock over a 15-day period. Write a program that reads these prices and sorts them into increasing order, using the insertion sort scheme described in the preceding exercise. The program should display the trading range, that is, the lowest and highest prices recorded, and also the median price.

18. One problem with bubble sort is that while larger values move rapidly toward their proper positions, smaller values move slowly in the other direction. **Shell sort** (named after Donald Shell) attempts to improve this. A series of compare-interchange scans are made, but consecutive items are not compared on each scan. Instead, there is a fixed "gap" between the items that are compared. When no more interchanges can be made for a given gap, the gap is cut in half, and the compare-interchange scans continue. The initial gap is commonly taken to be $n/2$ for a list of n items. For example, for the list

$$6,1,5,2,3,4,0$$

the following sequence of gaps and scans would be used:

Scan #	Gap	Rearranged List	Interchanges
1	3	2,1,4,0,3,5,6	(6,2), (5,4), (6,0)
2	3	0,1,4,2,3,5,6	(2,0)
3	3	0,1,4,2,3,5,6	none
4	1	0,1,2,3,4,5,6	(4,2), (4,3)
5	1	0,1,2,3,4,5,6	none

Write a program to sort a list of items, using the Shell sort method.

19. Peter the postman became bored one night and to break the monotony of the night shift, he carried out the following experiment with a row of mailboxes in the post office. These mailboxes were numbered 1 through 150, and beginning with mailbox 2, he opened the doors of all the even-numbered mailboxes. Next, beginning with mailbox 3, he went to every third mail box, opening its door if it was closed, closing it if it was open. Then he repeated this procedure with every fourth mailbox, then every fifth mailbox, and so on. When he finished, he was surprised at the distribution of open mailboxes. Write a program to determine which mailboxes these were.

20. A *prime number* is an integer greater than 1 whose only positive divisors are 1 and the integer itself. One method for finding all the prime numbers in the range from 1 through n is known as the *Sieve of Eratosthenes*. Consider the list of numbers from 2 through n. Two is the first prime number, but the multiples of 2 (4, 6, 8, . . .) are not, and so they are crossed out in the list. The first number after 2 that was not crossed out is 3, the next prime. We then cross out from the list all higher multiples of 3 (6, 9, 12, . . .). The next number not crossed out is 5, the next prime, and so we cross out all higher multiples of 5 (10, 15, 20, . . .). We repeat this procedure until we reach the first number in the list that has not been crossed out and whose square is greater than n. All the numbers that remain in the list will be the primes from 2 through n. Write a program that uses this sieve method to find all the prime numbers from 2 through n. Run it for $n = 50$ and for $n = 500$.

21. Write a program to add two large integers of length up to 300 digits. One approach is to treat each number as a list, each of whose elements is a block of digits of the number. For example, the integer 179,534,672,198 might be stored with $Block[1] = 198$, $Block[2] = 672$, $Block[3] = 534$, $Block[4] = 179$. Then add the integers (lists) element by element, carrying from one element to the next when necessary.

22. Proceeding as in Exercise 21, write a program to multiply two large integers of length up to 300 digits.

23. Write a recursive procedure to carry out the binary search method described in this section.

8.4 String Processing

The word *compute* usually suggests arithmetic operations performed on numeric data; thus, computers are sometimes thought to be mere "number-crunchers," devices whose only function is to process numeric information. We know that this is not the case, however, for in Chapter 1 we considered coding schemes used to represent character as well as boolean information, and in subsequent chapters we introduced some of the capabilities of Pascal for processing character and boolean data. We have also seen examples of problems that required processing character data. For example, the program in Figure 7.4 was designed to remove extra blanks from lines in a text file, and that in Figure 8.3 counted the occurrences of characters in a text file. In each of these examples, the data were processed as individual characters, and in this section we extend our study to problems in which the characters are grouped together in finite sequences called *strings*.

The basic string-processing operations include concatenating two strings, determining the location of one string in another string, extracting a substring from a string, and so on. Many versions of Pascal provide a predefined string data type together with predefined functions and procedures such as *length, concat, pos,* and *copy* to implement the basic operations (see the Variations and Extensions section at the end of this chapter). Standard Pascal, as we have seen, does provide the *char* type for processing single characters and does allow **string constants,** strings of characters enclosed in single quotes, which we have used in many of our sample programs to label output or to prompt the user to enter appropriate data. It does not, however, provide a predefined string data type, and strings must therefore be processed using some other structure. Arrays of character type are commonly used for this purpose, with each array element storing a single character of the string. For example, a one-dimensional array *Name* having five components of character type might be used to store the string SMITH; *Name*[1] would have the value S, *Name*[2] the value M, and so on.

In our discussion in Section 1.3 of the internal representation of data, we noted that the commonly used coding schemes ASCII and EBCDIC require only 8 bits (or 1 byte) to store a single character. In many computers, the length of each memory word is more than 8 bits and thus a word can store more than one character. Some Pascal compilers, however, allocate an entire memory word for each variable, in particular for variables of character type. Because the values assigned to such variables require only 8 bits for storage, this is an inefficient use of memory. For example, in a 32-bit word machine, only 8 bits of a 32-bit word are used to store a character, and thus three fourths of each such word is wasted. Memory utilization in such machines can be improved by using **packed arrays** in which several array elements or characters are stored in a single word.

To illustrate the difference between unpacked and packed arrays, suppose that arrays U and P are declared by

```
type
    UnpackedCharArray = array[1..8] of char;
    PackedCharArray = packed array[1..8] of char;

var
    U : UnpackedCharArray;
    P : PackedCharArray;
```

For some computers, the array U would be allocated eight memory words:

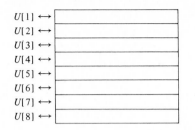

For a 32-bit machine, however, the packed array need be allocated only two memory words, since each word can store four characters:

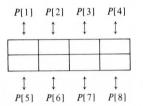

Memory is obviously used more efficiently in the second case than in the first, but the address translation that must be performed to locate an array element is more complex. Not only must the address of the memory word in which that element is stored be calculated, but the number of the byte within that word containing the component must also be determined.

The usual array operations can also be applied to packed arrays.[2] For example, packed arrays of the same type may appear in an assignment statement of the form

 array1 := *array2*

This assignment statement would not be valid, however, if one of *array1* or *array2* was packed and the other was not.

Although arrays of any type may be specified as packed arrays, the most important use of packed arrays is to process strings. Thus we restrict our attention to packed arrays of characters in this chapter. (Packed arrays of other types are considered in Appendix F.)

A packed array of type *char* whose index type is a subrange of the form $1..n$ for some integer $n > 1$ will be called a ***string*** type.[3] For example, consider the following type definitions:

---

[2] One exception is that a component of a packed array may not be an actual parameter that corresponds to a variable formal parameter.

[3] Most versions of Pascal that provide a predefined string type also allow packed character arrays for processing strings. The two string types may or may not be compatible.

type
 A = **packed array**[1..10] **of** *char*;
 B = **array**[1..10] **of** *char*;
 C = **packed array**[0..9] **of** *char*;
 D = **packed array**[1..10] **of** 'A'..'Z';
 E = **packed array**[1..1] **of** *char*;

Only type *A* is a string type. *B, C, D,* and *E* are not string types because arrays of type *B* are not packed, the subscript type for *C* does not begin with 1, the component type for *D* is not *char,* and the index type for *E* does not have two or more values.

A string constant may be used to assign a value to an array of string type, provided its length (number of characters) is the same as the number of array elements. For example, if the array *Name* is declared by

type
 NameString = **packed array**[1..10] **of** *char*;

var
 Name : *NameString*;

then the assignment statement

 Name := 'John Smith'

is valid. The string constant 'J. Doe' cannot be assigned to *Name* since it has only six characters. If four blanks are appended to this string, however, the resulting string may be assigned to *Name:*

 Name := 'J. Doe   '

Similarly, the string constant 'Johann VanderDoe' cannot be assigned to *Name* because it has more than ten characters. Thus we see one of the drawbacks of using arrays to process strings; strings need not have a fixed length, but arrays must have a fixed number of elements. (In versions of Pascal that provide a predefined string data type, lengths of strings are allowed to vary dynamically.)

This difficulty also arises in comparing strings. Two values of string type may be compared with the relational operators $<, >, =, <=, >=$, and $<>$, *provided they have the same length.* Thus,

 'cat' $<$ 'dog'

is a valid boolean expression and is evaluated by comparing, character by character, the strings cat and dog, using the collating sequence described in Section 4.2. Thus this boolean expression is true because c precedes d in the collating sequence. Similarly, the boolean expression

 'cat' $>$ 'car'

is true because t follows r in the collating sequence. Note, however, that the string constants 'apples' and 'oranges' cannot be compared because they have different lengths; that is, they do not have the same number of characters. The boolean expression

'apples ' < 'oranges'

is valid, however, and is true. Similarly, if each of *Name1* and *Name2* is of type *NameString,* then the following are valid boolean expressions:

Name1 < 'John Smith'

Name2 <> 'apples   '

Name1 >= *Name2*

String values may also appear in the output list of a *write* or *writeln* statement. We have already used this feature when string constants appeared in an output statement such as

writeln ('Mean of the scores is ', *MeanScore*:3:1);

The name of an array of string type may also appear in the output list. Thus if *Name* and *EmpNumber* are declared by

const
    StringLimit = 12;

type
    String = **packed array**[1..*StringLimit*] **of** *char*;

var
    Name : *String*;
    EmpNumber : *integer*;

and have values JohnbDoebbbb and 13520, respectively, then the statement

writeln (*Name, EmpNumber*:6)

produces the output

<u>John Doe   13520</u>

Some Pascal compilers do not allow the name of an array of string type to appear in the input list of a *read* or *readln* statement. Thus, a statement such as

readln(Name)

would not be allowed. Instead, the array elements must be read individually:

> **for** $i := 1$ **to** 12 **do**
> *read* (*Name*[*i*])

If the string

    John♭Doe♭♭♭♭

is entered, then the value assigned to *Name* is the string John♭Doe♭♭♭♭. The value of *Name*[1] is the character J, the value of *Name*[2] is o, and so on.[4]

In this example, twelve characters must be read. Although we may prefer to enter only the name John Doe, we must also enter characters for the other four elements of the array. Thus we entered four trailing blanks to be assigned to *Name*[9], . . . , *Name*[12].

Entering blanks or some other characters to fill up the positions of a character array is rather tedious. We prefer to enter only the characters in which we are interested and have the program assign blanks to the remaining positions. If we signal the end of the string being read with an end-of-line character (carriage return), we can use the *eoln* function as indicated in the following procedure. Recall that *eoln* has the value true if the end of the current input line has been reached and is false otherwise.

> **procedure** *ReadString* (**var** *Str* : *String*; *MaxString* : *integer*);
>
>   (∗ Procedure to read characters into string variable *Str* until an end of
>   line is encountered or the upper limit *MaxString* on the length of
>   *Str* is reached. Any positions for which no characters are read will
>   be filled with blanks. ∗)
>
> **var**
>   *i* : *integer*;
>
> *begin* (∗ *ReadString* ∗)
>   **for** $i := 1$ **to** *MaxString* **do**
>   **if not** *eoln* **then**
>   *read* (*Str*[*i*])
>   **else**
>   *Str*[*i*] := ' ';
>   *readln*
> **end** (∗ *ReadString* ∗);

Suppose, for example, that *Name* has been delcared by

> **const**
>   *StringLimit* = 12;
>
> **type**
>   *String* = **packed array**[1..*StringLimit*] **of** *char*;
>
> **var**
>   *Name* : *String*;

---

[4] Some compilers do not allow the elements of a packed array to be read. In this case, values can be read into an unpacked array, and these elements then must be copied into the packed array.

and consider the procedure call

   ReadString (Name, StringLimit);

If the string

   John Doe

is entered, the eight characters J, o, h, n, ♭, D, o, and e are read and assigned
to *Name*[1], *Name*[2], . . . , *Name*[8]. Because the end of the input line is now
encountered, the value of *eoln* is true. No more characters are read, and blanks
are assigned to *Name*[9], . . . , *Name*[12].

In our discussion of input in Chapter 6, we observed that values for the
variables in the list of an input statement are obtained from the standard system
file *input*. When this file is loaded from data cards or from data lines entered
by the user during execution, a data pointer is positioned at the beginning of
the file and advances through the file as the values are read. When the end of
an input line is reached, an **end-of-line-mark** is entered into the input file. For
example, the two lines of input

   John Doe
   Mary Smith

produce the following contents in the file *input*

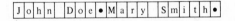

where, as before, ● denotes an end-of-line mark and ↑ represents the data
pointer. When the procedure *ReadString* is executed, characters are read until
the data pointer reaches the first end-of-line mark; then blank filling begins.

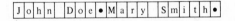

The *readln* statement then advances the data pointer beyond the end-of-line
mark so that *eoln* becomes false. If this statement were omitted, *eoln* would
remain true and subsequent calls to procedure *ReadString* would return strings
consisting of all blanks.

Many text-processing problems involve strings of various lengths, and for
such applications the number of characters read into the character array used
to store each string must be determined during execution. This can be done by
initializing a counter to 0 and then incrementing it by 1 each time a character
is read, as illustrated in the following modified version of procedure *Read-
String*.[5]

---

[5] Versions of Pascal that allow an array of string type in an input list may also allow a second
parameter, for example,

   readln (EmpName : Length)

Length will be assigned the number of characters that are read.

procedure *ReadString* (**var** *Str* : *String*; *MaxString* : *integer*;
                                    var *Length* : *integer*);

(* Procedure to read characters into the string array *Str* until an end-
   of-line mark is encountered or the upper limit *MaxString* on the
   size of *Str* is reached. Any positions for which no characters are
   read are filled with blanks. *Length* is assigned the number of
   characters read. *)

var
    i : *integer*;

begin (* *ReadString* *)
    Length := 0;
    for *i* := 1 **to** *MaxString* **do**
        if not *eoln* **then**
            begin
                read (*Str*[*i*]);
                Length := *Length* + 1
            end (* **if** *)
        else
            Str[*i*] := ' ' ;
    readln
end (* *ReadString* *);

In some situations it may not be necessary to blank fill a character array, as we have been doing in these examples. Characters may be read into the first positions of the array, and only those characters are processed. In the preceding example, *Length* is the number of positions of the array into which characters have been read, and if we confine all subsequent processing to positions 1, 2, . . . , *Length*, no values previously assigned to the array positions *Length* + 1, . . . , *MaxString* will be used.

To read values for only the first part of an array without blank filling the remaining positions, we could simply remove the **else** clause in the preceding procedure. However, the resulting sequence of statements is not very efficient because the **for** loop is executed *MaxString* times in every case. An alternative set of statements in which the repetition structure is executed only *Length* times is the following:

Length := 0;
while (**not** *eoln*) **and** (*Length* < *MaxString*) **do**
    begin
        Length := *Length* + 1;
        read (*Str*[*Length*])
    end (* **while** *);

As noted in Chapter 6, an attempt to read the end-of-line character does not result in an error. Rather, the end-of-line character is read as a blank. For example, if the preceding set of statements is executed twice and the file *input* has the contents

the first execution assigns the characters J, o, h, n, ƀ, D, o, and e to the array elements *Str*[1], *Str*[2], . . . , *Str*[8] and advances the data pointer to the first end-of-line mark. The second execution of these statements then assigns the characters ƀ, M, a, r, y, ƀ, S, m, i, and t to *Str*[1], *Str*[2], . . . , *Str*[10]. The source of the extra leading blank is the end-of-line mark that is read as a blank for *Str*[1]. Once again, the problem is solved by using a *readln* statement to advance the data pointer past the end-of-line mark before reading another string.

The program in Figure 8.7 uses the techniques described in this section to implement a simple cryptographic scheme, that is, a scheme for coding a message as a scrambled sequence of characters, known as a ***cryptogram.***

```
PROGRAM Coder (input, output);

(*******************************************************************

    This program scrambles a message by converting each character of
    the message to its numeric code, adding an integer to this code,
    then converting the resulting number back to a character.

********************************************************************)

CONST
    StringLength = 80;     (* upper limit on lengths of strings *)

TYPE
    String = PACKED ARRAY [1..StringLength] OF char;

VAR
    Message : String;      (* message to be scrambled *)
    NumChars,              (* number of characters in message *)
    Scrambler,             (* integer to be added to scramble message *)
    i : integer;           (* index *)

PROCEDURE ReadString (VAR Str : String; MaxString : integer;
                      VAR Length : integer);

    (*******************************************************************

        Procedure to read characters into string variable Str until
        an end-of-line mark is encountered or the upper limit
        MaxString on the length of Str is reached.  Any positions
        for which no characters are read will be filled with blanks.
        Length is assigned the number of characters read.

    ********************************************************************)

    VAR
        i : integer;       (* index *)
```

Figure 8.7

Figure 8.7 (Cont.)

```
   BEGIN (* ReadString *)
      Length := 0;
      FOR i := 1 TO MaxString DO
         IF NOT eoln THEN
            BEGIN
               read (Str[i]);
               Length := Length + 1
            END (* IF *)
         ELSE
            Str[i] := ' '
   END (* ReadString *);

BEGIN (* main program *)
   writeln ('Enter message to be scrambled:');
   ReadString (Message, StringLength, NumChars);
   write ('Enter (small) integer to use in scrambling:  ');
   readln (Scrambler);
   FOR i := 1 TO NumChars DO
      Message[i] := chr(ord(Message[i]) + Scrambler);
   writeln;
   writeln ('Coded message:');
   writeln (Message)
END (* main program *).


Sample run (assuming ASCII):


Enter message to be scrambled:
THE REDCOATS ARE COMING.
Enter (small) integer to use in scrambling:  5

Coded message:
YMJ%WJIHTFYX%FWJ%HTRNSL3
```

Because access to elements of a packed array may be more time-consuming than that of an unpacked array, the method used to input the elements of the packed array *TextLine* in the program of Figure 8.7 may be inefficient and, as we have noted, may not be allowed with some compilers. This difficulty can be avoided by reading each character into a temporary character variable and then assigning it to the appropriate array element. For example, the procedure *ReadString* of Figure 8.7 could be modified by declaring a local variable *TempChar* of type *char* and replacing the **if** statement with

> **if not** *eoln* **then**
>   **begin**
>   *read (TempChar)*;
>   *Str*[*i*] := *TempChar*;
>   *Length* := *Length* + 1
>   **end** (* **if** *)
>   **else**
>   *Str*[*i*] : = ' '

Alternatively, we could use the predefined Pascal procedures *pack* and *unpack* to transfer elements between an unpacked array and a packed array. These procedures are described in Appendix F.

8.5   Application: Text Editing

The preparation of textual material such as letters, books, and computer programs often involves the insertion, deletion, and replacement of parts of the text. The software of most computer systems includes an ***editing*** package that makes it easy to carry out these operations. To illustrate how these text-editing functions can be implemented in Pascal, we consider the problem of replacing a specified substring with another string in a given line of text. A solution to this problem is given in the program in Figure 8.8. The sample run shows that in addition to string replacements, the program can be used to make insertions and deletions.[5] For example, changing the substring

A N

in the line of text

A NATION CONCEIVED IN LIBERTY AND AND DEDICATED

to

A NEW N

yields the edited line

A NEW NATION CONCEIVED IN LIBERTY AND AND DEDICATED

Entering the edit change

AND / /

changes the substring

ANDb

(where b denotes a blank) in the line of text to an empty string containing no characters, and so the edited result is

A NEW NATION CONCEIVED IN LIBERTY AND DEDICATED

---

[5] The program can be greatly simplified in versions of Pascal that provide predefined string functions and procedures (see Figure 8.10).

```
PROGRAM TextEditor (input, output, TextFile, NewTextFile);

(*******************************************************************

   Program to perform some basic text-editing functions on lines of
   text.  The basic operation is that of replacing a substring of
   the text by another string.  This replacement is accomplished
   by a command of the form
                       OldString/NewString/
   where OldString specifies the substring in the text to be replaced
   by the specified string NewString; NewString may be an empty
   string which then causes the substring OldString (if found) to be
   deleted.  The text lines are read from TextFile, and after editing
   has been completed, the edited lines are written to NewTextFile.

   *****************************************************************)

CONST
   StringLimit = 80;        (* maximum length of lines of text *)

TYPE
   String = PACKED ARRAY[1..StringLimit] OF char;

VAR
   TextFile,                (* file of original text *)
   NewTextFile : text;      (* file of edited text *)
   TextLine : String;       (* line of text to be edited *)
   LineLength : integer;    (* length of TextLine *)

PROCEDURE GetTextLine (VAR TextLine : String; VAR CharCount : integer);

   (*******************************************************************

      Procedure to read a line of text from TextFile and count the
      number of characters in it.

      *****************************************************************)

   VAR
      i : integer;  (* index *)

   BEGIN (* GetTextLine *)
      CharCount := 0;
      FOR i := 1 TO StringLimit DO
         IF NOT eoln(TextFile) THEN
            BEGIN
               CharCount := CharCount + 1;
               read (TextFile, TextLine[CharCount])
            END (* IF *)
         ELSE
            TextLine[i] := ' ';
      readln (TextFile);
      writeln;
      writeln (TextLine: CharCount)
   END (* GetTextLine *);
```

Figure 8.8

Figure 8.8 (Cont.)

```pascal
PROCEDURE Edit (TextLine : String; LineLength : integer);

   (*****************************************************************

      Procedure to carry out the editing operations on TextLine.
      After editing is completed, edited line is written to
      NewTextFile.

   *****************************************************************)

   VAR
      OldString,              (* old string in edit change *)
      NewString : String;     (* new string in edit change *)
      OldLength,              (* length of oldstring *)
      NewLength,              (* length of newstring *)
      Location : integer;     (* location of OldString in TextLine *)
      Response : char;        (* user response *)

PROCEDURE GetEditChange (VAR OldString, NewString : String;
                         VAR OldLength, NewLength : integer);

   (*****************************************************************

      Procedure to read the edit change of the form
                  OldString/NewString/
      It returns OldString, NewString, and their lengths.

   *****************************************************************)

   VAR
      Symbol : char;          (* a symbol in edit change *)
      EndOfOld,               (* indicates end of OldString *)
      EndOfNew : boolean;     (* indicates end of NewString *)

   BEGIN (* GetEditChange *)
      writeln ('Edit change:  ');
      OldLength := 0;
      EndOfOld := false;
      WHILE NOT EndOfOld DO
         BEGIN
            read (Symbol);
            IF Symbol = '/' THEN
               EndOfOld := true
            ELSE
               BEGIN
                  OldLength := OldLength + 1;
                  OldString[OldLength] := Symbol
               END (* ELSE *)
         END (* WHILE *);
      NewLength := 0;
      EndOfNew := false;
      WHILE NOT EndOfNew DO
         BEGIN
            read (Symbol);
            IF Symbol = '/' THEN
               EndOfNew := true
            ELSE
               BEGIN
                  NewLength := NewLength + 1;
                  NewString[NewLength] := Symbol
               END (* ELSE *)
         END (* WHILE *);
      readln
   END (* GetEditChange *);
```

Figure 8.8 (Cont.)

```
FUNCTION Index (TextLine, SubString : String;
                LineLength, SubLength : integer) : integer;

   (*******************************************************************

      Function to determine the first occurrence of SubString in the
      specified line of text.  The value of Index is the position in
      TextLine of the first character of the first occurrence of
      SubString, or 0 if SubString does not appear in TextLine.
      Textlength and SubLength are the number of characters in
      TextLine and SubString, respectively.

   *******************************************************************)

   VAR
      TextPos,              (* position in TextLine *)
      SubPos : integer;     (* position in SubString *)
      Found : boolean;      (* indicates if SubString found *)

   BEGIN (* Index *)
      TextPos := 1;
      Found := false;
      WHILE (TextPos <= LineLength) AND (NOT Found) DO
         BEGIN
            Index := TextPos;
            SubPos := 1;
            WHILE (SubString[SubPos] = TextLine[TextPos]) AND
                  (SubPos <= SubLength) AND (TextPos <= LineLength) DO
               BEGIN
                  TextPos := TextPos + 1;
                  SubPos := SubPos + 1
               END (* WHILE *);
            IF SubPos > SubLength THEN
               Found := true;
            TextPos := TextPos + 1
         END (* WHILE *);
      IF NOT Found THEN
         Index := 0
   END (* Index *);

PROCEDURE Replace (VAR TextLine: String; VAR LineLength : integer;
                   NewString : String; OldLength, NewLength,
                   Start : integer);

   (*******************************************************************

      Procedure to replace a substring of length OldLength beginning
      at position Start of TextLine with NewString of length
      NewLength; LineLength will be the length of the modified string.

   *******************************************************************)

   VAR
      Shift,                (* amount to shift end of TextLine *)
      i : integer;          (* index *)
```

Figure 8.8 (Cont.)

```
    BEGIN (* Replace *)
        Shift := NewLength - OldLength;
        IF (Shift + LineLength) > StringLimit THEN
            writeln ('*** Change makes line of text too long ***')
        ELSE
            BEGIN
                IF Shift > 0 THEN  (* shift last part to the right *)
                    FOR i := LineLength DOWNTO Start + OldLength DO
                        TextLine[i + Shift] := TextLine[i];

                IF Shift < 0 THEN  (* shift last part to the left *)
                    FOR i := Start + OldLength TO LineLength DO
                        TextLine[i + Shift] := TextLine[i];

                (* Now insert the new string *)
                FOR i := 1 TO NewLength DO
                    TextLine[Start + i - 1] := NewString[i];
                LineLength := LineLength + Shift;
            END (* ELSE *);
        writeln (TextLine:LineLength);
    END (* Replace *);

    BEGIN (* Edit *)
        writeln ('Edit this line?  ');
        readln (Response);
        WHILE Response = 'Y' DO
            BEGIN
                GetEditChange (OldString, NewString, OldLength, NewLength);
                Location := Index (TextLine, OldString, LineLength, OldLength);
                IF Location = 0 THEN
                    writeln (OldString:OldLength, ' not found')
                ELSE
                    Replace (TextLine, LineLength, NewString, OldLength,
                             NewLength, Location);
                writeln ('More editing (Y or N)?  ');
                readln (Response)
            END (* WHILE *);
        writeln (NewTextFile, TextLine:LineLength)
    END (* Edit *);

BEGIN (* main program *)
    reset (TextFile);
    rewrite (NewTextFile);
    WHILE NOT eof (TextFile) DO
        BEGIN
            GetTextLine (TextLine, LineLength);
            Edit (TextLine, LineLength)
        END (* WHILE *)
END (* main program *).
```

Figure 8.8 (Cont.)

Listing of TestFile:

FOURSCORE AND FIVE YEARS AGO, OUR MOTHERS
BROUGHT FORTH ON CONTINENT
A NATION CONCEIVED IN LIBERTY AND AND DEDICATED
TO THE PREPOSITION THAT ALL MEN
ARE CREATED EQUAL.

Sample run:

FOURSCORE AND FIVE YEARS AGO, OUR MOTHERS
Edit this line?
Y
Edit change:
FIVE/SEVEN/
FOURSCORE AND SEVEN YEARS AGO, OUR MOTHERS
More editing (Y or N)?
Y
Edit change:
MOTHERS/FATHERS/
FOURSCORE AND SEVEN YEARS AGO, OUR FATHERS
More editing (Y or N)?
N

BROUGHT FORTH ON CONTINENT
Edit this line?
Y
Edit change:
ON C/ON THIS C/
BROUGHT FORTH ON THIS CONTINENT
More editing (Y or N)?
N

A NATION CONCEIVED IN LIBERTY AND AND DEDICATED
Edit this line?
Y
Edit change:
A N/A NEW N/
A NEW NATION CONCEIVED IN LIBERTY AND AND DEDICATED
More editing (Y or N)?
Y
Edit change:
AND //
A NEW NATION CONCEIVED IN LIBERTY AND DEDICATED
More editing (Y or N)?
N

TO THE PREPOSITION THAT ALL MEN
Edit this line?
Y
Edit change:
PRE/PRO/
TO THE PROPOSITION THAT ALL MEN
More editing (Y or N)?
N

Figure 8.8 (Cont.)

```
ARE CREATED EQUAL.
Edit this line?
N


Listing of NewTextFile:


FOURSCORE AND SEVEN YEARS AGO, OUR FATHERS
BROUGHT FORTH ON THIS CONTINENT
A NEW NATION CONCEIVED IN LIBERTY AND DEDICATED
TO THE PROPOSITION THAT ALL MEN
ARE CREATED EQUAL.
```

Exercises

1. Assume that the following declarations have been made:

type
   Color = (*red, yellow, blue, green, white, black*);
   ColorCodeArray = **packed array**[*Color*] **of** *char*;
   ArrayOfCharacters = **array**[1..10] **of** *char*;
   StringType = **packed array**[1..10] **of** *char*;

var
   ColorCode : *ColorCodeArray*;
   CharArray : *ArrayOfCharacters*;
   TextLine : *StringType*;
   Col : *Color*;
   i, j : *integer*;

Assume also that the following data are entered:

   ABCDEFG
   HI$

For each of the following, tell what value (if any) will be assigned to each array element, or explain why an error occurs.

(a) **for** *i* := 1 **to** 7 **do**
      read (*TextLine*[*i*]);
   readln;
   for *i* := 8 **to** 10 **do**
      read (*TextLine*[*i*];

(b) **for** *Col* := *black* **downto** *red* **do**
      read (*ColorCode*[*Col*]);

(c) **for** *i* := 1 **to** 10 **do**
      read (*TextLine*[*i*]);

(d) **for** *i* := 10 **downto** 1 **do**
      read (*TextLine*[*i*]);

(e) **for** *Col* := *red* **to** *black* **do**
    read (*ColorCode*[*Col*]);
for *Col* := *red* **to** *black* **do**
    TextLine[*ord*(*Col*) + 1] := *ColorCode*[*Col*];
for *i* := 7 **to** 10 **do**
    read (*TextLine*[*i*]);

(f) **for** *Col* := *red* **to** *black* **do**
    read (*ColorCode*[*Col*]);
TextLine := *ColorCode*;

(g) **for** *i* := 1 **to** 10 **do**
    read (*CharArray*[*i*]);
TextLine := *CharArray*;

(h) **for** *i* := 1 **to** 10 **do**
    read (*CharArray*[*i*]);
write (*CharArray*);

(i) **for** *i* := 1 **to** 10 **do**
    if not *eoln* **then**
      read (*TextLine*[*i*])
    else
      TextLine[*i*] := '¢';

(j) **for** *i* := 1 **to** 10 **do**
    if not *eoln* **then**
      read (*TextLine*[*i*])
    else
      readln;

(k) **for** *i* := 1 **to** 5 **do**
    if not *eoln* **then**
      read (*CharArray*[*i*], *CharArray*[*i* + 5])
    else
      begin
        CharArray[*i*] := '\$';
        CharArray[*i* + 5] := '¢'
      end;

(l) *i* := 0;
for *j* := 1 **to** 2 **do**
    begin
      while not *eoln* **do**
        begin
          i := *i* + 1;
          read (*TextLine*[*i*])
        end (* **while** *);
      readln
    end (* **for** *);

(**m**) $i := 0$;
  repeat
    while not *eoln* **do**
      begin
        $i := i + 1$;
        read (*TextLine*[*i*])
      end (* **while** *);
    readln
  until *TextLine*[*i*] = '\$';

2. Write a procedure to convert a string of lower- and upper-case letters into all upper-case.

3. Write a program to count all double-letter occurrences in a given line of text.

4. Develop a procedure to concatenate two strings. Then use this procedure in a program that reads two strings, calls the procedure to concatenate them, and then displays the resulting string.

5. The local chapter of the Know-Nothing party maintains a file of names and addresses of its contributors. Each line of the file contains the following items of information in the order indicated:

    Last Name: a string of length 12
    First name: a string of length 10
    Middle initial: a character
    Street address: a string of length 15
    City and state: a string of length 20
    Zip code: an integer

Each of the strings is assumed to be padded with blanks as necessary; for example,

DoeƀƀƀƀƀƀƀƀƀJohnƀƀƀƀƀƀQ123ƀSomeStreetƀAnyTown,ƀAnyStateƀƀƀ12345

Write a program that reads each line of the file and produces a mailing label having the format

    John Q. Doe
    123 SomeStreet
    AnyTown, AnyState 12345

6. Repeat Exercise 5 but assume that the strings are not padded with blanks in the file; rather, all of the items in each line are separated by some delimiter such as #; for example,

    Doe#John#Q#123 SomeStreet#AnyTown, AnyState#12345

7. Write a program to print a "personalized" contest letter like those frequently received in the mail. It might have a format like that of the

following sample, with the underlined locations filled in with appropriate data:

Mr. John Q. Doe
123 SomeStreet
AnyTown, AnyState 12345

Dear Mr. Doe:

How would you like to see a brand new Cadillac parked in front of 123 SomeStreet in AnyTown, AnyState? Impossible, you say? No, it isn't, Mr. Doe. Simply keep the enclosed raffle ticket and validate it by sending a $100.00 tax-deductible political contribution and 10 labels from Shyster & Sons chewing tobacco. Not only will you become eligible for the drawing to be conducted on Februrary 29 by the independent firm of G.Y.P. Shyster, but you will also be helping to reelect Sam Shyster. That's all there is to it, John. You may be a winner!!!

8. Write a program that permits the input of a name consisting of a first name, a middle name or initial, and a last name, in that order, and then prints the last name, followed by a comma, and then the first and middle initials, each followed by a period. For example, the input John H. Doe should produce Doe, J. H.

9. The encoding scheme used in this section to produce a cryptogram consists simply of adding a specified integer to the code of each character of the message. This is a special case of the technique known as *keyword* encoding, in which a sequence of integers corresponding to the characters of a specified keyword is added in order to the codes of the message characters. To illustrate, if the keyword is ABC and the message is MEETATNOON, the codes for A, B, and C are added to the codes for M, E, and E, respectively, and then added to the codes for T, A, and T, respectively, and so forth, producing the cryptogram NGHUCWOQRO (assuming this is an ASCII machine). Write a program to implement this keyword method of encoding.

10. Another method of encoding uses substitutions, for example:

letter: A B C D E F G H I J K L M N O P Q R S T U V W X Y Z
substitute: T F H X Q J E M U P I D C K V B A O L R Z W G N S Y

Each letter of the input message is then replaced with its substitute, for example:

message: T H E R E D C O A T S A R E C O M I N G
cryptogram: R M Q O Q X H V T R L T O Q H V C U K E

Write a program that permits the input of either a message or a cryptogram and then encodes or decodes it by using substitutions.

11. There are 3 teaspoons in a tablespoon, 4 tablespoons in a quarter of a cup, 2 cups in a pint, and 2 pints in a quart. Write a program to

convert units in cooking. The program should call for the input of the amount, the units used, and the new units desired. For example, the input 0.5, CUPS, TEASPOONS asks for the conversion of one-half cup to teaspoons.

12. Frequency counts can be graphically displayed by using a *histogram.* For example if the frequency counts of persons in three education levels, high school, college, and graduate, were 15, 8, 12, respectively, these could be displayed by the following histogram:

   High School: XXXXXXXXXXXXXXX
       College: XXXXXXXX
      Graduate: XXXXXXXXXXXX

Write a program to read several pairs of strings and frequencies and to plot a histogram displaying the information.

13. Write a program to convert ordinary Hindu-Arabic numerals into Roman numerals and vice versa. (I = 1, V = 5, X = 10, L = 50, C = 100, D = 500, and M = 1,000.)

14. A string is said to be a *palindrome* if it does not change when the order of characters in the string is reversed. For example,

   MADAM

   463364

   ABLE WAS I ERE I SAW ELBA

are palindromes. Write a program to read a string and then determine whether it is a palindrome.

15. Repeat Exercise 14, but this time use a recursive procedure to determine whether a string is a palindrome.

16. Graphs of equations can also be plotted by using the computer. For example, Figure 8.9 shows computer-generated plots of

$$Y = X^2 \text{ for } -3 \le X \le 3$$

and

$$Y = X^3 \text{ for } -2 \le X \le 2$$

using an X increment of 0.25 in each case. Note that for convenience, the X axis has been printed vertically and the Y axis horizontally. Write a program to produce a similar plot of a given equation, using a packed character array with the number of array elements equal to the width of the page. For each X value, set all of the array elements equal to blanks, or equal to the marks comprising the Y axis if $X = 0$; then set one array element equal to the X axis mark and another equal to the plotting character; the position of this latter array element should correspond to the Y coordinate of the point on the graph for that X value.

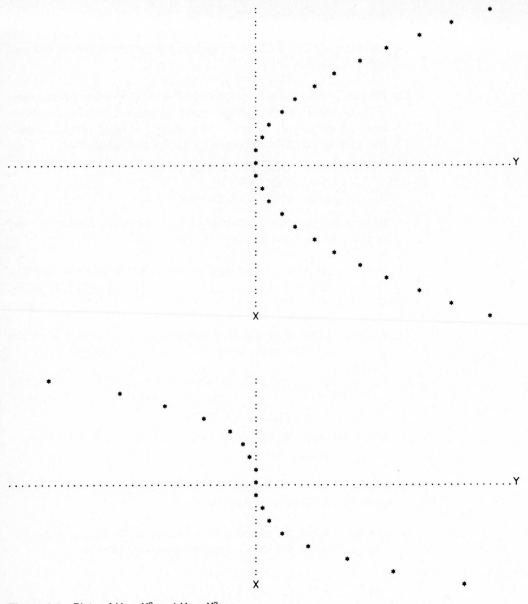

Figure 8.9   Plots of $Y = X^2$ and $Y = X^3$.

17. Write a program that uses the Sieve Method of Eratosthenes to find all prime numbers from 2 through some integer n. (See Exercise 20 of Section 8.3.) Use a packed array *Sieve* of boolean type in which *Sieve*[i] is true if i is in the list, false if i has been crossed out.

18. Write a program to determine whether a specified string occurs in a given string, and if so, print an asterisk (*) under the first position of each occurrence.

19. Write a program to count the number of occurrences of a specified string in several lines of text.

20. Write a program that accepts two strings and determines whether one string is an ***anagram*** of the other, that is, whether one string is a permutation of the characters in the other string. For example, "dear" is an anagram of "read," as is "dare."

Programming Pointers

In this chapter we discussed one-dimensional arrays. It is quite common for beginning programmers to have some difficulty when using arrays. The following are some of the major points to remember.

1. *The types of the components of an array may be any predefined or user-defined type. The types of the indices may be any ordinal data type.*

2. *In an indexed variable the index must be compatible with the type specified in the array declaration.* The most common error is that of an index getting out of range. For example, suppose that the array *Number* is declared by

> **type**
>   *ListOfNumbers* = **array**[1..10] **of** *integer*;

> **var**
>   *Number* : *ListOfNumbers*;

and consider the following statements designed to read and count the elements of this array, where *i* is assumed to be of integer type, *Temp* is of integer type, and −999 is an end-of-data flag:

> *i* := 0;
> **repeat**
>   *i* := *i* + 1;
>   *read* (*Temp*);
>   **if** *Temp* <> −999 **then**
>   *Number*[*i*] := *Temp*
> **until** *Temp* = −999;

These statements correctly read values for the entries of *Number*, provided that there are no more than ten values preceding the end-of-data flag. But if there are more than ten values, an error results when the value of *i* reaches 11, because an attempt is made to read a value for *Number*[11], and an error message such as the following may be displayed:

> *** Value 11 out of range, must be <= 10 ***

As this example demonstrates, it is important to check ***boundary conditions*** when processing the elements of arrays, that is, to check to make sure that the index is not out of range. Thus, the preceding set of statements could better be written as

```
i := 0;
repeat
   i := i + 1;
   read (Temp);
   if Temp <> -999 then
      Number[i] := Temp
until (Temp = -999) or (i = 10);
if Temp <> -999 then
   writeln ('End-of-data flag not encountered');
```

3. *When reading the elements of an array of characters, remember that end-of-line marks are read as blanks.*

4. *Assignment of one array to another requires that the arrays have the same type.*

5. *Values of string type may be compared with the standard relational operators, provided they have the same length. They may also be output using the write and writeln procedures.* This is not the case, however, for unpacked arrays. Also, the elements of arrays cannot usually be read by including the array name in the input list of a *read* or *readln* statement. This must be accomplished by reading the individual elements of the arrays, and in some versions of Pascal, these may not be elements of a packed array.

6. *To utilize memory efficiently, it is usually advisable to specify as variable parameters the formal parameters of functions and procedures that represent arrays (especially if they are large).* If value parameters are used for arrays, two copies of the array are stored in memory; also, the elements of the actual array must be copied to that of the subprogram, and this is quite time-consuming for large arrays.

Variations and Extensions

As an extension to the array-processing features of standard Pascal, some versions of Pascal (UCSD) allow arrays of the same type to be compared with the relational operators = and <>, and some (Turbo) allow arrays to be initialized in the declaration part of a program. By far the most useful and most common extension, however, is the inclusion of a predefined string data type and a number of predefined functions and procedures for manipulating strings. What follows are some of the string-processing features provided in those versions of Pascal that have a predefined string type:

- *String declarations*. A string declaration commonly has the form

  string[*length-limit*]

  where *string* is a predefined identifier (Macintosh, UCSD) or a reserved word (Turbo); *length-limit* is a positive integer constant no greater than some specified value such as 80 (UCSD) or 255 (Macintosh, Turbo); it specifies the maximum length (number of characters) that a string of this type may have. Examples of variable declarations using this type are

  var
      Name : *string*[20];   (* maximum length is 20 *)
      Sentence : *string*[255];   (* maximum length is 255 *)
      Initial : *string*[1];   (* string of length 1 *)

  Some versions (Macintosh, UCSD) also allow string declarations of the form *string* with no specification of a length limit. In this case, a default maximum length is assumed.

- *String*[#] vs. **packed array**[1 . . #] **of** *char*. The lengths of strings assigned to a variable of a predefined string type are *dynamic*, whereas strings assigned to a variable declared to be a packed character array have *constant* length. Because of this fundamental difference, these two types may not be compatible. For the same reason, types *string*[1] and *char* may be incompatible. The following list illustrates some of the similarities and differences between these two string types. It assumes the declarations:

  var
      Ident : **packed array**[1..20] **of** *char*;
      Name : *string*[20];

- *Lengths of strings*. Values for *Ident* will be strings of length exactly equal to 20, but the actual lengths of strings assigned to *Name* may vary from a minimum length of 0 (the **empty string** is a legal value) to a maximum length of 20. Thus, in the assignment statements

  Name := 'John Doe';
  Ident := 'John Doeƀƀƀƀƀƀƀƀƀƀƀƀ';

  the string 'John Doe' of length 8 is assigned to *Name*; padding with twelve blanks is required in the similar assignment to *Ident*.

- *Input of strings*. A value can be read for *Name* by simply using the string variable in an input statement; for example,

  readln (*Name*);   Input: John Doe

When the end-of-line character (carriage return) is encountered, the assignment of the string 'John Doe' of length 8 to *Name* is complete; no padding with blanks occurs.

● *Output of strings*. The default field width used to display the value of *Name* is the current length (8) of this value:

  writeln (*Name*, '-11/29/38');   Output: John Doe-11/29/38

If *Name* were replaced by *Ident,* a default field width of 20 would be used and the blanks used to pad the string would be displayed.

● *Use of indices*. The individual characters in the value of a variable of a predefined string type can be accessed in the same manner as for packed character arrays by using an index that can range from 1 up through the current length. For example, the following **if** statement could be used to display the value of *Name* if it begins with the letter J:

  if *Name* [1] = 'J' **then**
    writeln (*Name*);

● *Comparison of strings*. Values of type *string*[#] need not have the same length to be compared. For example, if *Name1* and *Name2* are of type *string*[20] and have the values 'Doe' and 'Smith', respectively, then the following is a valid boolean expression and has the value true:

  Name1 < *Name2*

● *Predefined string functions and procedures*. Four predefined functions are provided for manipulating strings, *concat, copy, length,* and *pos*. A function reference of the form

  concat(*str-1, str-2, . . . , str-n*)

returns the string formed by concatenating the strings *str-1, str-2, . . . , str-n* in this order. The function reference

  copy(*str, index, size*)

returns a substring of the specified *size* from the string *str,* beginning at position *index*. A reference to the *length* function

  length(*str*)

returns the current length (integer) of the specified string. A function reference of the form

  pos(*str-1, str-2*)

returns the position of the first character of the first occurrence of string *str-1* within the string *str-2* or 0 if *str-1* is not found in *str-2*.

Two predefined procedures, *delete* and *insert*, are also provided:

delete (str, index, size)

modifies the value of string *str* by removing a substring of the specified size, starting at position *index*;

insert (str-1, str-2, index)

modifies string *str-2* by inserting the string *str-1* at position *index*.

The program in Figure 8.10 is a modification of the text editor program in Figure 8.8. It uses the predefined string type and string functions and procedures of Turbo Pascal to carry out the basic text-editing operations.

```
PROGRAM TextEditor;

(*************************************************************************

   Program to perform some basic text-editing functions on lines of
   text.  The basic operation is that of replacing a substring of
   the text by another string.  This replacement is accomplished
   by a command of the form
                    OldString/NewString/
   where OldString specifies the substring in the text to be replaced
   by the specified string NewString; NewString may be an empty
   string which then causes the substring OldString (if found) to be
   deleted.  The text lines are read from TextFile, and after editing
   has been completed, the edited lines are written to NewTextFile.

*************************************************************************)

CONST
   MaxString = 80;              (* maximum length of lines in TextFile *)

TYPE
   StringType = STRING[MaxString];

VAR
   TextFile,                    (* file of original text *)
   NewTextFile : text;          (* file of edited text *)
   OldFileName,                 (* actual name of text file *)
   NewFileName : STRING[20];    (* actual name for new file *)
   TextLine : StringType;       (* line of text to be edited *)
```

Figure 8.10

Figure 8.10 (Cont.)

```
PROCEDURE GetTextLine (VAR TextLine : StringType);

   (****************************************************************

      Procedure to read and echo a line of text from TextFile.

   ****************************************************************)

   BEGIN (* GetTextLine *)
      readln (TextFile, TextLine);
      writeln;
      writeln (TextLine)
   END (* GetTextLine *);

PROCEDURE Edit (TextLine : StringType);

   (****************************************************************

      Procedure to carry out the editing operations on TextLine.
      After editing is completed, edited line is written to
      NewTextFile.

   ****************************************************************)

   VAR
      OldString,                  (* old string in edit change *)
      NewString : StringType;     (* new string in edit change *)
      Location : integer;         (* location of OldString in TextLine *)
      Response : char;            (* user response *)

   PROCEDURE GetEditChange (VAR OldString, NewString : StringType);

      (****************************************************************

         Procedure to read the edit change of the form
                     OldString/NewString/
         It returns OldString and NewString.

      ****************************************************************)

      VAR
         EditChange : StringType;  (* editing change *)
         OldLength,                (* length of OldString *)
         NewLength : integer;      (* length of NewString *)

      BEGIN (* GetEditChange *)
         writeln ('Edit change:  ');
         readln (EditChange);
         OldLength := pos('/', EditChange) - 1;
         OldString := copy(EditChange, 1, OldLength);
         delete(EditChange, 1, OldLength + 1);
         NewLength := length(EditChange) - 1;
         NewString := copy(EditChange, 1, NewLength)
      END (* GetEditChange *);
```

Figure 8.10 (Cont.)

```pascal
PROCEDURE Replace (VAR TextLine: StringType;
                       OldString, NewString : StringType; Start : integer);

   (***************************************************************

      Procedure to replace a substring OldString beginning at
      position Start of TextLine with NewString.

      *************************************************************)

   BEGIN (* Replace *)
      delete(TextLine, Start, length(OldString));
      IF Start < length(TextLine) THEN
         insert(NewString, TextLine, Start)
      ELSE
         TextLine := concat(TextLine, NewString);
      writeln (TextLine)
   END (* Replace *);

BEGIN (* Edit *)
   writeln ('Edit this line?  ');
   readln (Response);
   WHILE Response = 'Y' DO
      BEGIN
         GetEditChange (OldString, NewString);
         Location := pos (OldString, TextLine);
         IF Location = 0 THEN
            writeln (OldString, ' not found')
         ELSE
            Replace (TextLine, OldString, NewString, Location);
         writeln ('More editing (Y or N)?  ');
         readln (Response)
      END (* WHILE *);
   writeln (NewTextFile, TextLine)
END (* Edit *);

BEGIN (* main program *)
   write ('Name of file to be edited?  ');
   readln (OldFileName);
   assign (TextFile, OldFileName);
   write ('Name of new file to be produced?  ');
   readln (NewFileName);
   assign (NewTextFile, NewFileName);
   reset (TextFile);
   rewrite (NewTextFile);
   WHILE NOT eof (TextFile) DO
      BEGIN
         GetTextLine (TextLine);
         Edit (TextLine)
      END (* WHILE *);
   close (TextFile);
   close (NewTextFile)
END (* main program *).
```

9

Multidimensional Arrays

Everyone knows how laborious the usual Method is of attaining to Arts and Sciences; whereas by his Contrivance, the most ignorant Person at a reasonable Charge, and with a little bodily Labour, may write Books in Philosophy, Poetry, Politicks, Law, Mathematicks, and Theology, without the least Assistance from Genius or Study. He then led me to the Frame, about the sides whereof all his Pupils stood in Ranks. It was Twenty Foot square . . . linked by slender Wires. These Bits . . . were covered on every Square with Paper pasted upon them; and on These Papers were written all the Words of their Language. . . .

The Professor then desired me to observe, for he was going to set his Engine at work. The Pupils at this Command took each of them hold of an Iron Handle, whereof there were Forty fixed round the Edges of the Frame; and giving them a sudden Turn, the whole Disposition of the Words was entirely changed. . . .

JONATHAN SWIFT, *Gulliver's Travels*

In the preceding chapter we considered one-dimensional arrays and used them to process lists and strings. We also observed that Pascal allows arrays of more than one dimension, and that two-dimensional arrays are useful when the data being processed can be arranged in rows and columns. Similarly, a three-dimensional array is appropriate when the data can be arranged in rows, columns, and ranks. When there are several characteristics associated with the data, still higher dimensions may be appropriate, with each dimension corresponding to one of these characteristics. In this chapter we consider how such multidimensional arrays are processed in Pascal programs.

9.1 Introduction to Multidimensional Arrays; Multiply Indexed Variables

There are many problems in which the data being processed can be naturally organized as a table. For example, suppose that water temperatures are recorded four times a day at each of three locations near the discharge outlet of the cooling system of a nuclear power plant. These temperature readings can be arranged in a table having four rows and three columns:

Time	Location 1	2	3
1	65.5	68.7	62.0
2	68.8	68.9	64.5
3	70.4	69.4	66.3
4	68.5	69.1	65.8

In this table, the three temperature readings at time 1 are in the first row, the three temperatures at time 2 are in the second row, and so on.

These 12 data items can be conveniently stored in a ***two-dimensional array.*** The array declaration

```
const
    MaxTimes = 4;
    MaxLocations = 3;

type
    TemperatureTable = array[1..MaxTimes, 1..MaxLocations] of real;

var
    TempTab : TemperatureTable;
```

reserves 12 memory locations for these data items. The doubly indexed variable

$TempTab[2, 3]$

then refers to the entry in the second row and third column of the table, that is, to the temperature 64.5 recorded at time 2 at location 3. In general,

$TempTab[i, j]$

refers to the entry in the ith row and jth column, that is, to the temperature recorded at time i at location j.

To illustrate the use of an array with more than two dimensions, suppose that the temperature readings are made for one week, so that seven such tables are collected:

Time	Location 1	2	3	
1	66.5	69.4	68.4	
2	68.4	71.2	69.3	Day 7
3	70.1	71.9	70.2	
4	69.5	70.0	69.4	

Time	Location 1	2	3	
1	63.7	66.2	64.3	
2	64.0	66,8	64.9	Day 2
			66.3	
			65.8	

Time	Location 1	2	3	
1	65.5	68.7	62.0	
2	68.8	68.9	64.5	Day 1
3	70.4	69.4	66.3	
4	68.5	69.1	65.8	

A *three-dimensional array* Temp declared by

```
const
    MaxTimes = 4;
    MaxLocations = 3;
    MaxDays = 7;

type
    ListOfTempTables =
        array[1..MaxTimes, 1..MaxLocations, 1..MaxDays] of real;

var
    Temp : ListOfTempTables;
```

can be used to store these 84 temperature readings. The value of the triply indexed variable

Temp[1, 3, 2]

is the temperature recorded at time 1 at location 3 on day 2, that is, the value 64.3 in the first row, third column, second rank. In general,

Temp[Time, Loc, Day]

is the temperature recorded at time *Time* at location *Loc* on day *Day*.

In some problems, even higher-dimensional arrays may be useful. For example, suppose that a retailer maintains an inventory of jeans. He carries several different brands of jeans and for each brand stocks a variety of styles, waist sizes, and inseam lengths. A four-dimensional array can be used to record the inventory, with each element of the array being the number of jeans of a particular brand, style, waist size, and inseam length currently in stock. The first index represents the brand; thus it might be of type

$$BrandType = (Levi, Wrangler, CalvinKlein, Lee, BigYank);$$

The second index represents style and is of type

$$StyleType = 'A'..'F';$$

The third and fourth indices represent waist size and inseam length, respectively. Their types might be given by

$$WaistSize = 28..40;$$
$$InseamSize = 28..36;$$

In a Pascal program for maintaining this inventory, the following type section is thus appropriate:

type
    BrandType = (*Levi, Wrangler, CalvinKlein, Lee, BigYank*);
    StyleType = 'A'..'F';
    WaistSize = 28..40;
    InseamSize = 28..36;
    JeansArray = **array**[*BrandType, StyleType, WaistSize, InseamSize*]
                 of *integer*;

The four-dimensional array *JeansInStock* having indices of the types just described can then be declared by

var
    JeansInStock : *JeansArray*;

The value of the quadruply indexed variable

$$JeansInStock\ [Levi,\ 'B',\ 32,\ 31]$$

is the number of Levi style-B 32 X 31 jeans in stock. The statement

$$JeansInStock[b,\ s,\ w,\ i] := JeansInStock[b,\ s,\ w,\ i] - 1$$

records the sale of one pair of jeans of brand b, style s, waist size w, and inseam length i.

The Pascal standard places no limit on the number of dimensions of an array, but the type of each index must be declared. The general form of the declaration of an **n-dimensional array** is

$$\textbf{array}[index\text{-}type\text{-}1,\ index\text{-}type\text{-}2,\ \ldots\ ,\ index\text{-}type\text{-}n]\ \textbf{of}\ component\text{-}type$$

where *index-type-i* specifies the type of the ith index and may be any ordinal type. The syntax diagram for array declarations is

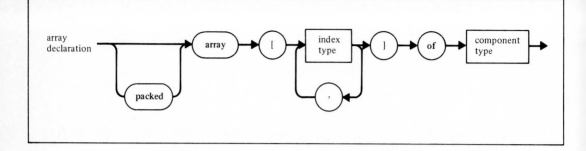

An equivalent method of declaring a multidimensional array is as an **array of arrays,** that is, an array whose elements are other arrays. To illustrate, reconsider the table of temperatures given earlier:

Time	Location 1	Location 2	Location 3
1	65.5	68.7	62.0
2	68.8	68.9	64.5
3	70.4	69.4	66.3
4	68.5	69.1	65.8

For each time there is an array of temperatures corresponding to one row of the table. The entire table might then be viewed as an array of these temperature arrays. Thus, if we define the types *Temperatures* and *ArrayOfTemperatures* by

>**type**
> *Temperatures* = **array**[1..*MaxLocations*] **of** *real*;
> *ArrayOfTemperatures* = **array**[1..*MaxTimes*] **of** *Temperatures*;

or

>**type**
> *ArrayOfTemperatures* =
>   **array**[1..*MaxTimes*] **of array**[1..*MaxLocations*] **of** *real*;

then the declaration

>**var**
> *Table* : *ArrayOfTemperatures*;

establishes 12 memory locations for these data items. The singly indexed variable

>*Table*[2]

refers to the second row of the table, that is, to the list of temperatures at time 2:

>68.8   68.9   64.5

The doubly indexed variable

Table[2][3]

or equivalently,

Table[2, 3]

then refers to the third temperature in this row, that is, the temperature 64.5 recorded at time 2 at location 3. In general, either of

Table[*i*][*j*]   or   *Table*[*i*, *j*]

refers to the *j*th entry in the *i*th row of the table, that is, to the temperature recorded at time *i* at the *j*th location.

Another problem in which it might be natural to structure the data as an array of arrays arises in processing pages of text. A book can be thought of as an array of pages and each page as an array of lines of text; thus a book can be viewed as an array of arrays of lines. Similarly, a line is an array of characters; consequently, a page is an array of arrays of characters, and a book is an array of arrays of arrays of characters.

To illustrate, if the types *Line, Page,* and *Book* are defined by

type
    Line = **packed array**[1..70] **of** *char*;
    Page = **packed array**[1..45] **of** *Line*;
    Book = **packed array**[1..30] **of** *Page*;

and the array name *PascalText* is declared as

var
    PascalText : *Book*;

then

PascalText[30]

denotes the thirtieth page;

PascalText[30][5]

or

PascalText[30, 5]

denotes the fifth line on that page; and

PascalText[30][5][10]

or

    PascalText[30, 5, 10]

denotes the tenth character on that line. This character could also be denoted
by

    PascalText[30, 5][10]

or

    PascalText[30][5, 10]

but these notations are seldom used.

9.2 Processing Multidimensional Arrays

In the preceding section we gave several examples of multidimensional arrays
and showed how such arrays are declared in a Pascal program. We also noted
that any element of the array can be accessed directly by using a multiply
indexed variable consisting of the array name followed by the indices that
indicate that item's location in the array. In this section we consider the processing of multidimensional arrays, including the input and output of arrays or parts
of arrays, copying the elements of one array into another array, and using
multidimensional arrays as parameters in subprograms.

    As we observed in the preceding chapter, the most natural order for processing
the elements of a one-dimensional array is the usual sequential order, from first
item to last. For multidimensional arrays there are several different orders in
which the indices may be varied when processing the array elements.

    Two-dimensional arrays are often used when the data can be organized as
a table consisting of rows and columns. This leads to two natural orders for
processing the entries of a two-dimensional array, *rowwise* and **columnwise.**
Rowwise processing means that the array elements in the first row are processed
first, then those in the second row, and so on, as shown in Figure 9.1(a) for
the 3 × 4 array *A* having three rows and four columns. In columnwise processing, the entries in the first column are processed first, then those in the second
column, and so on, as illustrated in Figure 9.1(b).

    In the list of array elements shown in Figure 9.1(b), we observe that in
the columnwise processing of a two-dimensional array, it is the first index that
varies first and the second index second; that is, the first index must vary over
its entire set of values before the second index changes. For arrays of three or
more dimensions, the same pattern of processing is commonly used; that is,
the first index varies first, followed by the second index, and then by the third,
and so on. This is illustrated in Figure 9.2 for the 2 × 4 × 3 array *B* having
two rows, four columns, and three ranks.

    The elements of a multidimensional array can be read by using nested
repetition structures; we simply place an input statement within a pair of nested
for (or **while** or **repeat**) loops, each of whose control variables controls one

(a) A[1,1]
     A[1,2]
     A[1,3]
     A[1,4]
     A[2,1]
     A[2,2]
     A[2,3]
     A[2,4]
     A[3,1]
     A[3,2]
     A[3,3]
     A[3,4]

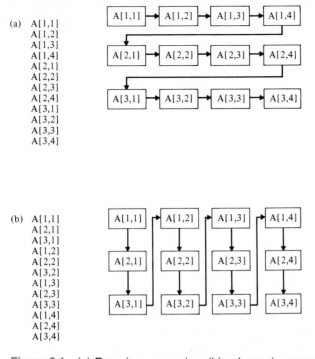

(b) A[1,1]
     A[2,1]
     A[3,1]
     A[1,2]
     A[2,2]
     A[3,2]
     A[1,3]
     A[2,3]
     A[3,3]
     A[1,4]
     A[2,4]
     A[3,4]

Figure 9.1   (a) Rowwise processing; (b) columnwise processing.

B[1,1,1]
B[2,1,1]
B[1,2,1]
B[2,2,1]
B[1,3,1]
B[2,3,1]
B[1,4,1]
B[2,4,1]
B[1,1,2]
B[2,1,2]
B[1,2,2]
B[2,2,2]
B[1,3,2]
B[2,3,2]
B[1,4,2]
B[2,4,2]
B[1,1,3]
B[2,1,3]
B[1,2,3]
B[2,2,3]
B[1,3,3]
B[2,3,3]
B[1,4,3]
B[2,4,3]

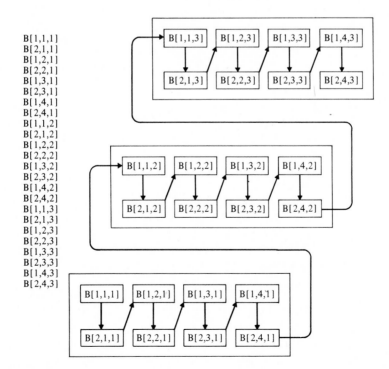

Figure 9.2

of the indices of the array. For example, to read the twelve entries of a
3×4 integer array A in rowwise order so that it has the value

$$\begin{bmatrix} 22 & 37 & 0 & 0 \\ 0 & 1 & 17 & 32 \\ 6 & 18 & 4 & 12 \end{bmatrix}$$

we could use the nested **for** statements

    for *row* := 1 **to** 3 **do**
      for *column* := 1 **to** 4 **do**
        read (*A*[*row, column*]);

When these statements are executed, the outer **for** loop sets the value of the
control variable *row* to 1 and the inner **for** loop is then executed, using 1 as
the value for *row;* the effect, therefore, is the same as executing

    for *column* := 1 **to** 4 **do**
      read (*A*[1, *column*]);

which is equivalent to the following four *read* statements:

    read (*A*[1, 1]);
    read (*A*[1, 2]);
    read (*A*[1, 3]);
    read (*A*[1, 4]);

The first pass through the outer **for** loop thus reads values for the first row of
A, so the first four values entered must be 22, 37, 0, and 0.
    Now the outer **for** loop sets the value of the control variable *row* to 2,
and the inner **for** loop is executed again:

    for *column* := 1 **to** 4 **do**
      read (*A*[2, *column*]);

which is equivalent to the four *read* statements

    read (*A*[2, 1]);
    read (*A*[2, 2]);
    read (*A*[2, 3]);
    read (*A*[2, 4]);

so that the next four values entered must be those in the second row of *A*, 0,
1, 17, and 32.
    Finally, the outer **for** loop sets the value of *row* to 3, and the inner **for**
loop is executed again:

    for *column* := 1 **to** 4 **do**
      read (*A*[3, *column*]);

which has the same effect as

> *read* (*A*[3, 1]);
> *read* (*A*[3, 2]);
> *read* (*A*[3, 3]);
> *read* (*A*[3, 4]);

for which the values in the third row of *A* must be entered: 6, 18, 4, and 12.

The entries in this table must thus be entered in the order 22, 37, 0, 0, 0, 1, 17, 32, 6, 18, 4, 12 for rowwise processing. They can all be read from the same line

> 22 37 0 0 0 1 17 32 6 18 4 12

or from three lines each containing four values

> 22 37 0 0
> 0 1 17 32
> 6 18 4 12

or from as many lines as desired. Note that if *readln* had been used instead of *read*, it would have been necessary to enter the values one per line, thus requiring twelve separate lines of data.

Columnwise input is also possible. We need only reverse the order of the two **for** loops

> **for** *column* := 1 **to** 4 **do**
>   **for** *row* := 1 **to** 3 **do**
>   *read* (*A*[*row, column*]);

and enter the values in the order 22, 0, 6, 37, 1, 18, 0, 17, 4, 0, 32, 12.

Special care must be taken when reading values for a character array. For example, consider the 3 × 3 table

$$\begin{bmatrix} A & B & C \\ D & E & F \\ G & H & I \end{bmatrix}$$

To read these nine characters into the 3 × 3 character array *CharArray* in rowwise order, we could use the statement

> **for** *row* := 1 **to** 3 **do**
>   **for** *column* := 1 **to** 4 **do**
>   *read* (*CharArray*[*row, column*]);

and enter all the data on one line

> ABCDEFGHI

But the data cannot be entered on separate lines because an end-of-line character is read and stored as a blank. Thus, if the data are entered as

    ABC
    DEF
    GHI

then the table actually stored in the array *CharArray* is

$$\begin{bmatrix} A & B & C \\ b & D & E \\ F & b & G \end{bmatrix}$$

because the end-of-line character is read for *CharArray*[2, 1] and *CharArray*[3, 2] and stored as a blank (b) in these locations. If the preceding nested **for** statements are changed to

```
for row := 1 to 3 do
    begin
        for column := 1 to 3 do
            read (CharArray[row, column]);
        readln
    end (* for *);
```

the data can be entered as

    ABC
    DEF
    GHI

because in this case the *readln* statement with no input list advances the data pointer past the next end-of-line mark.

The elements of an array can be displayed by using repetition structures similar to those used for input. For example, the statement

```
for row := 1 to 3 do
    begin
        for column := 1 to 4 do
            write (A[row, column]:4);
        writeln
    end (* for *);
```

where *A* is the integer array just considered produces as output

   22 37   0   0
    0   1 17 32
    6 18   4 12

Note that the *write* statement displays the values in each row on the same line and that a *writeln* statement is used to terminate this line.

These same input/output techniques can be applied to higher-dimensional arrays. For example, values could be read into the 2 × 4 × 3 array *B* in the order indicated in Figure 9.2 by the nested **for** statements

```
for rank := 1 to 3 do
    for column := 1 to 4 do
        for row := 1 to 2 do
            read (B[row, column, rank]);
```

Other types of array processing can also be carried out using nested repetition structures. To illustrate, consider the 4 × 3 array *TempTab* used in Section 9.1 to store the following table of temperature readings:

Time	Location 1	2	3
1	65.5	68.7	62.0
2	68.8	68.9	64.5
3	70.4	69.4	66.3
4	68.5	69.1	65.8

To calculate the average temperature at each of the four times, it is necessary to calculate the sum of the entries in each row and to divide each of these sums by 3. The following program segment can be used to carry out this computation and to display the average temperature at each time:

```
for Time := 1 to 4 do
    begin
        Sum := 0;
        for Loc := 1 to 3 do
            Sum := Sum + TempTab[Time, Loc];
        MeanTemp := Sum / 3;
        writeln ('Mean temperature at time ', Time:1, ' is ', MeanTemp:3:1)
    end (* for *);
```

Nested repetition structures can also be used to copy the entries of one array into another array. For example, if *A* and *B* are 5 × 10 arrays, the nested **for** statements

```
for row := 1 to 5 do
    for column := 1 to 10 do
        B[row, column] := A[row, column];
```

will copy the entries of *A* into the corresponding locations of array *B*, assuming, of course, that the component type of *A* is compatible with the component type of *B*. If *A* and *B* have the *same types* (see Section 8.2), this can be done more simply with the array assignment statement

```
B := A;
```

Multidimensional arrays may also be used as parameters for functions and procedures. The rules governing the use of arrays as parameters, which were described in detail in Section 8.2 for one-dimensional arrays, also apply to multidimensional arrays. These rules are summarized as follows:

1. The types of formal parameters in a function or procedure heading must be specified by type identifiers. Thus, for example, the array declaration *Grades* : **array**[1..25, 1..4] **of** *real* may not be used to declare the type of a formal parameter in a procedure or function heading. It may be given in the form *Grades* : *Table* where *Table* is a type identifier associated with **array**[1..25, 1..4] **of** *real*.
2. The types of arrays used as actual parameters must be the same as the types of the corresponding arrays used as formal parameters.
3. The type of a function value may not be an array.

9.3   Application to String Processing

In Section 8.4 we examined in detail the use of packed arrays to process strings. A collection of such strings can be processed using an array of strings. To illustrate, suppose that a list of names, each consisting of a first name followed by a blank followed by a last name, is to be sorted so that the last names are in alphabetical order. The names in this sorted list are then to be displayed in the form last name, first name.

Each name to be processed can be stored in an array of string type. Thus we might define the type identifier *NameString* by

> **const**
>   *NameLength* = 30;
>   *ListLimit* = 100;
>
> **type**
>   *NameString* = **packed array**[1..*NameLength*] **of** *char*;

where *NameLength* is a constant specifying the number of characters (including trailing blanks) in each name. If the type identifier *List* is then defined by

> *List* = **array**[1..*ListLimit*] **of** *NameString*;

it may be used to declare arrays that store the list of names; for example,

> **var**
>   *Name* : *List*;

The singly indexed variable *Name*[*i*] then refers to the *i*th name in the list. The *j*th character of the *i*th name can be accessed by the doubly indexed variable *Name*[*i, j*] or *Name*[*i*][*j*].

The following algorithm solves this problem, and the program in Figure 9.3 implements the algorithm.

ALGORITHM TO SORT A LIST OF NAMES

1. Repeat the following until all the names have been read.
   a. Read a name and store it in the temporary one-dimensional array *Buffer*.
   b. Search *Buffer* to find the first name and last name in this string and interchange them.
   c. Store this reversed name in the array *Name*.
2. Alphabetize the array *Name* using the bubble sort method.
3. Display the sorted list of names in the desired format.

```
PROGRAM NameSort (input, output);

(*********************************************************************

  Program to read a list of first and last names, sort them so
  the last names are in alphabetical order, and display them
  in the form:    Last-name, First-name.

*********************************************************************)

CONST
   NameLength = 30;         (* maximum length of names *)
   ListLimit = 100;         (* limit on length of list *)

TYPE
   NameString = PACKED ARRAY[1..NameLength] of char;
   List = ARRAY[1..ListLimit] of NameString;

VAR
   Name : List;             (* list of names *)
   i,                       (* index *)
   NumNames : integer;      (* number of names in list *)

PROCEDURE ReadAndReverseNames (VAR Name : List; VAR Count : integer);

   (*****************************************************************

       Procedure to read and count the names, reverse them so they have
       the form
                      Last-Name, First-Name
       and store these reversed names in the array Name.

   *****************************************************************)

   VAR
      Buffer : NameString;  (* temporary array for name *)
      i : integer;          (* index *)
```

Figure 9.3

Figure 9.3 (Cont.)

```
PROCEDURE Reverse (VAR Buffer : NameString);

    (********************************************************************

    Procedure to reverse the order of the first and last names in
    each name, and insert a comma so each has the form
                        Last-name, First-name

    *****************************************************************)

    VAR
        BlankPos,               (* position of first blank in name *)
        i,                      (* index *)
        First,                  (* index to scan first name *)
        Last : integer;         (* index to scan last name *)
        FirstName : NameString; (* first name *)

    BEGIN (* Reverse *)

        (* Locate position of first blank and store first name *)

        BlankPos := 0;
        REPEAT
            BlankPos := BlankPos + 1;
            FirstName[BlankPos] := Buffer[BlankPos]
        UNTIL Buffer[BlankPos] = ' ';

        (* Move last name to beginning of Buffer *)

        First := 0;
        REPEAT
            First := First + 1;
            Last := First + BlankPos;
            Buffer[First] := Buffer[Last]
        UNTIL (Buffer[Last] = ' ') OR (Last = NameLength);

        (* Insert comma and copy first name to end of Buffer *)

        Buffer[First] := ',';
        First := First + 1;
        Buffer[First] := ' ';
        FOR i := 1 TO BlankPos - 1 DO
            Buffer[i + First] := FirstName[i]
    END (* Reverse *);
```

Figure 9.3 (Cont.)

```
BEGIN (* ReadAndReverseNames *)
   writeln ('Enter the names, 1 per line.   Enter * to stop.');
   writeln;
   Count := 0;
   REPEAT
      FOR i := 1 TO NameLength DO
         IF NOT eoln THEN
            read (Buffer[i])
         ELSE
            Buffer[i] := ' ';
      readln;
      IF Buffer[1] <> '*' THEN       (* not the end-of-data flag *)
         BEGIN
            Reverse (Buffer);
            IF Count < ListLimit THEN
               BEGIN
                  Count := Count + 1;
                  Name[Count] := Buffer
               END (* IF *)
            ELSE
               BEGIN
                  writeln ('*** Too many names — processing first ',
                           ListLimit:1, ' names ***');
                  Buffer[1] := '*'    (* force end of data *)
               END (* ELSE *)
         END (* IF *)
   UNTIL Buffer[1] = '*';
END (* ReadAndReverseNames *);

PROCEDURE BubbleSort (VAR Item : List; N : integer);

   (***********************************************************************

   Procedure to sort Item[1], ..., Item[N] into ascending order
   using the bubble sort algorithm.  For descending order,
   change > to < in the boolean expression Item[i] > Item[i+1].

   ***********************************************************************)

   VAR
      i,                     (* index *)
      NumPairs : integer;    (* number of pairs examined in current scan *)
      Temporary : NameString; (* used to interchange two items *)
      Done : boolean;        (* indicates if sorting completed *)
```

Figure 9.3 (Cont.)

```
BEGIN (* BubbleSort *)
   NumPairs := N - 1;

   (* Scan the list comparing consecutive items *)

   REPEAT
      Done := true;
      FOR i := 1 TO NumPairs DO
         IF Item[i] > Item[i+1] THEN
            BEGIN
               Temporary := Item[i];
               Item[i] := Item[i+1];
               Item[i+1] := Temporary;
               Done := false  (* interchange occurred, so scan again *)
            END (* IF *);

      (* Largest Item has sunk into place, so eliminate
         it from the next scan *)

      NumPairs := NumPairs - 1
   UNTIL Done
END (* BubbleSort *);

BEGIN (* main program *)
   ReadAndReverseNames (Name, NumNames);
   BubbleSort (Name, NumNames);
   FOR i := 1 TO NumNames DO
      writeln (Name[i])
END (* main program *).
```

Sample run:

Enter the names, 1 per line. Enter * to stop.

John Doe
Mary Smith
Johann VanderVan
Fred Jones
Jesse James
Merry Christmas
*
Christmas, Merry
Doe, John
James, Jesse
Jones, Fred
Smith, Mary
VanderVan, Johann

9.4 Numeric Applications: Automobile Sales, Matrix Multiplication, Inventory Control

EXAMPLE 1: Automobile Sales.   Suppose that a certain automobile dealership sells fifteen different models of automobiles and employs ten salesmen.

A record of sales for each month can be represented by a table, the first row of which contains the number of sales of each model by salesman 1, the second row contains the number of sales of each model by salesman 2, and so on. For example, suppose that the sales table for a certain month is the following:

```
0  0  2  0  5  6  3  0  10  0  3  2  5  7  5
5  1  9  0  0  2  3  2   1  1  3  1  5  3  0
0  0  0  1  0  0  0  0   0  0  2  0  8  2  3
1  1  1  0  2  2  2  1   1  0  2  0  3  0 12
5  3  2  0  0  2  5  5   7  0  0  2  0  0  2
2  2  1  0  1  1  0  0   6  8  0  0  0  2  0
3  2  5  0  1  2  0  4   8  0  0  2  2  2  1
3  0  7  1  3  5  2  4   4  3  5  1  7  2  4
0  2  6  1  0  5  2  1   4  3  0  0  4  0  5
4  0  2  0  3  2  1  0   9  0  1  4  5  4  8
```

A program is to be written to produce a monthly sales report, displaying the monthly sales table in the form

MODEL

SALESMAN:	1	2	3	4	5	6	7	8	9	10	11	12	13	14	15
1 :	0	0	2	0	5	6	3	0	10	0	3	2	5	7	5
2 :	5	1	9	0	0	2	3	2	1	1	3	1	5	3	0
3 :	0	0	0	1	0	0	0	0	0	0	2	0	8	2	3
4 :	1	1	1	0	2	2	2	1	1	0	2	0	3	0	12
5 :	5	3	2	0	0	2	5	5	7	0	0	2	0	0	2
6 :	2	2	1	0	1	1	0	0	6	8	0	0	0	2	0
7 :	3	2	5	0	1	2	0	4	8	0	0	2	2	2	1
8 :	3	0	7	1	3	5	2	4	4	3	5	1	7	2	4
9 :	0	2	6	1	0	5	2	1	4	3	0	0	4	0	5
10 :	4	0	2	0	3	2	1	0	9	0	1	4	5	4	8

and which also displays the total number of automobiles sold by each salesman and the total number of each model sold by all salesmen.

The input to the program is to be a sales table, as just described, and the output is to be a report of the indicated form. The required processing is given by the following algorithm:

ALGORITHM FOR SALES REPORT

1. Read the sales table into a 10×15 array *Sales* so that each of the ten rows contains the sales information for one of the ten salesmen, and each of the fifteen columns contains the information for one of the fifteen models.
2. Print the array *Sales* with appropriate headings.
3. Calculate and print the totals of the entries in each of the rows. These totals are the sales totals for each of the ten salesmen.
4. Calculate and print the totals of the entries in each of the columns. These totals are the total sales for each of the fifteen models.

The program in Figure 9.4 implements this algorithm using the four procedures
indicated in the following structure diagram:

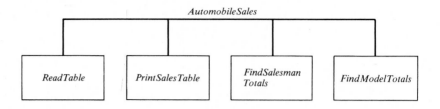

```
PROGRAM AutomobileSales (input, output, SalesFile);

(*****************************************************************************

  Program to read in a sales table and calculate total sales for
  each salesman and total sales of each model of automobile.

****************************************************************************)
CONST
    RowLimit = 25;        (* limit on number of rows in table *)
    ColumnLimit = 25;     (* limit on number of columns in table *)

TYPE
    Table = ARRAY[1..RowLimit, 1..ColumnLimit] OF integer;

VAR
    Rows,                 (* number of rows (salesmen) in sales table *)
    Columns : integer;    (* number of columns (models) in sales table *)
    Sales : Table;        (* sales table *)
    SalesFile : text;     (* file containing the sales data *)

PROCEDURE ReadTable (VAR Sales : Table; VAR Rows, Columns : integer);

   (****************************************************************************

     Procedure to read the number of rows and columns in the sales
     table and then read the table.  The data is read from the
     text file SalesFile.

   **************************************************************************)

   VAR
       Man,              (* row index — salesman number *)
       Model : integer;  (* column index — model number *)

   BEGIN (* ReadTable *)
       reset (SalesFile);
       readln (SalesFile, Rows, Columns);
       FOR Man := 1 TO Rows DO
           FOR Model := 1 TO Columns DO
               read (SalesFile, Sales[Man, Model])
   END (* ReadTable *);
```

Figure 9.4

Figure 9.4 (Cont.)

```
PROCEDURE PrintSalesTable (VAR Sales : Table; Rows, Columns : integer);

   (*****************************************************************

     Procedure to print the sales table in the desired format.

   *****************************************************************)

   VAR
      Man,                   (* salesman number *)
      Model : integer;   (* model number *)

   BEGIN (* PrintSalesTable *)
      writeln ('MODEL' : 2*Columns + 9);
      write ('SALESMAN:');
      FOR Model := 1 TO Columns DO
         write (Model:4);
      writeln;
      FOR Model := 1 TO 4*Columns + 9 DO
         write('-');
      writeln;
      FOR Man := 1 TO Rows DO
         BEGIN
            write (Man:5, '   :');
            FOR Model := 1 TO Columns DO
               write (Sales[Man, Model]:4);
            writeln
         END (* FOR *)
   END (* PrintSalesTable *);

PROCEDURE FindSalesmanTotals (VAR Sales : Table; Rows, Columns : integer);

   (*****************************************************************

     Procedure to find and display sum of each row of sales table.

   *****************************************************************)

   VAR
      Man,                   (* row index — salesman number *)
      Model,                 (* column index — model number *)
      RowTotal : integer;   (* row total *)

   BEGIN (* FindSalesmanTotals *)
      writeln;
      FOR Man := 1 TO Rows DO
         BEGIN
            RowTotal := 0;
            FOR Model := 1 TO Columns DO
               RowTotal := RowTotal + Sales[Man, Model];
            writeln ('Sales of salesman', Man:3, ':', RowTotal:4)
         END (* FOR *);
   END (* FindSalesmanTotals *);
```

Figure 9.4 (Cont.)

```
PROCEDURE FindModelTotals (VAR Sales : Table; Rows, Columns : integer);

   (*****************************************************************

      Procedure to find and display sum of each column of sales table.

   *****************************************************************)

   VAR
      Man,                    (* row index — salesman number *)
      Model,                  (* column index — model number *)
      ColTotal : integer;     (* column total *)

   BEGIN (* FindModelTotals *)
      writeln;
      FOR Model := 1 TO Columns DO
         BEGIN
            ColTotal := 0;
            FOR Man := 1 TO Rows DO
               ColTotal := ColTotal + Sales[Man, Model];
            writeln ('Sales of model   ', Model:3, ':', ColTotal:4)
         END (* FOR *)
   END (* FindModelTotals *);

BEGIN (* main program *)
   ReadTable (Sales, Rows, Columns);
   PrintSalesTable (Sales, Rows, Columns);
   FindSalesmanTotals (Sales, Rows, Columns);
   FindModelTotals (Sales, Rows, Columns)
END (* main program *).
```

Sample run:

							MODEL								
SALESMAN:	1	2	3	4	5	6	7	8	9	10	11	12	13	14	15
1 :	0	0	2	0	5	6	3	0	10	0	3	2	5	7	5
2 :	5	1	9	0	0	2	3	2	1	1	3	1	5	3	0
3 :	0	0	0	1	0	0	0	0	0	0	2	0	8	2	3
4 :	1	1	1	0	2	2	2	1	1	0	2	0	3	0	12
5 :	5	3	2	0	0	2	5	5	7	0	0	2	0	0	2
6 :	2	2	1	0	1	1	0	0	6	8	0	0	0	2	0
7 :	3	2	5	0	1	2	0	4	8	0	0	2	2	2	1
8 :	3	0	7	1	3	5	2	4	4	3	5	1	7	2	4
9 :	0	2	6	1	0	5	2	1	4	3	0	0	4	0	5
10 :	4	0	2	0	3	2	1	0	9	0	1	4	5	4	8

```
Sales of salesman  1:   48
Sales of salesman  2:   36
Sales of salesman  3:   16
Sales of salesman  4:   28
Sales of salesman  5:   33
Sales of salesman  6:   23
Sales of salesman  7:   32
Sales of salesman  8:   51
Sales of salesman  9:   33
Sales of salesman 10:   43
```

Figure 9.4 (Cont.)

```
Sales of model    1:   23
Sales of model    2:   11
Sales of model    3:   35
Sales of model    4:    3
Sales of model    5:   15
Sales of model    6:   27
Sales of model    7:   18
Sales of model    8:   17
Sales of model    9:   50
Sales of model   10:   15
Sales of model   11:   16
Sales of model   12:   12
Sales of model   13:   39
Sales of model   14:   22
Sales of model   15:   40
```

EXAMPLE 2: Matrix Multiplication.   A two-dimensional array having m rows and n columns is called an **$m \times n$ matrix**. An important operation of matrix algebra is matrix multiplication, defined as follows: Suppose that *Mat1* is an $m \times n$ matrix and *Mat2* is an $n \times p$ matrix. The product *Prod* of *Mat1* with *Mat2* will then be an $m \times p$ matrix with the entry *Prod*[i, j], which appears in the ith row and the jth column given by

$Prod[i, j]$ = the sum of the products of the entries in row i of *Mat1*
     with the entries of column j of *Mat2*
   $= Mat1[i, 1] * Mat2[1, j] + Mat1[i, 2] * Mat2[2, j] + \cdots$
     $+ Mat1[i, n] * Mat2[n, j]$

Note that the number of columns (n) in *Mat1* is equal to the number of rows in *Mat2*, which must be the case for the product of *Mat1* with *Mat2* to be defined.

For example, suppose that *Mat1* is the 2×3 matrix

$$\begin{bmatrix} 1 & 0 & 2 \\ 3 & 0 & 4 \end{bmatrix}$$

and that *Mat2* is the 3×4 matrix

$$\begin{bmatrix} 4 & 2 & 5 & 3 \\ 6 & 4 & 1 & 8 \\ 9 & 0 & 0 & 2 \end{bmatrix}$$

Because the number of columns (3) in *Mat1* equals the number of rows in *Mat2*, the product matrix *Prod* is defined. The entry in the first row and first column, *Prod*[1, 1], is

$$1 * 4 + 0 * 6 + 2 * 9 = 22$$

Similarly, the entry *Prod*[1, 2] in the first row and second column is

$$1 * 2 + 0 * 4 + 2 * 0 = 2$$

The complete product matrix *Prod* is the 2 × 4 matrix given by

$$\begin{bmatrix} 22 & 2 & 5 & 7 \\ 48 & 6 & 15 & 17 \end{bmatrix}$$

In general, the algorithm for multiplying matrices is:

MATRIX MULTIPLICATION ALGORITHM

(* Algorithm for multiplying a *Rows1* × *Cols1* matrix *Mat1* with *Rows2* × *Cols2* matrix *Mat2*. *)

1. If *Cols1* ≠ *Rows2*, then the product *Prod* = *Mat1* * *Mat2* is not defined; terminate the algorithm. Otherwise proceed with the following steps:
2. For an index *i* ranging from 1 to the number of rows *Rows1* of *Mat1*, do the following:
   For an index *j* ranging from 1 to the number of columns *Cols2* of *Mat2*, do the following:
   (i) Set *Sum* equal to 0.
   (ii) For an index *k* ranging from 1 to the number of columns *Cols1* of *Mat1* (= the number of rows *Rows2* of *Mat2*), add *Mat1*[*i*, *k*] * *Mat2*[*k*, *j*] to *Sum*.
   (iii) Set *Prod*[*i*, *j*] equal to *Sum*.

The program in Figure 9.5 reads two matrices and uses this algorithm to calculate and display their product.

```
PROGRAM MatrixMultiplication (input, output);

(*******************************************************************

   Program to read two matrices and calculate their product.

*******************************************************************)
CONST
   RowLimit = 20;     (* limit on number of rows in a matrix *)
   ColumnLimit = 20;  (* limit on number of columns in a matrix *)

TYPE
   Matrix = ARRAY[1..RowLimit, 1..ColumnLimit] OF integer;
```

Figure 9.5

Figure 9.5 (Cont.)

```
VAR
    Mat1, Mat2,                     (* matrices being multiplied *)
    Prod : Matrix;                  (* product of Mat1 with Mat2 *)
    Rows1, Cols1,                   (* dimensions of Mat1 *)
    Rows2, Cols2 : integer;         (* dimensions of Mat2 *)
    ProductDefined : boolean;       (* true if Cols1 = Rows2, else false *)

PROCEDURE ReadMatrix (VAR Mat : Matrix; VAR Rows, Columns : integer);

    (************************************************************************

        Procedure to read number of rows and columns in a matrix and
        then read a matrix of those dimensions.

    ************************************************************************)

    VAR
        i, j : integer;    (* row, column indices *)

    BEGIN (* ReadMatrix *)
        write ('Enter number of rows & columns:   ');
        readln (Rows, Columns);
        writeln ('Enter the matrix rowwise:');
        FOR i := 1 TO Rows DO
            FOR j := 1 to Columns DO
                read (Mat[i,j]);
        readln
    END (* ReadMatrix *);

PROCEDURE PrintMatrix (VAR Mat : Matrix; Rows, Columns : integer);

    (************************************************************************

        Procedure to display an integer Rows X Columns matrix.

    ************************************************************************)

    CONST
        FieldWidth = 5;    (* width of field used to display an entry *)

    VAR
        i, j : integer;    (* row, column indices *)

    BEGIN (* PrintMatrix *)
        writeln;
        FOR i := 1 TO Rows DO
            BEGIN
                FOR j := 1 TO Columns DO
                    write (Mat[i,j]:FieldWidth);
                writeln;
                writeln
            END (* FOR *)
    END (* PrintMatrix *);
```

Figure 9.5 (Cont.)

```
PROCEDURE MatMultiply (VAR Mat1, Mat2, Prod : Matrix;
                       Rows1, Cols1, Rows2, Cols2 : integer;
                       VAR ProductDefined : boolean);

   (******************************************************************

      Procedure to multiply the Rows1 X Cols1 matrix Mat1 and the
      Rows2 X Cols2 matrix Mat2; Cols1 must equal Rows2 for the
      product Prod to be defined.

   ******************************************************************)

   VAR
      i, j, k,           (* indices *)
      Sum : integer;     (* used to calculate product matrix *)

   BEGIN (* MatMultiply *)
      ProductDefined := (Cols1 = Rows2);
      IF ProductDefined THEN
         BEGIN
            FOR i := 1 TO Rows1 DO
               FOR j := 1 to Cols2 DO
                  BEGIN
                     Sum := 0;
                     FOR k := 1 to Cols1 DO
                        Sum := Sum + Mat1[i,k] * Mat2[k,j];
                     Prod[i,j] := Sum
                  END (* FOR j *)
         END (* IF *)
   END (* MatMultiply *);

BEGIN (* main program *)
   ReadMatrix (Mat1, Rows1, Cols1);
   writeln ('First Matrix:');
   PrintMatrix (Mat1, Rows1, Cols1);
   ReadMatrix (Mat2, Rows2, Cols2);
   writeln ('Second Matrix:');
   PrintMatrix (Mat2, Rows2, Cols2);
   MatMultiply (Mat1, Mat2, Prod, Rows1, Cols1, Rows2, Cols2,
                ProductDefined);
   IF ProductDefined THEN
      BEGIN
         writeln ('Product:');
         PrintMatrix (Prod, Rows1, Cols2)
      END (* IF *)
   ELSE
      BEGIN
         writeln ('Product undefined — number of columns ', Cols1:1,
                  ' in first matrix');
         writeln (' is not equal to number of rows ', Rows2:1,
                  ' in second matrix')
      END (* ELSE *)
END (* main program *).
```

Figure 9.5 (Cont.)

Sample run:

```
Enter number of rows & columns:   2 3
Enter the matrix rowwise:
1 2 3
4 0 1
First Matrix:

    1    2    3

    4    0    1

Enter number of rows & columns:   3 4
Enter the matrix rowwise
1 0 0 1
2 1 1 2
3 0 1 1
Second Matrix:

    1    0    0    1

    2    1    1    2

    3    0    1    1

Product:

   14    2    5    8

    7    0    1    5
```

EXAMPLE 3: Inventory Control.   In Section 9.1 we noted that a higher-dimensional array *JeansInStock* might be used in a program that maintains an inventory of jeans of various brands, styles, and sizes. In this example, unlike the two-dimensional arrays considered thus far, the indices are of different types. The type of the first index is an enumerated type

BrandType = (Levi, Wrangler, CalvinKlein, Lee, BigYank);

the type of the second index is a subrange of *char,*

StyleType = 'A'..'F';

and the types of the third and fourth indices are subranges of integers

WaistSize = 28..40;
InseamSize = 28..36;

The structure of the program in Figure 9.6 is given by the following diagram:

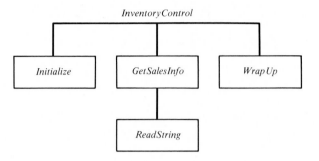

It first calls the procedure *Initialize* to read entries for the array *JeansInStock* from the file *InventoryFile*. The procedure *GetSalesInfo* is then called repeatedly to gather information regarding sales of jeans of a particular brand, style, and size, and this information is used in the main program to update the array *JeansInStock*. Finally, the procedure *WrapUp* is called to copy the updated entries of this array into the file *NewInventoryFile*.

```
PROGRAM InventoryControl (input, output, InventoryFile, NewInventoryFile);

(*****************************************************************************

    Inventory control program that demonstrates use of a
    four-dimensional array with different types of indices.

*****************************************************************************)

CONST
    StringLength = 11;                  (* lengths of strings *)
    FirstStyle = 'A'; LastStyle = 'F'; (* first, last values of StyleType *)
    SmallWaist = 28; LargeWaist = 40;  (*    "       "       "    " WaistSize *)
    ShortInseam = 28; LongInseam = 36; (*    "       "       "    " InseamSize *)

TYPE
    BrandType = (Levi, Wrangler, CalvinKlein, Lee, BigYank);
    StyleType = FirstStyle..LastStyle;
    WaistSize = SmallWaist..LargeWaist;
    InseamSize = ShortInseam..LongInseam;
    JeansArray = ARRAY[BrandType, StyleType, WaistSize, InseamSize] OF integer;
    String = PACKED ARRAY[1..StringLength] OF char;
    BrandNameArray = ARRAY[BrandType] OF String;
```

Figure 9.6

Figure 9.6 (Cont.)

```
VAR
    JeansInStock : JeansArray;     (* array that maintains jeans inventory *)
    BrandName : BrandNameArray;    (* array of strings — names of brands *)
    InventoryFile,                 (* original inventory file *)
    NewInventoryFile : text;       (* inventory file produces by program *)
    Brand : BrandType;             (* index *)
    Style : StyleType;             (*   "   *)
    Waist : WaistSize;             (*   "   *)
    Inseam : InseamSize;           (*   "   *)
    NumSold,                       (* number sold *)
    InStock : integer;             (* number in stock *)
    Response : char;               (* user response *)

PROCEDURE Initialize (VAR InventoryFile : text;
                      VAR JeansInStock : JeansArray;
                      VAR BrandName : BrandNameArray);

    (*****************************************************************

        Procedure to initialize array JeansInStock from InventoryFile
        and to initialize the array BrandName of names of brands.

    *****************************************************************)

    VAR
        Brand : BrandType;     (* index *)
        Style : StyleType;     (*   "   *)
        Waist : WaistSize;     (*   "   *)
        Inseam : InseamSize;   (*   "   *)

    BEGIN (* Initialize *);
        (* Initialize array JeansInStock from InventoryFile *)
        reset (InventoryFile);
        FOR Brand := Levi TO BigYank DO
            FOR Style := FirstStyle TO LastStyle DO
                FOR Waist := SmallWaist TO LargeWaist DO
                    FOR Inseam := ShortInseam To  LongInseam DO
                        read (InventoryFile,
                              JeansInStock[Brand, Style, Waist, Inseam]);

        (* Initialize array of brand names *)
        BrandName[Levi]        := 'LEVI       ';
        BrandName[Wrangler]    := 'WRANGLER   ';
        BrandName[CalvinKlein] := 'CALVINKLEIN';
        BrandName[Lee]         := 'LEE        ';
        BrandName[BigYank]     := 'BIGYANK    '
    END (* Initialize *);

PROCEDURE GetSalesInfo (VAR BrandName : BrandNameArray;
                        VAR Brand : BrandType; VAR Style : StyleType;
                        VAR Waist : WaistSize; VAR Inseam : InseamSize;
                        VAR NumSold : integer);

    (*****************************************************************

        Procedure to read the Brand, Style, Waist, Inseam, and
        number  sold (NumSold) of a particular kind of jeans

    *****************************************************************)
```

Figure 9.6 (Cont.)

```
VAR
    Name : String;          (* name of brand entered by user *)
    NameFound : boolean;    (* signals if name found in array BrandName *)
    b : BrandType;          (* index *)

PROCEDURE ReadString (VAR Str : String; MaxString : integer);

    (*********************************************************************

        Procedure to read characters into string variable Str until
        an end-of-line mark is encountered or the upper limit
        MaxString on the length of Str is reached.  Any positions
        for which no characters are read will be filled with blanks.

    *********************************************************************)

    VAR
        i : integer;        (* index *)

    BEGIN (* ReadString *)
        FOR i := 1 TO MaxString DO
            IF NOT eoln THEN
                read (Str[i])
            ELSE
                Str[i] := ' ';
        readln
    END (* ReadString *);

    BEGIN (* GetSalesInfo *)
        REPEAT
            write ('BRAND (use all CAPS)?  ');
            ReadString (Name, StringLength);
            NameFound := false;
            FOR b := Levi TO BigYank DO
                IF BrandName[b] = Name THEN
                    BEGIN
                        Brand := b;
                        NameFound := true
                    END (* IF *);
        UNTIL NameFound;
        write ('Style (', FirstStyle, '-', LastStyle, ')?  ');
        readln (Style);
        write ('Waist size (', SmallWaist:1, '-', LargeWaist:1, ')?  ');
        readln (Waist);
        write ('Inseam (', ShortInseam:1, '-', LongInseam:1, ')?  ');
        readln (Inseam);
        write ('Number sold?  ');
        readln (NumSold)
    END (* GetSalesInfo *);

PROCEDURE WrapUp (VAR NewInventoryFile : text;
                  VAR JeansInStock : JeansArray);

    (*********************************************************************

        Procedure to copy array JeansInStock to NewInventoryFile

    *********************************************************************)
```

Figure 9.6 (Cont.)

```
    VAR
        Brand : BrandType;      (* index *)
        Style : StyleType;      (*    "    *)
        Waist : WaistSize;      (*    "    *)
        Inseam : InseamSize;    (*    "    *)

    BEGIN (* WrapUp *)
        rewrite (NewInventoryFile);
        FOR Brand := Levi TO BigYank DO
            FOR Style := FirstStyle TO LastStyle DO
                FOR Waist := SmallWaist TO LargeWaist DO
                    BEGIN
                        FOR Inseam := ShortInseam To  LongInseam DO
                            write (NewInventoryFile,
                                    JeansInStock[Brand, Style, Waist, Inseam]:3);
                        writeln(NewInventoryFile)
                    END (* FOR *)
    END (* WrapUp *);

BEGIN (* main program *)
    Initialize(InventoryFile, JeansInStock, BrandName);
    REPEAT
        GetSalesInfo (BrandName, Brand, Style, Waist, Inseam, NumSold);
        InStock := JeansInStock[Brand, Style, Waist, Inseam] - NumSold;
        IF InStock < 0 THEN
            BEGIN
                writeln ('Not enough in stock; backorder ', abs(Instock):1);
                InStock := 0
            END (* IF *);
        JeansInStock[Brand, Style, Waist, Inseam] := InStock;
        writeln;
        write ('More sales (Y or N)?  ');
        readln (Response);
    UNTIL (Response <> 'Y') AND (Response <> 'y');
    WrapUp (NewInventoryfile, JeansInStock)
END (* main *).
```

InventoryFile:

```
  3   3   0  12   1  12  19  17   0
  4  15  18   2  14   2   0  14  19
 18   7  19  10  11   3   2  18  12
                    .
                    .
                    .
 12  18  11  12  16  14   9  12   9
```

Sample run:

```
BRAND (use all CAPS)?  LEVI
Style (A–F)?  A
Waist size (28–40)?  28
Inseam (28–36)?  28
Number sold?  10
Not enough in stock; backorder 7
```

Figure 9.6 (Cont.)

```
More sales (Y or N)?   Y
BRAND (use all CAPS)?   BIGYANK
Style (A-F)?   F
Waist size (28-40)?   40
Inseam (28-36)?   36
Number sold?   1

More sales (Y or N)?   N

NewInventoryFile:
```

```
  0   3   0  12   1  12  19  17   0
  4  15  18   2  14   2   0  14  19
 18   7  19  10  11   3   2  18  12
                 .
                 .
                 .
 12  18  11  12  16  14   9  12   8
```

Exercises

1. Consider the following type declarations:

   type

   $Color$ = (*red, yellow, blue, green, white, black*);
   $BigTable$ = **array**[1..50, 1..100] **of** *integer*;
   $PointTable$ = **array**[−10..10, −10..10] **of** *real*;
   $CharTable$ = **packed array**['A'..'Z', 'A'..'Z'] **of** *char*;
   $BooleanTable$ = **array**[*boolean, boolean*] **of** *boolean*;
   $BitArray$ = **array**[0..1, 0..1, 0..1, 0..1] **of** 0..1;
   $Shirt$ = **array** [*Color,* 14..18, 32..36] **of** *integer*;
   $MixedArray$ = **array** [*Color,* 'A'..'F', 0..10, *boolean*] **of** *real*;
   $InStockArray$ = **array**['A'..'F'] **of array**[*Color*] **of** *boolean*;
   $ShirtStock$ = **array**[1..5] **of** *Shirt*;

   How many elements can be stored in an array of each of the following types?

(a) *BigTable*	**(b)** *PointTable*	**(c)** *CharTable*
(d) *BooleanTable*	**(e)** *BitArray*	**(f)** *Shirt*
(g) *MixedArray*	**(h)** *InStockArray*	**(i)** *ShirtStock*

2. Assume that the following declarations have been made:

   type

   $String$ = **packed array**[1..6] **of** *char*;
   $Array3X3$ = **array**[1..3, 1..3] **of** *integer*;
   $ArrayOfStrings$ = **array**[1..2] **of** *String*;

var
    TextLine : *ArrayOfStrings*;
    Matrix : *Array3X3*;
    i, j : *integer*;

and that the following data are entered for those of the following statements that involve input:

ABCD
EFGH
IJKL
MNOP
QRST
UVWX

For each of the following, tell what value (if any) is assigned to each array element, or explain why an error results.

(a) **for** $i := 1$ **to** 3 **do**
    for $j := 1$ **to** 3 **do**
        Matrix[i, j] $:= i + j$;

(b) **for** $i := 1$ **to** 2 **do**
    begin
        for $j := 1$ **to** 6 **do**
            read (*TextLine*[i, j]);
        readln
    end (∗ **for** ∗);

(c) **for** $i := 1$ **to** 2 **do**
    begin
        for $j := 1$ **to** 6 **do**
            read (*TextLine*[i][j]);
        readln
    end (∗ **for** ∗);

(d) **for** $i := 1$ **to** 2 **do**
    for $j := 1$ **to** 6 **do**
        read (*TextLine*[i, j]);

(e) **for** $j := 1$ **to** 6 **do**
    begin
        for $i := 1$ **to** 2 **do**
            read (*TextLine*[i, j]);
        readln
    end (∗ **for** ∗);

(f) **for** $j := 1$ **to** 6 **do**
    begin
        for $i := 1$ **to** 2 **do**
            read (*TextLine*[j, i]);
        readln
    end (∗ **for** ∗);

(g) for $i := 1$ **to** 2 **do**
      for $j := 6$ **downto** 1 **do**
          if not *eoln* **then**
             read (TextLine[i, j])
          else
             readln;

(h) for $i := 1$ **to** 3 **do**
      for $j := 3$ **downto** 1 **do**
          if $i = j$ **then**
             Matrix[i, j] $:= 0$
          else
             Matrix[i, j] $:= 1;$

(i) for $i := 1$ **to** 3 **do**
      for $j := 1$ **to** 3 **do**
          if $i < j$ **then**
             Matrix[i, j] $:= -1$
          else if $i = j$ **then**
             Matrix[i, j] $:= 0$
          else
             Matrix[i, j] $:= 1;$

(j) for $i := 1$ **to** 3 **do**
      begin
          for $j := 1$ **to** i **do**
             Matrix[i, j] $:= 0;$
          for $j := i + 1$ **to** 3 **do**
             Matrix[i, j] $:= 2$
      end (* **for** *);

3. Modify the program segment on page 351 so that it calculates and displays the average temperature at each of the three locations.

4. In procedure *GetSalesInfo* of the inventory control program in Figure 9.6, a **for** loop is used to search the array *BrandNames* for the *Name* entered by the user. This means that the entire array is examined for each *Name*. Rewrite this program segment so the search terminates as soon as *Name* is found in the array. (*Hint:* Be careful not to "fall off the end" of the enumerated type *BrandType*. You may find it convenient to add a dummy last value in this type.)

5. Like one-dimensional arrays, multidimensional arrays are stored in a block of consecutive memory locations, and address translation formulas are used to determine the location in memory of each array element. To illustrate, consider an array A of type **array**[1..3, 1..4] **of** *integer,* and suppose that an integer can be stored in one memory word. If A is allocated memory in a rowwise manner and b is its **base address,** then the first row of A, $A[1,1]$, $A[1,2]$, $A[1,3]$, $A[1,4]$ is stored in words b, $b + 1$, $b + 2$, $b + 3$, the second row in words

$b + 4$ through $b + 7$, and the third row in words $b + 8$ through $b + 11$.

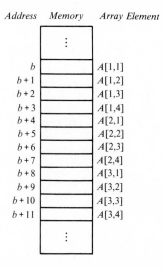

Address	Memory	Array Element
	⋮	
b		$A[1,1]$
$b+1$		$A[1,2]$
$b+2$		$A[1,3]$
$b+3$		$A[1,4]$
$b+4$		$A[2,1]$
$b+5$		$A[2,2]$
$b+6$		$A[2,3]$
$b+7$		$A[2,4]$
$b+8$		$A[3,1]$
$b+9$		$A[3,2]$
$b+10$		$A[3,3]$
$b+11$		$A[3,4]$
	⋮	

In general, $A[i, j]$ is stored in word $b + 4(i - 1) + (j - 1)$.

(a) Give a similar diagram and formula for $A[i, j]$, assuming columnwise allocation.

(b) Give diagrams and formulas for both rowwise and columnwise allocation if A is of type **array**$[0..3, -1..1]$ **of** *integer*.

(c) Repeat part b for A of type **array**$[0..2, 4..7]$ **of** *real* where real values require two words for storage.

6. A certain company has a product line that includes five items that sell for $100, $75, $120, $150, and $35. There are four salespersons working for this company, and the following table gives the sales report for a typical week:

Salesperson Number	Item Number				
	1	2	3	4	5
1	10	4	5	6	7
2	7	0	12	1	3
3	4	9	5	0	8
4	3	2	1	5	6

Write a program to

(a) Compute the total dollar sales for each salesperson.

(b) If the sales commission is 10 percent, compute the total commission for each salesperson.

(c) If each salesperson receives a fixed salary of $200 per week in addition to commission payments, find the total income for each salesperson for the week.

7. Write a program to calculate and display the first ten rows of *Pascal's triangle*. The first part of the triangle has the form

where each row begins and ends with 1, and each of the other entries in a row is the sum of the two entries just above it. If this form for the output seems too challenging, you might display the triangle as

```
1
1  1
1  2  1
1  3  3  1
1  4  6  4  1
```

8. A demographic study of the metropolitan area around Dogpatch divided it into three regions, urban, suburban, and exurban, and published the following table showing the annual migration from one region to another (the numbers represent percentages):

	Urban	Suburban	Exurban
Urban	1.1	0.3	0.7
Suburban	0.1	1.2	0.3
Exurban	0.2	0.6	1.3

For example, 0.3 percent of the urbanites (0.003 times the current population) move to the suburbs each year. The diagonal entries represent internal growth rates. Using a two-dimensional array with an enumerated type for the indices to store this table, write a program to determine the population of each region after 10, 20, 30, 40, and 50 years. Assume that the current populations of the urban, suburban, and exurban regions are 2.1, 1.4, and 0.9 million, respectively.

9. Suppose that the prices for the fifteen automobile models in the first example of Section 9.4 are as follows:

Model #	Model Price
1	$ 7,450
2	$ 9,995
3	$26,500
4	$ 5,999
5	$10,400
6	$ 8,885
7	$11,700
8	$14,440
9	$17,900
10	$ 9,550
11	$10,500
12	$ 8,050
13	$ 7,990
14	$12,300
15	$ 6,999

Write a program to read this list of prices and the sales table given in Section 9.4 and calculate the total dollar sales for each salesman and the total dollar sales for all salesmen.

10. If A and B are two $m \times n$ matrices, their **sum** is defined as follows: If A_{ij} and B_{ij} are the entries in the ith row and jth column of A and B, respectively, then $A_{ij} + B_{ij}$ is the entry in the ith row and jth column of their sum, which will also be an $m \times n$ matrix. Write a program using procedures to read two $m \times n$ matrices, display them, and calculate and display their sum.

11. The inventory control program in Example 3 of Section 9.4 simply updates the array *JeansInStock* with sales figures entered during execution. Extend the program by adding other user options such as the following:

    (a) Search the array *JeansInStock* to determine how many of a particular kind of jeans are currently in stock.
    (b) Print a reorder list of all brand names, styles, and sizes of jeans for which the number in stock is below some specified reorder point.
    (c) Do the same as in (b), but print an overstocked list of jeans for which the number in stock is above some specified overstocked point.

12. Write an inventory control program like that in Example 3 of Section 9.4 (see also the preceding exercise), but for an automobile dealership and using a five-dimensional array. The first index is the make of a car (*Chrysler, Dodge, Plymouth*), the second is style (*TwoDoor, FourDoor, StationWagon, Van*), the third is color (*blue, brown, green, red, silver, yellow*), the fourth is the year of the vehicle (a small subrange of integers), and the fifth is a sales code (A, B, C).

13. The *Morse Code* is a standard encoding scheme that uses substitutions similar to those in the scheme described in Exercise 10 of Section 8.5. The substitutions used in this case are shown in the following table. Write a program to read a message either in plain text or in Morse Code and then encode or decode the message.

A ·−	M −−	Y −·−−
B −···	N −·	Z −−··
C −·−·	O −−−	1 ·−−−−
D −··	P ·−−·	2 ··−−−
E ·	Q −−·−	3 ···−−
F ··−·	R ·−·	4 ····−
G −−·	S ···	5 ·····
H ····	T −	6 −····
I ··	U ··−	7 −−···
J ·−−−	V ···−	8 −−−··
K −·−	W ·−−	9 −−−−·
L ·−··	X −··−	0 −−−−−

14. A *magic square* is an $n \times n$ matrix in which each of the integers 1, 2, 3, . . . , n^2 appears exactly once and all column sums, row sums, and diagonal sums are equal. For example, the following is a 5×5 magic square in which all the rows, columns, and diagonals add up to 65:

17	24	1	8	15
23	5	7	14	16
4	6	13	20	22
10	12	19	21	3
11	18	25	2	9

The following is a procedure for constructing an $n \times n$ magic square for any odd integer n. Place 1 in the middle of the top row. Then after integer k has been placed, move up one row and one column to the right to place the next integer $k + 1$, unless one of the following occurs:

  (i) If a move takes you above the top row in the jth column, move to the bottom of the jth column and place the integer there.

 (ii) If a move takes you outside to the right of the square in the ith row, place the integer in the ith row at the left side.

(iii) If a move takes you to an already filled square or if you move out of the square at the upper-right-hand corner, place $k + 1$ immediately below k.

Write a program to construct an $n \times n$ magic square for any odd value of n.

15. The famous mathematician G. H. Hardy once mentioned to the brilliant young Indian mathematician Ramanujan that he had just ridden

in a taxi whose number he considered to be very dull. Ramanujan promptly replied that on the contrary, the number was very interesting because it was the smallest positive integer that could be written as the sum of two cubes (that is, written in the form $x^3 + y^3$, with x and y integers) in two different ways. Write a program to find the number of Hardy's taxi.

16. A **directed graph** or **digraph** consists of a set of **vertices** and a set of **directed arcs** joining certain of these vertices. For example, the following diagram pictures a directed graph having five vertices numbered 1, 2, 3, 4, and 5, and seven directed arcs joining vertices 1 to 2, 1 to 4, 1 to 5, 3 to 1, 3 to itself, 4 to 3, and 5 to 1:

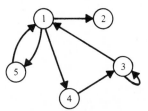

A directed graph having n vertices can be represented by its **adjacency matrix**, which is an $n \times n$ matrix, with the entry in the ith row and jth column a 1 if vertex i is joined to vertex j, 0 otherwise. The adjacency matrix for the preceding graph is

$$\begin{bmatrix} 0 & 1 & 0 & 1 & 1 \\ 0 & 0 & 0 & 0 & 0 \\ 1 & 0 & 1 & 0 & 0 \\ 0 & 0 & 1 & 0 & 0 \\ 1 & 0 & 0 & 0 & 0 \end{bmatrix}$$

If A is the adjacency matrix for a directed graph, then the entry in the ith row and jth column of A^k gives the number of ways that vertex j can be reached from vertex i by following k edges. Write a program to read the number of vertices in a directed graph and a collection of ordered pairs of vertices representing directed arcs; construct the adjacency matrix; and then find the number of ways that each vertex can be reached from every other vertex by following k edges for some value of k.

17. The game of **Life,** invented by the mathematician John H. Conway, is intended to model life in a society of organisms. Consider a rectangular array of cells, each of which may contain an organism. If the array is considered to extend indefinitely in both directions, then each cell has eight neighbors, the eight cells surrounding it. Births and deaths occur according to the following rules:
    (i) An organism is born in any empty cell having exactly three neighbors.

(ii) An organism dies from isolation if it has fewer than two neighbors.

(iii) An organism dies from overcrowding if it has more than three neighbors.

(iv) All other organisms survive to the next generation.

To illustrate, the following shows the first five generations of a particular configuration of organisms:

Write a program to play the game of Life and investigate the patterns produced by various initial configurations. Some configurations die off rather rapidly; others repeat after a certain number of generations; others change shape and size and may move across the array; and still others may produce "gliders" that detach themselves from the society and sail off into space.

18. The game of Nim is played by two players. There are usually three piles of objects, and on his or her turn, each player is allowed to take any number (at least one) of objects from one pile. The player taking the last object loses. Write a program that allows the user to play Nim against the computer. You might have the computer play a perfect game, or you might design the program to "teach" the computer. One way for the computer to "learn" is to assign a value to every possible move, based on experience gained from playing games. The value of each possible move is stored in some array; initially, each value is 0. The value of each move in a winning sequence of moves is increased by 1, and those in a losing sequence are decreased by 1. At each stage, the computer selects the best possible move (that having the highest value).

19. The game of Hangman is played by two persons. One person selects a word and the other person tries to guess the word by guessing individual letters. Design a program to play Hangman. You might store a list of words in an array or file and have the program randomly select a word for the user to guess (see Section 5.4).

20. Write a program that allows the user to play Tic-Tac-Toe against the computer.

Programming Pointers

Many of the difficulties encountered when using multidimensional arrays are similar to those for one-dimensional arrays considered in the preceding chapter. The first five of the programming pointers that follow are simply restatements of some of the programming pointers in Chapter 8, and the reader should refer to those for an expanded discussion.

1. *The types of the components of an array may be any predefined or user-defined data type, and the type of each index may be any ordinal type.*

2. *When processing the elements of a multidimensional array, each index must be compatible with the type specified for that index in the array declaration.*

3. *When reading the elements of an array of characters, remember that end-of-line marks are read as blanks.*

4. *Assignment of one array to another requires that the arrays have the same type.*

5. *Multidimensional arrays that are parameters of procedures or functions should be variable parameters so that memory is utilized more efficiently.*

6. *The amount of memory required to store a multidimensional array may be quite large, even though each index is restricted to a small range of values.* For example, the three-dimensional array *ThreeD* declared by

    type
        ThreeDimArray = **array**[1..20, 1..20, 1..20] **of** *integer*;
    var
        ThreeD : *ThreeDimArray*;

    requires $20 \times 20 \times 20 = 8{,}000$ memory locations. This memory requirement may be much too large for small computer systems.

7. *When processing the elements of a multidimensional array by using nested repetition structures, these structures must be arranged so that the indices vary in the intended order.* To illustrate, suppose that the two-dimensional array *Table* is declared by

    type
        Array3X4 = **array**[1..3, 1..4] **of** *integer*;
    var
        Table : *Array3X4*;

and the following data are to be read into the array:

    11   22   27   35   39   40   48   51   57   66   67   92

If these values are to be read and assigned in a rowwise manner so that the value is the matrix

$$\begin{bmatrix} 11 & 22 & 27 & 35 \\ 39 & 40 & 48 & 51 \\ 57 & 66 & 67 & 92 \end{bmatrix}$$

then the following nested **for** statements are appropriate:

> **for** *row* := 1 **to** 3 **do**
>   **for** *col* := 1 **to** 4 **do**
>   *read* (*Table*[*row*,*col*]);

If the values are to read and assigned in a columnwise manner so that *Table* is

$$\begin{bmatrix} 11 & 35 & 48 & 66 \\ 22 & 39 & 51 & 67 \\ 27 & 40 & 57 & 92 \end{bmatrix}$$

then the statements should be

> **for** *col* := 1 **to** 4 **do**
>   **for** *row* := 1 **to** 3 **do**
>   *read* (*Table*[*row*,*col*]);

Variations and Extensions

As in the case of one-dimensional arrays, there are only a few variations from or extensions to the array-processing features of standard Pascal in other versions of Pascal. Two that we noted at the end of Chapter 8 were:

- Arrays of the same type may be compared with the relational operators = and <> (UCSD).

- Arrays may be initialized in the declaration part of the program. (Turbo)

See Appendix G for additional details.

10

Records

Yea, from the table of my memory
I'll wipe away all trivial fond records.

WILLIAM SHAKESPEARE, *Hamlet*

In Chapters 8 and 9, we introduced one of Pascal's structured data types, the array, which may be used to store elements of the same type. In many situations, however, we need to process items that are related in some way but that are not all of the same type. For example, a date consists of a month name (of string type), a day (of type 1..31), and a year (of type 1900..2000 perhaps); an employee record might contain, among other items, an employee name (string), age (integer), number of dependents (integer), and an hourly pay rate (real). Such related data items of different types can be organized in a *record*. In this chapter we consider how records are implemented and processed in Pascal.

10.1 Introduction to Records and Fields

A *record* is a data structure in which a collection of related data items of possibly different types may be stored. The positions in which these data items are stored are called the *fields* of the record. Thus, an employee record might contain a name field, an age field, a dependents field, and an hourly rate field.

Records can be implemented in Pascal by using the structured data type **record.** A record declaration has the form

> **record**
>   *field-list*
> **end**;

where *field-list* is of the form

> *list-1* : *type-1*;
> *list-2* : *type-2*;
>   ⋮
> *list-m* : *type-m*

Each *list-i* is a single identifier or a list of identifiers, separated by commas, that name the fields of the record, and *type-i* specifies the type of each of these fields. This is summarized in the following syntax diagrams.

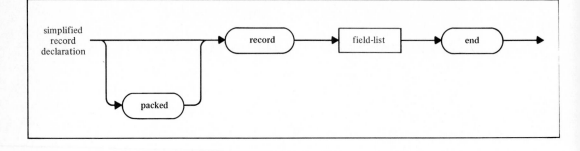

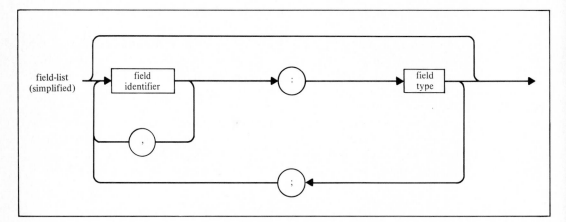

To illustrate, an employee record, as we have described it, could be declared by

> **record**
>   *Name* : **packed array**[1..20] **of** *char*;
>   *Age, Dependents* : *integer*;
>   *HourlyRate* : *real*
> **end**;

Such declarations of records, like those of other data types, may be used in the variable section of the declaration part of a program to specify the types of variables. But as with other structured types, it is preferable to assign them to type identifiers in the type section and use these identifiers to declare record variables. For example, consider

```
type
    NameString = packed array[1..20] of char;
    NameOfMonth = packed array[1..8] of char;
    EmployeeRecord = record
                        Name : NameString;
                        Age, Dependents : integer;
                        HourlyRate : real
                    end;
    BirthRecord = record
                        Month : NameOfMonth;
                        Day : 1..31;
                        Year : 1900..2000
                    end;

var
    Employee : EmployeeRecord;
    Birth : BirthRecord;
```

The variable *Employee* may have as a value any record of type *Employee-Record*. The first field of the record is of type *NameString* and is named with the field identifier *Name;* the second and third fields are of type *integer* and have the names *Age* and *Dependents;* and the fourth field is of type *real* and is named *HourlyRate*. The variable *Birth* may have as a value any record of type *BirthRecord*. The first field of the record is of type *NameOfMonth* and is named *Month;* the second field is of subrange type 1..31 and is named *Day;* and the third field is of type 1900..2000 and is named *Year*. Typical values for *Employee* and *Birth* might be pictured as follows:

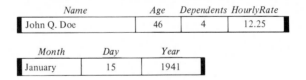

Name	Age	Dependents	HourlyRate
John Q. Doe	46	4	12.25

Month	Day	Year
January	15	1941

We have seen that each element of an array can be accessed directly by using an indexed variable formed by attaching an index enclosed in brackets to the array name. In a similar manner, one can access each field of a record directly by using a ***field-designated variable,*** which we abbreviate to ***fielded variable,*** of the form

record-name.field-name

in which a period followed by the field name is attached to the record name. Thus *Employee.Name* designates the first field of the record variable *Employee*. For the record displayed here, the value of *Employee.Name* would be the string JohnbQ.ЬDoebbbbbbbbbb (where ƀ denotes a blank). Similarly, *Employee.Age,*

Employee.Dependents, and *Employee.HourlyRate* refer to the second, third, and fourth fields and would have the values 46, 4, and 12.25, respectively. If the second record is the value of the record variable *Birth,* then *Birth.Month* has the value January♭, *Birth.Day* has the value 15, and *Birth.Year* has the value 1941.

The scope of a field identifier is the record in which that identifier is declared. This means that the same identifier may not be used to specify two different fields within the same record, but an identifier that names a field may be used elsewhere in the program for some other purpose.

The fields that comprise a record may be of any data type; in particular, they may be other records. For example, the declarations

```
type
    NameString = packed array[1..20] of char;
    NameOfMonth = packed array[1..8] of char;
    Date = record
                Month : NameOfMonth;
                Day : 1..31;
                Year : 1900..2000
          end;
    PersonnelRecord = record
                          Name : NameString;
                          Birth : Date;
                          Age, Dependents : integer;
                          HourlyRate : real
                      end;

var
    Employee : PersonnelRecord;
```

specify that variable *Employee* may have as a value any record of type *PersonnelRecord.* Such a record consists of five fields: the first field is of type *NameString* and is identified by *Name;* the second field is of type *Date* and is itself a record having three fields (*Month, Day,* and *Year*); the third and fourth fields are named *Age* and *Dependents* and are of type *integer;* and the fifth field is of type *real* and is named *HourlyRate.* A typical value for *Employee* might be pictured as follows:

Name	Birth			Age	Dependents	HourlyRate
	Month	*Day*	*Year*			
John Q. Doe	January	15	1941	46	4	12.25

The fields within such a **nested record** or **hierarchical record** may be accessed by simply affixing a second field identifier to the name of the larger record. Thus, *Employee.Birth.Month* refers to the first field in the inner record of type *Date;* for this record, its value would be the string January♭. Similarly, the values of *Employee.Birth.Day* and *Employee.Birth.Year* would be 15 and 1941, respectively.

The records considered in this section all consist of a fixed number of fields, each of which has a fixed type. It is also possible to declare records in which some of the fields are fixed but the number and types of other fields may vary. Thus, the number and types of fields in a variable of this record type may change during program execution. Such **variant records** are discussed in Section 10.5.

10.2 Processing Records

In the previous section we saw that records may be used to store several related data items that may be of different types and that each item or field in a record can be accessed with a fielded variable of the form

record-name.field-name

In this section we discuss how values can be assigned to the fields within a record, how these values can be read and displayed, and how the value of one record variable can be copied to another.

Because fielded variables and indexed variables both serve to specify a particular item in a structure, they are used in much the same way. To illustrate, consider the record type *ClassRecord* and the record variable *Student* declared by

```
const
    NameLength = 15;
    NumScores = 5;
    MaxScore = 100;

type
    NameString = packed array[1..NameLength] of char;
    ListOfScores = array[1..NumScores] of 0..MaxScore;
    ClassRecord = record
                        Snumb : integer;
                        Name : NameString;
                        Sex : char;
                        TestScore : ListOfScores
                  end;

var
    Student : ClassRecord;
```

Because the fielded variable *Student.Snumb* is of integer type, it may be assigned an integer value in an assignment statement

Student.Snumb := 12345;

or by an input statement

readln (Student.Snumb);

and its value can be displayed by using an output statement

writeln ('Student number: ', *Student.Snumb*);

Similarly, because *Student.TestScore* is an array, *Student.TestScore*[1] may be used to reference the first test score for this particular student.

Because records are structured data types, the value of a record variable can be neither read as a unit from the system file *input* (or any other text file) nor written as a unit to the system file *output* (or any other text file). Instead, input or output of records is done by reading or displaying the value of each field in the record. For example, to read a value for the record variable *Student* from the file *input,* the following statements might be used:

readln (*Student.Snumb*);
ReadString (*Student.Name, NameLength*);
readln (*Student.Sex*);
for *i* := 1 **to** *NumScores* **do**
   read (*Student.TestScore*[*i*]);
readln;

where *ReadString* is a procedure for reading strings (see Section 8.4).

The statements

Sum := 0;
for *i* := 1 **to** *NumScores* **do**
   Sum := *Sum* + *Student.TestScore*[*i*];
AveScore := *Sum* / *NumScores*

could then be used to calculate the average of the test scores.

The program in Figure 10.1 uses similar statements to read several records of type *ClassRecord,* by reading values from the text file *StudentInfoFile* for the individual fields. For each record, it calculates the average test score and then displays the student's number, name, sex, and average test score.

```
PROGRAM StudentAverages (input, output, StudentInfoFile);

(*******************************************************************

    Program to read student records each of which includes a student's
    number, name, sex, 5 test scores; calculate the average of the
    test scores; display this average together with the student's
    number, name, and sex.  The student records are read from the
    text file StudentInfoFile.

*******************************************************************)
CONST
    NameLength = 15;
    NumScores = 5;
    MaxScore = 100;
```

Figure 10.1

Figure 10.1 (Cont.)

```
TYPE
    String = PACKED ARRAY[1..NameLength] OF char;
    ListOfScores = ARRAY[1..NumScores] OF 0..MaxScore;
    ClassRecord = RECORD
                        Snumb : integer;
                        Name : String;
                        Sex : char;
                        TestScore :  ListOfScores
                  END;

VAR
    StudentInfoFile : text;   (* file containing student records *)
    Student : ClassRecord;    (* record for current student *)
    i,                        (* index *)
    Sum : integer;            (* sum of test scores *)
    AveScore : real;          (* average test score *)

PROCEDURE ReadString (VAR TextFile : text; VAR Str : String;
                      MaxString : integer);

    (***********************************************************

        Procedure to read characters into string variable Str from
        TextFile until an end-of-line mark is encountered or the upper
        limit MaxString on the length of Str is reached.  Any positions
        for which no characters are read will be filled with blanks.

    ***********************************************************)

    VAR
        i : integer;          (* index *)

    BEGIN (* ReadString *)
        FOR i := 1 TO MaxString DO
            IF NOT eoln(TextFile) THEN
                read (TextFile, Str[i])
            ELSE
                Str[i] := ' ';
        readln (TextFile)
    END (* ReadString *);

BEGIN (* main program *)
    reset (StudentInfoFile);

    (* Print headings *)

    writeln ('Student                    Test');
    writeln ('Number      Name      Sex Average');
    writeln ('------      ----      --- -------');
```

Figure 10.1 (Cont.)

```
WHILE NOT eof(StudentInfoFile) DO
   BEGIN
      (* Read student's record *)

      readln (StudentInfoFile, Student.Snumb);
      ReadString (StudentInfoFile, Student.Name, NameLength);
      readln (StudentInfoFile, Student.Sex);
      FOR i := 1 TO NumScores DO
         read (StudentInfoFile, Student.TestScore[i]);
      readln (StudentInfoFile);

      (* Calculate average test score *)

      Sum := 0;
      FOR i := 1 TO NumScores DO
         Sum := Sum + Student.TestScore[i];
      AveScore := Sum / NumScores;

      (* Display desired information *)

      writeln (Student.Snumb:5, Student.Name:17, Student.Sex:2,
               AveScore:8:1)
   END (* WHILE *)
END (* main program *).
```

Listing of StudentInfoFile:
_____

```
12345
John Doe
M
44 55 78 83 72
15651
Mary Smith
F
94 85 62 66 83
22001
Pete Vandervan
M
34 44 29 51 47
```

Sample run:
_____

Student Number	Name	Sex	Test Average.
12345	John Doe	M	66.4
15651	Mary Smith	F	78.0
22001	Pete Vandervan	M	41.0

Sometimes it is necessary to copy the fields of one record into another record. This can be done with a series of assignment statements that copy the individual fields, but it can be done more conveniently with a single assignment statement of the form

record-variable-1 := *record-variable-2*

In this case the two record variables must have the same type, which means that they must be declared using the same or equivalent type identifiers (see Section 8.2).

Recall that the value of a function may not be a structured type; in particular, it may not be a record. Records may, however, be used as parameters of functions and procedures, and in this case, the corresponding records must have the same type.

To illustrate the use of records as parameters for subprograms, consider the problem of finding the length of the segment joining two points in a plane and finding the equation of the line that passes through these points. The length of the segment joining P_1 with coordinates (x_1, y_1) and point P_2 with coordinates (x_2, y_2) is given by

$$\sqrt{(x_2 - x_1)^2 + (y_2 - y_1)^2}$$

The **slope-intercept** form of the equation of the line through P_1 and P_2 is

$$y = mx + b$$

where m is the **slope** of the line and is calculated by

$$m = \frac{y_2 - y_1}{x_2 - x_1}$$

(provided that $x_1 \neq x_2$); and b is the **y-intercept** of the line, that is, $(0,b)$ is the point where the line crosses the y axis. Using the slope m, we can calculate b as

$$b = y_1 - mx_1$$

In case $x_1 = x_2$, there is no y-intercept and the slope is not defined; the line through P_1 and P_2 is the vertical line having the equation

$$x = x_1$$

The program in Figure 10.2 uses the function *Length* to calculate the length of the segment joining points *P1* and *P2* and calls the procedure *FindLine* to find the equation of the line passing through *P1* and *P2*. Points are represented as records having two fields of real type named x and y, which represent the x and y coordinates, respectively:

```
Point = record
           x, y : real
        end;
```

```
PROGRAM PointsAndLines (input, output);

(*****************************************************************

   Program to read two points represented as records, calculate
   the length of the line segment joining them, and find the
   slope-intercept equation of the line passing through them.

*****************************************************************)

TYPE
   Point = RECORD
              x, y : real
           END;

VAR
   P1, P2 : Point;    (* 2 points being processed *)
   Response : char;   (* user response *)

FUNCTION Length (P1, P2 : Point) : real;

   (*****************************************************************

      Function to calculate the length of the line segment joining
      the two points P1 and P2.

   *****************************************************************)

   BEGIN (* Length *)
      Length := sqrt(sqr(P2.x - P1.x) + sqr(P2.y - P1.y))
   END (* Length *);

PROCEDURE FindLine (P1, P2 : Point);

   (*****************************************************************

      Procedure to find the slope-intercept equation  y = mx + b
      of the line passing though points P1 and P2.

   *****************************************************************)

   VAR
      m,          (* slope of line *)
      b : real;   (* y intercept of line *)

   BEGIN (* FindLine *)
      IF P1.x = P2.x THEN
         writeln ('Line is vertical line  x = ', P1.x:4:2)
      ELSE
         BEGIN
            m := (P2.y - P1.y) / (P2.x - P1.x);
            b := P1.y - m * P1.x;
            writeln ('Equation of line is y = ', m:4:2, 'x + ', b:4:2)
         END (* ELSE *)
   END (* FindLine *);
```

Figure 10.2

Figure 10.2 (Cont.)

```
BEGIN (* main program *)
   REPEAT
      write ('Enter coordinates of points P1 and P2:   ');
      readln (P1.x, P1.y, P2.x, P2.y);
      writeln ('For points (', P1.x:4:2, ',', P1.y:4:2, ') and (',
               P2.x:4:2, ',', P2.y:4:2, '):');
      writeln ('Length of segment joining P1 & P2 is ',
               Length(P1,P2):4:2);
      FindLine (P1, P2);
      writeln;
      write ('More (Y or N)?   ');
      readln (Response)
   UNTIL Response <> 'Y'
END (* main program *).
```

Sample run:

```
Enter coordinates of points P1 and P2:   0 0   1 1
For points (0.00,0.00) and (1.00,1.00):
Length of segment joining P1 & P2 is 1.41
Equation of line is y = 1.00x + 0.00

More (Y or N)?   Y
Enter coordinates of points P1 and P2:   1 1   1 5
For points (1.00,1.00) and (1.00,5.00):
Length of segment joining P1 & P2 is 4.00
Line is vertical line   x = 1.00

More (Y or N)?   Y
Enter coordinates of points P1 and P2:   3.1 4.2   -5.3 7.2
For points (3.10,4.20) and (-5.30,7.20):
Length of segment joining P1 & P2 is 8.92
Equation of line is y = -0.36x + 5.31

More (Y or N)?   N
```

10.3   The *with* Statement

Writing out the complete fielded variable for each of a record's fields can be quite cumbersome. For example, consider the record type *PersonnelRecord* of the preceding section:

```
type
    NameString = packed array[1..20] of char;
    NameOfMonth = packed array[1..8] of char;
    Date = record
              Month : NameOfMonth;
              Day : 1..31;
              Year : 1900..2000
           end;
```

Personnel Record = **record**
                                    Name : *NameString*;
                                    Birth : *Date*;
                                    Age, Dependents : *integer*;
                                    HourlyRate : *real*
                          end;

var
    CompanyName : *NameString*;
    Employee : *PersonnelRecord*;
    StartingDate : *Date*;

To display the values of *StartingDate* and *Employee,* we must display the values of each of their fields:

write ('Date of first employment: ');
writeln (*StartingDate.Month, StartingDate.Day*:3, ',',
            StartingDate.Year:5);
writeln;
writeln (*Employee.Name*);
writeln ('Birthday: ', *Employee.Birth.Month,*
            Employee.Birth.Day:3, ',', *Employee.Birth.Year*:5,
            ' Age = ', *Employee.Age*:1);
writeln ('# of dependents: ', *Employee.Dependents*:1);
writeln ('Hourly pay rate: $', *Employee.HourlyRate*:4:2);

To simplify references to the fields in a record, Pascal provides an option in which it is not necessary to specify the record name each time that a field within that record is referenced. This is accomplished by using the **with** statement of the form

with *record-name* **do**
    statement

The record name is automatically combined with each field identifier in the specified statement to form a complete fielded variable. Thus the statement

with *StartingDate* **do**
    writeln (*Month, Day*:3, ',', *Year*:5);

attaches the record name *StartingDate* to the field identifiers *Month, Day,* and *Year* to form the fielded variables *StartingDate.Month, StartingDate.Day,* and *StartingDate.Year.* It is thus equivalent to the second statement above.

Identifiers in a **with** statement that are not field identifiers are not combined with the record name but rather are treated in the usual way. Thus, in the statement

> **with** *StartingDate* **do**
>   *writeln* (*Month, Day*:3, ',', *Year*:5, *CompanyName*:30);

the identifier *CompanyName* is not a field identifier in the record *StartingDate* and hence is not modified by the **with** statement. This statement is equivalent, therefore, to

> *writeln* (*StartingDate.Month, StartingDate.Day*:3, ',',
>   *StartingDate.Year*:5, *CompanyName*:30);

With statements may also be ***nested;*** that is, one **with** statement may appear within another **with** statement. To illustrate, the preceding statements to display the value of the record variable *Employee* could be replaced by the **with** statement

> **with** *Employee* **do**
>   **begin**
>   *writeln* (*Name*);
>   *writeln* ('Birthday: ', *Birth.Month, Birth.Day*:3, ',',
>   *Birth.Year*:5, ' Age = ', *Age*:1);
>   *writeln* ('# of dependents: ', *Dependents*:1);
>   *writeln* ('Hourly pay rate: $', *HourlyRate*:4:2)
>   **end** (* **with** *);

or nested **with** statements might be used:

> **with** *Employee* **do**
>   **begin**
>   *writeln* (*Name*);
>   **with** *Birth* **do**
>   *writeln* ('Birthday: ', *Month, Day*:3, ',', *Year*:5,
>   ' Age = ', *Age*:1);
>   *writeln* ('# of dependents: ', *Dependents*:1);
>   *writeln* ('Hourly pay rate: $' *HourlyRate*:4:2)
>   **end** (* **with** *);

In this case, the inner **with** statement first attaches the record name *Birth* to the field identifers *Month, Day,* and *Year* to form the fielded variables *Birth.Month, Birth.Day,* and *Birth.Year;* but it does not attach *Birth* to the identifier *Age*, because this is not a field identifier within the record *Birth*. The outer **with** statement then attaches the record name *Employee* to form the fielded variables *Employee.Name, Employee.Birth.Month, Employee.Birth.Day, Employee.Birth.Year,* and *Employee.Age*.

An extended form of the **with** statement allows several record names to be listed:

> **with** *record-name-1, record-name-2, . . . , record-name-n* **do**
>   *statement*

This form is equivalent to

> **with** *record-name-1* **do**
>   **with** *record-name-2* **do**
>
>   .
>
>   .
>
>   **with** *record-name-n* **do**
>   *statement*

For example, the preceding nested **with** statement could also be written

> **with** *Employee, Birth* **do**
>   **begin**
>   *writeln* (*Name*);
>   *writeln* ('Birthday: ', *Month, Day*:3, ',', *Year*:5, ' Age = ', *Age*:1);
>   *writeln* ('# of dependents: ', *Dependents*:1);
>   *writeln* ('Hourly pay rate: $', *HourlyRate*:4:2)
>   **end** (* **with** *);

The program in Figure 10.1 to read student records and display them together with an average test score can be simplified using **with** statements. Figure 10.3 shows the resulting program.

```
PROGRAM StudentAverages (input, output, StudentInfoFile);

(*********************************************************************

   Program to read student records each of which includes a student's
   number, name, sex, 5 test scores; calculate the average of the
   test scores; display this average together with the student's
   number, name, and sex.  The student records are read from the
   text file StudentInfoFile.

*********************************************************************)

CONST
   NameLength = 15;
   NumScores = 5;
   MaxScore = 100;
```

Figure 10.3

Figure 10.3 (Cont.)

```
TYPE
    String = PACKED ARRAY[1..NameLength] OF char;
    ListOfScores = ARRAY[1..NumScores] OF 0..MaxScore;
    ClassRecord = RECORD
                     Snumb : integer;
                     Name : String;
                     Sex : char;
                     TestScore :  ListOfScores
                  END;

VAR
    StudentInfoFile : text;   (* file containing student records *)
    Student : ClassRecord;    (* record for current student *)
    i,                        (* index *)
    Sum : integer;            (* sum of test scores *)
    AveScore : real;          (* average test score *)

PROCEDURE ReadString (VAR TextFile : text; VAR Str : String;
                       MaxString : integer);

    (*********************************************************************

        Procedure to read characters into string variable Str from
        TextFile until an end-of-line mark is encountered or the upper
        limit MaxString on the length of Str is reached.  Any positions
        for which no characters are read will be filled with blanks.

    *********************************************************************)

    VAR
        i : integer;          (* index *)

    BEGIN (* ReadString *)
        FOR i := 1 TO MaxString DO
            IF NOT eoln(TextFile) THEN
                read (TextFile, Str[i])
            ELSE
                Str[i] := ' ';
        readln (TextFile)
    END (* ReadString *);

BEGIN (* main program *)
    reset (StudentInfoFile);

    (* Print headings *)

    writeln ('Student                      Test');
    writeln ('Number     Name        Sex  Average');
    writeln ('------     ----        ---  -------');
```

Figure 10.3 (Cont.)

```
WHILE NOT eof(StudentInfoFile) DO
    BEGIN
        (* Read student's record *)
        WITH Student DO
            BEGIN
                readln (StudentInfoFile, Snumb);
                ReadString (StudentInfoFile, Name, NameLength);
                readln (StudentInfoFile, Sex);
                FOR i := 1 TO NumScores DO
                    read (StudentInfoFile, TestScore[i]);
                readln (StudentInfoFile);
            END (* WITH *);

        (* Calculate average test score *)

        Sum := 0;
        FOR i := 1 TO NumScores DO
            Sum := Sum + Student.TestScore[i];
        AveScore := Sum / NumScores;

        (* Display desired information *)

        WITH Student DO
            writeln (Snumb:5, Name:17, Sex:2, AveScore:8:1)
    END (* WHILE *)
END (* main program *).
```

In some cases it may not be desirable to use **with** statements. For example, the statement

readln (*P1.x, P1.y, P2.x, P2.y*);

in the program of Figure 10.2 to read coordinates of points *P1* and *P2* cannot be written

with *P1, P2* **do**
readln (*x, y, x, y*);

since this would attach the record variable *P2* to the field identifiers *x* and *y* and is thus equivalent to

readln (*P2.x, P2.y, P2.x, P2.y*);

which reads a value only for the record *P2* (twice). The statement could be written

with *P1* **do**
readln (*x, y, P2.x, P2.y*);

or

> **with** *P1* **do**
>   *read* (*x*, *y*);
> **with** *P2* **do**
>   *readln* (*x*, *y*);

but neither of these seems better than the original. Similarly, replacing the statement

$$Length := sqrt(sqr(P2.x - P1.x) + sqr(P2.y - P1.y))$$

with

> **with** *P1, P2* **do**
>   *Length* := *sqrt(sqr(x − x) + sqr(y − y))*

is obviously incorrect since this is equivalent to the statement

$$Length := sqrt(sqr(P2.x - P2.x) + sqr(P2.y - P2.y))$$

which would always assign 0 to *Length*.

10.4 Application: Grading on the Curve and Sorting an Array of Records

Consider the problem of assigning letter grades to students by using the grading scheme commonly called "grading on the curve." In this scheme, a letter grade is assigned to a numerical grade according to the following table:

x = Numeric Score	Letter Grade
$x < m - \dfrac{3}{2}\sigma$	F
$m - \dfrac{3}{2}\sigma \le x < m - \dfrac{1}{2}\sigma$	D
$m - \dfrac{1}{2}\sigma \le x < m + \dfrac{1}{2}\sigma$	C
$m + \dfrac{1}{2}\sigma \le x < m + \dfrac{3}{2}\sigma$	B
$m + \dfrac{3}{2}\sigma \le x$	A

where *m* is the mean numeric score and σ is the standard deviation (see Exercises 14 and 15 of Section 8.3).

For each student we have the following information: student number and name and three numeric scores, one for homework, another for tests, and the third for the final examination. The final numeric grade is a weighted average of these scores and is to be calculated by

.2 × (homework score) + .5 × (tests score) + .3 × (exam score)

The output is to be a list of student numbers, final numeric scores, and final letter grades, arranged so that the scores are in descending order.

One alternative for storing this information would be to use seven **parallel arrays,** one of integer type to store the student numbers, another of string type to store the names, four arrays of real type to store the numeric scores, and an array of character type to store the letter grades. However, since the fields of a record may be of different types, it is much more convenient to use a single array whose components are records containing these items of information.

In the program in Figure 10.4, the given information, together with the calculated numeric score and letter grade for each student, is stored in a record having the structure:

```
StudentRecord = record
                  Snumb : integer;
                  Name : NameString;
                  Scores : record
                             HomeWork, Tests, Exam : real
                           end;
                  FinalNumScore : real;
                  LetterGrade : char
                end;
```

There is one record for each student, and the array *Student* is used to store these records so that *Student[i]* refers to the record of the *i*th student.

The structure of the program is displayed by the following structure diagram:

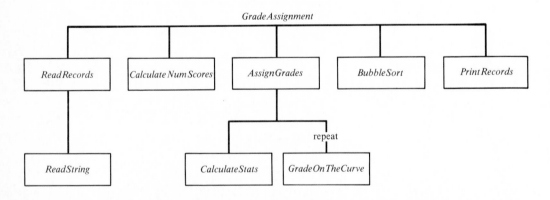

The procedure *ReadRecords* is first called to read each student's number, name, and three scores, storing these in the array *Student*. This array is then passed to the procedure *CalculateNumScore,* which calculates the final numeric score

for each student and inserts it in the field *FinalNumScore* of his or her record. The array of records is then passed to the procedure *AssignGrades*, which inserts the final letter grade in the field *LetterGrade* of each record. The procedure *AssignGrades* uses the procedure *CalculateStats* to calculate the mean and standard deviation of the final scores needed by the function *GradeOn-TheCurve*, which calculates the final letter grade. Finally, the program calls the procedure *BubbleSort* to arrange the records so that final numeric grades are in descending order and then calls the procedure *PrintRecords* to display the desired information. The procedure *BubbleSort* uses the bubble sort algorithm described in Section 8.3 with the modification that entire records are interchanged when necessary.

```
PROGRAM GradeAssignment (input, output, ScoresFile);

(******************************************************************

   Program to read students' records, each of which contains a
   student's number, name, and three numeric scores, one for
   homework, another for tests, and a third for the final exam.
   It calculates the final numeric grade as a weighted average of
   these scores using the weighting constants HomeworkWeight,
   TestWeight, and Examweight.  A letter grade is then calculated by
   "grading on the curve."  A list of student numbers with final
   numeric and letter grades is then displayed with numeric grades
   in descending order.  The student information is read from the
   text file ScoresFile.

******************************************************************)

CONST
   NameLength = 15;
   ListLimit = 100;

TYPE
   String = PACKED ARRAY[1..NameLength] OF char;
   StudentRecord = RECORD
      Snumb : integer;
      Name : String;
      Scores : RECORD
         Homework, Tests, Exam : real
         END;
      FinalNumScore : real;
      LetterGrade : char
   END;
   StudentRecordList = ARRAY[1..ListLimit] of StudentRecord;

VAR
   ScoresFile : text;                (* file of student scores *)
   Student : StudentRecordList;      (* list of student records *)
   NumStudents,                      (* number of students *)
   i : integer;                      (* index *)
```

Figure 10.4

Figure 10.4 (Cont.)

```
PROCEDURE ReadRecords (VAR Student : StudentRecordList;
                       VAR Count : integer);

   (*****************************************************************

      Procedure to read and count the list Student[1], Student[2], ...
      Student[Count] of student records.

   *****************************************************************)

   VAR
      i : integer;    (* index *)

   PROCEDURE ReadString (VAR TextFile : text; VAR Str : String;
                         MaxString : integer);

      (*************************************************************

         Procedure to read characters into string variable Str from
         TextFile until an end-of-line mark is encountered or the upper
         limit MaxString on the length of Str is reached.  Any positions
         for which no characters are read will be filled with blanks.

      *************************************************************)

      VAR
         i : integer;         (* index *)

      BEGIN (* ReadString *)
         FOR i := 1 TO MaxString DO
            IF NOT eoln(TextFile) THEN
               read (TextFile, Str[i])
            ELSE
               Str[i] := ' ';
         readln (TextFile)
      END (* ReadString *);

BEGIN (* ReadRecords *)
   reset (ScoresFile);
   Count := 0;
   WHILE NOT eof(ScoresFile) DO
      BEGIN
         Count := Count + 1;
         WITH Student[Count], Scores DO
            BEGIN
               readln (ScoresFile, Snumb);
               ReadString (ScoresFile, Name, NameLength);
               readln (ScoresFile, Homework, Tests, Exam)
            END (* WITH *)
      END (* WHILE *)
END (* ReadRecords *);
```

Figure 10.4 (Cont.)

```
PROCEDURE CalculateNumScores (VAR student : StudentRecordList;
                                  NumStudents : integer);

   (************************************************************

      Procedure to calculate final numeric grades for each student
      as a weighted average and insert it into his/her record.

   ************************************************************)

   CONST
      HomeWorkWeight = 0.2;
      TestWeight = 0.5;
      ExamWeight = 0.3;

   VAR
      i : integer;  (* index *)

   BEGIN (* CalculateNumScores *)
      FOR i := 1 TO NumStudents DO
         WITH Student[i], Scores DO
            FinalNumScore := HomeWorkWeight * Homework + TestWeight * Tests
                             + ExamWeight * Exam
   END (* CalculateNumScores *);

PROCEDURE AssignGrades (VAR student : StudentRecordList;
                        NumStudents : integer);

   (************************************************************

      Procedure to insert letter grades in the students' records.

   ************************************************************)

   VAR
      i : integer;                (* index *)
      Mean,                       (* mean of final numeric scores *)
      StandardDeviation : real;   (* standard deviation of final scores *)

   PROCEDURE CalculateStats (VAR Student : StudentRecordList;
                             NumStudents : integer;
                             VAR Mean,  StandardDeviation : real);

      (************************************************************

         Procedure to find the mean and standard deviation of the
         students' final numeric grades.

      ************************************************************)

      VAR
         i : integer;       (* index *)
         Sum,               (* used to calculate necessary totals *)
         Variance : real;   (* variance of the scores *)
```

Figure 10.4 (Cont.)

```
BEGIN (* CalculateStats *)

   (* Find the mean *)

   Sum := 0;
   FOR i := 1 TO NumStudents DO
         Sum := Sum + Student[i].FinalNumScore;
   Mean := Sum / NumStudents;

   (* Find the variance and standard deviation *)

   Sum := 0;
   FOR i := 1 TO NumStudents DO
      Sum := Sum + sqr(Student[i].FinalNumScore - Mean);
   Variance := Sum / NumStudents;
   StandardDeviation := sqrt(Variance)
END (* CalculateStats *);

FUNCTION GradeOnTheCurve (Score, Mean, StDev : real) : char;

   (*****************************************************************

      Function using "grading on the curve" to assign letter grade to
      numeric Score; Mean is the mean score, StDev is the standard
      deviation.

   *****************************************************************)

   BEGIN (* GradeOnTheCurve *)
      IF Score < (Mean - 1.5 * StDev) THEN
         GradeOnTheCurve := 'F'
      ELSE IF Score < (Mean - 0.5 * StDev) THEN
         GradeOnTheCurve := 'D'
      ELSE IF Score < (Mean + 0.5 * StDev) THEN
         GradeOnTheCurve := 'C'
      ELSE IF Score < (Mean + 1.5 * StDev) THEN
         GradeOnTheCurve := 'B'
      ELSE
         GradeOnTheCurve := 'A'
   END (* GradeOnTheCurve *);

BEGIN (* AssignGrades *)
   CalculateStats (Student, NumStudents, Mean, StandardDeviation);
   FOR i := 1 TO NumStudents DO
      WITH Student[i] DO
         LetterGrade :=
               GradeOnTheCurve (FinalNumScore, Mean, StandardDeviation)
END (* AssignGrades *);
```

Figure 10.4 (Cont.)

```
PROCEDURE BubbleSort (VAR Student : StudentRecordList;
                      NumStudents : integer);

   (***********************************************************************

      Procedure to sort Student[1], ..., Student[NumStudents] using
      the bubble sort algorithm so that key fields FinalNumScore
      are in descending order.

   **********************************************************************)

   VAR
      i,                        (* index *)
      NumPairs : integer;       (* number of pairs examined in current scan *)
      Temporary : StudentRecord; (* used to interchange two items *)
      Done : boolean;           (* indicates if sorting completed *)

   BEGIN (* BubbleSort *)
      NumPairs := NumStudents - 1;

      (* Scan the list comparing consecutive items *)

      REPEAT
         Done := true;
         FOR i := 1 TO NumPairs DO
            IF Student[i].FinalNumScore > Student[i+1].FinalNumScore THEN
               BEGIN
                  Temporary := Student[i];
                  Student[i] := Student[i+1];
                  Student[i+1] := Temporary;
                  Done := false  (* interchange occurred, so scan again *)
               END (* IF *);

         (* Record with largest key has sunk into place, so
            eliminate it from the next scan *)

         NumPairs := NumPairs - 1
      UNTIL Done
   END (* BubbleSort *);

PROCEDURE PrintRecords (VAR student : StudentRecordList;
                        NumStudents : integer);

   (***********************************************************************

      Procedure to print the final grades for all students.

   **********************************************************************)

   VAR
      i : integer;   (* index *)
```

Figure 10.4 (Cont.)

```
    BEGIN (* PrintRecords *)
        writeln ('Student      Final      Final');
        writeln ('Number       Score      Grade');
        writeln ('————       ————      ————');
        FOR i := 1 TO NumStudents DO
            WITH Student[i] DO
                writeln (Snumb:5, FinalNumScore:11:2, LetterGrade:8)
    END (* PrintRecords *);

BEGIN (* main program *)
    ReadRecords (Student, NumStudents);
    CalculateNumScores (Student, NumStudents);
    AssignGrades(Student, NumStudents);
    BubbleSort (Student, NumStudents);
    PrintRecords (Student, NumStudents)
END (* main *).
```

Listing of ScoresFile:


```
1234
John Doe
50 53 57
1441
Mary Smith
62 59 65
1531
Fred Jones
72 65 70
1554
Pete Vander
100 100 100
1638
Jane Doe
22 15 19
1734
Al Johnson
62 58 55
```

Sample run:

Student Number	Final Score	Final Grade
1638	17.60	F
1234	53.60	C
1734	57.90	C
1441	61.40	C
1531	67.90	C
1554	100.00	A

10.5 Variant Records

As we noted in Section 10.2, records may have a **variant part** in addition to a **fixed part.** The number and types of the fields in the fixed part of a record variable do not change during program execution, but those in the variant part may change in number and/or in type. In this section we discuss such **variant records.**

To illustrate variant records, consider the employee record described by

```
EmployeeRecord1 = record
                     Name : NameString;
                     Age, Dependents : integer;
                     DeptCode : char;
                     HourlyRate : real
                  end;
```

where *NameString* is a user-defined type such as **packed array**[1..20] **of** *char*. Such records are appropriate for factory employees who are paid on an hourly basis. For office employees, the records might have the following structure:

```
EmployeeRecord2 = record
                     Name : NameString;
                     Age, Dependents : integer;
                     Salary : real
                  end;
```

and for salespersons, an appropriate record structure might be

```
EmployeeRecord3 = record
                     Name : NameString;
                     Age, Dependents : integer;
                     MileageAllowance : integer;
                     BasePay, CommissionRate : real
                  end;
```

All of these record structures can be incorporated into a single record by using a record with a variant part:

```
EmployeeRecord = record
                    Name : NameString;
                    Age, Dependents : integer;
                    case EmpCode : char of
                        'F' : (DeptCode : char;
                               HourlyRate : real);
                        'O' : (Salary : real);
                        'S' : (MileageAllowance : integer;
                               BasePay, CommissionRate : real)
                 end;
```

This record has a fixed part that is the same for all values of type *EmployeeRecord*, and this fixed part consists of the fields *Name*, *Age*, and *Dependents*. In addition to these three fields, some values have *DeptCode* and *HourlyRate* fields; others have only a *Salary* field; and still others have *MileageAllowance*, *BasePay*, and *CommissionRate* fields. If *EmpCode* has the value F, then the fields *DeptCode* and *HourlyRate* are in effect; if *EmpCode* has the value O, then the field *Salary* is in effect; and if the value of *EmpCode* is S, then the *MileageAllowance*, *BasePay*, and *CommissionRate* fields are in effect.

The field *EmpCode* is called the **tag field** in this record. The values it may have are used to label the variant fields of the record and to determine the structure of a particular value of type *EmployeeRecord*. Thus, if the value of *EmpCode* is F, which labels the variant for a factory employee, the structure of the record is the same as one of type *EmployeeRecord1*. If the value of *EmpCode* is O, which labels the variant for an office employee, the structure of the record is that of type *EmployeeRecord2*. Finally, if the value of *EmpCode* is S, which labels the variant for a salesperson, the structure is the same as that of type *EmployeeRecord3*. Note that the variant part of a record follows the fixed part and that each variant field list is enclosed in parentheses.

In a variant record, several tag field values may label the same variant field list. It is also permissible for tag field values to label empty variant field lists. To illustrate, suppose that the following type declarations have been made:

```
type
    NameString = packed array[1..20] of char;
    TransactionType = (Deposit, Withdrawal, LoanPayment, Transfer,
                        Void);
    Date = record
                Month, Day, Year : integer
           end;
```

and consider the following definition of a record to store certain items of information related to banking transactions:

```
Transaction = record
                CustomerName : NameString;
                Number : integer;
                TransDate : Date;
                case TransType : TransactionType of
                    Deposit, Withdrawal : (Amount : real);
                    LoanPayment         : (LoanNumber : integer;
                                            Payment, Interest,
                                            NewBalance : real);
                    Transfer            : (TransferAccount : integer;
                                            AmountOfTransfer : real;
                                            Code : char);
                    Void                : ()
              end;
```

Note that the tag field *TransType* may have any of the five values specified by the enumerated type *TransactionType*. If the value of *TransType* is either *De-*

posit or *Withdrawal*, the field in effect is the single real field *Amount*. If the value of *TransType* is *LoanPayment*, then four fields are in effect: one integer field *LoanNumber* and three real fields, *Payment*, *Interest*, and *NewBalance*. For the value *Transfer* of *TransType*, there are three effective fields: *TransferAccount* of integer type, *AmountOfTransfer* of real type, and *Code* of character type (which indicates whether the transfer is to or from *Transfer-Account*). Finally, the value of *TransType* may be *Void*, in which case no information is required and thus no field is in effect.

Now suppose that the following variables have been declared:

```
var
     Account : Transaction;
     TransactionCode : char;
```

To read information into the record variable *Account*, one typically first reads values for the fixed field identifiers:

```
with Account do
   begin
      for i : = 1 to 20 do
         read (CustomerName[i]);
      readln;
      readln (Number);
      with TransDate do
         readln (Month, Day, Year)
   end (* with *);
```

Next, a value is read for *TransactionCode* that indicates whether the transaction is a deposit (D), withdrawal (W), loan payment (L), transfer (T), or void (V). This value can then be used to set the corresponding value of the tag field *TransType*. These codes of type *char*, rather than the actual values of *TransType*, are read, because values of the enumerated type *TransactionType* cannot be read from the system file *input* (or from any other text file). A **case** statement within a **with** statement might be used to set the tag field and read the values for items in the corresponding field list:

```
with Account do
   case TransactionCode of
      'D' : begin
               TransType : = Deposit;
               readln (Amount)
            end;
      'W' : begin
               TransType : = Withdrawal;
               readln (Amount)
            end;
      'L' : begin
               TransType : = LoanPayment;
               readln (LoanNumber, Payment)
            end;
```

```
'T' : begin
          TransType := Transfer;
          readln (TransferAccount, AmountOfTransfer, Code)
      end;
   'V' : TransType := Void
end (* case *);
```

As this example illustrates, a record structure may be quite complex, since there may be records nested within records (e.g., *TransDate* of record type *Date* nested within *Account* of record type *Transaction*); and although our example does not illustrate it, these nested records may themselves have variant parts.

The general form of a record structure is

record
   field-list
end

where *field-list* has one of the following forms:

fixed-part	*fixed-part;*	*variant-part*
	variant-part	

Here *fixed-part* has the form described in preceding sections:

```
list-1 : type-1;
list-2 : type-2;
     ⋮
list-m : type-m
```

where each *list-i* is a single identifier or a list of identifiers, separated by commas, that name the fields of the record, and *type-i* specifies the type of these fields. The *variant-part* has the form

```
case tag-field : tag-type of
   tag-list-1 : (variant-1);
   tag-list-2 : (variant-2);
        ⋮
   tag-list-n : (variant-n)
```

where each *variant-i* is a field list of the form previously described; thus, the syntax of each *variant-i* is the same as for a record, but parentheses are used to enclose it rather than the reserved words **record** and **end.** The type of the *tag-field* may be any ordinal type, and each of the possible values of the tag field must appear in exactly one *tag-list-i*. This general form of a record is displayed in the following syntax diagrams.

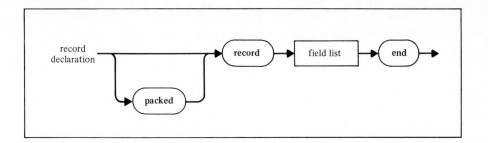

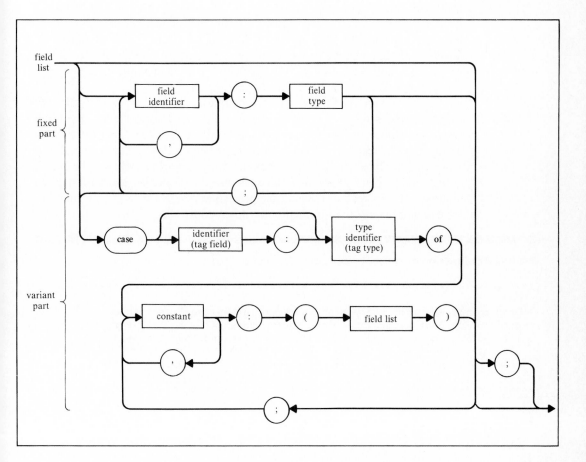

Note that a record may have both a fixed part and a variant part, only a fixed part, or only a variant part. It might also be noted that the tag field identifier, but not its type identifier, may be omitted. In this case, access to the items in a variant field list is still possible, but because no tag field identifier is used, the tag field itself cannot be accessed. Such records might be used when it is possible to determine by some other means which variant field list is in effect, for example, when the first fifty records in an array of one hundred records all use the same variant field list and the remaining fifty records involve some other variant field list. Omitting the tag field identifier, however, can easily lead to subtle errors and should normally be avoided (see Programming

Pointer 8 at the end of this chapter). Finally, as the syntax diagram indicates, records may be packed to permit the compiler to minimize the amount of storage required for a record.

10.6 Application: Information Retrieval

Records are frequently used in problems that require storing and retrieving information, since in many such problems the items of information are not all of the same type. For example, consider a file of employee records as described in the preceding section. Each record contains the name, age, and number of dependents for an employee and other information determined by the job classification of the employee. A department code and an hourly rate are stored for factory employees, a salary for office employees, and a mileage allowance, a base pay, and a commission rate for salespersons.

The program in Figure 10.5 reads these records from the text file *EmployeeFile*, using the procedure *ReadRecords*, and stores them in the array *Employee*, whose components are variant records of type *EmployeeRecord*. We assume that the records in *EmployeeFile* have been sorted so that the employee names are in alphabetical order. Thus the array *Employee* will also be sorted so that the procedure *BinarySearch* can be used to locate the record for a given employee. If this record is found, the procedure *PrintRecords* is then called to retrieve and display the information in this record.

```
PROGRAM InfoRetrieval (input, output, EmployeeFile);

(*******************************************************************

   Program to copy the information in the file EmployeeFile into an
   array of variant records and then search this array to retrieve
   information about a given employee.  The file and thus the array
   also are assumed to be sorted so employee names are in alphabetical
   order; a binary search is then used to retrieve an employee's record.

*******************************************************************)

CONST
   MaxString = 20;               (* upper limit on lengths of strings *)
   ArrayLimit = 100;             (* limit on size of array *)

TYPE
   String = PACKED ARRAY[1..MaxString] OF char;
   EmployeeRecord = RECORD
                       Name : String;
                       Age, Dependents : integer;
                       CASE EmpCode : char OF
                          'F' : (DeptCode : char; HourlyRate : real);
                          'O' : (Salary : real);
                          'S' : (MileageAllowance : integer;
                                 BasePay, CommissionRate : real)
                    END;
   ArrayOfRecords = ARRAY [1..ArrayLimit] of EmployeeRecord;
```

Figure 10.5

Figure 10.5 (Cont.)

```
VAR
    Employee : ArrayOfRecords;      (* array of employee records *)
    EmployeeFile : text;            (* file containing employee information *)
    Count,                          (* number of records *)
    Location : integer;             (* location of specified record in the array *)
    NameSought : String;            (* name of employee to be searched for *)
    Found : boolean;                (* indicates if record is found *)

PROCEDURE ReadRecords (VAR EmployeeFile : text;
                       VAR Employee: ArrayOfRecords; VAR Count : integer);

    (**************************************************************

        Procedure to read and Count array Employee of employee records
        from the text file EmployeeFile.

    **************************************************************)

    VAR
        i : integer;      (* index *)

    BEGIN (* ReadRecords *)
        reset (EmployeeFile);
        Count := 0;
        WHILE NOT eof(EmployeeFile) DO
            BEGIN
                Count := Count + 1;
                WITH Employee[Count] DO
                    BEGIN
                        FOR i := 1 TO MaxString DO
                            read (EmployeeFile, Name[i]);
                        readln (EmployeeFile, Age, Dependents);
                        read (EmployeeFile, EmpCode);
                        CASE EmpCode OF
                            'F' : readln (EmployeeFile, DeptCode, HourlyRate);
                            'O' : readln (EmployeeFile, Salary);
                            'S' : readln (EmployeeFile, MileageAllowance,
                                            BasePay, CommissionRate)
                        END (* CASE *)
                    END (* WITH *)
            END (* WHILE *)
    END (* ReadRecords *);

PROCEDURE ReadString (VAR Str : String; MaxString : integer);

    (**************************************************************

        Procedure to read characters into string variable Str until an
        end-of-line mark is encountered or the upper limit MaxString
        on the length of Str is reached.  Any positions for which no
        characters are read will be filled with blanks.

    **************************************************************)
```

Figure 10.5 (Cont.)

```
    VAR
        i : integer;          (* index *)

    BEGIN (* ReadString *)
        FOR i := 1 TO MaxString DO
            IF NOT eoln THEN
                read (Str[i])
            ELSE
                Str[i] := ' ';
        readln
    END (* ReadString *);

PROCEDURE BinarySearch (VAR Employee : ArrayOfRecords; n : integer;
                        NameSought : String;
                        VAR Mid : integer; VAR Found : boolean);

    (*********************************************************************

        Procedure to binary search the array Employee of size n for the
        record containing a specified employee name.  True is returned
        for Found if the search is successful and Mid is then the
        location of this record; else Found is set to false.

    *********************************************************************)

    VAR
        First, Last : integer;   (* first and last positions of
                                     the sublist being searched *)

    BEGIN (* BinarySearch *)
        Found := false;
        First := 1;
        Last := n;
        WHILE (First <= Last) AND NOT Found DO
            BEGIN
                Mid := (First + Last) DIV 2;
                WITH Employee[Mid] DO
                    IF NameSought < Name THEN
                        Last := Mid - 1
                    ELSE IF NameSought > Name THEN
                        First := Mid + 1
                    ELSE
                        Found := true
            END (* WHILE *)
    END (* BinarySearch *);

PROCEDURE PrintRecord (Employee : EmployeeRecord);

    (*********************************************************************

        Procedure to print the record of Employee.

    *********************************************************************)
```

Figure 10.5 (Cont.)

```
    BEGIN (* PrintRecord *)
       WITH Employee DO
          BEGIN
             writeln ('Age . . . . . . . . . .', Age:2);
             writeln ('Dependents . . . . . .', Dependents:2);
             CASE EmpCode OF
                'F' : BEGIN
                        writeln ('Department code . . . . ', DeptCode);
                        writeln ('Hourly rate  . . .', HourlyRate:7:2)
                      END;
                'O' : writeln ('Salary . . . . .', Salary:7:2);
                'S' : BEGIN
                        writeln ('Mileage allowance . . ', MileageAllowance:3);
                        writeln ('Base pay . . . . ', BasePay:7:2);
                        writeln ('Commission rate . . ', CommissionRate:5:3)
                      END
             END (* CASE *)
          END (* WITH *)
    END (* PrintRecord *);

BEGIN (* main program *)
   ReadRecords (EmployeeFile, Employee, Count);
   writeln ('Enter names in the form   Last-name, First-name');
   writeln ('using all upper case letters.  To quit, enter * for name.');
   writeln;
   write ('Employee''s Name?  ');
   ReadString (NameSought, MaxString);
   WHILE NameSought[1] <> '*' DO
      BEGIN
         BinarySearch (Employee, Count, NameSought, Location, Found);
         IF Found THEN
            PrintRecord (Employee[Location])
         ELSE
            writeln ('Employee''s record not found');
         writeln;
         write ('Employee''s Name?  ');
         ReadString (NameSought, MaxString)
      END (* WHILE *)
END (* main program *).
```

```
Listing of EmployeeFile used in sample run:


DOE, JOHN          35 3
O 35000
JONES, FRED        58 4
FM 13.55
SMITH, MARY        22 0
O 31150
VANDERVAN, PETER   29 1
S 500 12000 0.15
```

Figure 10.5 (Cont.)

```
Sample run:

Enter names in the form   Last-name, First-name
using all upper case letters.  To quit, enter * for name.

Employee's Name?  DOE, JOHN
Age . . . . . . . . . .35
Dependents  . . . . . . 3
Salary  . . . . .35000.00

Employee's Name?  VANDER, PETER
Employee's record not found

Employee's Name?  VANDERVAN, PETER
Age . . . . . . . . . .29
Dependents  . . . . . . 1
Mileage allowance . . 500
Base pay . . . . 12000.00
Commission rate . . 0.150

Employee's Name?  JONES, FRED
Age . . . . . . . . . .58
Dependents  . . . . . . 4
Department code . . . . M
Hourly rate  . . . 13.55

Employee's Name?  *
```

Exercises

1. For each of the following, develop an appropriate record structure for the given information, and then write type declarations for the records:

   (a) Cards in a deck of playing cards.
   (b) Time measured in hours, minutes, and seconds.
   (c) Length measured in yards, feet, and inches.
   (d) Listings in a telephone directory.
   (e) Description of an automobile (make, model, style, color, and the like).
   (f) Description of a book in a library's card catalogue (author, publisher, and the like).
   (g) Teams in a baseball league (name, won-lost record, and the like).
   (h) Position of a checker on a checker board.

2. The data files *StudentFile, InventoryFile,* and *UsersFile* are described in Appendix E. Write appropriate record declarations to describe the information in these files.

3. For each of the following, develop a record structure using variant records for the given information, and then write type declarations for the records:

(a) Information about a person: name; birthday; age; sex; social security number; height; weight; hair color; eye color; marital status and, if married, number of children.

(b) Statistics about a baseball player: name; age; birth date; position (pitcher, catcher, infielder, outfielder); for a pitcher: won-lost record, earned-run average, number of strikeouts, number of walks; if a starting pitcher, number of complete games; and if a relief pitcher, number of innings pitched and number of saves; for the other positions: batting average; slugging average; bats right, left, or is a switch hitter; fielding percentage; also, for an infielder, the positions he can play; for a catcher, whether he can catch a knuckleball.

(c) Weather statistics: date; city and state, province, or country; time of day; temperature; barometric pressure; weather conditions (clear skies, partly cloudy, cloudy, stormy); if cloudy conditions prevail, cloud level and type of clouds; for partly cloudy, percentage of cloud cover; for stormy conditions, snow depth if it is snowing; amount of rainfall if it is rainy; size of hail if it is hailing.

4. Like the elements of an array, the fields of a record can be stored in consecutive memory locations, and address translation is required to determine the location of a particular field. To illustrate, suppose that integers are stored in one memory word, real values require two words, and strings of characters are packed two characters per word. The declaration of the record variable *Employee* in Section 10.1 instructs the compiler to reserve a block of fourteen consecutive memory words to store such a record. As for arrays, the address of the first word in this block is called the **base address**. If the base address for *Employee* is b, then the field *Employee.Name* is stored in ten consecutive memory words beginning at b, *Employee.Age* is stored in word $b + 10$, *Employee.Dependents* in word $b + 11$, and *Employee.HourlyRate* in words $b + 12$ and $b + 13$.

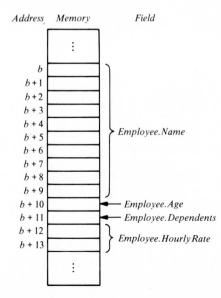

Assuming these storage requirements for integers, reals, and strings, and assuming that values of type *char* require an entire word, give a similar picture showing where each field of the following record types would be stored:

(a) *Point* in Figure 10.2.
(b) *StudentRecord* in Figure 10.4.
(c) *ClassRecord* in Figure 10.3.
(d) *Transaction* in Section 10.5. (See also Programming Pointer 8 following this set of exercises.)

5. Extend the program in Figure 10.2 to find

   (a) The midpoint of the line segment joining two points.
   (b) The equation of the perpendicular bisector of this line segment.

6. The **point-slope** equation of a line having slope m and passing through the point P with coordinates (x_1, y_1) is

$$y - y_1 = m(x - x_1)$$

   (a) Write a record description for a line, given its slope and a point on the line.
   (b) Write a program that reads the slope of a line and the coordinates of a point on the line and that then
   (i) Finds the point-slope equation of the line.
   (ii) Finds the slope-intercept equation of the line.

   (c) Write a program to read the point and slope information of two lines and determine whether they intersect or are parallel. If they intersect, find the point of intersection and also determine whether they are perpendicular.

7. Write a program that accepts a time of day in military format and finds the corresponding usual representation in hours, minutes and A.M./P.M. or accepts the time in the usual format and finds the corresponding military representation. For example, the input 0100 should produce 1:00 A.M. as output, and the input 3:45 P.M. should give 1545.

8. Write a record declaration for cards in a standard deck having fifty-two cards and two jokers. Then write a program to deal two ten-card hands from such a deck. (See Section 5.4 regarding a random number generator.) Be sure that the same card is not dealt more than once.

9. Write a declaration of a record having only a variant part for four geometric figures: circle, square, rectangle, and triangle. For a circle, the record should store its radius; for a square, the length of a side;

for a rectangle, the lengths of two adjacent sides; and for a triangle, the lengths of the three sides. Then write a program that reads one of the letters C (circle), S (square), R (rectangle), T (triangle) and the appropriate numeric quantity or quantities for a figure of that type and then calculates its area. For example, the input R 7.2 3.5 represents a rectangle with length 7.2 and width 3.5, and T 3 4 6.1 represents a triangle having sides of lengths 3, 4, and 6.1. (For a triangle the area can be found by using **Hero's formula:** area = $\sqrt{s(s - a)(s - b)(s - c)}$, where a, b, and c are the lengths of the sides and s is one half of the perimeter.

10. Write a program to read the records in *InventoryFile* (see Appendix E) and store them in an array of records, read a stock number entered by the user, and then search this array for the item having that stock number. If a match is found, the item name and number currently in stock should be displayed; otherwise, a message indicating that it was not found should be displayed.

11. Write a program to read the records in *StudentFile* and store them in an array of records, sort them so that cumulative GPAs are in descending order, and then display the student numbers, names, majors, and GPAs of the records in this sorted array.

12. A *complex number* has the form $a + bi$, where a and b are real numbers and $i^2 = -1$. The four basic arithmetic operations for complex numbers are defined as follows:

addition: $(a + bi) + (c + di) = (a + c) + (b + d)i$.

subtraction: $(a + bi) - (c + di) = (a - c) + (b - d)i$.

multiplication: $(a + bi) * (c + di) = (ac - bd) + (ad + bc)i$

division: $\dfrac{a + bi}{c + di} = \dfrac{ac + bd}{c^2 + d^2} + \dfrac{bc - ad}{c^2 + d^2} i$

provided $c^2 + d^2 \neq 0$.

Write a program to read two complex numbers and a symbol for one of these operations and to perform the indicated operation. Use a record to represent complex numbers, and use procedures to implement the operations.

13. A *rational number* is of the form a/b where a and b are integers with $b \neq 0$. Write a program to do rational number arithmetic, representing each rational number as a record with a numerator field and a denominator field. The program should read and display all rational numbers in the format a/b, or simply a if the denominator is 1. The following examples illustrate the menu of commands that the user should be allowed to enter:

Input	Output	Comments
3/8 + 1/6	13/24	$a/b + c/d = (ad + bc)/bd$ reduced to lowest terms.
3/8 − 1/6	5/24	$a/b − c/d = (ad − bc)/bd$ reduced to lowest terms.
3/8 * 1/6	1/16	$a/b * c/d = ac/bd$ reduced to lowest terms.
3/8 / 1/6	9/4	$a/b / c/d = ad/bc$ reduced to lowest terms.
3/8 I	8/3	Invert a/b.
8/3 M	2 + 2/3	Write a/b as a mixed fraction.
6/8 R	3/4	Reduce a/b to lowest terms.
6/8 G	2	Greatest common divisor of numerator and denominator.
1/6 L 3/8	24	Lowest common denominator of a/b and c/d.
1/6 < 3/8	true	$a/b < c/d$?
1/6 <= 3/8	true	$a/b \le c/d$?
1/6 > 3/8	false	$a/b > c/d$?
1/6 >= 3/8	false	$a/b \ge c/d$?
3/8 = 9/24	true	$a/b = c/d$?
2/3 X + 2 = 4/5	X = −9/5	Solution of linear equation $(a/b)X + c/d = e/f$.

Programming Pointers

A record is a collection of related data items called fields that may be of different types. In some situations, such as in assignment statements and subprogram references, records may be processed as single units. In other situations it is necessary to process the fields of a record separately by using field designated variables. The following are some of the important points to remember when using records:

1. *The reserved word **end** must be used to mark the end of each record declaration.*

2. *A field in a record is accessed with a field-designated variable, or fielded variable, of the form record-name.field-name.*

3. *The scope of each field identifier is the record in which it appears.* This scope rule has the following consequences:

   - *The same identifier may not be used to name two different fields within the same record.*
   - *An identifier that names a field within a record may be used for some other purpose outside that record (but see Programming Pointer 5).*

4. *Records cannot be read or written as units to or from text files; instead individual fields must be read or written.* For example, if *InfoRec* is a record of type *InformationRecord* defined by

type
    String20 = **packed array** [1..20] **of** *char*;
    String12 = **packed array** [1..12] **of** *char*;
    AddressRecord = **record**
                      StreetAddress : *String20*;
                      City, State : *String12*;
                      ZipCode : *integer*
              end;
    InformationRecord = **record**
                    Name : *String20*;
                    Address : *AddressRecord*;
                    Age : *integer*;
                    MaritalStatus : *char*
              end;

its fields can be displayed as follows:

    writeln (InfoRec.Name);
    writeln (InfoRec.Address.StreetAddress);
    writeln (InfoRec.Address.City, ', ', InfoRec.Address.State,
                InfoRec.Address.ZipCode);
    writeln ('Age: ', InfoRec.Age);
    writeln ('Marital Status: ', InfoRec.MaritalStatus);

5. *The* **with** *statement attaches a given record name(s) to each identifier within the statement that names a field within the specified record(s).* For example, the output statements in Programming Pointer 4 could be replaced with ●

    with *InfoRec* **do**
      begin
        writeln (Name);
        writeln (Address.StreetAddress);
        writeln (Address.City,', ', Address.State, Address.ZipCode);
        writeln ('Age: ', Age);
        writeln ('Marital Status:●', MaritalStatus)
      end (* **with** *);

    The **with** statement attaches a record name to *every* identifier appearing in the **with** statement that names a field within the specified record. Consequently, if one of these identifiers is used for some other purpose outside the record, the **with** statement attaches the record name to this identifier so that the field within the record is processed and not the value of the identifier outside the record.

    A **with** statement of the form

    with *record-name-1, record-name-2* **do**
      statement

is equivalent to

    with *record-name-1* **do**
      with *record-name-2* **do**
        statement

(and similarly for **with** statements with more than two record names). This means that *record-name-2* will first be attached to all identifiers that name fields within it before *record-name-1* is attached. Thus, the preceding **with** statement to display the fields within *InfoRec* could also be written

> **with** *InfoRec, Address* **do**
>   **begin**
>   *writeln (Name)*;
>   *writeln (StreetAddress)*;
>   *writeln (City,', ', State, ZipCode)*;
>   *writeln ('Age:' ', Age)*;
>   *writeln ('Marital Status: ', MaritalStatus)*
>   **end** (* **with** *);

One result of this order of attachment is that if an identifier names a field in *record-name-1* and a field in *record-name-2*, then *record-name-2* will be attached to this field identifier.

6. *The value of a record may be copied into another record by using an assignment statement, provided that the two records have the same type, which means that they must be declared by the same or equivalent type identifiers* (see Section 8.2). Thus, if the type *PersonRecord* is defined by

> *PersonRecord* = *InformationRecord*;

where *InformationRecord* is as described in Programming Pointer 3, then the record variables *RecA* and *RecB* declared by

> **var**
>   *RecA* : *InformationRecord*;
>   *RecB* : *PersonRecord*;

have the same type because *InformationRecord* and *PersonRecord* are equivalent type identifiers.

7. *Records may be used as parameters in functions or procedures, but each actual parameter must have the same type as the corresponding formal parameter. The value of a function may not be a record.*

8. *When variant records are used, sufficient memory is usually allocated to store the variant that requires the most memory, and all other variants of that record are stored using this same portion of memory.* To illustrate, consider declarations of the form

> **type**
>   *EmployeeRecord* = **record**
>   :   (* fixed part of record *)
>   **case** *EmpCode* : *char* **of**
>   'F': *(DeptCode* : *char*;
>   *HourlyRate* : *real)*;
>   'O': *(Salary* : *real)*
>   **end**;

Because the first variant is the larger, sufficient memory is allocated to store it, but the same memory locations are used for the second variant:

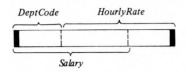

If values such as M and 11.25 are assigned to the fields of the first variant, a subsequent reference to this same record with the second variant is improper. An error or a "garbage" value for *Salary* may result, because an attempt is made to interpret the internal representation of the character M as part of a real value for *Salary*.

9. *The tag field in a variant record must be of ordinal type; each possible value of the tag field must appear in exactly one tag value list; the value of the tag field may not be passed to a variable formal parameter.*

Variations and Extensions

As with arrays, there are only a few variations from or extensions to the record-processing features of standard Pascal in other versions of Pascal. Two of these are:

● Records of the same type may be compared with the relational operators = and <> (UCSD).

● Records may be initialized in the declaration part of the program. (Turbo)

See Appendix G for additional details.

11

Sets

No one shall expel us from the paradise which Cantor has created for us.

DAVID HILBERT

In mathematics and computer science the term *set* denotes an unordered collection of objects called the *elements* or *members* of the set. For example, the set of digits contains the elements 0, 1, 2, 3, 4, 5, 6, 7, 8, and 9; the set of upper-case letters consists of the letters A, B, C, . . . , Z; the set of even prime numbers contains the single element 2; and the set of all females who were U.S. presidents before 1987 is the empty set, that is, the set of containing no elements.

Sets differ from arrays in that the elements of an array are ordered in a certain sequence, but the elements of a set are unordered. Thus we can speak of the first, second, third, . . . elements of an array, but it does not make sense to refer to the first, second, third, . . . elements of a set. For example, the set whose elements are the even digits 0, 2, 4, 6, and 8 is the same as the set whose elements are 4, 8, 0, 2, and 6 or the set whose elements are 8, 0, 6, 4, and 2. The ordering of array elements makes it possible to access an element directly by specifying its location in the array. Because sets are unordered, no such direct access to the elements of a set is possible.

Sets differ from records in two important ways. Data items stored in a record are directly accessible and may be of different types. In Pascal, however, the elements of a set must be of the same type, and as we have noted, they are not directly accessible.

In this chapter we discuss how sets are implemented in Pascal using the predefined data type **set** and how they are processed using the operations of set assignment, union, intersection, and difference, the membership relation, and the set relations of subset and equality.

11.1 Set Declarations, Set Constants, Set Assignment

In a problem involving sets, the elements are selected from some given set called the ***universal set*** for that problem. For example, if the set of vowels or the set whose elements are X, Y, and Z are being considered, the universal set might be the set of all letters. If the universal set is the set of names of months of the year, then one might use the set of summer months: June, July, August; the set of months whose names do not contain the letter r: May, June, July, August; or the set of all months having fewer than 30 days: February.

In a Pascal program, all of the elements of a set must be of the same type, called the ***base type*** of the set. This base type must be an ordinal type; thus sets of real elements or sets of arrays, strings, or records are not allowed. A ***set declaration*** has the form

> **set of** *base-type*

For example, if the ordinal types *Digits* and *Months* are defined by

> **type**
> *Digits* = 0..9;
> *Months* = (*January, February, March, April, May, June, July,*
> *August, September, October, November, December*);

then

> **set of** *Digits*
> **set of** *Months*
> **set of** *char*

are valid set declarations for most Pascal compilers.

Many Pascal compilers, however, impose certain restrictions on sets. The most common restriction is a limit on the number of elements that a set may have. This limit usually excludes *integer* as a base type and, for some compilers, also excludes *char*. In these cases, subranges of integers and/or subranges of characters must be used.

To illustrate set declarations, consider the following:

> **type**
> *Digits* = 0..9;
> *Months* = (*January, February, March, April, May, June, July,*
> *August, September, October, November, December*);
> *DigitSet* = **set of** *Digits*;
> *MonthSet* = **set of** *Months*;
> *CapLetterSet* = **set of** 'A'..'Z';
> *MonthArray* = **array**[1..4] **of** *MonthSet*;
>
> **var**
> *Dig1, Dig2* : *Digits*;
> *Numbers, Evens, Odds* : *DigitSet*;
> *Winter* : *MonthSet*;
> *Vowels, Consonants* : *CapLetterSet*;
> *Season* : *MonthArray*;

The variables *Numbers, Evens,* and *Odds* may have as values any sets of elements chosen from 0, 1, 2, . . . , 9; the value of *Winter* may be any set of elements selected from *January, February,* . . . , *December;* the variables *Vowels* and *Consonants* have values that are sets of capital letters. The array *Season* has four components, each of which is a set of months.

A *set constant* in Pascal has the form

[*element-list*]

where *element-list* is a list (possibly empty) of constants, variables, or expressions of the same type, separated by commas and enclosed in brackets [and]. Thus, for the base types just defined,

[0, 2, 4, 6, 8]

is a valid set constant that might be the value of *Evens.* This same set constant could also be denoted by

[4, 0, 8, 2, 6]

or

[8, 6, 4, 2, 0]

or by using any other arrangement of the elements. If *Dig1* has the value 0 and *Dig2* has the value 4, then

[*Dig1, Dig1* + 2, *Dig1* + 4, *Dig1* + 6, *Dig1* + 8]

is another representation of this same set constant, as is

[*Dig1, Dig2* **div** 2, *Dig2, Dig2* + 2, 2 * *Dig2*]

When some or all of the elements of a set are consecutive values of the base type, it is permissible to use subrange notation to specify them. For example, the set constant

[0, 1, 2, 3, 4]

can also be expressed as

[0..4]

or

[*Dig1..Dig2*]

and the set constant

[0, 1, 2, 5, 7, 8, 9]

can be expressed in any of the following ways:

[0..2, 5, 7..9]
[0..2, *Dig2* + 1, 7..9]
[*Dig1*..2, 5, (*Dig2* + 3)..(2 * *Dig2* + 1)]

To assign a value to a variable of set type, an assignment statement of the form

set-variable := *set-value*

may be used where *set-value* may be a set constant, a set variable, or a set expression (as described in the next section). The base type of *set-value* must be compatible with the base type of *set-variable*. (Recall that two types are compatible if they are the same type, one is a subrange of the other, or both are subranges of the same type.) Thus, for the base types defined earlier, the statement

Evens := [0, 2, 4, 6, 8];

is a valid assignment statement and assigns the set constant [0, 2, 4, 6, 8] to the set variable *Evens*. Similarly, the statements

Winter := [*December, January..March*];
Season[1] := [*December, January, February*];
Consonants := *Vowels*;
Numbers := [*Dig1*];

are valid assignment statements. The assignment statement

Winter := ['D', 'J', 'F', 'M'];

is not valid, however, because the base type of the set constant is not compatible with the base type of *Winter*. Similarly, the assignment statement

Season[1] := ['D', 1, *February*];

is not valid because this is not a valid set constant (the types of the elements are not the same).

The **empty set** is denoted in Pascal by the set constant

[ ]

and may be assigned to a set variable of any base type. Thus

Number := [ ];
Winter := [ ];

are both valid assignment statements, even though the set variables *Number* and *Winter* have different base types.

11.2 Set Operations and Relations

Because sets are collections of elements, it is important to be able to determine whether a particular element belongs to a given set. This test for set membership is implemented in Pascal by the relational operator **in.** Boolean expressions used to test set membership have the form

> *element* **in** *set*

where *set* is a set constant, set variable, or set expression, and the type of *element* and the base type of *set* are compatible. For example, if set variables *Vowels, Evens, Numbers,* and *Bits* are declared by

> **type**
> $\quad$ *DigitSet* = **set of** 0..9;
> $\quad$ *BinarySet* = **set of** 0..1;
> $\quad$ *SetOfCharacters* = **set of** *char*;
>
> **var**
> $\quad$ *Evens, Numbers* : *DigitSet*;
> $\quad$ *Bits* : *BinarySet*;
> $\quad$ *Vowels* : *SetOfCharacters*;
> $\quad$ *Num* : *integer*;

and have been assigned values by

> *Evens* := [0, 2, 4, 6, 8];
> *Bits* := [0, 1];
> *Numbers* := [0..2, 6..9];
> *Vowels* := ['A', 'E', 'I', 'O', 'U'];

then

> 2 **in** *Evens*
> 3 **in** *Numbers*
> 'I' **in** *Vowels*

are valid boolean expressions and have the values *true, false,* and *true,* respectively. Similarly, if *Num* has the value 3,

> *Num* **in** *Evens*
> 'B' **in** [ ]
> *Num* + 3 **in** *Numbers*

are valid boolean expressions that have the values *false, false,* and *true,* respectively. The expressions

> 5 **in** *Vowels*
> 'B' **in** *Numbers*

are not valid boolean expressions because of type incompatibility.

The relational operator **in** is used to determine whether a single element is a member of a given set, but sometimes it is necessary to determine whether all of the elements of some set *set1* are also members of another set *set2,* that is, to determine whether *set1* is a **subset** of *set2* as pictured in the following **Venn Diagram:**

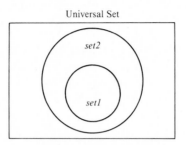

Universal Set

This subset relationship is indicated in Pascal by using the relational operators <= and >= to construct boolean expressions of the form

    set1 <= *set2*   or equivalently   *set2* >= *set1*

where *set1* and *set2* are set constants, variables, or expressions with compatible base types. These expressions are true if *set1* is a subset of *set2* and are false otherwise. The following table shows some valid boolean expressions and their values, given that the variables have the values previously assigned:

Boolean Expression	Value
[0,1,4] <= [0,1,2,3,4]	*true*
[2,4] <= *Evens*	*true*
Bits >= *Evens*	*false*
Vowels <= *Vowels*	*true*
Numbers <= *Bits*	*false*
['A', 'B'] >= ['A','C']	*false*
[ ] <= *Numbers*	*true*

Two sets are said to be **equal** if they contain exactly the same elements. Set equality can be checked in Pascal with a boolean expression of the form

    set1 = *set2*

where again *set1* and *set2* must have compatible base types. The relational operator <> may be used to check set inequality:

    set1 <> *set2*

and is equivalent to the boolean expression

    not (*set1* = *set2*)

For example,

    Bits = [0, 1]
    Bits <> *Evens*

are valid boolean expressions, and both have the value *true*.

In addition to the relational operators **in,** $<=$, $>=$, $=$, and $<>$, there are three binary set operations that may be used to combine two sets to form another set. These are the operations of union, intersection, and difference, which are denoted in Pascal by $+$, $*$, and $-$, respectively. The **union** of two sets *set1* and *set2* is the set of elements that are in *set1* or *set2* or both and is denoted by a set expression of the form

    set1 + *set2*

This can be pictured by the following Venn Diagram:

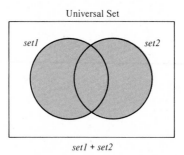

set1 + *set2*

The **intersection** of *set1* and *set2* is the set of elements that are in both sets and is denoted by

    set1 * *set2*

and can be pictured as

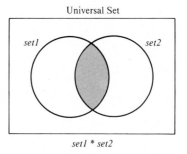

set1 * *set2*

The set **difference**

    set1 − *set2*

is the set of elements that are in *set1* but are not in *set2,* as indicated in the following diagram:

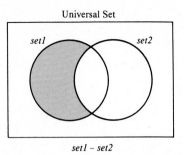

setl – set2

For each of these set expressions, the base types of *set1* and *set2* must be compatible. The following table illustrates these set operations:

Set Expression	Value
[1,2,3] + [4,5,6]	[1,2,3,4,5,6]
[1,2,3,4] + [2,4,6]	[1,2,3,4,6]
[1,2,3] + [ ]	[1,2,3]
[1,2,3,4] * [2,4,6]	[2,4]
[1,2,3] * [4,5,6]	[ ]
[1,2,3] * [ ]	[ ]
[1,2,3,4] − [2,4]	[1,3]
[1,2,3,4] − [2,4,6]	[1,3]
[1,2,3] − [4,5,6]	[1,2,3]
[1,2,3] − [1,2,3,4]	[ ]
[1,2,3] − [ ]	[1,2,3]

When a set expression contains two or more of these operators, it is evaluated according to the following priorities:

    *   ----------------   high priority
    + , − ----------------   low priority

Thus in the expression

   [2,3,5] + [2,4,7] * [2,4,6,8]

the intersection operation is performed first, giving the set [2,4], and

   [2,3,5] + [2,4]

is then evaluated, yielding

   [2,3,4,5]

Operations having the same priority are evaluated in the order in which they appear in the expression, from left to right. For example,

$$[1,2,3,4] - [1,3] + [1,2,5] = [2,4] + [1,2,5]$$
$$= [1,2,4,5]$$

and

$$[2,3,5] + [2,4,7] * [2,4,6,8] = [2,3,5] + [2,4]$$
$$= [2,3,4,5]$$

Parentheses may be used in the usual way to alter the standard order of evaluation; thus,

$$([2,3,5] + [2,4,7]) * [2,4,6,8] = [2,3,4,5,7] * [2,4,6,8]$$
$$= [2,4]$$

Compound boolean expressions that are formed using these operators and the boolean operators **not, and,** and **or** are evaluated according to the following precedence levels:

Operator	Priority
not	1 (highest)
$*$, $/$, **div, mod, and**	2
$+$, $-$, **or**	3
$<$, $<=$, $>$, $>=$, $=$, $<>$, **in**	4 (lowest)

The operators $+$, $-$, and $*$ may refer to either arithmetic or set operations, and the relational operators $<$, $<=$, $>$, $>=$, $=$, and $<>$ may be used with numeric, character, ordinal, string, or set data (except that $<$ and $>$ may not be used with sets). Thus the expression

0 **in** *Evens* **and** 0 **in** *Bits*

is not a valid boolean expression because **and** has higher priority than **in;** consequently, the first operation attempted is evaluation of *Evens* **and** 0, which results in an error because *Evens* and 0 are not of boolean type. Parentheses must be used in the usual way to modify the standard order of evaluation:

(0 **in** *Evens*) **and** (0 **in** *Bits*)

Set relations and operations may be used to simplify complex boolean expressions. For example, the boolean expression

$(ch = $ 'A') **or** $(ch = $ 'L') **or** $(ch = $ 'M') **or** $(ch = $ 'N')

can be expressed more compactly as

ch **in** ['A', 'L'..'N']

The boolean expression

$((ch >= $ 'a') **and** $(ch <= $ 'z')) **or** $((ch >= $ 'A') **and** $(ch <= $ 'Z')) to determine whenever the value of *ch* is a lower-case or upper-case letter (assuming ASCII representation) can be expressed equivalently as

> *ch* **in** *Lower* + *Upper*

where *Lower* and *Upper* are set variables whose values are ['a'..'z'] and ['A'..'Z'], respectively.

One situation in which such boolean expressions are useful is in checking the value of a selector in a **case** statement to ensure that it is in the correct range. For example, consider the **case** statement

```
case Num of
    5, 10, 15 : writeln ('Multiple of 5');
    7, 14     : writeln ('Multiple of 7');
    11        : writeln ('Multiple of 11')
end (* case *)
```

If the value of *Num* is not one of the integers listed as case labels, execution of the **case** statement results in an error. The following statement avoids this error:

```
if Num in [5,7,10,11,14,15] then
    case Num of
        5, 10, 15 : writeln ('Multiple of 5');
        7, 14     : writeln ('Multiple of 7');
        11        : writeln ('Multiple of 11')
    end (* case *)
```

11.3 Processing Sets

In the preceding section we used the assignment statement to assign a value to a set variable. In this section we show how to construct a set by reading its elements, how to display the elements of a set, and how to use sets as parameters for subprograms.

To construct a set, we first initialize it to the empty set, and then read each element and add it to the set, using the union operation. This process is described in the following algorithm.

ALGORITHM TO CONSTRUCT A SET

(* Algorithm to construct a set *S* by repeatedly reading an element *x* of *S* and adding it to S. *)

1. Initialize *S* to the empty set: S := [ ].
2. While there are more data, do the following:
   a. Read a value for a variable *x* whose type is that of the base type of *S*.
   b. Add *x* to *S* using the union operation: S := S + [x].

To display the elements of a set, we can use the following algorithm:

ALGORITHM TO DISPLAY A SET

(* Algorithm to display a set S by repeatedly finding an element x of S, displaying it, and removing it from S. Note that the set S is destroyed since it is reduced to the empty set. *)

1. Let x be a variable of the base type of S and initialize x to be the first element of this base type.
2. While S <> [ ], do the following:
   a. While x is not in S, replace x with its successor.
   b. Display x.
   c. Remove x from S, using the difference operation: S := S − [x].

If the set to be displayed with this algorithm is to be preserved, it should first be copied to some temporary set

   TempSet := S;

whose elements are then displayed.

Sets may also be used as parameters of functions and procedures. Remember, however, that the type of a function must be a simple data type and hence may not be of set type. The program in Figure 11.1 illustrates the use of sets as parameters. It determines which of a set of upper-case letters appear in a given text file. The procedures *ReadSet* and *DisplaySet* implement the preceding algorithms for constructing and displaying a set, respectively.

```
PROGRAM FindLetters (output, TextFile);

(*********************************************************************

   Program to determine which of a set of upper case letters
   entered by the user appear in a given text file.

*********************************************************************)

TYPE
    ElementType = 'A'..'Z';
    TypeOfSet = SET OF ElementType;

VAR
    TextFile : text;        (* text file to be analyzed *)
    Symbol : char;          (* a character in text file *)
    LetterSet,              (* set of letters to be found *)
    FoundSet : TypeOfSet;   (* set of letters found in TextFile *)
```

Figure 11.1

Figure 11.1 (Cont.)

```
PROCEDURE ReadSet (VAR S : TypeOfSet);

   (****************************************************************

       Procedure to read the elements of a set S of type TypeOfSet;
       the base type of the elements of S is ElementType which is
       char or a subrange of character or integer type.

   ****************************************************************)

   VAR
      x : ElementType;

   BEGIN (* ReadSet *)
      S := [];
      WHILE NOT eoln DO
         BEGIN
            read (x);
            S := S + [x]
         END (* WHILE *)
   END (* ReadSet *);

PROCEDURE SearchFile (VAR TextFile : text;
                      VAR LetterSet, FoundSet : TypeOfSet);

   (****************************************************************

       Procedure to search TextFile for letters in LetterSet
       and add them to FoundSet

   ****************************************************************)

   BEGIN (* SearchFile *)
      reset (TextFile);
      WHILE NOT eof(TextFile) DO
         BEGIN
            WHILE NOT eoln(TextFile) DO
               BEGIN
                  read (TextFile, Symbol);
                  IF Symbol IN LetterSet THEN
                     FoundSet := FoundSet + [Symbol]
               END (* WHILE NOT eoln *);
            readln (TextFile)
         END (* WHILE NOT eof *);
   END (* SearchFile *);

PROCEDURE PrintSet (S : TypeOfSet; FirstElement : ElementType);

   (****************************************************************

       Procedure to display the elements of a set S of type TypeOfSet;
       the base type of the elements of S is ElementType which is
       char or a subrange of character or integer type.  FirstElement
       is the first element in this base type.

   ****************************************************************)
```

Figure 11.1 (Cont.)

```
    VAR
        x : ElementType;

    BEGIN (* PrintSet *)
        x := FirstElement;
        WHILE S <> [] DO
            BEGIN
                WHILE NOT (x IN S) DO
                    x := succ(x);
                writeln (x);
                S := S - [x]
            END (* WHILE *)
    END (* PrintSet *);

BEGIN (* main program *)
    writeln ('Enter letters to search for:');
    ReadSet (LetterSet);
    FoundSet := [];
    SearchFile (TextFile, LetterSet, FoundSet);
    writeln ('Letters found:');
    PrintSet (FoundSet, 'A')
END (* main program *).
```

Listing of TextFile:
_____

     This program finds which UPPER CASE letters such as A, B, and C
appear in the file TextFile. It uses the procedure PrintSet to
display these letters after execution of the program is
completed.

Sample run:
_____

```
Enter letters to search for:
AEIOUY
Letters found:
A
E
I
U
```

11.4   Applications: Sieve of Eratosthenes, Simple Lexical Analyzer

EXAMPLE 1: Sieve of Eratosthenes.   A *prime number* is defined to be an integer n greater than 1 whose only divisors are 1 and n itself. Thus, 2, 3, 5, 7, 11, 13, 17, and 19 are prime numbers, whereas 4, 6, 8, and 9 are not primes because 2 divides 4, 6, and 8, and 3 divides 9. The Greek mathematician Eratosthenes developed an algorithm for finding all prime numbers less than or equal to a given number n, that is, all primes in the range 2 . . . n. This algorithm was described in Exercise 20 of Section 8.3 and can be rephrased using sets, as follows:

ALGORITHM FOR SIEVE METHOD

1. Initialize the set *Sieve* to contain the integers from 2 through n.
2. Select the smallest element *Prime* in *Sieve*.
3. While $Prime^2 \leq n$, do the following:
   a. Remove from *Sieve* all elements of the form $Prime * k$ for $k > 1$.
   b. Replace *Prime* with the smallest element in *Sieve* that is greater than *Prime*.

The elements remaining in *Sieve* when this algorithm terminates are the primes in the range 2 through n.

To illustrate Eratosthenes' algorithm, consider the problem of finding all primes in the range from 2 through 30. The following diagram shows the processing of the set *Sieve* using this algorithm:

Sieve

[2,3,4,5,6,7,8,9,10,11,12,13,14,15,16,17,18,19,20,21,22,23,24,25,26,27,28,29,30]

↓

Prime = 2

↓

[2,3,5,7,9,11,13,15,17,19,21,23,25,27,29]

↓

Prime = 3

↓

[2,3,5,7,11,13,17,19,23,25,29]

↓

Prime = 5

↓

[2,3,5,7,11,13,17,19,23,29]

↓

Prime = 7; terminate since $Prime^2 > 30$

The program in Figure 11.2 implements this algorithm. It uses the set *Sieve* that is declared to have elements in the subrange 2..*LargestNumber*. Because most Pascal compilers limit the size of sets, this program is restricted to small values of *LargestNumber*. For large values, the algorithm can be modified to use an array of sets; this modification is left as an exercise.

```
PROGRAM SieveofEratosthenes (input, output);

(*******************************************************************

   Program to find all prime numbers in the range from 2 through n
   using the Sieve Method of Eratosthenes.

*******************************************************************)

CONST
   LargestNumber = 100;   (* limit on largest value of n *)

TYPE
   ElementType = 2..LargestNumber;
   TypeOfSet = SET OF ElementType;

VAR
   Sieve : TypeOfSet;   (* set of numbers used in the algorithm *)
   n : integer;         (* 2, 3, 4, ..., n are numbers considered *)

PROCEDURE Eratosthenize (VAR Sieve : TypeOfSet; n : integer);

   (*******************************************************************

      Apply the sieve method of Eratosthenes to remove all nonprimes
      from Sieve.

   *******************************************************************)

   VAR
      Prime,         (* prime whose multiples are removed *)
      k : integer;   (* used to form multiples  Prime*k  *)

   BEGIN (* Eratosthenize *)
      Prime := 2;
      WHILE sqr(Prime) <= n DO
         BEGIN
            FOR k := 2 TO n DIV Prime DO
               Sieve := Sieve - [Prime * k];
            REPEAT
               Prime := Prime + 1
            UNTIL Prime IN Sieve
         END (* WHILE *)
   END (* Eratosthenize *);

PROCEDURE PrintSet (S : TypeOfSet; FirstElement : ElementType);

   (*******************************************************************

      Procedure to display the elements of a set S of type TypeOfSet;
      the base type of the elements of S is ElementType which is
      char or a subrange of character or integer type.  FirstElement
      is the first element in this base type.

   *******************************************************************)

   VAR
      x : ElementType;
```

Figure 11.2

Figure 11.2 (Cont.)

```
   BEGIN (* PrintSet *)
      x := FirstElement;
      WHILE S <> [] DO
         BEGIN
            WHILE NOT (x IN S) DO
               x := succ(x);
            writeln (x);
            S := S - [x]
         END (* WHILE *)
   END (* PrintSet *);

BEGIN (* main program *)
   write ('To find primes in range 2 through n, enter n:  ');
   readln (n);
   Sieve := [2..n];
   Eratosthenize (Sieve, n);
   writeln ('Primes in the range 2 .. ', n:1, ' are:');
   PrintSet (Sieve, 2)
END (* main program *).
```

Sample run:

```
To find primes in range 2 through n, enter n:   30
Primes in the range 2 .. 30 are:
      2
      3
      5
      7
     11
     13
     17
     19
     23
     29
```

EXAMPLE 2: Simple Lexical Analyzer.   In our discussion of system software in Chapter 1, we mentioned *compilers*, which are programs whose function is to translate a source program written in some high-level language, such as Pascal, into an object program in machine code. This object program is then executed by the computer.

The input to a compiler is a stream of characters that comprise the source program. Before the translation can actually be carried out, this stream of characters must be broken up into meaningful groups, such as identifiers, reserved words, constants, and operators. For example, the assignment statement

$$\text{alpha} := 200*\text{beta} + 5$$

is input as the string of characters

$$\text{alpha}\flat := \flat 200*\text{beta}\flat + \flat 5$$

and must be broken down into the following units:

alpha	----------------	identifier
:=	----------------	assignment operator
200	----------------	integer constant
*	----------------	arithmetic operator
beta	----------------	identifier
+	----------------	arithmetic operator
5	----------------	integer constant

These units are called **tokens,** and the part of the compiler that recognizes these tokens is called the **lexical analyzer.** It is then the task of the **parser** to group these tokens together to form the basic structures determined by the syntax rules of the language.

The program in Figure 11.3 implements a simple lexical analyzer that processes Pascal assignment statements involving only identifiers, integer constants, and the operators $+$, $-$, $*$, $/$, and $:=$, and ; which marks the end of the statement. Blanks may be used as separators in these assignment statements.

```
PROGRAM LexicalAnalyzer (input, output);

(********************************************************************

   This program implements a simple lexical analyzer for Pascal
   assignment statements involving only identifiers, integer
   constants, and operators +, -, *, /, :=, and ; (which marks
   the end of the statement).

********************************************************************)

CONST
   EndOfStatementMark = ';';   (* marks end of assignment statement *)
   MaxLength = 80;             (* maximum length of statement *)

TYPE
   CharacterSet = SET OF char;
   TextLine = PACKED ARRAY[1..MaxLength] OF char;
   String = PACKED ARRAY[1..21] OF char;

VAR
   Statement : TextLine;         (* assignment statement being processed *)
   LetterSet,                    (* set of letters *)
   DigitSet,                     (* set of digits *)
   ArithmeticOperators,          (* set of arithmetic operators *)
   Delimiters : CharacterSet;    (* set of delimiters *)
   i : integer;                  (* index *)
   Response : char;              (* user response *)
```

Figure 11.3

Figure 11.3 (Cont.)

```
PROCEDURE ReadStatement (VAR Statement : TextLine;
                          EndOfStatementMark : char);

   (***************************************************************

      Read characters in Statement until EndOfStatementMark.

   ***************************************************************)

   VAR
      i : integer;  (* index *)

   BEGIN (* ReadStatement *)
      writeln ('Enter assignment statement:');
      i := 0;
      REPEAT
         i := i + 1;
         read (Statement[i])
      UNTIL (Statement[i] = EndOfStatementMark) OR (i = MaxLength);
      readln;
   END (* ReadStatement *);

PROCEDURE IllegalCharacter (VAR Statement : TextLine; VAR i : integer;
                            Delimiters : CharacterSet);

   (***************************************************************

      Procedure to handle processing when i-th character in Statement
      is not a legal character.  All characters up to the next
      delimiter will be skipped.

   ***************************************************************)

   BEGIN (* IllegalCharacter *)
      write (Statement[i]);
      writeln ('   <** Illegal character:  ', Statement[i], ' **>');
      WHILE NOT (Statement[i] IN Delimiters) DO
         i := i + 1;
   END (* IllegalCharacter *);

PROCEDURE Process (Statement : TextLine; VAR i : integer; TokenSet,
                   Delimiters : CharacterSet; TokenType : String);

   (***************************************************************

      Process characters until not in the specified TokenSet; then
      check if next character (i-th) is a delimiter, and if so
      recognize the specified TokenType, else an illegal character.

   ***************************************************************)
```

Figure 11.3 (Cont.)

```
BEGIN (* Process *)
   REPEAT
      write (Statement[i]);
      i := i + 1
   UNTIL NOT (Statement[i] IN TokenSet);
   IF Statement[i] IN Delimiters THEN
      writeln ('      ', TokenType)
   ELSE
      IllegalCharacter (Statement, i, Delimiters)
END (* Process *);

PROCEDURE CheckForOperator (Statement : TextLine; VAR i : integer;
                            Delimiters : CharacterSet; NextSymbol : char;
                            TokenType : String);

(************************************************************************

   Check for arithmetic operator or assignment operator and
   advance to next character (i-th) in Statement.

 ************************************************************************)

VAR
   LegalOperator : boolean;     (* indicates if a legal operator *)

BEGIN (* CheckForOperator *)
   write (Statement[i]);
   i := i + 1;
   LegalOperator := true;
   IF NextSymbol = '=' THEN
      IF Statement[i] <> '=' THEN
         BEGIN
            LegalOperator := false;
            IllegalCharacter (Statement, i, Delimiters)
         END (* IF *)
      ELSE
         BEGIN
            write (Statement[i]);
            i := i + 1
         END (* ELSE *);
   IF LegalOperator THEN
      writeln ('      ', TokenType)
END (* CheckForOperator *);

BEGIN (* main program *)
   LetterSet := ['a'..'z', 'A'..'Z'];
   DigitSet := ['0'..'9'];
   ArithmeticOperators := ['+', '-', '*', '/'];
   Delimiters := ArithmeticOperators + [EndOfStatementMark, ' ', ':'];
```

Figure 11.3 (Cont.)

```
    REPEAT
        ReadStatement (Statement, EndOfStatementMark);

        (* Now process the statement *)

        writeln;
        i := 1;
        WHILE Statement[i] <> EndOfStatementMark DO
            BEGIN
                (* skip blanks *)
                WHILE Statement[i] = ' ' DO
                    i := i + 1;

                (* check for identifier *)
                IF Statement[i] IN LetterSet THEN
                    Process (Statement, i, LetterSet + DigitSet, Delimiters,
                             '<identifier>        ')

                (* check for integer constant *)
                ELSE IF statement[i] IN DigitSet THEN
                    Process (Statement, i, DigitSet, Delimiters,
                             '<integer constant>   ')

                (* check for arithmetic operator *)
                ELSE IF Statement[i] IN ArithmeticOperators THEN
                    CheckForOperator (Statement, i, Delimiters, ' ',
                                      '<arithmetic operator>')

                (* check for assignment operator *)
                ELSE IF Statement[i] = ':' THEN
                    CheckForOperator (Statement, i, Delimiters, '=',
                                      '<assignment operator>')

                (* check for illegal character *)
                ELSE IF Statement[i] <> EndOfStatementMark THEN
                    IllegalCharacter (Statement, i, Delimiters)
            END (* WHILE *);
        writeln;
        write ('More statements (Y or N)?  ');
        readln (Response)
    UNTIL NOT (Response IN ['Y', 'y'])
END (* main program *).
```

Sample run:

```
Enter assignment statement:
alpha := 37*BETA - gamma/delta     -3;

alpha       <identifier>
:=      <assignment operator>
37      <integer constant>
*       <arithmetic operator>
BETA        <identifier>
-       <arithmetic operator>
gamma       <identifier>
/       <arithmetic operator>
delta       <identifier>
-       <arithmetic operator>
3       <integer constant>
```

441

Figure 11.3 (Cont.)

```
More statements (Y or N)?  Y
Enter assignment statement:
X123 : z456*456ZETA - 8&9;

X123      <identifier>
:    <** Illegal character:    **>
z456      <identifier>
*      <arithmetic operator>
456Z    <** Illegal character:   Z **>
-      <arithmetic operator>
8&    <** Illegal character:   & **>

More statements (Y or N)?  N
```

Exercises

1. Given that A, B, C, and D are set variables assigned values as follows: $A := [3, 5..9, 11]$; $B := [1..5, 11, 12]$; $C := [2, 4, 6, 8]$; $D := [6..10]$; calculate the following:

   (a) $A * B$
   (b) $A + B$
   (c) $A - B$
   (d) $B - A$
   (e) $A + D$
   (f) $A - D$
   (g) $A * D$
   (h) $D - A$
   (i) $C + C$
   (j) $C * C$
   (k) $C - C$
   (l) $C - [ ]$
   (m) $A + B + C + D$
   (n) $(A - B) - C$
   (o) $A - (B - C)$
   (p) $A * B * C * D$
   (q) $A + B * C$
   (r) $A * B + C$
   (s) $A * B - C * D$
   (t) $(A - (B + C)) * D$
   (u) $A * B - (A + B)$
   (v) $A - B - C - D$
   (w) $B - B - C$
   (x) $B - (B - C)$

2. Write appropriate declarations for the following set type identifiers:

   (a) *SmallIntegers:* set of integers from 1 through 99.
   (b) *FirstLetters:* set of letters in the first half of the alphabet.
   (c) *Days:* the set of names of days of the week.
   (d) *Suit:* set of 13 cards in a suit.

3. Write appropriate variable declarations for the following set variables, and write statements to assign to each the specified value.

   (a) *Evens:* the set of all even integers from 1 through 99; and *Odd:* the set of all odd integers in the range from 1 through 99.
   (b) *OneModThree:* the set of all numbers of the form $3k + 1$ in the range from 1 through 99 with k as an integer.
   (c) *Null:* the empty set.
   (d) *LargeFactors:* the set of all numbers in the range 1 through 99 that are not divisible by 2, 3, 5, or 7.
   (e) *Divisors:* the set of all divisors of a given integer *Number*.
   (f) *Vowels:* the set of all vowels; and *Consonants:* the set of all consonants.

(g) *WeekDays:* the set of all weekdays.

(h) *FaceCards:* the set of all face cards in a suit; and *NumberCards:* the set of all number cards in a suit.

4. Write a procedure to print any set of characters or integers using the usual mathematical notation in which the elements are enclosed in braces { and } and are separated by commas. For example, the set of numbers 2, 5, and 7 should be displayed as {2, 5, 7}, the set whose element is 4 as {4}, and the empty set as { }.

5. Write a function to calculate the **cardinal number** of a set, that is, the number of elements in the set.

6. Sets are commonly stored in computer memory as **bit strings.** The length of these bit strings is the number of elements in the universal set, each bit corresponding to exactly one element of the universal set. Thus sets of base type 0..9 are represented by bit strings of length 10, the first bit corresponding to 0, the second to 1, and so on. A given set S is then represented by a bit string in which the bits corresponding to the elements of S are 1 and all other bits are 0. For example, the set [1, 3, 7..9] would be represented by the bit string

$$0101000111$$

(a) Assuming this same universal set, give the bit string representations of the following sets:

(i) the set of odd digits.

(ii) the set of prime digits.

(iii) the set of digits divisible by 1.

(iv) the set of digits not divisible by 1.

(b) For the base type 'A'..'Z', describe bit strings for the following sets:

(i) the set of vowels

(ii) ['A'..'E', 'X', 'Y', 'Z']

7. Write a program to find the set of all vowels and the set of all consonants that appear in a given line of text.

8. Write a program to read two lines of text, and find all characters that appear in both lines.

9. Write a program to find all letters that are not present in a given line of text and display them in alphabetical order.

10. Write a program to read several lines of text, and find all words having three or more distinct vowels.

11. Write a program to deal two ten-card hands from a standard deck of fifty-two cards. Use a random number generator (see Section 5.4), and use sets to ensure that the same card is not dealt twice.

12. A real number in Pascal has one of the forms $m.n$, $+m.n$, or $-m.n$, where m and n are nonnegative integers; or it may be expressed in exponential form xEe, $xE+e$, $xE-e$, where x is an integer or a real number not in exponential form and e is a nonnegative integer. Write a program that accepts a string of characters and then checks to see if it represents a valid real constant.

13. Write a program for a lexical analyzer to process assignment statements of the form *identifier* := *string-constant*. Have it recognize the following tokens: identifier, assignment operator (:=), and string constant.

14. Write a program for a lexical analyzer that processes assignment statements of the form *set-variable* := *set-value*. Have it recognize the following tokens: identifier, set constant, set operation (+, *, −), and assignment operator (:=).

15. Write a program that uses the Sieve Method of Eratosthenes to find all primes in the range 2 through n for large values of n. (*Hint:* Use an array *Sieve* of sets, *Sieve*[0], *Sieve*[1], *Sieve*[2], . . . , whose elements are integers in the range 0 through 99. Each element of *Sieve*[1] must be interpreted as 100 plus its value, each element of *Sieve*[2] as 200 plus its value, and so on.)

Programming Pointers

In this chapter we considered sets and their implementation in Pascal with the set data type. Some of the key points to remember when using this structured data type are as follows:

1. *All of the elements of a set must be of the same type, called the base type for that set. This base type must be an ordinal type.*

2. *Most versions of Pascal limit the size of sets, that is, the number of elements a set may have.* In particular, the declaration

    set of *integer*

    is usually not allowed, and in some versions,

    set of *char*

    is also not allowed. In such cases, to use sets whose elements are integers or characters, a subrange must be specified for these elements, for example,

    set of 1..100
    set of 'A'..'Z'

3. *The only standard set operations are* + *(union)*, * *(intersection), and* − *(difference)*. Some versions of Pascal may also allow a unary minus to denote the complement of a set.

4. *The only standard relational operators that may be used to compare sets are* <= *(subset),* >= *(superset),* = *(equal),* <> *(not equal)*. Some versions of Pascal may also allow the relational operators < (proper subset) and > (proper superset).

5. *The* **in** *relation for set membership can be used to simplify complex boolean expressions and to determine whether the value of the selector in a* **case** *statement is one of the case labels.* The examples at the end of Section 11.2 illustrate.

6. *A set value cannot be read by including the name of the set in the input list of a read or readln statement.* Instead, each element of the set must be read and added to the set. See the algorithm for constructing a set in Section 11.3.

7. *A set value cannot be displayed by including the name of the set in the output list of a write or writeln statement.* Instead, each element must be displayed individually. The algorithm for displaying a set in Section 11.3 indicates how this can be done.

Variations and Extensions

In the various versions of Pascal, there are few variations from or extensions to the set processing features of standard Pascal. One that we have already noted is the imposition of an upper limit on the size of sets (e.g., 255 in Turbo). Also, versions (Turbo) that allow initialization of arrays and records in the declaration part of a program also allow initialization of sets (see Appendix G for details).

12

Files

It became increasingly apparent to me that, over the years, Federal agencies have amassed vast amounts of information about virtually every American citizen. This fact, coupled with technological advances in data-collecting and dissemination, raised the possibility that information about individuals conceivably could be used for other than legitimate purposes and without the prior knowledge or consent of the individuals involved.

PRESIDENT GERALD R. FORD

The right of the people to be secure in their persons, houses, papers, and effects, against unreasonable searches and seizures, shall not be violated. . . .

FOURTH AMENDMENT OF THE U.S. CONSTITUTION

The programs that we have written up to this point have involved relatively small amounts of input/output data. In most of our examples, we have assumed that the input data were read from the standard system file *input*, which refers to an input device such as a terminal or card reader. For the most part, output has been directed to the standard system file *output*, referring to a system output device such as a terminal or printer. However, many applications involve large data sets, and these may be processed more conveniently if stored on magnetic tape or a magnetic disk or some other **secondary (auxiliary)** memory. Once data have been stored on such media, they may be used as often as desired without being reentered from a terminal or from a set of data cards. Also, several different data sets can be processed by a program, and the output produced by one program can be stored and used as input to another program.

Data stored in secondary memory can be processed in a Pascal program by using the structured data type **file.** Files may be the predefined Pascal files *input* and *output*, or they may be user-defined files. The programmer usually need not be concerned with the details of the actual external medium on which the data are stored because these details are handled by the operating system. Instead, the programmer deals with the logical structure of the file, that is, with the relationship among the items stored in the file, and with the algorithms needed to process these items. In this chapter we discuss how the file data structure is implemented in Pascal and illustrate some common file-processing techniques.

12.1   Review of Text Files

A *file* is a collection of related data items (usually stored on some external medium) for input to or output by a program. In contrast to arrays, sets, and records, the size of this collection is not fixed and is limited only by the amount of secondary memory available. Consequently, files are commonly used when there is too much data to store in main memory.

Files can be classified as sequential or direct access. In a *sequential file,* the components must be accessed in order, beginning with the first one. To access the nth component, one must go through the first $n - 1$ components of the file. In a *direct* or *random access file,* each component can be accessed directly by specifying its location in the file. Although many versions of Pascal allow both kinds of files (see the Variations and Extensions section at the end of this chapter), standard Pascal allows only sequential files.

The items in a file may be of any data type, simple or structured, except that they may not be of file type. The simplest files are those in which all the items are of type *char*. Such files are called *text files*. The standard Pascal files *input* and *output* are text files, and we considered user-defined text files in Chapter 6. Much of that discussion also applies to the other types of files that are considered in this chapter.

The principal rules governing the use of text files in standard Pascal programs as discussed in Chapter 6 may be summarized as follows:

1. *Program heading:* Pascal permits the use of **temporary** files and **permanent** files. Temporary files exist only during the execution of a program, whereas permanent files exist before and/or after program execution as well. The names of all permanent files used in a program (including the standard text files *input* and *output*) must appear in the file list of the program heading.
2. *Declaration:* All user-defined files must be declared in the declaration part of the program. For text files, the predefined type identifier *text* can be used to specify the types of file variables.
3. *Opening files for input:* Each file from which data are to be read must be opened for input by using the predefined procedure *reset* in a statement of the form

    reset (file-variable)

    Each such procedure call resets the data pointer to the beginning of the specified file. (The standard system file *input* need not be opened for input).
4. *Opening files for output:* Each file to which data are to be written must be opened for output with the predefined procedure *rewrite,* using a statement of the form

    rewrite (file-variable)

Each such procedure call empties the specified file, so any previous contents of the file are destroyed. (The standard system file *output* need not be opened for output.)

5. *File input:* Information can be read from a text file by using the predefined procedures *read* and *readln* in the forms

> read *(file-variable, input-list)*
> readln *(file-variable, input-list)*

If *file-variable* is omitted, values are read from the standard system file *input*.

6. *File output:* Output can be directed to a text file by using the predefined procedures *write* and *writeln* in the forms

> write *(file-variable, output-list)*
> writeln *(file-variable, output-list)*

If *file-variable* is omitted, output is directed to the standard file *output*.

7. *Copying files:* Copying the contents of one file to another cannot be accomplished by using an assignment statement of the form *file-variable-1* := *file-variable-2*. Rather, the components must be copied one at a time.

8. *Files as parameters:* Formal parameters that represent files must be variable parameters. This is a consequence of rule 7, since value parameters require copying the values of the corresponding actual parameters.

12.2 Files of Other Types

The files reviewed in the preceding section were text files, that is, files whose elements were of type *char*. The elements of a file, called the **file components,** may, however, be of any predefined or user-defined data type except another file type.

The general file declaration has the form

> **file of** *component-type*

where *component-type* specifies the type of the components of the file. The following illustrate some file declarations:

> **type**
>   *DaysOfWeek* = (*Sunday, Monday, Tuesday, Wednesday,*
>   *Thursday, Friday, Saturday*);
>   *String* = **packed array**[1..20] **of** *char*;
>   *List* = **array**[1..100] **of** *integer*;
>   *EmployeeRecord* = **record**
>   *Name : String*;
>   *Number, Dependents : integer*;
>   *HourlyRate : real*
>   **end**;
>   *FileOfNumbers* = **file of** *integer*;
>   *FileOfDays* = **file of** *DaysOfWeek*;
>   *LongStringsFile* = **file of packed array**[1..80] **of** *char*;
>   *FileOfLists* = **file of** *List*;
>   *EmployeeFile* = **file of** *EmployeeRecord*;

var

    CharacterSetFile : *text*;
    NumberFile : *FileOfNumbers*;
    DayFile : *FileOfDays*;
    AddressFile : *LongStringsFile*;
    ListFile : *FileOfLists*;
    EmpFile : *EmployeeFile*;

Files of type other than *char* usually can be created only with a program, and their components can be accessed only within a program. Attempting to list the contents of such a file by using the system text editor or some other system command usually causes "garbage" or some error message to be displayed. The characters that comprise a text file are stored using a standard coding scheme such as ASCII and EBCDIC, and when a text file is listed, these codes are automatically converted to the corresponding characters by the terminal, printer or other output device. On the other hand, the components of other types of files are stored using the internal representation scheme for the particular computer being used, and this representation usually cannot be correctly displayed in character form by the output device. Figure 12.1 illustrates this difference for the integer 32767.

There are, however, some advantages in using files other than text files. The primary advantage is that values of structured data types, such as arrays and records, and values of enumerated data types can be read from or written to nontext files. Another advantage is that the information in such files can be transferred more rapidly, since it is already in a form that requires no decoding or encoding. A third advantage is that data are usually stored more compactly if they are stored using their internal representation rather than their external representation in one of the standard coding schemes.

Recall that the name of each permanent file used in the program must be included in the file list of the program heading. Also, each file from which values are to be read (except *input*) must be opened by using the procedure *reset* before any of its components may be accessed. The statement

    reset (*file-variable*)

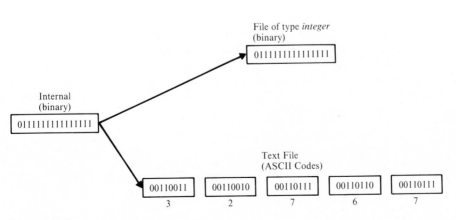

Figure 12.1

calls this procedure and opens the specified file for input. Because this procedure has a single argument, a separate procedure call is required for each file being opened for input. Similarly, each file to be used for output (except *output*) must be opened by using a *rewrite* procedure reference of the form

rewrite (file-variable)

Because in most computer systems nontext files must be created by a Pascal program, we first consider the *write* and *put* procedures that are used for this purpose. Values can be written into a file by using an output statement of the form

write (file-variable, output-list)

where *output-list* is an expression (constant, variable, or formula) or a list of expressions separated by commas, each of which must be compatible with the type of the components of *file-variable*. Note that the procedure *writeln* may *not* be used for files that are not text files.[1]

As a simple illustration, suppose that a comparison of high school and college grade point averages (GPAs) is to be made and we wish to create a data file containing pairs of such GPAs, one pair for each student. This file can be created by a program in which pairs of real values representing GPAs are entered by the user and each pair is then written into a file *GPAFile* whose components are of type

```
GPARecord = record
                HighSchool, College : real
            end;
```

Because this file is to be a permanent file, we must list it in the program heading

program *CreateGPAFile (input, output, GPAFile)*;

The type definitions and variable declarations required to declare the file *GPAFile* with components of type *GPARecord* are

```
type
    GPARecord = record
                    HighSchool, College : real
                end;
    FileOfGPARecords = file of GPARecord;

var
    GPAPair : GPARecord;
    GPAFile : FileOfGPARecords;
```

[1] As was noted in Chapter 6, file processing is quite different in some versions of Pascal. It may not be necessary or even permissible to list names of permanent files in the program heading. Modified forms of reference to procedures *reset* and *rewrite* or use of a special auxiliary procedure such as *assign* may be required to associate a file variable with the name of an actual data file in secondary memory. It may also be necessary to call a special *close* procedure to close files before program execution terminates. See Appendix G and the Variations and Extensions sections of Chapter 6 and this chapter for details.

The program in Figure 12.2 creates the desired file. It first opens file *GPAFile* for output and then reads pairs of real numbers representing pairs of GPAs, writing each pair to *GPAFile*.

```
PROGRAM CreateGPAFile (input, output, GPAFile);

(*********************************************************************

    Program to create the nontext file GPAFile having components
    of type GPARecord.  Pairs of grade point averages are input
    by the user during execution.

********************************************************************)

TYPE
    GPARecord = RECORD
                    HighSchool, College: real
                END;
    FileOfGPARecords = FILE OF GPARecord;

VAR
    GPAPair : GPARecord;            (* pair of grade point averages *)
    GPAFile : FileOfGPARecords;     (* file of GPA records created *)

BEGIN
    rewrite (GPAFile);
    writeln ('Enter negative GPA''s to stop.');
    write ('GPA pair?  ');
    readln (GPAPair.HighSchool, GPAPair.College);
    WHILE (GPAPair.HighSchool >= 0) DO
        BEGIN
            write (GPAFile, GPAPair);
            write ('GPA pair?  ');
            readln (GPAPair.HighSchool, GPAPair.College);
        END (* WHILE *);
    writeln ('Creation of GPAFile completed')
END.


Sample run:


Enter negative GPA's to stop.
GPA pair?   4.00 3.95
GPA pair?   3.64 3.15
GPA pair?   2.89 3.01
GPA pair?   3.18 2.85
GPA pair?   2.21 2.33
GPA pair?   1.55 0.76
GPA pair?   1.94 2.04
GPA pair?   4.00 4.00
GPA pair?   2.25 2.25
GPA pair?   3.01 2.99
GPA pair?   -1-1
Creation of GPAFile completed
```

Figure 12.2

Transfer of information between main memory and secondary memory is considerably slower than a transfer from one location in main memory to another. If execution of a program must be suspended while data items are transferred to or from secondary memory, program execution may be slowed dramatically. For this reason, special holding areas in main memory called **buffers** are commonly used. To illustrate, consider the output statement

write (GPAFile, GPAPair);

The transfer of information to the file *GPAFile* caused by execution of this statement actually takes place in two stages. The value of the record variable *GPAPair* is first copied into a special variable called a **file buffer variable** or a **file window,** which has the same type as the file components.

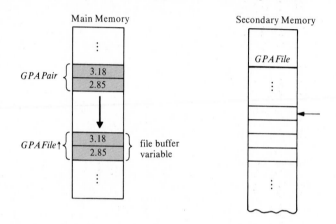

The second stage of output to *GPAFile* consists of transferring this value from the file buffer variable into the file itself. While this is being done, processing of other statements in the program can continue.

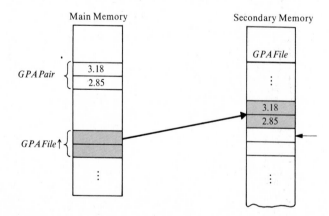

Declaration of a file automatically creates this file buffer variable. If *file-variable* is the name of the file, this buffer variable is denoted by

file-variable↑   or   *file-variable*^

In our example, therefore, the variable

> *GPAFile*↑

is the buffer variable associated with the file *GPAFile*. It is of type *GPARecord*, since this is the component type of the file *GPAFile*, and it may be used in the same manner as any other variable of type *GPARecord*. For example, the assignment statement

> *GPAFile*↑ := *GPAPair*;

assigns the value of the record variable *GPAPair* to *GPAFile*↑. The statement

> *readln (GPAFile↑.HighSchool, GPAFile↑.College)*;

or

> **with** *GPAFile*↑ **do**
> *readln (HighSchool, College)*;

reads values for the two fields in *GPAFile*↑.
    Assignment of a value to a file buffer variable carries out only the first stage of output to a file. It does not actually write this value into the associated file; rather, it merely copies the value into the memory location assigned to this buffer variable. The second stage can then be performed using the predefined procedure *put*. This procedure is called with a statement of the form

> *put (file-variable)*

and transfers the value of the buffer variable *file-variable*↑ to the associated file *file-variable*. This value is actually *transferred* rather than copied, and consequently, after execution of this statement, *file-variable*↑ is undefined.
    As an illustration, the program in Figure 12.3 is a modification of the program in Figure 12.2 for creating a file of GPA pairs. Each pair of real numbers is read directly into the fields of the buffer variable with the statement

> *readln (GPAFile↑.HighSchool, GPAFile↑.College)*;

and the statement

> *put (GPAFile)*;

then transfers this pair from the buffer variable *GPAFile*↑ to the file. This program thus bypasses the first stage of the file output process and will therefore execute slightly faster than that in Figure 12.2.

```
PROGRAM CreateGPAFile (input, output, GPAFile);

(*******************************************************************

    Program to create the nontext file GPAFile having components
    of type GPARecord.  Pairs of grade point averages are input
    directly into the file buffer variable the user during execution.

********************************************************************)

TYPE
    GPARecord = RECORD
                    HighSchool, College: real
                END;
    FileOfGPARecords = FILE OF GPARecord;

VAR
    GPAFile : FileOfGPARecords;   (* file of GPA records created *)

BEGIN
    rewrite (GPAFile);
    writeln ('Enter negative GPA''s to stop.');
    write ('GPA pair?  ');
    readln (GPAFilet.HighSchool, GPAFilet.College);
    WHILE (GPAFilet.HighSchool >= 0) DO
        BEGIN
            put (GPAFile);
            write ('GPA pair?  ');
            readln (GPAFILEt.HighSchool, GPAFILEt.College);
        END (* WHILE *);
    writeln ('Creation of GPAFile completed')
END.
```

Figure 12.3

In general, an output statement of the form

write (*file-variable, item-1, item-2, . . . , item-n*)

is equivalent to the following *n* pairs of statements:

> *file-variable↑* := *item-1;*
> *put* (*file-variable*);
> *file-variable↑* := *item-2;*
> *put* (*file-variable*);
> $\vdots$
> *file-variable↑* := *item-n;*
> *put* (*file-variable*)

The statements in each pair correspond to the two stages involved in producing output to a file.[2]

---

[2] Some versions of Pascal do not allow the use of *write* with nontext files; *put* must be used. In others, *put* is not allowed and *write* must be used.

Once a file has been created, it can be opened for input with the procedure *reset*, as described earlier. A component of this file can then be read by using an input statement of the form

read (file-variable, input-list)

where *input-list* is a single variable or a list of variables separated by commas. The type of each variable in the input list and the type of the file components must be compatible. Note that the procedure *readln* may *not* be used for files that are not text files, since such files have no line structure.

As an illustration of input from files, suppose that we wish to examine the contents of the file *GPAFile* created by the program in Figure 12.2 or Figure 12.3. This file must first be opened for input by using the statement

reset (GPAFile);

Each component of the file can then be read and assigned to the variable *GPAPair* of record type *GPARecord* by using the procedure *read:*

read (GPAFile, GPAPair);

and the values of the two fields of *GPAPair* can then be displayed:

writeln (GPAPair.HighSchool:4:2, GPAPair.College:7:2)

In the program in Figure 12.4, these two statements are repeated until the end-of-file mark in *GPAFile* is encountered. This end-of-file mark is automatically placed at the end of each file created by a Pascal program.

```
PROGRAM ReadGPAFile (output, GPAFile);

(*****************************************************************

   Program to read and display the contents of the permanent file
   GPAFile created by the program of Figure 12.2 or 12.3.

****************************************************************)

TYPE
   GPARecord = RECORD
                  HighSchool, College: real
               END;
   FileOfGPARecords = FILE OF GPARecord;

VAR
   GPAFile : FileOfGPARecords;    (* file of GPA records created *)
   GPAPair : GPARecord;           (* pair of grade point averages *)
```

Figure 12.4

Figure 12.4 (Cont.)

```
BEGIN
   reset (GPAFile);
   writeln ('Contents of GPAFile:');
   WHILE NOT eof(GPAFile) DO
      BEGIN
         read (GpaFile, GPAPair);
         writeln(GPAPair.HighSchool:4:2, GPAPair.College:7:2)
      END (* WHILE *)
END.
```

Sample run:

```
Contents of GPAFile:
4.00    3.95
3.64    3.15
2.89    3.01
3.18    2.85
2.21    2.33
1.55    0.76
1.94    2.04
4.00    4.00
2.25    2.25
3.01    2.99
```

File input, like file output, is a two-stage process that uses the file buffer variable or file window. When a file such as *GPAFile* is opened for input with the procedure *reset,* the first file component is copied into the file buffer variable *GPAFile* ↑ . Later, when the statement

   read (GPAFile, GPAPair);

is executed, the value of this buffer variable is copied to the record variable *GPAPair:*

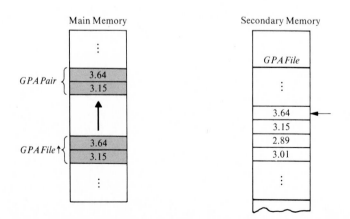

Then, while execution of the program continues, the next file component is copied from the file into the file buffer variable in preparation for the next time a value must be read:

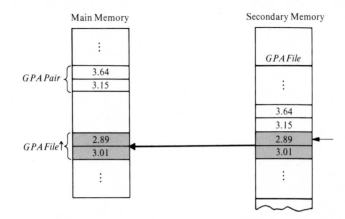

This buffer variable thus always contains a copy of the next component of the associated file, providing a "window" through which the *next* file component may be accessed.

The statement

read (GPAFile, GPAPair);

is equivalent to the pair of statements

GPAPair := GPAFile↑;
get (GPAFile);

where *get* is a predefined procedure that copies the next file component into the associated buffer variable.[3] In general, *get* is called with a statement of the form

get (file-variable)

and an input statement of the form

read (file-variable, variable-1, variable-2, . . . , variable-n)

is equivalent to the *n* pairs of statements

variable-1 := file-variable↑;
get (file-variable);
variable-2 := file-variable↑;
get (file-variable);
      ⋮
variable-n := file-variable↑;
get (file-variable)

---

[3] Some versions of Pascal do not provide a file buffer variable and thus do not provide procedure *get* either. Input must then be carried out using *read*.

The program in Figure 12.5 is a modification of the program in Figure 12.4 for reading the file *GPAFile*. The statement

writeln (GPAFile↑.HighSchool:4:2, GPAFile↑.College:7:2);

displays each file component directly rather than first transferring it to a record variable *GPAPair* and then displaying its value. The statement

get (GPAFile)

then copies the next file component into the file buffer variable.

```
PROGRAM ReadGPAFile (output, GPAFile);

(*********************************************************************

   Program to read and display the contents of the permanent file
   GPAFile created by the program of Figure 12.2 or 12.3.

*********************************************************************)

TYPE
   GPARecord = RECORD
                     HighSchool, College: real
                 END;
   FileOfGPARecords = FILE OF GPARecord;

VAR
   GPAFile : FileOfGPARecords;   (* file of GPA records created *)

BEGIN
   reset (GPAFile);
   writeln ('Contents of GPAFile:');
   WHILE NOT eof(GPAFile) DO
      BEGIN
         writeln(GPAFile↑.HighSchool:4:2, GPAFile↑.College:7:2);
         get (GPAFile)
      END (* WHILE *)
END.
```

Figure 12.5

In the examples of this section, we used one program to create *GPAFile* and a separate program to read the file. In the first program, *GPAFile* was opened for output by using the procedure *rewrite*. After the file was created, this same program could have opened it for input by using the procedure *reset* and then read and displayed the contents. The program in Figure 12.6 does precisely this and thus combines the functions of the programs in Figures 12.3 and 12.5 into a single program. Recall that opening a file for input and reading its contents does not alter the contents of the file but that opening a file for output does destroy any previous contents of the file.

```
PROGRAM CreateAndVerifyGPAFile (input, output, GPAFile);

(************************************************************************

    Program to create the nontext file GPAFile having components
    of type GPARecord.  Pairs of grade point averages are input
    directly into the file buffer variable the user during execution.
    The contents of the file are then verified by opening it for
    input, reading the contents, and displaying each pair of GPAs.

    ***********************************************************************)

TYPE
    GPARecord = RECORD
                    HighSchool, College: real
                END;
    FileOfGPARecords = FILE OF GPARecord;

VAR
    GPAFile : FileOfGPARecords;   (* file of GPA records created *)

BEGIN
    (* Create GPAFile *)

    rewrite (GPAFile);
    writeln ('Enter negative GPA''s to stop.');
    write ('GPA pair?  ');
    readln (GPAFile↑.HighSchool, GPAFile↑.College);
    WHILE (GPAFile↑.HighSchool >= 0) DO
        BEGIN
            put (GPAFile);
            write ('GPA pair?  ');
            readln (GPAFILE↑.HighSchool, GPAFILE↑.College);
        END (* WHILE *);

    (* Verify the contents of GPAFile *)

    reset (GPAFile);
    writeln;
    writeln ('Contents of GPAFile:');
    WHILE NOT eof(GPAFile) DO
        BEGIN
            writeln(GPAFile↑.HighSchool:4:2, GPAFile↑.College:7:2);
            get (GPAFile)
        END (* WHILE *)
END.
```

Figure 12.6

Figure 12.6 (Cont.)

Sample run:

```
Enter negative GPA's to stop.
GPA pair?   4.00 3.95
GPA pair?   3.64 3.15
GPA pair?   2.89 3.01
GPA pair?   3.18 2.85
GPA pair?   2.21 2.33
GPA pair?   1.55 0.76
GPA pair?   1.94 2.04
GPA pair?   4.00 4.00
GPA pair?   2.25 2.25
GPA pair?   3.01 2.99
GPA pair?   -1-1
```

```
Contents of GPAFile:
4.00     3.95
3.64     3.15
2.89     3.01
3.18     2.85
2.21     2.33
1.55     0.76
1.94     2.04
4.00     4.00
2.25     2.25
3.01     2.99
```

As we have seen, the procedures *read* and *get* copy the next file component into the file window unless the end of the file has been reached, in which case the value of

$$eof \, (\textit{file-variable})$$

is true (it is false otherwise), and the file buffer variable is undefined. Any subsequent calls to the procedures *read* or *get* result in an error, since an attempt is made to access information beyond the end of the file.

The procedures *get* and *put* may be used with files of any type, including text files. Because text files are files of type *char,* the corresponding file buffer variables store single characters.

When an end-of-line mark is encountered in a text file, the value of

$$eoln \, (\textit{file-variable})$$

becomes true (it is false otherwise), and a blank is placed in the file window. It is this blank that is read as the next file component, unless it is bypassed by using a statement of the form

$$get \, (\textit{file-variable})$$

A statement of the form

readln (file-variable)

may also be used to bypass an end-of-line mark, since it is equivalent to

while not *eoln (file-variable)* **do**
  get (file-variable);
get (file-variable)

Note that in either case the file window *file-variable↑* then contains the first character of the next line.

Our examples in this section have thus far dealt only with permanent files, which exist before and/or after as well as during program execution. The comments in this section regarding files also apply to temporary files, that is, to files that exist only during execution of the program. One exception, however, is that names of temporary files are not listed in the program heading.

A data-processing problem in which it is convenient to use temporary files is that of appending data to an existing permanent file. Because opening a file for output erases its previous contents, it is not possible to add the data by simply writing to the existing file. Instead, we must first copy the permanent file to a temporary work file, then add the additional data to this file, and finally, copy the resulting work file back to the permanent file. Because the work file is needed only during program execution, it may be a temporary file. The program in Figure 12.7 uses the temporary file *WorkFile* to append data entered by the user to the file *GPAFile.* created earlier. Note that although *WorkFile* is not listed in the program heading, it is declared and opened in the usual manner.

In this example, it is necessary to copy the contents from one file into another file, and this is accomplished with the following statements in procedure *CopyFile:*

while not *eof(FromFile)* **do**
  begin
    ToFile↑ := FromFile↑;
    put (ToFile);
    get (FromFile)
  end (* **while** *)

These statements copy one record at a time from the file *FromFile* into *ToFile*. This is necessary because the contents of a file can be accessed only one component at a time; it is *not* possible to copy one file into another file by using an assignment statement of the form *file-1 := file-2*.

One consequence of this is that files used as parameters, as in procedure *CopyFile, must be variable parameters.* Using value parameters for files is *not* allowed, because this would require copying an entire actual file into the corresponding formal file parameter. Corresponding actual file parameters and formal file parameters must have the **same type,** and as for the other structured data types, this means that they must be declared by the same or equivalent type identifiers (see Section 8.2).

```
PROGRAM AppendToGPAFile (input, output, GPAFile);

(***********************************************************************

   Program to read pairs of GPA's entered by the user and add
   these pairs to the end of the previously created GPAFile.
   The contents of GPAFile are first copied into the temporary
   file WorkFile, the new pairs are appended to WorkFile, and
   the contents of WorkFile are then copied back to GPAFile.
   The contents of GPAFile are then verified by reading and
   displaying each pair in it.

***********************************************************************)

TYPE
   GPARecord = RECORD
                    HighSchool, College : real
               END;
   FileOfGPARecords = FILE OF GPARecord;
   FileType = FileOfGPARecords;

VAR
   WorkFile,                           (* temporary file of GPA records *)
   GPAFile : FileOfGPARecords;         (* file of GPA records created *)

PROCEDURE CopyFile (VAR FromFile, ToFile : FileType);

   (**********************************************************************

      Procedure to copy the contents of FromFile into ToFile.

   **********************************************************************)

   BEGIN (* CopyFile *)
      reset (FromFile);
      rewrite (ToFile);
      WHILE NOT eof(FromFile) DO
         BEGIN
            ToFile↑ := FromFile↑;
            put (ToFile);
            get (FromFile)
         END (* WHILE *)
   END (* CopyFile *);
```

Figure 12.7

Figure 12.7 (Cont.)

```
BEGIN (* main program *)

   (* Copy contents of GPAFile to WorkFile *)

   CopyFile (GPAFile, WorkFile);

   (* Append new points to the end of WorkFile *)

   writeln ('Enter negative GPA''s to stop.');
   write ('GPA pair?  ');
   readln (WorkFile↑.HighSchool, WorkFile↑.College);
   WHILE (WorkFile↑.HighSchool >= 0) DO
      BEGIN
         put (WorkFile);
         write ('GPA pair?  ');
         readln (WorkFILE↑.HighSchool, WorkFILE↑.College);
      END (* WHILE *);

   (* Now copy the contents of WorkFile to GPAFile *)

   CopyFile (WorkFile, GPAFile);

   (* Finally, verify the contents of GPAFile *)

   reset (GPAFile);
   writeln;
   writeln ('Contents of GPAFile:');
   WHILE NOT eof(GPAFile) DO
      BEGIN
         writeln (GPAFile↑.HighSchool:5:1, GPAFile↑.College:7:1);
         get (GpaFile)
      END (* WHILE *)
END (* main program *).
```

Sample run:
_____

```
Enter negative GPA's to stop.
GPA pair?   3.3 3.3
GPA pair?   2.9 2.4
GPA pair?   1.1 1.3
GPA pair?   -1 -1

Contents of GPAFile:
   4.0      3.9
   3.6      3.1
   2.9      3.0
   3.2      2.8
   2.2      2.3
   1.5      0.8
   1.9      2.0
   4.0      4.0
   2.3      2.3
   3.0      3.0
   3.3      3.3
   2.9      2.4
   1.1      1.3
```

12.3   Application: Updating a File

To illustrate the file-processing techniques discussed in this chapter, we consider the important problem of updating a master file with the contents of a transaction file. For example, the master file may be an inventory file that is to be updated with a transaction file containing the day's sales; or the master file may be a file of students' records and the transaction file a file containing the students' grades for the semester just concluded.

In this section we consider the problem of updating a master file containing information regarding the users of a university's computing system. Suppose that components of the master file *UsersFile* are records containing the following information about each system user: identification number, name, password, limit on resources, and resources used to date. A daily log of the system's activity is also maintained. Among the other items of information, this log contains a list of user identification numbers and resources used for each job entered into the system. This list is maintained in the transaction file *UpdateFile*. At the end of each day, the master file *UsersFile* must be updated with the contents of *UpdateFile* to incorporate the activities of that day. We assume that both *UsersFile* and *UpdateFile* have been sorted so that the identification numbers are in ascending order. An algorithm for performing the file update is as follows:

FILE UPDATE ALGORITHM

(∗ Algorithm to update records in *UsersFile* with information from *UpdateFile* to produce *NewUsersFile*. It is assumed that records in these files are ordered so that identification numbers are in ascending order and that all identification numbers in *UpdateFile* are valid. ∗)

1. Read the first record from *UsersFile* and assign it to *UserRec*.
2. Read the first record from *UpdateFile* and assign it to *UpdateRec*.
3. Set a boolean variable *EndOfUpdate* to *false*.
4. While not *EndOfUpdate*, do the following updating:
   Compare the identification number in *UserRec* with that in *UpdateRec*. If they match, do the following:
   a. Update *UserRec* by adding the value of *ResourcesUsed* from *UpdateRec* to *UsedToDate* in *UserRec*.
   b. If the end of *UpdateFile* has been reached, set *EndOfUpdate* to *true;* otherwise, read the next value for *UpdateRec* from *UpdateFile*.
   If the identification numbers do not match, do the following:
   a. Write *UserRec* to *NewUsersFile*.
   b. Read a new value for *UserRec* from *UsersFile*.
5. Because the last updated user record has not been written, write *UserRec* to *NewUsersFile*.
6. Copy any remaining records in *UsersFile* into *NewUsersFile*.

The program in Figure 12.8 implements this algorithm. Also shown are the contents of two small files used in a test run and the output file produced.

●

These listings were obtained by executing a program that reads each record from a nontext file and then displays each field of the record by using a program segment of the form

> *reset (NonTextFile)*;
> **while not** *eof(NonTextFile)* **do**
>   **begin**
>   **with** *NonTextFile↑* **do**
>   *writeln (field-1, field-2, . . .)*;
>   *get (NonTextFile)*
>   **end**

```
PROGRAM UserFileUpdate (UsersFile, UpdateFile, NewUsersFile);

(***********************************************************************

    Program to update the entries in the master file UsersFile with
    the entries in the transactions file UpdateFile.  The records
    in UsersFile contain the id-number, name, password, resource
    limit, and resources used to date for each system user;
    UpdateFile represents the log of a day's activities; each
    record contains a user's id-number and resources used for a
    job entered into the system.  Both files are sorted so that
    id-numbers are in ascending order, and all id-numbers in
    UsersFile are assumed to be valid.  The updated records are
    written to the output file NewUsersFile.

***********************************************************************)

CONST
    NameLength = 20;                (* lengths of names *)
    PasswordLength = 4;             (* lengths of passwords *)

TYPE
    NameString = PACKED ARRAY[1..NameLength] OF char;
    PasswordString = PACKED ARRAY[1..PasswordLength] OF char;
    UserRecord = RECORD
                    IdNumber : integer;
                    Name : NameString;
                    Password : PasswordString;
                    ResourceLimit,
                    UsedToDate : integer
                 END;
    UserUpdateRecord = RECORD
                          UpdateNumber,
                          ResourcesUsed : integer
                       END;
    MasterFile = FILE OF UserRecord;
    TransactionFile = FILE OF UserUpdateRecord;
```

Figure 12.8

Figure 12.8 (Cont.)

```
VAR
    UserRec : UserRecord;                    (* record from UsersFile *)
    UpdateRec : UserUpdateRecord;            (* record from UpdateFile *)
    UsersFile,                               (* file containing user information *)
    NewUsersFile : MasterFile;               (* updated user file *)
    UpdateFile : TransactionFile;            (* file to update UsersFile *)
    EndOfUpdate : boolean;                   (* signals end of UpdateFile *)

BEGIN
    reset (UsersFile);
    reset (UpdateFile);
    rewrite (NewUsersFile);

    (* Read first record from each file *)

    read (UsersFile, UserRec);
    read (UpdateFile, UpdateRec);

    (* Update records of UsersFile with records of UpdateFile *)

    EndOfUpdate := false;
    WHILE NOT EndOfUpdate DO
        BEGIN
            WITH UserRec, UpdateRec DO
                IF IdNumber = UpdateNumber THEN      (* id-numbers match *)
                    BEGIN
                        UsedToDate := UsedToDate + ResourcesUsed;
                        IF eof(UpdateFile) THEN
                            EndOfUpdate := true
                        ELSE
                            read (UpdateFile, UpdateRec)
                    END (* IF *)
                ELSE                                  (* no match *)
                    BEGIN
                        write (NewUsersFile, UserRec);
                        read (UsersFile, UserRec)
                    END (* ELSE *)
        END (* WHILE *);

    (* Write UserRec to NewUsersFile; then copy any
       remaining records from UsersFile *)

    write (NewUsersFile, UserRec);
    WHILE NOT eof (UsersFile) DO
        BEGIN
            read (UsersFile, UserRec);
            write (NewUsersFile, UserRec)
        END (* WHILE *)
END.
```

Figure 12.8 (Cont.)

Contents of UsersFile:
```
12300JOHN DOE          GERM 200 125
12310MARY SMITH        SNOW 200  75
13320PETE VANDERVAN    RAIN 300 228
13400FRED JONES        FROM 100   0
13450JANE TARZAN       JUST 200  63
13490JACK JACKSON      DATE 300 128
14000ALBERT ALBERTS    LIST 400 255
14010JESSE JAMES       GUNS 100  38
14040DIRTY GERTIE      MESS 100  17
14100PRINCE ALBERT     CANS 300 185
```

Contents of UpdateFile:
```
12300 10
12300 24
12310 17
12310 3
12310 5
12310 10
13400 28
13450 25
13450 3
13450 1
13450 13
14010 22
14010 5
14010 12
14010 7
```

Contents of NewUsersFile:
```
12300JOHN DOE          GERM 200 159
12310MARY SMITH        SNOW 200 110
13320PETE VANDERVAN    RAIN 300 228
13400FRED JONES        FROM 100  28
13450JANE TARZAN       JUST 200 105
13490JACK JACKSON      DATE 300 128
14000ALBERT ALBERTS    LIST 400 255
14010JESSE JAMES       GUNS 100  84
14040DIRTY GERTIE      MESS 100  17
14100PRINCE ALBERT     CANS 300 185
```

Exercises

In these exercises, the files *UsersFile*, *InventoryFile*, *StudentFile*, *InventoryUpdate*, and *StudentUpdate* should be processed as files of records. For descriptions of these files, see Appendix E.

1. Each of the following program segments is intended to read a text file *InFile* in which each line contains an integer and to find the sum of all the integers in the file. Explain why each fails to do so.

(a) *reset (InFile)*;
   Sum := 0;
   while not *eof(InFile)* **do**
      begin
         read (InFile, Number);
         Sum := *Sum* + *Number*
      end (* **while** *)

(b) *reset (InFile)*;
   Sum := 0;
   readln (InFile, Number);
   while not *eof(InFile)* **do**
      begin
         Sum := *Sum* + *Number*;
         readln (InFile, Number)
      end (* **while** *)

(c) *reset (InFile)*;
   Sum := 0;
   repeat
      get (InFile);
      Sum := *Sum* + *InFile*↑
   until *eof(InFile)*

2. Each of the following program segments is intended to display all nonblank characters in the text file *InFile*, with no error resulting. For each, describe a text file for which it fails.

(a) *reset (InFile)*;
   read (InFile, Ch);
   repeat
      if *InFile*↑ = ' ' **then**
         get (InFile)
      else
         begin
            writeln (InFile↑);
            get (InFile)
         end (* **else** *)
   until *eof(InFile)*

(b) *reset (InFile)*;
   read (InFile, Ch);
   while not *eof(InFile)* **do**
      begin
         while *Ch* = ' ' **do**
            read (InFile, Ch);
         writeln (Ch);
         read (InFile, Ch)
      end (* **while** *)

(c) *reset (InFile)*;
   read (InFile, Ch);
   while not *eof(InFile)* **do**
      begin
         if *Ch* <> ' ' **then**
            writeln (Ch);
         read (InFile, Ch);
      end (* **while** *)

3. Write a procedure to concatenate two files of identical type.

4. The file update algorithm in this section assumes that all identification numbers in *UpdateFile* are valid. Modify this algorithm and the program in Figure 12.8 so they work correctly even if *UpdateFile* has not been previously validated.

5. Modify Exercise 7 of Section 8.5 to print "personalized" junk-mail letters in which certain blanks in a form letter are filled in with personal information obtained from a file containing that information.

6. Write a program to read *UsersFile* to find and display the password for a specified user's identification number.

7. Write a program to read *StudentFile* and produce a report for all freshmen with GPAs below 2.0. This report should include the student's first name, middle initial, last name, major, and cumulative GPA, with appropriate headings.

8. At the end of each month, a report is produced that shows the status of the account of each user in *UsersFile*. Write a program to read the current date and produce a report of the following form:

USER ACCOUNTS—09/30/87

USER NAME	USER-ID	RESOURCE LIMIT	RESOURCES USED
Joseph Miltgen	100101	$750	$380
Isaac Small	100102	$650	$598***
⋮	⋮	⋮	⋮

where the three asterisks (***) indicate that the user has already used 90 percent or more of the resources available to him or her.

9. Write a program to update *InventoryFile* with *InventoryUpdate* to produce a new inventory file. Each record in *InventoryFile* for which there is no record in *InventoryUpdate* with a matching item number should remain unchanged. Each record with one or more corresponding records in *InventoryUpdate* should be updated with the entries in the update file. For transaction code R, the number of items returned should be added to the number in stock. For transaction code S, the number of items sold should be subtracted from the number currently in stock; if more items are sold than are in stock, display a message showing the order number, stock number, item name, and how many should be back-ordered (that is, the difference between the number ordered and the number in stock), and set the number currently in stock to zero.

10. Write a program to read the files *StudentFile* and *StudentUpdate* and produce an updated grade report. This grade report should show

(a) the current date.

(b) the student's name and student number.

(c) a list of the names, grade, and credits for each of the current courses under the headings COURSE, GRADE, and CREDITS.

(d) current GPA (multiply credits by numeric grade—A = 4.0, A− = 3.7, B+ = 3.3, B = 3.0, . . . , D− = 0.7, F = 0.0—for each course to find honor points earned for that course, sum these to find total new honor points, and then divide total new honor points by total new credits to give the current GPA, rounded to two decimal places).

(e) total credits taken (old credits from *StudentFile* plus total new credits).

(f) new cumulative GPA (first calculate old honor points = old credits times old cumulative GPA and then new cumulative GPA = sum of old honor points and new honor points divided by updated total credits.)

11. Write a simple ***text-formatting*** program that reads a text file and produces another text file in which no lines are longer than some given length. Put as many words as possible on the same line. You will have to break some lines of the given file, but do not break any words or put punctuation marks at the beginning of a new line.

12. Extend the text-formatting program of Exercise 11 to right-justify each line in the new text file by adding evenly distributed blanks in lines where necessary. Also, preserve all indentation of lines in the given text file that begin a new paragraph.

13. Most system text formatters also allow command lines to be placed within the unformatted text. These command lines might have forms like the following:

.P *m n*	Insert *m* blank lines before each paragraph and indent each paragraph *n* spaces.
.W *n*	Width of page (line length) is *n*.
.L *n*	Page length (number of lines per page) is *n*.
.I *n*	Indent all lines following this command line *n* spaces.
.U	Undent all following lines and reset to previous left margin.

Extend the program of Exercises 11 and 12 to implement command lines.

14. A ***pretty-printer*** is a special kind of text formatter that reads a text file containing a program and then prints it in a "pretty" format. For example, a pretty-printer for Pascal programs might insert blank lines between procedures and indent and align statements within other statements, such as **if** statements, compound statements, type declarations, variable declarations, and the like to produce a format similar to that used in the sample programs of this text. Write a pretty-print program

for Pascal programs to indent and align statements in a pleasing format.

15. Write a menu-driven program that uses *Studentfile* and *StudentUpdate* and allows (some of) the following options. For each option, write a separate procedure so that options and corresponding procedures can be easily added or removed.

   1. Locate a student's permanent record when given his or her student number and print it in a nicer format than that in which it is stored.

   2. Same as Option 1, but locate the record when given his or her name.

   3. Print a list of all student names and numbers in a given class (1, 2, 3, 4, 5).

   4. Same as Option 3, but for a given major.

   5. Same as Option 3, but for a given range of cumulative GPAs.

   6. Find the average cumulative GPAs for all
      (a) females   (b) males   (c) students with a specified major
      (d) all students. (These are suboptions of Menu Option 6.)

   7. Produce updated grade reports having the following format:

      GRADE REPORT—SEMESTER #1
      12/23/87

      DISPATCH UNIVERSITY

      10103   James L. Johnson

	GRADE	CREDITS
ENGL 176	C	4
EDUC 268	B	4
EDUC 330	B+	3
P E 281	C	3
ENGR 317	D	4

      Cumulative Credits: 33
      Current GPA: 2.22
      Cumulative GPA: 2.64

   (See Exercise 10 for descriptions of these last items.)

   8. Same as Option 7, but instead of producing grade reports, produce a new permanent file containing the updated total credits and new cumulative GPAs.

   9. Produce an updated file when a student (a) drops or (b) adds a course.

   10. Produce an updated file when a student (a) transfers to or (b) withdraws from the university.

Programming Pointers

In this chapter we reviewed text files and introduced files of other types. Many of the programming pointers at the end of Chapter 6 regarding text files apply to files in general. These are summarized here; for additional details, see the Programming Pointers of Chapter 6.

1. *Each file variable that names a permanent file must appear in the file list of the program heading and must be declared to be of file type in the variable section of the program.*

2. *Before any input operation can be attempted from a file, that file must be opened for input by using the procedure reset. Similarly, before any output to a file is attempted, the file must be opened for output by using the procedure rewrite.*

3. *Each call of the procedure reset loads the file window with the first component of the file.*

4. *Each call of the procedure rewrite empties the file, and any previous contents the file may have had are destroyed.*

5. *After values have been obtained for each variable in the input list, the procedure read loads the file window with the next file component to be read unless the end of the file is encountered, in which case the file buffer variable is undefined.*

6. *Nontext files have no line structure, and thus the procedures readln and writeln and the function eoln cannot be used with them.*

7. *Assignment statements of the form file-variable-1 := file-variable-2 are not allowed. The components of one file must be copied to another file individually.*

8. *File variables used as formal parameters in functions and procedures must be variable parameters.*

9. *The file window for an input file always contains the next file component, if there is one.* For text files, the file components are characters. Consequently, if *Number* is a numeric variable, an assignment statement of the form

    Number := *TextFile*↑

   is an error, because it attempts to assign a character to *Number*.

10. *The procedure get replaces the contents of the file window with the next file component.* Thus, *get* should not be referenced before the processing of the file component currently in the file window has been completed.

11. *The procedure put transfers (does not copy) the component currently in the file window to the specified file.* Thus, *put* should not be called until the processing of the file component currently in the file window has been completed. After the procedure *put* has been executed, the file window is undefined.

Variations and Extensions

Text files were introduced in Chapter 6, and the file processing features described in the Variations and Extensions section at the end of that chapter should be reviewed at this point. Here we consider *direct access* or *random access* files which, as we have noted, are provided in addition to sequential files in many versions of Pascal (e.g., Macintosh, Turbo, and UCSD). These are files in which each component can be accessed directly by specifying its location in the file, thus allowing components to be read/written anywhere in the file. Such files cannot usually be text files, but any other type of file is allowed. What follows are descriptions of the common features for processing direct access files. Each version of Pascal may also provide its own special features, and some of these are described in Appendix G.

- *Program heading.* The program heading may be optional (Turbo), or a modified form may be allowed or required (Macintosh, UCSD). It is not always used to specify permanent files used in the program.
- *Opening for input/output.* In some versions of Pascal, the procedure *reset* used to open sequential files for input is also used to open direct access files for both input and output:

      reset (file-variable, file-name);   (∗ UCSD ∗)

  or

      assign (file-variable, file-name);   (∗ Turbo ∗)
      reset (file-variable);

  Some versions (Macintosh), however, require a special predefined procedure to open a direct access file; for example,

      open (file-variable, file-name);

- *The procedure seek.* The components in a file are assumed to be numbered, beginning with 0, and the predefined procedure *seek* is used to locate a particular component. It is called with a statement of the form

      seek (file-variable, component number)

  where *component-number* is an integer expression specifying the number of the component in the file to be located. The result of a call to *seek* with a component number too small (negative) or too large is system dependent. Commonly, seeking a component whose number is one more than the number of the last component sets *eof(file-variable)* to true and positions the data pointer just past the last component, thus making it possible to append new components to the file.

- *Writing to a file.* Once a component in a direct access file has been located, the procedure *put* can be used to replace this component with the contents of the file buffer variable (Macintosh, UCSD),

      seek (file-variable, component-number);
      file-variable↑ := expression;
      put (file-variable);

  or the procedure *write* can be used to carry out this replacement (Macintosh, Turbo, UCSD):

      seek (file-variable, component-number);
      write (file-variable, new-component);

- *Reading from a file.* When *seek* is called, the component of the file that is located is *not* copied into the file buffer, since it is not known at that time whether the next operation will be to read from the file or to write to it. Consequently, if this component is to be read, the procedure *get* must first be called to copy this component into the file buffer (Macintosh, UCSD):

      seek (file-variable, component-number);
      get (file-variable);
      variable := file-variable↑;

  Alternatively, the procedure *read* may be used to read this component (Macintosh, Turbo, UCSD):

      seek (file-variable, component-number);
      read (file-variable, variable);

- *Closing a file.* It may be necessary to invoke a special *close* procedure to close a file before program execution is completed (Macintosh, Turbo, UCSD).

The program in Figure 12.9 illustrates the use of direct access files in Turbo Pascal. It is a file update program in which component numbers correspond to part numbers in an inventory file.

```
PROGRAM InventoryUpdate;

(*************************************************************************

    Program to update a direct access file PartsFile in which the
    numbers of records in the file are interpreted as part numbers.
    A part number is entered by the user, the corresponding record
    is retrieved and displayed, modifications are made, and the
    updated record then rewritten to the file.

**********************************************************************)

CONST
    MaxNumRecords = 100;              (* upper limit on record numbers *)

TYPE
    InvRecord = RECORD
                     ItemName : STRING[20];
                     NumInStock : integer;
                     Price : real;
                END;
    InventoryFile = FILE OF InvRecord;

VAR
    PartsFile : InventoryFile; (* file to be updated *)
    FileName : STRING[20];     (* actual name of  file *)
    PartsRec : InvRecord;      (* a record from PartsFile *)
    NumSold,                   (* number sold/returned *)
    PartNum : integer;         (* part number *)
BEGIN
    (* open PartsFile *)
    write ('Name of file to be updated?  ');
    readln (FileName);
    assign (PartsFile, FileName);
    reset (PartsFile);

    (* update the file *)
    writeln ('Enter negative part number to stop.');
    writeln;
    write ('Part #?  ');
    readln (PartNum);
```

Figure 12.9

Figure 12.9 (Cont.)

```
    WHILE (PartNum >= 0) DO
        BEGIN
            IF PartNum <= MaxNumRecords THEN
                BEGIN
                    seek (PartsFile, PartNum);
                    read (PartsFile,PartsRec);
                    WITH PartsRec DO
                        BEGIN
                            writeln (ItemName);
                            writeln (NumInStock:1, ' in stock');
                            writeln ('Price:   $', Price:4:2);
                            write ('# sold (negative if returned)?  ');
                            readln (NumSold);
                            NumInStock := NumInStock - NumSold
                        END (* WITH *);
                    seek (PartsFile, PartNum);
                    write (PartsFile, PartsRec)
                END (* IF *)
            ELSE
                Writeln ('Part # > ', MaxNumRecords:1, ' — out of range');
            writeln;
            write ('Part #?  ');
            readln (PartNum)
        END (* WHILE *);
    writeln;
    writeln ('File updating completed');
    close (PartsFile)
END.
```

Sample run:

Name of file to be updated? PARTSFILE
Enter negative part number to stop.

Part #? 1
V-378 FAN BELT
30 in stock
Price: $7.95
sold (negative if returned)? 5

Part #? 72
HALOGEN HEADLIGHT PR-378
82 in stock
Price: $13.90
sold (negative if returned)? 12

Part #? 30
FORD MUFFLER MF-3668
10 in stock
Price: $25.95
sold (negative if returned)? -2

Part #? -1

File updating completed

13

Pointers and Linked Lists

> *[Pointers] are like jumps, leaping wildly from one part of a data structure to another. Their introduction into high-level languages has been a step backward from which we may never recover.*
>
> C. A. R. HOARE
>
> *I've got a little list, I've got a little list.*
>
> GILBERT AND SULLIVAN, *The Mikado*

Variables are symbolic addresses of memory locations. This relationship between a variable and the memory location it names is a static one that is established when the program is compiled and remains fixed throughout the execution of the program. Although the contents of a memory location associated with a variable may change during execution, that is, the value of the variable may change, variables themselves can be neither created nor destroyed during execution. Consequently, these variables are called *static variables.*

In some situations, however, the memory requirements will be known only while the program is executing, so that static variables are not adequate. In such cases, a method for acquiring additional memory locations as needed during execution and for releasing them when they are no longer needed is required. Variables that are created and disposed of during execution are called *dynamic variables.* At one point during execution, there may be a particular memory location associated with a dynamic variable, and at a later time, no memory location or a different one may be associated with it. Pascal provides for such dynamic memory allocation and deallocation by using *pointers* and the predefined procedures *new* and *dispose.*

Unlike *static data structures* such as arrays whose sizes and associated memory locations are fixed at compile time, *dynamic data structures* expand or contract as required during execution and their associated memory locations change. A dynamic data structure is a collection of elements called *nodes* of

477

the structure—usually of record type—that are linked together. This linking is established by associating with each node a pointer that points to the next node in the structure. One of the simplest linked structures is a *linked list* that might be pictured as follows:

Dynamic data structures are especially useful in storing and processing data sets whose sizes change during program execution, for example, the collection of jobs that have been entered into a computer system and are awaiting execution or the collection of passenger names and seat assignments on a given airplane flight. In this chapter we consider pointers and the procedures *new* and *dispose* and how they can be used to construct and process dynamic data structures.

13.1   Pointers; The Procedures *new* and *dispose*

As noted in the introduction, construction of a dynamic data structure requires the ability to allocate memory locations as needed during program execution. Because the number of locations is not known in advance, they cannot be allocated in the usual manner using variable declarations, since such allocations are made at compile time. Instead the predefined procedure *new* is used for this purpose. When it is called, it returns the address of a memory location in which a node of the data structure can be stored. To reference this memory location so that data may be stored in it or retrieved from it, a special kind of variable called a ***pointer variable,*** or simply a ***pointer,*** is used. The value of a pointer is thus the address of some memory location.

The nodes of a dynamic data structure may be of any type but are most often of some record type. The type of a pointer that is used to reference the memory location storing one of these nodes must be specified by

$\uparrow$*type-identifier*   or $\wedge$*type-identifier*

where *type-identifier* specifies the type of the nodes. The pointer is said to be ***bound*** to this type, since it may not be used for nodes of any other type. For example, if the nodes are records defined by

type
        EmployeeRecord = **record**
                                Number : *integer*;
                                HourlyRate : *real*
                        end;

then the type of a pointer *EmployeePointer* for such nodes is

$\uparrow$*EmployeeRecord*

Such a pointer type declaration may be used in the variable section to declare that a variable is a pointer of this type

var
　　EmployeePointer : ↑*EmployeeRecord*;

but it is usually preferable to assign it to a type identifier that is then used to specify the pointer type:

type
　　EmployeeRecord = **record**
　　　　　　　　　　　Number : *integer*;
　　　　　　　　　　　HourlyRate : *real*
　　　　　　　　end;
　　PointerToEmployeeRecord = ↑*EmployeeRecord*;

var
　　EmployeePointer : *PointerToEmployeeRecord*;

In either case, *EmployeePointer* is bound to the type *EmployeeRecord* and may be used only for nodes of this type.

The procedure *new* may then be used during program execution to acquire a memory location in which an employee record may be stored. This procedure is called with a statement of the form

　　new (*pointer*)

which assigns the address of a memory location to *pointer* and is thus equivalent to a statement of the form

　　pointer := *memory-address*

Thus the statement

　　new (*EmployeePointer*)

assigns to *EmployeePointer* a memory address, say 1074; that is, the value of *EmployeePointer* is this memory address:

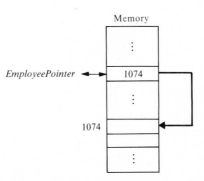

This is the address of a memory location where a value of type *EmployeeRecord* can be stored. We say that *EmployeePointer* "points" to this memory location and picture this by a diagram such as

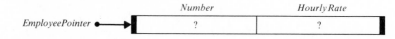

The contents of boxes representing fields of an employee record are shown here as question marks to indicate that these fields are initially undefined.[1]

Each call of the procedure *new* acquires a new memory location and assigns its address to the specified pointer. Thus, if *TempPointer* is also a pointer of type *PointerToEmployeeRecord*, the statement

> *new (TempPointer)*

acquires a new memory location pointed to by *TempPointer*:

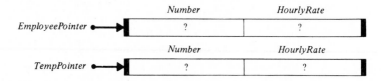

The value of a pointer is the address of a memory location. The value stored in this memory location is denoted by

> *pointer*↑   or   *pointer*^

For the pointer *EmployeePointer* of type *PointerToEmployeeRecord*, the value of *EmployeePointer*↑ is therefore the employee record pointed to by *EmployeePointer*. Thus, *EmployeePointer*↑ is a variable of type *Employee-Record* and may be used in the same manner as is any other record variable of this type. For example, values can be assigned to the fields of this record by the input statement

> *readln (EmployeePointer↑.Number, EmployeePointer↑.HourlyRate)*

or

> **with** *EmployeePointer*↑ **do**
> *readln (Number, HourlyRate)*

If the values

> 35331 7.50

---

[1] An alternative form of reference to the procedure *new* may be used for variant records, which allows the system to allocate memory locations more efficiently. This form is described in Appendix F.

are read, we then have

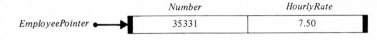

The statement

$$TempPointer\uparrow := EmployeePointer\uparrow$$

is a valid assignment statement, since both *EmployeePointer* and *TempPointer* are bound to the type *EmployeeRecord*, and so *EmployeePointer*↑ and *TempPointer*↑ are of the same type. It copies the contents of the record pointed to by *EmployeePointer* into the location pointed to by *TempPointer*:

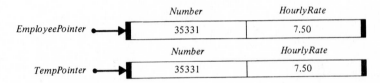

Similarly, if *NewEmpRecord* is a static variable of type *EmployeeRecord*, the statement

$$NewEmpRecord := EmployeePointer\uparrow$$

is valid.

Because the values of pointers are addresses of memory locations, the operations that may be performed on them are limited: only assignment and comparison using the relational operators $=$ and $<>$ are allowed. If *pointer1* and *pointer2* are bound to the same type, an assignment statement of the form

$$pointer1 := pointer2$$

assigns the value of *pointer2* to *pointer1* so that both point to the same memory location. The previous location (if any) pointed to by *pointer1* can no longer be accessed unless pointed to by some other pointer. The following diagrams illustrate:

Before assignment:

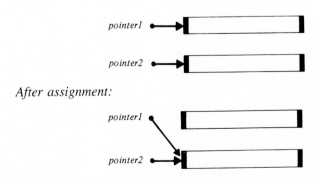

Before assignment:

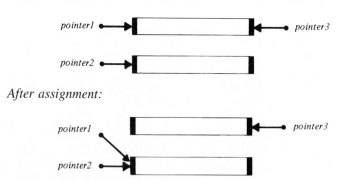

After assignment:

Because inaccessible nodes may be unusable by the system, the situation pictured in the first set of diagrams should be avoided.

As an illustration, suppose that *TempPointer* and *EmployeePointer* are pointers of type *PointerToEmployeeRecord,* pointing to the following employee records:

	Number	HourlyRate
TempPointer →	35331	7.50

	Number	HourlyRate
EmployeePointer →	44622	9.25

The assignment statement

   TempPointer := *EmployeePointer*

causes *TempPointer* to point to the same employee record as does *EmployeePointer,* and so the first employee record can no longer be accessed (unless pointed to by some other pointer of type *PointerToEmployeeRecord*):

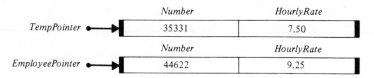

Note that this result is very different from that produced by the assignment statement

   TempPointer↑ := *EmployeePointer*↑

which copies the employee record pointed to by *EmployeePointer* into the memory location pointed to by *TempPointer:*

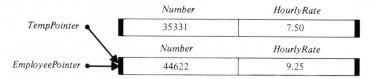

The relational operators = and <> can be used to determine whether two pointers *bound to the same type* point to the same memory location. Thus the boolean expression

TempPointer = EmployeePointer

is true only if *TempPointer* and *EmployeePointer* point to the same memory location

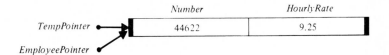

Note that this is *not* equivalent to the boolean expression

TempPointer↑ = EmployeePointer↑

since this is an attempt to compare the record pointed to by *TempPointer* with the record pointed to by *EmployeePointer,* and records cannot be compared with relational operators; thus this is *not* a valid boolean expression. Obviously, if *TempPointer = EmployeePointer* is true, then the records pointed to by *TempPointer* and *EmployeePointer,* that is, the values of *TempPointer↑* and *EmployeePointer↑,* are identical. The converse is not true, however. These two records may be identical, that is, *TempPointer↑* and *EmployeePointer↑* may have the same value, but *TempPointer = EmployeePointer* may be false.

In some situations it may be necessary to assign a value to a pointer variable that indicates that it does not point to any memory location. This can be done by assigning the pointer constant **nil** in an assignment statement of the form

pointer := **nil**

This value **nil** may be assigned to a pointer of any type. We picture a nil pointer as simply a dot with no arrow emanating from it:

pointer •

It should be noted that a pointer having the value **nil** is *not* the same as its being undefined. For example, if *TempPointer* is undefined, any attempt to use its value, as in the boolean expression

TempPointer = EmployeePointer

is an error, as is any reference to *TempPointer↑.* If *TempPointer* has the value **nil,** however, this boolean expression is valid. Any reference to *TempPointer↑* would still be an error, however, since *TempPointer* points to no memory location.

If the memory location pointed to by a pointer is no longer needed, it may be released and made available for later allocation by calling the procedure *dispose* with a statement of the form

    dispose (pointer)

This procedure frees the memory location pointed to by *pointer* and leaves *pointer* undefined.[2]

Pointers may also be used as parameters in user-defined functions and procedures. These parameters may be either value or variable parameters, but corresponding pointer parameters must be bound to the same type. The value of a function may also be a pointer.[3] Pointers are used as parameters in several examples of the next section.

13.2   Introduction to Linked Lists

Pointer variables, which we introduced in the preceding section, are not very useful by themselves. Their importance lies in the fact that they make it possible to implement dynamic data structures. As we noted in the introduction to this chapter, dynamic structures are more appropriate than static structures for modeling a data set whose size changes during processing. In this section we consider a simple dynamic structure, a linked list, and show how it can be constructed using pointers.

A *linked list* consists of a collection of elements called *nodes* linked together by pointers, together with a pointer to the first node in the list. The nodes contain two different kinds of information: (1) the actual data item being stored and (2) a *link* or pointer to the next node in the list. A linked list containing the integers 95, 47, and 83 with 95 as the first element might thus be pictured as follows:

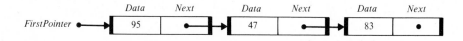

In this diagram, *FirstPointer* is a pointer to the first node in the list. The *Data* field of each node stores one of the integers, and the *Next* field is a pointer to the next node; the dot in the last node having no arrow emanating from it represents a nil pointer and indicates that there is no next node.

The nodes in a linked list are represented in Pascal as records having two kinds of fields, *data fields* and *link fields.* The data fields have types that are appropriate for storing the necessary information, and the link fields are of pointer type. For example, the nodes in the preceding linked list may be declared by

---

    [2] An alternative form of reference to the procedure *dispose* may be used for variant records; see Appendix F.

    [3] If *f* is a pointer-valued function, a function reference of the form *f(actual-parameters)*↑ is not permitted. The value of the function must be assigned to a pointer variable, and this variable used to access the contents of the memory location to which it points.

type
    ListPointer = ↑*ListNode*;
    ListNode = **record**
               Data : *integer*;
               Next : *ListPointer*
       end;

Each node in this list is a record of type *ListNode* consisting of two fields. The first field *Data* is of integer type and is used to store the data. The second field *Next* is a pointer of type *ListPointer* and points to the next node in the list. Note that the definition of the pointer type *ListPointer*

    ListPointer = ↑*ListNode*;

precedes the definition of the record type *ListNode*. This is the only situation in which it is permissible to use an identifier (*ListNode*) before it is defined.

    In addition to the nodes of the list in which to store the data items, a pointer to the first node is needed. Thus we declare a pointer variable *First-Pointer* by

    var
      FirstPointer : *ListPointer*;

    To illustrate the basic steps in the construction of a linked list, suppose that the integers 83 and 47 have already been stored in a linked list

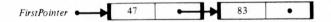

and we wish to add 95 to this list. In the construction, we use two pointers, *FirstPointer* to point to the first node in the list and *TempPointer* as a temporary pointer.

    var
      FirstPointer, TempPointer : *ListPointer*;

We first acquire a new node temporarily pointed to by *TempPointer*,

    new (TempPointer);

and store 95 in the data field of this record:

    TempPointer↑.*Data* := 95;

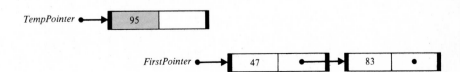

This node can then be joined to the list by setting its link field so that it points to the first node:

$TempPointer\uparrow.Next := FirstPointer;$

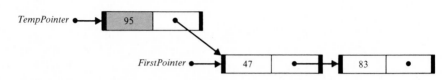

The pointer *FirstPointer* is then updated to point to this new node:

$FirstPointer := TempPointer;$

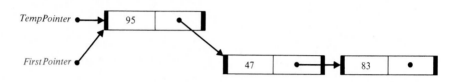

To construct the entire list, we could first initialize an empty list:

$FirstPointer :=$ **nil**;

and then repeat the preceding four statements three times, replacing 95 by 83 in the second assignment statement, then by 47, and finally using the value 95. In practice, however, such linked lists are usually constructed by reading the data values rather than assigning them by means of assignment statements. In this example, the linked list could be constructed by using the following program segment:

```
(* Initially the list is empty *)
FirstPointer := nil;

(* Read the data values and construct the list *)
while not eof do
  begin
    new (TempPointer);
    readln (TempPointer↑.Data);
    TempPointer↑.Next := FirstPointer;
    FirstPointer := TempPointer
  end (* while *);
```

Once a linked list has been constructed, we may want to **_traverse_** the list from beginning to end and display each element in it. In Chapter 8 we saw that to traverse a list stored in an array, we could easily move through the list from one element to the next by varying an array index in some repetition structure. The analog for a linked list is to move through the list by varying a pointer variable in a repetition structure.

To illustrate, suppose we wish to display the integers stored in the linked list

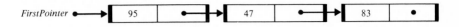

We begin by initializing a pointer variable *CurrPointer* to point to the first node

CurrPointer := *FirstPointer*;

and display the integer stored in this node:

writeln (*CurrPointer*↑.*Data*);

To move to the next node, we follow the link from the current node:

CurrPointer := *CurrPointer*↑.*Next*;

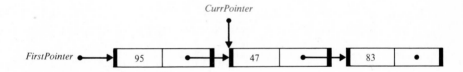

After displaying the integer in this node, we move to the next node

CurrPointer := *CurrPointer*↑.*Next*;

and display its data. Since we have now reached the last node, we need some way to signal this condition. But this is easy, for if we attempt to move to the next node, *CurrPointer* becomes nil:

The boolean condition *CurrPointer* <> **nil** can thus be used to control repetition in a **while** loop:

> *CurrPointer* := *FirstPointer*;
> **while** *CurrPointer* <> **nil do**
>   **begin**
>   *writeln* (*CurrPointer↑.Data*);
>   *CurrPointer* := *CurrPointer↑.Next*
>   **end** (* **while** *)

Also note that this program segment correctly traverses an empty list, since in this case, *FirstPointer* is nil and the **while** loop is bypassed.

The program in Figure 13.1 uses these techniques for constructing and traversing a linked list to reverse the characters in a string. It reads a sequence of characters and stores them in a linked list, adding each character to the beginning of the list as it is read. When the special symbol $ is read, signaling the end of the string, the list is traversed. Since the last characters read are at the beginning of the list, they are displayed in reverse order. (The Last-In-First-Out processing suggests an alternative to the array implementation of stacks described in Exercise 8 of Section 8.3. Linked stacks and queues are considered in the next chapter.)

```
PROGRAM ReverseAString (input, output);

(***********************************************************************

    Program to reverse a string by reading characters and adding them
    to the beginning of a linked list until the end-of-string mark ($)
    is read, then traversing the list and displaying the characters.

***********************************************************************)

CONST
    EndMark = '$';                    (* marks the end of the string *)

TYPE
    DataType = char;
    ListPointer = ↑ListNode;
    ListNode = RECORD
                    Data : DataType;
                    Next : ListPointer
                END;

VAR
    FirstPointer : ListPointer;   (* pointer to first node in linked list *)
    Symbol : char;                (* current character from string or list *)
```

Figure 13.1

Figure 13.1 (cont.)

```
PROCEDURE AddToList (VAR FirstPointer : ListPointer; Element : DataType);

   (*********************************************************************

      Procedure to add Element at beginning of linked list pointed
      to by FirstPointer.  New value of FirstPointer is returned.

   *********************************************************************)

   VAR
      TempPointer: ListPointer;  (* temporary pointer *)

   BEGIN (* AddToList *)
      new (TempPointer);
      TempPointer↑.Data := Element;
      TempPointer↑.Next := FirstPointer;
      FirstPointer := TempPointer
   END (* AddToList *);

PROCEDURE Traverse (FirstPointer : ListPointer);

   (*********************************************************************

      Procedure to traverse linked list pointed to by FirstPointer,
      displaying each element in the list.

   *********************************************************************)

   VAR
      CurrPointer: ListPointer;  (* temporary pointer *)

   BEGIN (* Traverse *)
      CurrPointer := FirstPointer;
      WHILE CurrPointer <> NIL DO
         BEGIN
          write (CurrPointer↑.Data);
          CurrPointer := CurrPointer↑.Next
         END (* WHILE *);
       writeln
   END (* Traverse *);

   BEGIN (* main program *)

      (* Initialize empty list *)

      FirstPointer := NIL;

      (* Read the string, adding each character at front of the list *)

      writeln ('Enter the string to be reversed:');
      read (Symbol);
      WHILE Symbol <> EndMark DO
         BEGIN
            AddToList (FirstPointer, Symbol);
            read (Symbol)
         END (* WHILE *);
      readln;
```

Figure 13.1 (cont.)

```
    (* Now traverse the list and display the characters *)

    writeln;
    writeln ('Reversed string:');
    Traverse (FirstPointer)
END (* main program *).
```

Sample runs:

```
Enter the string to be reversed:
Kelloggs Cornflakes$

Reversed string:
sekalfnroC sggolleK



Enter the string to be reversed:
able was I ere I saw elba$

Reversed string:
able was I ere I saw elba
```

13.3   Processing Unordered Linked Lists

In Chapter 8 we used arrays to store and process lists, and observed that although this was a good implementation for static lists, it was not efficient for dynamic ones. The fixed size of an array limits the size of the list and the array may become full, so that no more insertions are possible. We also noted that inserting a new item into a list required moving array elements to make room for it, and deleting an item required shifting array elements to fill the position vacated by this item. In this section we show how these problems of size limitation and movement of list elements can be avoided by using linked lists.

The type declarations we have used to define linked lists have had the general form

```
type
    DataType = . . . ; (* type of data to be stored in list nodes *)
    ListPointer = ↑ListNode;
    ListNode = record
                     Data : DataType;
                     Next : ListPointer
               end;
```

Here *DataType* represents the type of the data items to be stored in the linked list. It might be a simple type like *integer* or *char,* as in the examples of the preceding section, but it may in fact be any type. In particular, it may be a record if several items of information are to be stored in each node. For example, to define a linked list of employee records containing an employee number and an hourly rate, we might use the following declarations:

```
type
    EmployeeRecord = record
                         Number : integer;
                         HourlyRate : real
                     end;
    DataType = EmployeeRecord;
    ListPointer = ↑ListNode;
    ListNode = record
                   Data : DataType;
                   Next : ListPointer
               end;
```

Suppose also that the following variables have been declared;

```
var
    FirstPointer, CurrPointer : ListPointer;
    EmpNumber : integer;
    NewRate : real;
    Found : boolean;
```

Access to this list of records is by means of the pointer *FirstPointer*, which points to the first employee record:

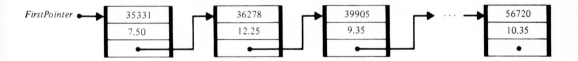

To traverse this list and display the employee records, we might use

```
CurrPointer := FirstPointer;
while CurrPointer <> nil do
    begin
        with CurrPointer↑.Data do
            writeln ('Number:', EmpNumber:6,'   Rate: $', HourlyRate:4:2);
        CurrPointer := CurrPointer↑.Next
    end (* while *)
```

Searching a linked list for a given item is done similarly. We initialize an auxiliary pointer to the first node and move through the list via the link fields until the desired node is found or we reach the end of the list. For example, to search the preceding linked list for the record of the employee whose number is *EmpNumber*, the following statements may be used:

```
Found := false;
CurrPointer := FirstPointer;
while (CurrPointer <> nil) and (not Found) do
   if CurrPointer↑.Data.Number = EmpNumber then
      Found := true
   else
      CurrPointer := CurrPointer↑.Next;
```

The preceding **while** loop is terminated when the desired record is found, in which case *CurrPointer* points to the node containing that record or the end of the list is reached and the record is not found; in this last case, *CurrPointer* has the value **nil.** If the record is found, the information in this record can be displayed:

```
if Found then
   writeln ('Hourly rate for employee ', EmpNumber:1, ' is ',
            CurrPointer↑.Data.HourlyRate:4:2)
else
   writeln ('Employee ', EmpNumber:1, ' not found')
```

or perhaps modified, for example, by changing the hourly rate:

```
if Found then
   CurrPointer↑.Data.HourlyRate := NewRate
else
   writeln ('Employee ', EmpNumber:1, ' not found')
```

The search technique we have used here is a ***linear search*** and is the only feasible searching strategy for linked lists. The more efficient binary search described in Section 8.3 for ordered lists implemented as arrays is not a real option for linked lists. Although ordered linked lists can be constructed, as we show in the next section, binary search is still not practical since it requires repeatedly accessing the middle element of the part of the list being searched, and this can be done efficiently only when each list element can be accessed directly. For a linked list, however, we have direct access only to the first node; to access any other node, we must traverse the first part of the list, following the links, until we reach that node. (In the next chapter we describe a ***multiply linked structure*** called a ***binary search tree*** in which a binary-like search is possible.)

In general, linked lists are preferred over arrays for processing dynamic lists whose sizes vary as items are added and deleted. This is because the number of nodes that a linked list may have is limited only by the available memory and because the insertion and deletion operations are easy to implement. Since we are considering unordered linked lists in this section, that is, lists in which the elements need not be arranged in a particular order, we can insert a new element at any convenient location in the list. And as we observed in the preceding section, inserting it at the beginning of the list is easy:

1. Obtain a new node and store the element in its data field.
2. Set the link field of this node to point to the first node in the list.
3. Reset the pointer *FirstPointer* to point to this new node.

The following procedure implements these steps.

> **procedure** *Insert* (**var** *FirstPointer* : *ListPointer*; *Element* : *DataType*);
>
> > (∗ Procedure to insert *Element* at the beginning of the linked list
> > pointed to by *FirstPointer*. The new pointer to the linked list is
> > returned. ∗)
>
> **var**
> > *TempPointer* : *ListPointer*; (∗ temporary pointer to a new node ∗)
>
> **begin** (∗ *Insert* ∗)
> > *new* (*TempPointer*);
> > *TempPointer*↑.*Data* := *Element*;
> > *TempPointer*↑.*Next* := *FirstPointer*;
> > *FirstPointer* := *TempPointer*
> **end** (∗ *Insert* ∗);

For deletion, there are two cases to consider: (1) deleting the first element
in the list and (2) deleting an element that has a predecessor. The first case is
easy and consists of the following steps, assuming that *CurrPointer* points to
the node to be deleted:

1. Set *FirstPointer* to point to the second node in the list.
2. Dispose of the node pointed to by *CurrPointer*.

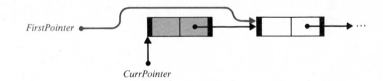

For the second case, suppose that the predecessor of the node to be deleted
is pointed to by *PredPointer:*

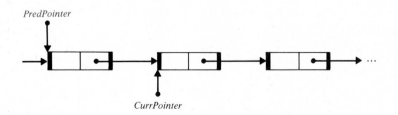

Deletion is accomplished by setting the link field of the node pointed to by
PredPointer so that it points to the successor of the node to be deleted:

$PredPointer\uparrow.Next := CurrPointer\uparrow.Next;$

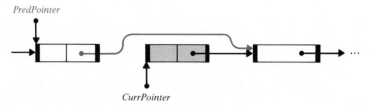

CurrPointer

As these diagrams illustrate, a delete procedure requires the two pointers *CurrPointer* to the node to be deleted and *PredPointer* to its predecessor. These pointers can be positioned with the following procedure *Search*, which advances *CurrPointer* through a linked list until it points to the desired item or reaches the end of the list; *PredPointer* follows *CurrPointer* through the list, always pointing to the predecessor of the node pointed to by *CurrPointer*.

procedure *Search* (*FirstPointer* : *ListPointer*; *Item* : *DataType*;
      var *PredPointer*, *CurrPointer* : *ListPointer*;
      var *Found* : *boolean*);

(∗ Procedure to search a linked list having first node pointed to by
   FirstPointer for a node containing *Item*. If the item is not found,
   Found is returned as false; otherwise, *CurrPointer* points to the
   first node containing the item and *PredPointer* points to its
   predecessor or is nil if there is none. ∗)

begin (∗ *Search* ∗)
   CurrPointer := *FirstPointer*;
   PredPointer := **nil**;
   Found := *false*;
   while (**not** *Found*) **and** (*CurrPointer* <> **nil**) **do**
     if *CurrPointer*↑.*Data* = *Item* **then**
       Found := *true*
     else
       begin
         PredPointer := *CurrPointer*;
         CurrPointer := *CurrPointer*↑.*Next*
       end (∗ **else** ∗)
end (∗ *Search* ∗);

The following procedure *Delete* can then be used to implement the delete operation for general lists.

procedure *Delete* (**var** *FirstPointer* : *ListPointer*; *Item* : *DataType*);

(∗ Procedure to delete a specified *Item* from a linked list with first
   node pointed to by *FirstPointer*. ∗)

var
   CurrPointer,   (∗ pointer to node containing *Item* ∗)
   PredPointer : *ListPointer*;   (∗ pointer to its predecessor ∗)
   Found : *boolean*;   (∗ indicates if *Item* found ∗)

```
begin (* Delete *)
    Search (FirstPointer, Item, PredPointer, CurrPointer, Found);
    if Found then
        begin
            if PredPointer = nil then (* first node to be deleted *)
                FirstPointer := FirstPointer↑.Next
            else                              (* node has a predecessor *)
                PredPointer↑.Next := CurrPointer↑.Next;
            dispose (CurrPointer)
        end (* if *)
    else
        writeln ('Item not found in the list')
end (* Delete *);
```

13.4 Ordered Linked Lists

One of the important data-processing problems we have considered on several occasions is that of sorting a list of items. In each of our examples, these items were stored in an array, since direct access to each element of the array was required to use the sorting techniques we considered. As we have seen, however, an array is not the best data structure to use for dynamic lists; for if an item is inserted into a sorted array, all the array elements following it must be moved to make room for it, and when an element is deleted, all elements following it must be moved forward, or a "hole" results. Maintaining an ordered list whose contents change frequently because of insertions and deletions is done more efficiently by using an ordered linked list.

An **ordered linked list** is a linked list in which the nodes are linked in such a way that the items stored in the nodes occur in ascending (or descending) order as the list is traversed. If the data part of a node is a record, then one of the fields in this record is designated as the **key field,** and the ordering is based on the values that appear in this field.

To insert an element into a linked list, we first obtain a new node temporarily accessed via a pointer *TempPointer*

```
new (TempPointer);
```

and store the element in its data field

```
TempPointer↑.Data := Element;
```

There are now two cases to consider: (1) inserting the element at the beginning of the list and (2) inserting it after some specified element in the list. The first case is simply the insert operation considered in the preceding section. For the second case, suppose that the new node is to be inserted between the nodes pointed to by *PredPointer* and *CurrPointer:*

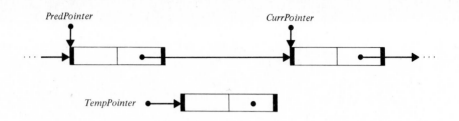

Insertion is accomplished by setting the pointer in the link field of the new node to point to the node pointed to by *CurrPointer*

$$TempPointer\uparrow.Next := CurrPointer;$$

and then resetting the pointer in the link field of the node pointed to by *PredPointer* to point to the new node

$$PredPointer\uparrow.Next := TempPointer;$$

The following diagram illustrates:

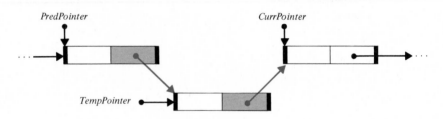

Assuming type declarations of the form

```
type
    DataType = record (* type of data part of nodes *)
                  ⋮
                  Key : KeyType;
                  ⋮
               end;
    ListPointer = ↑ListNode;
    ListNode = record
                  Data : DataType;
                  Next : ListPointer
               end;
```

we can use the following procedure *OrderedSearch* to position the pointers *PredPointer* and *CurrPointer*. It advances *CurrPointer* through an ordered linked list until either it reaches the first node containing a value in its key field that is greater than or equal to the item sought or it reaches the end of the list.

```
procedure OrderedSearch (FirstPointer : ListPointer; Item : KeyType;
                         var PredPointer, CurrPointer : ListPointer;
                         var Found : boolean);
```

(∗ Procedure to search an ordered linked list having first node pointed
to by *FirstPointer* for a node containing *Item* in its key field or for
a position to insert a new node. *CurrPointer* points to the first
node containing key value >= *Item* or is **nil** if *Item* follows all
keys in the list. *PredPointer* points to its predecessor or is **nil** if
Item precedes all keys in the list. *Found* is returned as true if *Item*
is already in the list. This procedure assumes that the key fields
are in ascending order; for descending order, change >= to <=
in the **if** statement. ∗)

```
var
    DoneSearching : boolean; (* indicates when search is complete *)
begin (* OrderedSearch *)
    CurrPointer := FirstPointer;
    PredPointer := nil;
    Found := false;
    DoneSearching := false;
    while (not DoneSearching) and (CurrPointer <> nil) do
        if CurrPointer↑.Data.Key >= Item then
            begin
                DoneSearching := true;
                Found := (CurrPointer↑.Data.Key = Item)
            end (* if *)
        else
            begin
                PredPointer := CurrPointer;
                CurrPointer := CurrPointer↑.Next
            end (* else *)
end (* OrderedSearch *);
```

The following procedure *Insert* uses this procedure to position the required
pointers correctly and then inserts a specified element using the techniques
described earlier.

procedure *Insert* (**var** *FirstPointer* : *ListPointer*; *Element* : *DataType*);

(∗ Procedure to insert *Element* into an ordered linked list having first
node pointed to by *FirstPointer*. This element is to be inserted
between the nodes pointed to by *PredPointer* and *CurrPointer*. A
nil value for *PredPointer* indicates insertion at the beginning of the
list. A value of true for *Found* indicates that there is already a
node containing *Element.Key* in its key field; no new node is then
inserted into the list. ∗)

```
var
    PredPointer,
    CurrPointer,
    TempPointer : ListPointer; (* pointer to new node *)
    Found : boolean;
```

```
begin (* Insert *)
    OrderedSearch (FirstPointer, Element.Key,
                        PredPointer, CurrPointer, Found);
    if Found then
        writeln ('Item already in the list')
    else
        begin
            new (TempPointer);
            TempPointer↑.Data := Element;
            if PredPointer = nil then (* insert at beginning of list *)
                begin
                    TempPointer↑.Next := FirstPointer;
                    FirstPointer := TempPointer
                end (* if *)
            else                              (* there is a predecessor *)
                begin
                    TempPointer↑.Next := CurrPointer;
                    PredPointer↑.Next := TempPointer
                end (* else *)
        end (* else *)
    end (* Insert *);
```

For an ordered linked list, the deletion operation is essentially the same as for unordered lists. The procedure *Delete* of the preceding section can be used if we replace the call to procedure *Search* with a call to *OrderedSearch*.

```
procedure Delete ( var FirstPointer : ListPointer; Item : KeyType);

    (* Procedure to delete a specified Item from an ordered linked list with
       first node pointed to by FirstPointer. *)

    var
        CurrPointer,                  (* pointer to node containing Item *)
        PredPointer : ListPointer;    (* pointer to its predecessor *)
        Found : boolean;              (* indicates if Item found *)

    begin (* Delete *)
        OrderedSearch (FirstPointer, Item, PredPointer, CurrPointer,
                        Found);
        if Found then
            begin
                if PredPointer = nil then (* first node to be deleted *)
                    FirstPointer := FirstPointer↑.Next
                else                          (* node has a predecessor *)
                    PredPointer↑.Next := CurrPointer↑.Next;
                dispose (CurrPointer)
            end (* if *)
        else
            writeln ('Item not found in the list')
    end (* Delete *);
```

The program in Figure 13.2 uses the procedures *OrderedSearch, Insert,* and *Delete* to maintain an ordered linked list of employee records, each of which contains an employee's number, age, number of dependents, and hourly pay rate. This list is ordered so that employee numbers are in ascending order. The program first calls the procedure *Initialize* to create the ordered linked list by reading the records from the file *EmpFile* and repeatedly calling procedure *Insert* to construct the initial ordered linked list. The user then selects from a menu of options for deleting, inserting, or modifying an employee record or for terminating processing. When the last option is selected, the updated list is copied back into *EmpFile*. The structure of the program is displayed in the following structure diagram. (Recall that a shaded corner in a box indicates a procedure that is shared by two or more program units.)

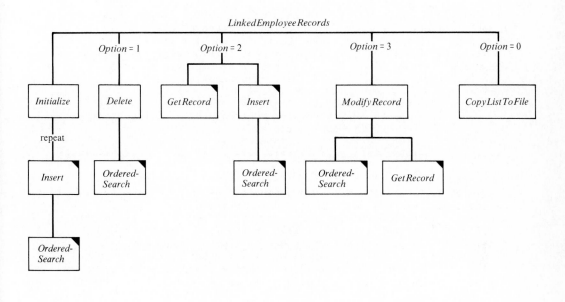

```
PROGRAM LinkedEmployeeRecords (input, output, EmpFile);

(********************************************************************

    Program to process employee records.  Options are displayed
    by procedure PrintMenu.  The records are stored in an ordered
    linked list; employee names are in alphabetical order.

*****************************************************************)

CONST
    NumberOfOptions = 3;            (* number of options in menu *)
```

Figure 13.2

Figure 13.2 (cont.)

```
TYPE
   EmployeeRecord = RECORD
                          Number, Age, Dependents : integer;
                          HourlyRate : real
                     END;
   EmployeeFile = FILE of EmployeeRecord;
   DataType = EmployeeRecord;
   KeyType = integer;
   ListPointer = ↑ListNode;
   ListNode = RECORD
                   Data : DataType;
                   Next : ListPointer
              END;

VAR
   FirstPointer : ListPointer;      (* pointer to first employee record *)
   Option : integer;                (* option selected by user *)
   EmpRecord : EmployeeRecord;      (* record for an employee *)
   EmpFile : EmployeeFile;          (* permanent file of employee records *)
   EmpNumber : integer;             (* number of an employee *)
   Response : char;                 (* user response *)

PROCEDURE OrderedSearch (FirstPointer : ListPointer; Item : KeyType;
                         VAR PredPointer, CurrPointer : ListPointer;
                         VAR Found : boolean);

   (************************************************************************

      Procedure to search an ordered linked list having first node
      pointed to by FirstPointer for a node containing Item in its key
      (employee) field or for a position to insert a new node.
      CurrPointer points to the first node containing key value >= Item
      or is NIL if Item follows all keys in the list.  PredPointer
      points to its predecessor or is NIL if Item precedes all keys
      in the list.  Found is returned as true if Item is already in the
      list.  This procedure assumes that the key fields are in ascending
      order; for descending order, change >= to <= in the IF statement.

   ************************************************************************)

   VAR
      DoneSearching : boolean;  (* indicates when search is complete *)

   BEGIN (* OrderedSearch *)
      CurrPointer := FirstPointer;
      PredPointer := NIL;
      DoneSearching := false;
      Found := false;
      WHILE (NOT DoneSearching) AND (CurrPointer <> NIL) DO
         IF CurrPointer↑.Data.Number >= Item THEN
            BEGIN
               DoneSearching := true;
               Found := CurrPointer↑.Data.Number = Item
            END (* If *)
         ELSE
            BEGIN
               PredPointer := CurrPointer;
               CurrPointer := CurrPointer↑.Next
            END (* ELSE *)
   END (* OrderedSearch *);
```

Figure 13.2 (cont.)

```
PROCEDURE Insert (VAR FirstPointer : ListPointer; Element : DataType);

   (*******************************************************************

       Procedure to insert Element into an ordered linked list having
       first node pointed to by FirstPointer.  This element is to be
       inserted between the nodes pointed to by PredPointer and
       CurrPointer.  A NIL value for PredPointer indicates insertion
       at the beginning of the list.  A value of true for Found
       indicates that there is already a node containing Element.Key
       in its key field; no new node is then inserted into the list.

   *******************************************************************)

   VAR
      PredPointer,
      CurrPointer,
      TempPointer: ListPointer;   (* pointer to new node *)
      Found : boolean;

   BEGIN (* Insert *)
      OrderedSearch (FirstPointer, Element.Number,
                     PredPointer, CurrPointer, Found);
      IF Found THEN
         writeln ('Item already in the list')
      ELSE
         BEGIN
            new (TempPointer);
            TempPointer↑.Data := Element;
            IF PredPointer = NIL THEN  (* insert at beginning of list *)
               BEGIN
                  TempPointer↑.Next := FirstPointer;
                  FirstPointer := TempPointer
               END (* IF *)
            ELSE                         (* there is a predecessor *)
               BEGIN
                  TempPointer↑.Next := CurrPointer;
                  PredPointer↑.Next := TempPointer
               END (* ELSE *)
         END (* ELSE *)
   END (* Insert *);

PROCEDURE Initialize (VAR EmpFile : EmployeeFile;
                      VAR FirstPointer : ListPointer);

   (*******************************************************************

       Procedure to read employee records from EmpFile and construct
       linked list of these records with first record pointed to by
       FirstPointer.

   *******************************************************************)
```

Figure 13.2 (cont.)

```
BEGIN (* Initialize *)
    reset (EmpFile);
    FirstPointer := NIL;
    WHILE NOT eof(EmpFile) DO
        BEGIN
            Insert (FirstPointer, EmpFile↑);
            get (EmpFile)
        END (* WHILE *)
END (* Initialize *);

PROCEDURE Delete (VAR FirstPointer : ListPointer; Item : KeyType);

    (**************************************************************

        Procedure to delete a specified Item from an ordered linked
        list with first node pointed to by FirstPointer.

    **************************************************************)

    VAR
        CurrPointer,                (* pointer to node containing Item *)
        PredPointer : ListPointer; (* pointer to its predecessor *)
        Found : boolean;            (* indicates if Item found *)

    BEGIN (* Delete *)
        OrderedSearch (FirstPointer, Item, PredPointer, CurrPointer, Found);
        IF Found THEN
            BEGIN
                IF PredPointer = NIL THEN     (* first node to be deleted *)
                        FirstPointer := FirstPointer↑.Next
                    ELSE                       (* node has a predecessor *)
                        PredPointer↑.Next := CurrPointer↑.Next;
                dispose (CurrPointer)
            END (* IF *)
        ELSE
            writeln ('Item not found in the list')
    END (* Delete *);

PROCEDURE GetRecord (VAR EmpRecord : EmployeeRecord);

    (**************************************************************

        Procedure to get record of an employee from the user

    **************************************************************)

    BEGIN (* GetRecord *)
        writeln ('Enter employee''s number, age, dependents, and hourly rate:');
        WITH EmpRecord DO
            readln (Number, Age, Dependents, HourlyRate)
    END (* GetRecord *);

PROCEDURE ModifyRecord (FirstPointer : ListPointer);

    (**************************************************************

        Procedure to modify record of a specified employee

    **************************************************************)
```

Figure 13.2 (cont.)

```
    VAR
        EmpNumber : integer;              (* employee's number *)
        CurrPointer,                      (* pointer to old record *)
        PredPointer : ListPointer;        (* and its predecessor *)
        Found : boolean;                  (* indicates if record was found *)

    BEGIN (* ModifyRecord *)
        write ('Employee''s number?  ');
        readln (EmpNumber);
        OrderedSearch (FirstPointer, EmpNumber, PredPointer, CurrPointer, Found);
        IF Found THEN
            WITH CurrPointer↑.Data DO
                BEGIN
                    writeln ('Age: ', Age:1, '    Dependents: ', Dependents:1,
                                '    Hourly Rate:  $', HourlyRate:4:2);
                    write ('Enter new age, dependents, and hourly rate:  ');
                    readln (Age, Dependents, HourlyRate)
                END (* WITH *)
        ELSE
            writeln ('Employee ', EmpNumber:1, ' not found')
    END (* ModifyRecord *);

PROCEDURE CopyListToFile (FirstPointer: ListPointer;
                          VAR EmpFile : EmployeeFile);

    (*******************************************************************

        Procedure to write the list pointed to by FirstPointer to EmpFile

        *****************************************************************)

    VAR
        CurrPointer: ListPointer;    (* pointer to current node *)

    BEGIN (* CopyListToFile *)
        rewrite (EmpFile);
        CurrPointer := FirstPointer;
        WHILE CurrPointer <> NIL DO
            BEGIN
                write (EmpFile, CurrPointer↑.Data);
                CurrPointer := CurrPointer↑.Next
            END (* WHILE *)
    END (* CopyListToFile *);

    BEGIN (* main program *)
        Initialize (EmpFile, FirstPointer);
        REPEAT
            writeln ('To delete, add, or modify an employee''s record, enter');
            write   ('    1       2    or   3    (0 to quit):  ');
            readln (Option);
```

Figure 13.2 (cont.)

```
        IF Option in [0..NumberOfOptions] THEN
            CASE Option OF
                0 : CopyListToFile (FirstPointer, EmpFile);
                1 : BEGIN
                        write ('Number of employee to be deleted:  ');
                        readln (EmpNumber);
                        write ('Sure (Y or N)?  ');
                        readln (Response);
                        IF Response in ['Y', 'y'] THEN
                            Delete (FirstPointer, EmpNumber);
                    END (* case 1 *);
                2 : BEGIN
                        GetRecord (EmpRecord);
                        Insert (FirstPointer, EmpRecord)
                    END (* case 2 *);
                3 : ModifyRecord (FirstPointer)
            END (* CASE *)
        ELSE
            writeln ('*** Illegal Option ***');
        writeln
    UNTIL Option = 0
END (* main program *).
```

```
Sample run:


To delete, add, or modify an employee's record, enter
      1      2   or   3     (0 to quit):  3
Employee's number?  1112
Employee 1112 not found

To delete, add, or modify an employee's record, enter
      1      2   or   3     (0 to quit):  3
Employee's number?  1111
Age: 39   Dependents: 3   Hourly Rate:  $10.50
Enter new age, dependents, and hourly rate:  4439 3 10.75

To delete, add, or modify an employee's record, enter
      1      2   or   3     (0 to quit):  2
Enter employee's number, age, dependents, and hourly rate:
3137 44 2 11.25

To delete, add, or modify an employee's record, enter
      1      2   or   3     (0 to quit):  1
Number of employee to be deleted:  2222
Sure (Y or N)?  Y

To delete, add, or modify an employee's record, enter
      1      2   or   3     (0 to quit):  4
*** Illegal Option ***

To delete, add, or modify an employee's record, enter
      1      2   or   3     (0 to quit):  0
```

Exercises

In these exercises, the files *InventoryFile, StudentFile,* and *UsersFile* should be processed as files of records. For descriptions of these files, see Appendix E.

1. Assume the following declarations:

> **var**
>> *X : integer;*
>> *P1, P2 :* ↑*integer;*
>> *Q1, Q2 :* ↑*real;*

What (if anything) is wrong with each of the following statements?

(a) *writeln (P1);*   **(b)** *readln (P1*↑*);*

(c) *P1 := Q1;*   **(d)** *new (X);*

(e) if *P1*↑ = **nil then**   **(f) begin**
       Q1 := Q2;   *P1*↑ *:=* 17*;*
                                    new (P1)
                                end

2. Write type declarations needed to construct a linked list of records from

(a) *InventoryFile*   **(b)** *StudentFile*   **(c)** *UsersFile*

3. Write a function to count the nodes in a linked list.

4. Write a boolean-valued function that determines whether the data items in a linked list are arranged in ascending order.

5. Write a function that returns a pointer to the last node in a linked list having first node pointed to by *FirstPointer.*

6. Write a procedure to reverse a linked list; that is, the last node becomes the first node and all links between nodes are reversed.

7. Modify procedures *Insert* and *Delete* so that they require only the pointer *PredPointer* to the predecessor of the item to be inserted or deleted rather than the two pointers *PredPointer* and *CurrPointer.* Also, write a function *Predecessor* that searches the linked list and returns this pointer.

8. The procedures *Insert* and *Delete* given in the text require checking to see whether the item to be inserted or deleted has a predecessor in the list. These procedures can be shortened if we require every linked list to have a dummy node, called a **head node,** at the beginning of the list so that the first node that stores the actual data has the head node as a predecessor. Modify the procedures *Insert* and *Delete* for linked lists having head nodes.

9. The method of successive division for converting a base-10 number to base b described in Exercise 12 of Section 1.3 produces the digits of the base-b representation in reverse order. Write a program implementing this algorithm to convert a base-10 integer to base b; use a linked list to store the digits so they can be printed in the usual left-to-right order.

10. Suppose that jobs entering a computer system are assigned a job number and a priority from 0 through 9. The numbers of jobs awaiting execution by the system are kept in a *priority queue.* A job entered into this queue is placed ahead of all jobs of lower priority but after all those of equal or higher priority. Write a program to read one of the letters R (remove), A (add), or L (list). For R, remove the first item in the queue; for A, read a job number and priority and then add it to the priority queue in the manner just described; for L, list all the job numbers in the queue. Maintain the priority queue as a linked list.

11. Write a program to read the records from *StudentFile* and construct five linked lists of records containing a student's name, number, and cumulative GPA, one list for each class. Each list is to be an ordered linked list in which the names are in alphabetical order. After the lists have been constructed, print each of them with appropriate headings.

12. A *polynomial of degree n* has the form

$$a_n x^n + a_{n-1} x^{n-1} + \cdots + a_1 x + a_0$$

where $a_0, a_1, \ldots, a_n$ are numeric constants called the *coefficients* of the polynomial and $a_n \neq 0$. For example,

$$5x^4 - 7x^3 + 3x + 1$$

is a polynomial of degree 4 with integer coefficients.

(a) Develop an ordered linked list that can represent any such polynomial. Let each node store a nonzero coefficient and the corresponding exponent.

(b) Write a program to read the nonzero coefficients and exponents of a polynomial, construct its linked representation, and then print it using the usual mathematical format with x^n written as $x \uparrow n$. The program should then read values for x and evaluate the polynomial for each of them.

13. Write a program that reads the nonzero coefficients and exponents of two polynomials, possibly of different degrees, stores them in linked lists (as described in Exercise 12), and then calculates and displays their sum and product.

14. The number of elements in an ordered list may grow so large that searching the list, always beginning with the first node, is not efficient. One way to improve efficiency is to maintain several smaller linked lists with an array of pointers to the first nodes of these lists. Write a

program to read several lines of upper-case text and to produce a ***text concordance,*** which is a list of all distinct words in the text. Store distinct words beginning with A alphabetically ordered in one linked list, those beginning with B in another, and so on. Use an array with subscripts of type 'A'..'Z', with each array element being a pointer to the first node in the list of words that begin with the corresponding subscript. After all the text lines have been read, print a listing of all these words in alphabetical order.

15. Modify the program of Exercise 14 so that the concordance also includes the frequency with which each word occurs in the text.

16. ***Directed graphs*** and their representations using adjacency matrices were described in Exercise 16 of Section 9.4.

(**a**) Imitating the construction in Exercise 14, develop a representation of a directed graph by using an array of pointers (one for each vertex) to linked lists containing the vertices that can be reached directly (following a single directed arc) from the vertex corresponding to the subscript.

(**b**) Draw a diagram showing the linked representation for the following directed graph:

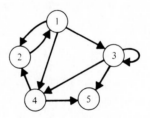

(**c**) Write a program to read the numbers (or names) of the vertices of a directed graph and ordered pairs of vertices representing the directed arcs, construct the linked representation for the digraph, and then use it to display the adjacency matrix.

17. In Chapter 9 we represented matrices by two-dimensional arrays. For a ***sparse matrix,*** that is, one with few nonzero entries, this is not an efficient representation.

(**a**) Imitating the construction in Exercise 14, develop a representation for a sparse matrix by using one ordered linked list for each row and an array of pointers to the first nodes in these lists. Do not store zero entries of the matrix. (*Hint:* Store a matrix entry and the number of the column in which it appears.)

(**b**) Write a program to read the nonzero entries of a sparse matrix and their locations in the matrix, and construct its linked representation. Then print the matrix in the usual table format with all entries (including 0's) displayed.

18. Extend the program of Exercise 17 to read two sparse matrices and calculate their sum and product. (see Section 9.4).

Programming Pointers

The variables that we have considered in previous chapters have as values specific data items such as integers, real numbers, characters, strings, sets, and records. Pointer variables, however, have memory addresses as values. Consequently, the manner in which pointer variables are used is quite different from that in which other kinds of variables are processed; thus, pointers can cause special difficulties for both beginning and experienced programmers. Pointers are used to create dynamic data structures, such as linked lists, which are processed in a way quite different from that in which static data structures, such as sets and arrays, are processed. The following are some of the main features to remember when using pointer variables and dynamic structures in Pascal programs.

1. *Each pointer variable is bound to a certain type; a pointer is the address of a memory location in which only a value of that type can be stored.* For example, if *P* and *Q* are pointer variables declared by

    type
        String = **packed array**[1..20] **of** *char*;

    var
        P : ↑*integer;*
        Q : ↑*String;*

    then *P* is bound to the type *integer* and *Q* to the specified type *String*. Memory locations pointed to by *P* can store only integers, whereas those to which *Q* points can store only strings of length 20.

2. *Because pointers have memory addresses as values, the operations that can be performed on them are limited.* Some of these limitations are as follows:

    - *The only values that may be assigned to a pointer variable using an assignment statement are the value* **nil** *or the value of another pointer variable bound to the same type.* Other values are assigned to pointers by using the procedure *new*, which obtains a memory location in which a value of the type to which the pointer is bound can be stored and assigns the address of this location to the pointer.
    - *Arithmetic operations cannot be performed on pointers.* For example, the values (memory addresses) of two pointer variables cannot be added, nor can a numeric value be added to the value of a pointer variable.
    - *Pointer values cannot be compared with the relational operators* <, <=, >, *and* >=. Only the relational operators = and <> are allowed, and then only to determine whether two pointers bound to

the same type point to the same memory location or to determine whether a pointer is nil.

- *Pointer values cannot be read or displayed.*
- *Pointers may be used as parameters in functions and procedures, but corresponding actual and formal parameters cannot be bound to different types.* Also, if pointer variable *P* of type ↑*integer* is used as a formal parameter of a function or procedure, it cannot be declared in the subprogram heading using

    . . . *P* : ↑*integer*; . . .

because the types of formal parameters must be specified using type identifiers. A type identifier must be associated with the pointer type ↑*integer*

    type
        IntegerPointer = ↑*integer*;

and this type identifier used to specify the type of *P*:

    . . . *P* : *IntegerPointer*; . . .

Similarly, the value of a function may be a pointer, but it must also be specified by a type identifier.

3. *The value of a pointer P is the address of a memory location, whereas the value of P↑ is the data item stored in that location.* For example, suppose that the pointer variable *P* is declared by

    var
        P : ↑*integer*;

The statement *writeln* (*P*) is not allowed, because the value (memory address) of a pointer cannot be displayed. The statement *writeln* (*P*↑) is valid, however, provided that *P* has been assigned to a memory location and a value has been stored in that location. This statement displays the integer stored in the location pointed to by *P*. Similarly, the statement *P* := *P* + 1 is not valid, but *P*↑ := *P*↑ + 1 is valid, assuming again that *P* has been assigned some memory location.

4. *An undefined pointer is not the same as a nil pointer.* A pointer becomes defined when it is assigned the address of a memory location or the value **nil.** Assigning a pointer the value **nil** is analogous to "blanking out" a character (or string) variable or "zeroing out" a numeric variable.

5. *If P is a pointer that is undefined or nil, then an attempt to use P↑ is an error.*

6. *Memory locations that were once associated with a pointer variable and that are no longer needed should be returned to the "storage pool" of available locations by using the procedure dispose.* Special care is required so that inaccessible memory locations are avoided. For example, if *P* and *Q* are pointer variables bound to the same type, the

assignment statement

$P := Q$

causes P to point to the same memory location as that pointed to by Q. Any memory location previously pointed to by P becomes inaccessible and cannot be disposed of properly unless it is pointed to by some other pointer. One should always use temporary pointers when necessary to maintain access, as in the following statements:

TempPointer := P;
$P := Q$;
dispose (*TempPointer*)

7. *Processing linked structures requires attention to special cases and to the problem of losing access to nodes.* Some errors commonly made when using linked lists include the following:

● *Attempting to process data items beyond the end of a linked list.* For example, consider the following attempt to search a nonempty linked list for a given item:

CurrPointer := *FirstPointer*;
while *CurrPointer*↑.*Data*<> *ItemSought* **do**
    CurrPointer := *CurrPointer*↑.*Next*;

If the item is not present in any node of the linked list, *CurrPointer* eventually reaches the last node in the list. *CurrPointer* then becomes nil, and an attempt is made to examine the *Data* field of a nonexistent node, resulting in an error message such as

*** Attempted access via NIL pointer ***

An attempted solution to the problem might be the following:

CurrPointer := *FirstPointer*;
while (*CurrPointer* <> **nil**) **and**
        (*CurrPointer*↑.*Data* <> *ItemSought*) **do**
    CurrPointer := *CurrPointer*↑.*Next*;

In most versions of Pascal this also results in an error if the item is not in the list. The reason is that boolean expressions are usually evaluated in their entirety. Thus, when the end of the list is reached and *CurrPointer* becomes nil, the second part of the boolean expression is evaluated, and an error results when an attempt is made to access the *Data* field of a nonexistent node.

Another attempt to avoid running past the end of a nonempty list might be the following:

Found := *false*;
CurrPointer := *FirstPointer*;
while *CurrPointer*↑.*Next* <> **nil do**
    if *CurrPointer*↑.*Data* = *ItemSought* **then**
        Found := *true*
    else
        CurrPointer := *CurrPointer*↑.*Next*;

Although this avoids the problem of moving beyond the end of the list, it fails to locate the desired item (that is, set *Found* to *true*) if this item is the last one in the list. When *CurrPointer* reaches the last node, the value of *CurrPointer↑.Next* is nil, and repetition is terminated without examining the *Data* field of this last node. Another problem is that if the item is found in the list, the remaining nodes (except the last) are also examined.

One solution is to use a boolean variable together with an end-of-list check to control the repetition:

Found := *false*;
CurrPointer := *FirstPointer*;
while (*CurrPointer*<> **nil**) **and** (**not** *Found*) **do**
   if *CurrPointer↑.Data* = *ItemSought* **then**
      Found := *true*
   else
      CurrPointer := *CurrPointer↑.Next*;

If the item is found in the list, then *Found* is set to *true* and repetition is terminated. If it is not in the list, *CurrPointer* eventually becomes nil and repetition terminates.

- *Attempting to access items in an empty list.* An example of this is the set of statements

CurrPointer := *FirstPointer*;
while *CurrPointer↑.Data* <> *ItemSought* **do**
   CurrPointer := *CurrPointer↑.Next*;

An error results if the list is empty—that is, if *FirstPointer* is nil—because the first value of *CurrPointer* is then nil and an attempt is made to examine a field in a nonexistent node. This is also the case with the following example:

Found := *false*;
CurrPointer := *FirstPointer*;
while *CurrPointer↑.Next* <> **nil do**
   if *CurrPointer↑.Data* = *ItemSought* **then**
      Found := *true*
   else
      CurrPointer := *CurrPointer↑.Next*;

For an empty list, *CurrPointer* is initially nil, and the *Next* field of a nonexistent node cannot be examined.

- *"Burning bridges before they are crossed,"* more precisely, *changing some link in a list before certain other links have been reset.* As an example, suppose that a node pointed to by *NewNodePointer* is to be inserted at the beginning of a list with first node pointed to by *FirstPointer*. The statements

FirstPointer := *NewNodePointer*;
NewNodePointer↑.Next := *FirstPointer*

are not used in the correct order. As soon as *FirstPointer* is set to

NewNodePointer, access to the remaining nodes in the list (those previously pointed to by *FirstPointer*) is lost. The second statement then simply sets the *Next* field of the node pointed to by *New-NodePointer* (and by *FirstPointer*) to point to the node itself. The new node must first be linked into the list before *FirstPointer* is reset:

NewNodePointer↑.Next : = *FirstPointer*;
FirstPointer : = *NewNodePointer*

Variations and Extensions

Most versions of Pascal process pointer variables as described for standard Pascal in this chapter. One exception is that some versions (Turbo) do not allow the special forms of reference to procedures *new* and *dispose* mentioned in the footnotes of Section 13.1 and described in Appendix F. Some versions (UCSD) may not even provide the procedure *dispose*, but rather require the use of other special predefined procedures for dynamic memory management.

14

Data Structures
and Algorithms

Algorithms + Data Structures = Programs

NIKLAUS WIRTH

*There is nothing more difficult to take in hand, more perilous to conduct,
or more uncertain in its success, than to take the lead in the introduction
of a new order of things.*

NICCOLÒ MACHIAVELLI, *The Prince*

We have now considered all of the Pascal statements, data types, procedures,
and functions, with the exception of a few seldom-used features that are described in Appendix F. The first seven chapters dealt mainly with designing
algorithms to solve problems and implementing these algorithms with Pascal
programs and subprograms. In Chapter 8 we noted that in many problems it is
necessary to organize the data in an appropriate data structure, and thus we
undertook a study of the **predefined data structures** provided in Pascal: arrays,
records, sets, and files. We have also seen that there are useful **user-defined**
or **higher-level data structures** that are not provided in the programming language being used and must therefore be implemented using those structures
that are available. In particular, in the preceding chapter we considered linked
lists and showed how they can be implemented in Pascal using pointers and
records. There are many other important user-defined data structures, and quite
often there are several ways to implement them. In this chapter we describe
some of the simpler ones and a few of their applications.

An important aspect of implementing a data structure is the design of
algorithms for the basic operations used to process the data. Although some
attention was paid to the efficiency of the algorithms in the preceding chapters,
most of them were designed to show as simply as possible the various features

513

of the Pascal language. In situations in which there are several algorithms that might be used, for example, in sorting and searching problems, some means of comparing them is necessary. Thus, in this chapter we also consider more carefully the design and analysis of algorithms and introduce some techniques for measuring their efficiency more precisely.

14.1 Stacks and Queues

To illustrate how the analysis of a problem leads to the organization of the data into a data structure, consider the following problems:

> *Problem 1.* A program is to be written to simulate a certain card game. One aspect of this simulation is to maintain a discard pile. On any turn, a player may discard a single card from his hand to the top of this pile or he may retrieve the top card from this discard pile. What data structure is needed to model this discard pile?

> *Problem 2.* A program is to be written to model a railroad switching yard. One part of the switching network consists of a main track and a siding onto which cars may be shunted and removed at any time (see Figure 14.1). What data structure can be used to model the operation of this siding?

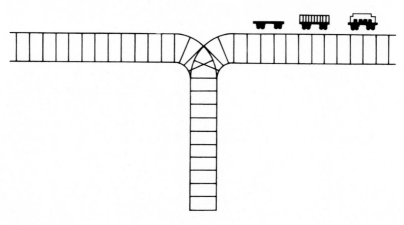

Figure 14.1

> *Problem 3.* One task that must be performed by a compiler is to scan an arithmetic expression containing parentheses to determine if these parentheses balance, that is, if each left parenthesis has exactly one matching right parenthesis. What data structure will facilitate this syntax checking?

Each of these problems involves a collection of related data items, a deck of cards in Problem 1, a set of railroad cars in Problem 2, and a collection of left and right parentheses in Problem 3. In Problem 1, the basic operations that must be performed are adding to and removing from the top of the discard pile. In Problem 2, the basic operations are pushing a car onto the siding and removing the last car placed on the siding. To solve Problem 3, we must scan the expression and temporarily store each left parenthesis until a right parenthesis is encountered. This right parenthesis matches the last left parenthesis that was stored, and thus that left parenthesis is removed from storage and the scan is continued.

In each case, we are led to a data structure in which items can be stored and retrieved in a *Last-In-First-Out* (*LIFO*) order, that is, the last item stored is the first item to be retrieved. Such a data structure is called a *stack* (or *push-down stack*) because it functions in the same manner as does a spring-loaded stack of plates or trays used in a cafeteria. Plates are added to the stack by pushing them onto the *top* of the stack. When a plate is removed from the top of the stack, the spring causes the next plate to pop up. For this reason, the store and retrieve operations for a stack are commonly called *push* and *pop,* respectively.

A stack can be viewed as a special kind of list in which one of the ends is designated as the top of the stack and access to the data items is restricted to this end of the list. Since we have used arrays to process lists, it should also be possible to implement this new data structure using arrays. Thus we might define a new type *StackType* and declare a stack variable *Stack* by

```
const
    StackLimit = 50;

type
    DataType = . . . ; (* type of data items *)
    StackType = array[1..StackLimit] of DataType;

var
    Stack : StackType;
```

and store the data items in the array *Stack*.

In an array, however, each item can be accessed directly, whereas in a stack, only the top item can be accessed. One way to make the array *Stack* operate as a stack is to designate the first position in the array as the top of the stack and adopt the convention that data items will be stored in and retrieved from only this position. For example, if the data items are characters, the sequence of stack operations

Push 'A', Push 'B', Push 'C', Pop

might be traced as follows:

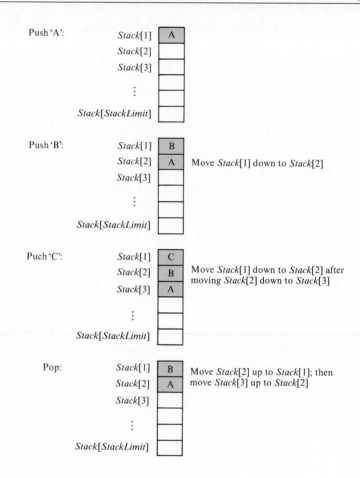

One drawback with implementing a stack with an array in this manner is one that we noted for array implementations of lists in general: the array elements must be moved each time a push (insert) or pop (delete) operation is performed. This difficulty can be eliminated by letting the stack grow from position 1 toward position *StackLimit,* but keeping a "pointer" *Top* to the current top of the stack and pushing and popping at this location. For this improved method of implementing a stack, we can use the declarations

const
    StackLimit = 50;

type
    DataType = . . . ; (* type of data items *)
    StackType = **array**[1..*StackLimit*] **of** *DataType*;

var
    Stack : *StackType*;
    Top : *integer*;

(An alternative approach would be to use a record containing two fields, *Top* and *Stack*.) An empty stack is signaled by *Top* = 0 and a full stack by *Top* = *StackLimit*. The preceding sequence of stack operations can then be pictured as follows:

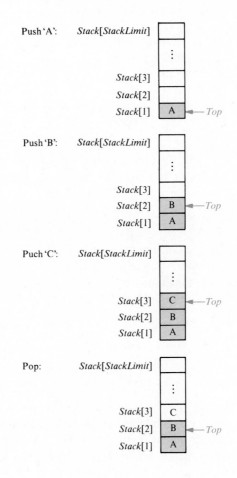

This implementation of a stack makes procedures for the stack operations push and pop easy to write. No movement of array elements is required; instead, the value of the variable *Top* need only be incremented or decremented appropriately. Since the array has a fixed size, however, one must check that the stack is not full before a push operation is performed. It is also necessary to check that the stack is not empty before performing a pop operation. Procedures for the push and pop operations are as follows:

procedure *Push* (**var** *Stack* : *StackType*; **var** *Top* : *integer*;
     Item : *DataType*; **var** *StackFull* : *boolean*);

 (* Procedure to push *Item* onto *Stack; Top* is the top of the stack.
 StackFull is set to true if stack is full. *)

```
begin (* Push *)
   if Top = StackLimit then
      StackFull := true
   else
      begin
         StackFull := false;
         Top := Top + 1;
         Stack[Top] := Item
      end (* else *)
end (* Push *);


procedure Pop (var Stack : StackType; var Top : integer;
                  var Item : DataType; var StackEmpty : boolean);
```

(* Procedure to pop and retrieve *Item* from *Top* of *Stack*. *StackEmpty* is set to true if the stack is empty. *)

```
begin (* Pop *)
   if Top = 0 then
      StackEmpty := true
   else
      begin
         StackEmpty := false;
         Item := Stack[Top];
         Top := Top - 1
      end (* else *)
end (* Pop *);
```

In some applications of stacks, a stack-full condition may be a nuisance or may even be intolerable, and we would prefer an implementation in which the stack can grow to any size. Since a linked list is a dynamic structure and a stack is a special kind of list, it should be possible to implement stacks using linked lists. In fact, it is more natural to use a linked list rather than an array to implement a stack, since only the first node in a linked list may be accessed directly.

To define such a **linked stack,** we can use type definitions similar to those in the preceding chapter

```
type
   DataType = . . . ; (* type of data part of nodes *)
   StackPointer = ↑StackNode;
   StackNode = record
                  Data : DataType;
                  Next : StackPointer
               end;
```

and declare a pointer to the top of the stack:

> **var**
>   *TopPointer* : *StackPointer*;

A linked stack of integers, for example, might then be pictured as follows:

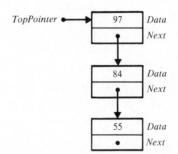

To push an item onto a linked stack, we simply insert it at the beginning of this linked list. A procedure to implement the push operation is therefore a simple modification of the procedure *Insert* described for unordered linked lists in Chapter 13:

> **procedure** *Push* (**var** *TopPointer* : *StackPointer*; *Item* : *DataType*);
>
>   (* Procedure to push *Item* onto the stack pointed to by *TopPointer*.
>   The new pointer to the top of the stack is returned. *)
>
> **var**
>   *TempPointer* : *StackPointer*; (* temporary pointer to new node *)
>
> **begin** (* *Push* *)
>   *new* (*TempPointer*);
>   *TempPointer↑.Data* := *Item*;
>   *TempPointer↑.Next* := *TopPointer*;
>   *TopPointer* := *TempPointer*
> **end** (* *Push* *);

The following diagram illustrates the procedure reference

> *Push* (*TopPointer*, 77)

for the preceding linked stack of integers:

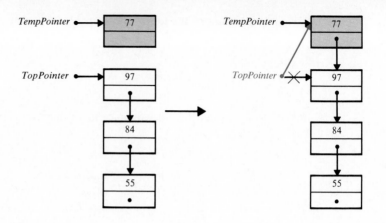

To pop an element from a linked stack, we first retrieve the data in the top node

$$Item := TopPointer\uparrow.Data;$$

and then remove this node from the stack by first setting a temporary pointer to it

$$TempPointer := TopPointer;$$

so that it can be properly disposed of later, and then resetting *TopPointer* to point to the next node in the stack:

$$TopPointer := TopPointer\uparrow.Next;$$

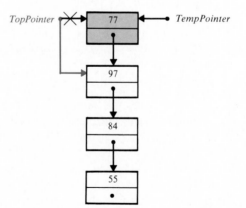

The procedure *dispose* can now be used to free this node for later allocation:

    dispose (*TempPointer*);

The following procedure uses these four statements to implement the pop operation:

    procedure *Pop* (**var** *TopPointer* : *StackPointer*; **var** *Item* : *DataType*;
                  var *StackEmpty* : *boolean*);

      (∗ Procedure to pop and return the top *Item* from the stack pointed to
      by *TopPointer*. If the stack is empty, true is returned for
      StackEmpty; otherwise false is returned as well as the new pointer
      to the top of the stack. ∗)

    var
      TempPointer : *StackPointer*;

    begin (∗ *Pop* ∗)
      if *TopPointer* = **nil then**
        StackEmpty := *true*
      else
        begin
          StackEmpty := *false*;
          Item := *TopPointer*↑.*Data*;
          TempPointer := *TopPointer*;
          TopPointer := *TopPointer*↑.*Next*;
          dispose (*TempPointer*)
        end (∗ **else** ∗)
    end (∗ *Pop* ∗);

Another important data structure is a *queue,* which is a list in which items may be added only at one end, called the *rear* or *back*, and removed only at the other end, called the *front* or *head.* This *First-In-First-Out* (*FIFO*) structure functions like a waiting line at a service facility; arriving customers enter the line at the rear, and when a customer reaches the front of the line, he or she is removed from the line and serviced.

In addition to many applications of queues to model waiting lines, queues play an important role in the design of computer systems, for example, in *input/output buffering.* Transfer of information from an input device or to an output device is a relatively slow operation. If processing of a program must be suspended while data items are transferred, program execution is slowed dramatically. The most common solution is to use sections of main memory known as *buffers* and to transfer data between the program and the buffers rather than between the program and the input/output device directly.

In particular, consider the problem in which data being processed by a program must be read from a file stored on a disk. This information is transferred from the disk file to an input buffer in main memory while the central processing unit (CPU) is performing some other task. When the program requires data, the next values stored in this buffer are retrieved. While these data items are being processed, additional data values can be transferred from the disk file to the buffer. Clearly, the buffer must be organized as a first-in-first-out structure, that is, as a queue. A queue-full condition signals that the buffer is full and no more data can be transferred from the disk file to it. A queue-empty condition indicates that the input buffer is empty and program execution is suspended while the operating system attempts to load more data into the buffer or signals the end of input.

Implementing queues with arrays requires a bit more ingenuity than for stacks. A first attempt might be to imitate what we did for stacks, using an array *Queue* indexed 1..*QueueLimit* and two integer variables *Front* and *Rear* to keep track of the front and rear of the queue, respectively. To add a new item to the queue, we would simply increment *Rear* by 1 and store the item in *Queue*[*Rear*]. Similarly, to remove an item, we would increment *Front* by 1. Eventually, however, *Rear* would "go off the end" of the array, and we would be forced to move all of the elements back to the beginning. A better implementation is to index the array beginning with 0 and increment *Front* and *Rear* using addition **mod** *QueueLimit*. The array might thus be viewed as being circular, with the first element following the last. (See Exercise 9 in Section 8.3.)

To implement a queue as a linked list, we might use two pointers, *FirstPointer* and *RearPointer,* declared as follows:

> **type**
> > *DataType* = . . . ; (* Type of data part of nodes *)
> > *QueuePointer* = ↑*QueueNode*;
> > *QueueNode* = **record**
> > > *Data* : *DataType*;
> > > *Next* : *QueuePointer*
> > **end**;
>
> **var**
> > *FrontPointer, RearPointer* : *QueuePointer*;

To illustrate, a linked queue containing the integers 573, 29, and 616 in this order might be pictured as follows:

Inserting the number 127 produces the following queue:

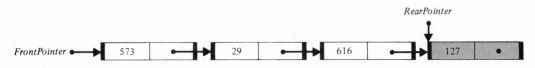

Procedures to implement the insert and delete operations for linked queues are left as exercises.

14.2   Application of Stacks: Reverse Polish Notation

The task of a compiler is to generate the machine language instructions required to carry out the instructions of the source program written in a high-level language (see Section 1.3). One part of this task is to generate the machine instructions for evaluating arithmetic expressions like that in the assignment statement

$$X := A * B + C$$

The compiler must generate machine instructions to:

1. Retrieve the value of A from the memory location where it is stored and load it into the accumulating register.
2. Retrieve the value of B and multiply it by the value in the accumulating register.
3. Retrieve the value of C and add it to the value in the accumulating register.
4. Store the value in the accumulating register in the memory location associated with X.

Arithmetic expressions are ordinarily written using **infix** notation like that above, in which the symbol for each binary operation is placed between the operands. In many compilers, the first step in evaluating such infix expressions is to transform them into **postfix** notation in which the operation symbol follows the operands; machine instructions are then generated to evaluate this postfix expression. Likewise, calculators commonly evaluate arithmetic expressions using postfix notation. The reason for this is that conversion from infix to postfix is straightforward and postfix expressions are in general easier to evaluate mechanically than infix expressions.

When infix notation is used for arithmetic expressions, parentheses are often needed to indicate the order in which operations are to be carried out. For example, parentheses are placed in the expression $2 * (3 + 4)$ to indicate that the addition is to be performed before the multiplication. If the parentheses were omitted, giving $2 * 3 + 4$, the standard priority rules would dictate that the multiplication is to be performed before the addition.

In the early 1950s, the Polish logician Jan Lukasiewicz observed that parentheses are not necessary in postfix notation, also called **Reverse Polish Notation** (**RPN**). For example, the infix expression

$$2 * (3 + 4)$$

can be written in RPN as

$$2 \ 3 \ 4 \ + \ *$$

To illustrate how such RPN expressions are evaluated, consider

$$1 \ 5 \ + \ 8 \ 4 \ 1 \ - \ - \ *$$

which corresponds to the infix expression $(1 + 5) * (8 - (4 - 1))$. This expression is scanned from left to right until an operator is found. At that point, the last two preceding operands are combined, using this operator. For our example, the first operator encountered is $+$, and its operands are 1 and 5, as indicated by the underline in the following:

$$\underline{1\ 5\ +}\ 8\ 4\ 1\ -\ -\ *$$

Replacing this subexpression with its value 6 yields the reduced RPN expression

$$6\ 8\ 4\ 1\ -\ -\ *$$

Resuming the left-to-right scan, we next encounter the operator $-$ and determine its two operands:

$$6\ 8\ \underline{4\ 1\ -}\ -\ *$$

Applying this operator then yields

$$6\ 8\ 3\ -\ *$$

The next operator encountered is another $-$ and its two operands are 8 and 3:

$$6\ \underline{8\ 3\ -}\ *$$

Evaluating this difference gives

$$6\ 5\ *$$

The final operator is $*$,

$$\underline{6\ 5\ *}$$

and the value 30 is obtained for this expression.

This method of evaluating an RPN expression requires that the operands be stored until an operator is encountered in the left-to-right scan; at this point, the last two operands must be retrieved and combined using this operation. This suggests that a LIFO structure, that is, a stack, should be used to store the operands. Each time an operand is encountered, it is pushed onto the stack. When an operator is encountered, the top two values are popped from the stack, the operator applied to them, and the result pushed back onto the stack. The following algorithm summarizes this procedure:

ALGORITHM TO EVALUATE RPN EXPRESSIONS

1. Initialize an empty stack.
2. Repeat the following until the end of the expression is encountered:
   a. Get the next *Token* (constant, variable, arithmetic operator) in the RPN expression.

b. If *Token* is an operand, push it onto the stack. If it is an operator, do the following:

(i) Pop the top two values from the stack. (If the stack does not contain two items, an error due to a malformed RPN expression has occurred and evaluation is terminated.)

(ii) Apply the operator *Token* to these two values.

(iii) Push the resulting value back onto the stack.

3. When the end of the expression is encountered, its value is on top of the stack (and in fact must be the only value in the stack).

Figure 14.2 illustrates this algorithm for the RPN expression

$$2\ 4\ *\ 9\ 5\ +\ -$$

The up-arrow ($\uparrow$) indicates the current token.

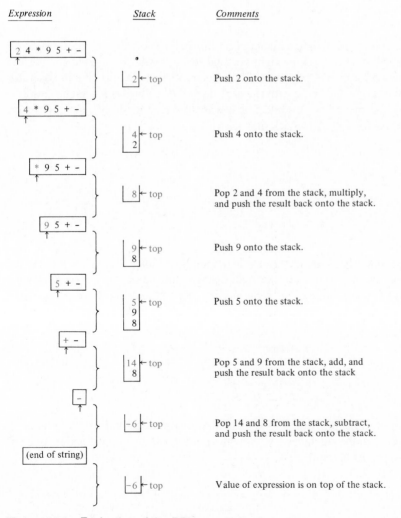

Figure 14.2   Evaluation of the RPN expression 2 4 $*$ 9 5 + −

To illustrate how a stack is also used in the conversion from infix to RPN, consider the infix expression

$$7 + 2 * 3$$

In a left-to-right scan of this expression, 7 is encountered and may be immediately displayed. Next, the operator + is encountered, but since its right operand has not yet been displayed, it must be stored and thus is pushed onto a stack of operators:

Output   Stack

7

Next, the operand 2 is encountered and displayed. At this point, it must be determined whether 2 is the right operand for the preceding operator + or the left operand for the next operator. This is determined by comparing the operator + on the top of the stack with the next operator *. Since * has higher priority than +, the preceding operand 2 that was displayed is the left operand for *; thus we push * onto the stack and search for its right operand:

Output   Stack

7 2   ⌊ * ⌋
                          ⌊ + ⌋

The operand 3 is encountered .next and displayed. Since the end of the expression has now been reached, the right operand for the operator * on the top of the stack has been found, so * can now be popped and displayed:

Output   Stack

7 2 3 *   ⌊ + ⌋

The end of the expression also signals that the right operand for the remaining operator + in the stack has been found, so it too can be popped and displayed, yielding the RPN expression

7 2 3 * +

Parentheses within infix expressions present no real difficulties. A left parenthesis indicates the beginning of a subexpression, and when encountered, it is pushed onto the stack. When a right parenthesis is encountered, operators are popped from the stack until the matching left parenthesis rises to the top. At this point, the subexpression originally enclosed by the parentheses has been converted to RPN, so the parentheses may be discarded and conversion continues. All of this is contained in the following algorithm:

ALGORITHM TO CONVERT INFIX EXPRESSIONS TO RPN

1. Initialize an empty stack.
2. Repeat the following until the end of the infix expression is reached.
   a. Get the next input *Token* (constant, variable, arithmetic operator, left parenthesis, right parenthesis) in the infix expression.
   b. If *Token* is

(i) a left parenthesis:	Push it onto the stack.
(ii) an operand:	Display it.
(iii) an operator:	If the stack is empty or *Token* has higher priority than the top stack element, push *Token* onto the stack.
	Otherwise, pop an operator from the stack and display it; then repeat the comparison of *Token* with the new top stack item.
	Note: a left parenthesis in the stack is assumed to have a lower priority than that of operators.
(iv) a right parenthesis:	Pop and display stack elements until a left parenthesis is on top of the stack. Pop it also, but do not display it.

3. When the end of the infix expression is reached, pop and display stack items until the stack is empty.

Figure 14.3 illustrates this algorithm for the infix expression

$$7 * 8 - (2 + 3)$$

An up-arrow ($\uparrow$) has been used to indicate the current input symbol and the symbol displayed by the algorithm. The program in Figure 14.4 implements this algorithm, using an array to store the stack of operators.

Expression	Stack	Output	Comments
7 * 8 − (2 + 3)			
	(empty)	7	Display 7
* 8 − (2 + 3)			
	* ← top	7	Stack *
8 − (2 + 3)			
	* ← top	7 8	Display 8
− (2 + 3)			
	(empty)	7 8 *	Pop and display *
	− ← top	7 8 *	Stack −
(2 + 3)			
	(← top	7 8 *	Stack (
2 + 3)			
	(← top / −	7 8 * 2	Display 2
+ 3)			
	+ ← top / (/ −	7 8 * 2	Stack +
3)			
	+ ← top / (/ −	7 8 * 2 3	Display 3
)			
	(← top / −	7 8 * 2 3 +	Pop and display +
	− ← top	7 8 * 2 3 +	Pop (
(end of string)			
	(empty)	7 8 * 2 3 + −	Pop and display −

Figure 14.3   Converting infix expression 7 * 8 − (2 + 3) to RPN.

```
PROGRAM InfixToRPN (input, output);

(*********************************************************************

    Program to convert an infix expression to Reverse Polish Notation.

*********************************************************************)

CONST
    MaxExpression = 80;         (* limit on expression length *)
    StackLimit = 50;            (* limit on stack size *)
    EndMark = ';';              (* marks end of infix expression *)

TYPE
    Expression = PACKED ARRAY[1..MaxExpression] OF char;
    DataType = char;
    StackType = PACKED ARRAY[0..StackLimit] OF DataType;

VAR
    Exp : Expression;           (* infix expression *)
    i : integer;                (* index of a token in Exp *)
    Response : char;            (* user response *)

PROCEDURE ConvertToRPN (Exp : Expression);

    (*******************************************************************

            Procedure to convert infix expression Exp to RPN.

    *******************************************************************)

    VAR
        Stack : StackType;          (* stack represented by an array *)
        Top,                        (* Stack[Top] is the top of the stack *)
        i : integer;                (* index *)
        StackFull,                  (* signals stack overflow *)
        StackEmpty,                 (* signals stack underflow *)
        Error,                      (* signals error in expression *)
        DonePopping : boolean;      (* signals when stack-popping is completed *)
        Token,                      (* a character in the expression *)
        TempToken : char;           (* temporary token *)

FUNCTION Priority (Operator : char) : integer;

    (*****************************************************************

        Function to find the priority of an arithmetic operator or (.

    *****************************************************************)

    BEGIN  (* Priority *)
        CASE Operator OF
                '(' : Priority := 0;
            '+', '-' : Priority := 1;
            '*', '/' : Priority := 2
        END (* CASE *)
    END (* Priority *);
```

Figure 14.4

Figure 14.4 (cont.)

```
PROCEDURE Push (VAR Stack : StackType; VAR Top : integer;
                Item : DataType; VAR StackFull : boolean);

   (*****************************************************************

       Procedure to push Item onto Stack; Top is the top of the
       the stack.  StackFull is set to true if stack is full.

   ****************************************************************)

   BEGIN (* Push *)
      IF Top = StackLimit THEN
         StackFull := true
      ELSE
         BEGIN
            StackFull := false;
            Top := Top + 1;
            Stack[Top] := Item
         END (* ELSE *)
   END (* Push *);

PROCEDURE Pop (VAR Stack : StackType; VAR Top : integer;
               VAR Item : DataType; VAR StackEmpty : boolean);

   (*****************************************************************

       Procedure to pop and retrieve Item from Top of Stack.
       StackEmpty is set to true if the stack is empty.

   ****************************************************************)

   BEGIN (* Pop *)
      IF Top = 0 THEN
         StackEmpty := true
      ELSE
         BEGIN
            StackEmpty := false;
            Item := Stack[Top];
            Top := Top - 1
         END (* ELSE *)
   END (* Pop *);

BEGIN (* ConvertToRPN *)

   (* Initialize an empty stack *)
   Top := 0;
   StackEmpty := true;
   Error := false;

   (* Begin the conversion to RPN *)
   i := 1;
   Token := Exp[1];
   WHILE (Token <> EndMark) AND NOT Error DO
      BEGIN
         IF Token <> ' ' THEN                     (* skip blanks *)
            IF Token = '(' THEN                    (* left parenthesis *)
               Push (Stack, Top, Token, Error)
```

Figure 14.4 (cont.)

```
      ELSE IF Token = ')' THEN                (* right parenthesis *)
         REPEAT
            Pop (Stack, Top, TempToken, StackEmpty);
            IF StackEmpty THEN
               Error := true
            ELSE IF TempToken <> '(' THEN
               write (TempToken:2)
         UNTIL (TempToken = '(') OR Error
      ELSE IF (Token = '+') OR               (* arithmetic operator *)
              (Token = '-') OR
              (Token = '*') OR
              (Token = '/') THEN
         BEGIN
            DonePopping := false;
            REPEAT
               Pop (Stack, Top, TempToken, StackEmpty);
               IF StackEmpty THEN
                  DonePopping := true
               ELSE IF (Priority(Token) <= Priority(TempToken)) THEN
                  write (TempToken:2)
               ELSE
                  BEGIN
                     Push (Stack, Top, TempToken, Error);
                     DonePopping := true
                  END (* ELSE *)
            UNTIL DonePopping;
            Push (Stack, Top, Token, Error)
         END (* ELSE IF *)
      ELSE                                    (* operand *)
         write (Token:2);

   (* Now get next Token and process it *)
   i := i + 1;
   Token := Exp[i]
END (* WHILE *);

      (* If no error detected, pop and display any operands on the stack *)
      IF NOT Error THEN
         BEGIN
            Pop (Stack, Top, Token, StackEmpty);
            WHILE NOT StackEmpty DO
               BEGIN
                  write (Token:2);
                  Pop (Stack, Top, Token, StackEmpty)
               END (* WHILE *);
            writeln
         END (* IF *)
      ELSE
         writeln ('*** Error in infix expression ***')
   END (* ConvertToRPN *);

BEGIN (* main program *)
   REPEAT
     (* read infix expression *)

     write ('Enter infix expression: ');
     i := 0;
```

Figure 14.4 (cont.)

```
      REPEAT
         i := i + 1;
         read (Exp[i])
      UNTIL Exp[i] = EndMark;
      readln;

      (* convert to RPN *)

      writeln;
      write ('RPN Expression:             ');
      ConvertToRPN (Exp);
      writeln;
      write ('More (Y or N)?  ');
      readln (Response)
   UNTIL Response <> 'Y'
END (* main program *).
```

Sample run:
___

```
Enter infix expression: A + B

RPN Expression:           A B +

More (Y or N)?  Y
Enter infix expression: A - B - C

RPN Expression:           A B - C -

More (Y or N)?  Y
Enter infix expression: A - (B - C)

RPN Expression:           A B C - -

More (Y or N)?  Y
Enter infix expression: ((A + 5)/B - 2)*C

RPN Expression:           A 5 + B / 2 - C *

More (Y or N)?  N
```

Exercises

1. Write procedures to insert in and delete from linked queues.

2. Write a program that reads a question from a file, displays it, and accepts an answer from the user. If the answer is correct, go on to the next question. If it is not correct, put the question into a linked queue. Then when the file of questions is exhaused, the questions that were missed are displayed again. Keep a count of the correct answers and display the final count. Also, display the correct answer when necessary in the second round of questioning.

3. A *deque* (double-ended queue) is a list in which insertion and deletion are allowed at either end. Write procedures to insert and delete items in a linked list representing a deque.

4. Suppose that $A = 7.0, B = 4.0, C = 3.0$, and $D = -2.0$. Evaluate the following RPN expressions:

   (a) $A\ B\ +\ C/D\ *$ (b) $A\ B\ C\ +\ /D\ *$
   (c) $A\ B\ C\ D\ +\ /*$ (d) $A\ B\ +\ C\ +\ D\ +$
   (e) $A\ B\ +\ C\ D\ +\ +$ (f) $A\ B\ C\ +\ +\ D\ +$
   (g) $A\ B\ C\ D\ +\ +\ +$ (h) $A\ B\ -\ C\ -\ D\ -$
   (i) $A\ B\ -\ C\ D\ -\ -$ (j) $A\ B\ C\ -\ -\ D\ -$
   (k) $A\ B\ C\ D\ -\ -\ -$

5. Convert the following infix expressions to RPN:

   (a) $A * B + C - D$ (b) $A + B/C + D$
   (c) $(A + B)/C + D$ (d) $A + B/(C + D)$
   (e) $(A + B)/(C + D)$ (f) $(A - B) * (C - (D + E))$
   (g) $(((A - B) - C) - D) - E$ (h) $A - (B - (C - (D - E)))$

6. Convert the following RPN expressions to infix notation:

   (a) $A\ B\ C\ +\ -\ D\ *$ (b) $A\ B\ +\ C\ D\ -\ *$
   (c) $A\ B\ C\ D\ +\ -\ *$ (d) $A\ B\ +\ C\ -\ D\ E\ */$
   (e) $A\ B/C/D/$ (f) $A\ B/C\ D//$
   (g) $A\ B\ C/D//$ (h) $A\ B\ C\ D///$

7. The symbol $-$ cannot be used for the unary minus operation in postfix notation. For example, $5\ 3\ -\ -$ could be interpreted as either $5 - (-3) = 8$ or $-(5 - 3) = -2$. Suppose that $\sim$ is used for unary minus.

   (a) Evaluate the following RPN expressions if $A = 7, B = 5$, and $C = 3$:

      (i) $A \sim B\ C\ +\ -$ (ii) $A\ B \sim C\ +\ -$
      (iii) $A\ B\ C \sim\ +\ -$ (iv) $A\ B\ C\ +\ \sim\ -$
      (v) $A\ B\ C\ +\ -\ \sim$ (vi) $A\ B\ C\ -\ -\ \sim\ \sim\ \sim$

   (b) Convert the following infix expressions to RPN:

      (i) $A * (B + \sim C)$ (ii) $\sim(A + B/(C - D))$
      (iii) $(\sim A) * (\sim B)$ (iv) $\sim(A - (\sim B * (C + \sim D)))$

8. Convert the following boolean expressions to RPN:

   (a) A **and** B **or** C
   (b) A **and** $(B$ **or not** $C)$
   (c) **not** $(A$ **and** $B)$
   (d) $(A$ **or** $B)$ **and** $(C$ **or** $(D$ **and not** $E))$
   (e) $(A = B)$ **or** $(C = D)$
   (f) $((A < 3)$ **and** $(A > 9))$ **or not** $(A > 0)$
   (g) $((B * B - 4 * A * C) >= 0)$ **and** $((A > 0)$ **or** $(A < 0))$

9. An alternative to postfix notation is **prefix** notation, in which the symbol for each operation precedes the operands. For example, the infix expression 2 ∗ 3 + 4 would be written in prefix notation as + ∗ 2 3 4 and 2 ∗ (3 + 4) would be written as ∗ 2 + 3 4. Convert each of the infix expressions in Exercise 5 to prefix notation.

10. Suppose that $A = 7.0$, $B = 4.0$, $C = 3.0$, and $D = -2.0$. Evaluate the following prefix expressions (see Exercise 9):

   (a) ∗ A / + B C D   (b) ∗ / + A B C D
   (c) − A − B − C D   (d) − − A B − C D
   (e) − A − − B C D   (f) − − − − A B C D
   (g) + A ∗ B − C D   (h) + ∗ A B − C D
   (i) + ∗ − A B C D

11. Convert the following prefix expressions to infix notation (see Exercise 9):

   (a) ∗ + A B − C D   (b) + ∗ A B − C D
   (c) − − A B − C D   (d) − − − A − B C D
   (e) − − − − A B C D   (f) / + ∗ A B − C D E
   (g) / + ∗ A B C − D E   (h) / + A ∗ B C − D E

12. Write a procedure to implement the algorithm for evaluating RPN expressions that involve only one-digit integers and the binary operators +, −, and ∗.

13. Write a program that reads an RPN expression and determines whether it is well formed, that is, whether each binary operator has two operands and the unary operator ~ has one (see Exercise 7).

14. Write a program that converts an integer expression involving the operators +, −, ∗, **div, mod,** and integer constants from infix notation to RPN.

15. For prefix notation as described in Exercise 9, write procedures to:

   (a) Convert infix expressions into prefix.
   (b) Evaluate prefix expressions containing only one-digit integers and the binary operators +, −, and ∗.

14.3 Evaluating Data Structures and Algorithms

Problem solving requires not only the design of an algorithm but also the selection of an appropriate data structure to organize the data of the problem. Both aspects of program development, algorithm design and data structure selection, are equally important. Indeed, Niklaus Wirth, the originator of the Pascal language, entitled one of his books

> *Algorithms + Data Structures = Programs*

In this section we describe some of the factors that should be taken into consideration when selecting a data structure and show how the efficiency of algorithms to process the data can be measured.

For each of the data structures we have considered, both predefined and user-defined, the data structure consists of a collection of data items together with certain basic operations to be performed on these items. For a user-defined data structure, an ***implementation*** of that structure must be designed if it is to be used in a program. Such an implementation consists of one or more ***storage structures*** to store the items and ***algorithms*** to carry out the operations. Since these storage structures and algorithms must be implemented in some programming language, they must be designed to take advantage of the features of that language. This means that, where possible, they should be based on the predefined data types, operations, functions, and procedures available in that language.

For example, in our first attempt to implement a stack, we used an array for the storage structure, with the top of the stack being the first position of the array. In this case, however, we observed that algorithms for the push and pop operations required moving the array elements each time one of these operations was performed. By storing the stack items differently in the array and using an integer variable *Top* to keep track of the top item, we found that the push and pop algorithms did not require shifting array elements and thus were more efficient. Then we described yet another implementation of a stack using a linked list in which the push algorithm, unlike the implementation using arrays, did not require checking for stack overflow. Thus we see the interdependence of storage structures and algorithms. Selection of the data structure must always be made in conjunction with design of the algorithms, since these are inextricably linked.

In choosing an implementation of a data structure, it is important to evaluate the efficiency of the various alternatives. Efficiency is usually measured according to two criteria. The first is ***space utilization,*** which is the amount of memory required for the storage structure; the second is ***time efficiency,*** which is the amount of time required to execute the algorithms. Unfortunately, it is usually not possible to minimize both the space and time requirements for an implementation. The algorithms for those storage structures that require the least memory are often slower than the algorithms for which the storage structures use more memory. For example, the push algorithm for a linked stack does not require checking if the stack is full, whereas for an array implementation, it does. The linked stack does require more space, however, since in addition to the data items, a link must also be stored for each item. Thus the programmer is usually faced with a trade-off between space efficiency and time efficiency. When forced to choose which of these to optimize, the time efficiency of algorithms is usually considered to be the more important of the two. In this chapter, we will concentrate on how time efficiency can be measured.

In addition to the space–time trade-off that often faces a programmer choosing between alternative implementations, there is also frequently a trade-off between efficiency and clarity. Ideally, algorithms should be efficient, easy to understand, and easily translated into programs. Again, these goals are sometimes in conflict, since the most efficient algorithms may not be the most understandable or the easiest to program. If a program is to be used only a few times or with only a small amount of input data, it is usually appropriate to select a less efficient but simpler algorithm over a more efficient but complicated one. The time saved in writing, debugging, and maintaining the program will compensate for the less efficient execution.

There are many factors that influence the execution time of a program. The first of these is the size of the input. Obviously, the number of input items usually affects the time required to process them. For example, the time required to sort a list of items surely depends on how many there are. This means that the execution time T of an algorithm must be expressed as a function $T(n)$ of the size n of the input.

In many cases, T may depend not only on the size of the input but on the arrangement of the input items as well. For example, it may take less time to sort a list of items that are nearly in order initially than to sort a list in which the items are in reverse order. Thus we might attempt to measure T in the **worst case** or in the **best case,** or we might attempt to compute the **average** value of T over all possible cases. The best-case performance of an algorithm is usually not very informative, and the average performance is often quite difficult to determine; thus $T(n)$ is commonly taken as a measure of the algorithm's performance in the worst case.

The kinds of instructions and the speed with which the machine can execute them also influence execution time. These factors, however, depend on the particular computer being used; consequently, we cannot expect to express the value of $T(n)$ meaningfully in real time units such as seconds. Instead, $T(n)$ will be the (approximate) number of instructions executed.

Another factor that influences computing time is the quality of the code generated by the compiler. The fact that not all compilers generate equally efficient code implies that $T(n)$ cannot be computed as the number of machine instructions executed. Thus, $T(n)$ is taken to be the number of times the instructions in the algorithm (or in the source program) are executed.

To illustrate how the computing time of an algorithm is measured, we first consider the two methods for searching a list described in Chapter 8, linear search and binary search. There we claimed that binary search is more efficient than linear search, and we will now substantiate this claim.

Recall that a linear search is carried out by examining each element in a list sequentially, beginning with the first element, until either the desired item is found or the end of the list is reached. The algorithm given in Section 8.3 can be summarized as follows:

LINEAR SEARCH ALGORITHM

(∗ Algorithm to linear search a list of items $X[1], X[2], \ldots, X[n]$ for a specified *Item*. *Found* is set to true and *Location* to the position of *Item* if the search is successful; otherwise, *Found* is false. ∗)

(1) Set *Found* to false.
(2) Set *Location* equal to 1.
(3) While *Location* $\leq n$ and not *Found* do the following:
(4)   If *Item* = $X[Location]$ then
(5)   Set *Found* to true.
(6)   Else
            Increment *Location* by 1.

(In this algorithm, the statements have been numbered for easy reference.)

The worst case for the linear search algorithm obviously occurs when *Item* is not in the list; thus, to measure the performance of this algorithm, we will count the number of times each statement is executed in this case. Clearly, statements 1 and 2 are executed only once. The boolean expression in statement 3 will be evaluated $n + 1$ times, once for each value of *Location* from 1 through $n + 1$. Statements 4 and 6 will be executed n times, once on each pass through the **while** loop, and statement 5 is never executed, since *Item* is not in the list. The following table summarizes these statement counts:

Statement	Count
1	1
2	1
3	$n + 1$
4	n
5	0
6	n
Total:	$3n + 3$

Thus the total number of statements expressed as a function of the size n of input is

$$T(n) = 3n + 3$$

For sufficiently large values of n ($n \geq 3$), we see that

$$T(n) \leq 4n$$

and so we say that $T(n)$ has **order of magnitude n** and denote this using the "big Oh" notation by

$$T(n) = O(n)$$

In general, the execution time $T(n)$ of an algorithm is said to have **order of magnitude $g(n)$,** denoted

$$T(n) = O(g(n))$$

if there exists some constant C so that

$$T(n) \leq C \cdot g(n)$$

for all sufficiently large values of n.

The binary search algorithm for ordered lists given in Section 8.3 can be summarized as follows:

BINARY SEARCH ALGORITHM

(∗ Algorithm to binary search a list $X[1], X[2], \ldots, X[n]$ that has been ordered so the elements are in ascending order. *Found* is set to true and *Location* to the position of the *Item* being sought if the search is successful; otherwise, *Found* is set to false. ∗)

(1) Set *First* equal to 1.
(2) Set *Last* equal to n.

(3) Set *Found* equal to false.
(4) While *First* ≤ Last and not *Found* do the following:
(5)   a. Calculate *Location* = integer quotient when
                                   (*First* + *Last*) is divided by 2.
(6)   b. If *Item* < X[*Location*] then
(7)   set *Last* equal to *Location* − 1.
(8)   Else if *Item* > X[*Location*] then
(9)   set *First* equal to *Location* + 1.
(10)   Else
                set *Found* equal to true.

In this algorithm, it is clear that statements 1, 2, and 3 will be executed exactly once, and to determine the worst-case performance, we must determine the number of times the loop composed of statements 4 through 10 is executed when *Item* is not in the list. This is not as easy to determine as it is for linear search, and so we first consider some particular values of *n*.

First, consider a list containing only one element X[1], and suppose that *Item* is greater than X[1]. After statements 1, 2, and 3 are executed, the boolean expression in statement 4 is evaluated and found to be true (*First* = 1, *Last* = 1, and *Found* = false). Thus the body of the **while** loop is executed; statement 5 calculates the value 1 for *Location*, and statements 8 and 9 set *First* equal to 2. The boolean expression in statement 4 is then evaluated again and found to be false (*First* = 2, *Last* = 1), causing repetition to terminate. Thus we see that for *n* = 1, one pass through the loop is made and one additional evaluation of the boolean expression is made to terminate repetition.

Next, consider a list of size *n* = 2, X[1], X[2], and suppose that *Item* is greater than both elements of this list. A first pass through the loop sets *First* equal to 2 so that the sublist yet to be searched is reduced from two elements to one, X[2]. As we have just seen, a list of size 1 requires one pass through the loop and one more evaluation of the boolean expression in statement 4 to terminate repetition. Thus, for *n* = 2, the loop is executed twice and statement 4 one additional time.

Now consider a list of size *n* = 4, X[1], X[2], X[3], X[4], with *Item* greater than each list element. A first pass through the loop reduces the list to one of size 2, X[3], X[4]. From what we have just determined for a list of two elements, we see that for a list of size 4, the loop is executed three times and the boolean expression in statement 4 is evaluated one additional time.

Continuing this analysis with values 8, 16, . . . for *n*, we obtain the following table:

n	Number of Passes Through the Loop
$1 = 2^0$	1
$2 = 2^1$	2
$4 = 2^2$	3
$8 = 2^3$	4
$\vdots$	$\vdots$
2^k	$k + 1$

Thus we see that a list of size 2^k requires $k + 1 = \log_2(2^k) + 1$ passes through the loop. In general, a list of size n requires no more than $\log_2 n + 1$ passes through the loop.

Since only statements 5, 8, and 9 are executed in the worst case and statement 4 is executed one more time than the number of loop repetitions, we obtain the following (approximate) counts for executions of the statements in the binary search algorithm:

Statement	Count
1	1
2	1
3	1
4	$\log_2 n + 2$
5	$\log_2 n + 1$
6	0
7	0
8	$\log_2 n + 1$
9	$\log_2 n + 1$
10	0
Total:	$4\log_2 n + 8$

Thus we see that in the worst case, the computing time of binary search is $T(n) = 4\log_2 n + 8$, and since

$$T(n) \leq 5\log_2 n$$

for large n ($n \geq 2^8$), we see that $T(n)$ has order of magnitude $\log_2 n$,

$$T(n) = O(\log_2 n)$$

In summary, we have the following measures of worst-case performance of the linear search and binary search algorithms (which also measure the average case performance):

Linear search: $O(n)$
Binary search: $O(\log_2 n)$

Since the function $\log_2 n$ grows less rapidly than n as the number n of inputs increases, it follows that binary search is more efficient than linear search for large lists. For small lists, however, linear search may, and in fact does, outperform binary search. Empirical studies indicate that linear search is more efficient than binary search for lists of up to 20 elements. Moreover, binary search is applicable only to ordered lists; consequently, it may be necessary to sort the list before it can be used. We are thus led to consider the efficiency of sorting algorithms.

In Section 8.3 we described the bubble sort algorithm, which can be summarized as follows:

BUBBLESORT ALGORITHM

(* Algorithm to bubble sort the list $X[1]$, $X[2]$, . . . , $X[n]$ so they are in ascending order. *)

(1) Set *NumPairs* equal to $n - 1$.
(2) Repeat the following until *Done:*
(3)   a. Set *Done* to true.
(4)   b. For i ranging from 1 to *NumPairs* do:
(5)   If $X[i] > X[i + 1]$ then
(6)   (i) Interchange $X[i]$ and $X[i + 1]$.
(7)   (ii) Set *Done* to false.
(8)   c. Decrease *NumPairs* by 1.

The worst case for this algorithm occurs when the items are in reverse order, since in this case only one item (the largest) is positioned correctly on each pass through the repeat loop. Statements 3 and 8 are each executed $n - 1$ times, once on each pass through the loop. On the first pass with *NumPairs* $= n - 1$, statement 4 is executed n times. On the second pass with *NumPairs* $= n - 2$, it is executed $n - 1$ times, and so on. Thus statement 4 is executed a total of $n + (n - 1) + \cdots + 1$ times. This sum is equal to $n(n + 1)/2$. Similarly, statements 5, 6, and 7 are each executed a total of $(n - 1) + (n - 2) + \cdots + 1 = (n - 1)n/2$ times. Since statement 1 is executed only once and statement 2 is executed $n - 1$ times, the total computing time for this bubble sort algorithm is given by $T(n) = n^2 + 3n - 2$, so that in the worst case we have

$$T(n) = O(n^2)$$

On the average, we also have $T(n) = O(n^2)$, but this is considerably more difficult to show.

In addition to $O(\log_2 n)$, $O(n)$, and $O(n^2)$, other computing times that frequently arise in algorithm analysis are $O(\log_2(\log_2 n))$, $O(n \cdot \log_2 n)$, $O(n^3)$, and $O(2^n)$. The following table displays values of these seven functions for several values of n:

$\log_2(\log_2 n)$	$\log_2 n$	n	$n \cdot \log_2 n$	n^2	n^3	2^n
—	0	1	0	1	1	2
0	1	2	2	4	8	4
1	2	4	8	16	64	16
1.58	3	8	24	64	512	256
2	4	16	64	256	4096	65536
2.32	5	32	160	1024	32768	2147483648
2.6	6	64	384	4096	2.6×10^5	1.85×10^{19}
3	8	256	4.48×10^2	6.55×10^4	1.68×10^7	1.16×10^{77}
3.32	10	1024	1.02×10^4	1.05×10^6	1.07×10^9	1.8×10^{308}
4.32	20	1048576	2.1×10^7	1.1×10^{12}	1.1×10^{18}	6.0×10^{315652}

It should be clear from this table that algorithms whose computing times are exponential are practical only for solving problems in which the number of inputs is small. To demonstrate this, suppose that each instruction in some algorithm can be executed in 1 microsecond (0.000001 second). The following table shows the time required for each of the common computing times with $n = 256$ inputs:

Function	Time
$\log_2(\log_2 n)$	3 microseconds
$\log_2 n$	8 microseconds
n	0.25 millisecond (0.001 second)
$n \cdot \log_2 n$	2 milliseconds
n^2	65 milliseconds
n^3	17 seconds
2^n	3.7×10^{61} centuries

Exercises

1. Which of the orders of magnitude given in this section is the best O-notation to describe the following computing times?

   (a) $T(n) = n^3 + 100n \cdot \log_2 n + 5000$ (b) $T(n) = 2^n + n^{99} + 7$

   (c) $T(n) = \dfrac{n^2 - 1}{n + 1} + 8\log_2 n$ (d) $T(n) = 1 + 2 + 4 + \cdots + 2^{n-1}$

2. What would it mean to say that an algorithm has computing time $T(n) = O(1)$? Give an example of such an algorithm.

3. Using one of the "big Oh" computing times given in the text, give the worst-case computing time for each of the following program segments as a function of n.

   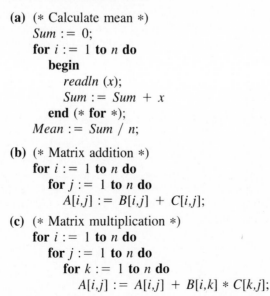

   (a) (* Calculate mean *)
   ```
   Sum := 0;
   for i := 1 to n do
       begin
           readln (x);
           Sum := Sum + x
       end (* for *);
   Mean := Sum / n;
   ```

   (b) (* Matrix addition *)
   ```
   for i := 1 to n do
       for j := 1 to n do
           A[i,j] := B[i,j] + C[i,j];
   ```

   (c) (* Matrix multiplication *)
   ```
   for i := 1 to n do
       for j := 1 to n do
           for k := 1 to n do
               A[i,j] := A[i,j] + B[i,k] * C[k,j];
   ```

(d) (* Selection sort *)
    for $i := 1$ **to** $n - 1$ **do**
      begin
        $Loc := i$;
        $Temp := X[Loc]$;
        for $j := i + 1$ **to** n **do**
          if $X[j] < Temp$ **then**
          begin
            $Loc := j$;
            $Temp := X[Loc]$
          end (* **if** *);
      $X[Loc] := X[i]$;
      $X[i] := Temp$
    end (* **for** *);

(e) **while** $n \geq 1$ **do**
    $n := n$ **div** 2;

(f) $x := 1$;
    for $i := 1$ **to** $n - 1$ **do**
      begin
        for $j := 1$ **to** x **do**
          $writeln$ (j);
        $x := 2 * x$
      end (* **for** *);

14.4 Quicksort

On several occasions we have considered the important data-processing problem of sorting a list of items. In several examples we used the bubble sort algorithm, and in the preceding section we showed that it has worst-case computing time $O(n^2)$ and noted that this is also its average computing time. The *quicksort* method of sorting described in this section is more efficient; although its worst-case computing time is $O(n^2)$, its average computing time is $O(n \cdot \log_2 n)$. It is in fact one of the fastest methods of sorting and is most often implemented by a recursive algorithm. In our description of this method, we assume, for the sake of simplicity, that the items being sorted are simple items. If they are records, sorting is carried out using a key field in the records.

The basic idea of quicksort for sorting a list of items into ascending order is to select one item from the list and then rearrange the list so that this item is in its proper position; that is, all list elements that precede it are less than this item, and all those that follow it are greater than the item. This divides the original list into two sublists, each of which may then be sorted independently in the *same* way. As might be expected, this divide-and-conquer strategy leads naturally to a recursive algorithm for quicksort.

To illustrate this splitting of a list into two sublists, consider the following list of integers:

50, 30, 20, 80, 90, 70, 95, 85, 10, 15, 75, 25

If we select the first number as the item to be properly positioned, we must rearrange the list so that 30, 20, 10, 15, and 25 are placed before 50, and 80, 90, 70, 95, 85, and 75 are placed after it. To carry out this rearrangement, we search from the right end of the list for an item less than 50 and from the left end for an item greater than 50.

50 , 30 , 20 , 80 , 90 , 70 , 95 , 85 , 10 , 15 , 75 , 25

This locates the two numbers 25 and 80, which we now interchange to obtain

We then resume the search from the right for a number less than 50 and from the left for a number greater than 50:

This locates the numbers 15 and 90, which are then interchanged:

50 , 30 , 20 , 25 , 90 , 70 , 95 , 85 , 10 , 15 , 75 , 80

A continuation of the searches locates 10 and 70:

50 . 30 , 20 , 25 , 15 , 70 , 95 , 85 , 10 , 90 , 75 , 80

Interchanging these gives

When we resume our search from the right for a number less than 50, we locate the value 10, which was found on the previous left-to-right search. This signals the end of the two searches, and we interchange 50 and 10, thus giving

10 , 30 , 20 , 25 , 15 , 50 , 95 , 85 , 70 , 90 , 75 , 80

The two underlined sublists now have the required properties: all items in the first sublist are less than 50, and all those in the right sublist are greater than 50. Consequently, 50 has been properly positioned.

Both the sublist

10, 30, 20, 25, 15

consisting of the numbers in positions 1 through 5 and the sublist

95, 85, 70, 90, 75, 80

consisting of numbers in positions 7 through 12 can now be sorted independently. For this, a procedure is needed to split a list of items in the array positions given by two parameters *Low* and *High,* denoting the beginning and end positions of the sublist, respectively. If we assume declarations of the form

const
    ListLimit = . . . ; (* limit on length of list *)

type
    DataType = . . . ; (* type of elements in the list *)
    List = **array**[1..*ListLimit*] **of** *DataType*;

then the following procedure carries out the desired splitting of the (sub)list *X*[*Low*], . . . , *X*[*High*].

    procedure *Split* (**var** *X* : *List*; *Low, High* : *integer*; **var** *Mid* : *integer*);

        (* Procedure to rearrange *X*[*Low*], . . . , *X*[*High*] so that one item is properly positioned; it returns the rearranged list and the final position *Mid* of that item. *)

    var
        Left,   (* index for searching from the left *)
        Right : *integer*;   (* index for searching from the right *)
        TempItem : *DataType*;(* temporary item used for interchanging *)

    begin (* *Split* *)
        (* Initialize indices for left and right searches *)
        Left := *Low*;
        Right := *High*;

        (* Carry out the searches *)
        while *Left* < *Right* **do**   (* While searches haven't met *)
          begin
            (* Search from the right *)
            while *X*[*Right*] > *X*[*Low*] **do**
              Right := *Right* − 1;

            (* Search from the left *)
            while (*Left* < *Right*) **and** (*X*[*Left*] <= *X*[*Low*]) **do**
              Left := *Left* + 1;

            (* Interchange items if searches have not met *)
            if *Left* < *Right* **then**
              begin
                TempItem := *X*[*Left*];
                X[*Left*] := *X*[*Right*];
                X[*Right*] := *TempItem*
              end (* **if** *)
          end (* **while** *);

        (* End of searches; place selected item in proper position *)
        Mid := *Right*;
        TempItem := *X*[*Mid*];
        X[*Mid*] := *X*[*Low*];
        X[*Low*] := *TempItem*
    end (* *Split* *);

A recursive procedure to sort a list is now easy to write:

> **procedure** *QuickSort* (**var** *X* : *List*; *Low, High* : *integer*);
>
> (* Procedure to quicksort *X*[*Low*], . . . , *X*[*High*] *)
>
> **var**
>   *Mid* : *integer*;   (* final position of selected item *)
>
> **begin** (* *QuickSort* *)
> (*1*)   **if** *Low* < *High* **then**   (* list has more than one item *)
>   **begin**
> (*2*)   *Split* (*X, Low, High, Mid*);   (* split into two sublists *)
> (*3*)   *QuickSort* (*X, Low, Mid* − 1); (* sort first sublist *)
> (*4*)   *QuickSort* (*X, Mid* + 1, *High*) (* sort second sublist *)
>   **end** (* **if** *)
> (*5*)   **end** (* *QuickSort* *);

(Some of the statements have been numbered for later reference.) This procedure is called with a statement of the form

> *QuickSort* (*Item*, 1, *NumItems*)

where *NumItems* is the number of elements in the given list *Item* to be sorted.
　　To demonstrate this procedure, suppose that the following list of integers is to be sorted:

> 8, 2, 13, 5, 14, 3, 7

We can use tree-like diagrams to display the action of *Quicksort*. In each tree, a circle indicates an item placed in its proper position, with a shaded circle indicating the item being positioned at this step. Rectangles represent sublists to be sorted, and a shaded rectangle indicates the next sublist to be sorted. In the list of comments, a label such as II.3 indicates the level (II) in the tree of the sublist being processed and the statement (3) in *QuickSort* currently being executed.

Tree	Comments
8,2,13,5,14,3,7	First call to *QuickSort* (*Low* = 1, *High* = 7).
8,2,13,5,14,3,7 → 3,2,7,5 ⑧ 14,13	I.1: 1 < 7 so I.2: Split the list and position 8. I.3: Call *QuickSort* on left sublist (*Low* = 1, *High* = 4)

Tree	Comments

II.1: $1 < 4$ so
II.2: Split the sublist and position 3.
II.3: Call *QuickSort* on left sublist
     ($Low = 1$, $High = 1$)

III.1: $1 \not< 1$ (one-element sublist) so
III.5: Return to previous level.

II.4: Call *QuickSort* on right sublist
     ($Low = 3$, $High = 4$).

III.1: $3 < 4$ so
III.2: Split the sublist and position 7.
III.3: Call *QuickSort* on left sublist
     ($Low = 3$, $High = 3$).

IV.1: $3 \not< 3$ (one-element sublist) so
IV.5: Return to previous level.

III.4: Call *QuickSort* on right sublist
     ($Low = 5$, $High = 4$).

Tree	Comments
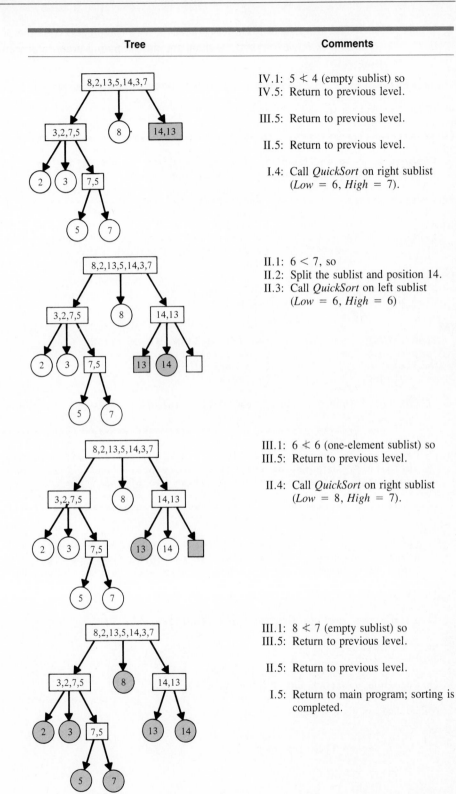	IV.1: 5 ≮ 4 (empty sublist) so IV.5: Return to previous level. III.5: Return to previous level. II.5: Return to previous level. I.4: Call *QuickSort* on right sublist (*Low* = 6, *High* = 7). II.1: 6 < 7, so II.2: Split the sublist and position 14. II.3: Call *QuickSort* on left sublist (*Low* = 6, *High* = 6) III.1: 6 ≮ 6 (one-element sublist) so III.5: Return to previous level. II.4: Call *QuickSort* on right sublist (*Low* = 8, *High* = 7). III.1: 8 ≮ 7 (empty sublist) so III.5: Return to previous level. II.5: Return to previous level. I.5: Return to main program; sorting is completed.

The program in Figure 14.5 reads a list of numbers, calls the procedures *Split* and *QuickSort* to sort the numbers into ascending order, and then displays the sorted list.

```pascal
PROGRAM SortWithQuickSort (input, output);

(************************************************************************

    Program to read and count a list of items, sort them using the
    quicksort algorithm, and then display the sorted list.

*************************************************************************)

CONST
    ListLimit = 100;            (* upper limit onlength of list *)
              = -9999;          (* signals end of data *)

TYPE
    DataType = integer;
    List = ARRAY[1..ListLimit] OF DataType;

VAR
    Item : List;                (* list of items to be sorted *)
    Temp : DataType;            (* temporary item read *)
    NumItems,                   (* number of items *)
    i : integer;                (* index *)

PROCEDURE Split (VAR X : List; Low, High : integer; VAR Mid : integer);

        (************************************************************************

    Procedure to rearrange X[Low], ..., X[High] so that one item
    (originally in position Low) is properly positioned; it returns
    rearranged list and the final position Mid of that item.

    *************************************************************************)

    VAR
        Left                    (* index for searching from the left *)
        Right : integer;        (* index for searching from the right *)
        TempItem : DataType;    (* temporary item used for interchanging *)

BEGIN (* Split *)

    (* Initialize indices for left and right searches *)

    Left := Low;
    Right := High;

    (* Continue searches until they meet *)

    WHILE Left < Right DO
        BEGIN

            (* search from the right *)

            WHILE X[Right] > X[Low] DO
                Right := Right - 1;
```

Figure 14.5

Figure 14.5 (cont.)

```
                (* search from the left *)

            WHILE (Left < Right) AND (X[Left] <= X[Low]) DO
                Left := Left + 1;

            (* interchange items if searches haven't met *)

            IF Left < Right THEN
                BEGIN
                    TempItem := X[Left];
                    X[Left] := X[Right];
                    X[Right] := TempItem
                END (* IF *)
            END (* WHILE *);

        (* End of search; place selected item in proper position *)

        Mid := Right;
        TempItem := X[Mid];
        X[Mid] := X[Low];
        X[Low] := TempItem
    END (* Split *);

PROCEDURE QuickSort (VAR X : List; Low, High : integer);

    (************************************************************************

            Procedure to QuickSort X[Low], ..., X[High]

    ************************************************************************)

    VAR
        Mid : integer;   (* final position of selected item *)

    BEGIN (* QuickSort *)
        IF Low < High THEN                   (* list has more than one item *)
            BEGIN
                Split (X, Low, High, Mid);       (* split into two sublists *)
                QuickSort (X, Low, Mid - 1);     (* sort first sublist *)
                QuickSort (X, Mid + 1, High)     (* sort second sublist *)
            END (* IF *)
    END (* QuickSort *);

BEGIN (* main program *)
    NumItems := 0;
    writeln ('Enter the items (', EndDataFlag:1,
            ' to signal the end of data).');
    read (Temp);
    WHILE (Temp <> EndDataFlag AND (NumItems < ListLimit) DO
        BEGIN
            NumItems := NumItems + 1;
            Item[NumItems] := Temp;
            read (Temp)
        END (* WHILE *);
    QuickSort (Item, 1, NumItems);
    writeln ('Sorted list:');
    FOR i := 1 TO NumItems DO
        writeln (Item[i])
END (* main program *).
```

Figure 14.5 (cont.)

```
Sample run:


Enter the items (−9999 to signal the end of data).
54 67 34 99 27 5 62 45 83
−9999
Sorted list:
        5
       27
       34
       45
       54
       62
       67
       83
       99
```

The worst-case computing time for quicksort is $O(n^2)$ and the average time is $O(n \cdot \log_2 n)$. Although a rigorous derivation of these computing times is quite difficult, it is possible to see intuitively why these are correct by using tree diagrams like those we have used to describe the operation of quicksort. At each level of the tree, the split procedure is applied to several sublists whose total size is at most n; hence, each of the statements in the **while** loop of procedure *Split* is executed at most n times on each level. The computing time for quicksort is thus $O(n \cdot (\text{number of levels in the tree}))$. In the worst case, one of the sublists produced by *Split* is always empty; consequently, the tree has n levels. It follows that quicksort has computing time $O(n^2)$ in this case. If, however, the two sublists produced by *Split* are approximately of equal size, the number of levels will be approximately $\log_2 n$, giving $O(n \cdot \log_2 n)$ as the computing time for quicksort.

Exercises

1. Draw a sequence of trees like those in the text to illustrate the actions of *Split* and *QuickSort* while sorting the following lists:

   (a) 5, 1, 6, 4, 3, 2   **(b)** 1, 2, 3, 6, 5, 4
   (c) 6, 5, 4, 3, 2, 1   **(d)** 1, 2, 3, 4, 5, 6

2. One of the lists in Exercise 1 shows why the condition *Left* < *Right* is needed to control the search from the left in procedure *Split*. Which is it? What would happen if this condition were omitted?

3. Modify the procedures *Split* and *QuickSort* to sort a list of records so that the values in a key field are in ascending order. Use these procedures in a program to read the student names and student numbers and addresses from *StudentFile* and then quicksort them so that the students' last names are in alphabetical order. (See Appendix E for a description of *StudentFile*.)

4. The procedure *QuickSort* always sorts the left sublist before the right. Its performance improves slightly if the shorter of the two sublists is the first to be sorted. Modify *QuickSort* to sort the shorter sublist first.

5. Another improvement of the quicksort method is to use some other sorting algorithm to sort small sublists. For example, insertion sort is usually better than quicksort when the list has fewer than 20 items. Modify the quicksort scheme to use insertion sort (see Exercise 16 of Section 8.3) if the sublist has fewer than *LBound* items for some constant *LBound* and otherwise use quicksort.

6. The procedure *Split* always selects the first element of the sublist to position. Another common practice is to use the "median-of-three" rule in which the median of the three numbers $X[Low]$, $X[Middle]$, and $X[High]$ is selected, where $Middle = (Low + High)$ **div** 2. (The median of three numbers a, b, and c, arranged in ascending order, is the middle number b.) Modify *Split* to use this median-of-three rule.

14.5 Mergesort

All of the sorting algorithms we have considered thus far are *internal* sorting schemes; that is, the entire collection of items to be sorted must be stored in main memory. In many data-processing problems, however, the data sets are too large to store in main memory and must be stored in external memory. To sort such collections of data, an *external* sorting algorithm is required. One popular and efficient external sorting method is the *mergesort* technique, a variation of which, called *natural mergesort,* is examined in this section.

As the name mergesort suggests, the basic operation in this sorting scheme is merging data files. The merge operation combines two files that have previously been sorted so that the resulting file is also sorted. To illustrate, suppose that *File1* has been sorted and contains the integers

File1 :   2   4   5   7   9   15   16   20

and *File2* contains

File2 :   1   6   8   10   12

To merge these files to produce *File3*, we read one element from each file, say X from *File1* and Y from *File2*.

File1 :   <u>2</u>   4   5   7   9   15   16   20
        ↑
        X

File2 :   <u>1</u>   6   8   10   12
        ↑
        Y

We write the smaller of these values, in this case Y, into *File3*:

File3 : 1

and then read another value for Y from *File2*:

File2 : |2| 4 5 7 9 15 16 20
        ↑
        X

File2 : 1 |6| 8 10 12
        ↑
        Y

Now X is smaller than Y, and so it is written to *File3*, and a new value for X is read from *File1*:

File1 : 2 |4| 5 7 9 15 16 20
        ↑
        X

File2 : 1 |6| 8 10 12
        ↑
        Y

File3 : 1 2

Again X is less than Y, and so X is written to *File3*, and a new X value is read from *File1*:

File1 : 2 4 |5| 7 9 15 16 20
        ↑
        X

File2 : 1 |6| 8 10 12
        ↑
        Y

File3 : 1 2 4

Continuing in this manner, we eventually reach the value 15 for X and the value 12 for Y:

File1 : 2 4 5 7 9 |15| 16 20
        ↑
        X

File2 : 1 6 8 10 |12|
        ↑
        Y

File3 : 1 2 4 5 6 7 8 9 10

Because Y is smaller than X, we write Y to *File3*:

File3 : 1 2 4 5 6 7 8 9 10 12

Because the end of *File2* has been reached, we simply copy the remaining values in *File1* to *File3* to obtain the final sorted file *File3*:

File3 : 1 2 4 5 6 7 8 9 10 12 15 16 20

The general algorithm to merge two sorted files *File1* and *File2* is as follows:

MERGE ALGORITHM

1. Open *File1* and *File2* for input, *File3* for output.
2. Read the first element X from *File1* and the first element Y from *File2*.
3. Repeat the following until the end of either *File1* or *File2* is reached:
   If $X < Y$, then
     (i) Write X to *File3*.
     (ii) Read a new X value from *File1*.
   Otherwise:
     (i) Write Y to *File3*.
     (ii) Read a new Y value from *File2*.
4. If the end of *File1* was encountered, copy any remaining elements from *File2* into *File3*. If the end of *File2* was encountered, copy the rest of *File1* into *File3*.

In this algorithm, we have assumed that the file components are simple components. If the files contain records that are sorted on the basis of some key field, the key field of X is compared with the key field of Y in Step 3.

To see how the merge operation is used in sorting a file, consider the following file F containing fifteen integers:

F : 75 55 15 20 80 30 35 10 70 40 50 25 45 60 65

Notice that several segments of F contain elements that are already in order:

F : | 75 | 55 | 15 20 80 | 30 35 | 10 70 | 40 50 | 25 45 60 65 |

These segments, enclosed by the vertical bars, are called **subfiles** or **runs** in F and subdivide F in a natural way.

We begin by reading these subfiles of F and alternately writing them to two other files, $F1$ and $F2$:

$F1$: | 75 | 15 20 80 | 10 70 | 25 45 60 65 |
$F2$: | 55 | 30 35 | 40 50 |

and then identifying the sorted subfiles in $F1$ and $F2$.

$F1$: | 75 | 15 20 80 | 10 70 | 25 45 60 65 |
$F2$: | 55 | 30 35 40 50 |

Note that although the subfiles of $F1$ are the same as those copied from F, two of the original subfiles written into $F2$ have combined to form a larger subfile.

We now merge the first subfile of $F1$ with the first subfile of $F2$, storing the elements back in F.

F : |55 75 |

Next, the second subfile of *F1* is merged with the second subfile of *F2* and written to *F*.

> *F* : | 55 75 | 15 20 30 35 40 50 80 |

This merging of corresponding subfiles continues until the end of either or both of the files *F1* and *F2* is reached. If either file still contains subfiles, these are simply copied into *F*. Thus, in our example, because the end of *F2* has been reached, the remaining subfiles of *F1* are copied back into *F*.

> *F* : | 55 75 | 15 20 30 35 40 50 80 | 10 70 | 25 45 60 65 |

Now file *F* is again split into files *F1* and *F2* by copying its subfiles alternately into *F1* and *F2*.

> *F1* : | 55 75 | 10 70 |
> *F2* : | 15 20 30 35 40 50 80 | 25 45 60 65 |

Identifying the sorted subfiles in each of these files, we see that for this splitting, none of the original subfiles written into either *F1* or *F2* combine to form larger ones. Once again we merge corresponding subfiles of *F1* and *F2* back into *F*.

> *F* : | 15 20 30 35 40 50 55 75 80 | 10 25 45 60 65 70 |

When we now split *F* into *F1* and *F2*, each of the files *F1* and *F2* contains a single sorted subfile, and each is, therefore, completely sorted.

> *F1* : | 15 20 30 35 40 50 55 75 80 |
> *F2* : | 10 25 45 60 65 70 |

Thus, when we merge *F1* and *F2* back into *F*, *F* will also contain only one sorted subfile and hence will be sorted.

> *F* : | 10 15 20 25 30 35 40 45 50 55 60 65 70 75 80 |

From this example we see that the mergesort method has two steps: (1) splitting file *F* into two other files, *F1* and *F2*, and (2) merging corresponding subfiles in these two files. These steps are repeated until each of the smaller files contains a single sorted subfile, and when these are merged, the resulting file is completely sorted.

The splitting operation is carried out by the following algorithm:

SPLITTING ALGORITHM

1. Open file *F* for input and files *F1* and *F2* for output.
2. While the end of *F* has not been reached, do the following:
   a. Copy a sorted subfile of *F* into *F1* as follows: Repeatedly read an element of *F* and write it into *F1* until the next element in *F* is smaller than this copied item or the end of *F* is reached.

    b. If the end of *F* has not been reached, copy the next sorted subfile
      of *F* into *F2* in a similar manner.

In this algorithm we have assumed that the elements of file *F* are simple. If they are records, the key field on which the sorting is based is used in comparing file elements.

The following algorithm implements the merge operation illustrated in the example.

ALGORITHM TO MERGE SORTED SUBFILES

1. Open files *F1* and *F2* for input; open *F* for output.
2. While neither the end of *F1* nor the end of *F2* has been reached, do the following:
   a. While the end of no subfile in *F1* or *F2* has been reached, do the following:
      If the next element in *F1* is less than the next element in *F2*, then copy the next element from *F1* into *F*; otherwise, copy the next element from *F2* into *F*.
   b. If the end of a subfile in *F1* has been reached, then copy the rest of the corresponding subfile in *F2* to *F*; otherwise, copy the rest of the corresponding subfile in *F1* to *F*.
3. Copy any remaining subfiles remaining in *F1* or *F2* to *F*.

In this algorithm, the copying of a subfile from *F1* to *F* can be done by using the technique described in the splitting algorithm if the roles of *F* and *F1* are interchanged. A similar modification can be used to copy a subfile from *F2* to *F*.

The program in Figure 14.6 implements the mergesort algorithm and has the structure shown in the following diagram:

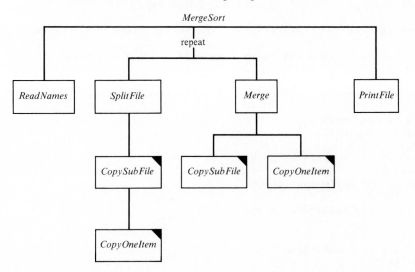

(Recall that a shaded corner in a box indicates a procedure that is shared by two or more program units.) This program reads names from *NameFile*, displaying them in their original order, and copies them into file *F*, using the procedure *ReadNames*. It then calls the procedures *SplitFile* and *Merge* to sort the file of names, using the mergesort algorithm, and finally calls *PrintFile* to display the contents of the sorted file. *SplitFile* and *Merge* use the procedures *CopyOneItem* and *CopySubFile* to copy one item or a sorted subfile, respectively, from one file to another.

```
PROGRAM MergeSort (input, output, NameFile);

(*********************************************************************

    Program to sort the external file NameFile using the natural
    mergesort algorithm.

*********************************************************************)

CONST
    MaxString = 30;              (* upper limit on lengths of strings *)

TYPE
    String = PACKED ARRAY[1..MaxString] OF char;
    FileType = String;
    DataFile = FILE OF FileType;

VAR
    NumSubFiles : integer;      (* number of subfiles merged at each stage *)
    F1, F2, F,                  (* files to be used in mergesort *)
    NameFile : DataFile;        (* external file to be sorted *)

PROCEDURE ReadNames (VAR F, NameFile : DataFile);

    (*****************************************************************

        Procedure to read the names from NameFile and copy them
        to file F.

    *****************************************************************)

    BEGIN (* ReadNames *)
        reset (NameFile);
        rewrite (F);
        writeln ('Contents of original file:');
        writeln;
        WHILE NOT eof(NameFile) DO
            BEGIN
                read (NameFile, F↑);
                writeln (F↑);
                put (F);
            END (* WHILE *);
        writeln
    END (* ReadNames *);
```

Figure 14.6

Figure 14.6 (cont.)

```
PROCEDURE CopyOneItem (VAR FileA, FileB : DataFile;
                       VAR NextItemSmaller : boolean);

   (*****************************************************************

       Procedure to copy one item from FileA to FileB and to check
       if the next item in FileA is smaller than the one just copied
       (indicating the end of a subfile in FileA).

    ****************************************************************)

   BEGIN (* CopyOneItem *)
      IF NOT eof(FileA) THEN
         BEGIN
            read (FileA, FileB↑);
            IF eof(FileA) THEN
               NextItemSmaller := true
            ELSE
               NextItemSmaller := (FileA↑ < FileB↑);
            put (FileB)
         END (* IF *)
   END (* CopyOneItem *);

PROCEDURE CopySubFile (VAR FileA, FileB: DataFile; VAR EndSubfile : boolean);

   (*****************************************************************

       Procedure to copy a sorted subfile from FileA to FileB.

    ****************************************************************)

   BEGIN (* CopySubFile *)
      EndSubfile := false;
      WHILE NOT EndSubfile DO
         CopyOneItem (FileA, FileB, EndSubfile)
   END (* CopySubFile *);

PROCEDURE SplitFile (VAR F, F1, F2 : DataFile);

   (*****************************************************************

       Procedure to read sorted subfiles from file F and write them
       alternately to files F1 and F2.

    ****************************************************************)

   VAR
      FileNum : 1..2;            (* # of file being written to *)
      EndSubfile : boolean;      (* indicates end of subfile *)

   BEGIN (* SplitFile *)

      (* Open the files *)

      reset (F);
      rewrite (F1);
      rewrite (F2);
```

Figure 14.6 (cont.)

```
     (* Split the file *)

     FileNum := 1;
     WHILE NOT eof(F) DO
         BEGIN
             CASE FileNum OF
                     1 : CopySubFile (F, F1, EndSubfile);
                     2 : CopySubFile (F, F2, EndSubfile)
             END (* CASE *);

             (* Switch to other file *)

             FileNum := 3 - FileNum
         END (* WHILE *)
  END (* SplitFile *);

PROCEDURE Merge (VAR F, F1, F2 : DataFile; VAR NumSubFiles : integer);

  (*********************************************************************

     Procedure to merge sorted subfiles in F1 and F2 and write these
     to file F; NumSubFiles is the number of subfiles written to F.

  *********************************************************************)

  VAR
     FileNum :    1..2;              (* # of file being used *)
     EndSubfile : ARRAY[1..2] OF boolean;
                                     (* indicate end of subfiles in F1 and F2 *)

  BEGIN (* Merge *)

     (* Open the files *)

     reset (F1);
     reset (F2);
     rewrite (F);

     (* Now merge subfiles of F1 & F2 into F *)

     NumSubFiles := 0;
     WHILE NOT (eof(F1) OR eof(F2)) DO
         BEGIN

             (* set end-of-subfile indicators *)

             EndSubfile[1] := false;
             EndSubfile[2] := false;

             (* merge two subfiles *)

             WHILE NOT (eof(F1) OR eof(F2) OR
                         EndSubfile[1] OR EndSubfile[2]) DO
                 IF F1↑ < F2↑ THEN
                     CopyOneItem (F1, F, EndSubfile[1])
                 ELSE
                     CopyOneItem (F2, F, EndSubfile[2]);
```

Figure 14.6 (cont.)

```
                (* copy rest of other subfile *)

                IF EndSubfile[1] THEN
                   CopySubFile (F2, F, EndSubfile[2])
                ELSE
                   CopySubFile (F1, F, EndSubfile[1]);
                NumSubFiles := NumSubFiles + 1
            END (* WHILE *);

        (* Now copy any remaining subfiles in F1 or F2 to F *)

        WHILE NOT eof(F1) DO
            BEGIN
                CopySubFile (F1, F, EndSubfile[1]);
                NumSubFiles := NumSubFiles + 1
            END (* WHILE *);
        WHILE NOT eof(F2) DO
            BEGIN
                CopySubFile (F2, F, EndSubfile[2]);
                NumSubFiles := NumSubFiles + 1
            END (* WHILE *);
    END (* Merge *);

PROCEDURE PrintFile (VAR F : DataFile);

    (********************************************************************

            Procedure to print the contents of file F.

    ********************************************************************)

    BEGIN (* PrintFile *)
        reset (F);
        WHILE NOT eof(F) DO
            BEGIN
                writeln (F↑);
                get (F)
            END (* WHILE *)
    END (* PrintFile *);

    BEGIN (* main program *)
        ReadNames (F, NameFile);

        (* Now split and merge subfiles until number of sorted subfiles is 1 *)

        REPEAT
            SplitFile (F, F1, F2);
            Merge (F, F1, F2, NumSubFiles)
        UNTIL NumSubFiles = 1;

        (* Display sorted file *)

        writeln ('Contents of sorted file:');
        writeln;
        PrintFile (F)
    END (* main program *).
```

Figure 14.6 (cont.)

```
Sample run:
```

```
Contents of original File:
```

```
Doe, John Q.
Smith, Mary J.
Jones, Frederick N.
Vandervan, Peter F.
Adams, John Q.
Zzcyk, Stanislaw S.
Gertie, Dirty
James, Jesse
Terrific, Tom T.
Jackson, R.
```

```
Contents of sorted File:
```

```
Adams, John Q.
Doe, John Q.
Gertie, Dirty
Jackson, R.
James, Jesse
Jones, Frederick N.
Smith, Mary J.
Terrific, Tom T.
Vandervan, Peter F.
Zzcyk, Stanislaw S.
```

Mergesort can also be used as an internal sorting method for lists. The splitting and merge algorithms can easily be modified to use arrays or linked lists in place of files F, $F1$, and $F2$. However, in contrast to the other internal sorting schemes we have considered in which only one copy of the list is used, the extra storage required by mergesort makes it less space efficient, although its time efficiency is comparable to that of quicksort.

The worst case for mergesort occurs when the items are in reverse order. In this case the subfiles have sizes 1, 2, 4, 8, and so on. It follows that to sort a file or list of n items, $\log_2 n$ split and merge operations are required, and each of the n items must be examined in each of them. Hence, in the worst case, and as can be shown for the average case as well, the computing time for mergesort is O $(n \cdot \log_2 n)$.

Exercises

1. Following the example of the text, show the various splitting-merging stages of mergesort for the following lists of numbers:

    (a) 1, 5, 3, 8, 7, 2, 6, 4
    (b) 1, 8, 2, 7, 3, 6, 5, 4
    (c) 1, 2, 3, 4, 5, 6, 7, 8
    (d) 8, 7, 6, 5, 4, 3, 2, 1

2. Modify mergesort to sort a file of records so that the values in a key field are in order. Then write a program to read records from *UsersFile* (see Appendix E) and sort them so that the resources used to date are in increasing order.

3. One variation of the mergesort method is obtained by modifying the splitting operation as follows: copy some fixed number of elements into main memory, sort them using an internal sorting method such as insertion sort (see Exercise 16 of Section 8.3), and write this sorted list to *F1*; then read the same number of elements from *F* into main memory, sort them internally, and write this sorted list to *F2*, and so on, alternating between *F1* and *F2*. Write procedures for this modified merge-sort scheme, using insertion sort to sort internally the sublists containing *Size* elements for some constant *Size*.

4. Write a program that uses mergesort, appropriately modified, to sort a list stored in an array.

5. Proceed as in Exercise 4, but for a list stored in a linked list. For the merge operation, merge the two linked lists by simply changing links rather than actually copying the list elements into a third list.

14.6 Multiply Linked Structures: Trees

In Section 14.3 we analyzed the linear and binary search algorithms and showed that binary search is significantly more efficient than linear search. For each of these algorithms, however, the list was assumed to be stored in an array rather than in a linked list, as described in the preceding chapter. As we observed there, a linear search can be carried out with a linked list, but binary search is not feasible since it requires direct access to each item in the list. In this section we describe another data structure, a **binary search tree**, which makes a binary search possible while maintaining the flexibility of a linked structure. A binary search tree is a special kind of **tree**, an important data structure that is commonly implemented as a **multiply linked structure**, that is, one in which the nodes have more than one link field. In addition to their use in representing trees, such structures have many other applications; some of these are explored in the exercises.

A tree is a special case of a more general structure called a **directed graph**. A directed graph consists of a finite set of elements called **vertices** or **nodes** and a finite set of **directed arcs** that connect pairs of vertices. For example, a directed graph having five vertices numbered 1, 2, 3, 4, 5 and seven directed arcs joining vertices 1 to 2, 1 to 4, 1 to 5, 2 to 3, 2 to 4, 3 to itself, 4 to 2, and 4 to 3 might be pictured as

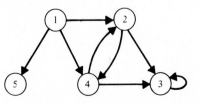

A *tree* is a directed graph in which one of the nodes, called the *root,* has no incoming arcs but from which each node in the tree can be reached by exactly one path, that is, by following a unique sequence of consecutive arcs. Thus the preceding directed graph is not a tree. The only vertex having no incoming arcs is vertex 1, and hence it is the only possibility for a root. However, because there are many different paths from vertex 1 to vertex 3 ($1 \rightarrow 2 \rightarrow 3$, $1 \rightarrow 4 \rightarrow 3$, $1 \rightarrow 4 \rightarrow 2 \rightarrow 3$, $1 \rightarrow 4 \rightarrow 2 \rightarrow 4 \rightarrow 3$, $1 \rightarrow 2 \rightarrow 3 \rightarrow 3 \rightarrow 3$, and so on), this directed graph is not a tree.

Trees are so named because they have a tree-like appearance, except that they are usually drawn upside down with the root at the top. For example,

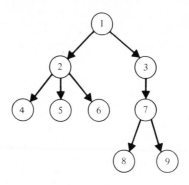

shows a tree having nine vertices in which vertex 1 is the root. Vertices having no outgoing arcs are called *leaves;* in this example, vertices 4, 5, 6, 8, and 9 are the leaves of the tree. Nodes that can be reached directly from a given node—that is, by using only one directed arc—are called the *children* of that node, and a node is said to be the *parent* of each of its children. For example, in the tree just shown, vertex 2 is the parent of vertices 4, 5, and 6, and these vertices are the children of vertex 2.

Applications of trees are many and varied. For example, a *genealogical tree* such as the following is a convenient way to picture a person's descendants:

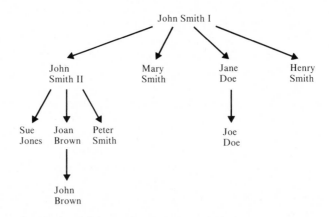

Game trees like the following, which shows the various configurations possible in the Tower of Hanoi problem with two disks (see Section 5.7), are used to analyze games and puzzles.

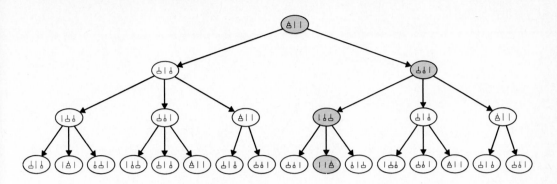

Parse trees constructed during compilation of a program are used to check the program's syntax; for example, the following parse tree might be produced for the Pascal statement

if $x < 0$ **then**
    Flag := 1

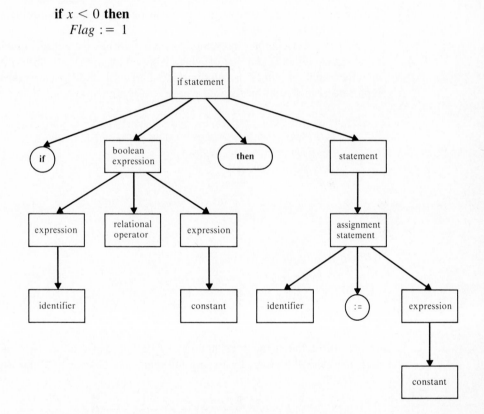

Binary trees, in which each node has at most two children, are especially useful in modeling processes in which an activity proceeds in stages, and at each stage there are two possible outcomes, on or off, 0 or 1, Yes or No, . or ＿, and so on. For example, a binary tree can be used to decode a message transmitted in Morse Code (see Exercise 13 of Section 9.4). In this case, the nodes represent the characters being encoded, and each directed arc is labeled with a dot or a dash. Thus, part of the tree for Morse Code is

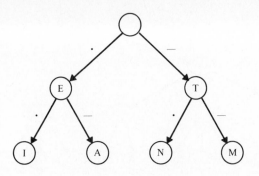

The sequence of dots and dashes labeling a path from the root to a particular node corresponds to the Morse Code for that character; for example, .. is the code for I and _. is the code for N.

In this section we confine our attention to binary trees. This is not a serious limitation, however, because any tree can be represented by a binary tree, as described in the exercises.

Binary trees can be represented as multiply linked structures in which each node has two link fields, one of which is a pointer to the left child of that node and the other of which is a pointer to the right child. Such nodes can be represented in Pascal by records whose declarations have the form

```
type
    DataType = . . . ; (* type of data items in the nodes *)
    TreePointer = ↑TreeNode;
    TreeNode = record
                    Data : DataType;
                    LChild, RChild : TreePointer
               end;
```

The two link fields *LChild* and *RChild* are pointers to nodes representing the left and right children, respectively,

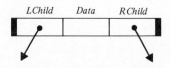

or are nil if the node does not have a left or right child. A leaf node is characterized, therefore, by having nil values for both *LChild* and *RChild*.

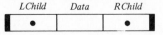

The binary tree

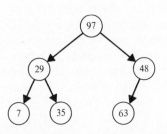

can thus be represented as the following linked tree of records:

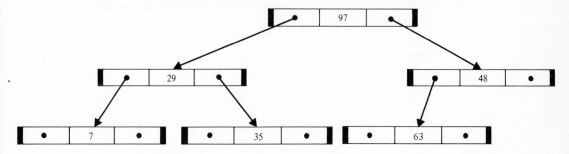

This binary tree has directed arcs from the root node containing 97 to the nodes containing 29 and 48. Each of these nodes is itself the root of a binary *subtree:*

In the same way, there are arcs from the node containing 29 to the nodes containing 7 and 35. Each of these may be thought of as the root of a binary subtree consisting of a single node (its left and right subtrees are empty):

This leads to the following ***recursive definition of a binary tree:***

A binary tree either
1. is empty or
2. consists of a node called the ***root,*** which has pointers to two disjoint binary (sub)trees called the ***left subtree*** and the ***right subtree.***

This recursive definition suggests that it may be easy to develop recursive algorithms for processing binary trees.

The first operation for binary trees that we consider is ***traversing*** the tree, that is, visiting each node in the binary tree exactly once. There are three basic steps in traversing a binary tree recursively: (1) visit a node, (2) traverse the left subtree of that node and (3) traverse the right subtree of that node. These three steps can be performed in any order. If we denote these steps by

    N: visit a node
    L: traverse the left subtree
    R: traverse the right subtree

then the six different orders are

    NLR
    LNR
    LRN
    NRL
    RNL
    RLN

We can reduce this list to the first three orders if we agree always to traverse the left subtree before the right subtree. The traversals that result from these three orders are given special names:

NLR: *preorder traversal*
LNR: *inorder traversal*
LRN: *postorder traversal*

To illustrate these traversals, consider the following binary tree:

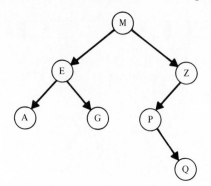

The three types of traversals visit the nodes in the following sequences:

preorder: M E A G Z P Q
inorder: A E G M P Q Z
postorder: A G E Q P Z M

The postorder traversal is obtained as follows: We begin at the root M, but before we list it, we must traverse its left and right subtrees. These subtrees are highlighted in the following diagram:

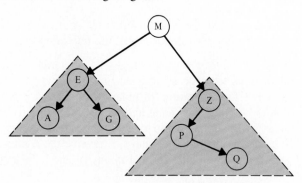

The left subtree has root E, but before listing it, we must traverse its left and right subtrees.

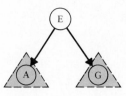

The left subtree has root A, but again we must first traverse its left and right subtrees before listing it.

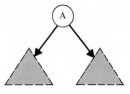

Because these subtrees are empty, A may now be listed. The right subtree of E has root G, which also has empty left and right subtrees,

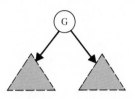

and thus G may be listed. Because both the left and right subtrees of E have been traversed, E may now be listed. The sequence of nodes visited thus far is

A G E

Because the left subtree of M has been traversed, we consider its right subtree having root Z. Before listing Z, we must traverse its left and right subtrees.

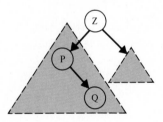

The left subtree has root P, and before listing P, we must traverse its left and right subtrees.

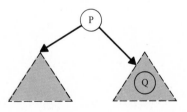

The left subtree is empty, and the right subtree has root Q.

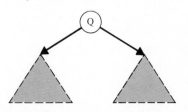

Because the left and right subtrees of Q are empty, Q may now be listed:

A G E Q

The left and right subtrees of P have now been traversed, and so P is listed:

A G E Q P

The left subtree of Z has now been traversed, and because its right subtree is empty, Z may now be listed:

A G E Q P Z

Finally, we may list the vertex M, as both its left and right subtrees have been traversed:

A G E Q P Z M

The reader should derive the preorder and inorder traversals in a similar manner.

The names *preorder, inorder,* and *postorder* for traversals of a binary tree are appropriate because they correspond to the prefix, infix, and postfix forms for an arithmetic expression. (See Section 14.2 and Exercise 9 in that section.) To illustrate, consider the arithmetic expression

A − B ∗ C + D

This can be represented as a binary tree by representing each operand as a child of a node that represents the corresponding operator:

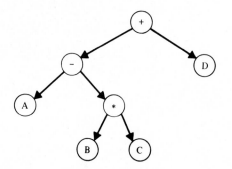

An inorder traversal of this binary tree produces the infix expression

A − B ∗ C + D

a preorder traversal yields the prefix expression

+ − A ∗ B C D

and a postorder traversal gives the postfix (RPN) expression

A B C ∗ − D +

The method we have used for traversing a binary tree is a recursive one, since traversing a tree (or subtree) requires traversing each of the subtrees pointed to by its root. Thus it is natural to use recursive procedures to traverse a binary tree. For example, a recursive procedure for inorder traversal is as follows:

procedure *InOrder* (*RootPointer* : *TreePointer*);

(∗ Procedure for inorder traversal of a binary tree ∗)

begin (∗ *InOrder* ∗)
   if *RootPointer* <> **nil then**   (∗ tree is not empty ∗)
     begin
       InOrder (*RootPointer*↑.*LChild*);   (∗ L operation ∗)
       Visit (*RootPointer*);   (∗ N operation ∗)
       InOrder (*RootPointer*↑.*RChild*)   (∗ R operation ∗)
     end (∗ **if** ∗)
  end (∗ *InOrder* ∗);

Here *Visit* is a procedure to process the data field *RootPointer*↑.*Data* of the node pointed to by *RootPointer*. Procedures for the preorder and postorder traversals are obtained by simply changing the order of the statements representing the L, N, and R operations, and are left as exercises.

To demonstrate how this procedure operates, suppose that the procedure *Visit* simply displays the data stored in a node, and consider the following binary tree:

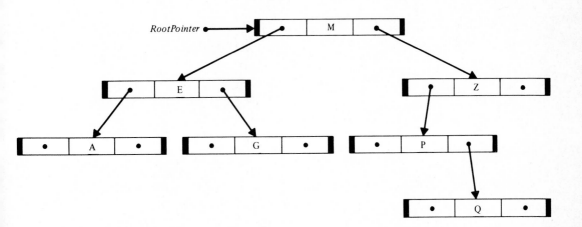

The statement

   InOrder (*RootPointer*)

calls the procedure *InOrder* to perform an inorder traversal of this tree. The action of this procedure while traversing the tree is indicated by the following table:

Contents of Current Node	Level in the Tree	Action	Output
M	1	Call *InOrder* with pointer to root (E) of the left subtree.	
E	2	Call *InOrder* with pointer to root (A) of left subtree.	
A	3	Call *Inorder* with pointer (nil) to root of left subtree.	
None	4	None; return to parent node.	
A	3	Display contents of node.	A
A	3	Call *InOrder* with pointer (nil) to root of right subtree	
None	4	None; return to parent node.	
A	3	Return to parent node.	
E	2	Display contents of node.	E
E	2	Call *InOrder* with pointer to root (G) of right subtree.	
G	3	Call *InOrder* with pointer (nil) to root of left subtree.	
None	4	None; return to parent node.	
G	3	Display contents of node.	G
G	3	Call *InOrder* with pointer (nil) to root of right subtree.	
None	4	None; return to parent node.	
G	3	Return to parent node.	
E	2	Return to parent node.	
M	1	Display contents of node.	M
M	1	Call *InOrder* with pointer to root (Z) of right subtree.	
Z	2	Call *InOrder* with pointer to root (P) of left subtree.	
P	3	Call *InOrder* with pointer (nil) to root of left subtree.	
None	4	None; return to parent node.	
P	3	Display contents of node.	P
P	3	Call *InOrder* with pointer to root (Q) of right subtree.	
Q	4	Call *InOrder* with pointer (nil) to root of left subtree.	
None	5	None; return to parent node.	
Q	4	Display contents of node.	Q
Q	4	Call *InOrder* with pointer (nil) to root of right subtree.	

Contents of Current Node	Level in the Tree	Action	Output
None	5	None; return to parent node.	
Q	4	Return to parent node.	
P	3	Return to parent node.	
Z	2	Display contents of node.	Z
Z	2	Call *InOrder* with pointer (nil) to root of right subtree.	
None	3	None; return to parent node.	
Z	2	Return to parent node.	
M	1	Terminate procedure; traversal complete.	

In the preceding example, the output produced by *InOrder* was

A E G M P Q Z

Note that the letters are in alphabetical order. This is because this binary tree has the special property that the items in the left subtree of each node are less than the item in that node, which in turn is less than all items in the right subtree. A binary tree having this property is called a ***binary search tree*** **(BST)** because it can be searched using an algorithm much like the binary search algorithm for arrays.

To illustrate, suppose we wish to search the following BST for 41:

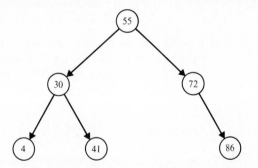

We begin at the root, and since 41 is less than the value 55 in the root, we know that the desired value is located in the left subtree of the root:

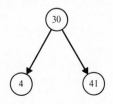

Now we continue the search by comparing the desired value with the value in the root of this subtree. Since 41 > 30, we know that the right subtree should be searched:

Examining the value in the root of this one-node subtree locates the desired value.

Similarly, in searching for the value 64, we are led to the right subtree after comparing 64 with the value 55 in the root:

Now, because 64 < 72, if the desired value is in the tree, it would be in the left subtree of the node containing 72; however, since this left subtree is empty, we conclude that the value 64 is not in the tree.

The following procedure *BSTSearch* for searching a binary search tree incorporates these techniques. The pointer *CurrPointer* begins at the root of the BST and then is repeatedly replaced by its left or right link, depending on whether the item for which we are searching is less than or greater than the value stored in the current node. This continues until either the desired item is found or *CurrPointer* becomes nil, indicating an empty subtree, in which case the item is not in the tree.

```
procedure BSTSearch (RootPointer : TreePointer; Item : DataType;
                     var CurrPointer : TreePointer;
                     var Found : boolean);

   (* Procedure to search the BST with root pointed to by RootPointer
      for a specified Item. Found is returned as true and CurrPointer
      points to a node containing Item if the search is successful;
      otherwise, Found is returned as false. *)

begin (* BSTSearch *)
   CurrPointer := FirstPointer;      (* begin at the root *)
   Found := false;
   while not Found and (CurrPointer <> nil) do
       with CurrPointer↑ do
           if Item < Data then        (* search left subtree *)
               CurrPointer := LChild
           else if Item > Data then   (* search right subtree *)
               CurrPointer := RChild
           else                        (* Item found *)
               Found := true
end (* BSTSearch *);
```

Since each time we move down to a subtree we search it in the same manner as the preceding (sub)tree, we could have written this procedure recursively (as the exercises ask you to do). This recursive procedure, however, is no shorter or easier to understand than the nonrecursive one given here.

For **balanced** binary search trees like that in this example, in which the left and right subtrees of each node contain approximately the same number of nodes, the elements are searched in a manner much like that of binary search for arrays of elements. At each stage, the number of elements in the subtree still to be searched is approximately one-half that of the current subtree. Binary search trees need not, however, have such a balanced structure. For example, the following is a BST containing the same values:

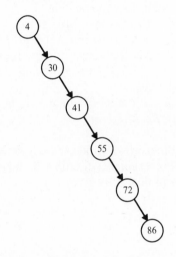

For such unbalanced BSTs, search times increase since the search procedure degenerates into a linear search.

A binary search tree can be constructed by repeatedly calling the following procedure to insert elements into a BST that is initially empty (*RootPointer* = **nil**). The method used to determine where an element is to be inserted is similar to that used in *BSTSearch*. We move down to a left or right subtree of a node, beginning at the root, depending on whether the element is less than or greater than the value in that node. (In the case of elements that are records, a key field within these records is the basis for comparison.) If the element is not already in the tree, we eventually reach an empty subtree in which the item is to be inserted. As in the case of the search procedure, an insert procedure can be written either recursively or nonrecursively; in this case, the recursive formulation is considerably shorter and easier to understand.

    procedure *RecBSTInsert* (**var** *RootPointer* : *TreePointer*;
                                  Element : *DataType*);

      (∗ Recursive procedure to insert *Element* into the BST with root pointed
        to by *RootPointer* ∗)

```
begin (* RecBSTInsert *)
    if RootPointer = nil then                    (* insert in empty tree *)
        begin
            new (RootPointer);
            with RootPointer↑ do
                begin
                    Data := Element;
                    LChild := nil;
                    RChild := nil
                end (* with *)
        end (* if *)
    else
        with RootPointer↑ do
            if Element < Data then                (* insert in left subtree *)
                RecBSTInsert (LChild, Element)
            else if Element > Data then           (* insert in right subtree *)
                RecBSTInsert (RChild, Element)
            else                                  (* Element already in tree *)
                writeln ('Item already in the tree')
end (* RecBSTInsert *);
```

The order in which items are inserted into a BST determines the shape of the tree. For example, inserting the letters C, A, B, L, and E into a BST of characters in this order gives

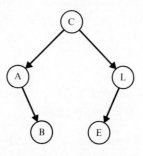

but inserting them in the order A, B, C, E, L yields

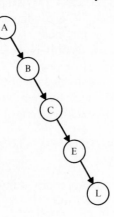

As we noted earlier, search time increases for such unbalanced trees. Insertion algorithms that avoid construction of such unbalanced trees are known, but are beyond the level of this introductory text.

If we combine this method of constructing a binary search tree with that for performing an inorder traversal, we obtain a new scheme for sorting a list of elements. We simply insert the list items into a BST, initially empty, and then use an inorder traversal to copy them back into the list. The following algorithm uses this technique to sort a list stored in an array.

TREESORT ALGORITHM

(∗ Algorithm that uses a BST to sort a list of n items stored in an array X so they are in ascending order. ∗)

1. Initialize an empty BST.
2. For i ranging from 1 to n:
   Insert $X[i]$ into the BST.
3. Initialize an index i to 0.
4. Perform an inorder traversal of the BST, where visiting a node consists of the following two steps:
   a. Increment i by 1.
   b. Set $X[i]$ equal to the data item in the current node

Deleting a leaf node in a binary search tree is easy to do, but deleting an interior node (one having at least one child) is more complicated. The exercises explore the deletion operation in more detail.

Exercises

1. For each of the following lists of letters,

   (a) Draw the binary search tree that is constructed when the letters are inserted in the order given.
   (b) Perform inorder, preorder, and postorder traversals of the tree and show the sequence of letters that results in each case.

   (i) M, I, T, E, R   **(ii)** T, I, M, E, R
   (iii) R, E, M, I, T   **(iv)** C, O, R, N, F, L, A, K, E, S

2. For the trees in Exercise 1, traverse each tree, using the following orders:

   (a) NRL   (b) RNL   (c) RLN

3. For each of the following arithmetic expressions, draw a binary tree that represents the expression, and then use tree traversals to find the

equivalent prefix and postfix (RPN) expressions:

(a) $A + B + C/D$
(b) $(A + B)/C - D$
(c) $(A + B) * ((C + D)/(E + F))$
(d) $A - (B - (C - (D - E)))$

4. Write procedures for preorder and postorder traversals of a binary tree.

5. **(a)** Preorder traversal of a certain binary tree produced

      A D F G H K L P Q R W Z

    and inorder traversal produced

      G F H K D L A W R Q P Z

    Draw the binary tree.

    (b) Postorder traversal of a certain binary tree produced

      F G H D A L P Q R Z W K

    and inorder traversal gave the same result as in (a). Draw the binary tree.

    (c) Show by example that knowing the results of a preorder traversal and a postorder traversal does not uniquely determine the binary tree; that is, give an example of two different binary trees for which a preorder traversal of each gives the same result, and so does a postorder traversal.

6. As noted in the text, every tree can be represented by a binary tree. This can be done by letting node x be a left child of node y in the binary tree if x is the leftmost child of y in the given tree, and by letting x be the right child of y if x and y are siblings (have the same parent) in the original tree. For example, the tree

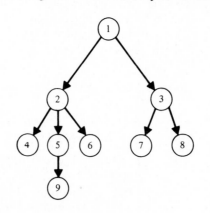

can be represented by the binary tree

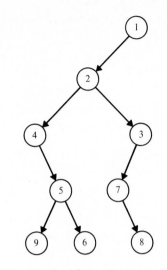

Represent each of the following by binary trees:

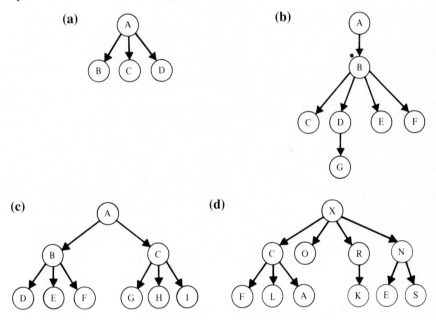

(a)

(b)

(c)

(d)

7. Write a recursive version of procedure *BSTSearch*.

8. Write a recursive function to count the number of leaves in a binary tree. (*Hint:* How is the number of leaves in the entire tree related to the number of leaves in the left and right subtrees of the root?)

9. Write a recursive function to find the depth of a binary tree. The depth of an empty tree is 0, and for a nonempty tree it is one more than the larger of the depths of the left and right subtrees of the root.

10. Write a recursive function to find the level in a BST at which a given item is located. The root is at level 0 and its children are at level 1.

11. Repeat Exercise 10, but do not assume that the binary tree is a BST.

12. Write a program to process a BST whose nodes contain characters. The user should be allowed to select from the following menu of options:

> I followed by a character: To insert a character
> S followed by a character: To search for a character
> TI: for inorder traversal
> TP: for preorder traversal
> TR: for postorder traversal
> QU: to quit

13. Write a procedure *TreeSort* that implements the treesort algorithm for sorting a list of items stored in (a) an array and (b) a linked list. You may assume that procedures *Inorder* and *BSTInsert* have been previously defined.

14. Write a program that reads a collection of records consisting of student numbers and names, and then uses the procedure *TreeSort* of Exercise 13 to sort them so that the student numbers are in ascending order.

15. Complete the binary tree begun in this section for decoding messages in Morse Code for the table of characters and codes in Exercise 13 of Section 9.4.

16. Write a program that uses a binary tree as described in Exercise 15 to decode messages in Morse Code.

17. To delete a node *x* from a BST, three cases must be considered: (1) *x* is a leaf; (2) *x* has only one subtree; (3) *x* has two subtrees. Case 1 is handled easily. For Case 2, simply replace *x* by the root of its subtree by linking the parent of *x* to this root. For Case 3, *x* must be replaced by its inorder successor (or predecessor). The following diagram illustrates this case:

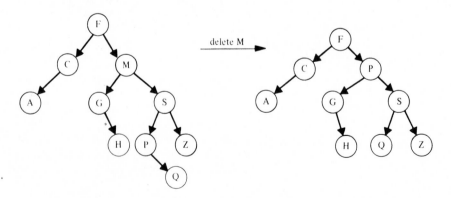

Write a procedure to delete an item from a BST. A procedure like *BSTSearch* can be used to locate the item and its parent in the tree.

18. For a certain company, the method by which the pay for each employee is computed depends on whether that employee is classified as an *Office* employee, a *Factory* employee, or a *Salesman*. Suppose that a file of employee records is maintained in which each record is a variant record containing the following information for each employee:

> Name (20 characters)
> Social security number (integer)
> Age (integer)
> Number of dependents (integer)
> Employee code (character O, F, S representing *Office, Factory,* and *Salesman,* respectively)
> Hourly rate if employee is *Factory*
> Annual salary if employee is *Office*
> A base pay (real) and a commission percentage (real) if employee is *Salesman*

Write a menu-driven program that allows at least the following options to be selected by the user of the program:

> GET :   Get the records from the employee file and store them in a binary search tree, sorted so that the names are in alphabetical order.
>
> INS :   Insert the record for a new employee into the BST.
>
> UPD :   Update the record of an employee already in the tree.
>
> RET :   Retrieve and display the record for a specified employee (by name or by social security number)
>
> LIS :   List the records (or perhaps selected items in the records) in order. This option should allow suboptions
> > ALL—to list for all employees
> > OFF—to list for only *Office* employees
> > FAC—to list for only *Factory*
> > SAL—to list for only *Salesman*
>
> SAV :   Copy the records from the BST into a permanent file.
>
> DEL :   Delete the record of an employee from the BST.

19. An alternative storage structure for a BST is an array. We simply number each of the possible positions in the BST from top to bottom, numbering from left to right on each level

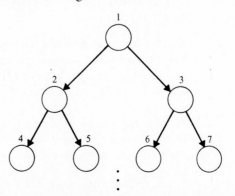

and then store an item in the *i*th position of the BST in the *i*th location of an array B.

a. Show what each element of array *B* would be for the BSTs in Exercise 1.

b. In general, why is this an inefficient way to store BSTs? For what kinds of BSTs is this a good storage structure to use?

20. Assume that array B is used to store a BST containing positive integers, as described in Exercise 19. Write a procedure to perform *BSTSearch* for this implementation.

21. In a ***doubly*** or ***symmetrically linked list,*** each node has two link fields, one containing a pointer to the predecessor of that node and the other containing a pointer to its successor. It might be pictured as follows

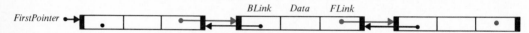

FirstPointer

and is especially useful when it is necessary to traverse a linked list or a part of it in either direction.

(a) Write the necessary type declarations for such a doubly linked list.

(b) Write a procedure for traversing the list from left to right.

(c) Write a procedure for traversing the list from right to left.

(d) Write a procedure for inserting an item (1) after or (2) before some other given element in a doubly linked list.

(e) Write a procedure to delete an item from a doubly linked list.

22. A ***doubly linked ring*** or ***doubly linked circular list*** is a doubly linked list in which the nil right pointer in the last node is replaced with a pointer to the first node, and the nil left pointer in the first node is replaced with a pointer to the last node.

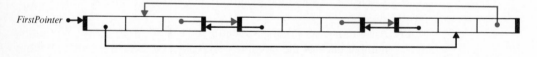

FirstPointer

Assuming that *FirstPointer* points to the first node, write procedures to

(a) Traverse the list from left to right.

(b) Traverse the list from right to left.

(c) Insert an item (1) after or (2) before a given element in the list.

(d) Delete an item from the list.

23. Another application of multiply linked lists is to maintain a list sorted in two or more different ways. For example, consider the following multiply linked list having two links per node:

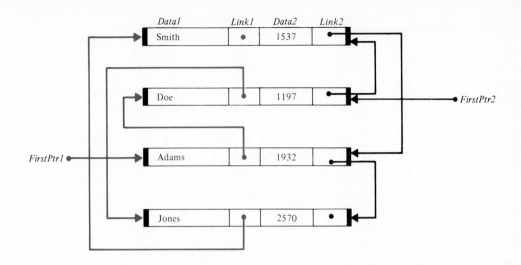

If this list is traversed and the data fields displayed by using *FirstPtr1* to point to the first node and following the pointers in the field *Link1*, the names are in alphabetical order:

Adams	1932
Doe	1197
Jones	2570
Smith	1537

A traversal using *FirstPtr2* to point to the first node and following pointers in the field *Link2* gives the identification numbers in ascending order:

Doe	1197
Smith	1537
Adams	1932
Jones	2570

This list is logically ordered, therefore, in two different ways. Write a program to read the first ten records from *UsersFile* (see Appendix E), and store them in a multiply linked list that is logically sorted so that the user identification numbers are in ascending order and the resources used to date are in descending order. Traverse the list and display the records so that the identification numbers are in ascending order. Then traverse the list and display the records so that the resources used to date are in descending order.

24. In Exercise 12 of Chapter 13, a linked list representation for a polynomial in x,

$$P(x) = a_n x^n + a_{n-1} x^{n-1} + \cdots + a_1 x + a_0$$

was described. A ***polynomial in two variables*** x and y can be viewed as a polynomial in one variable y, with coefficients that are polynomials in x; that is, it has the form

$$P(x,y) = A_m(x)y^m + A_{m-1}(x)y^{m-1} + \cdots + A_1(x)y + A_0(x)$$

where each $A_i(x)$ is a polynomial in x. For example,

$$7x^5y^3 + 5x^2y^3 + 4x^5y^2 - 3xy^2 + y^2 + 7x + 1$$

can be rewritten as

$$(7x^5 + 5x^2)y^3 + (4x^5 - 3x + 1)y^2 + (7x + 1)$$

A multiply linked representation for such polynomials is obtained by representing each term of the form $A_k(x)y^k$ by a node that stores the exponent of y and two links, one containing a pointer to a linked list representing the polynomial $A_k(x)$ and the other a pointer to the next term. For example, the first term in the preceding example can be represented as

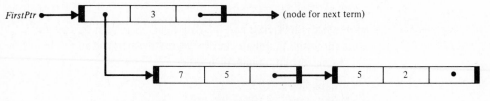

(a) Draw a multiply linked representation for

$$P(x,y) = 3x^9y^5 + 5x^7y^5 - 7x^5y^5 + 6x^2y^4$$
$$+ xy^4 + 2xy + 9y + x^2 + 4x + 1$$

(b) Write a program to read triples of the form

(coefficient, x-exponent, y-exponent)

for a polynomial in x and y and construct its linked representation. Then read values for x and y and find the corresponding value of the polynomial.

(c) Modify the program in part (b) so that the exponents of x and the exponents of y need not be read in decreasing order.

A

ASCII and EBCDIC

Decimal	Binary	Octal	Hexadecimal	ASCII	EBCDIC
0	00000000	0	0	NUL	NUL
.	.	.	.	.	.
.	.	.	.	.	.
.	.	.	.	.	.
32	00100000	40	20	space	
33	00100001	41	21	!	
34	00100010	42	22	"	
35	00100011	43	23	#	
36	00100100	44	24	$	
37	00100101	45	25	%	
38	00100110	46	26	&	
39	00100111	47	27	'	
40	00101000	50	28	(	
41	00101001	51	29	)	
42	00101010	52	2A	*	
43	00101011	53	2B	+	
44	00101100	54	2C	,	
45	00101101	55	2B	−	
46	00101110	56	2E	.	
47	00101111	57	2F	/	
48	00110000	60	30	0	
49	00110001	61	31	1	
50	00110010	62	32	2	
51	00110011	63	33	3	
52	00110100	64	34	4	
53	00110101	65	35	5	
54	00110110	66	36	6	
55	00110111	67	37	7	
56	00111000	70	38	8	
57	00111001	71	39	9	
58	00111010	72	3A	:	
59	00111011	73	3B	;	
60	00111100	74	3C	<	
61	00111101	75	3D	=	
62	00111110	76	3E	>	
63	00111111	77	3F	?	
64	01000000	100	40	@	blank

Decimal	Binary	Octal	Hexadecimal	ASCII	EBCDIC
65	01000001	101	41	A	
66	01000010	102	42	B	
67	01000011	103	43	C	
68	01000100	104	44	D	
69	01000101	105	45	E	
70	01000110	106	46	F	
71	01000111	107	47	G	
72	01001000	110	48	H	
73	01001001	111	49	I	
74	01001010	112	4A	J	¢
75	01001011	113	4B	K	.
76	01001100	114	4C	L	<
77	01001101	115	4D	M	(
78	01001110	116	4E	N	+
79	01001111	117	4F	O	|
80	01010000	120	50	P	&
81	01010001	121	51	Q	
82	01010010	122	52	R	
83	01010011	123	53	S	
84	01010100	124	54	T	
85	01010101	125	55	U	
86	01010110	126	56	V	
87	01010111	127	57	W	
88	01011000	130	58	X	
89	01011001	131	59	Y	
90	01011010	132	5A	Z	!
91	01011011	133	5B	[	$
92	01011100	134	5C	\	*
93	01011101	135	5D	]	)
94	01011110	136	5E	$\wedge$ (or $\uparrow$)	;
95	01011111	137	5F	_ (or $\leftarrow$)	¬
96	01100000	140	60	`	−
97	01100001	141	61	a	/
98	01100010	142	62	b	
99	01100011	143	63	c	
100	01100100	144	64	d	
101	01100101	145	65	e	
102	01100110	146	66	f	
103	01100111	147	67	g	
104	01101000	150	68	h	
105	01101001	151	69	i	
106	01101010	152	6A	j	
107	01101011	153	6B	k	
108	01101100	154	6C	l	%
109	01101101	155	6D	m	—
110	01101110	156	6E	n	>
111	01101111	157	6F	o	?
112	01110000	160	70	p	
113	01110001	161	71	q	
114	01110010	162	72	r	
115	01110011	163	73	s	
116	01110100	164	74	t	
117	01110101	165	75	u	
118	01110110	166	76	v	
119	01110111	167	77	w	
120	01111000	170	78	x	

Decimal	Binary	Octal	Hexadecimal	ASCII	EBCDIC
121	01111001	171	79	y	
122	01111010	172	7A	z	:
123	01111011	173	7B	{	#
124	01111100	174	7C	|	@
125	01111101	175	7D	}	'
126	01111110	176	7E	~	=
127	01111111	177	7F	DEL	"
128	10000000	200	80		
129	10000001	201	81		a
130	10000010	202	82		b
131	10000011	203	83		c
132	10000100	204	84		d
133	10000101	205	85		e
134	10000110	206	86		f
135	10000111	207	87		g
136	10001000	210	88		h
137	10001001	211	89		i
.	.	.	.		.
.	.	.	.		.
.	.	.	.		.
145	10010001	221	91		j
146	10010010	222	92		k
147	10010011	223	93		l
148	10010100	224	94		m
149	10010101	225	95		n
150	10010110	226	96		o
151	10010111	227	97		p
152	10011000	230	98		q
153	10011001	231	99		r
		.	.		.
		.	.		.
		.	.		.
162	10100010	242	A2		s
163	10100011	243	A3		t
164	10100100	244	A4		u
165	10100101	245	A5		v
166	10100110	246	A6		w
167	10100111	247	A7		x
168	10101000	250	A8		y
169	10101001	251	A9		z
.	.	.	.		.
.	.	.	.		.
.	.	.	.		.
192	11000000	300	C0		}
193	11000001	301	C1		A
194	11000010	302	C2		B
195	11000011	303	C3		C
196	11000100	304	C4		D
197	11000101	305	C5		E
198	11000110	306	C6		F
199	11000111	307	C7		G
200	11001000	310	C8		H
201	11001001	311	C9		I
.		.	.		.
.		.	.		.
.		.	.		.

Decimal	Binary	Octal	Hexadecimal	ASCII	EBCDIC
208	11010000	320	D0		}
209	11010001	321	D1		J
210	11010010	322	D2		K
211	11010011	323	D3		L
212	11010100	324	D4		M
213	11010101	325	D5		N
214	11010110	326	D6		O
215	11010111	327	D7		P
216	11011000	330	D8		Q
217	11011001	331	D9		R
.	.	.	.		.
.	.	.	.		.
.	.	.	.		.
224	11100000	340	E0		\
225	11100001	341	E1		
226	11100010	342	E2		S
227	11100011	343	E3		T
228	11100100	344	E4		U
229	11100101	345	E5		V
230	11100110	346	E6		W
231	11100111	347	E7		X
232	11101000	350	E8		Y
233	11101001	351	E9		Z
.	.	.	.		.
.	.	.	.		.
.	.	.	.		.
240	11110000	360	F0		0
241	11110001	361	F1		1
242	11110010	362	F2		2
243	11110011	363	F3		3
244	11110100	364	F4		4
245	11110101	365	F5		5
246	11110110	366	F6		6
247	11110111	367	F7		7
248	11111000	370	F8		8
249	11111001	371	F9		9
.	.	.	.		
.	.	.	.		
.	.	.	.		
255	11111111	377	FF		

Note: Entries for which there is no character shown indicate that these codes have not been assigned or are used for control.

B

Reserved Words, Standard Identifiers, and Operators

Reserved Words

and	end	mod	repeat
array	file	nil	set
begin	for	not	then
case	forward	of	to
const	function	or	type
div	goto	packed	until
do	if	procedure	var
downto	in	program	while
else	label	record	with

Standard Identifiers

Predefined Constants
false   *true*   *maxint*

Predefined Types
boolean   *char*   *integer*   *real*   *text*

Predefined Files
input   *output*

Predefined Functions

abs	*exp*	*sin*
arctan	*ln*	*sqr*
chr	*odd*	*sqrt*
cos	*ord*	*succ*
eof	*pred*	*trunc*
eoln	*round*	

Predefined Procedures

dispose	*put*	*unpack*
get	*read*	*write*
new	*readln*	*writeln*
pack	*reset*	
page	*rewrite*	

Operators

Unary Arithmetic Operators

Operator	Operation	Type of Operand	Type of Result
+	unary plus	integer	integer
		real	real
–	unary minus	integer	integer
		real	real

Binary Arithmetic Operators

Operator	Operation	Type of Operands	Type of Result
+	addition	integer or real	integer if both operands are integer, otherwise real
–	subtraction	integer or real	integer if both operands are integer, otherwise real
*	multiplication	integer or real	integer if both operands are integer, otherwise real
/	division	integer or real	real
div	integer division	integer	integer
mod	modulo	integer	integer

Relational Operators

Operator	Operation	Type of Operands	Type of Result
=	equality	simple, string, set, or pointer	boolean
<>	inequality	simple, string, set, or pointer	boolean
<	less than	simple or string	boolean
>	greater than	simple or string	boolean
<=	less than or equal to, or subset	simple, string, or set	boolean
>=	greater than or equal to, or superset	simple, string, or set	boolean
in	set membership	first operand: ordinal type second operand: set type	boolean

Boolean Operators

Operator	Operation	Type of Operands	Type of Result
and	conjunction	boolean	boolean
not	negation	boolean	boolean
or	disjunction	boolean	boolean

Set Operators

Operator	Operation	Type of Operands	Type of Result
+	set union	set type	same as operands
−	set difference	set type	same as operands
*	set intersection	set type	same as operands

Assignment Operator

Operator	Operation	Type of Operands
:=	assignment	any type except file types

C

Syntax Diagrams

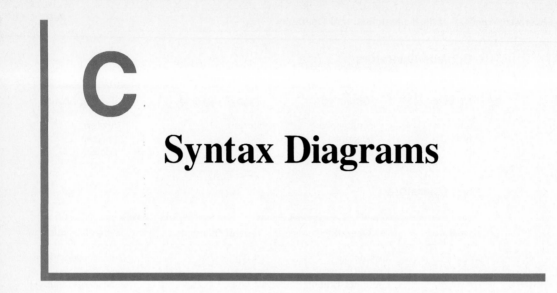

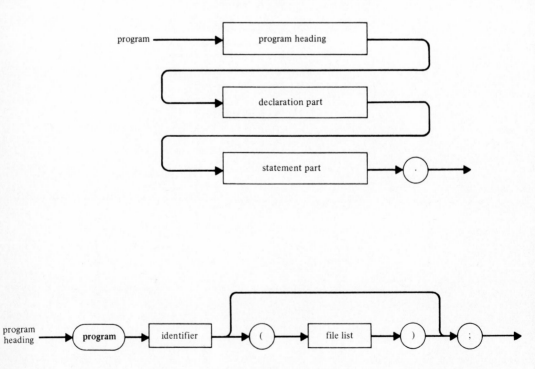

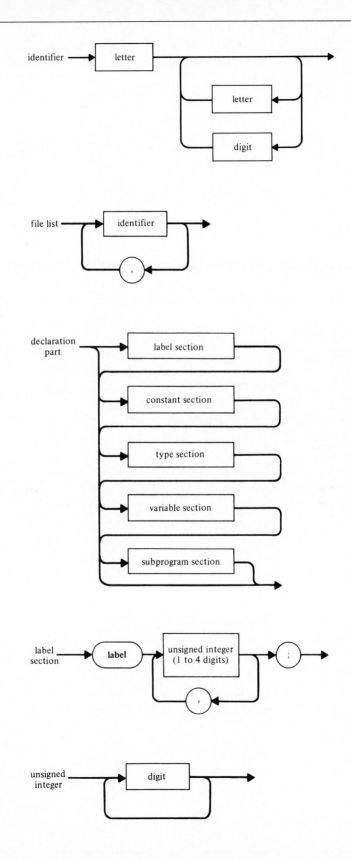

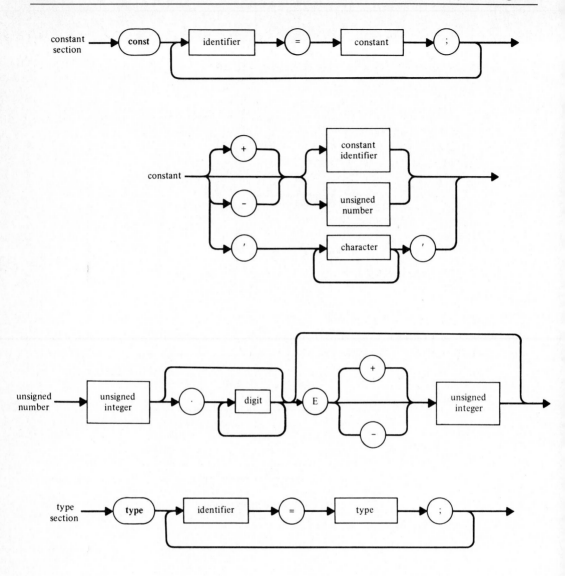

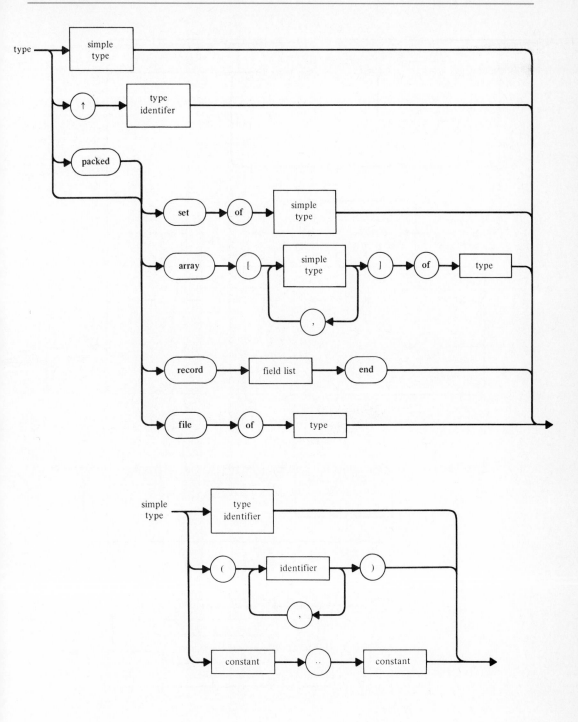

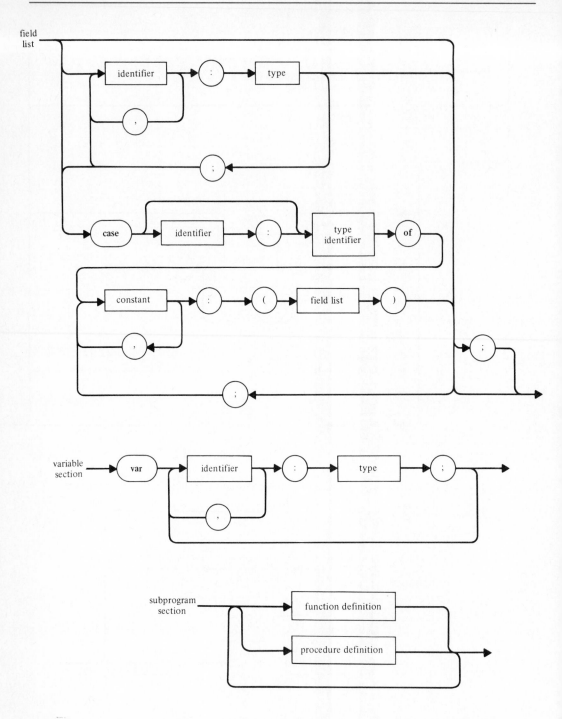

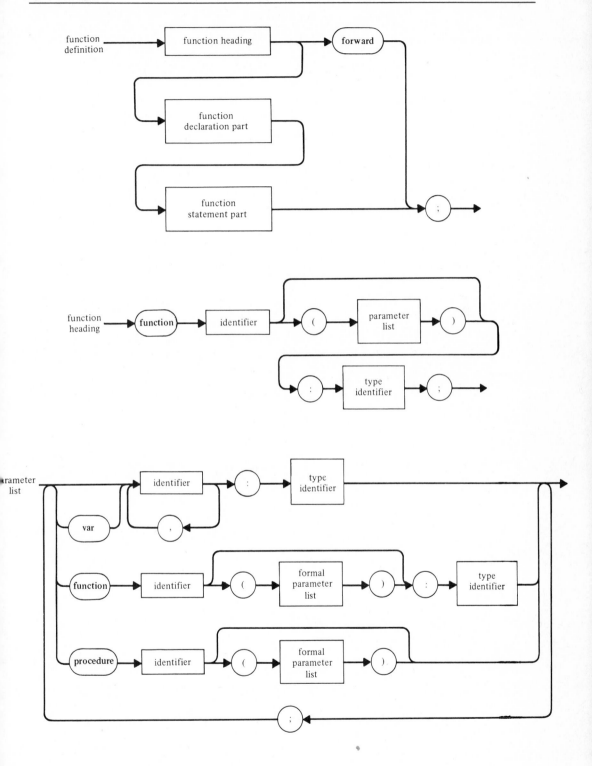

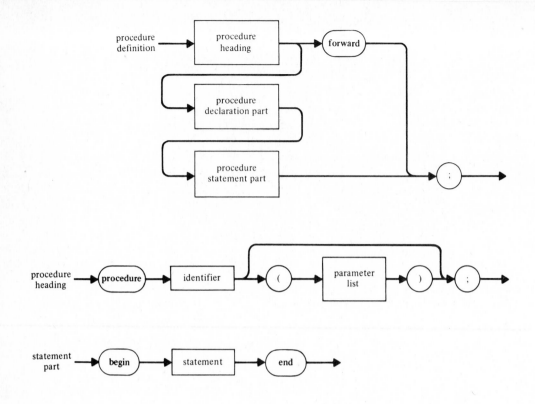

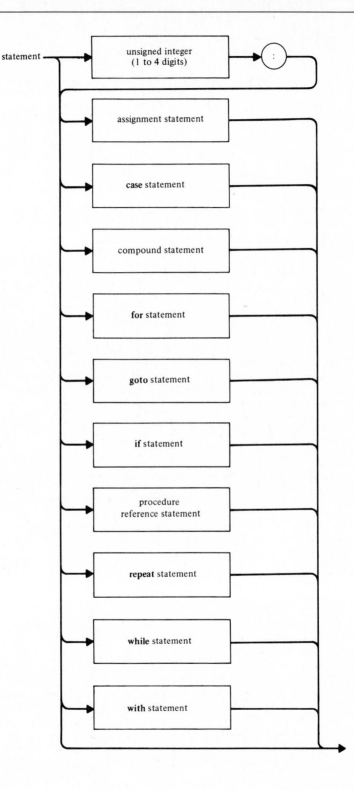

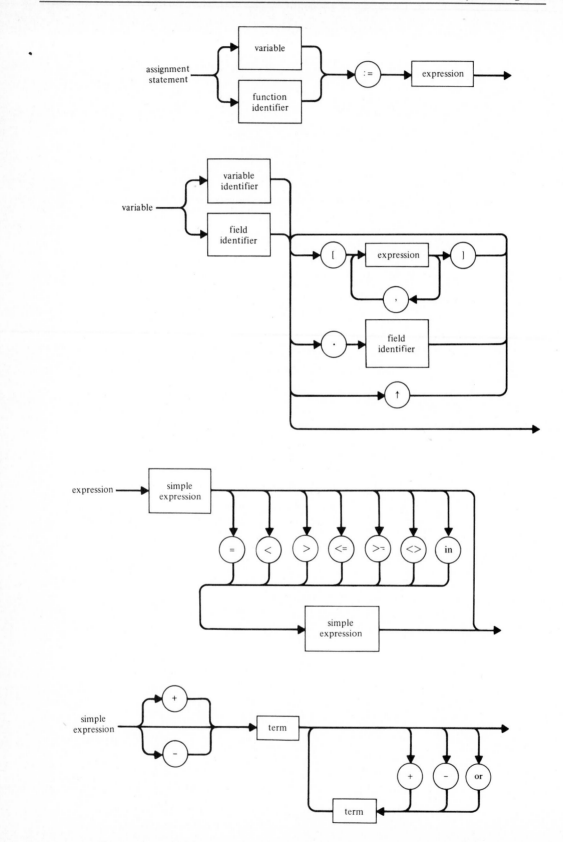

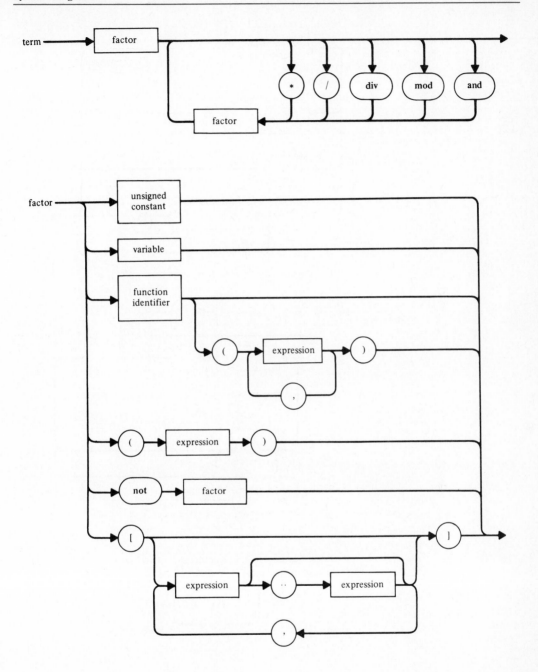

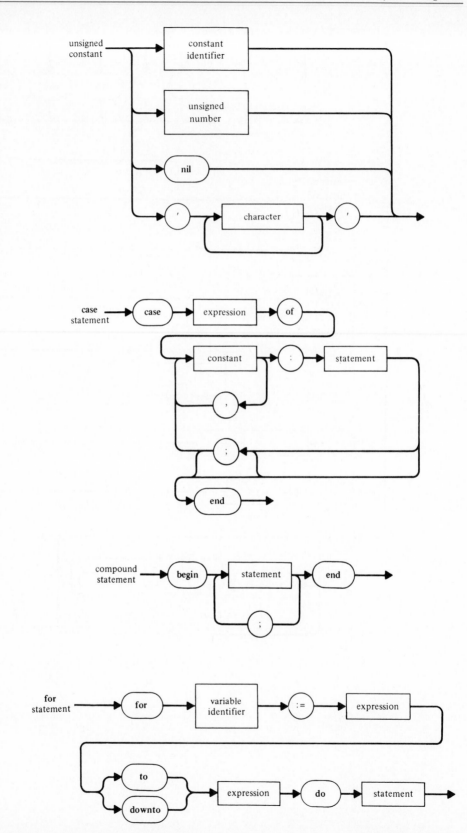

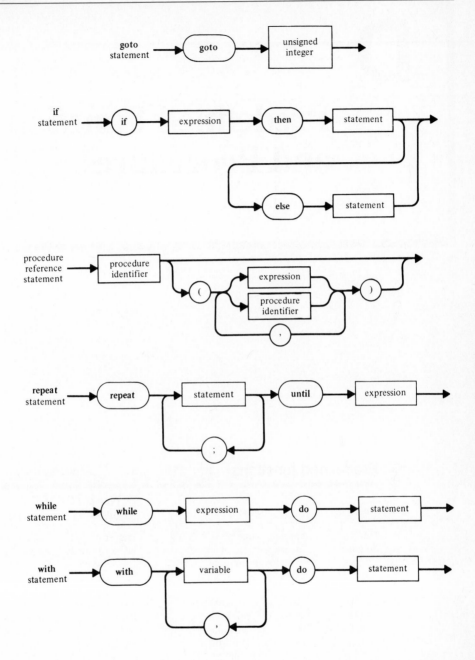

D

Predefined Functions and Procedures

Predefined functions

Function	Description	Type of Argument	Type of Value
$abs(x)$	absolute value of x	integer or real	same as arguments
$arctan(x)$	inverse tangent of x (value in radians)	integer or real	real
$chr(x)$	character whose ordinal number is x	integer	character
$cos(x)$	cosine of x (in radians)	integer or real	real
$eof(f)$	end-of-file function	file	boolean
$eoln(f)$	end-of-line function	text	boolean
$exp(x)$	exponential function e^x	integer or real	real
$ln(x)$	natural logarithm of x	integer or real	real
$odd(x)$	true if x is odd, false otherwise	integer	boolean
$ord(x)$	ordinal number of x	ordinal	integer
$pred(x)$	predecessor of x	ordinal	ordinal
$round(x)$	x rounded to nearest integer	real	integer
$sin(x)$	sine of x (in radians)	integer or real	real
$sqr(x)$	x^2	integer or real	same as argument
$sqrt(x)$	square root of x	integer or real	real
$succ(x)$	successor of x	ordinal	ordinal
$trunc(x)$	x truncated to its integer part	real	integer

Predefined procedures

Procedure	Description
dispose (*P*) *dispose* (*P, tag-value-list*)	Releases the memory location pointed to by pointer variable *P*, leaving *P* undefined. The second form may be used for variant records.
get (*F*)	Advances the data pointer in file *F* to the next component and assigns this component to the file buffer variable *F*↑.
new (*P*) *new* (*P, tag-value-list*)	Acquires a memory location and assigns its address to pointer variable *P*. The second form may be used for variant records.
pack (*U, First, P*)	Copies the elements of the unpacked array *U* beginning at position *First* to the packed array *P*.
page (*F*)	Causes a system-dependent effect on the text file *F* such that subsequent text written to *F* will be on a new page if *F* is printed on a suitable output device.
put (*F*)	Transfers the contents of the buffer variable *F*↑ to the file *F*.
read (*F, input-list*)	Reads values from the file *F* and assigns these to the variables in the input list. If *F* is not specified, the standard file *input* is assumed.
readln (*F, input-list*)	Reads values from the text file *F*, assigns these to the variables in the input list, and then advances the data pointer in *F* past the next end-of-line mark. If *F* is not specified, the standard file *input* is assumed.
reset (*F*)	Opens the file *F* for input, positions the data pointer in *F* at the first file component, and assigns this component to the file buffer variable *F*↑.
rewrite (*F*)	Creates the empty file *F* and opens it for output. Any previous contents of *F* are destroyed.
unpack (*P, U, First*)	Copies the elements of the packed array *P* beginning at position *First* to the unpacked array *U*.
write (*F, output-list*)	Writes the values of the items in the output list to file *F*. If *F* is not specified, the standard file *output* is assumed.
writeln (*F, output-list*)	Writes the values of the items in the output list to text file *F* followed by an end-of-line mark. If *F* is not specified, the standard file *output* is assumed.

E

Sample Data Files

Several exercises in the text use the files *InventoryFile, InventoryUpdate, Least-SquaresFile, StudentFile, StudentUpdate,* and *UsersFile.* This appendix describes the contents of these files and gives a sample listing for each.

InventoryFile
Item number: a six-digit integer
Number currently in stock: an integer in the range 0 through 999
Unit price: a real value
Minimum inventory level: an integer in the range 0 through 999, followed by a blank
Item name: a 25-character string

File is sorted so that item numbers are in increasing order.

Sample InventoryFile:

```
101001  20   54.95   15 TELEPHOTO POCKET CAMERA
101002  12   24.95   15 MINI POCKET CAMERA
102001  20   49.95   10 POL. ONE-STEP CAMERA
102002  13  189.95   12 SONAR 1-STEP CAMERA
102003  15   74.95    5 PRONTO CAMERA
103001   9  279.99   10 8MM ZOOM MOVIE CAMERA
103002  15  310.55   10 SOUND/ZOOM 8MM CAMERA
104001  10  389.00   12 35MM SLR XG-7 MINO. CAM.
104002  11  349.95   12 35MM SLR AE-1 PENT. CAM.
104003  20  319.90   12 35MM SLR ME CAN. CAM.
104101  13  119.95   12 35MM HI-MATIC CAMERA
104102  20   89.99   12 35MM COMPACT CAMERA
151001   7  129.95    5 ZOOM MOVIE PROJECTOR
151002   9  239.99    5 ZOOM-SOUND PROJECTOR
152001  10  219.99    5 AUTO CAROUSEL PROJECTOR
152002   4  114.95    5 CAR. SLIDE PROJECTOR
201001   4   14.95    5 POCKET STROBE
201002  12   48.55   10 STROBE SX-10
201003  10   28.99   15 ELEC.FLASH SX-10
301001  13   32.99   15 TELE CONVERTER
301002  14   97.99   15 28MM WIDE-ANGLE LENS
301003  13   87.95   15 135MM TELEPHOTO LENS
301004   8  267.95    5 35-105 MM ZOOM LENS
301005   7  257.95    5 80-200 MM ZOOM LENS
311001   4   67.50    5 HEAVY-DUTY TRIPOD
311002  10   19.95    5 LIGHTWEIGHT TRIPOD
351001  10  159.99    5 35MM ENLARGER KIT
401001   4   35.98    5 40X40 DELUXE SCREEN
401002  10   44.98    5 50X50 DELUXE SCREEN
501001  17    4.29   25 120-SLIDE TRAY
501002  33    2.95   25 100-SLIDE TRAY
502001  12    6.25   15 SLIDE VIEWER
503001  12   55.95   10 MOVIE EDITOR
601001  10   59.95    5 CONDENSER MICROPHONE
611001  80    0.89  100 AA ALKALINE BATTERY
701001  19   19.79   20 GADGET BAG
801001  45    1.49   50 135-24 COLOR FILM
802001  60    0.99   50 110-12 COLOR FILM
802002  42    1.45   50 110-24 COLOR FILM
802003  37    0.59   25 110-12 B/W FILM
802004  43    0.95   25 110-24 B/W FILM
803001  44    0.89   50 126-12 COLOR FILM
803002  27    0.59   25 126-12 B/W FILM
804001  39    6.89   50 8MM FILM CASSETTE
```

InventoryUpdate
Order number: three letters followed by four digits
Item number: a six-digit integer (same as those in *InventoryFile*)
Transaction code: a character (S = sold, R = returned)
Number of items sold or returned: an integer in the range 0 through 999

File is sorted so that item numbers are in increasing order. (Some items in *InventoryFile* may not have update records; others may have more than one.)

Sample InventoryUpdate:

CCI7543	101002S	2		BTP5396	301003S	1
LTB3429	101002S	7		GFL4913	301003S	8
DJS6762	102001S	9		EHQ7510	301003S	7
NQT1850	102002S	1		QQL6472	301003S	5
WYP6425	102003S	4		SVC6511	301004S	4
YOK2210	102003R	2		XJQ9391	301004S	4
QGM3144	102003S	1		ONO5251	311001S	3
NPQ8685	103001S	5		CXC7780	311001S	1
MAP8102	103001S	13		VGT8169	311002S	8
JRJ6335	103001S	1		IMK5861	351001S	2
UWR9386	103002S	3		QHR1944	351001S	1
TJY1913	103002S	11		ZPK6211	401001S	2
YHA9464	104001S	5		VDZ2970	401002S	6
SYT7493	104001S	3		BOJ9069	501001S	6
FHJ1657	104002S	7		MNL7029	501001S	9
OJQ2215	104003S	8		MRG8703	502001S	10
UOX7714	104003S	2		DEM9289	502001S	1
ERZ2147	104003S	7		BXL1651	503001S	2
MYW2540	104101S	1		VAF8733	611001S	65
UKS3587	104102S	2		UYI0368	701001S	2
AAN3759	104102S	2		VIZ6879	801001S	16
WZT4171	104102S	12		GXX9093	801001S	19
TYR9475	151001S	1		HHO5605	802001S	41
FRQ4184	151001S	1		BOL2324	802001S	49
TAV3604	151002S	2		PAG9289	802003S	15
DCW9363	152002S	1		MDF5557	802003S	17
EXN3964	152002R	1		IQK3388	802004S	12
OIN5524	152002S	1		OTB1341	802004S	28
EOJ8218	152002S	1		SVF5674	803001S	24
YFK0683	201001S	2		ZDP9484	803001S	15
PPX4743	201002S	4		OSY8177	803002S	15
DBR1709	201003S	4		GJQ0185	803002S	8
JOM5408	201003S	3		VHW0189	804001S	20
PKN0671	201003S	1		WEU9225	804001S	6
LBD8391	301001S	9		YJO3755	804001S	8
DNL6326	301002S	9				

LeastSquaresFile

This is a text file in which each line contains a pair of real numbers representing the *x* coordinate and the *y* coordinate of a point.

Sample LeastSquaresFile:

2.18	1.06		7.5	12.32
7.46	12.04		7.49	11.74
5.75	8.68		7.62	12.07
3.62	4.18		7.39	12.17
3.59	3.87		1.88	0.58

(cont.)

6.31	10.09	9.59	15.82
2.53	2.04	1.81	0.45
5.44	8.25	0.99	-0.71
1.21	-0.76	4.82	6.91
9.07	15.5	9.68	16.24
3.95	5.0	1.21	-0.22
9.63	17.01	4.54	5.64
9.75	16.91	1.48	0.3
9.99	16.67	6.58	9.8
3.61	4.69	3.05	3.56
9.06	15.0	6.19	9.62
5.03	6.62	6.47	9.83
4.45	6.12	8.13	10.75
4.54	5.89	7.31	11.73
0.92	-1.02	0.33	-1.93
0.82	-1.5	5.12	7.41
2.62	2.1	5.23	7.73
5.66	8.53	7.14	11.02
8.05	13.05	1.27	-0.21
8.99	14.85	2.51	1.59
5.12	7.03	5.26	7.86
3.85	4.43	4.74	6.19
6.08	9.21	2.1	2.12
1.42	0	5.27	7.73
2.58	2.38	2.85	2.63
5.99	9.42	1.99	1.09
0.63	-1.63	8.91	15.03
9.98	17.25	2.19	1.21
5.63	8.58	1.6	-0.05
8.94	15.27	8.93	15.12
7.34	11.48	3.19	3.56
6.55	9.92	3.37	3.64
4.89	7.07		

StudentFile
Student number: a six-digit integer
Student's last name: a 15-character string
Student's first name: a 10-character string
Student's middle initial: a character
Hometown: 25-character string
Phone number: a seven-digit integer
Sex: a character (M or F)
Class level: a one-digit integer (1, 2, 3, 4, or 5 for special)
Major: a four-character string
Total credits earned to date: an integer
Cumulative GPA: a real value

File is arranged so that student numbers are in increasing order.

Sample StudentFile:

```
010103JOHNSON           JAMES     L
WAUPUN, WISCONSIN            7345229M1ENGR 15 3.15
010104ANDREWS           PETER     J
GRAND RAPIDS, MICHIGAN   9493301M2CPSC 42 2.78
010110PETERSON          SAMUEL    L
LYNDEN, WASHINGTON          3239550M5ART  63 2.05
010113VANDEN KLOP       MARILYN   K
FREMONT, MICHIGAN           5509237F4HIST110 3.74
010126BROOKS            SUSAN     R
CHINO, CALIFORNIA           3330861F3PHIL 78 3.10
010144LUCKETT           FREDERICK M
GRANDVILLE, MICHIGAN        7745424M5HIST 66 2.29
010179DE VRIES          NANCY     L
THREE RIVERS, MICHIGAN   6290017F1MATH 15 3.83
010191NAKAMURA          BENJAMIN  C
CHICAGO, ILLINOIS           4249665M1SOCI 12 1.95
010226MORRIS            REBECCA   J
LYNDEN, WASHINGTON          8340115F1PSYC 15 1.85
010272JEFFERSON         GREGORY   W
GRAND RAPIDS, MICHIGAN   2410744M5ENGL102 2.95
010274JACKOWSKI         MICHELLE  M
BYRON CENTER, MICHIGAN   8845115F3MUSC 79 2.75
010284ORANGE            WILLIAM   B
GRAAFSCHAAP, MICHIGAN    3141660M2ENGR 42 2.98
010297KING              RODNEY    L
DENVER, COLORADO            4470338M4HIST117 3.25
010298BLAINE            DAWN      J
DE MOTTE, INDIANA           5384609F4PSYC120 2.99
010301ELDER             KENNETH   L
GALLUP, NEW MEXICO          6632997M1EDUC 14 1.95
010302PATRICK           ELIZABETH A
SHEBOYGAN, WISCONSIN        5154997F2CHEM 40 3.85
010304OLSON             KATHLEEN  E
SPARTA, MICHIGAN            8861201F5GERM 14 3.05
010307ANDREWS           STEVEN    J
PEORIA, ILLINOIS            2410744M3MUSC 76 2.87
010310ISMOND            SIDNEY    O
LAKEWOOD, CALIFORNIA     7172339M2CPSC 46 3.83
010319HOPKINS           GREGORY   L
YORKTOWN, PENNSYLVANIA   3385494M2MATH 41 3.00
010323HOLMES            JILL      D
TRAVERSE CITY, MICHIGAN  6763991F3MATH 77 2.75
010330JACOBSON          MARSHA    A
SILVER SPRINGS, MD          4847932F5HIST 25 2.98
010339NOOYER            ROCHELLE  J
SALT LAKE CITY, UTAH        6841129F2EDUC 41 3.83
010348BRINK             ALBERT    J
SAGINAW, MICHIGAN           6634401M4CPSC115 3.25
010355ZYLSTRA           CATHERINE E
DOWNS, KANSAS               7514008F1ENGL 16 1.95
010377WORKMAN           RONALD    K
COLUMBUS, OHIO              4841771M2SOCI 44 2.78
010389YOUNG             GLORIA    L
CHEYENNE, WYOMING           7712399F4EDUC115 2.99
```

(cont.)

```
010395MENDELSOHN      DOUGLAS   M
WHITINSVILLE, MA          9294401M3ENGR 80 3.10
010406KRAMER          CHERYL    L
SEATTLE, WASHINGTON       5582911F1CPSC 15 2.99
010415ANDERSON        DANIEL    R
GRANDVILLE, MICHIGAN      5325912M2ENGR 43 2.79
010422BROUWER         DAVID     J
WHEATON, ILLINOIS         6631212M2PSYC 42 2.48
010431VAN DER PLOEG   THOMAS    K
CAWKER CITY, KANSAS       6349971M1CPSC 15 4.00
010448SMITTER         DEBORAH   S
SIOUX CENTER, IOWA        2408113F1ART  77 2.20
010458LOTTERMAN       ALICE     H
REDLANDS, CALIFORNIA      9193001F1POLS 15 3.15
010467HUITING         THEODORE  A
HAWTHORNE, NEW JERSEY     5513915M3ECON 78 2.75
010470PARKS           SANDRA    L
TROY, MICHIGAN            8134001F4MUSC118 3.25
010482NYENBERG        WILLIAM   K
ROCHESTER, NEW YORK       7175118M1ENGL 15 3.15
010490CHAPMAN         ROBERT    J
CHINO, CALIFORNIA         3132446M2P E  43 2.78
010501COOPER          REBECCA   J
WINDOW ROCK, ARIZONA      4245170F1BIOL 16 3.10
010519HOUSEMAN        JANICE    A
BOZEMAN, MONTANA          8183226F3SPEE 77 3.40
010511RIDDERING       ELIZABETH L
NEW ERA, MICHIGAN         6461125F4E SC114 3.37
010515ALLENHOUSE      GERALD    T
BOISE, IDAHO              5132771M5EDUC 87 1.99
010523VOS             ROGER     D
FARMINGTON, MICHIGAN      9421753M1BIOL 13 1.77
010530VERMEER         SHARLENE  M
OKLAHOMA CITY, OK         3714377F5ENGL 95 2.66
010538ROSSMAN         STEVEN    G
ST LOUIS, MISSOURI        8354112M3ENGR 74 2.75
010547PATTERSON       SHIRLEY   A
PETOSKEY, MICHIGAN        4543116F5CPSC 55 2.95
010553SMITH           GERRIT    C
BURKE, VIRGINIA           2351881M1HIST 15 1.77
010560VELDERMAN       MARILYN   K
FT LAUDERDALE, FLORIDA    4421885F1SOCI 13 1.95
010582JEMISON         JONATHAN  B
RUDYARD, MICHIGAN         3451220M3MATH 76 2.99
010590STRONG          ELLEN     M
SPRINGFIELD, ILLINOIS     6142449F1CPSC 14 1.88
010597QUIST           MICHAEL   J
PORTLAND, OREGON          4631744M4P E 116 1.98
010610BLACK           CALVIN    R
SPRING LAKE, MICHIGAN     9491221M5E SC135 2.95
010623ENGELSMA        CAROL     J
CINCINATTI, OHIO          3701228F4GREE119 3.25
010629COOPER          FREDERICK A
BOULDER, COLORADO         5140228M1MATH 13 1.95
010633BROWN           CAROLYN   J
RIPON, CALIFORNIA         4341883F5GEOG 89 2.29
010648PETERSON        PAMELA    J
ALBANY, NEW YORK          7145513F1EDUC 14 1.75
010652JACKSON         FREDERICK R
RAPID CITY, SD            3335910M3LATI 77 2.87
```

(cont.)

```
010657WILSON         STEVEN    L
DETROIT, MICHIGAN        4841962M4PHIL115 2.99
010663LONG           ALIDA    C
LINCOLN, NEBRASKA        7120111F5EDUC100 2.70
010668FREDRICKSON    ALBERT   M
NEWARK, NEW JERSEY       3710225M2ENGR 41 2.78
010675GREGORY        ROBERT   L
NASHVILLE, TENNESSEE     4921107M4MATH115 3.25
010682HEERES         STEPHANIE M
AUSTIN, TEXAS            5132201F4ART 117 3.74
010688STONE          DANIEL   E
BROOKLYN, NEW YORK       7412993M1CPSC 15 1.98
```

StudentUpDate
Student number: a six-digit integer (same as those used in *StudentFile*)
For each of five courses:
    Course name: a seven-character string (e.g., CPSC131)
    Letter grade: a two-character string (e.g., A−, B+, Cb)
    Course credit: an integer

The file is sorted so that student numbers are in increasing order. There is one update record for each student in *StudentFile*.

Sample StudentUpdate:

```
010103ENGL176C 4EDUC268B 4EDUC330B+3P E 281C 3ENGR317D 4
010104CPSC271D+4E SC208D-3PHIL340B+2CPSC146D+4ENGL432D+4
010110ART 520D 3E SC259F 1ENGL151D+4MUSC257B 4PSYC486C 4
010113HIST498F 3P E 317C+4MUSC139B-3PHIL165D 3GEOG222C 3
010126PHIL367C-4EDUC420C-3EDUC473C 3EDUC224D-3GERM257F 4
010144HIST559C+3MATH357D 3CPSC323C-2P E 246D-4MUSC379D+4
010179MATH169C-4CHEM163C+4MUSC436A-3MATH366D-2BIOL213A-4
010191SOCI177F 4POLS106A 4EDUC495A-3ENGR418B+2ENGR355A 4
010226PSYC116B 3GERM323B-4ART 350A 4HIST269B+4EDUC214C+3
010272ENGL558A-4EDUC169D+3PSYC483B+4ENGR335B+2BIOL228B 4
010274MUSC351B 4PSYC209C-4ENGR400F 1E SC392A 4SOCI394B-3
010284ENGR292D 4PSYC172C 4EDUC140B 4MATH274F 4MUSC101D+4
010297HIST464F 1HIST205F 1ENGR444F 1MATH269F 1EDUC163F 1
010298PSYC452B 3MATH170C+4EDUC344C-2GREE138C-2SPEE303A-3
010301EDUC197A 4P E 372B 3ENGR218D 4MATH309C 4E SC405C-4
010302CHEM283F 1P E 440A 2MATH399A-3HIST455C-4MATH387C-3
010304GERM526C-2CHEM243C 4POLS331B-4EDUC398A 3ENGR479D+4
010307MUSC323B+3MATH485C 4HIST232B+4EDUC180A 3ENGL130B+4
010310CPSC264B 2POLS227D+3ENGR467D-3MATH494D-4ART 420C+4
010319MATH276B 2E SC434A 3HIST197B-4GERM489B-2ART 137C-3
010323MATH377D-4EDUC210D 4MATH385D-4ENGR433C 2HIST338A-4
010330HIST546C+3E SC440B+3GREE472C+3BIOL186B 4GEOG434C+2
010339EDUC283B 3CPSC150B 3ENGR120D 4CPSC122F 4ART 216B 4
```

(cont.)
```
010348CPSC411C-3HIST480C+4PSYC459B 4BIOL299B+4ECON276B+3
010355ENGL130C-3CPSC282C+4CPSC181A-4CPSC146C-4SOCI113F 1
010377SOCI213D+3PSYC158D 4MUSC188C 3PSYC281D-4ENGR339B+4
010389EDUC414B+4PSYC115C+2PSYC152C-4ART 366A-3ENGR366B+4
010395ENGR396B 4HIST102F 3ENGL111A 4PSYC210D-2GREE128A 4
010406CPSC160C+4CPSC233C 1LATI494C+3ENGL115C-3MATH181A 3
010415ENGR287C 4EDUC166B-4EDUC106A-3P E 190F 3MATH171B-3
010422PSYC275A-4MATH497A 4EDUC340F 1GERM403C-4MATH245D+4
010431CPSC187D-4CPSC426F 4ENGR476B-4BIOL148B+3CPSC220F 3
010448ART 171D+3CPSC239C-3SOCI499B-4HIST113D+3PSYC116C 4
010458POLS171F 1CPSC187C+4CHEM150B 2PHIL438D-4PHIL254D 4
010467ECON335D-3E SC471B+4MATH457C+3MATH207C 2BIOL429D 4
010470MUSC415C+3POLS177C 3CPSC480A 4PSYC437B 3SOCI276D 4
010482ENGL158D-4EDUC475B 3HIST172B-2P E 316F 4ENGR294A-3
010490P E 239F 4ENGL348F 3LATI246F 4CPSC350F 4MATH114F 1
010501BIOL125F 4CPSC412F 3E SC279F 4ENGR153F 2ART 293F 1
010519SPEE386B+4HIST479C 4PSYC249B-2GREE204B-4P E 421A 1
010511E SC416B 3MATH316D-4MATH287C 2MATH499A-4E SC288D 3
010515EDUC563D+3PHIL373D-3ART 318B 4HIST451F 1ART 476C+3
010523BIOL183D-2HIST296D+4HIST380B+4ENGR216C 4MATH412B-2
010530ENGL559F 1EDUC457D+4CPSC306A 3ENGR171B+1CPSC380A 4
010538ENGR328A-4ENGR336C 3EDUC418D+3PHIL437B+4CPSC475D 4
010547CPSC537A-4ART 386C 4HIST292D-4ENGR467A-4P E 464B+4
010553HIST170A-4SOCI496D-3PHIL136B+4CPSC371D-4CPSC160A-1
010560SOCI153D+3MATH438D+4CPSC378C 4BIOL266F 3EDUC278D+3
010582MATH388A-3P E 311B 3ECON143D 4MATH304C+3P E 428C+4
010590CPSC134B-3E SC114B+3CPSC492C 4ENGL121C 4ENGR403A-4
010597P E 423A-3BIOL189D+3PHIL122D-4ENGL194C-4SOCI113D+3
010610E SC594C-3PHIL344F 4CPSC189B+2ENGR411D-3MATH241A 4
010623GREE412B-4ENGL415D-3ENGL234D-4MATH275F 1SOCI124B+3
010629MATH137D 2MATH481F 3E SC445F 1MATH339D 4ART 219B+4
010633GEOG573B 4ENGL149C+4EDUC113B+4ENGR458C-2HIST446D+4
010648EDUC132D+4MUSC103D-4ENGL263C 4ENGL134B+4E SC392A 3
010652LATI363F 3BIOL425F 1CPSC267C 4EDUC127C+3MATH338B 4
010657PHIL429F 1ART 412D-4MUSC473B-4SOCI447C-4MATH237D+2
010663EDUC580B-4ENGR351B+4SOCI283D 4ART 340C 4PSYC133D+3
010668ENGR274B+4SOCI438C 1P E 327C 4BIOL158A 4EDUC457A-4
010675MATH457A 4ENGR114C 4CPSC218C 3E SC433C-3PSYC243C+1
010682ART 483D+3GERM432C 3ENGL103B+4MUSC169C-3SOCI381C-2
010688CPSC182F 1HIST371C+4PSYC408F 1MUSC214B+4MATH151C 3
```

UsersFile
Identification number: a six-digit integer
User's name: A 30-character string in the form Last Name, First Name
Password: a 5-character string
Resource limit (in dollars): an integer of up to four digits
Resources used to date: a real value

This file is arranged so that identification numbers are in increasing order.

Sample UsersFile:

```
100101MILTGEN, JOSEPH                    MOE
 750 380.81
100102SMALL, ISAAC                       LARGE
 650 598.84
100103SNYDER, LAWRENCE                   R2-D2
 250 193.74
100104EDMUNDSEN, RONALD                  ABCDE
 250 177.93
100105BRAUNSCHNEIDER, CHRISTOPHER        BROWN
 850 191.91
100106PIZZULA, NORMA                     PIZZA
 350 223.95
100107VANDERPOL, HENRY                   VAN
 750 168.59
100108VANZWALENBERG, FLORENCE            VANZ
 450  76.61
100109ALEXANDER, ALVIN                   AL
 650 405.04
100110COSTEMAN, MICHAEL                  MICKY
  50  42.57
100111WYZOREK, GEORGE                    ZIGGY
 350  73.50
100112NAWSADIS, BARBARA                  HAPPY
 850  33.28
100113SINKE, LAUREL                      SWIM
 750 327.53
100114VELTEMA, DONALD                    DONV
 550 382.03
100115KENIEWSKI, KEN                     KEKEN
 550  28.82
100116BEECHEM, WILLIAM                   BOAT
 950 256.18
100117DOYLE, YVONNE                      CONAN
 450 337.01
100118ZWIER, ALEXANDER                   GREAT
 350 249.48
100119JESTER, MICHELLE                   JOKER
 450 281.16
100120MCCONNEL, STEPHEN                  STEVE
 250  35.00
100121WITCZAK, ROGER                     WITTY
 650  38.36
100122VRIESMAN, BENJAMIN                 DUTCH
 850  37.32
100123JAGER, JEFFREY                     TIGER
 250 246.73
100124TRAVIS, DANIEL                     XXXXX
 150 100.19
100125BRYANT, MARY                       CUTIE
 250   0.03
100126BRINK, MARILEE                     LEE
 750  67.35
100127ARMSTRONG, KENNETH                 JACK
 550 392.00
```

```
(cont.)
100128ENGELS, BARBARA            HOUSE
 150   16.39
100129DYKSEN, DIRK               DD
 950   89.57
100130FELTON, GEORGE             JAWGE
 850  466.95
100131ZEILSTRA, LAWRENCE         LARRY
 750  332.12
100132SMITH, ALEXANDER           RADIO
 850  337.43
200101VITO, ANTHONY              TONY
  50   32.81
200102VENEMA, VERNON             VEVE
 250  109.34
200103STOB, SIMON                SLIM
 350  269.93
200104KUIPERS, JESSAMINE         JESSE
 950  183.93
200105BROWN, CALVIN              GREEN
 350  128.69
200106RHODES, LAWRENCE           HIWAY
 150  100.31
200107NYHOFF, JOEL               NIGHT
 350   63.63
200108LEESTMA, SAM               SANDY
 850  202.24
200109MULLER, CHRISTOPHER        KRIS
 550  168.49
200110JOHNSON, JANET             JJ
 550  333.47
200111STEVENS, JEFFREY           CONNY
 950   37.02
200112BOONSTRA, ALFRED           BOON
 750  337.74
200113HARRISON, BENJAMIN         BEN
 550  262.97
200114JAMES, JESSE               GUNS
 250   58.81
200115SCOTT, FRANCINE            FLAG
 350  168.11
200116PHILLIPS, JAMES            GAS66
 650  322.22
200117BROOKS, ANN-MARIE          WATER
 350   26.34
200118SANDERS, PETER             BEACH
 350   22.86
200119LEWIS, GEORGE              LULU
 950  460.30
200120NEWMANN, ALFRED            MAD
 450  116.00
200121VAN, GEORGE                VAN
 550  486.05
200122PETERSON, STEVEN           PETE
 250   35.31
200124JANSMA, BENJAMIN           SMOKE
 150  127.70
```

Miscellany

In the main part of this text we mentioned some special features of Pascal that were not described in detail because they are not usually covered in an introductory programming course. For completeness they are briefly described in this appendix.

Random Number Generation

As we noted in Section 5.4, a random number generator is not a predefined function/procedure in standard Pascal. Consequently, some versions of Pascal may not provide a function like *Random* assumed in the text. In such cases, the following function may be used to generate random numbers. Details of this and other techniques for generating random numbers can be found in *The Art of Computer Programming: Seminumerical Algorithms,* vol. 2, by Donald Knuth (Reading, Mass.: Addison-Wesley, 1981).

>   **function** *Random* : *real*;
>
>   (* This function generates a random real number in the interval from 0
>   to 1. It uses the global variable *Seed* which is initialized by the user
>   and should be an odd positive integer; thereafter, it is the random
>   integer generated on the preceding reference to *Random*.
>   *Note:* The constant 65536 used in this function is appropriate for a
>   machine having 32-bit words. For a machine having M-bit words, it
>   should be replaced by the value of 2 to the power $M/2$. *)
>
>   **const**
>   *Modulus* = 65536;
>   *Multiplier* = 25173;
>   *Increment* = 13849;

begin (* *Random* *)
  Seed := (*Multiplier* * *Seed* + *Increment*) **mod** *Modulus*;
  Random := *Seed* / *Modulus*
end (* *Random* *);

Indirect Recursion

The examples of recursion given in the main part of the text have illustrated *direct recursion* in which the functions and procedures reference themselves directly. *Indirect recursion* occurs when a subprogram references other subprograms, and some chain of subprogram references eventually results in a reference to the first subprogram again. For example, function *A* may reference function *B*, which references procedure *C*, which references *A* again. Since Pascal requires that a subprogram be defined before it is referenced, *B* would have to be defined before *A*, since *A* references *B*, and *C* must be defined before *B*, since *B* references *C*. However, since *C* references *A*, *A* would have to be defined before *C*. Thus it would seem that indirect recursion is not possible in Pascal programs.

To allow indirect recursion without violating Scope Rule 4 in Section 5.4, Pascal allows *dummy definitions* of functions and procedures in addition to actual definitions. A dummy definition consists only of the subprogram heading followed by the reserved word **forward** that is a *directive* to the compiler that the actual definition appears later in the subprogram section of the program. It thus has the form

  function *name* (*formal-parameter-list*) : *result-type*; **forward**;

or

  procedure *name* (*formal-parameter-list*); **forward**;

In the heading of the corresponding actual definition of the subprogram, the formal parameter list and the result type for a function are omitted so that it has the form

  function *name*;

or

  procedure *name*;

Now consider again the situation of function *A* referencing function *B* referencing procedure *C* which references *A* again. The following arrangement of dummy and actual subprogram definitions makes this indirect recursion possible without violating Scope Rule 4:

> **function** A *(formal-parameter-list)* : *result-type*; **forward**;
>   (∗ Dummy definition of A ∗)

> **procedure** C *(formal-parameter-list)* ; **forward**;
>   .
>   .
>   .
>   (∗ Actual definition of C ∗)
>   .
>   .
>   .

> **function** B *(formal-parameter-list)* : *result-type*;
>   .
>   .
>   .
>   (∗ Actual definition of B ∗)
>   .
>   .
>   .

> **function** A;
>   .
>   .
>   .
>   (∗ Actual definition of A ∗)
>   .
>   .
>   .

A can reference B (in its actual definition), since B has already been defined. Similarly, B can reference C since C has been defined earlier. And C can reference A since A is defined before C (albeit in a dummy fashion).

The directive **forward** is the only compiler directive in standard Pascal, but many versions of Pascal also provide others. Another common directive is **external**, which specifies that the actual definition of a subprogram is external to the program.

Functions and Procedures as Parameters

Subprograms considered in the main part of the text have involved two kinds of formal parameters, value parameters and variable parameters. In addition to these kinds of parameters, Pascal also allows functions and procedures as parameters.

To illustrate the use of *function parameters*, consider a function *Integral* to approximate the area of the region under the graph of a function $f(x)$ for $a \leq x \leq b$, by subdividing this region into n rectangles and summing the areas of these rectangles, as described in Section 5.4. This subprogram *Integral* must have the formal parameters *a*, *b*, and *n*, which are ordinary value parameters, and a function parameter *f*. When *Integral* is referenced, actual parameters of real type are associated with the formal parameters *a* and *b*, an actual parameter of integer type is associated with the formal parameter *n*, and an actual function will be associated with the formal parameter *f*.

Function parameters are designated as such by a function heading (without the closing semicolon) within the formal parameter list.[1] Thus an appropriate heading for *Integral* is

> **function** *Integral* (**function** *f*(*x* : *real*) : *real*;
> *a*, *b* : *real*; *n* : *integer*) : *real*;

Here **function** *f*(*x* : *real*) : *real* specifies that *f* is a function parameter denoting a function whose formal parameter and value are of real type. The corresponding actual function parameter must be a function having a real formal parameter and a real value. For example, if *Integrand* is a real-valued function with a real parameter,

> *Area* := *Integral*(*Integrand*, 0, 1.5, 20)

is a valid function reference. Note that only the name of the actual function parameter is given; it is not accompanied by its own actual parameters.

Figure F.1 shows a program that uses the function *Integral* to calculate the area under the graph of the function *Integrand* defined by *Integrand*(*x*) = $x^2 + 3x + 2$ for $0 \leq x \leq 4$.

Procedures may also be used as parameters in subprograms. In this case, a formal parameter is designated as a ***procedure parameter*** by including a procedure heading (without the closing semicolon) in the formal parameter list.

If *F* is a formal function or procedure parameter and *A* is the corresponding actual parameter, then the following rules apply:

1. *A* must be defined within the program; it may not be a predefined function or procedure.
2. If *F* denotes a function whose value is of type *T*, then *A* must also denote a function whose value is of type *T*.
3. If

> *Flist-1* : *type-1*; *Flist-2* : *type-2*; . . . ; *Flist-n* : *type-n*

is the formal parameter list of *F*, then the formal parameter list of *A* must have the form

> *Alist-1* : *type-1*; *Alist-2* : *type-2*; . . . ; *Alist-n* : *type-n*

---

[1]This is the standard form for specifying a function parameter and is different from that given by Wirth. In implementations of Pascal that use Wirth's form, the heading for the function *Integral* would be

> **function** *Integral* (**function** *f* : *real*; *a*, *b* : *real*; *n* : *integer*) : *real*;

```
PROGRAM AreaUnderCurve (input, output);

(*******************************************************************

   Program that uses the function Integral to calculate the area
   under the graph of the function Integrand.

 ***************************************************************** *)

VAR
    Left, Right : real;         (* endpoints of intervals *)
    NumSubintervals : integer;  (* number of subintervals *)

FUNCTION Integrand (x : real) : real;

   (*******************************************************************

      The function for which area is being calculated.

    ***************************************************************** *)

   BEGIN (* Integrand *)
      Integrand := sqr(x) + 3 * x + 2;
   END (* Integrand *);

FUNCTION Integral (FUNCTION f(x : real): real;
                  a, b : real; n : integer) : real;

   (*******************************************************************

      Approximates definite integral of function f over the interval
      [a, b] using n subintervals.  The function is evaluated at the
      midpoints of the subintervals.

    ***************************************************************** *)

   VAR
      x,            (* midpoint of a subinterval *)
      Deltax,       (* size of subintervals *)
      Sum : real;   (* sum of areas of rectangles *)

   BEGIN (* Integral *)
      Deltax := (b - a) / n;
      Sum := 0;
      x := a + Deltax / 2;
      WHILE x <= b DO
         BEGIN
            Sum := Sum + f(x);
            x := x + Deltax
         END (* WHILE *);
      Integral := Sum * Deltax
   END (* Integral *);
```

Figure F.1

Figure F.1 (cont.)

```
BEGIN (* main program *)
   writeln ('Endpoints and number of subintervals:');
   readln (Left, Right, NumSubintervals);
   writeln ('Approximate integral = ',
            Integral(Integrand, Left, Right, NumSubintervals):8:6)
END (* main program *).

Sample runs:


Endpoints and number of subintervals:
0 4 4
Approximate integral = 53.000000


Endpoints and number of subintervals:
0 4 8
Approximate integral = 53.250000


Endpoints and number of subintervals:
0 4 500
Approximate integral = 53.333312
```

where each *Flist-i* and *Alist-i* contain the same number of parameters, and all of these parameters are value parameters, all are variable parameters, all are function parameters, or all are procedure parameters. (In the case of function or procedure parameters, they must also satisfy these same rules.)

To illustrate Rule 2, consider the following procedure heading:

procedure *Demo* (**procedure** *F*(*x, y* : *integer*; **var** *V* : *real*));

The heading of the procedure defining the actual procedure *A* corresponding to *F* could be

procedure *A* (*Num1, Num2* : *integer*; **var** *Alpha* : *real*);

but it could not be any of the following:

procedure *A* (*Num1, Num2* : *integer*; **var** *Num3* : *integer*);
procedure *A* (*Num1* : *integer*; **var** *Alpha* : *real*);
procedure *A* (*Num1, Num2* : *integer*; *Alpha* : *real*);
procedure *A* (*Num1* : *integer*; *Num2* : *integer*; **var** *Alpha* : *real*);

Statement Labels and the *goto* Statement

All programs can be written using the three control structures we considered in Chapter 4: sequence, selection, and repetition. In some unusual situations, however, it may be awkward or inefficient to use only these structures. A typical example is a program for which the input data may contain errors, and in this case, provision should be made for detecting these errors. When such an error occurs, control might be passed to some other part of the program for error handling and/or execution of the program terminated. The processing of these abnormal situations can be handled easily by using statement labels and the **goto** statement. For example, if all of the data processed by a program are no greater than 100, the following **if** statement might be used to trap invalid data items:

> *read (Data)*;
> **if** *Data* > 100 **then**
>   **begin**
>   *writeln* ('*** Input data error ***');
>   **goto** 50
>   **end** (* **if** *);
>   ⋮
> 50:
> **end** (* main program *).

In this example, 50 is a ***statement label.*** Such labels must be declared in the label section in the declaration part of the program. This section has the form

> **label**
>   *label-1, label-2, . . . label-n*;

and must be the first section in the declaration part. Each *label-i* must be a positive integer of up to four digits and can be used to label only one statement. Control can then be transferred to that statement by using a **goto** statement of the form

> **goto** *label-i*

In the preceding example, if a data value greater than 100 is read, an error message is to be displayed and control then transferred to the statement with label 50. A label section such as the following must therefore be used to define this statement label:

> **label** 50;

The statement label 50 followed by a colon (:) can then be attached as a prefix to any statement in the program unit in which this label section appears. In our example, it is attached to an empty statement preceding the reserved word **end** that marks the end of the program and thus serves to terminate execution.

The scope rules considered in Section 5.5 dealt only with identifiers and did not mention statement labels. The scope rules for labels may be obtained by simply replacing the word "identifier" with "statement label" in the fundamental scope principle and in the first three scope rules. Thus the ***fundamental scope principle for labels*** is

> The scope of a statement label is the program unit in which it is declared.

and the three **scope rules for labels** are:

1. A statement label declared in a program unit is not accessible outside that unit.
2. A global statement label is accessible in any subprogram in which that label is not declared locally.
3. Statement labels declared in a subprogram can be accessed by any subprogram defined within it, provided that the label is not declared locally in the internal subprogram.

The Procedure *page*

The procedure *page* is designed to insert page breaks into the output produced by a program. This procedure is called with a statement of the form

>   *page* (*file-name*)

or

>   *page*

In the second form, the standard file *output* is assumed. The effect of a call to procedure *page* is system dependent, and the details must be determined by consulting the system reference manuals. The Pascal standard states only that

> *Page* (*f*) shall cause an implementation-defined effect on the textfile *f*, such that subsequent output to *f* will be on a new page if the textfile is printed on a suitable device and shall perform an implicit *writeln*. . . .

Alternate Forms of Procedures *new* and *dispose*

Alternate forms of reference to the procedures *new* and *dispose* may be used for variant records. The procedure *new* may be called with a statement of the form

>   *new* (*pointer, tag-value-1, tag-value-2, . . . , tag-value-n*)

Here *tag-value-1, tag-value-2, . . . , tag-value-n* represent values of tag fields in increasingly nested variant parts of the record; that is, this procedure reference may be used to allocate a memory location for a record having the structure

```
record
    fixed-part-1;
    case tag-field-1 : tag-type-1 of
                    .
                    .
                    .

        tag-value-1 : (fixed-part-2;
                        case tag-field-2 : tag-type-2 of
                                        .
                                        .
                                        .

                tag-value-2 : (fixed-part-3;
                                case tag-field-3 : tag-type-3 of
                                                .
                                                .
                                                .

                        tag-value-3 : ( . . .
                                    .
                                    .
                                    .


end;
```

When a memory location is allocated for a variant record with a procedure call of the form

new (pointer)

it is sufficiently large to store the largest variant in that record. If it is known that a record with a particular variant is being processed, the alternative form of the procedure call may be used. This allows the system to allocate a location whose size is appropriate for that variant. To illustrate, consider the following declarations:

```
type
    NameString = packed array[1..20] of char;
    EmployeeRecord = record
                        Name : NameString;
                        Age, Dependents : integer;
                        case EmpCode : char of
                            'F' : (* Factory employee *)
                                    (DeptCode : char;
                                    HourlyRate : real);
                            'O' : (* Office employee *)
                                    (Salary : real);
                            'S' : (* Salesperson *)
                                    (MileageAllowance : integer;
                                    BasePay, CommissionRate : real)

    end;
```

If it is known that a location is needed to store the record of an office employee (*EmpCode* is O) and *P* is to point to this location, the procedure reference

   new (*P*, 'O')

may be used.

When a memory location is allocated in this manner, however, it may then be used only for a record with this particular structure, that is, to store a record for an office employee. Also, to dispose of this memory location, an alternate form of reference to the procedure *dispose* is required. For this example, it would be

   dispose (*P*, 'O')

The form for *dispose* that corresponds to the general form of the procedure reference for *new* is

   dispose (*pointer, tag-value-1, tag-value-2, . . . , tag-value-n*)

The alternate forms of procedure references to *new* and *dispose* allow the system (but do not require it) to allocate memory more efficiently for variant records. When each of the variant parts is about the same size, however, there is no real advantage in using these alternate forms.

The Procedures *pack* and *unpack*

The procedures *pack* and *unpack* transfer elements between unpacked arrays and packed arrays. The procedure *pack* is called with a statement of the form

   pack (*unpackedarray, first, packedarray*)

where *unpackedarray* is the unpacked array and *first* is the position of the first element of *unpackedarray* to be transferred to the packed array *packedarray*. To illustrate, the technique used in procedure *ReadString* of Section 8.4 for reading a string into a packed array could be modified to declare an unpacked array *Buffer*,

   Buffer : **array**[1..*StringLimit*] **of** *char;*

read characters into *Buffer*,

```
for i: = 1 to StringLimit do
   if not eoln then
      read (Buffer[i])
   else
      Buffer[i]) := ' ';
readln;
```

and then transfer these to the string variable *Str* of type **packed array**[1 . . *StringLimit*] **of** *char*;

   pack (*Buffer*, 1, *Str*);

The procedure *unpack* transfers the elements from a packed array to an unpacked array. This procedure is called with a statement of the form

   unpack (*packedarray*, *unpackedarray*, *first*)

where *packedarray* is the packed array whose elements are to be transferred to the unpacked array *unpackedarray; first* denotes the position in *unpackedarray* where the first element of *packedarray* is to be placed.

For both of the procedures *pack* and *unpack*, the component-type of the two arrays must be the same, but the indices may be of different ordinal types. The number of array elements transferred is the number of elements in the packed array. Consequently, the segment of the unpacked array to which or from which values are being transferred must be at least as large as the number of elements in the packed array.

Arrays of any type may be packed. In particular, packing may be useful in processing boolean arrays since the boolean constants *false* and *true* are normally represented internally as 0 and 1, each of which may be stored in a single bit. A 32-bit memory word can, therefore, store 32 boolean constants. The declaration

   type
      Barray = **packed array**[1..100] **of** *boolean*;

therefore, allows memory to be allocated more efficiently than

   type
      Barray = **array**[1..100] **of** *boolean*;

The beginning programmer should not be overly concerned with the details of how data is stored internally but instead should expect the computer to utilize the memory as efficiently as possible. Consequently, the procedures *pack* and *unpack* and the packed array specification are seldom used except for character arrays.

G

Other Versions of Pascal

As we have noted, there are several popular versions of Pascal that vary somewhat from the ANSI/IEEE standard version of Pascal described in this text. In this appendix we summarize the major variations and extensions in three such dialects of Pascal.

Turbo Pascal

Turbo Pascal is a popular version of Pascal for microcomputers. It was developed and marketed by Borland International. The following is a summary of the major Turbo variations and extensions, organized by chapters for easy reference.

Chapter 3

- *Additional data types*. The predefined type *byte* is equivalent to the subrange 0..255 of *integer*.
- *Alternative representations of numbers*. Integers may be expressed in hexadecimal notation consisting of a dollar sign ($) followed by up to four hexadecimal digits.
- *Predefined constants. Maxint* has the value 32767. *Pi* is a predefined real constant with the value 3.1415926536E+00.
- *Reserved words*. The following are additional reserved words in Turbo Pascal: **absolute, external, inline, shl, shr, string,** and **xor**.
- *Identifiers*. An identifier consists of a letter or underscore (_) followed by up to 126 additional letters, digits, or underscores, all of which are significant.
- *Arithmetic operators*. The shift operators **shl** and **shr** shift the bits in the binary representation of an integer a specified number of positions to the left or right, respectively. For example, 4 **shl** 6 = 256 and 256

256 **shr** 6 = 4. **Shl** and **shr** have the same priorities as the multipication and division operators. The boolean operators **not, and, or,** and **xor** may also be used to perform bitwise boolean operations on integer values (see the Turbo Pascal notes for Chapter 4).

- *Arithmetic functions. Frac* and *int* are predefined arithmetic functions; *frac (x)* returns the fractional part of the real or integer parameter *x* and *int (x)* returns the integer part.
- *Program heading.* In Turbo Pascal, the program heading is optional.
- *Declaration part.* The sections of the declaration part may appear any number of times and in any order.
- *Typed constants.* Turbo Pascal allows typed constants. These are not true constants but are, in fact, variables whose initial values are specified in a modified form of the usual constant declaration. For example,

```
const
    Sum : integer = 0;
    Radius : real = 2.5;
    Code : char = 'A';
```

declares the integer variable *Sum* and initializes it to 0, the real variable *Radius* and initializes it to 2.5, and the character variable *Code*, initializing it to 'A'.

Chapter 4

- *Boolean operators.* In addition to **not, and,** and **or,** the exclusive-or operator **xor** is provided; *P* **xor** *Q* is true if exactly one of *P* or *Q* is true and is false otherwise. Also, these four boolean operators may be applied bitwise to integer values (0 = false, 1 = true). For example,

$$14 \text{ and } 23 = 0000000000001110_2 \text{ and } 0000000000010111_2$$
$$= 0000000000000110_2 = 6$$

Similarly, 14 **or** 23 = 31 and 14 **xor** 23 = 25.

- **case** *statement.* A **case** statement may have an **else** clause; for example,

```
case Class of
      1 : writeln ('Freshman');
      2..4 : writeln ('Upperclassman')
    else
          writeln ('Special')
end (* case *)
```

If the value of the selector is not in any of the label lists, the statement in the **else** clause is executed; if no **else** clause is present, execution "falls through" the **case** statement and continues with the next statement. As this example also illustrates, subrange notation may be used in label lists to indicate a range of consecutive values.

- **for** *statement.* When execution of a **for** statement is completed, the control variable retains its last value.

Chapter 5

In addition to the standard predefined Pascal procedures and functions, Turbo Pascal provides a number of others. Some of the more useful of these are:

- *Delay (Time)*. This procedure creates a ''busy-wait'' loop that executes for approximately *Time* (integer) milliseconds.
- *GoToXY (XPos, YPos)*. This procedure moves the cursor to the position on the screen whose coordinates are *(XPos, YPos)*; (1,1) represents the upper-left corner (home position).
- *KeyPressed*. This function returns the value true if a key has been depressed and false otherwise.
- *Random, Random (Num)*. This function generates random numbers. The first form returns a random real number in the interval [0, 1), and the second returns a random integer value in the interval [0, *Num*).
- *Randomize*. This procedure initializes the random number generator with a random value.

The string functions *concat, copy, length*, and *pos* and the string procedures *delete* and *insert* described in the Variations and Extensions section at the end of Chapter 8 are also provided. In addition, there are a number of special graphics subprograms designed for use with the IBM PC or compatibles. These include:

- *Draw (X1, Y1, X2, Y2, Color)*. This procedure draws a line between the points whose integer screen coordinates are *(X1, Y1)* and *(X2, Y2)* in a specified color (an integer code in the range 0 through 15).
- *Plot (X, Y, Color)*. This procedure plots a point of the specified color at integer screen coordinates *(X, Y)*. (0, 0) represents the upper-left corner of the screen. The ranges of X and Y are 0..319 and 0..199, respectively (0..639 and 0.199 for high resolution).
- *WhereX, WhereY*. These functions return integers representing the x and y coordinates, respectively, of the current cursor position.
- *Window (X1, Y1, X2, Y2)*. This procedure defines the rectangular region whose upper-left screen coordinates are *(X1, Y1)* and lower-right screen coordinates are *(X2, Y2)* as the active window.

Chapter 6

- *Opening a file*. Before a permanent file can be opened with the procedures *reset* or *rewrite*, a name must be assigned to it with the procedure *assign*. This procedure is called with a statement of the form

    assign (file-variable, file-name)

    where *file-name* is the actual name of the data file stored in secondary memory to be associated with *file-variable*.
- *Closing a file*. When input from or output to a file is completed, the file should be closed by calling the procedure *close* with a statement of the form

    close (file-variable)

Failure to do so may result in loss of data in the file, inability to access it, or some other misfortune.

Chapter 7

- *Type conversion.* Any ordinal type identifier *OrdType* may be used as a function to convert a value of any other ordinal type to the value of type *OrdType* having the same ordinal number. For example, for the declarations

    type
    　　DaysOfWeek = (*Sunday, Monday, Tuesday, Wednesday,*
    　　　　　　　　　　　　Thursday, Friday, Saturday);
    　　FaceCard = (*Jack, Queen, King*);
    　　CardRange = 1..13;

    integer (*Queen*) = *CardRange* (*Queen*) = 1, *DaysOfWeek*(2) = *Tuesday*, and *FaceCard* (*Sunday*) = *Jack*.
- *Range-checking.* A special compiler directive may be required to enable range-checking.

Chapters 8 and 9

In Turbo Pascal, there are only a few variations from and extensions to the array-processing features of standard Pascal:

- *Array constants.* An array variable may be initialized as a typed constant by using a declaration of the form

    const
    　　array-name : *array-type* = (*list-of-array-elements*);

    For example, the declarations

    type
    　　DigitType = 0..9;
    　　NumeralType = '0'..'9';
    　　NumeralArray = **array**[*DigitType*] **of** *NumeralType*;
    const
    　　Numeral : *NumeralArray* = ('0', '1', '2', '3', '4',
    　　　　　　　　　　　　　　'5', '6', '7', '8', '9');

    initialize the array *Numeral* with *Numeral*[0] = '0', *Numeral*[1] = '1', ..., *Numeral*[9] = '9'. An alternative form of constant section could also have been used:

    const
    　　Numeral : *NumeralArray* = '0123456789';

Similar declarations can be used to initialize multidimensional arrays. In this case, nested parentheses enclose the array elements in each dimension with the innermost constants corresponding to the rightmost dimensions. For example, to initialize a two-dimensional array A so that

$$A = \begin{bmatrix} 1 & 2 & 3 \\ 2 & 4 & 6 \\ 3 & 6 & 9 \end{bmatrix}$$

we could use

```
const
    RowLimit = 3;
    ColumnLimit = 3;

type
    Matrix = array [1..RowLimit, 1..ColumnLimit] of integer;

const
    Mat : Matrix = ((1, 2, 3), (2, 4, 6), (3, 6, 9));
```

- *Packed Arrays.* Although the reserved word **packed** is allowed, it has no effect, since packing of arrays is done automatically whenever possible. In particular, the array declarations **array** [*index-type*] **of** *char* and **packed array** [*index-type*] **of** *char* are equivalent. Consequently, the procedures *pack* and *unpack* are not provided in Turbo Pascal.

As noted at the end of Chapter 8, many versions of Pascal include a predefined string type and a number of predefined string functions and procedures. In particular, this is true of Turbo Pascal, which also has the following variations and extensions.

- *String type.* String declarations using the predefined type *string* have the form *string*[#], where # is an integer constant in the range 1 through 255 indicating the maximum length of strings of this type. This maximum length must always be specified; no default value is provided. Strings are implemented as character arrays having index type 0..#. The individual characters are stored in positions 1 through #, and position 0 stores *chr(length)*, where *length* is the current length of the string. Thus, if *Str* is a string variable, *length(Str)* is equivalent to *ord(Str* [0]).
- *Strings and characters.* Characters and strings of length 1 are compatible, and character arrays may be viewed as strings of constant length. When a character array appears in a string expression, it is converted to a string with length equal to the (fixed) size of the array. As in standard Pascal, a string constant may be assigned to a character array, provided they have the same length, but string variables and computed values of string expressions may not be.
- *String functions.* In addition to the string functions *concat, copy, length*, and *pos* and the string procedures *delete* and *insert* described in the

Variations and Extensions section of Chapter 8, Turbo Pascal provides the following:

- **+** *operator*. Concatenation may also be accomplished by using the + operator. For example, 'John' + ' Henry' + 'Doe' yields the string 'John Henry Doe'.
- *val procedure*. The procedure call *val(numeral, number, error)* converts the value of the string expression *numeral* representing an integer or real numeral into the corresponding numeric value *number*. For example, val('123', *Number, Error*) assigns the integer value 123 to *Number*. *Error* is an integer variable for which a value of 0 is returned if there is no conversion error; if an error occurs, *number* is undefined and the value of *error* is the position of the first erroneous character in *numeral*.
- *str procedure*. The procedure call *str(number, numeral)* converts the integer or real value *number* into the string of characters representing the corresponding *numeral*. For example, *str(123, Numeral)* assigns the string '123' to string variable *Numeral*.

Chapter 10

- *Record constants*. A record variable may be initialized as a typed constant by using a declaration of the form

  const
      record-name : *record-type* = (*list-of-field-constants*);

  where each field constant has the form *field-name* : *field-value*. For example, the declarations

  type
      Point = **record**
                X, Y : *real*
          end;
  const
      Origin : *Point* = (*X* : 0, *Y* : 0);

  initializes the record variable *Origin* with both *Origin.X* and *Origin.Y* equal to 0.

Chapter 11

- *Restrictions on sets*. The maximum number of elements in a set is 256. The ordinal values of the base type must be in the range 0..255.
- *Set constants*. A set variable may be initialized as a typed constant by using a declaration of the form

  const
      set-name : *set-type* = *set constant*;

for example,

type
    LetterSet = **set of** 'a'..'z';

const
    Vowels : *LetterSet* = ['a', 'e', 'i', 'o', 'u'];

Chapter 12

- *Opening/closing files*. As described in the Turbo Pascal notes for Chapter 6, a file must be assigned a name with the procedure *assign* before it is opened with *reset* or *rewrite*, and a file should be closed with the procedure *close* when input from or output to it has been completed.
- *get* and *put*. The standard predefined procedures *get* and *put* are not provided. Instead, all file i/o is done using *read* and *write*. Consequently, file buffer variables are not used in Turbo Pascal.
- *Direct access files*. Direct access files are opened in the usual manner using the *assign*, *reset*, and *rewrite* procedures. The procedure *seek* is used to position the file pointer as described in the Variations and Extensions section of Chapter 12.
- *Additional procedures and functions*. There are a number of other predefined procedures for processing files. These include:
  - **erase.** *erase* (*file-variable*) erases the specified file. The file should be closed before it is erased.
  - **flush.** *flush* (*file-variable*) empties the buffer associated with the specified file.
  - **rename.** *rename* (*file-variable, str*) renames the specified file with the string *str*.

  Two additional predefined functions, **filepos** and **filesize**, are also provided:
  - *filepos* (*file-variable*) is the current position of the file pointer in the specified file.
  - *filesize* (*file-variable*) is the number of components in the specified file. Since components are numbered beginning with zero, the value of this function is one more than the number of the last component in the file.

Chapters 13 and 14

Pointer variables can be processed as in standard Pascal except that the alternative forms of reference to procedures *new* and *dispose* for variant records as described in Appendix F are not allowed.

Miscellany

- *Procedure page*. This procedure is not provided in Turbo Pascal.
- *Procedures new and dispose*. The alternative forms of reference to procedures *new* and *dispose* for variant records described in Appendix F are not allowed.
- *Function and procedure parameters*. Functions and procedures may not be used as parameters.

Macintosh Pascal

Macintosh Pascal is that version of Pascal distributed by Apple Computer, Inc., for use with its Macintosh personal computers. It conforms very closely to standard Pascal with the following variations and extensions.

Chapter 3

- *Additional data types*. The predefined types *longint* (long integer), *double extended*, and *computational* (fixed point decimal) are provided. The range of *integer* values is $-2^{15} = 32768$ through $2^{15} - 1 = 32767$; the range of values of type *longint* is $-2^{31} = -2147483648$ through $2^{31} - 1 = 2147483647$, and these may be used wherever integers are used, provided they fall in the smaller range. In integer expressions that involve both types, all operands are converted to *longint* before any integer arithmetic is performed, and the result is always of type *longint*. The range of positive *real* values is $1.5E-45$ through $3.4E+38$ with 7–8 significant decimal digits. The range of positive values of type *double* is $5.0E-324$ through $1.7E+308$ with 15–16 significant decimal digits. The range of positive values of type *extended* is $1.9E-4951$ through $1.1E+4932$ with 19–20 significant decimal digits. In mixed mode expressions, all *integer* and *real* operands are converted to *extended* before any real arithmetic is performed and the result is always *extended*. An extended value may be used wherever *real, double,* or *computational* values are used, provided it falls within the range of permissible values.
- *Alternative representations of numbers*. Integers may be expressed in hexadecimal notation consisting of a dollar sign ($) followed by up to four hexadecimal digits for type *integer*, eight for type *longint*.
- *Predefined constants*. *Maxint* has the value 32767. *MaxLongInt* is a predefined *longint* constant with the value 2147483647.
- *Reserved words*. The following are additional reserved words in Macintosh Pascal: **otherwise, string,** and **uses.**
- *Identifiers*. An identifier consists of a letter followed by up to 255 additional letters, digits, or underscores (_), all of which are significant.
- *Program heading*. Only *input* and *output* may appear in the file list of the program heading.

Chapter 4

- *case* statement. A **case** statement may have an **otherwise** clause; for example,

```
case Class of
      1 : writeln ('Freshman');
   2,3,4 : writeln ('Upperclassman')
otherwise
         writeln ('Special')
end (* case *)
```

If the value of the selector is not in any of the label lists, the statement in the **otherwise** clause is executed.

Chapter 5

In addition to the standard predefined Pascal procedures and functions, Macintosh Pascal provides a large number of others. Some of the more useful functions are:

- *Random.* This function generates random integers in the range -32768 through 32767. (Another random number generator is available in the SANE library.)
- *BitNot(Long1), BitAnd(Long1, Long2), BitOr(Long1, Long2), BitXor (Long1, Long2).* These functions perform bitwise **not, and, or,** and exclusive-or operations on the *longint* values *Long1* and *Long2*; the result is of type *longint*. For example, *BitAnd*(14, 23) = 6, *BitOr*(14, 23) = 31, *BitXor*(14, 23) = 25 (see notes on Chapter 4 for Turbo Pascal).
- *BitShift(Long, Number).* This function shifts the bits in the binary representation of the *longint* value *Long* the specified number of bits to the left or right according to whether *Number* is positive or negative; the result is of type *longint*. For example, *BitShift*(4, 6) = 256 and *BitShift*(256,6) = 4.

The string functions and procedures described in the Variations and Extensions section at the end of Chapter 8 are provided in Macintosh Pascal. Two additional functions are *omit* and *include*; these are described in the Macintosh Pascal notes for Chapters 8 and 9. A large number of other predefined functions and procedures are provided for memory management, event management, screen management, sound generation, graphics, and advanced numerical applications. Some of these are in the special libraries *QuickDraw1*, *QuickDraw2*, and *SANE*, and attaching a clause of the form **uses** *library-name* to the program heading makes them accessible in a program.

Chapter 6

- *Program heading.* Only *input* and *output* may appear in the file list of the program heading.
- *reset and rewrite.* These procedures for opening files may be referenced in the standard manner with a single parameter or with the alternative forms

      reset (file-variable, file-name)
      rewrite (file-variable, file-name)

  where *file-name* is an expression with a string value. These extended forms with two parameters associate the file variable used in the program with the name of an actual data file stored in secondary memory and are needed for permanent files. The standard one-parameter forms are used for temporary ("anonymous") files.

- *Closing a file.* When input from or output to a permanent file is completed, the file should be closed by calling the procedure *close* in a statement of the form

    close (file-variable)

    Failure to do so many result in loss of data in the file, inability to access it, or some other misfortune.

Chapter 7

- *Input of enumerated types.* Values of an enumerated type can be read from text files. The longest string of characters that form an identifier of that type (ignoring the case of the letters) is read and the corresponding identifier assigned.
- *Output of enumerated types.* Values of an enumerated type can be written to text files. If a format descriptor of the form :*w* is used to specify the field width, the field will be extended if necessary.
- *ord* function. The *ord* function returns a value of type *longint*.

Chapters 8 and 9

As noted at the end of chapter 8, many versions of Pascal include a predefined string type and a number of predefined string functions and procedures. In particular, this is true of Macintosh Pascal.

- *String type.* String declarations have the form

    string or *string[#]*

    where # is an integer constant in the range 1 through 255 indicating the maximum length of strings of this type; in the first form, the default maximum length 255 is used.
- *Strings and characters.* Characters and strings of length 1 are assignment-compatible. Also, a packed array of type *char* with index type 1..# may be assigned to a variable of type *string* provided its length does not exceed the maximum length specified for that string variable. Conversely, a string value may be assigned to such a packed character array, provided they have the same length.
- *String functions.* In addition to the string functions *concat, copy, length,* and *pos* and the string procedures *delete* and *insert,* Macintosh Pascal provides the following string functions:
  - **Omit(str, index, size).** This function returns the string formed by deleting a substring of the specified *size,* starting at position *index,* from the string *str.* Unlike procedure *delete, omit* leaves *str* unchanged.
  - **Include(str-1, str-2, index).** This function returns the string formed by inserting the string *str-1* into the string *str-2* at position *index.* Unlike procedure *insert, include* leaves *str-2* unchanged.

Chapters 10 and 11

Record and set processing are the same as in standard Pascal.

Chapter 12

- *Program heading*. Permanent files are not listed.
- *Opening/Closing files*. As described earlier, alternative forms of reference to procedures *reset* and *rewrite* are necessary to associate names with permanent files. Also, permanent files should be closed with the procedure *close* when input from or output to them has been completed.
- *Direct access files*. Direct access files are opened using the procedure *open*:

    open (file-variable, file-name)

  The procedure *seek* is used to position the file pointer as described in the Variations and Extensions section of Chapter 12.
- The ***filepos*** *function. filepos (file-variable)* is the component number of the position of the file pointer in the specified file.

Chapters 13 and 14

Pointer variables can be processed as in standard Pascal.

UCSD Pascal

UCSD Pascal was developed at the University of California at San Diego. Its variations and extensions of standard Pascal have been incorporated into many of the popular dialects of Pascal.

Chapter 3

- ***Maxint***. The value of *maxint* is usually 32767.
- *Identifiers*. Identifiers consist of a letter followed by any number of letters and digits, but only the first eight characters are significant.
- *Arithmetic Functions*. Two additional predefined arithmetic functions are:
  - ***log:*** *log (x)* returns the base-10 logarithm of the integer or real parameter *x*.
  - ***pwroften:*** *pwroften(n)* returns the real value of 10 raised to the integer power *n*.
- *Program heading*. The file list is not required in the program heading; if present, it is ignored.
- *Output of boolean values*. Boolean values cannot be displayed.

Chapter 4

- ***case*** *statement*. If the value of the selector is not in any of the label lists, execution "falls through" to the next statement.

Chapter 5

In addition to the standard predefined Pascal functions, UCSD Pascal provides the arithmetic functions *log* and *pwroften* (see the notes on Chapter 3 for UCSD Pascal). It also provides the string functions described in the Variations and Extensions section of Chapter 8.

Chapter 6

- *Output of boolean values.* Boolean values cannot be written to text files.
- *Program heading.* The file list is not required in the program heading; if present, it is ignored.
- *Input from the keyboard.* The *read* and *readln* procedures may be called with statements of the form

  read (keyboard, input-list)

  or

  readln (keyboard, input-list)

  to read values from the keyboard without echoing them on the screen.
- *Interactive files.* The difficulty caused by the look-ahead property of the data pointer described in Programming Pointer 4 in Chapter 6 does not arise because the file *input* is a special file type called *interactive* and is not a text file. When an interactive file is opened with the *reset* procedure, the functions *eoln* and *eof* are intialized to false, and they remain false until the end-of-line character (carriage return) or a special end-of-file character is entered.
- *Procedures reset and rewrite.* Files are opened with the modified references to procedures *reset* and *rewrite*

  reset (file-variable, file-name)
  rewrite (file-variable, file-name)

  (See the Macintosh Pascal notes for Chapter 6.)
- *Closing files.* Any file to which output has been directed must be closed after output is completed with a statement of the form

  close (file-variable, **lock**)

  if the file is to be retained after execution or

  close (file-variable, **purge**)

  if it is to be deleted.

Chapter 7

UCSD Pascal is consistent with standard Pascal in the use of ordinal types.

Chapters 8 and 9

- *Comparison of arrays.* Arrays of the same type may be compared with the relational operators = and <>.
- **Pack** *and* **unpack.** Procedures *pack* and *unpack* are not provided; packing of arrays is done automatically when necessary.
- *String type and string functions.* String declarations have the form

    string or *string*[#]

  where # is an integer constant in the range 1 through 255 indicating the maximum length of strings of this type; in the first form, the default maximum length 255 is used. Also, UCSD Pascal provides the string functions *concat*, *copy*, *length*, and *pos* together with procedures *delete* and *insert* as described in the Variations and Extensions at the end of Chapter 8.

Chapters 10 and 11

Records and sets of the same type may be compared with = and <>.

Chapter 12

In addition to the variations and extensions for file processing described in the notes for Chapter 6, UCSD also provides the following:

- *Interactive files.* For a file of type *interactive*, a statement of the form

    read (*file-variable, character*)

  is equivalent to

    get (*file-variable*);
    character := *file-variable*↑;

  which is the reverse of the order for ordinary text files.
- *Direct access files.* UCSD Pascal supports direct access files as described in the Variations and Extensions section of Chapter 8.

Chapters 13 and 14

- **dispose** *procedure.* The *dispose* procedure may not be provided.

Miscellany

- **goto** *statement.* The **goto** statement may not transfer control outside the program unit in which the statement appears.
- **exit** *procedure.* UCSD Pascal provides the predefined procedure *exit* for this purpose to provide a ''clean'' exit from a program unit. It is called with a statement of the form *exit* (*name*) where *name* is the name of the function or subprogram to be exited.
- *Function and procedure parameters.* Functions and procedures may not be used as parameters.

H

Answers to
Selected Exercises

Section 1.3 (P. 21)

5. (a) 9   (c) 64   (e) 1.5

6. (a) 83   (c) 4096   (e) 7.25

7. (a) 18   (c) 2748   (e) 8.75

8. (a) 1010011   (c) 1000000000000   (e) 111.01

9. (a) 10010   (c) 101010111100   (e) 1000.11

10. (a) 11   (c) 100   (e) 1.4

11. (a) 9   (c) 40   (e) 1.8

12. (a) (i) $(11011)_2$ (ii) $(33)_8$ (iii) $(1B)_{16}$
     (c) (i) $(100111010)_2$ (ii) $(472)_8$ (iii) $(13A)_{16}$

13. (a) (i) $(0.1)_2$ (ii) $(0.4)_8$ (iii) $(0.8)_{16}$
     (d) (i) $(10000.0001)_2$ (ii) $(20.04)_8$ (iii) $(10.1)_{16}$

14. (a) (i) $(0.0\overline{1001})_2$ (ii) $(0.2\overline{3146})_8$ (iii) $(0.4\overline{C})_{16}$
     (c) (i) $(0.00\overline{0011})_2$ (ii) $(0.0\overline{3146})_8$ (iii) $(0.0\overline{C})_{16}$

15. (a) 64   (c) -65 (e) -256

16. (a) 0000000011111111
(c) 1111111100000001
(e) 1100011010001001

18. (a) (i) 0110000000010001 (ii) Same as (i)
(c) (i) 0101000000010001 (ii) Same as (i)
(e) (i) 0110011001111101 (ii) Same as (i)

19. (a) (i)

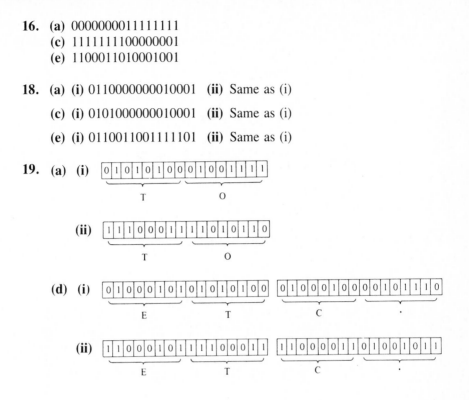

Section 2.5 (P. 47)

2. Given information: Two temperature scales. Celsius and Fahrenheit, with 0° Celsius corresponding to 32° Fahrenheit, 100° Celsius corresponding to 212° Fahrenheit, and that a linear relationship of the form $F = aC + b$ holds in general. Also given some temperature C on the Celsius scale.

To find: The corresponding number F of degrees on the Fahrenheit scale.

We first must find the specific linear relationship between the two scales. In general, $C°$ Celsius corresponds to $F°$ Fahrenheit, where $F = aC + b$ for some constants a and b. Because 0° Celsius corresponds to 32° Fahrenheit, we must have

$$32 = a \cdot 0 + b$$

so that $b = 32$. This means, then, that

$$F = aC + 32$$

Because 100° Celsius corresponds to 212° Fahrenheit, we must have

$$212 = a \cdot 100 + 32$$

which gives $a = 9/5$, so that our equation becomes

$$F = \frac{9}{5}C + 32$$

The algorithm for solving the problem is now straightforward;

(∗ This algorithm converts a temperature of *DegreesC* on the Celsius scale to the corresponding *DegreeF* on the Fahrenheit scale. ∗)
1. Enter *DegreesC*.
2. Calculate
    $DegreesF = (9 * DegreesC)/5 + 32$.
3. Display *DegreesF*.

7. Given information: A list of scores in the range 50 through 100 and a method for assigning letter grades: A if score $\geq$ 90, B if 75 $\leq$ score < 90, and C if 50 $\leq$ score < 75.

To find: The corresponding letter grades for the scores in the list.

An algorithm for solving this problem is the following:

(∗ Algorithm to assign letter grades to numeric scores. A negative score is used to signal the end of data. ∗)
1. Initialize *ALine, BLine,* and *CLline* to 90, 75, and 50, respectively.
2. Enter first value for *Score*.
3. While *Score* $\geq$ 0, do the following:
    a. If *Score* $\geq$ *ALine*, display 'A'; else if *Score* $\geq$ *BLine*, display 'B'; else if *Score* $\geq$ *CLine*, display 'C'; else display 'Erroneous score'.
    b. Enter next value for *Score*.

14. **program** *CelsiusToFahrenheit* (*input, output*);

(∗ Program to convert a temperature on the Celsius scale to the corresponding temperature on the Fahrenheit scale. ∗)

var
```
DegreesC,          (* degrees Celsius *)
DegreesF : real;   (* degrees Fahrenheit *)
```
begin
```
write ('Enter temperature in degrees Celsius: ');
readln (DegreesC);
DegreesF := (9 * DegreesC) / 5 + 32;
writeln ('Corresponding temperature in degrees Fahrenheit is ',
        DegreesF:8:2)
```
end.

Section 3.2 (P. 56)

2. **(a)** 12 is an integer constant.

    (b) 12. is not a valid constant (real constants may not end in a period).

    (c) 12.0 is a real constant.

3. **(a)** 'X' is legal.

   (c) IS' is not legal (missing first quote)

   (e) 'DO''ESNT' is legal.

4. **(c) var**
      Mileage : *real*;
      Cost, Distance : *integer*;

5. **(c) const**
      Year = 1984;
      Female = 'F';
      Blank = ' ';

Section 3.3 (P. 60)

1. **(a)** 1

   (d) Not a valid expression. 9 / 2 is a real value, and **div** requires integer operands.

   (g) 2

   (j) 2

   (m) 0

   (p) 18.0

   (s) 3.25

   (v) 4.0

2. **(a)** 8.0   **(c)** 2.$\overline{6}$ **(e)** 5.1   **(g)** 6.25

3. **(a)** $10 + 5 * B - 4 * A * C$

   (c) $sqrt(a + 3 * sqr(b))$

Section 3.4 (P. 66)

1. **(a)** Valid

   (d) Valid

   (g) Not valid; variable must be to the left of an assignment operator.

   (j) Valid

   (m) Not valid; string constant may not be assigned to a boolean variable.

2. **(a)** 15.0

   (d) 6

(g) Not valid; an integer value may not be assigned to a character variable.

(j) Not valid; a real value may not be assigned to a character variable.

(m) Not valid; a character value may not be assigned to a real variable.

(p) 2

3. **(a)** *Distance* := *Rate* ∗ *Time*

(d) *Area* := (*b* ∗ *h*) / 2

4. **(a)** For *a* = 2, *b* = 4, *c* = 8, *a* ∗ (*b* **div** *c*) = 0, *a* ∗ *b* **div** *c* = 1.

Section 3.5 (P. 77)

1. **(d)** `__436__872`   **(e)** `___-567.4__436_____`
   `___0.00040`   `Tolerance:_0.00040`

2. **(a)** `__New_balance_=_2559.50`
   `____C____8.02_____`

3. **(a)** *writeln* (*R1*:9:4, *C*:4, *N1*:5);
   writeln (*N2*:5, 'PDQ', *R2*:8:5)

4. **(a)** *A* ← 1, *B* ← 2, *C* ← 3, *X* ← 4.0, *Y* ← 5.5, *Z* ← 6.6

(e) Same as (a).

Section 3.8 (P. 86)

6. **program** *RightTriangle* (*input, output*);

(∗ Program to read the lengths of two legs of a right triangle and calculate the area of the triangle and the length of the hypotenuse. ∗)

var
   Leg1, Leg2,
   Area,
   Hypotenuse : *real*;

begin
   write ('Enter the lengths of the two legs of right triangle: ');
   readln (*Leg1, Leg2*);
   Area := (*Leg1* ∗ *Leg2*)/2;
   Hypotenuse := *sqrt*(*sqr*(*Leg1*) + *sqr*(*Leg2*));
   writeln ('Area = ', *Area*:4:2);
   writeln ('Hypotenuse = ', *Hypotenuse*:4:2)
end.

Section 4.2 (p. 101)

1. (a)

a	b	a or not b
true	true	true
true	false	true
false	true	false
false	false	true

(d)

a	true	(1 + 2 = 4)	a and true or (1 + 2 = 4)
true	true	false	true
false	true	false	false

Section 4.4 (P. 114)

1. (b) **if** *Code* = 1 **then**
    begin
        readln (*X, Y*);
        Sum := *X* + *Y*;
        writeln ('X = ', *X*, 'Y = ', *Y*, 'Sum = ', *Sum*)
    end (* **if** *)

(e) **if** (*Distance* >= 0) **and** (*Distance* <= 100) **then**
    Cost := 5.00
else if *Distance* <= 500 **then**
    Cost := 8.00
else if *Distance* < 1000 **then**
    Cost := 10.00
else
    Cost := 12.00

Section 4.8 (P. 136)

1. (d) 6
    4
    5
    6
    7

2. (a) **while** *x* > 0 **do**
    begin
        writeln ('x = ', *x*);
        x := *x* − 0.5
    end (* **while** *)

(d) **for** *Number* := 1 **to** 100 **do**
    writeln (*sqr*(*Number*))

Section 5.2 (P. 169)

1. **(a)** Can be used.

   (d) Cannot be used; a constant ('M') cannot be passed to a variable parameter.

4. **procedure** *Switch* (**var** *VarA, VarB : integer*);

   (∗ Procedure to interchange the values of *VarA* and *VarB*. ∗)

   var
      TempVar : integer;

   begin (∗ *Switch* ∗)
      TempVar := *VarA*;
      VarA := *VarB*;
      VarB := *TempVar*
   end (∗ *Switch* ∗);

Section 5.3 (P. 177)

1. **(a)** Can be used.

   (d) Cannot be used; illegal function reference. (*f* is a function, not a procedure.)

   (g) Can be used.

   (j) Cannot be used; invalid boolean expression since there is no value associated with a procedure.

   (m) Can be used.

4. **function** *IsADigit(Character : char) : boolean*;

   (∗ Function to determine if *Character* is a digit. ∗)

   begin (∗ *IsADigit* ∗)
      IsADigit := (*Character* >= '0') **and** (*Character* <= '9')
   end (∗ *IsADigit* ∗);

Section 6.1 (P. 235)

1. **(a)** The values assigned to *Num1*, *Num2*, *Num3*, and *Num4* will be 1, −2, 3, and 4, respectively.

   (d) The values assigned to *Num1*, *Num2*, *Num3*, and *Num4* will be 1, −2, 4, and −5, respectively.

2. (a) $N1 \leftarrow 123$ (d) $C1 \leftarrow X$
    $R1 \leftarrow 45.6$ $N1 \leftarrow 78$
    $C1 \leftarrow X$ $C2 \leftarrow b$ (blank)
    $N2 \leftarrow 78$ $R1 \leftarrow -909.8$
    $R2 \leftarrow -909.8$ $R2 \leftarrow 7.0$
    $C2 \leftarrow -$ $N2 \leftarrow -65$
    $N3 \leftarrow 65$ $C3 \leftarrow \$$
    $C3 \leftarrow \$$ $R3 \leftarrow 432.10$

(g) 123 is read and assigned to $N1$; 45.6 is read and assigned to $R1$; the end-of-line mark is read, and a blank is assigned to $C1$; then an error occurs because X is nonnumeric and thus cannot be read for $N2$.

3. (a) $N1 \leftarrow 54$
    $N2 \leftarrow 32$
    $C1 \leftarrow E$
    $C2 \leftarrow 1$
    $R1 \leftarrow -6.78$
    $C3 \leftarrow \$$
    $N3 \leftarrow 90$

```
| 5 | 4 |   | 3 | 2 | E | 1 | ● | - | 6 | . | 7 | 8 | $ | 9 | 0 | ● | ● |   | 1 | ● |
                                                  ↑
```

(d) Same as (a).

(g) $R1 \leftarrow 54.0$
    $R2 \leftarrow 32E1$
    $C1 \leftarrow -$
    $N1 \leftarrow 6$
    $C2 \leftarrow .$
    $N2 \leftarrow 78$
    $C3 \leftarrow \$$
    $N3 \leftarrow 90$

```
| 5 | 4 |   | 3 | 2 | E | 1 | ● | - | 6 | . | 7 | 8 | $ | 9 | 0 | ● | ● |   | 1 | ● |
                                              ↑
```

Section 6.2 (P. 250)

1. (a) I think that I shall never see
    A poem lovely as a tree.

        —JOYCE KILMER (1914)

Section 7.3 (P. 273)

1. (a) **type**
        MonthAbbrev = (*Jan, Feb, Mar, Apr, May, Jun, Jul, Aug,*
                   Sep, Oct, Nov, Dec);
       MonthNumber = 1..12;

3. (a) *true*   (d) *Mar*   (g) *Mar*   (j) 8

Section 8.3 (P. 305)

1. (a) *Number*[1] ← 0   **(d)** *Number*[1] ← 1
     Number[2] ← 1   *Number*[2] ← 2
     Number[3] ← 1   *Number*[3] ← 4
     Number[4] ← 2   *Number*[4] ← 8
     Number[5] ← 2   *Number*[5] ← 16
     Number[6] ← 3   *Number*[6] ← 32
     Number[7] ← 3   *Number*[7] ← 64
     Number[8] ← 4   *Number*[8] ← 128
     Number[9] ← 4   *Number*[9] ← 256
     Number[10] ← 5   *Number*[10] no value assigned

(g) *Price*[*red*] ← 19.95
     Price[*yellow*] ← 12.75
     Price[*blue*] ← 19.95
     Price[*green*] ← 14.50
     Price[*white*] no value assigned
     Price[*black*] ← 14.50

2. (a) Declarations:

> **type**
>   *SmallNumberArray* = **array**[0..5] **of** [0..5];
>
> **var**
>   *Number* : *SmallNumberArray*;
>   *i* : *integer*;

Statement:

> **for** *i* := 0 **to** 5 **do**
>   *Number*[*i*] := *i*;

(d) Declarations:

> **type**
>   *BooleanArray* = **array**[1..20] **of** *boolean*;
>
> **var**
>   *TFQuestion* : *BooleanArray*;
>   *Num* : *integer*;

Statement:

> **for** *Num* := 1 **to** 20 **do**
>   *TFQuestion*[*Num*] := **not** *odd*(*Num*);

3. (b)

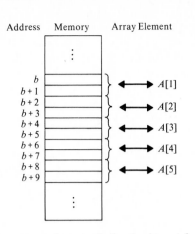

Address   Memory   Array Element

$A[i]$ is stored in two consecutive words beginning at $b + 2(i - 1)$

4. function *Max* (**var** *Number* : *NumberArray*; *NumElements* : *integer*) : *integer*;

> (* Returns the largest element in the integer array *Number* which has *NumElements* elements *)

var
> *i*,   (* index *)
> *Largest* : *integer*;   (* Largest element found so far *)

begin (* *Max* *)
> **if** *NumElements* = 0 **then**
> > *writeln* ('Empty array')
> **else**
> > **begin**
> > > *Largest* := *Number*[1];
> > > **for** *i* := 2 **to** *NumElements* **do**
> > > > **if** *Number*[*i*] > *Largest* **then**
> > > > > *Largest* := *Number*[*i*];
> > > *Max* := *Largest*
> > **end** (* **else** *)
end (* *Max* *);

Section 8.5 (P. 327)

1. (a) *TextLine*[1] ← A
       TextLine[2] ← B
       TextLine[3] ← C
       TextLine[4] ← D
       TextLine[5] ← E
       TextLine[6] ← F
       TextLine[7] ← G
       TextLine[8] ← H
       TextLine[9] ← I
       TextLine[10] ← $

(d) *TextLine*[1] ← I
       TextLine[2] ← H
       TextLine[3] ← b
       TextLine[4] ← G
       TextLine[5] ← F
       TextLine[6] ← E
       TextLine[7] ← D
       TextLine[8] ← C
       TextLine[9] ← B
       TextLine[10] ← A

(g) *CharArray*[1] ← A
   CharArray[2] ← B
   CharArray[3] ← C
   CharArray[4] ← D
   CharArray[5] ← E
   CharArray[6] ← F
   CharArray[7] ← G
   CharArray[8] ← ♭
   CharArray[9] ← H
   CharArray[10] ← I

Error occurs when the assignment statement

   TextLine := *CharArray*

is encountered since an unpacked array may not be assigned to a
packed array.

(j) Same as (a).   **(m)** Same as (a).

Section 9.4 (P. 370)

1. (a) 5000   **(d) 4**   **(g) 792**

2. (a) $\begin{bmatrix} 2\ 3\ 4 \\ 3\ 4\ 5 \\ 4\ 5\ 6 \end{bmatrix}$ **(d)** $\begin{bmatrix} A\ B\ C\ D\ ♭\ E \\ F\ G\ H\ ♭\ I\ J \end{bmatrix}$

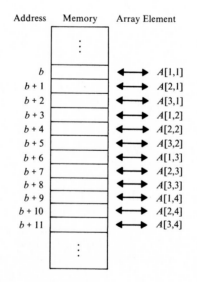

Address	Memory	Array Element
	⋮	
b		A[1,1]
b + 1		A[2,1]
b + 2		A[3,1]
b + 3		A[1,2]
b + 4		A[2,2]
b + 5		A[3,2]
b + 6		A[1,3]
b + 7		A[2,3]
b + 8		A[3,3]
b + 9		A[1,4]
b + 10		A[2,4]
b + 11		A[3,4]
	⋮	

$A[i, j]$ is stored in the word with address $b + 3(j - 1) + (i - 1)$

Figure H.1

(g) $\begin{bmatrix} E & ? & D & C & B & A \\ J & I & ? & H & G & F \end{bmatrix}$ (? = undefined) **(j)** $\begin{bmatrix} 0 & 2 & 2 \\ 0 & 0 & 2 \\ 0 & 0 & 0 \end{bmatrix}$

5. See Figure H.1, p. 648.

Section 10.6 (P. 414)

1. (a) type
      CardSuit = (*Hearts, Diamonds, Spades, Clubs*);
      PlayingCard = **record**
                Suit : *CardSuit*;
                CardValue : 1..13
           end;

(d) type
      String7 = **packed array**[1..7] **of** *char*;
      String20 = **packed array**[1..20] **of** *char*;
      Listing = **record**
                 Name, Address : *String20*;
                 PhoneNumber : *String7*
            end;

3. (a) type
      NameString = **packed array** [1..20] **of** *char*;
      NumberString = **packed array**[1..11] **of** *char*;
      Color = (*blue, brown, green, other*);
      MaritalStatus = (*Married, Single*);
      Date = **record**
                Month : 1..12;
                Day : 1..31;
                Year : 1900..2000
           end;

      PersonalInfo = **record**
                 Name : *NameString*;
                 BirthDay : *Date*;
                 Age : *integer*;
                 Sex : *char*;
                 SocSecNumber : *NumberString*;
                 Height, Weight : *integer*;
                 EyeColor : *Color*;
                 case *MarStat* : *MaritalStatus* **of**
                    Married : (*NumChildren* : *integer*);
                    Single : ()
            end;

4. (a)   Address Memory Record Field

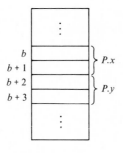

Here *P* is a record of type *Point*.

Section 11.4 (P. 442)

1. (a) [3, 5, 11]   **(d)** [1, 2, 4, 12]   **(g)** [6..9]
   (j) [2, 4, 6, 8]   **(m)** [1..12]   **(p)** [ ]
   (s) [3, 5, 11]   **(v)** [ ]

2. (a) type
       SmallIntegers = **set of** 1..99;

   (c) type
       DaysOfWeek = (*Sunday, Monday, Tuesday, Wednesday,*
                       Thursday, Friday, Saturday);
       Days = **set of** *DaysOfWeek*;

3. (a) Declarations:

       type
           SetOfNumbers = **set of** 1..99;

       var
           Even, Odd : *SetOfNumbers*;
           Number : *integer*;

   Statements:

       Even := [ ];
       for *Number* := 1 **to** 49 **do**
           Even := *Even* + [2 * *Number*];
       Odd := [1..99] − *Even*;

   (f) Declarations:

       type
           LetterSet = **set of** *char*;

       var
           Vowels, Consonants : *LetterSet*;

   Statements:

       Vowels := ['A', 'E', 'I', 'O', 'U', 'a', 'e', 'i', 'o', 'u'];
       Consonants := ['A'..'Z', 'a'..'z'] − *Vowels*;

(g) Declarations:

type
  DaysOfWeek = (*Sunday, Monday, Tuesday,*
                Wednesday, Thursday, Friday,
                Saturday);

  SetOfDays = **set of** *DaysOfWeek*;

var
  WeekDays : *SetOfDays*;

Statements:

  WeekDays := [*Monday..Friday*];

6. (a) (i) 0101010101

   (b) (i) 100010001000001000001000000

Section 12.3 (P. 468)

1. (a) Attempts to read beyond the end of the file when the data pointer is positioned at the last end-of-line mark.

2. (a) Fails for all text files whose first character is not a blank.

Section 13.4 (P. 505)

1. (a) Values of pointer variables cannot be displayed.

   (d) The procedure *new* is used only to assign a value to a pointer variable.

3. **function** *CountNodes*(*FirstPointer* : *ListPointer*) : *integer*;

   (∗ Function to count the nodes in a linked list with first node pointed to by *FirstPointer*. ∗)

   var
     TempPointer : *ListPointer*;
     Count : *integer*;

   begin (∗ *CountNodes* ∗)
     Count := 0;
     TempPointer := *FirstPointer*;
     while *TempPointer* <> **nil do**
       begin
         Count := *Count* + 1;
         TempPointer := *TempPointer*↑.*Next*
       end (∗ **while** ∗);
     CountNodes := *Count*
   end (∗ *CountNodes* ∗);

Section 14.2 (P. 532)

4. **(a)** $-7.\overline{3}$ **(d)** 12.0   **(g)** 12.0   **(j)** 8.0

5. **(a)** $A\ B * C + D -$ **(d)** $A\ B\ C\ D + / +$
    (g) $A\ B - C - D - E -$

6. **(a)** $(A - (B + C)) * D$ **(d)** $((A + B) - C) / (D * E)$
    (g) $A / ((B / C) / D)$

7. **(a) (i)** -15 **(iv)** 15
    (b) (i) $A\ B\ C \sim + *$ **(iii)** $A \sim B \sim *$

8. **(a)** $A\ B$ **and** C **or**   **(e)** $A\ B = C\ D =$ **or**

9. **(a)** $- + * A\ B\ C\ D$ **(d)** $+ A / B + C\ D$
    (g) $- - - - A\ B\ C\ D\ E$

10. **(a)** -24.5 **(d)** -2.0 **(g)** 55.0

11. **(a)** $(A + B) * (C - D)$ **(d)** $A - (B - C) - D$
    (g) $(A * B + C) / (D - E)$

Section 14.3 (P. 541)

1. **(a)** $O(n^3)$
    (c) $O(n)$

3. **(a)** $O(n)$
    (d) $O(n^2)$

Section 14.4 (P. 550)

1. **(a)**

$$\boxed{5, 1, 6, 4, 3, 2}$$

First call to *QuickSort*
$(Low = 1, High = 6)$

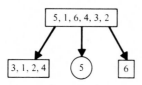

I.1: $1 < 6$ so
I.2: Split the list and position 5.
I.3: Call *QuickSort* on left sublist
$(Low = 1, High = 4)$.

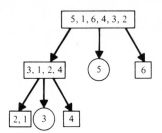

II.1: $1 < 4$ so
II.2: Split sublist and position 3.
II.3: Call *QuickSort* on left sublist
($Low = 1$, $High = 2$).

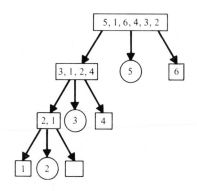

III.1: $1 < 2$ so
III.2: Split sublist and position 2.
III.3: Call *QuickSort* on left sublist
($Low = 1$, $High = 1$).

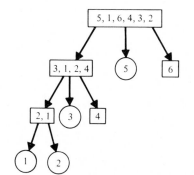

IV.1: $1 \not< 1$ (one-element sublist) so
IV.5: Return to previous level.

III.4: Call *QuickSort* on right sublist
($Low = 4$, $High = 3$).

IV.1: $4 \not< 3$ (empty sublist) so
IV.5: Return to previous level.

III.5: Return to previous level.

II.4: Call *QuickSort* on right sublist
($Low = 4$, $High = 4$).

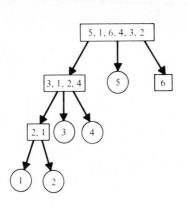

III.1: $4 \ll 4$ (one-element sublist) so
III.5: Return to previous level.

II.5: Return to previous level.

I.4: Call *QuickSort* on right sublist
     (*Low* = 6, *High* = 6).

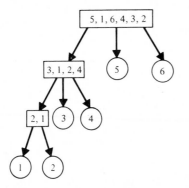

II.1: $6 \ll 6$ (one-element sublist) so
II.5: Return to previous level.

I.5: Return to main program;
     sorting is completed.

Section 14.5 (P. 560)

1. (a)   F: |1   5 | 3   8 | 7 | 2   6 | 4 |

        F1: |1   5   7 | 4 |
        F2: |3   8 | 2   6 |

         F: |1   3   5   7   8 | 2   4   6 |

        F1: |1   3   5   7   8 |
        F2: |2   4   6 |

         F: |1   2   3   4   5   6   7   8|

Section 14.6 (P. 575)

1. (a) (i)

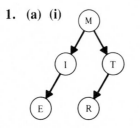

(b) (i) Inorder: E I M R T
        Preorder: M I E T R
        PostOrder: E I R T M

2. (a) (i) M T R I E

   (b) (i) T R M I E

   (c) (i) R T E I M

3. (a)

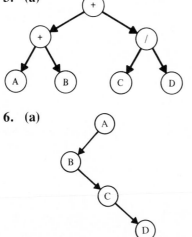

Prefix: + + A B / C D
Postfix: A B + C D / +

6. (a)

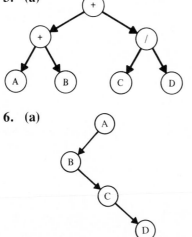

8. function *LeafCount(RootPointer : TreePointer) : integer*;

  (∗ Function to count the number of leaves in a binary tree with root
note pointed to by *RootPointer*. ∗)

     begin (∗ *LeafCount* ∗)
       if *RootPointer* = **nil then**
         LeafCount := 0
       else if (*RootPointer↑.Left* = **nil**) **and**
           (*RootPointer↑.Right* = **nil**) **then**
         LeafCount := 1
      else
        LeafCount := *LeafCount(RootPointer↑.Left)*
             + *LeafCount(RootPointer↑.Right)*
     end (∗ *LeafCount* ∗);

19. (a) (i) $B[1] \leftarrow$ 'M'
           $B[2] \leftarrow$ 'I'
           $B[3] \leftarrow$ 'T'
           $B[4] \leftarrow$ 'E'
           $B[5] \leftarrow$?
           $B[6] \leftarrow$ 'R'
           $B[7] \leftarrow$?
           (All other array elements are undefined; also, ? = undefined.)

Glossary

actual parameter A parameter that appears in a procedure/function reference and is associated with the corresponding formal parameter in the procedure/function heading.

address A label associated with a memory location. Each word in memory has a unique address that makes it possible to access its contents.

address translation A computation that must be performed to determine the address of the location in memory where a particular item in a structured data type is stored.

algorithm A sequence of clearly stated simple steps for solving a problem in a finite amount of time.

ALU See *arithmetic logic unit*

anchor A part of a recursive definition in which one or more values of a function (or parameters being returned by a procedure) are specified.

arithmetic-logic unit (ALU) That part of the central processing unit that performs basic arithmetic and logical operations.

array A data structure consisting of a fixed number of data items, all of the same type, organized in a sequence, and accessed directly by specifying their locations in this sequence.

ASCII American Standard Code for Information Interchange. One of the standard coding schemes for characters.

assembler System software that translates programs written in assembly language into machine language.

assembly language A language that is closely related to machine language but that uses instruction mnemonics (names) in place of numeric opcodes and symbolic addresses (variables) in place of numeric addresses.

assignment operator An operator denoted in Pascal by := that assigns a value to a variable or to a function identifier.

assignment statement A Pascal statement that uses an assignment operator to assign a value to a variable or to a function identifier.

auxiliary memory See *secondary memory*.

base address   The address of the first memory word in a block of consecutive words used to store the elements of an array or record.

base of a number system   In a positional number system, the digits in a numeral are coefficients of powers of the base of that number system. For example, in the *decimal* or *base-10* number system, each digit in a numeral is a coefficient of a power of 10; thus $234 = 2 \times 10^2 + 3 \times 10^1 + 4 \times 10^0$.

base type   An ordinal type used in defining subrange and set types. For a subrange type it specifies the larger collection of values containing the subrange. For a set type it specifies the type of elements in the universal set.

batch processing   A mode of processing in which a file containing a program, data, and certain command lines is submitted to the system, and execution proceeds without any user interaction.

big Oh notation   See *order of magnitude*.

binary digit   A digit, 0 or 1, in the binary number system.

binary number system   A number system, using only the binary digits 0 and 1, that is commonly used for internal computer representation.

binary search   A scheme for searching an ordered list by repeatedly examining the middle item in the (sub)list to determine which half of the (sub)list contains the desired item, and then continuing the search with that sublist.

binary search tree   A binary tree in which the data item stored in each node is greater than the data item in its left child but less than the data item in its right child.

binary tree   A tree in which each node has at most two children.

bit   See *binary digit*.

boolean   A predefined Pascal data type in which the only possible values are *true* and *false*.

bubble sort   A simple sorting scheme based on comparisons and interchanges of consecutive list items.

buffer   Portion of main memory used for temporary storage of data values being transferred between main memory and secondary memory. Buffers are used to reduce the effects of differences in operating speeds of various devices.

bug   A progam error.

byte   A group of bits, usually eight.

call   A reference to a procedure or function.

case **statement**   A Pascal statement implementing a multialternative selection structure in which the selection is based on the value of a selector variable or expression. Cases specifying the alternative courses of action are labeled with lists of possible values of this selector.

central processing unit (CPU)   Controls the operation of the entire computer system, performs arithmetic/logic operations, stores and retrieves instructions and data.

char   A predefined Pascal data type in which the values are single characters.

character   Any symbol in the Pascal character set including letters, both upper-case and lower-case, digits, and various special symbols.

character constant   A constant of type *char*. In Pascal, this character must be enclosed within single quotes (apostrophes).

children of a node Nodes in a tree pointed to by a given node called their *parent*.

coding Writing a program or subprogram in a high-level language.

collating sequence A sequence used in a particular computer to establish an ordering of the character set.

comments Used to provide documentation within a Pascal program and enclosed between the comment delimiters (* and *) or { and }.

compatible types Two simple data types are said to be compatible if they are the same type, one is a subrange of the other, or both are subranges of the same type.

compile-time error See *syntax error*.

compiler System software used to translate source programs written in a high-level language into object programs in machine or assembly language.

component An element of a data structure such as an array or file.

compound statement A Pascal statement formed by combining several statements into a block by enclosing them between the reserved words **begin** and **end** and separating them by semicolons.

concatenation A string operation that appends one string to another.

constant A quantity that does not change during program execution.

constant section That section of the declaration part of a Pascal program in which named constants are defined.

control structure Structures that control the logical flow in an algorithm or program. Structured algorithms and programs use only the control structures: *sequence, repetition,* and *selection*.

control unit That part of the central processing unit that fetches instructions from memory, decodes them, and directs the system to execute the operations indicated by the instructions.

control variable A variable used to control repetition in a for loop.

CPU See central processing unit.

data structure A collection of related data items together with basic operations defined on this collection. They may be *predefined* data structures such as arrays and records, or they may be *user-defined* structures such as linked lists and trees.

debug To locate and correct errors (bugs) in a program.

declaration part That part of a Pascal program in which variables are declared and constants, types, functions, procedures, and labels are defined.

deque Double-ended queue.

desk-checking Tracing the execution of a program segment by hand to locate logical errors. The values of all or certain key variables are recorded in a trace table as the program segment is traced step by step.

digraph See *directed graph*.

direct access (also called *random access*) Accessing a given component in a data structure by specifying its position in the structure without examining other components, as in sequential access.

direct access file A file in which each component can be accessed directly. Standard Pascal provides only sequential access files, but some versions provide both sequential and direct access files.

direct recursion Recursion in which a function or procedure references itself directly.

directed graph   A structure consisting of a finite set of vertices (nodes) together with a finite set of directed arcs that connect pairs of vertices.

disk   See *magnetic disk*.

divide-and-conquer   An algorithm design strategy in which problems are repeatedly divided into simpler subproblems until a solution to each subproblem is straightforward.

documentation   Information that explains what a program does, how it works, what variables it uses, any special algorithms it implements, and so on.

dummy definition   A definition of a function or procedure that consists of only a heading together with the **forward** directive that indicates that the actual definition of the subprogram appears later. This Pascal feature makes indirect recursion possible.

dynamic data structure   A data structure whose size changes during processing.

dynamic variables   Variables that are created and disposed of during program execution. Dynamic variables are accessed by means of a pointer rather than by a variable name; they are created by using the procedure *new* and are disposed of with the procedure *dispose*.

EBCDIC   Extended Binary Coded Decimal Interchange Code. One of the standard coding schemes for characters.

editor   System software used to create and modify files.

empty statement   A Pascal statement used to indicate that no action is required.

end-of-file-mark   A special control character used to indicate the end of a file.

end-of-line-mark   A special control character used to indicate the end of a line of text.

enumerated type   A user-defined ordinal data type. The definition consists of listing the values of this data type, separated by commas, and enclosed within parentheses.

equivalent type identifiers   Type identifiers whose definitions can be traced back to a common type identifier.

external file   See *permanent file*.

external memory   See *secondary memory*.

external sorting   A sorting scheme appropriate for sorting large files stored in secondary memory.

field (of a record)   An element of a record.

field-designated variable   A variable used to access the value stored in a field within a record. It has the form *record-name. field name*.

fielded variable   See *field-designated variable*.

FIFO structure   See *queue*.

file   A collection of data items, usually stored in secondary memory, that are input to or output by a program.

file buffer   A buffer associated with a given file.

file buffer variable   A variable of the form *file-variable*↑ used to access the file buffer.

file window   Synonym for *file buffer variable*.

fixed part (of a record)   Those fields in a variant record that occur in all variants.

flag   See *sentinel*.

floating point number   Synonym for *real number*.

floating point representation   See *scientific representation*.

flowchart   A graphic representation of an algorithm.

for statement   A Pascal statement implementing a repetition structure in which the body of the loop is repeated once for each value of a control variable in some specified range of values.

formal parameter   A parameter used in a subprogram heading to transfer information to or from the subprogram.

format descriptor   An expression used in an output statement to specify the format in which values are to be displayed.

forward **directive**   See *dummy definition*.

function   A subprogram that (ordinarily) returns a single value via the function name.

function heading   A function definition begins with a function heading of the form

function *function-name (formal-parameter-list) : result-type*;

function parameter   A parameter that is a function.

Fundamental Scope Principle   *The scope of an identifier is the program unit in which it is declared.*

global variable   A variable declared in the main program and therefore accessible in the main program and in all subprograms in which it is not declared locally.

goto **statement**   A seldom-used statement that transfers control to a statement with a specified label.

hardware   The actual physical components of a computer system such as disk drives, printers, central processing unit, memory, and so on.

heading   See *function heading, procedure heading,* and *program heading*.

hexadecimal number system   A base-16 number system.

hierarchical records   See *nested*.

high-level language   A language such as Pascal that is similar to natural language and that is intended to facilitate program development. Programs written in such languages must be converted into machine language using a compiler (or interpreter) before they can be executed.

identifier   Names given to programs, constants, variables, functions, procedures, and other entities in a program.

if **statement**   A Pascal statement that implements a selection structure in which selection is controlled by a boolean expression.

if-else if **construct**   A compound form of an **if** statement that implements a multialternative selection struction.

implementation of a data structure   Selection of storage structures to store the data items and the design of algorithms to carry out the basic operations.

in parameter   See *value parameter*.

in-out parameter   See *variable parameter*.

index   An expression that indicates the position in an array of a particular component.

indexed variable A variable of the form *array-name[index]* used to access a particular component of an array.

indirect recursion Recursion in which a subprogram references other subprograms and in which some chain of subprogram references eventually results in a reference to the first subprogram again.

inductive step Part of a recursive definition of a function (or procedure) that specifies the value of a function (or parameters) in terms of previously defined values.

infinite loop A loop that does not terminate.

infix notation Notation for arithmetic expressions in which the symbol for each binary operation is placed between its operands.

inorder traversal Traversal of a binary tree in which the left subtree of a node is visited, then the node itself, and then the right subtree of that node.

input Data obtained by a program from an external source during execution.

input file A standard default input file in Pascal. It is a text file and usually refers to an external device such as a terminal.

integer A predefined Pascal data value in which the values are all of the integers in the range *−maxint* through *maxint* where the value of *maxint* is machine dependent.

interpreter System software that translates each statement in a source program into one or more machine language instructions. These instructions are executed before the next statement is translated.

interactive processing A mode of processing in which the user communicates with a program during execution.

internal memory See *memory unit*.

internal sorting A sorting scheme appropriate for lists stored in main memory.

key field A field in a record on which sorting or searching is based.

label section That section of the declaration part of a program in which statement labels are declared.

leaf node A tree node that has no children.

lexical analyzer The part of a compiler that groups characters in a source program into logical units such as identifiers, reserved words, operators, and so on.

LIFO structure See *stack*.

linear search A strategy for searching a list by examining the items sequentially, beginning with the first item.

link A field in a node of a linked structure that points to another node.

linked list A data structure consisting of nodes linked together by pointers, together with a pointer to the first node in the list. Each node contains two kinds of information: the actual data item being stored and a link (pointer) to the next node in the list.

local variable A variable whose scope is a subprogram.

logical error An error in the logical structure of a program (or algorithm). These errors usually do not prevent the program from executing, but incorrect results are produced.

loop See *repetition structure*.

machine language The language used directly by a particular computer for all calculations and processing.

magnetic disk   A secondary mass storage medium that stores information on rotating disks coated with a substance that can be magnetized.

magnetic tape   A secondary mass storage medium that stores information on plastic tape coated with a substance that can be magnetized.

main memory   See *memory unit*.

maxint   A predefined identifier representing a machine-dependent integer constant that is the largest integer value that can be stored in a particular computer's memory.

memory unit   That part of the computer hardware in which the instructions and data of the currently executing program are stored.

mergesort   A sorting scheme, usually external, based on the operations of creating and merging sorted subfiles.

modular programming   A programming strategy in which major tasks to be performed are identified and individual procedures/functions (called *modules*) for these tasks are designed and tested.

multialternative selection structure   A control structure in which one of several (usually more than two) actions is selected for execution.

multidimensional array   An array with two or more dimensions.

multiply indexed variable   A variable used to access a component of a multi-dimensional array. It is formed by attaching the appropriate number of indices enclosed within brackets to the array's name.

multiply linked structure   A linked structure in which each node has two or more link fields.

n-dimensional array   'An array having *n* dimensions.

named constant   A constant that has been named in the constant section of a Pascal program.

nested   A term describing the placement of one structure with another, e.g., nested **if** statements and nested records.

nil   A predefined pointer constant. Assigning this value to a pointer variable indicates that it does not point to any memory location.

nil pointer   A pointer to which the value **nil** has been assigned.

node   A component of a linked structure.

object program   A machine language program produced by a compiler.

octal number system   A base-8 number system.

one-dimensional array   Often used as a synonym for *array*.

opcode   A numeric code for a machine language instruction.

operating system   System software that controls the overall operation of the computer system.

order of magnitude   An approximate measure of the computing time of an algorithm. $T(n)$ is said to have order of magnitude $g(n)$, denoted $T(n) = O(g(n))$, if there exists a constant C such that $T(n) \leq g(n)$ for all sufficiently large values of n.

ordinal number   The number of the position of a value of ordinal type in the ordering for that type.

ordinal type   A simple data type in which the values of that type are ordered so that each one except the first has an immediate predecessor and each one except the last has an immediate successor.

output   Information produced by a program.

output **file**   A standard default output file in Pascal. It is a text file and usually refers to an external device such as a terminal or printer.

overflow A condition that results when a value is generated that is too large to be stored in the computer being used.

packed array An array in which more than one array component is stored in a single memory word.

parameter A variable used to pass information between program units.

parent of a node See *children of a node*.

parser The part of a compiler that groups tokens together according to the syntax rules of the language.

peripheral devices Hardware devices such as terminals, printers, disk drives, and tape drives that are not part of the central processing unit.

permanent file A file usually stored in secondary memory that exists not only during execution of a program but also before and/or after execution.

pointer, pointer variable A variable whose value is a memory address.

pop The deletion operation for a stack.

postfix notation Notation for arithmetic expressions in which the symbol for each binary operation is placed after its operands.

postorder traversal Traversal of a binary tree in which the left subtree of a node is visited, then the right subtree, and then the node itself.

precedence rules Rules that specify the order in which the operators in an expression are to be performed.

prefix notation Notation for arithmetic expressions in which the symbol for each binary operation is placed before its operands.

preorder traversal Traversal of a binary tree in which a node is visited, then its left subtree, and then its right subtree.

primary memory See *memory unit*.

priority See *precedence rules*.

procedure A subprogram that performs a particular task. Information is passed between a procedure and other program units by means of parameters.

procedure heading A procedure definition begins with a procedure heading of the form

    procedure *procedure-name* (*formal-parameter-list*);

procedure parameter A parameter that is a procedure.

procedure reference statement A Pascal statement of the form

    procedure-name (*actual-argument-list*)

that is used to call a procedure.

program heading Every Pascal program begins with a program heading of the form

    program *program-name* (*file-list*);

program stub Incomplete subprograms used temporarily in designing a program in a top-down manner.

pseudocode A loosely defined language that resembles a programming language and is used to describe algorithms.

pseudorandom numbers A sequence of numbers that are generated by an algorithm but that appear to be random, i.e., they appear to be uniformly distributed over some range.

push The insertion operation for a stack.

queue   A list in which items may be added only at one end, called the *back* or *rear,* and removed only at the other end, called the *front* or *head.* A queue is a *First-In-First-Out (FIFO)* structure.

quicksort   A recursive sorting scheme based on correctly positioning one element of a (sub)list so that all list items that precede it are less than this item and all those that follow it are greater than this item. The two sublists that result are then sorted independently in the same way.

random access file   See *direct access file.*

random number generator   A subprogram that generates pseudorandom numbers.

real   A predefined Pascal data type used for values that are real numbers. They may be represented either in decimal form or in scientific notation.

record   A data structure in which a collection of related data items of possibly different types may be stored. The positions in which these data items are stored are called the *fields* of the record.

recursion, recursive   A process of a function or procedure referencing itself.

relational operators   The operators $=$, $<$, $>$, $<>$, $<=$, $>=$, and **in**. They are used to form simple boolean expressions.

repeat loop   A posttest loop, i.e., a repetition structure in which the boolean expression that controls repetition is tested after the body of the loop is executed.

repeat **statement**   A Pascal statement that implements a repeat loop.

repetition structure   A control structure in which one or more statements are repeatedly executed. Repetition must be controlled so that these statements are executed only a finite number of times.

reserved words   Keywords such as **begin, end,** and **var** that have a special meaning in Pascal and may be used only in the special ways required by the syntax of the language.

Reverse Polish Notation (RPN)   See *postfix notation.*

root node   See *tree.*

roundoff error   The error that results in storing a real number because of the limited number of bits used to store its fractional part.

run-time error   An error such as division by zero that occurs during execution of a program.

same type   Two types are the *same* if they are declared by the same type identifier or by equivalent type identifiers.

scientific representation   Representation of a real number (also called *floating point representation*) that consists of an integer or a real constant in decimal form followed by the letter *E* (or *e*) followed by an integer constant that is intepreted as an exponent on the base 10.

scope (of an identifier)   That part of a program in which an identifier is accessible.

secondary memory   Storage devices such as magnetic disks and magnetic tapes that provide relatively inexpensive long-term storage for large collections of information.

selection structure   A control structure in which one of a number of alternative actions is selected.

semantics   The interpretation or meaning of the statements in a language.

sentinel   An artificial data value used to mark the end of a collection of input data.

sequential access   A method of access in which an item can be accessed only by examining all those items that precede it.

sequential file   A file in which the components must be accessed sequentially.

sequential structure   A control structure in which the statements comprising the structure are executed in the order in which they appear.

set   A predefined structured data type used to process unordered collections of items that are all of the same type.

simple data type   A data type in which each datum is atomic, i.e., it consists of a single entity that cannot be subdivided.

simulation   Modeling a dynamic process and using this model to study the behavior of the process.

software   Computer programs.

sorting   Arranging a list of items so that they are in either ascending or descending order.

source program   A program written in a high-level language such as Pascal.

stack (push-down stack)   A list in which elements may be inserted (*pushed*) and deleted (*popped*) at only one end, called the *top* of the stack. A stack is a *Last-In-First-Out* (*LIFO*) structure.

statement part   The part of a Pascal program that contains the statements that actually carry out the steps of an algorithm.

static data structure   A data structure whose size remains fixed during program execution.

static variable   A variable to which memory locations are allocated at compile time. This association does not change during program execution. (See also *dynamic variables*.)

string   A finite sequence of characters.

string constant   In Pascal, a string enclosed within single quotes (apostrophes).

string type   In Pascal, a packed array of type *char* whose index type is a subrange of the form $1..n$ for some integer $n > 1$.

structure diagram   A diagram that displays the structure of an algorithm by displaying the major tasks that must be performed and the relationship between them.

structured algorithm (program)   An algorithm (program) that is designed using only the three basic control structures: sequential, selection, and repetition.

structured data type   A data type in which a datum consists of a collection of items.

subprogram   A function or procedure.

subprogram section   That section of the declaration part of a Pascal program in which functions and procedures are defined.

subrange type   An ordinal type that is defined by specifying the first and last elements in the range of values for a datum of this type.

subscript, subscripted variable   See *index* and *indexed variable*.

successive refinement   See *divide-and-conquer*.

syntax   The grammar of a language, i.e., the set of rules for forming words and statements in that language.

syntax diagram   A diagram used to display the syntax of a particular statement or construct in a language.

syntax error   A violation of the syntax of the language that is detected during compilation of the program.

system software   A collection of programs such as editors, compilers, interpreters, debuggers, etc. supplied as part of the computer system.

tag field   A field within a variant record whose value determines which variant is in effect.

tape   See *magnetic tape*.

temporary file   A file that exists only during execution of a program.

text file   A file of characters that is organized into lines.

top-design design   See *divide-and-conquer*.

trace table   See *desk-checking*.

tree   A directed graph with a root node that has no incoming arcs but from which each node in the tree can be reached by exactly one path, i.e., by following a unique sequence of consecutive arcs.

type   A formal specification of the set of values that a variable may have.

type section   That section of the declaration part of a Pascal program in which data types are defined.

value parameter   A formal parameter of a subprogram that is used to pass information to the subprogram but not to return information from it.

variable   An identifier associated with a particular memory location. The value stored in this location is the value of the variable, and this value may be changed during program execution.

variable parameter   A formal parameter of a subprogram that is used both to pass information to and to return information from the subprogram. In Pascal, variable parameters must be indicated as such by preceding them with the reserved word **var**.

variant part   The last part of a variant record.

variable section   That section of the declaration part of a program in which variables are declared.

variant record   A record that may contain a variant part in addition to the usual fixed part. The number and types of the fields in the fixed part do not change during program execution, but those in the variant part may change in number and/or type.

walking through the code   See *desk-checking*.

while loop.   A pretest loop, i.e., a repetition structure in which the boolean expression that controls repetition is tested before the body of the loop is executed.

while **statement**   A Pascal statement that implements a while loop.

window   See *file window*.

with **statement**   A Pascal statement used to attach a record name to identifiers of fields within that record to form fielded variables.

word   A basic storage unit consisting of a machine-dependent number of bits (commonly 16 or 32) whose contents are directly accessible by means of its address.

Index of Examples
and Exercises

Examples

INDEX

Statements	Example
Assignment (61–66, 287–288, 313, 389, 425, 481, 483)	*Count* := 0; *Wages* := *RoundCents* (*Hours* * *Rate*); *DeptCode* := 'A'; *OverTime* := (*Hours* > 40); *ProductName* := 'Ford-Carburetor'; *Letters* := ['A'..'F', 'P', 'S']; *EmpRec* := *InFile*↑; *EmpRec.Number* := 12345; *TempPtr* := **nil**; *FirstPtr*↑.*Data* := *ProductName*;

Sequential (94–95)
  Compound (95)
	begin
	  Wages := *RoundCents* (*Hours* * *Rate*);
	  OverTime := *false*
	end;

Selection (102–117)
  case (109–114)
	case *DeptCode* **of**
	  'o', 'O' : *Dept* := *Office*;
	  'f', 'F' : *Dept* := *Factory*;
	  's', 'S' : *Dept* := *Sales*
	end (* **case** *);

if (102–110)	**if** *Hours* <= 40 **then**
	  Wages := *RoundCents* (*Hours* * *Rate*)
	else
	  begin
	    OverTime := *true*;
	    Wages := *RoundCents* (*HoursLimit* * *Rate* +
	      OTMult * *Rate* * (*Hours* − *HoursLimit*))
	  end (* **else** *);